In Anticipation of a Future Period of Incapacity

In Anticipation of a Future Period of Incapacity

The Dutch 'Levenstestament' from a Legal, Empirical and Comparative Perspective

Rieneke Stelma-Roorda

eleven

Published, sold and distributed by Eleven
P.O. Box 85576
2508 CG The Hague
The Netherlands
Tel.: +31 70 33 070 33
Fax: +31 70 33 070 30
e-mail: sales@elevenpub.nl
www.elevenpub.com

Sold and distributed in USA and Canada
Independent Publishers Group
814 N. Franklin Street
Chicago, IL 60610, USA
Order Placement: +1 800 888 4741
Fax: +1 312 337 5985
orders@ipgbook.com
www.ipgbook.com

Eleven is an imprint of Boom uitgevers Den Haag.

ISBN 978-90-4730-189-9
ISBN 978-94-0011-366-4 (e-book)
NUR 822

Table of Contents

1	**General introduction**	11
1.1	Introduction	11
1.2	Legal-normative context	13
1.3	Research questions	16
1.4	Research delineation	17
1.5	Research design	20
1.6	Research overview	23
1.7	Terminology	24
2	**A changing paradigm of protection of vulnerable adults and its implications for the Netherlands**	27
2.1	Introduction	27
2.2	Historical context – embedding the new human rights-based paradigm	28
2.3	Article 12 UNCRPD: Two conflicting interpretations	30
2.4	Beyond the two conflicting interpretations: the alternate framework	34
2.5	Support measures for adults unable to make their own decisions	35
2.6	The Dutch adult guardianship measures	38
2.7	The living will	42
2.8	Conclusion	45
3	**The misuse or abuse of continuing powers of attorney: what are appropriate safeguards?**	47
3.1	Introduction	47
3.2	The risk of abuse or misuse of CPAs	50
3.3	Appropriate safeguards in the context of the CPA	58
3.4	Safeguards in Belgium, England & Wales, Germany, the Netherlands, and Switzerland	66
3.5	Conclusion	73

4	**The legal basis and scope of the levenstestament in the Netherlands**	75
4.1	Origin of the levenstestament in the Netherlands	75
4.2	Regulation in the absence of a statutory framework	82
	4.2.1 An ambiguous legal basis	82
	4.2.2 The efforts of the notariate	94
	4.2.3 The judiciary	100
4.3	The levenstestament for health and medical affairs	106
	4.3.1 The legal status of treatment advance directives	107
	4.3.2 Research on treatment advance directives in the Netherlands	109
	4.3.3 Weighing the pros and cons	113
4.4	Conclusion	115
5	**The levenstestament in practice**	119
5.1	Introduction	119
5.2	The application of the levenstestament by the notariate	120
	5.2.1 Research questions	121
	5.2.2 Methods	122
	5.2.3 Results	123
	5.2.4 Discussion	138
5.3	An analysis of court cases featuring the levenstestament	141
	5.3.1 A brief overview of the legal framework	142
	5.3.2 Methods	143
	5.3.3 The deliberations of the court when issuing an adult guardianship measure	144
	5.3.4 Discussion	148
5.4	Overall conclusion	150
6	**Decision-making by and for adults with impaired capacity: the potential of the Dutch levenstestament**	153
6.1	Introduction	153
6.2	Decision-making by and on behalf of adults with impaired capacity	155
	6.2.1 The Dutch levenstestament	155
	6.2.2 The normative aspirations of the UNCRPD	157
	6.2.2 Supported and substitute decision-making in practice	160
6.3	Current study	163
6.4	Methods	164
	6.4.1 Research design	164
	6.4.2 Procedure	165
	6.4.3 Analytic strategy	166

6.5 Results 167
 6.5.1 Sample 168
 6.5.2 Expectations of adults who had recently made a levenstestament 168
 6.5.3 Expectations of nominated attorneys 172
 6.5.4 Experiences of active attorneys 174
6.6 Discussion and conclusion 177
 6.6.1 Discussion 177
 6.6.2 Limitations and strengths 180
 6.6.3 Conclusion 181

7 Continuing powers of attorney – different legal rules, similar problems and solutions: What can the Netherlands learn from Belgium, England and Wales, Germany and Switzerland? 183
7.1 Introduction 184
7.2 Methods 185
7.3 The Netherlands: an exploration of the existing problems 189
7.4 Belgium: the *zorgvolmacht* 192
 7.4.1 Regulatory framework 192
 7.4.2 Form and registration 193
 7.4.3 Entry into force and appointment of the attorney 194
 7.4.4 Rights and duties of the attorney 195
 7.4.5 Supervision 196
 7.4.6 Law in action 196
7.5 England and Wales: the lasting power of attorney 199
 7.5.1 Regulatory framework 199
 7.5.2 Form and registration 200
 7.5.3 Entry into force and appointment of the attorney 201
 7.5.4 Rights and duties of the attorney 202
 7.5.5 Supervision 203
 7.5.6 Law in action 204
7.6 Germany: the *Vorsorgevollmacht* 205
 7.6.1 Regulatory framework 205
 7.6.2 Form and registration 207
 7.6.3 Entry into force and appointment of the attorney 207
 7.6.4 Rights and duties of the attorney 209
 7.6.5 Supervision 210
 7.6.6 Law in action 210
7.7 Switzerland: the *Vorsorgeauftrag* 213
 7.7.1 Regulatory framework 213
 7.7.2 Form and registration 214
 7.7.3 Entry into force and appointment of the attorney 214

7.7.4 Rights and duties of the attorney 216
7.7.5 Supervision 217
7.7.6 Law in action 218
7.8 Comparative synthesis and best practices for the Netherlands 221
7.9 Conclusion 234

8 Conclusion 237
8.1 Introduction 237
8.2 Part I: a legal-normative perspective 238
8.3 Part II: an empirical perspective 245
8.4 Part III: a comparative perspective 249
8.5 Main conclusion 250
8.6 Methodological reflection: strengths and limitations 252
8.7 Recommendations 253
8.7.1 Implications for policy and practice 253
8.7.2 Suggestions for future research 263

References 265

Appendix 1: Questionnaire 'Experiences of notaries with the levenstestament' 277

Appendix 2: Interview schedule Adult cohort 1 – interview study 'The levenstestament in practice' 289

Appendix 3: Interview schedule Attorney cohort 1 – interview study 'The levenstestament in practice' 299

Appendix 4: Interview schedule Attorney cohort 2 – interview study 'The levenstestament in practice' 307

Appendix 5: Country report Belgium 315

Appendix 6: Country report England and Wales 343

Appendix 7: Country report Germany 387

Appendix 8: Country report Switzerland 421

Samenvatting / Dutch summary 459

Summary 463

Dankwoord / Acknowledgements 467

Curriculum Vitae and Publications 469

1 General introduction

1.1 Introduction

In some instances, the ability of adults to exercise their rights and duties and protect their own interests can be impaired. This inability to decide and act can result from a progressive condition, such as dementia, which can cause a gradual decline in decision-making capacity. It concerns a significant group here. Currently, more than 290.000 people in the Netherlands have dementia. This number will increase to over half a million in the next 25 years.[1] An inability to decide and act can also occur suddenly. A car accident, for example, can lead to a severe brain injury. Or a stroke may relatively suddenly cause a coma. During the Covid-19 pandemic, some adults were so severely ill that they had to be put in an induced coma to receive ventilation treatment in the intensive care unit.

As in many other countries, the law in the Netherlands provides protection for adults when their ability to decide and act is impaired. This protection has traditionally been offered through adult guardianship measures. In Dutch law, three adult guardianship measures can be distinguished: *curatele* (full guardianship), *beschermingsbewind* (financial guardianship or protective trust) and *mentorschap* (personal guardianship).[2] All three measures involve the appointment of a guardian to manage the adult's affairs (financial, personal or both) on the adult's behalf. However, these measures also result in a limitation or deprivation of the adult's legal capacity. In other words, adults are restricted in their ability to exercise their rights and duties themselves.[3]

1. Alzheimer Nederland, via: https://www.alzheimer-nederland.nl/factsheet-cijfers-en-feiten-over-dementie# (last accessed: 17-03-2023).
2. See section 16 (articles 378-391), section 19 (articles 431-449) and section 20 (articles 450-462) of Book 1 of the Dutch Civil Code.
3. As will be discussed more elaborately in subsequent chapters of this book, the words 'capacity' and its counterpart 'incapacity' can be used in different contexts and for various purposes. Ruck Keene notes that both terms can have a least two different meanings. The first, legal capacity, comprises both the ability to hold rights and duties (legal standing) and the ability to exercise those rights and duties (legal agency). The second, often referred to as mental capacity, concerns the decision-making skills of a person (A. Ruck Keene, 'Fundamental Definitions' in: R. Frimston,

In 2010, the Dutch Association for Notarial Estate Planners presented a format for a new instrument in the Netherlands called a 'levenstestament'. An instrument that allows adults to make their own provisions in advance for a future period of incapacity, thus avoiding an adult guardianship measure and a limitation of thweir legal capacity. The *levenstestament* has been designed and conceptualised by the Dutch notariate within the framework of existing law. As such, the word *levenstestament* does not appear in Dutch statutory law. In practice, the word is used as an umbrella term for several enduring documents often distinguished in other countries.[4] Adults can include in their *levenstestament* a continuing power of attorney (CPA), defined by the Council of Europe as 'a mandate given by a capable adult with the purpose that it shall remain in force, or enter into force, in the event of the granter's incapacity'.[5] Adults can also include advance directives in their *levenstestament*, defined as 'instructions given or wishes made by a capable adult concerning issues that may arise in the event of his or her incapacity'.[6] Such instructions or wishes can be addressed to the attorney but also to third parties in the form of a medical treatment advance directive (article 7:450(3) of the Dutch Civil Code) or a directive addressed to the court containing the adult's choice of representative in case the court deems an adult guardianship measure necessary.

Over the past decade, the *levenstestament* has become increasingly popular in the Netherlands.[7] As a result, more and more people are relying on their own provisions for a future period of incapacity. Importantly, however, the *levenstestament* becomes active when adults are likely less and less able to indicate whether the *levenstestament* is carried out according to their wishes and preferences. This calls for research exploring whether the adult's trust in the *levenstestament* is justified. More specifically, research exploring the adult's expectations when making a *levenstestament*, research into the attorney's experiences and problems encountered in practice and, in sum, research exploring whether the *levenstestament* lives up to its expectations. A gradual decline of cognitive abilities and incapacity often also means that the adult becomes

A. Ruck Keene, C. van Overdijk & A.D. Ward, *The International Protection of Adults*, Oxford: Oxford University Press 2015, pp. 3-7).

4. The literal translation of the word 'levenstestament' would be 'living will'. Since this phrase is abroad frequently used to denote treatment advance directives in which an adult can specify that certain (medical) treatment is under circumstances refused, the use of this phrase to denote the Dutch 'levenstestament' was not considered appropriate. As the *levenstestament* combines two instruments which are internationally often distinguished, it is difficult to find an appropriate translation in English, other than for example a general phrase such as 'anticipatory decision-making instrument'. In the end, I have decided not to use a translation, but to continue using the Dutch term 'levenstestament' instead.
5. Principle 2 of the Council of Europe Recommendation CM/Rec (2009)11.
6. Ibid.
7. KNB, Factsheet Testamenten, July 2021, via: https://www.knb.nl/actueel/factsheets (last accessed: 05-10-2021).

increasingly unable to supervise the execution of the *levenstestament*. In the absence of a specific regulatory framework, there are concerns about whether the adult is adequately protected against misuse or abuse of the *levenstestament* by the attorney.[8] This means research exploring whether there are sufficient safeguards against misuse or abuse of the *levenstestament* by the attorney is also important.

Through a multidisciplinary study (legal-normative, empirical and comparative research), this book aims to address the aforementioned research lacunae by looking at the legal regulation of the *levenstestament* and the application of the *levenstestament* in practice. In doing so, this study takes into account the legal-normative context in which instruments such as the *levenstestament* operate. The *levenstestament* becomes active in a particular context – a setting in which the adult experiences a (gradual) decline in cognitive abilities – to which specific human rights norms and principles apply.[9] These human rights norms and principles – in particular, article 12 of the United Nations Convention on the Rights of Persons with Disabilities – have been used in this book as a benchmark to determine whether the *levenstestament* is suited to the task of empowering adults in the exercise of their legal capacity.

1.2 Legal-normative context

Over the years, the perception of how the interests of adults who, due to an impairment or insufficiency of their personal faculties, are unable to protect their own interests should be protected has been subject to significant change. Some even use the phrase 'paradigm shift' to denote the amplitude of this change.[10] In the framework of this change the legitimacy of traditional measures involving the appointment, by the state, of a representative who is to take decisions on behalf

8. See e.g. K. Blankman, 'Een wettelijke regeling voor het levenstestament?', in: F.W.J.M. Schols & B.C.M. Waaijer, *Het levenstestament. Nader verfijnd*, The Hague: Sdu 2017, pp. 45-64. As will be explained in more detail in chapter 4 of this book, the phrase 'misuse' is used to refer to situations where the inappropriate use of the anticipatory decision-making instrument by the attorney is unintentional (e.g. a situation where inappropriate use occurs because the attorney is ill-informed or unaware of certain responsibilities). The phrase 'abuse' on the other hand refers to situations where the inappropriate use of the anticipatory decision-making instrument is intentional.
9. As I will discuss in more detail in section 1.4, the *levenstestament* can also be used for purposes other than making provisions for a future period of incapacity (e.g. adults who are in good health but simply prefer someone else to manage their affairs for them). However, this book focuses on the specific setting in which the *levenstestament* is used to make provisions for a future period of incapacity.
10. D. Lush, 'The civil law and the common law' in: R. Frimston, A. Ruck Keene, C. van Overdijk & A.D. Ward, *The International Protection of Adults*, Oxford: Oxford University Press 2015, pp. 37-52 (46); K. Booth-Glen, 'Changing Paradigms: Mental Capacity, Legal Capacity, Guardianship, and Beyond', *Columbia Human Rights Law Review* 2012 vol. 44, pp. 93-169. See also United Nations Committee on the Rights of Persons with Disabilities, General Comment No. 1. Article 12: Equal Recognition before the law, 2014.

of the adult – also referred to as a substitute decision-maker – and a limitation or deprivation of the adult's legal capacity is increasingly questioned.[11] This stark notion of protection as a starting point, where the state and the law aim to protect and secure the rights and interests of those, who cannot do so themselves, by restricting their legal capacity, is considered by many to be paternalistic.[12] Perhaps not surprisingly, given the extent to which such measures interfere with the adult's private life, the adult's right to autonomy and self-determination and the adult's right to be treated as equal before the law have come to the forefront in recent decades.[13]

Nowhere is this more clearly expressed than in the United Nations Convention on the Rights of Persons with Disabilities (UNCRPD), where article 3 UNCRPD lists 'respect for inherent dignity, individual autonomy including the freedom to make one's own choices, and independence of persons' as the first general principle of the Convention. Moreover, article 12(2) UNCRPD stipulates that persons with disabilities should be granted the right to enjoy legal capacity on an equal basis with others concerning all aspects of life. However, at the same time, states are also obliged under the Convention to protect adults. According to article 16 UNCRPD, states are obliged to take appropriate steps to protect adults from exploitation, violence and abuse. In addition, according to article 12(4) UNCRPD, states must ensure that all measures relating to the exercise of legal capacity come with appropriate and effective safeguards to prevent abuse.

Regarding the rights to autonomy and protection, there is no hierarchy where one right takes precedence over the other.[14] In other words, a proper balance must be struck between these two rights. Article 12(3) UNCRPD makes clear that support is the key to achieving this balance.[15] The article reads: 'States Parties shall take appropriate measures to provide access by persons with disabilities to the support they may require in exercising their legal capacity'. In other words, states should refrain from protection through a limitation or deprivation of legal capacity and instead empower adults to exercise their legal capacity through support.[16] However, the question of what this support should entail is subject to debate. As will be discussed more extensively in the subsequent chapters of this book,

11. United Nations Committee on the Rights of Persons with Disabilities, General Comment No. 1. Article 12: Equal Recognition before the law, 2014.
12. I. Doron, 'Mental incapacity, guardianship, and the elderly: An exploratory study of Ontario's consent and capacity board', *Canadian Journal of Law and Society* 2003, 18(1), pp. 131-145 (131).
13. E. Ryrstedt, 'Dementia and autonomy' in E. Numhauser-Henning, *Elder Law. Evolving European Perspectives*, Cheltenham: Edward Elgar Publishing 2017, pp. 358-378 (360).
14. Ryrstedt 2017, p. 365.
15. Ryrstedt 2017, p. 360 & 365.
16. A. Arstein-Kerslake & E. Flynn, 'The General Comment on Article 12 of the Convention on the Rights of Persons with Disabilities: a roadmap for equality before the law', *The International Journal of Human Rights* 2016 vol 20, no. 4, pp. 471-491 (475).

this discussion centres around two critical issues regarding the interpretation of article 12 UNCRPD. The first has already been mentioned above and concerns the legitimacy of measures involving the appointment of a substitute decision-maker and the restriction of the adult's legal capacity. It is argued, first and foremost by the Committee on the Rights of Persons with Disabilities (the Committee), that these so-called measures of substitute decision-making should be abandoned and that states should instead develop alternative instruments of supported decision-making.[17] The second issue concerns the weight to be accorded to the will and preferences of the adult. The Committee notes in this regard that while measures of substitute decision-making frequently amount to decisions being taken in the 'best interest' of the adult, supported decision-making alternatives should give primacy to the adult's own will and preferences.[18] To date, the discussion as to these two issues is still ongoing. Accordingly, the Netherlands has adopted the following stand, expressed through an interpretative statement concerning article 12 UNCRPD upon ratification of the UNCRPD:

> The Kingdom of the Netherlands recognizes that persons with disabilities enjoy legal capacity on an equal basis with others in all aspects of life. Furthermore, the Kingdom of the Netherlands declares its understanding that the Convention allows for supported and substitute decision-making arrangements in appropriate circumstances and in accordance with the law. The Kingdom of the Netherlands interprets Article 12 as restricting substitute decision-making arrangements to cases where such measures are necessary, as a last resort and subject to safeguards.[19]

Although the debate on the interpretation of Article 12(3) UNCRPD is still ongoing, there seems to be consensus that under this provision, measures and instruments that enable adults to exercise their legal capacity should be preferred. In other words, there has been a change of perspective in that the starting point has changed. Instead of providing adults with impaired capacity with protection through a restriction of their legal capacity, the emphasis should be put on measures empowering adults to exercise their legal capacity. The Netherlands has acknowledged this in its interpretative statement by declaring that substitute decision-making arrangements, which in the Netherlands include a limitation or deprivation of legal capacity, should only be used when necessary and as a last resort.[20] In other words, a setting where adults are empowered to exercise

17. United Nations Committee on the Rights of Persons with Disabilities, General Comment No. 1. Article 12: Equal Recognition before the law, 2014, p. 6.
18. Ibid.
19. United Nations Treaty Collection, Chapter IV-15 Convention on the Rights of Persons with Disabilities, via: https://treaties.un.org/Pages/ViewDetails.aspx?src=TREATY&mtdsg_no=IV-15&chapter=4&clang=_en#EndDec (last accessed: 06-01-2022).
20. This has again been acknowledged in the Initial report submitted by the Netherlands under article 35 of the UNCRPD, p. 19.

their legal capacity is required. The question is what this change of perspective means for the Netherlands. This is, first of all, a question that has to be answered concerning the system of adult protection measures and instruments in the Netherlands as a whole. Are the current measures and instruments aimed at the protection of adults with impaired capacity compliant with the UNCRPD, and is the interpretative statement made by the Dutch state adhered to in practice? In case of non-compliance, is this non-compliance remediable? Can current measures and instruments be adjusted, or must new ones be designed? How do current measures and instruments relate to each other? Are there particular measures or instruments preferable to others?[21]

The question of how adults can be empowered in the exercise of their legal capacity is not only a question that has to be asked on a systemic level but also on an instrumental level concerning specific measures and instruments aimed at the empowerment and protection of adults. With a levenstestament, adults remain legally able to decide and act for themselves. However, it is important to explore whether adults – through this instrument – also receive the support needed to exercise their legal capacity. Adults can only be supported in the exercise of their legal capacity in a setting where there is also sufficient protection against misuse and abuse of the *levenstestament*. Concerns in this regard have already been outlined above. Although cases of misuse or abuse of the *levenstestament* have come to light, research looking into the prevalence, nature and consequences of misuse or abuse of the *levenstestament* is currently lacking. More information is needed to develop tailored safeguards to counteract the misuse and abuse of the *levenstestament*. As noted above, a *levenstestament* is made to provide for a future period of incapacity and becomes applicable when the adult will most likely be increasingly less able to indicate whether the *levenstestament* is executed according to his wishes and preferences. This makes research addressing these questions all the more important.

1.3 Research questions

The central research question that will be answered in this book is:

Is the Dutch levenstestament, both in theory and in practice, suited to the task of empowering adults with impaired capacity in the exercise of their legal capacity by ensuring that both their right to autonomy and self-determination and their right to protection are balanced and, if not, how can it be improved?

21. In this book, these questions are addressed only in the margin of chapter 2. However, at the time of completion of this book, a six-year multidisciplinary research project exploring precisely these questions is ongoing in the Netherlands.

This main question will be answered through six sub-questions, which are in line with subsequent chapters:

1. How does the *levenstestament* fit within the changed and still changing international landscape concerning the empowerment and protection of adults with impaired capacity?

2. What is known from international and national research about the risk of misuse or abuse of continuing powers of attorney, such as the *levenstestament*? What do appropriate safeguards in this respect look like?

3. What is the regulatory framework in the Netherlands on which the *levenstestament* is based? And is this regulatory framework compliant with article 12 UNCRPD?

4. How is the *levenstestament* applied in practice?

5. What are the expectations adults have when they decide to make a *levenstestament*? What are the expectations of nominated attorneys regarding their (future) role? And what are the experiences of active attorneys with the *levenstestament* in practice?

6. What are the experiences of other jurisdictions with enduring documents? Which problems are experienced in other jurisdictions? Which solutions have been found? And what are best practices that might be adopted as a solution to similar problems experienced in the Netherlands?

1.4 Research delineation

As becomes apparent from the main research question and the sub questions, this book focuses on the theoretical and practical setting in which the *levenstestament* is used to provide for a future period of incapacity. International and national research shows that enduring documents are also used for purposes other than making provisions for a future period of incapacity.[22] Engelbertink refers to adults who, due to their physical condition, cannot take care of some or all of their affairs or adults, who are in good health, but prefer someone else to take care of their affairs.[23] However, the difference between these situations and the situation

22. J. Thurston, *A Practitioner's Guide to Powers of Attorney*, Croydon: Bloomsbury Publishing 2015; J. Wilson, C. Tilse, D. Setterlund, and L. Rosenman, 'Older People and Their Assets: A Range of Roles and Issues for Social Workers', *Australian Social Work* 2009 (62-2), pp. 155-167.
23. C.G.C. Engelbertink, 'Het levenstestament in de maatschappij', in: K. Blankman & C.G.C. Engelbertink, *Notariële bescherming ouderen*, Sdu Uitgevers: Den Haag 2013, pp. 59-110 (60 & 62-63). Examples of the first group of adults concern adults with hearing or visual impairments. Regarding the second group, Engelbertink refers to adults struggling with a society

in which an enduring document is used to provide for future incapacity is that adults, in the first instance, will generally be able to supervise the execution of the *levenstestament*, in particular the actions of the attorney themselves. Research shows that this becomes increasingly difficult for adults when their ability to act and decide is declining.[24] This makes the question of safeguards preventing the misuse or abuse of enduring documents a pressing one. In a situation of impaired capacity, different standards are required to ensure that the adult is empowered in the exercise of his legal capacity, and it is this setting on which this book focuses.

In addition to this first delineation of the research question, another delineation was made. Internationally two enduring documents are generally distinguished: the continuing power of attorney (CPA) and the advance directive (AD). The CPA concerns, as said, a conferral of authority to the attorney to act on behalf of the adult in the event of incapacity.[25] Whereas ADs consist of statements involving the adult's wishes, preferences and instructions in the event of his incapacity. The distinction between these two instruments can be considered somewhat arbitrary as a CPA will, in all likelihood, also include to some extent wishes, preferences and instructions addressed to the attorney, instructing him on how to act. In addition, studying the primarily medical literature on advance directives, one also finds the notion of proxy directives within advance directives, where an attorney is appointed to explain the adult's wishes and instructions as recorded in the advance directive.[26] Taking this into account, Ward makes a distinction between the two instruments based on the following presumption:

---

where more and more matters are being organised via the internet (e.g. transfer of money, filling in the tax form, etc.). In these situations, adults might prefer someone else to take care of their 'digital' affairs. See also S. Mos-Van Gool, 'Het levenstestament in de praktijk', in: A.R. Autar, J.P.M. Stubbé & L.C.A. Verstappen, *Compendium Levenstestament*, Sdu Uitgevers: Den Haag 2021, pp. 79-92 (81).

24. S. Davidson, P. Rossall, and S. Hart, *Financial Abuse Evidence Review*, Age UK 2015, p. 7; D. Bagshaw, S. Wendt, L. Zannettino, and V. Adams, 'Financial Abuse of Older People by Family Members: Views. and Experiences of Older Australians and their Family Members', *Australian Social Work* 2013 (66-1), pp. 86-103 (101); J. Manthorpe, K. Samsi, and J. Rapaport, 'Responding to the Financial Abuse of People with Dementia: A Qualitative Study of Safeguarding Experiences in England', *International Psychogeriatrics* 2012 (24-9), pp. 1454-1464 (1454).

25. K. Purser, T. Cockburn, C. Cross, and H. Jacmon, 'Alleged Financial Abuse of Those under an Enduring Power of Attorney: An Exploratory Study', *British Journal of Social Work* 2018 (48), pp. 887-905 (891).

26. C. Vezzoni, *The legal status and social practice of treatment directives in the Netherlands*, dissertation RUG, 2005, pp. 12-16.

> 'The instructions and wishes in a CPA are directed to the attorney, who is responsible for implementing them. The instructions and wishes in an advance directive apply directly as "the voice of the granter", without being directed through another party such as an attorney.'[27]

The distinction here is based on whether or not an intermediary is involved in conveying the adult's wishes and instructions. According to Ward's interpretation, an AD differs from a CPA in that wishes and instructions are not directed through another party but directly addressed to a third party. The most common examples in this regard are treatment directives, in which the adult can specify which medical treatment under certain conditions is desired or refused, and directives addressed to the court in the context of an adult guardianship procedure, nominating the person to be appointed as guardian.[28] Ward's interpretation is not undisputed, and to date, various terms and ways of demarcating the two instruments are still being used. Notwithstanding this ambiguity, it is clear that both instruments, as distinguished by Ward, can, in the Netherlands, be included in the *levenstestament*.[29] A *levenstestament* can, in other words, encompass the conferral of authority to the attorney, including wishes and instructions directed to the attorney as to how to act, as well as treatment directives and directives addressed to the court in the event of an adult guardianship procedure. That is, however, not to say that both the CPA and the AD do not exist 'in their own right' in the Netherlands. Indeed, the possibility of drafting a so-called non-treatment advance directive has existed since 1995. And with the enactment of the Euthanasia law in 2002, adults in the Netherlands obtained the possibility to draft a euthanasia advance directive. These treatment directives, as such, have already been the subject of considerable research in the Netherlands.[30] This research has not been replicated in the context of this book. The research featuring in this book focuses on what is internationally referred to as a CPA, including the wishes and instructions addressed to the attorney. This aspect of the *levenstestament* was considered insufficiently studied.

27. A.D. Ward, *Enabling citizens to plan for incapacity. A review of follow-up action taken by member states of the Council of Europe to Recommendation CM/Rec(2009)11 on principles concerning continuing powers of attorney and advance directives for incapacity*, Strasbourg: Council of Europe 2018, p. 20-21.
28. M.E. de Boer, *Advance directives in dementia care. Perspectives of people with Alzheimer's disease, elderly care physicians and relatives*, 2011, p. 14.
29. This is possible since the *levenstestament* in the Netherlands is, to date, not regulated by law. Instead, it is a 'product' developed by the notarial profession within the framework of the existing law.
30. Most notably, the studies conducted by Vezzoni (2005) focusing on treatment advance directives and De Boer focusing, among others, on euthanasia advance directives.

1.5 Research design

To answer the main research question and the sub-questions formulated in section 1.3, a multidisciplinary research design was adopted using a mixed methods approach combining legal-dogmatic, empirical and comparative research. To answer sub-questions 1, 2 and 3, relevant national and international legal literature was studied. A survey study among Dutch notaries and an analysis of relevant published court cases were used to examine how the *levenstestament* is applied in practice (sub-question 4). An important aim of this book was also to gain an impression of the perspective of those involved in using a *levenstestament*. To that end, an interview study in cohort design was conducted, looking at the expectations of adults and nominated attorneys when making the *levenstestament* and the experiences of active attorneys when executing the *levenstestament*. This interview study was used to answer sub-question 5. Finally, a legal-comparative study, involving a quick scan of European countries and a subsequent in-depth study of four jurisdictions (Belgium, Germany, England & Wales and Switzerland), was conducted to answer sub-question 6. Connecting the various research components in the conclusion, this book can be characterised as an 'empirical legal research' study.[31] Bijleveld describes empirical legal research as research studying the underlying assumptions on which laws and procedures are built, examining how the law is applied in practice and exploring the intended and unintended (side-)effects of the law.[32] The focus in research addressing the question of how (conflicting) rights should be balanced often lies on legal-dogmatic research. However, in the context of adult protection measures and instruments, it seems just as important to study the underlying assumptions on which adult protection measures and instruments are based, to explore how these measures and instruments function in practice and to examine the effects of these measures and instruments. The following observation by Donnelly highlights this:

> 'Normative choices always come at a cost. More relaxed legal frameworks make supported decision-making more accessible for people with impaired capacity, but they may also leave a potentially vulnerable person at greater risk of abuse. More stringent legal frameworks may reduce the possibility of abuse, but they also reduce the accessibility of support and are invasive in the private and family/relational lives of the person and his or her supporters. In this context, it is also worth noting that we lack empirical evidence regarding the link between stringent legal frameworks and reduced instances of abuse. We may have an instinct that stringent legal

---

31. The phrase 'empirical legal research' is frequently used interchangeably with 'empirical legal studies' (C.C.J.H. Bijleveld, *Research Methods for Empirical Legal Studies: An Introduction*, Den Haag: Eleven International Publishers 2019, p. 5).
32. Bijleveld 2019, pp. 3-4.

> frameworks reduce abuse, but we cannot say definitively that more people are abused when the framework is relaxed and fewer when it is stringent.'[33]

In other words, when it comes to answering the main research question of this book, it seems important to add some empirical colour to the study of how both the right to protection and the right to autonomy in the context of the *levenstestament* should be balanced. With regard to the right to protection, this means using the available information as to what is known on the risk of misuse and abuse of enduring documents to establish what appropriate safeguards look like (question 2). Regarding the right to autonomy, this means studying the expectations and experiences with the levenstestament of both adults and attorneys to better understand what the right to autonomy in practice entails. These insights are subsequently combined with the outcomes of the legal-dogmatic and the comparative study to provide an answer to the main research question.

A more detailed overview of the methods used is presented below.

Literature studies

A study of national and international (academic) literature and national parliamentary documents has been conducted to answer sub-questions 1, 2 and 3. Different national (Legal Intelligence and Rechtsorde) and international (Web of Science, PubMed and Google Scholar) search engines have been used to identify relevant literature. In addition, national (e.g. WPNR) and international (e.g. International Journal of Law and Psychiatry) journals have been checked for relevant publications. The snowball method was used to complement the identified literature with other relevant literature. References in the identified articles have been checked for other interesting literature. In addition, the option provided by several search engines, such as Google Scholar, to search for literature in which a particular article has been cited has been used to identify more recent articles. Relevant parliamentary documents have been identified using the search function on the website of the Dutch government.[34]

Study of published court cases

A study of court cases – published by the Council for the Judiciary – in which the *levenstestament* plays a significant role has been conducted to answer sub-questions 2 and 4.[35] All cases published since the emergence of the *levenstestament* until the completion of the study in mid-July 2021 have been included in the study.[36]

33. M. Donnelly, 'Deciding in dementia: The possibilities and limits of supported decision-making', *International Journal of Law and Psychiatry*, 2019, vol. 66, pp. 1-7 (p. 4).
34. zoek.officielebekendmakingen.nl (last accessed: 06-12-2020).
35. It concerns cases published on the website www.rechtspraak.nl.
36. The first court case included in this study was published on 14-08-2012.

Subsequently, a distinction between two types of court cases has been made. First, I looked at cases where the judiciary, in the absence of a statutory framework, has steered the development of the *levenstestament* by providing certain directions. For example, directions concerning the position of the *levenstestament* vis-à-vis the adult guardianship measures. This information has been used to answer sub-question three concerning the regulatory framework on which the *levenstestament* in the Netherlands is based. A second type of cases were cases where the court, notwithstanding the presence of a *levenstestament*, was confronted with a request for an adult guardianship measure. The expectation was that these cases might shed light on the problems with the *levenstestament* in practice. This information has been used to answer sub-question four concerning the application of the levenstestament in *practice.*

Survey study

In addition to the study of published court cases, a survey study among Dutch notaries was conducted to answer sub-question 4. Although the involvement of a professional is not required in the Netherlands, a significant number of adults use the services of a notary to make a *levenstestament*. The survey aimed to learn more about the experiences of this profession with the *levenstestament*. The study was conducted in 2018, and with the generous support of the Dutch Notarial Association (*Koninklijke Notariële Beroepsorganisatie* – KNB), all members of the KNB could be invited to participate. The survey consisted of both open and closed questions. The response to the open questions has been analysed using content analysis, while the response to the closed questions has been analysed through descriptive statistics using SPSS.

Interview study

To capture the experiences across different phases of the life-span of the *levenstestament* (sub-question 5), a so-called cohort study was conducted, consisting of interviews with both adults who had recently made a *levenstestament* and their nominated attorneys (cohort 1) and interviews with active attorneys (cohort 2). In cohort 1, interviews were conducted with 23 adults and six attorneys. In cohort 2, interviews were conducted with 16 attorneys. The method for these interviews was essentially the same. A semi-structured interview guide was used for each interview, which allowed the researcher to ask additional questions based on information brought up by the respondent during the interview. The interviews generally lasted between 30 minutes and 2 hours and were conducted face-to-face and online (via Zoom and Skype) during the Covid-19 pandemic. The interviews were recorded and transcribed by two interns. Atlas-TI was used to aid the analysis of the interviews.

Comparative law study
The sixth and final sub-question has been answered through a legal-comparative law study looking at the experiences of other jurisdictions with enduring documents, similar to the Dutch *levenstestament*. This study aimed to identify best practices abroad that might provide a solution to the problems identified in the regulation and application of the *levenstestament* in the Netherlands (sub-questions 1 to 5). A selection of jurisdictions was made with the help of a quickscan. The report 'Enabling citizens to plan for incapacity', a review of the follow-up action undertaken by member states of the Council of Europe on Recommendation CM/Rec(2009)11 on principles concerning continuing powers of attorney and advance directives for incapacity, produced by Adrian Ward, was used as a basis for this quickscan. This means the quickscan was confined to an assessment of European jurisdictions, specifically member states of the Council of Europe. Based on the quickscan, four jurisdictions (Belgium, England and Wales, Germany and Switzerland) were selected for an in-depth study. The study of each jurisdiction commenced with a desk study of relevant literature and case law at home. Thanks to a fellowship grant from the Dutch Alzheimer Society, I was subsequently able to visit each jurisdiction for three weeks to finalise my study of the law in the books and gain an impression of the law in action. During these research visits, interviews were conducted with scholars and practitioners, such as notaries, judges, government officials, lawyers and physicians, to gain an impression of the socio-legal context in which the enduring documents operate.

1.6 Research overview

This book consists of eight chapters. Chapters 2, 3, 6 and 7 contain articles that have been published, which means some repetition is unavoidable.[37] The text of these articles has not been changed, which means that some terms and phrases used in these articles do not correspond with the rest of the chapters in this book. Examples include the use of the phrase 'vulnerable adult' and 'living will' in chapter 2.[38] As noted above, the perception of how the interests of adults with impaired capacity should be protected has been subject to change. Instead of protection through a restriction of legal capacity, adults should be empowered, through support, in the exercise of their legal capacity. Chapter 2 sets the stage by discussing what this change of perspective means for the system of adult protection measures and instruments in the Netherlands. It outlines the legal-normative context in which the *levenstestament* operates. Chapter 3 provides an overview of what is known from international and national research on

37. Apart from minor textual amendments, no changes have been made to the content of these publications.
38. As footnote 4 and section 1.6 make clear I have changed my mind regarding using these phrases since the publication of the article included in chapter 2.

the risk of misuse and abuse of enduring documents. This information is then used to operationalise the requirement of article 12(4) UNCRPD to provide for appropriate safeguards to prevent abuse in the context of CPAs. Chapter 4 focuses on the legal nature and scope of the *levenstestament* in the Netherlands and whether this regulatory framework complies with Article 12 UNCRPD. Chapters 5 and 6 discuss empirical research findings on how the *levenstestament* functions in practice. Chapter 5 discusses the results of two studies looking into how the *levenstestament* is perceived by the notariate on the one hand and the judiciary on the other. Chapter 6 discusses the findings of a qualitative study focussing on the expectations of both adults who recently made a *levenstestament* and their nominated attorneys and the experiences of active attorneys with the *levenstestament* in practice. Chapter 7 focuses on the problems identified in chapters 2-6 and discusses the results of a comparative study looking at best practices adopted abroad, providing a potential solution to problems identified in the Netherlands. Chapter 8 comprises a general conclusion and a discussion of the practical implications that can be derived from the aforementioned studies. This is followed by recommendations to the relevant societal actors regarding possible improvements and recommendations for future research directions.

1.7 Terminology

Last but not least, it is necessary to say a few words about the terminology used in this book. In the past, various, sometimes derogatory, terms have been used to refer to the class of adults featured in this book. Examples are: incapacitated adults, mentally retarded adults, and vulnerable adults, etc. Given the variety of the terms used and the fact that some of these terms have been or are still being used to refer to adults who are considered as being less than a full legal actor, I have grappled with choosing an appropriate, respectful term to refer to the adults featured in this book. This is reflected, for example, in the expression 'vulnerable adults' used in chapter 2, an expression that I now no longer consider appropriate. In the end, I based my use of terminology on the factual description provided in article 1 of the Convention on the International Protection of Adults (the Hague 35): 'adults who, by reason of an impairment or insufficiency of their personal faculties, are not in a position to protect their interests'. In this book, I use the term' adult' when referring to this class of adults. In cases where it was necessary to distinguish between adults and adults as falling under the scope of article 1 of the Hague 35, I use the factual term 'adults with impaired capacity', as provided by the authors of the book *The International Protection of Adults*.[39] There is one exception to this rule, in cases where reference was made to international human rights documents, the

39. R. Frimston, A. Ruck Keene, C. van Overdijk & A.D. Ward, *The International Protection of Adults*, Oxford: Oxford University Press 2015.

language and terminology adopted by the particular treaty or convention have, in most cases, been used.

2 A changing paradigm of protection of vulnerable adults and its implications for the Netherlands

This chapter was published as: H.N. Stelma-Roorda, C. Blankman & M.V. Antokolskaia, 'A changing paradigm of protection of vulnerable adults and its implications for the Netherlands', Family & Law 2019.

2.1 Introduction

With the phrase 'protection of adults', the Convention on the International Protection of Adults refers in article 1(1) to 'adults who, by reason of an impairment or insufficiency of their personal faculties, are not in a position to protect their interests'. The perception of how the interests of these vulnerable adults should be protected has changed over time. There has been a shift in the protection paradigm, from paternalism and a substitute decision-making approach to autonomy and a supportive decision-making human rights-based approach. In the framework of this shift, in addition to traditional adult guardianship measures, new instruments have been developed allowing adults to play a greater role in the protection of their (future) interests. This has also been the case in the Netherlands, where adults in the course of the last decade have acquired the possibility to make a so-called living will, internationally better known as a continuing, enduring or lasting power of attorney. The aim of this article is to discuss this instrument, in comparison with the traditional adult guardianship measures currently in force in the Netherlands, from the perspective of the new protection paradigm based on a human rights approach. To this end, in the following paragraph, we will try to delineate the historical context of the new protection paradigm and the human rights approach. Then in paragraph 3, we will focus on the influence of article 12 of the Convention on the Rights of Persons with Disabilities (UNCRPD) and the controversy around its implications for the protection paradigm.[1] In paragraph 4, we will provide an outline of the attempt to go beyond this controversy – the so-called alternate framework developed by

1. https://www.un.org/development/desa/disabilities/convention-on-the-rights-of-persons-with-disabilities.html. The Convention has been ratified by 177 countries, including the Netherlands (14 June 2016).

Martin *et al.* In paragraph 5 we will elaborate on what kind of measures could meet the requirements of article 12 of the UNCRPD and what kind of safeguards should be incorporated therein. In paragraph 6, we will deal with the question whether the traditional adult guardianship measures in the Netherlands, based on substitute decision-making schemes, are compliant with the new protection paradigm. In paragraph 7, we will discuss the potential of the living will as an instrument of supportive decision-making. The conclusion will comprise some final remarks and suggestions for the future.

2.2 Historical context – embedding the new human rights-based paradigm

In many jurisdictions the concept of 'capacity' is used to determine when and how measures to protect the interests of adults with an intellectual impairment can be taken.[2] The term 'capacity' can be used in at least two different ways, both of which are used in the Netherlands. The term denotes either 'legal' capacity' or 'mental capacity'. The Committee on the Rights of Persons with Disabilities (the Committee) explains the difference between these two as follows: legal capacity involves 'the ability to hold rights and duties (legal standing) and to exercise those rights and duties (legal agency)', while mental capacity refers to 'the decision-making skills of a person'.[3] Over time the scope and meaning of both these concepts have changed. In this regard three models can be distinguished. The first and second model together with an overview of their historical context will be discussed in the remainder of this paragraph. The emergence of the third model will be discussed in the next paragraph.

One of the first, if not the first, provisions aimed at the protection of an adult with an intellectual impairment can be found in Old Roman law. Table V of the Twelve Tables, drawn up around 450-451 BC, reads: *Si furiosus escit, adgnatum gentiliumque in eo pecuniaque eius potestas esto.*[4] Or in English: 'a *furiosus* is placed under the guardianship of his family members with his person and money'.[5] Responsible for the guardianship of the *furiosus*, or incapacitated adult, was the *curator furiosi*, which was either the nearest relative in the male line or the nearest male relative

2. A. Ruck Keene, 'Fundamental Definitions', in: R. Frimston, A. Ruck Keene, C. van Overdijk & A.D. Ward (eds.), The International Protection of Adults, Oxford – New York: Oxford University Press 2015, pp. 5-6. In the Netherlands the term 'handelings(on)bekwaamheid' and 'wils(on)bekwaamheid' are customary.
3. United Nations Committee on the Rights of Persons with Disabilities, General Comment No. 1. Article 12: Equal Recognition before the law, 2014, p. 3.
4. M. Kaser, *Römisches Privatrecht. Ein Studienbuch.* 15 Auflage, München: C.H. Beck'sche Verlagsbuchhandlung 1989, p. 297.
5. K. Blankman, 'Guardianship Models in the Netherlands and Western Europe', *International Journal of Law and Psychiatry* 1997 vol. 20, no. 1, pp. 47-57.

from the wider family unit (*gentes*).[6] During the Roman era, in a timespan of almost a thousand years, the character of the *cura furiosi* was subject to change and the involvement of the State increased. Although in Old Roman law the main aim of the *cura furiosi* was to preserve the family fortune for the next generation, in Classical Roman law the interests of the individual became more important.[7] In Old Roman law there was no official procedure to confirm incapacity and the nearest male relative automatically became *curator furiosi*. This changed however, and in Classical Roman law a *curator furiosi* started to be appointed by the magistrate if the male relatives were not considered suitable.[8]

The Roman legal concept of the *cura furiosi* forms the basis of what can be described as the traditional model.[9] Within this model a status-based approach is used to determine whether a person has capacity. Once it is established that an individual has an intellectual impairment, a lack of legal capacity is consequently presumed.[10] This means that a binary approach is adopted; either a person has legal capacity or he has not, there is no area in between.[11] Another example of the status-based approach is the legal incapacity of married women, in the Netherlands in place as late as 1956. The incapacitated adult loses his legal capacity completely and a proxy or guardian is appointed to represent and protect the adult. This guardian is to act in the objectively presumed best interest of the incapacitated adult, the subjective wishes and preferences of the adult himself are considered less important.[12] Until the 1960s this model was prevailing in many West European countries.[13] These countries often had just one guardianship-like measure similar to the Roman *cura furiosi*.[14]

6. K. Blankman, *Curatele voor personen met een geestelijke stoornis en bescherming op maat*, Zwolle: Tjeenk Willink 1994, pp. 5-6; Kaser 1989, p. 197; D. Lush, 'The Civil Law and the Common Law', in: R. Frimston, A. Ruck Keene, C. van Overdijk & A.D. Ward (eds.), *The international Protection of Adults*, Oxford – New York: Oxford University Press 2015, pp. 37-52.
7. Blankman 1994, p. 8-9; Lush 2015, p. 38.
8. Lush 2015, p. 38.
9. W. Fuchs, *Systems of advocacies for the elderly in a comparative perspective*, Presentation at the Advocacies for frail and incompetent elderly in Europe (ADEL) project final conference on 24 September 2010 in Berlin.
10. A. Dhanda, 'Legal Capacity in the Disability Rights Convention: Stranglehold of the Past or Lodestar for the Future', *Syracuse Journal of International Law and Commerce* 2007 vol. 34, pp. 429-462.
11. K. Booth-Glen, 'Changing Paradigms: Mental Capacity, Legal Capacity, Guardianship, and Beyond', *Columbia Human Rights Law Review* 2012 vol. 44, pp. 93-169.
12. Fuchs 2010, p. 2.
13. Blankman 1997, p. 48.
14. Although we restrict ourselves in this article to a discussion of the Roman concept of cura furiosi which has formed the basis for adult guardianship legislation in many civil law jurisdictions, a status-based approach was also adopted in common law jurisdictions. An example is England where around 1270 the wardship of the estates of 'idiots' was placed in the hand of the king as the 'parens patriae'. For more information, we refer to Lush 2015, pp. 40-43.

The development of human rights in general and patient's rights in particular that commenced after World War II, brought change.[15] The so-called 'welfare model' emerged and the status-based approach was replaced by a functional approach.[16] The Mental Capacity Act 2005 in force in England and Wales provides a good example of this approach.[17] Section two of the Mental Capacity Act makes clear that legal capacity is decision-specific, stating that 'a person lacks capacity in relation to a matter if at the material time he is unable to make a decision for himself in relation to the matter because of an impairment of, or a disturbance in the functioning of, the mind or brain'. Section three of the Act numerates the circumstances in which this is the case. In order to make a decision for himself a person must be able: 'to understand the information relevant to the decision; to retain that information; to use or weigh that information as part of the process of making the decision, or to communicate his decision'.[18] In other words, legal incapacity is not automatically presumed upon an intellectual impairment, instead the focus lies on the person's decision-making capabilities. As said, such an assessment should be carried out in relation to a particular decision. Inherent to the functional approach is that although a person may lack the mental capacity to make for example financial decisions, he may be perfectly able to make decisions on other topics. From this it then follows that protection measures need to be tailor-made, maximizing the autonomy of the adult and only offering protection where necessary.[19] As in the traditional status-based model, the welfare model presupposes that a guardian is appointed to represent and protect the adult. The difference is that in the welfare model the guardian has to take into account the wishes and preferences of the adult, even if they run contrary to what is considered to be in the adult's objective best interest.[20]

2.3 Article 12 UNCRPD: Two conflicting interpretations

The adoption of the Convention on the Rights of Persons with Disabilities by the United Nations General Assembly in 2006 marked, according to many, the emergence of a third, new human rights-based model or paradigm.[21] The key

15. Blankman 1997, p. 48.
16. Fuchs 2010, p. 3.
17. Although the functional approach embedded within the Mental Capacity Act 2005 is used to illustrate this approach, it is by no means assumed that this approach can only be linked to the second model. Indeed Martin *et al.* (2014) provide a convincing argument that the functional approach of the Mental Capacity Act 2005 can also be used within the human rights approach.
18. Mental Capacity Act 2005, s 3.
19. Blankman 1997, p. 48.
20. Fuchs 2010, p. 3.
21. E.g. Booth-Glen 2012; Dhanda 2007; E. Flynn & A. Arstein-Kerslake, 'The Support Model of Legal Capacity: Fact, Fiction, or Fantasy?', *Berkeley Journal of International Law* 2014 vol. 32, no. 1, pp. 124-143.

article in relation to capacity law is Article 12 UNCRPD, in particular the first four paragraphs, which read as follows:

> 'Equal recognition before the law
> 1. States Parties reaffirm that persons with disabilities have the right to recognition everywhere as persons before the law.
> 2. States Parties shall recognize that persons with disabilities enjoy legal capacity on an equal basis with others in all aspects of life.
> 3. States Parties shall take appropriate measures to provide access by persons with disabilities to the support they may require in exercising their legal capacity.
> 4. States Parties shall ensure that all measures that relate to the exercise of legal capacity provide for appropriate and effective safeguards to prevent abuse in accordance with international human rights law. Such safeguards shall ensure that measures relating to the exercise of legal capacity respect the rights, will and preferences of the person, are free of conflict of interest and undue influence, are proportional and tailored to the person's circumstances, apply for the shortest time possible and are subject to regular review by a competent, independent and impartial authority or judicial body. The safeguards shall be proportional to the degree to which such measures affect the person's rights and interests.'[22]

According to Flynn and Arstein-Kerslake article 12 UNCRPD should be understood as both calling for the respect for legal capacity of adults with a disability on an equal basis with other persons, and at the same time putting an obligation on States Parties to provide access to the support that is needed for exercising this legal capacity.[23] In other words: '[I]f an individual is having difficulty making a decision or communicating a decision, the answer is not to deny legal capacity to the individual, it is instead to provide access to support for the exercise of legal capacity'.[24]

Article 12 UNCRPD has, however, led to much debate with regard to its precise interpretation. In the two models described above, the traditional model and the welfare model, the presumption of incapacity is followed by a form of substitute decision-making. In both cases an adult loses legal capacity and is appointed a guardian to represent and protect his interests. The only difference is that in the first case the guardian acts according to the objective best interests of the adult and in the second case has to take into consideration the adult's wishes and

22. http://www.ohchr.org/EN/HRBodies/CRPD/Pages/ConventionRightsPersonsWithDisabilities.aspx.
23. Flynn & Arstein-Kerslake 2014, p. 128.
24. A. Arstein-Kerslake & E. Flynn, 'The General Comment on Article 12 of the Convention on the Rights of Persons with Disabilities: a roadmap for equality before the law', *The International Journal of Human Rights* 2016 vol 20, no. 4, pp. 471-491 (p. 475).

preferences. It has been argued that article 12 UNCRPD calls for the abolition of both these systems of substitute decision-making and instead requires the development of supported decision-making alternatives.[25] This interpretation of article 12 UNCRPD has been promoted by disability advocacy groups and within academia, but more importantly, it has also been embraced by the Committee on the Rights of Persons with Disabilities. In its General Comment on article 12 UNCRPD the Committee states:

> '[T]he Committee on the Rights of Persons with Disabilities has repeatedly stated that States parties must review "the laws allowing for guardianship and trusteeship, and take action to develop laws and policies to replace regimes of substitute decision-making by supported decision-making, which respects the person's autonomy, will and preferences".'[26]

This opinion by the Committee adds another important element to the interpretation of article 12 UNCRPD, which is that the best interest approach is to be replaced by an approach that respects the rights, will and preferences of the individual and is tailored to the individual's needs.[27]

Although the interpretation of article 12 UNCRPD described above is advocated by many, there are also those who remain sceptical. Martin *et al.* note that the Convention itself does not call for the abolition of substitute decision-making. They argue that the analysis of the *travaux préparatoires* of the UNCRPD suggests that the absence of such a call was quite deliberate.[28] Lush expresses his fear that the stance calling for abolition of substitute decision-making could potentially undermine the system of existing safeguards and harm vulnerable adults. He notes that 'some profoundly disabled individuals lack the ability to make any decisions at all, even with support, and for them there is no viable alternative to substitute decision-making'.[29] But perhaps more importantly, the European Court of Human Rights also seems to accept that a limitation of legal capacity and a form of substitute decision-making is sometimes necessary as a last resort. In its judgement on Ivinović v. Croatia the Court states:

25. E.g. Arstein-Kerslake & Flynn 2016; C. de Bhailís & E. Flynn, 'Recognising legal capacity: commentary and analysis of Article 12 CRPD', *International Journal of Law in Context* 2017 vol. 13, no. 1, pp. 6-21; Flynn & Arstein-Kerslake 2014.
26. United Nations Committee on the Rights of Persons with Disabilities, *General Comment No. 1. Article 12: Equal Recognition before the law*, 2014, p. 6.
27. Arstein-Kerslake & Flynn 2016, p. 476. A point upon which we will elaborate in paragraph 5.
28. W. Martin, S. Michalowski, J. Stavert, A. Ward, A. Ruck Keene, C. Caughey, A. Hempsey & R. McGregor, *The Essex Autonomy Project. Three Jurisdictions Report. Towards Compliance with CRPD Art. 12 in Capacity/Incapacity legislation across the UK*, Essex: University of Essex 2016.
29. Lush 2015, p. 47.

> 'deprivation, even partial, of legal capacity should be a measure of last resort, applied only where the national authorities, after carrying out a careful consideration of possible alternatives, have concluded that no other, less restrictive measure would serve the purpose or where other, less restrictive measures, have been unsuccessfully attempted.'[30]

These two different interpretations of article 12 UNCRPD raise the question whether we are dealing with irreconcilable differences or whether the 'tension' between the two can somehow be lessened. Upon a closer study of the General Comment and the literature on article 12 UNCRPD it becomes apparent that even the proponents of the so-called supported decision-making paradigm seem to acknowledge that in some instances the appointment of a substitute decision-maker is called for.[31] Arstein-Kerslake and Flynn refer to the situation in which 'the individual's will and preferences are unknowable and a decision needs to be made',[32] for example if a person is in coma. They, however, also argue that we should not assume too soon that this is the case. Gooding notes:

> '[T]here will remain individuals for whom no relationships of trust exist and for whom not enough intention is expressed to guide decision-making. There are clear risks to stretching the meaning of the term "supported decision-making" to cover situations where decisions are being made "for" a person, rather than "by" a person.'[33]

Gooding, however, also argues that these situations should not be used as an example to legitimize measures of substitute decision-making in every instance.[34] The Committee does not address this issue in great detail, except in paragraph 21 of the General Comment on article 12 UNCRPD, where it states that: 'where, after significant efforts have been made, it is not practicable to determine the will and preferences of an individual, the "best interpretation of will and preferences" must replace the "best interests" determinations'.[35] Ruck Keene and Ward note in this regard that the actual issue in situations of what they call 'factual incapability'

30. ECHR 18 September 2014 (Ivinović v. Croatia), no. 13006/13.
31. According to paragraph 27 of General Comment No. 1 on article 12 the appointment of a substitute decision-maker by someone other than the person concerned is one of the characteristics of a regime of substitute decision-making. See however Martin *et al.* 2016, p. 12 & pp. 63-66 (Appendix C) and A. Ruck Keene & A.D. Ward, 'With and Without "Best Interests": the Mental Capacity Act 2005, the Adults with Incapacity (Scotland) Act 2000 and Constructing Decisions', *International Journal of Mental health and Capacity Law* 2016, pp. 17-37 (in particular pp. 18-19) for an analysis of the problems that exist with regard to this definition.
32. Arstein-Kerslake & Flynn 2016, p. 477.
33. P. Gooding, 'Navigating the 'Flashing Amber Lights' of the Right to Legal Capacity in the United Nations Convention on the Rights of Persons with Disabilities: Responding to Major Concerns', *Human Rights Law Review* 2015, vol. 15, pp. 45-71 (p. 53).
34. Gooding 2015, pp. 53-54.
35. United Nations Committee on the Rights of Persons with Disabilities, *General Comment No. 1. Article 12: Equal Recognition before the law*, 2014, p. 5.

does not seem to be whether or not a decision-maker should be appointed, but rather whether he should adopt the best interpretation approach instead of the best interest approach.[36]

It is important to note that ratification of the Convention on the Rights of Persons with Disabilities does not mean that States Parties are bound by the Committee's interpretation of the UNCRPD. States Parties are only bound by the text of the Convention itself.[37] That does not mean that the General Comment on article 12 UNCRPD should not be taken seriously, neither should it however be seen as unequivocal. The text of the Convention and the *travaux préparatoires* leave room for other interpretations.

2.4 Beyond the two conflicting interpretations: the alternate framework

In order to move beyond what can be described as the substitute versus supported decision-making impasse Martin *et al.* have provided an alternate framework that can be used to achieve compliance with article 12 UNCRPD on the bases of a compromise between these two conflicting interpretations. They propose to firstly ask the following overarching question:

> 'What measures should be taken to support the exercise of legal capacity, both by supporting persons with disabilities to make decisions themselves wherever possible, and by supporting their ability to exercise their legal agency even in circumstances when they lack the ability to make the requisite decisions themselves?'[38]

According to article 12(3) UNCRPD States Parties are obliged to make sure that adults with a disability have access to the support they require in exercising their legal capacity. However, the meaning of the term 'support' is not specified in article 12 UNCRPD nor in the General Comment on this article. The Committee defines it as 'a broad term that encompasses both informal and formal support arrangements of varying types and intensity'.[39] According to Arstein-Kerslake and Flynn the Committee deliberately chose not to create a rigid definition in order to take into account that new measures of support are still being developed and to show an understanding of the fact that the support provided can vary from one person to another due to the diversity of adults with a disability.[40] This means the

36. Ruck Keene & Ward 2016, pp. 18-19.
37. Martin *et al.* 2016, p. 10.
38. Martin *et al.* 2016, pp. 13-14.
39. United Nations Committee on the Rights of Persons with Disabilities, *General Comment No. 1. Article 12: Equal Recognition before the law*, 2014, p. 4.
40. Arstein-Kerslake & Flynn 2016, p. 476.

range of potential measures to support the exercise of legal capacity is considerably broad.

As becomes apparent from the overarching question cited above, two categories of support for the exercise of legal capacity have been distinguished by Martin *et al.* The first category of support consists of measures and instruments provided to help an adult to make a decision himself and to implement this decision with legal effect.[41] The presumption here is that the adult is still able to make his own decisions. The second category of support comes into play in those instances where the adult, notwithstanding the support that is provided, cannot make his own decision. Further, in this article we will predominantly focus on this second category of support measures.

2.5 Support measures for adults unable to make their own decisions

If we agree with Martin *et al.* that article 12 UNCRPD requires that support measures should be provided in situations where an adult is unable to make his own decision, it is necessary to specify what kind of measures these should be. It seems, therefore, necessary to come back to another requirement derived from article 12 UNCRPD, namely the duty to respect the legal capacity of adults with a disability on an equal basis with others.[42] In this paragraph, we will elaborate on the question what kind of support measures need to be in place and what kind of safeguards should be employed in order to meet the requirements of article 12 UNCRPD.

In order to ensure respect for the legal capacity of adults with a disability on an equal basis with others, article 12(3) UNCRPD calls on States Parties to take all appropriate measures to provide adults with access to the support they require in exercising their legal capacity. As was noted in paragraph 2, according to the Committee legal capacity involves both a legal standing ('the ability to hold rights and duties') as well as legal agency. The latter should be understood as 'the power to engage in transactions and create, modify or end legal relationships'.[43] According to Martin *et al.* the challenge with regard to the second category of support is to find ways to support the exercise of this legal agency, even in the absence of decision-making capacity.[44] They refer in this regard to instruments such as the continuing power of attorney, an instrument that with regard to the

41. Martin *et al.* 2016, p. 24.
42. Article 12(2) UNCRPD.
43. United Nations Committee on the Rights of Persons with Disabilities, *General Comment No. 1. Article 12: Equal Recognition before the law*, 2014, p. 3.
44. Martin *et al.* 2016, pp. 37 & 24-25.

Netherlands will be discussed in more detail in paragraph 7 of this article. By means of a continuing power of attorney, adults can make their own tailormade provisions for a future period of incapacity. An attorney is given the authority to act on the adult's behalf in accordance with the adult's wishes and instructions, thereby supporting the exercise of his legal agency.

Notwithstanding the challenge to find ways to enhance legal agency where possible, Martin *et al.* acknowledge that there are limits to the support provided for the exercise of legal capacity. They refer in this regard to the so-called 'hard cases', including for example comatose patients or adults who are in an advanced stage of dementia.[45] According to Martin *et al.*:

> 'In such circumstances, the law must provide for someone else to take the decisions that the affected individual is unable to take, while establishing the methodology to be employed, and the safeguards to protect persons who find themselves in that vulnerable position.'[46]

What this means for the traditional guardianship measures in force in the Netherlands will be discussed in paragraph 6. As the quote makes clear, any legislative intervention has to incorporate the safeguards of article 12(4) UNCRPD. The same applies to the measures and instruments aimed at providing both categories of support mentioned above. According to article 12(4) UNCRPD appropriate and effective safeguards to prevent abuse need to be in place. These safeguards can be divided in three categories: safeguards ensuring respect for the rights, will and preferences of the person, safeguards ensuring that measures are free of conflict of interest, and safeguards ensuring that measures are free of undue influence. In addition, several requirements to which every measure must comply are distinguished. Using the language of article 12(4) UNCRPD itself, Martin *et al.* distinguish:

- an overarching aim ('to prevent abuse in accordance with human rights law');
- a duration constraint ('for the shortest time possible');
- a review requirement ('subject to regular review by a competent independent and impartial authority or judicial body');
- a proportionality requirement;
- an effectiveness requirement;
- and the plurality of safeguards.[47]

Both the plurality of safeguards and the proportionality requirement are important in determining the weight that is to be accorded to the first category of safeguards: safeguards ensuring respect for the rights, will and preferences of the person. The

45. Martin *et al.* 2016, p. 35.
46. Martin *et al.* 2016, p. 37.
47. Martin *et al.* 2016, p. 38.

precise interpretation of the phrase 'respect for the rights, will and preferences' has led to much debate.[48] As was noted in paragraph 3, a second point of discussion in addition to the substitute-supported divide, is the replacement of the so-called 'best interests' paradigm by a 'will and preference paradigm', with the Committee stating:

> 'All forms of support in the exercise of legal capacity, including more intensive forms of support, must be based on the will and preference of the person, not on what is perceived as being in his or her objective best interests.'[49]

Martin *et al.* point out that both the plurality of the safeguards and the proportionality requirement entail that respect for the will and preferences of the person cannot be assured at any cost. The plurality of safeguards means that safeguards addressing conflict of interest and undue influence (the second and third category of safeguards) also need to be in place. The proportionality requirement makes clear that there are also other rights enshrined in the Convention that need to be respected and this might in exceptional cases require action contrary to the will and preference of the person.[50] That being said, the importance of respect for the will and preference of the person is acknowledged within the alternate framework. A middle ground between the mere consideration (often embedded within the 'best interest' approach) of will and preferences and the unqualified deference to will and preferences, by means of a 'rebuttable presumption approach' is proposed:

> '[W]herever an individual is authorised or obligated to construct a decision with or on behalf of a person whose decision-making is impaired or absent, that individual should operate with the rebuttable presumption that the reasonably ascertainable will and preferences of that person should be given effect in the matter.'[51]

In addition to safeguards ensuring respect for the rights, will and preferences of the adult (the first category of safeguards), article 12(4) UNCRPD requires the States Parties to establish safeguards ensuring that measures relating to the exercise of legal capacity are free from conflict of interest and undue influence. Although the question what safeguards ensuring respect for the will

48. See e.g. Arstein-Kerslake & Flynn 2016; Ruck-Keene & Ward 2016.
49. United Nations Committee on the Rights of Persons with Disabilities, *General Comment No. 1. Article 12: Equal Recognition before the law*, 2014, p. 5 & 7.
50. Martin et al. 2016, p. 39 & 41. See also ECHR 23 March 2017 (Case of A.-M.V. v. Finland), no. 53251/13, where the Court considers that a balance needs to be struck between the respect for the dignity and self-determination of the individual and the need to protect the individual and safeguards his interests, which in this case meant that action had to be taken contrary to the wishes and preferences of the adult.
51. Martin *et al.* 2016, pp. 40-41.

and preferences of the person should look like has been addressed extensively by the Committee, much less has been said about the second and third category of safeguards. This holds true in particular for the second category of safeguards. The phrase 'conflict of interest' is not mentioned at all in the General Comment on article 12 UNCRPD. With regard to this second category of safeguards, Martin *et al.* note that these safeguards should not be looking to eliminate conflicts of interest, but rather to manage (potential) conflicts of interest. They note that safeguards ensuring that measures are free from conflict of interest should not have the effect of excluding an individual who is best placed to support the adult in the exercise of legal capacity.[52]

With regard to the third category of safeguards, the Committee notes that although undue influence can be encountered by anyone, the risk is exacerbated for people relying on the support of others to make decisions. According to the Committee, undue influence occurs in situations, 'where the quality of the interaction between the support person and the person being supported includes signs of fear, aggression, threat, deception or manipulation'.[53] Safeguards addressing these situations should be balanced with respect for the rights, will and preferences of the adult, which is to include the right to take risks and make mistakes.[54] Both Martin *et al.* and Series note that it is difficult to determine when influence should be regarded as undue. In other words, which signs of fear or which level of manipulation justify an intervention by the State and how should safeguards in this respect look like?[55] To date no conclusive answers to these questions have been found. Further research looking at safeguards to protect the adult from situations of undue influence and safeguards managing situations of conflicts of interest, seems called for.

2.6 The Dutch adult guardianship measures

In the previous paragraphs we have focused on the emergence of the new paradigm based on the human rights approach. Such a long run-up is needed in order to thoroughly embed the Dutch situation into the framework of the historical and human rights developments. In the remaining paragraphs of this article we will examine whether the adult protection scheme currently in force in the Netherlands, is compliant with this new protection paradigm based on the human rights approach. Therefore, in this paragraph we will first give a brief

52. Martin *et al.* 2016, pp. 48-50.
53. United Nations Committee on the Rights of Persons with Disabilities, *General Comment No. 1. Article 12: Equal Recognition before the law*, 2014, p. 5.
54. United Nations Committee on the Rights of Persons with Disabilities, *General Comment No. 1. Article 12: Equal Recognition before the law*, 2014, p. 5.
55. Martin *et al.* 2016, pp. 44-45; L. Series, 'Relationships, autonomy and legal capacity: Mental capacity and support paradigms', *International Journal of Law and Psychiatry* 2015 vol. 40, pp. 80-91.

overview of the traditional adult guardianship measures in the Netherlands. After that, we will focus on both the role these measures play in the system of adult protection in the Netherlands and on their compliance with the safeguards of article 12(4) UNCRPD.[56]

There are currently three adult guardianship measures in the Netherlands; all three can be found in Book 1 of the Dutch Civil Code (CC). Plenary or full guardianship (in Dutch: *curatele*) is the oldest of the three. This measure is based on the Roman *cura furiosi* mentioned in paragraph 2, and was until 1982 the only adult guardianship measure in the Netherlands.[57] According to article 1:378 CC, a court can order *curatele* if a person, due to a mental or physical condition or habitual alcohol or drug abuse, is unable to take care of his own interests or is endangering his own safety or the safety of others.[58] A so-called *curator* (guardian) is subsequently appointed. *Curatele* covers the protection of both financial and personal interests. It entails a complete loss of legal capacity, which makes it the most far-reaching measure available in the Netherlands.[59]

A less intrusive adult protection measure is the protective trust (in Dutch: *beschermingsbewind*). The development of this adult guardianship measure, introduced in 1982, can be linked to the emergence of the welfare model discussed in paragraph 2.[60] In contrast with *curatele, beschermingsbewind* solely covers the protection of the financial interests of the adult. *Beschermingsbewind* may be ordered if a person, due to a mental or physical condition, prodigality or problematic debts, is unable to take care of his financial interests.[61] The introduction of the third and final adult guardianship measure can also be linked to the emergence of the welfare model. Personal guardianship (in Dutch: *mentorschap*) was introduced in 1995 and deals with the non-financial interests of the adult, which include decisions relating to care, nursing and

56. With regard to the compliance of the adult guardianship measures with article 12(4), we are referring to a study conducted by: Blankman & Vermariën, *Conformiteit van het VN-Verdrag inzake de rechten van personen met een handicap en het EVRM met de huidige voorgestelde wetgeving inzake vertegenwoordiging van wilsonbekwame personen in Nederland*, Amsterdam: Vrije Universiteit 2015, p. 9.
57. Blankman 1997, p. 49.
58. C. Blankman, 'Guardianship legislation in The Netherlands', in: K. Dayton (ed.), *Comparative Perspectives on Adult Guardianship*, Durham North Carolina: Carolina Academic Press 2014, pp. 181-190; R. Frimston, C. Engelbertink & A. Vrenegoor, 'Netherlands', in: R. Frimston, A. Ruck Keene, C. van Overdijk & A.D. Ward (eds.), *The international Protection of Adults*, Oxford – New York: Oxford University Press 2015, pp. 568-574 (p. 569).
59. Frimston, Engelbertink & Vrenegoor 2015, p. 569; P. Vlaardingerbroek, K. Blankman, A.P. van der Linden, E.C.C. Punselie & W.M. Schrama, *Het hedendaagse personen- en familierecht*, Deventer: Wolters Kluwer 2017, pp. 573-575. There are a few exceptions to this legal incapacity (article 1:381 CC).
60. Blankman 1997, p. 49.
61. Frimston, Engelbertink & Vrenegoor 2015, p. 569; Blankman 2014, p. 183.

treatment of the adult.[62] *Mentorschap* may be ordered if an adult, due to his mental or physical condition, is unable to take care of his non-financial interests.[63] According to Blankman, *mentorschap* can be seen as complementary to *beschermingsbewind*. Not surprisingly both measures are frequently ordered together.[64] Both *beschermingsbewind* and *mentorschap* entail a restriction of legal capacity. However, an important exception should be noted with regard to *mentorschap*. From article 1:453 CC follows that the legal capacity of the adult placed under *mentorschap* is restricted, unless the law or a treaty specifies otherwise. This section of article 1:453 CC is particularly relevant as several Dutch laws do specify otherwise. In line with the functional approach, article 7:465 CC for example, requires the medical professional to assess whether the adult is capable to make a decision with regard to treatment himself, even if personal guardianship is in place. It is only when the adult is not deemed capable that the guardian is asked to decide upon the matter in question.[65]

The adult guardianship measures described above can be classified as substitute decision-making.[66] Although according to the Committee systems of substitute decision-making should be abandoned in favour of supported decision-making alternatives, as discussed above, the UNCRPD leaves room for the interpretation that there are limits to the support that can be provided in order to facilitate the exercise of legal capacity. There are so-called 'hard cases' in which the individual, notwithstanding the provided support, simply is not able to exercise legal capacity. In those cases, the law must provide for a substitute entitled to take the decisions that the adult is unable to take.[67] However, in line with the ECHR judgment in the case Ivinović v. Croatia, the application of protection measures limiting legal capacity wholly or partly should be regarded as a last resort.[68] Martin *et al.* even go so far as to say that practicable support in decision-making must have been demonstrably provided before any such measures are permitted.[69]

The question that should be asked is whether the current adult guardianship measures are applied in the Netherlands as a last resort. In 2015 *beschermingsbewind* was ordered 36.341 times, 1.976 adults were placed under *curatele* and *mentorschap*

62. Article 1:453 CC.
63. Article 1:450 of the Dutch Civil Code; Frimston, Engelbertink & Vrenegoor, p. 569.
64. Blankman 2014, pp. 183-184.
65. Blankman 1997, p. 50.
66. See also list of characteristics that according to the Committee define a substitute decision-making regime, United Nations Committee on the Rights of Persons with Disabilities, *General Comment No. 1. Article 12: Equal Recognition before the law*, 2014, p. 6.
67. Martin *et al.* 2016, p. 37.
68. Martin *et al.* 2016, pp. 34-35; ECHR 18 September 2014 (Ivinović v. Croatia), no. 13006/13.
69. Martin *et al.* 2016, p. 35.

was ordered 7.398 times.[70] These figures suggest that the adult guardianship measures still seem to be the norm, rather than the exception.[71] In contrast to, for example, the different jurisdictions in the United Kingdom, in the Netherlands the court is not legally obligated to previously verify whether practicable support has been provided to an adult, or whether less intrusive alternatives such as the yet to be discussed living will are in place.[72] In a study conducted in 2015, Blankman and Vermariën concluded that the question whether, prior to application of measures of adult guardianship, enough has been done to support adults with a disability to make decisions themselves, could not be answered in the affirmative.[73] To date, this still seems to be the case.

According to article 12(4) UNCRPD all measures relating to the exercise of legal capacity need to comprise appropriate and effective safeguards. With regard to the first category of safeguards, respect for the rights, will and preferences of the adult, Martin *et al.* propose a 'rebuttable presumption approach'. The substitute decisionmaker 'should operate with the rebuttable presumption that the reasonably ascertainable will and preferences of that person should be given effect in the matter'.[74] The Dutch Civil Code devotes attention to the wishes and preferences of the adult in various ways. With regard to the appointment of a guardian in case of *curatele,* article 1:383(2) CC states that the court shall follow the preferences of the adult unless there are good reasons not to do so. A similar rule applies in case of *beschermingsbewind* (article 1:435(3) CC) and *mentorschap* (article 1:452(3) CC). In addition, both article 1:454 CC and article 1:381(4) CC applied to the provision of *mentorschap* and to the protection of personal interests by means of *curatele,* require the guardian to involve the adult as much as possible when taking decisions concerning the care, nursing and treatment of the adult. These articles also require the guardian to encourage the adult to act for himself when the adult has the mental capacity to do so. Although there is no such obligation with regard to *beschermingsbewind,* a certain degree of collaboration between the guardian and the adult is required. Article 441 CC obliges the guardian to ask the adults' consent for important financial decisions, such as the sale of property. This consent can however be replaced by the judge. Blankman

70. K. Blankman, 'Een wettelijke regeling voor het levenstestament?', in: *Het levenstestament. Nader verfijnd,* Den Haag: Sdu uitgevers 2017, pp. 45-64.
71. See also the annually increasing number of adult guardianship measures that are in place (Raad voor de Rechtspraak, I, https://www.rechtspraak.nl/SiteCollectionDocuments/Factsheettoezicht.pdf (last accessed: 7 January 2019)).
72. See for example section 1.3 of the Mental Capacity Act and section 1.6 of The Adults with Incapacity (Scotland) Act 2000.
73. Blankman & Vermariën, *Conformiteit van het VN-Verdrag inzake de rechten van personen met een handicap en het EVRM met de huidige voorgestelde wetgeving inzake vertegenwoordiging van wilsonbekwame personen in Nederland,* Amsterdam: Vrije Universiteit 2015, p. 9.
74. Martin *et al.* 2016, pp. 40-41.

and Vermariën note that the latter happens too often in practice.[75] They conclude that more can be done to ensure respect for the will and preferences of the adult and propose the adoption of an explicit guiding principle for substitute decision-makers.[76]

There are several safeguards in place with the aim to ensure that the adult guardianship measures are free from undue influence and that conflicts of interests are managed. Article 1:383 CC requires the judge to assess the suitability of the person to be appointed as guardian in cases of full guardianship.[77] In addition, certain persons, such as staff of the institution where the adult is placed, cannot be appointed as guardian.[78] This to avoid a potential conflict of interest. Finally, the law also provides for supervision by the judge, who in principle receives an annual report from the guardian.[79] To date, it is unknown whether these safeguards and the supervision by judge are sufficient in practice. Again, we note that this is a matter on which further research is required.

2.7 The living will

Beside the three traditional adult guardianship measures, there is also a new voluntary instrument in the Netherlands: the living will (in Dutch: *levenstestament*). By means of a *levenstestament* adults can make their own tailor-made arrangements for a future period of incapacity. The *levenstestament* is also well known in other countries and is internationally better known as a continuing, lasting or enduring power of attorney. The Council of Europe has provided the following definition: 'a mandate given by a capable adult with the purpose that it shall remain in force, or enter into force, in the event of the granter's incapacity'.[80] As this definition makes clear, a *levenstestament* can only be made by a 'capable adult'. In order to ensure legal effectiveness, living wills are therefore often notarised documents in the Netherlands.[81] The scope of the living will can be considerably broad and may include both financial, health and matters as well as the adult's wishes, preferences and instructions as to these matters.

As we mentioned previously, Martin *et al.* argue that article 12(3) UNCRPD includes the challenge to find ways to extend legal agency where possible, even

75. Blankman & Vermariën 2015, p. 26.
76. Blankman & Vermariën 2015, p. 5.
77. A similar article applies in case of the protective trust (article 1:453 CC) and personal guardianship (article 1:452 CC).
78. Article 1:383 CC, article 1:435 CC and article 1:452 CC.
79. Blankman & Vermariën 2015, p. 27; Article 1:386(1) CC, article 1:455 CC and article 1:459 CC.
80. Committee of Ministers of the Council of Europe, *Recommendation CM/Rec(2009)11. Principles concerning continuing powers of attorney and advance directives for incapacity*, 2009, p. 9.
81. R. Frimston, C. Engelbertink & A. Vrenegoor 2015, p. 572.

in the absence of decision-making capacity.[82] The *levenstestament* is an important instrument in the Netherlands with the potential to do so. By means of the *levenstestament* the attorney is given the authority to act on the granter's behalf in accordance with his/her wishes and instructions. The attorney is thereby supporting the granter in the exercise of his rights and duties. Unlike the adult guardianship measures, the *levenstestament* does not entail a loss or limitation of legal capacity. This means there can be a gradual increase of support provided by the attorney, taking into account the declining decision-making capacity of the granter. However, in order to fulfil this potential, the *levenstestament* must be embedded in the safeguards of article 12(4) UNCRPD.[83]

To date the *levenstestament* is not yet regulated by law in the Netherlands. In the absence of statutory regulation, the only regulation of the living will is provided by notarial practice. The Dutch government has taken a passive role.[84] Ensuring compliance with article 12(4) UNCRPD is thus left to the discretion of a notary and ultimately to the granter, as it is the granter who decides about the content of the living will and the safeguards that need to be incorporated. However, the *levenstestament* under the Dutch law is modelled upon the power of attorney, a traditional instrument employed for authorising an attorney by a legally capable grantor, who can execute supervision, replace or dismiss the attorney. As noted above, the *levenstestament* allows for a gradual increase of support by the attorney as the mental capacity of the grantor declines. This means there will come a time when the granter will not be able to supervise whether the attorney is acting according to his wishes and preferences, will probably be more vulnerable to undue influence and will not be able to assess whether there is any conflict between his interests and the interests of the attorney. All that makes the question of safeguards very pressing, especially as there is no supervision by the court or any other administrative body. There are, however, no legal rules obliging notaries to cease cooperation in cases where the granter is unwilling or unable to incorporate necessary safeguards.[85]

Although little is known about the application of the living will in practice, there are at least indications that the issue of safeguards is far from being a theoretical one. In a case before the Court of Appeal in Amsterdam, *mentorschap* was deemed necessary, notwithstanding the existence of a living will, in order to ensure respect for the will and preferences of the adult. In this case, the adult wanted to stay

82. Martin *et al.* 2016, p. 37 & 24-25.
83. Martin *et al.* 2016, p. 53.
84. Dutch Senate, *Wijziging van enige bepalingen van Boek 1 van het Burgerlijk Wetboek inzake curatele, onderbewindstelling ter bescherming van meerderjarigen en mentorschap ten behoeve van meerderjarigen en enige andere bepalingen* (*Wet wijziging curatele, beschermingsbewind en mentorschap*), Memorie van Antwoord 2013-2014, 33054-c.
85. Blankman 2017, p. 46.

home as long as possible which was considered possible by the caregivers. The attorney, the daughter of the granter, had however already taken steps to place her father in a care institution.[86] In addition, there have already been several cases where *beschermingsbewind* was deemed necessary due to a conflict of financial interest of the attorney and the grantor. In these cases, large sums of money were taken by the attorney, without explicit consent given by the granter in the *levenstestament*.[87] In two cases, the court ruled that the attorney had financially exploited the granter, which in both cases led to a criminal conviction of the attorney.[88] Taking the aforementioned into account, the passive role of the Dutch government does not seem to meet the requirements of article 12(4) UNCRPD. There is after all an obligation for the *State* to ensure the compliance with the human rights instruments and to provide for appropriate and effective safeguards preventing abuse of vulnerable citizens. This requires a more active approach on the part of the Dutch State than has been the case until now. In order to acquire a more complete picture of problems arising from the lack of safeguards more empirical research is needed.[89]

The question that remains then is how the State can ensure compliance with article 12(4) UNCRPD. Which safeguards can be best implemented in order to enforce respect for the rights, will and preferences and guarantee protection from undue influence and conflict of interest in the context of the living will? In its Recommendation on Principles concerning continuing powers of attorney and advance directives and the accompanying Explanatory Memorandum, the Committee of Ministers of the Council of Europe has addressed the question how safeguards addressing conflicts of interest could be implemented.[90] According to the Explanatory memorandum a conflict of interest could be presumed to arise in case of any transaction between the attorney acting for himself and the granter at the same time. Legislation dealing with conflict of interest should, according to the Recommendation, strive to establish a balance between protection and self-determination, which can be achieved by: 'having clear rules as to conflict of

86. Court of Appeal Amsterdam 2 March 2016, ECLI:NL:GHAMS:2016:346, s. 4.12.
87. Court of Appeal Amsterdam 2 February 2016, ECLI:NL:GHAMS:2016:333, s. 4.6; Court of Appeal Amsterdam 2 March 2016, ECLI:NL:GHAMS:2016:346, s. 4.11; District Court Midden-Nederland 14 September 2017: ECLI:NL:RBMNE:2017:4768.
88. District Court Overijssel 9 May 2017, ECLI:NL:RBOVE:2017:1932; District Court Noord-Nederland 8 April 2016, ECLI:NL:RBNNE:2016:1711.
89. An empirical study focusing on the application of the living will is currently ongoing as part of a comprehensive multidisciplinary PhD study aimed ad evidence-based proposals for improvement of the regulation and application of the living will in the Netherlands.
90. Committee of Ministers of the Council of Europe, *Recommendation CM/Rec(2009)11. Principles concerning continuing powers of attorney and advance directives for incapacity*, 2009.

interest but allowing the granter to permit – by express provision in the power of attorney – what would otherwise be a conflict of interest'.[91]

Several safeguards, aimed at avoiding or addressing potential situations of undue influence, have been proposed in the literature. In the context of the living will, these safeguards can be aimed either at avoiding situations of undue influence at the time when the living will is made or addressing situations of undue influence at the time when the living will has already come into effect.[92] A safeguard employed in several countries are requirements as to the choice of attorney. In Belgium, Germany and Austria for example, the attorney cannot be someone who is employed by the institution where the granter is living.[93] This in order to avoid a conflict of interest but also to avoid a situation in which a care provider is trying to persuade the granter, who is dependent on his support, to make a living will in his favour.[94] Further comparative research focusing on the effectiveness of these and other safeguards and assessing their suitability for implementation in the Netherlands seems required.[95]

2.8 Conclusion

The perception of how the interests of vulnerable adults should be protected has changed over time. Under the influence of the human rights approach, a profound shift of protection paradigms has taken place in the last decades. In line with these developments, the traditional adult guardianship measures are increasingly rendered inconsistent with the right to autonomy and self-determination of vulnerable adults. There seems to be a growing consensus that measures of substitute decision-making should be considered a last resort and need to be reserved for situations in which the individual, notwithstanding the support provided, lacks the ability to make any decisions at all.[96] The focus has thus shifted to instruments of supported decision-making, allowing adults to make decisions themselves and extending their legal agency in the absence of decision-making capacity. Even this brief analysis reveals that current emphasis on the traditional

91. Committee of Ministers of the Council of Europe, *Recommendation CM/Rec(2009)11. Principles concerning continuing powers of attorney and advance directives for incapacity*, 2009, pp. 52-53.
92. Blankman 2017, p. 56.
93. Committee of Ministers of the Council of Europe, *Recommendation CM/Rec(2009)11. Principles concerning continuing powers of attorney and advance directives for incapacity*, 2009, p. 40; A. van den Broeck, 'Inspiratie uit het buitenland voor het Nederlandse levenstestament', in: *Het levenstestament. Nader verfijnd*, Den Haag: Sdu uitgevers 2017, pp. 17-43.
94. A. van den Broeck, *Vermogensbescherming van kwetsbare meerderjarigen via lastgeving*, Antwerpen – Cambridge: Intersentia 2014, p. 120.
95. A comparative study of legislation and best practices abroad is currently ongoing as part of a comprehensive multidisciplinary PhD study aimed at evidence-based proposals for improvement of the regulation and application of the living will in the Netherlands.
96. Martin *et al.* 2016, p. 35.

adult guardianship measures in the Netherlands cannot be considered compliant with this approach. These measures still seem to be the norm rather than the exception. The overall conclusion is that both the traditional adult guardianship measures and the practice of their application should be adjusted according to the new human rights-based protection paradigm and the requirements of article 12 of the UNCRPD. Thereby vulnerable adults should be provided with practicable support to make decisions themselves and instruments extending legal agency in the absence of decision-making capacity should be stimulated and promoted. The *levenstestament* can be considered an addition to the arsenal of instruments in the Netherlands with the potential to play an important part in this adjustment.

In order to fulfil this potential, the *levenstestament* needs to be embedded in the robust safeguards of article 12(4) UNCRPD. As we have indicated throughout this article, the operationalization of these safeguards requires further research. Research is required on a number of issues including questions as to when influence should be regarded as undue and how situations of conflict of interest can best be managed. Another issue, not raised in this article, concerns the question how safeguards ensuring respect for the rights, will and preferences of the person, can provide for reflection on later changes in the will and preferences of the adult. This question seems particularly relevant in the context of the *levenstestament* where present wishes may collide with past wishes that have been laid down in the *levenstestament*.[97] Research focusing on these and other questions should be aimed at evidence-based improvement of the regulation and application of the *levenstestament* the Netherlands in order to ensure compliance with article 12 UNCRPD.

97. A.D. Ward, *Enabling Citizens to Plan for Incapacity. A review of follow-up action taken by member states of the Council of Europe to Recommendation CM/Rec(2009)11 on principles concerning continuing powers of attorney and advance directives for incapacity*, Strasbourg: Council of Europe 2018, p. 64-68.

3 The misuse or abuse of continuing powers of attorney: what are appropriate safeguards?

This chapter was published as: R. Stelma-Roorda, 'The Misuse or Abuse of Continuing Powers of Attorney: What Are Appropriate Safeguards', International Journal of Law, Policy and the Family, 2021, 35(1), pp. 1-25.

Abstract

With a continuing power of attorney adults may provide for a future period of incapacity. The misuse or abuse of CPAs is a growing concern in many countries, increasingly the question is asked whether CPAs should not be furnished with more safeguards. Article 12(4) UNCRPD requires states to ensure appropriate and effective safeguards are in place to prevent abuse. This article focuses on the question what appropriate safeguards preventing the misuse and abuse of CPAs are. The article starts with an overview of the research on the risk of misuse and abuse that to date has been conducted. This information is subsequently used to operationalise the three categories of safeguards mentioned in article 12(4) UNCRPD, providing directions as to how appropriate safeguards might look like. Based on these directions, the safeguards implemented in five European countries have been studied with a view to providing insight into how these countries have tried to meet the requirement to ensure appropriate safeguards are in place. It is concluded that more can be done to ensure adults who want to be involved in the running of their affairs are given the opportunity to do so. In addition, attorneys should be made aware of their rights and responsibilities upon entry into force of the CPA and provided with the necessary support.

3.1 Introduction

Over the years so-called anticipatory decision-making instruments, allowing adults to make their own provisions for an eventual future period of incapacity, have come to the forefront. The continuing power of attorney (CPA) is such an instrument. The Council of Europe has defined the CPA as 'a mandate given by a capable adult with the purpose that it shall remain in force or enter into force, in the event of the granter's incapacity.'[1] The main attraction of the CPA

1. Council of Europe, Recommendation CM/Rec (2009)11.

is that it promotes the autonomy of adults, as it allows adults themselves to appoint an attorney of their own choosing.[2] In contrast, in the framework of traditional guardianship measures, a deputy or guardian is being appointed for adults by a court or tribunal. However, the main concern with CPAs is that they do not, in general, provide the same level of safeguards as traditional guardianship measures, where a deputy or guardian is in most cases supervised by the court. The CPA is an instrument based on a premise of trust, namely the assumption that the adult will choose an attorney who is trustworthy and has the necessary skills to take care of the adult's affairs. Therefore, many countries have deliberately chosen not to build a substantial security framework surrounding the CPA, but rather to create a low-threshold, relatively cheap, and easy-to-use instrument. Yet, the CPA also requires at least some basic level of safeguards. Adults make CPAs with the intention to create provisions for a future period of incapacity, a time when they are generally no longer able to scrutinise and supervise the actions of the attorney themselves. In practice, adults frequently use CPAs for conferring broad powers to the attorney, without properly regulating the attorney's accountability or independent monitoring.[3] In these cases, there is a potential risk that the attorney might at a later stage misuse or abuse the CPA. The danger of misuse or abuse of CPAs by the attorney is a growing concern in many countries.[4] Increasingly, the question is asked whether CPAs should not be furnished with more safeguards.

Article 12(4) of the United Nations Convention on the Rights of Persons with Disabilities (UNCRPD) calls on states to ensure that 'appropriate and effective safeguards' are in place to prevent abuse. To date, there is no research data on the effectiveness of current safeguards aimed at the prevention of misuse or abuse of CPAs. As effectiveness can only be assessed through empirical research, nothing can be said at the moment of the conformity of current safeguards with Article 12(4) UNCRPDs requirement to ensure that effective safeguards are in place. Further (empirical) research is needed to establish this. Appropriateness is in contrast a normative rather than empirical notion, it can be assessed by means of a theoretical analysis. Assessing the appropriateness of (current) safeguards, therefore, seems the first step in the process of achieving compliance

2. The Council of Europe, eg has recommended its Member States by means of Recommendation CM/Rec (2009)11 to 'promote self-determination for capable adults by introducing legislation on continuing powers of attorney and advance directives.'
3. C. Tilse, J. Wilson, B. White, L. Wilmott, and A. McCawley, 'Enduring Powers of Attorney: Promoting Attorneys' Accountability as Substitute Decision Makers' (2014) 33 (3) *Australasian Journal on Ageing* 193-197.
4. As will be explained in more detail later on in this chapter, the phrase 'misuse' is used to refer to situations where the inappropriate use of the CPA by the attorney is unintentional (e.g. a situation where inappropriate use occurs because the attorney is ill-informed or unaware of certain responsibilities). The phrase 'abuse' on the other hand refers to situations where the inappropriate use of the CPA is intentional.

with the requirements of Article 12(4) UNCRPD. The theoretical assessment of the appropriateness of safeguards can be based on the guidance provided in Article 12(4) UNCRPD itself, where three categories of appropriate safeguards have been distinguished. Article 12(4) UNCRPD states that there should be: (i) safeguards ensuring that the rights, will, and preferences of the adult are respected; (ii) safeguards ensuring that measures and provisions are free from conflict of interest; and (iii) safeguards ensuring that measures and provisions are free from undue influence. Much has already been said about the interpretation of these safeguards in general and about the first category of safeguards in particular. Yet, Stelma-Roorda et al argue that the operationalisation of these safeguards with regard to the CPA, is a challenge that requires further research.[5] An important aspect to consider in this regard, is that the need to create safeguards should be balanced with the need to keep the CPA a simple and easy-to-use instrument. Lush points out that if anticipatory decision-making instruments become too restrictive and cease to be simple, effective, and inexpensive instruments, people will try to circumvent them and search for alternatives instead.[6] Mitchell et al refer in this regard to research that shows that people are less likely to make formal anticipatory decision-making arrangements if there is a family member whom they could trust to act as an informal decision-maker. This then removes the need for formal arrangements which are considered too restrictive and therefore not ideal.[7] McCawley et al note that if the task of attorney becomes an onerous one, attorney's might be unwilling to undertake it.[8] Safeguards should, in other words, not restrict either adult or attorney more than is necessary to ensure that the adult is sufficiently protected from misuse or abuse of the CPA. This means the need to offer the adult adequate protection should be carefully balanced with the need to retain an instrument, ie based on trust and informality.

This article aims to explore how the requirement of Article 12(4) UNCRPD to provide for appropriate safeguards against abuse, can be operationalised in the context of the CPA, keeping in mind striking the right balance between protection on the one hand and trust and informality on the other hand. This exploration

5. H.N. Stelma-Roorda, C. Blankman, and M.V. Antokolskaia, 'A Changing Paradigm of Protection of Vulnerable Adults and Its Implications for the Netherlands' (2019) *Family & Law* doi: 10.5553/FenR/.000037.
6. D. Lush, 'Adult Guardianship and Powers of Attorney in England and Wales' in L. Ho and R. Lee (eds.), *Special Needs Financial Planning: A Comparative Perspective* (Cambridge University Press, 2019) pp. 117-148.
7. L.K. Mitchell, N.A. Pachana, J. Wilson, K. Vearncombe, B. Massavelli, G.J. Byrne, and C. Tilse, 'Promoting the Use of Enduring Powers of Attorney in Older Adults: A Literature Review' (2014) 33 (1) *Australasian Journal on Ageing* 2-7.
8. A. McCawley, C. Tilse, J. Wilson, L. Rosenman, and D. Setterlund 'Access to Assets: Older People with Impaired Capacity and Financial Abuse' (2006) 8 (1) *The Journal of Adult Protection* 20-32. See also C. Tilse, D. Setterlund, J. Wilson, and L. Rosenman, 'Minding the Money: A Growing Responsibility for Informal Carers' (2005) 25 *Ageing and Society* 215-227.

will be made in three steps. As balancing protection and informality requires an assessment of the risk of misuse or abuse of CPAs, paragraph 2 will provide an outline of the available information on the risk of misuse and abuse of CPAs by attorneys. Building on this information, paragraph 3 will provide directions as to how the three categories of safeguards, included in Article 12(4) UNCRPD, can be operationalised in the context of the CPA. Using these directions as a starting point, paragraph 4 will look at the safeguards currently employed in five European jurisdictions (Belgium, Germany, England and Wales, the Netherlands, and Switzerland). The aim of this exercise is to use these five jurisdictions as an illustration of how European countries are trying to meet the Convention's requirement to provide for appropriate safeguards in order to prevent misuse or abuse of CPAs and how protection and informality are balanced in this regard.

In conclusion, I will try to delineate the steps that still need to be taken on the way to furnish the CPA with appropriate safeguards, as required by the UNCRPD.

3.2 The risk of abuse or misuse of CPAs

To date, there is a dearth of research into the nature, cause, and prevalence of abuse in the context of CPAs.[9] This lack of empirical evidence on the risks surrounding the CPA, means the CPA is advocated by some as a protective and safeguarding instrument, enabling adults to prepare for an eventual period when they are no longer able to protect their own interests. At the same time, others highlight the danger that CPAs might be misused or abused.[10] This paragraph aims to provide an overview of the available normative and empirical literature on the risk of misuse and abuse of CPAs. In addition to discussing the few studies that have been conducted in this area, it draws on the general literature and research on elder abuse and the abuse of older adults with cognitive impairments to find an answer to the following questions:

- who are at risk of misuse or abuse of CPAs by attorneys;
- what is the nature of misuse of abuse of CPAs;
- what is the profile of 'wrongdoers' and what triggers their misuse or abuse of CPAs;
- what is the response to the misuse or abuse of CPAs?

9. K. Purser, T. Cockburn, C. Cross, and H. Jacmon, 'Alleged Financial Abuse of Those under an Enduring Power of Attorney: An Exploratory Study' (2018) 48 *British Journal of Social Work* 887-905.
10. Ibid; Council of Europe Recommendation CM/Rec (2009)11; J. Manthorpe, K. Samsi, and J. Rapaport, 'Responding to the Financial Abuse of People with Dementia: A Qualitative Study of Safeguarding Experiences in England' (2012) 24 (9) *International Psychogeriatrics* 1454-1464; J. Chesterman, 'Taking: Control: Putting Older People at the Centre of Elder Abuse Response Strategies' (2016) 69 (1) *Australian Social Work* 115-124.

1 *Who Are at Risk of Misuse or Abuse of CPAs by Attorneys?*

Assuming that the CPA itself provides a potential vehicle for abuse in situations where the adult is no longer able to scrutinise the actions of the attorney, every adult with a CPA is upon execution of the instrument potentially at risk of abuse.[11] CPAs may after all be granted by adults of all ages as incapacity can suddenly occur at any age (eg a comatose state due to a car accident). Purser et al note, however, that there may be certain factors contributing to and heightening the risk of abuse of CPAs, such as 'dependence, disability, failing physical health, depression, socio-economic status, cognitive impairments, and social isolation'.[12] Although age does not automatically equate with the occurrence of these factors, there is an increased age-related risk with regard to several of these factors, such as increasing physical frailty and the development of cognitive impairments due to a disease such as dementia.[13] Research in the field of elder abuse demonstrates that the risk of abuse, financial abuse, in particular, is likely to increase with age. People with dementia or a reduced cognitive function are considered a group particular at risk of abuse.[14] Manthorpe et al note that individuals in these groups become increasingly less able to protect themselves, have declining abilities to identify and manage risks, and may not report concerns or are not taken seriously when doing so.[15]

This is particularly important to keep in mind when considering instances where CPAs are granted by adults whose cognitive abilities are already starting to deteriorate. Several research studies indicate that it is not an unlikely occurrence for adults to wait 'until the 11th hour' before making a CPA.[16] This can stem from a lack of knowledge about anticipatory decision-making instruments. In a study looking at the knowledge and experience of older adults with power of attorney arrangements, Setterlund et al identified lower-income and physical disability as two factors associated with a limited understanding of these kinds of arrangements.[17] But even in cases where people are aware of the possibility, they may be inclined to wait until there is an actual and concrete need to put in

11. D. Setterlund, C. Tilse, and J. Wilson, 'Older People and Substitute Decision-Making Legislation: Limits to Informed Choice' (2002) 21 (3) *Australasian Journal on Ageing* 128-133.
12. K. Purser, T. Cockburn, and E. Ulrick, 'Examining Access to Formal Justice Mechanisms for Vulnerable People in the Context of Enduring Powers of Attorney' (2019) 12 (1) *Elder Law Review* 1-32.
13. Ibid.
14. S. Davidson, P. Rossall, and S. Hart, *Financial Abuse Evidence Review* (Age UK, 2015); D. Bagshaw, S. Wendt, L. Zannettino, and V. Adams, 'Financial Abuse of Older People by Family Members: Views and Experiences of Older Australians and their Family Members' (2013) 66 (1) *Australian Social Work* 86-103.
15. Manthorpe et al (n 10).
16. Setterlund et al (n 11).
17. Ibid.

place anticipatory decision-making arrangements such as the CPA.[18] Samsi and Manthorpe have studied the experiences, opinions, and attitudes of older adults regarding planning for the future and concluded that although people in general thought planning would be a good idea, they were keen to postpone any future planning themselves for 'when they got older, in worse health or when it seemed "more appropriate" to do so'.[19]

As the next paragraph will explain in more detail, it is in keeping with Article 12 UNCRPD to not exclude adults with deteriorating cognitive abilities from establishing a CPA, if they still have the capacity, albeit diminished capacity, to do so.[20] The Council of Europe notes in this regard:

> Therefore, certain people with some degree of incapacity, including those with lifelong incapacities, may be able to grant a valid continuing power of attorney to appoint a person of their choice to deal with matters which they themselves would find very difficult to handle, if not beyond their capacity.[21]

The downside is, however, that adults facing a deterioration of their cognitive abilities may have a sense of urgency to establish a CPA, before it is too late. Mitchell et al point out that this urgency often leaves little time to consider who would be most suited as attorney.[22] They note in this regard: 'those involved in this process are often already experiencing a high level of distress, which does not necessarily form a sound basis upon which to make informed decisions.'[23] In these cases, there is also an increased risk that the adult may be unduly influenced by the prospective attorney to establish a CPA and does not fully appreciate the effect of the CPA as to the terms and scope of the authority being granted.[24] Bielanska notes with regard to England and Wales that it is in practice not uncommon for family members to contact a professional advisor in order to 'get' the authority to

18. Mitchell et al (n 7).
19. K. Samsi and J. Manthorpe, "I Live for Today': A Qualitative Study Investigating Older People's Attitudes to Advance Planning' (2011) 19 (1) *Health and Social Care in the Community* 52-59.
20. M. Donnelly, 'Deciding in Dementia: The Possibilities and Limits of Supported Decision-Making' (2019) 66 *International Journal of Law and Psychiatry* 1-7.
21. Council of Europe Recommendation CM/Rec (2009)11.
22. Mitchell et al (n 7).
23. Ibid.
24. The Law Commission of England and Wales, *The Incapacitated Principal* (Law Com. No. 122, 1983); T.L. Hafemeister, 'Financial Abuse of the Elderly in Domestic Settings' in R.J. Bonnie and R.B. Wallace (eds.), *Elder Mistreatment: Abuse, Neglect, and Exploitation in Aging America* (National Academies Press, 2003) pp. 382-445; See also the study conducted by C. Cross, K. Purser, and T. Cockburn, *Examining Access to Justice for Those with an Enduring Power of Attorney (EPA) Who Are Suffering Financial Abuse* (Crime and Justice Research Centre, Queensland University of Technology, 2017) pp. 1-61.

act on behalf of the adult, rather than wishing the authority to act to be 'given' by the adult.[25]

2 *What Is the Nature of Misuse or Abuse of CPAs?*

As noted above, older adults are a group considered particularly at risk of misuse or abuse of CPAs. In the literature, the misuse or abuse of CPAs is therefore frequently linked to elder abuse, where it is considered one of the forms in which elder abuse can be perpetrated.[26] Elder abuse has been defined by the World Health Organization (WHO) as:

> a single, or repeated act, or lack of appropriate action, occurring within any relationship where there is an expectation of trust which causes harm or distress to an older person.[27]

The emphasis on the phrase 'expectation of trust' seems apt given the relationship between adult and attorney underlying the CPA.[28] The WHO has distinguished several forms of elder abuse, including 'physical, sexual, psychological and emotional abuse, financial and material abuse; abandonment, neglect; and serious loss of dignity and respect'.[29] Although research conducted by Cross et al shows that various of these forms of abuse can occur in the context of a CPA, financial or material abuse seems the most likely to occur as in many cases substantial financial powers are conferred to the attorney.[30] In addition, other forms of abuse, such as physical, psychological, emotional abuse, and neglect, occurring by means of a CPA, can frequently be linked to an underlying financial motive guiding the actions of the attorney. Examples include not providing appropriate care, such as admission to a care home, with the intention to save money. Or the reverse, arranging premature admission to a care home so the attorney may sell the adult's property.[31]

25. Bielanska, *Can Legal Professionals Do More to Safeguard Against the Abuse of Lasting Powers?*, https://cbielanska.com/articles (last accessed 23 July 2019).
26. See, eg: Purser et al (n 9); Purser et al (n 12); D. Setterlund, C. Tilse, J. Wilson, A. McCawley, and L. Rosenman, 'Understanding Financial Elder Abuse in Families: The Potential of Routine Activities Theory' (2007) 27 (4) *Ageing and Society* 599-614.
27. WHO *Elder Abuse* (2020) https://www.who.int/en/news-room/fact-sheets/detail/elder-abuse (last accessed 6 July 2020).
28. Purser et al (n 12)
29. WHO (n 27).
30. Cross et al (n 24); Tilse et al (n 4).
31. F. Matthews, 'Doctors, Elder Abuse, and Enduring Powers of Attorney' (2004) 117 *The New Zealand Medical Journal* 1-8.; The Law Commission of New Zealand, *Misuse of Enduring Powers of Attorney* (Law Com. No. 40, 2000).

Two categories of elder abuse, related to the specific nature of the CPA, have been specified in the literature.[32] The first concerns so-called 'procedural abuse', where the adult either lacks sufficient capacity to grant the CPA or is unduly influenced by the attorney to grant the CPA.[33] As noted before, adults are particularly vulnerable to this form of abuse when their cognitive abilities are declining. The second category of abuse has been characterised by Gordon as a 'violation of trust' and concerns situations in which the attorney uses the CPA for purposes beyond those for which it was intended.[34] The two types of abuse are connected in a sense that 'procedural abuse' may serve as a prelude to the inappropriate use of the CPA by the attorney.[35] Although this categorisation is helpful in terms of distinguishing two important forms of abuse that can occur with regard to the CPA, the second category is considerably broad. Langan and Means note in this regard that in addition to a categorisation of the various types of abuse, attention should be given to the different levels or degrees of abuse.[36]

In distinguishing different levels or degrees of abuse, it is important to realise that the inappropriate use of the CPA is not necessarily intentional. Research shows that there may be various underlying reasons for the inappropriate use of CPAs by attorneys. Manthorpe et al note in this regard that people 'may not intend to abuse but may be confused when managing other people's money or hold "distorting" views about their "entitlement" to these assets.'[37] McCawley et al point out that the task of being an attorney for some people may not be so easy or straightforward after all.[38] Tilse et al argue that in addition to the trustworthiness and willingness to accept responsibility, it is of paramount importance that attorneys understand their responsibility and are capable of carrying out the responsibilities granted to them by means of the CPA.[39] Based on this the following distinction as to the nature of misuse and abuse of CPAs by attorneys could be made:

1. Misuse of the CPA because the attorney is ill-informed or unaware of (certain) responsibilities;

32. R.M. Gordon, 'Material Abuse and Powers of Attorney in Canada: A Preliminary Examination' (1993) 4 (1-2) *Journal of Elder Abuse and Neglect* 173-193.; Hafemeister (n 24).
33. Gordon (n 32).
34. Ibid; Hafemeister (n 24).
35. Ibid.
36. J. Langan and R. Means, 'Financial Management and Elderly People with Dementia in the UK: As Much a Question of Confusion as Abuse?' (1996) 16 *Ageing and Society* 287-314; See also Setterlund et al (n 26) who place financial elder abuse at the end of a continuum of familial asset-management practices.
37. Manthorpe et al (n 10) referring to Langan and Means (n 36); C. Tilse, J. Wilson, D. Setterlund, and L. Rosenman, 'Older People's Assets: A Contested Site' (2005) 24 *Australasian Journal on Ageing* S51-S56; Setterlund et al (n 26).
38. McCawley et al (n 8); See also Setterlund et al (n 26).
39. Tilse et al (n 4).

2. Misuse (or a neglect of duties) of the CPA because the attorney lacks the necessary time, skills, motivation, or capacity to act as attorney;
3. Abuse of the CPA because the attorney intentionally deviates from the powers conferred to him by means of the CPA, with a view to advancing his own interests.[40]

3 *What Is the Profile of 'Wrongdoers' and What Triggers Their Misuse or Abuse of CPAs?*

To date, few research studies have looked specifically into the profile of wrongdoers accused or guilty of misuse or abuse of a CPA. Research on financial elder abuse shows that although financial abuse may be committed by professionals such as care workers, financial advisors, or solicitors, in most cases, wrongdoers are close family members or relatives.[41] This seems to fit the particular context of the CPA, as often a close family member such as a son or daughter, is appointed as attorney.[42] When addressing the question what triggers the misuse or abuse of CPAs by family members acting as attorney, it should again be stressed that misuse of the CPA is not necessarily intentional. In their research on familial management of older adult's assets, Setterlund et al conceptualise financial abuse as being at the end of a continuum of familial asset-management practices.[43] They argue that in order to gain an understanding of what drives a person to abuse or misuse arrangements such as the CPA and to gain insight into why some practices may eventually turn into illegitimate or abusive practices, a contextual approach is needed.[44] Often several factors play a role in enabling misuse or abuse.[45] One example in this regard has already been mentioned before and concerns the attorney's ignorance of the rights and obligations under a CPA. Combined with the adult's complete and unfailing trust in the attorney, resulting in insufficient monitoring of the attorney's actions, these two factors can create a setting in which misuse of the CPA by the attorney may occur.[46] In some cases, the attorney's task of looking after the adult's affairs, is part of a whole range of caregiving tasks.[47] Misuse or abuse of the CPA in these cases may be underpinned by the attorney's desire 'to make tasks as easy as possible'.[48] Setterlund et al point out that an

40. A similar though slightly different differentiation has been made by Gordon (n 32).
41. Purser et al (n 12); Davidson et al (n 14) 8; Bagshaw et al (n 14); Setterlund et al (n 26).
42. Bagshaw et al (n 14); Setterlund et al (n 26).
43. Setterlund et al (n 26).
44. Ibid.
45. Ibid.
46. Setterlund et al (n 26). See also J. Wilson, C. Tilse, D. Setterlund, and L. Rosenman, 'Older People and Their Assets: A Range of Roles and Issues for Social Workers' (2009) 62 (2) *Australian Social Work* 155-167.
47. Tilse et al (n 37).
48. Wilson et al (n 46).

extensive caring role may also come with certain stress and the possibility of the caregiver getting overburdened, which may result in misuse of the CPA.[49]

These two examples show the context in which an attorney needs to manage the adult's affairs can be a complex one. Tilse et al note that this context may become even more complex by the competing interests of the state, service providers, and family members, when it comes to the use of the adult's assets to provide for their own (health)care expenses and accommodation.[50] They note in this regard:

> Whereas policy changes increasingly promote planning for self-provision of retirement incomes and the use of capital assets to fund care choices, families and older people often retain the view that income and care in older age should be primarily funded by the state.[51]

Both Bagshaw et al and Wilson et al point out that older adults are increasingly under pressure to use their assets to provide for their own healthcare costs and what else is needed to ensure a comfortable old age, but also for their children.[52] Linked to this, the attorney's so-called 'sense of entitlement' to the adult's assets is frequently mentioned as an underlying motive for the misuse or abuse of CPAs in the literature.[53] This sense of entitlement may be based on various underlying feelings. Purser et al note in this regard the 'early inheritance syndrome' where a child acting as attorney feels entitled to the adult's assets since 'he will inherit these anyway'.[54] This 'syndrome' might be exacerbated by the feeling that the adult no longer needs his financial assets or at least not all of it, whereas the attorney has good use for it. Or in cases where the attorney has an extensive caring role, the feeling of entitlement to assets as a reward for services rendered.[55] The attorney's sense of entitlement can lead to what is by Tilse et al referred to as 'asset-stripping', where the attorney is taking steps to ensure that his future inheritance is not exhausted to fund the care and accommodation expenses of the adult.[56] As noted before, misuse of this kind is not necessarily intentional. Conrad et al talk in this regard about 'honest confusion' as the desire to pass down assets may be mutually shared by both parent and child.[57] An attorney may act in the mistaken belief that

49. Setterlund et al (n 26).
50. Tilse et al (n 37); Tilse et al (n 8).
51. Tilse et al (n 37).
52. Bagshaw et al (n 14); Wilson et al (n 46).
53. Purser et al (n 12); Bagshaw et al (n 14); Davidson et al (n 14); K.J. Conrad, M. Iris, J.W. Ridings, K.P. Fairman, A. Rosen, and K.H. Wilber, 'Conceptual Model and Map of Financial Exploitation of Older Adults' (2011) 23 (4) *Journal of Elder Abuse and Neglect* 304-325; D.J. Rabiner, J. O'Keeffe, and D. Brown, 'A Conceptual Framework of Financial Exploitation of Older Persons' (2005) 16 (2) *Journal of Elder Abuse and Neglect* 53-73; Tilse et al (n 37).
54. Purser et al (n 12).
55. Davidson et al (n 14); Rabiner et al (n 53); See also Setterlund et al (n 26).
56. Tilse et al (n 8); Rabiner et al (n 53).
57. Conrad et al (n 53).

he acts appropriately as the adult would have wanted him to use the assets in this way.[58] Abuse of the CPA for this purpose can, however, also be intentional or become intentional over time. For instance, in cases where the attorney does not act in accordance with the wishes and instructions of the adult and is taking the adult's assets purely for his own interests, thereby reducing the inheritance of other heirs.

4 *What Is the Response to the Misuse or Abuse of CPAs?*

Based on the previous section, one must conclude that the basic premise of the CPA, ie the assumption that attorneys in all cases and situations act for the benefit of the adult, does not always hold true.[59] There are cases in which the adult's trust and confidence are betrayed by the attorney. The breadth of powers often conferred by means of CPAs, means that in these cases the attorney can, eg sell the adult's property or withdraw money from the adult's bank account to use these assets to his own advantage. As Gordon notes, this can be done 'virtually undetectable' unless a third party such as a friend, relative or professional is keeping a watchful eye and reports his suspicions to the authorities.[60] Bond notes that even in cases where the authorities become aware of the misuse or abuse, the full extent of this abuse might be difficult to uncover. For instance, in cases where the adult, due to physical frailty or a decline of cognitive capabilities, is no longer able to provide the authorities with the necessary information.[61] Alternatively, the adult might be unwilling to provide information out of fear of jeopardising the relationship with the attorney.[62] Moreover, as concluded by Purser et al, even in cases where adults want to report the misuse or abuse of their CPA, there are significant barriers to access justice.[63] The most predominant barrier in this regard is the ability of adults to obtain (legal) advice and assistance, especially in cases where the adult has been isolated by the attorney who is denying friends and family access to the adult and has taken away means of communication.[64] As to the impact of this abuse, Hafemeister notes that beside the risk of financial ruin, the abuse might also have psychological consequences. He notes in this regard: 'losing assets accumulated over a lifetime, often through hard work and deprivation, can be devastating.'[65]

The aforementioned underlines the importance of appropriate safeguards preventing misuse and abuse of CPAs from occurring. However, as has become

58. Bagshaw et al (n 14).
59. McCawley et al (n 8).
60. Gordon (n 32).
61. J.B. Bond, R. Cuddy, G.L. Dixon, K.A. Duncan, and D.L. Smith, 'The Financial Abuse of Mentally Incompetent Older Adults: A Canadian Study' (2000) 11 (4) *Journal of Elder Abuse & Neglect* 23-38.
62. Purser et al (n 9).
63. Purser et al (n 9); Purser et al (n 12).
64. Ibid.
65. Hafemeister (n 24).

clear in this paragraph, designing these safeguards cannot be considered an easy task. Not only can different levels and degrees of misuse and abuse be distinguished, but research also shows that often several factors play a role in enabling the abuse or misuse of CPAs.[66] In addition, the competing interests of actors such as the state, service providers, family members, and attorneys with regard to the financial assets of the adult, mean that what is considered abuse or misuse might also be dependent on the eye of the beholder. Further research looking into the various factors and underlying dynamics enabling misuse and abuse of the CPA remains therefore important in order to ensure that safeguards are as appropriate and targeted as possible.

3.3 Appropriate safeguards in the context of the CPA

In the previous paragraph, an overview of the literature on the misuse or abuse of CPAs has been presented. Bows and Penhale note that such a knowledge and understanding are necessary in order to determine which safeguards to prevent and address the various types of abuse are most appropriate.[67] As noted in the introduction, this article explores the question what appropriate safeguards preventing misuse or abuse of CPAs look like, within the framework of Article 12(4) UNCRPD. Article 12(4) UNCRPD entails an obligation for States Parties to provide for three categories of safeguards preventing abuse: respect for the rights, will, and preferences of the adult, avoiding undue influence, and managing conflicts of interest. After highlighting the literature on the operationalisation of these three categories of safeguards in general, each subparagraph focuses on the question how these safeguards can be operationalised in the context of the CPA. Building on the information presented in the previous paragraph, directions as to how appropriate safeguards look like in the context of the CPA are presented.

1 *Safeguards Ensuring Respect for the Rights, Will, and Preferences of the Adult*

Article 12(4) UNCRPDs requirement to provide for safeguards ensuring respect for the rights, will, and preferences of the adult is best understood in conjunction with Article 12(3) UNCRPD, requiring States Parties to take appropriate measures to provide persons with disabilities with the support they need in the exercise of their legal capacity. Article 12(3) UNCRPD has been the subject of much debate. Although it goes beyond the scope of this article to delve into the depths of this debate, it is necessary to provide a synopsis as a basis upon which further operationalisation of Article 12(4) UNCRPDs first category of safeguards in the

66. Setterlund et al (n 26).
67. H. Bows and B. Penhale, 'Editorial: Elder Abuse and Social Work: Research, Theory and Practice' (2018) 48 *British Journal of Social Work* 873-886.

context of the CPA, can take place.[68] With regard to Article 12(3) UNCRPD, a distinction is often made between substitute and supported decision-making. Substitute decision-making is frequently characterised as amounting to a situation in which 'a decision is made on behalf of a person who is unable to make that decision.'[69] This is then contrasted with supported decision-making where the adult is provided with the support needed to make a decision himself.[70] The Committee on the Rights of Persons with Disabilities (the Committee) has with regard to Article 12(3) UNCRPD noted that 'support in the exercise of legal capacity must respect the rights, will and preferences of persons with disabilities and never amount to substitute decision-making.'[71]

In this regard, it is necessary to clarify a misunderstanding with regard to CPAs. In the majority of the literature to date, the CPA is classified as an instrument of substitute decision-making and the aspect of representation including the appointment of an attorney, albeit by the adult himself, is emphasised.[72] However, this focus on representation creates the risk that the possibility for the adult to provide the attorney with instructions as to how to act and informing the attorney of his wishes and preferences, before or during use of the CPA, is overlooked. Martin et al and Stelma-Roorda et al argue that it is this aspect that signifies the potential value of the CPA as an instrument fulfilling the requirements of Article 12(3) UNCRPD.[73] Martin et al note in this regard, that the requirement of Article 12(3) UNCRPD is broader than support for decision-making. States are required to provide adults with the support in the exercise of their legal capacity. Two categories of support are distinguished by Martin et al in this regard:

- support enabling an adult to make a decision himself; and
- support in the absence of decision-making capacity of the adult.[74]

The CPA can play a role with regard to both these forms of support. When it comes to the first category of support, ie support enabling the adult to make a

68. The reader is for more information referred to, eg Stelma-Roorda et al (n 5) and W. Martin, S. Michalowski, J. Stavert, A. Ward, A. Ruck Keene, C. Caughey, A. Hempsey, and R. McGregor, *The Essex Autonomy Project Three Jurisdictions Report. Towards Compliance with CRPD Art. 12 in Capacity/Incapacity Legislation across the UK* (University of Essex, 2016).
69. P. Webb, G. Davidson, R. Edge, D. Falls, F. Keenan, B. Kelly, A. McLaughlin, L. Montgomery, C. Mulvenna, B. Norris, A. Owens, and R.S. Irvine, 'Key Components of Supporting and Assessing Decision Making Ability' (2020) 72 *International Journal of Law and Psychiatry* 1-9.
70. Ibid; UNCRPD, *General Comment No. 1. Article 12: Equal recognition before the law.*
71. Ibid. Although the phrase 'substitute' and 'supported decision-making' are used by the Committee, both phrases do not feature in the UNCRPD itself and it has been argued that a framing of the requirements of Article 12 UNCRPD in such a dichotomy is unhelpful as both phrases are mired with ambiguity.
72. See, eg McCawley et al (n 8); Purser et al (n 9); Purser et al (n 12).
73. Martin et al (n 68); Stelma-Roorda et al (n 5).
74. Martin et al (n 68).

decision himself, it is important to realise that the entry into force of a CPA not necessarily coincides with full or partial incapacity of the adult. Capacity is time and decision-specific, meaning that although a person may lack the capacity to take, eg a decision on the sale of the house, he may be perfectly able to decide on a birthday gift for his grandchild. In other words, there may be certain decisions an adult with declining decision-making capacity is still able, with support, to make himself. In these cases, the attorney can provide the adult with the support needed to make his own decisions. The second category of support becomes relevant when an adult lacks the ability to make his own decisions. With regard to this second category of support, Martin et al argue that the challenge is to find ways to support the adult in the exercise of his legal agency.[75] To demonstrate this, Martin et al disentangle the concept of legal capacity. Two components are generally distinguished: 'legal standing' and 'legal agency'. The first concerns the 'ability to hold rights and duties', the second concerns 'the power to engage in transactions and create, modify or end legal relationships'.[76] Martin et al note that even in cases where the decision-making capacity of the adult is impaired or absent, there might be ways to support the adult in the exercise of his legal agency.[77] The CPA might provide such a way. An attorney can take over the handling of those affairs for which the adult is no longer, or not at present, able to act and decide. By subsequently acting according to the previously recorded wishes and instructions of the adult, the attorney supports the adult in the exercise of his legal agency.[78]

Taking the aforementioned into account and building on the information presented in paragraph 2, three directions as to appropriate safeguards ensuring respect for the adult's rights, will, and preferences can be inferred.

A. The will, preferences, and instructions of the adult should be clearly documented

Emphasising the value of the CPA as an instrument providing the adult with support in the exercise of his legal capacity, not only ensures the adult's autonomy is as much as possible respected, but it also has an important advantage with regard to the adult's protection against the misuse or abuse of CPAs. As noted, misuse or abuse of CPAs is not necessarily intentional. Attorneys may act in the mistaken believe that their actions are perfectly legitimate because they are based on 'what the adult would have wanted'. Langan and Means argue that in determining whether actions should be classified as abuse, too little attention is paid to the view of the adult either before the onset of diseases impairing capacity

75. Ibid.
76. UNCRPD, *General Comment No. 1. Article 12: Equal recognition before the law.*
77. Martin et al (n 68).
78. Stelma-Roorda et al (n 5).

or during lucid intervals.[79] With regard to, eg gifts from the adult to the attorney, they note that older adults may indeed 'feel a strong drive to leave their money to their children rather than have it all consumed by the costs of services received in the last few years of their life.'[80] The issue here seems a lack of clear documentation as to the adult's wishes and instructions, with the result that it becomes unclear whether the attorney is acting on behalf of the adult or purely in his own interest. Clear documentation of the adult's wishes and instructions as to, eg gifts the attorney may give to himself or to others, seems a potential way forward in this regard.

B. Support of the first category (support enabling the adult to make a decision himself) should be ensured for adults who want to be involved in the execution of their CPA

As noted above, the entry into force of the CPA not necessarily coincides with full incapacity of the adult. Indeed, research shows that CPAs are sometimes also made by adults who due to physical frailty are less able to act themselves or adults who are not digitally proficient, therefore preferring someone else to take care of their affairs for them.[81] Linked to this, various types of CPAs can be distinguished. There are CPAs entering into force immediately after the adult's signature, remaining in force upon the adult's incapacity. There are also CPAs entering into force upon a specified time in the future, most commonly a time when the adult becomes less able to act and decide himself.[82] The advantage of the first type of CPA is that it provides more room for a gradual transfer of responsibilities from the adult to the attorney. However, regardless of which type of CPA is chosen, it is important that there are safeguards ensuring the adult's involvement in the execution of the CPA in cases where the adult desires involvement and still has decision-making capacity with regard to the affair at hand. Tilse et al conducted a study looking at the experiences of older adults who still had capacity but needed help with managing their financial affairs.[83] They found that although some adults were perfectly happy to relinquish complete control over their financial affairs to someone else and did not need to be kept informed, there were also adults seeking more involvement in the running of their (financial) affairs. These adults either found their carer or attorney unwilling or unable to involve them in the decision-making process or were afraid to ask due to fear of disrupting the relationship.[84] Change at this point naturally begins with the

79. Langan and Means (n 36).
80. Ibid; See also Conrad et al (n 53).
81. Stelma-Roorda et al (n 5); Wilson et al (n 46).
82. Council of Europe Recommendation CM/Rec (2009)11; Hafemeister (n 24).
83. C. Tilse, D. Setterlund, J. Wilson, and L. Rosenman, 'Managing the Financial Assets of Older People: Balancing Independence and Protection' (2007) 37 (3) *The British Journal of Social Work* 565-572.
84. Ibid.

attorney's willingness to involve the adult in the decision-making process when possible. However, a greater understanding and more awareness of the dynamic nature of the concept of capacity, may help attorneys to assess when to provide support of the first category (enabling the adult to make a decision himself) and when to act on behalf of the adult according to the adult's (previously expressed) wishes and instructions. This also applies to professionals. Gordon highlights the risk that professionals in cases where a CPA is in place, ignore the adult and instead turn to the attorney for all forms of decision-making.[85] Adequate training might help professionals to assess whether the adult is still able, with support, to make his own decision, instead of turning to the attorney by default.

C. States should ensure attorneys are 'up to the task' and receive sufficient support

As noted, misuse of the CPA is not necessarily intentional in cases where the attorney lacks the necessary time, skills, motivation, or capacity to act as attorney. A direction following from this is that countries should provide safeguards ensuring that upon entry into force of the CPA, the attorney is 'up to the task'. Preferably, adults themselves should, already at the time the CPA is made, consider the suitability of the attorney and discuss with the prospective attorney whether he or she is willing to undertake this task. Adults should have the opportunity to appoint a substitute or replacement attorney in case the prospective attorney is, upon entry into force of the CPA, unable or unwilling to carry out the task. States should ensure that attorneys who are 'up to the task' receive sufficient support with the execution of this task. This support can consist of professional assistance for attorneys helping them to assess the decision-making capabilities of the adult. Support can also include the availability of financial advice, in cases where the attorney is responsible for complex financial decisions. Or legal advice in cases, where the attorney is, eg experiencing difficulties in the execution of his task due to disturbed family relationships.[86]

2 *Safeguards Ensuring that There Is No Undue Influence*

Although a lot has been said about the operationalisation of the first category of safeguards, safeguards ensuring respect for the rights, will, and preferences of the adult, much less has been said about safeguards ensuring there is no undue influence. In General Comment No. 1, the Committee merely notes that undue influence occurs in situations 'where the quality of the interaction includes signs of fear, aggression, threat, deception or manipulation.'[87] Both Martin et al and Series note that it is difficult to determine what the precise turning point is; which

85. Gordon (n 32).
86. Tilse et al (n 8); Setterlund et al (n 26).
87. UNCRPD, *General Comment No. 1. Article 12: Equal recognition before the law.*

level of manipulation, eg makes influence undue?[88] The Committee leaves this question unanswered and confines itself to stating that safeguards addressing undue influence should be balanced with the rights, will, and preferences of the adult, which 'includes the right to take risks and make mistakes'.[89] Further research looking into, eg the question which levels of influence in practice amount to undue influence, seems in other words called for. The information presented in paragraph 2 cannot provide an answer to this question. However, it does provide information as to how situations of undue influence can potentially be avoided. In this regard, the following two directions as to appropriate safeguards can be inferred:

A. States should consider strategies promoting the timely drafting of CPAs

Although undue influence can be encountered by anyone, it seems evident that the risk is exacerbated in cases where the decision-making capabilities of the adult are declining.[90] As it is not an unlikely occurrence for adults to wait until the '11th hour', states should consider strategies ensuring that adults who want to make a CPA, do so 'on time'.[91] Education and awareness campaigns could promote the early drafting of CPAs, for instance, by pointing out to adults that timely drafting ensures that there is no rush to take decisions on the wishes and instructions to be included in the CPA and on the choice of attorney. In addition, states could provide training for professionals, helping them to find the 'right time' to introduce the notion of future planning in cases where the 11th hour is fast approaching. Samsi and Manthorpe note in this regard that professionals might find it difficult to determine the appropriate moment to introduce the idea of future planning in cases where the adult is still adjusting to a diagnosis of dementia.[92]

B. States should provide for safeguards ensuring that CPAs are made by adults with capacity, who are not unduly influenced by the attorney

As noted, undue influence can result in procedural abuse, where the attorney is using improper means to persuade the adult to make a CPA. In all cases, but especially in cases where CPAs are made at the 11th hour, it is therefore important that states provide for safeguards ensuring that CPAs are only made by adults who still have sufficient capacity. More specifically, adults who understand the scope and implications of the CPA and who are not unduly influenced by the prospective attorney or any other person. Unfortunately, it is not always the case

88. Martin et al (n 68); L. Series, 'Relationships, Autonomy and Legal Capacity: Mental Capacity and Support Paradigms' (2015) 40 *International Journal of Law and Psychiatry* 80-91.
89. UNCRPD, *General Comment No. 1. Article 12: Equal recognition before the law*; Stelma-Roorda et al (n 5).
90. Ibid.
91. Mitchell et al (n 7); Setterlund et al (n 11).
92. Samsi and Manthorpe (n 19).

that adults have sufficient capacity, eg in a small-scale exploratory study Cross et al identified several cases where CPAs had been signed by adults who did not fully understand the implications of their CPA.[93] In another small-scale study, Bagshaw et al found that many adults, especially adults with declining decision-making capabilities, were not mindful of potential risks to their (financial) wellbeing.[94] The involvement of a third party or person to assess whether an adult sufficiently understands the scope and implications of the CPA, seems essential in this regard. There are some who argue or imply that this third party should be a professional.[95] The advantage is that professionals may be better equipped or can receive training to adequately assess whether or not an adult has the capacity to make a CPA and may be in a better position to identify any signs of undue influence or other forms of procedural abuse occurring.[96] In addition, they can discuss the question of suitability of the attorney with the adult, advise on the scope of the authority being granted to the attorney and discuss with the adult which safeguards to supervise the attorney, should be included in the CPA.

3 *Safeguards Ensuring that Conflicts of Interest Are Managed*

Although the Committee has said little about safeguards ensuring that there is no conflict of interest, Martin et al highlight an important point, namely that safeguards should not be focussed on the elimination of conflicts of interest, but rather ensure that (potential) conflicts of interest are managed.[97] In other words, safeguards should not have the undesirable effect of excluding suitable attorneys.[98] In this regard, the following two directions as to appropriate safeguards can be inferred.

A. States should provide for safeguards ensuring attorneys are aware of their rights and responsibilities

Aside from situations where adults were insufficiently aware of the implications of their CPA, Cross et al also identified situations where attorneys did not fully understand their role and responsibilities.[99] Setterlund et al note in this regard that attorneys should be aware that 'although they act in private spaces and in the context of family relationships, whatever the circumstances legal and ethical obligations to others always apply.'[100] In order to combat the, eg distorting views attorneys may have about their 'entitlement' to assets and to avoid inadvertent

93. Cross et al (n 24).
94. Bagshaw et al (n 14).
95. Purser et al (n 12); Hafemeister (n 24).
96. Purser et al (n 12).
97. Martin et al (n 68).
98. Ibid.
99. Cross et al (n 24).
100. Setterlund et al (n 26).

misuse of the CPA, states should provide safeguards ensuring attorneys are aware of their rights and responsibilities.[101] These safeguards can once again take the form of training or awareness campaigns. A more stringent alternative is to provide attorneys, prior to the entry into force of the CPA, with information and require them to confirm they are aware of their rights and responsibilities.

B. States should provide for safeguards ensuring there is some form of 'oversight' on the actions of the attorney

A declining ability of the adult to manage his own affairs is often accompanied by a declining ability to supervise and monitor the attorney's actions. This means that some form of 'oversight' on the actions of the attorney is needed. This is particularly important in situations where there are conflicting interests, eg gifts made on behalf of the adult to the attorney. Oversight can be based on stringent safeguards, such as the obligation to submit a detailed annual financial statement to a supervisory institution such as a court or tribunal.[102] States should, however, ensure that safeguards are not too stringent. As already described in the introduction of this article, too stringent safeguards may result in adults choosing other (informal) anticipatory decision-making mechanisms, which offer less protection than the CPA. In addition, prospective attorneys might be unwilling to take up the position of attorney as this task is considered too burdensome. Donnelly notes in this regard that there is, as yet no empirical evidence regarding a link between stringent measures and reduced instances of abuse.[103] States could therefore also recommend or require the inclusion of safeguards in the CPA by the adult and the (prospective) attorney. As noted, professionals could play an important role in this regard by encouraging adult and attorney to put safeguards in place. Wilson et al justly note that the absence of safeguards not only creates a risk for the adult, but also for the attorney, namely being accused of the inappropriate management of the adult's affairs by others such as family members.[104]

4 *General Safeguards*

As the abuse or misuse of CPAs falls within the broader area of abuse of elderly and adults with cognitive impairments in general, more general safeguards moving beyond the specific context of the CPA, are also required. A few examples are mentioned here, although it should be noted that this list is by no means exhaustive. In addition to providing safeguards geared towards the prevention of misuse or abuse, states should also provide safeguards ensuring misuse or abuse is detected and stopped. Efforts in this regard could consist of public campaigns

101. McCawley et al (n 8).
102. Hafemeister (n 24).
103. Donnelly (n 20).
104. Wilson et al (n 46).

creating more awareness of the risk factors and indicators of abuse among professionals as well as the general public.[105] In addition, it should for both these groups be abundantly clear, where suspicions of misuse or abuse can be reported (eg the police or an adult protection authority). Finally, states should ensure that there is access to justice for the victims of the abuse or misuse. Chesterman warns in this regard against strategies focusing solely on the vulnerability of the victim. He points out that the standard response to abuse in cases where the adult has a cognitive impairment, often includes the appointment of a deputy or guardian and the removal of decision-making authority.[106] Chesterman notes in this regard:

> A number of factors render guardianship a problematic response to elder abuse. Key among these is that guardianship is a future protective response that focuses on the victim. It does not deal with past wrongdoing. Rather than focusing on the victim's vulnerability, elder abuse response strategies could be improved by prioritising what service responses, if any, the person wants even when the person has a significant cognitive impairment.[107]

In this paragraph, the information on the risk of misuse and abuse presented in paragraph 2 has been used to operationalise the three categories of safeguards mentioned in Article 12(4) UNCRPD and directions as to how appropriate safeguards should look like, have been presented. These directions remain, however, somewhat abstract. They are broadly phrased and leave room for implementation in various ways by means of a range of safeguards. The next paragraph will therefore focus on the safeguards currently employed in five European countries to examine how these countries are trying to meet the requirement of Article 12(4) UNCRPD to provide for appropriate safeguards, in the context of the CPA.

3.4 Safeguards in Belgium, England & Wales, Germany, the Netherlands, and Switzerland

Safeguards ensuring adequate protection for the adult against misuse or abuse of the CPA, are relevant at three different stages in the so-called 'life-span' of CPAs: (i) when the adult makes a CPA, (ii) when the CPA enters into force, and (iii) when the CPA has become 'active' and the attorney has started to act on behalf of the adult. This paragraph will look at the safeguards in each of these three phases, implemented in Belgium, England and Wales, Germany, the Netherlands and Switzerland. In these countries, adults have the opportunity to establish either a zorgvolmacht (Belgium), a lasting power of attorney (England and Wales), a Vorsorgevollmacht (Germany), a levenstestament (The Netherlands),

105. Bond et al (n 61).
106. Chesterman (n 10)
107. Ibid.

or a Vorsorgeauftrag (Switzerland). All countries were included in a comparative study looking at best practices as a solution to problems with the CPA in the Netherlands and the selection of legal systems was in first instance geared towards this. For the purpose of this article, an external normative approach has, however, been adopted. This means that neither the Netherlands, nor any of the other four countries, has been used as a starting point for the comparative study. Instead, all countries were looked at with a view to providing insight into how these countries try to meet the requirement of Article 12(4) UNCRPD, ensuring that appropriate safeguards are in place, and the steps that are in this regard still to be taken. Although the selection of legal systems may at first glance seem somewhat arbitrary in this regard, this is certainly not the case. Included are countries where the possibility to make a CPA has been in place for some time (England and Wales and Germany) and where legislation is more recent (Belgium and Switzerland). In addition, both common law (England and Wales) and civil law jurisdictions are included. Finally, included are countries where there is an extensive regulatory framework (Belgium, England and Wales, and Switzerland), a country where this regulatory framework is less extensive (Germany), and a country where there is no specific regulatory framework at all (the Netherlands).

1 *Safeguards at the time the CPA is made*

Several of the directions as to appropriate safeguards highlighted in the previous paragraph are important around the time the adult decides to make a CPA. It is first of all important that there are safeguards in place ensuring that the adult still has sufficient capacity to make the CPA and is not unduly influenced by the attorney. When the adult has sufficient capacity to make a CPA, it is subsequently important that wishes and instructions are clearly documented in the CPA.

A. States should provide for safeguards ensuring that CPAs are made by adults with capacity, who are not unduly influenced by the attorney

When studying the efforts undertaken in the various countries to incorporate this direction, the tension between ease of use and protection becomes clearly visible. Countries on the one hand do not want to create too big a hurdle for adults to make a CPA, but at the same time also want to ensure that sufficient protection is in place. Although adults are in most countries advised to use the services of a professional (often a notary) to draft a CPA, in Belgium, Germany, the Netherlands, and Switzerland, CPAs may also be drafted by adults themselves, without the involvement of a third party.[108] In order to provide some form of

108. Article 490 Belgian Civil Code; Article 167 German Civil Code (GCC); W. Zimmermann, *Vorsorgevollmacht, Betreuungsverfügung, Patientenverfügung für die Beratungspraxis* (Erich Schmidt Verlag, 2017) 50-54; Zimmerman notes that in Germany with regard to some affairs (eg registrations in the land register) a so-called 'beglaubigung' of the Vorsorgevollmacht is required. In these cases, a third party, such as a notary, has to confirm the signature is that of the person

safeguard and to prevent situations where the adult simply signs a document drafted by someone else, in Switzerland, the CPA has to be handwritten from beginning to end when drafted without the involvement of a third party.[109] The question is whether safeguards such as these offer sufficient protection in practice. As noted in the previous paragraph the involvement of a third party assessing whether the adult understands the scope and implications of the CPA seems essential. This third party can be a professional, but also someone who knows the adult well, as is the case in England and Wales where a so-called 'certificate provider' needs to confirm that the adult understands the significance of the CPA and has not been unduly influenced to make it. This certificate provider can be a professional such as a lawyer or physician, but also someone who has known the adult well for at least 2 years, such as a friend or colleague (family members cannot act as certificate provider).[110] Professionals must, when asked to assess the capacity of the adult, have the skills to do so. Significant efforts have been undertaken in the Netherlands to provide notaries with the tools and assistance to carry out such an assessment. A roadmap has been developed, offering notaries a framework for the assessment of capacity, not only with regard to CPAs, but other notarial deeds such as wills as well. In case a notary is unsure, the client can be referred to a so-called 'VIA-arts', an independent physician who can be approached to assess whether the adult still has sufficient capacity to make a CPA.[111]

B. The will, preferences, and instructions of the adult should be clearly documented

When the adult has sufficient capacity and is not unduly influenced the CPA can be made. At this stage, it is important that the adult's wishes and instructions are documented clearly and concise. When the adult, eg directs the attorney to consult a designated person with regard to 'major decisions', it should be clear which 'major decisions' the adult has in mind.[112] In addition, wishes and instructions

who made the CPA. A *beglaubigung*, however, does not involve a verification as to whether the will of the adult corresponds with what has been recorded in the CPA, meaning the involvement of the third party can be considered rather limited; C.G.C. Engelbertink, 'Het levenstestament in de maatschappij' in: Notariële bescherming ouderen, preadvies KNB (SDU Uitgevers, 2013) 69-74; Article 361(1) Swiss Civil Code (SCC).

109. Article 361(2) SCC; Botschaft zur Änderung des Schweizerischen Zivilgesetzbuches (Erwachsenenschutz, Personenrecht und Kindesrecht, 2006).

110. D. Lush and C. Bielanska, *Cretney & Lush on Lasting and Enduring Powers of Attorney* (LexisNexis, 2017); Office of the Public Guardian https://www.gov.uk/government/publications/make-a-lasting-power-of-attorney/lp12-make-and-register-your-lasting-power-of-attorney-a-guide-web-version#A10 (last accessed 26 October 2020).

111. A.R. Autar, 'Inleiding' in A.R. Autar, J.P.M. Stubbe´, and L.C.A. Verstappen (eds.), *Compendium Levenstestament* (Sdu, 2018) pp. 19-27; Vereniging Artsen Volksgezondheid https://vavolksgezondheid. nl/wilsbekwaamheid/ (last accessed 26 October 2020).

112. See, eg the case of Re Thrussell (Lush and Bielanska n 110).

may not be contrary to the law. In England and Wales, there are eg, restrictions regarding gifts the attorney may make on behalf of the adult and the adult cannot authorise the attorney to disregard these restrictions.[113] A third aspect that must be considered concerns the influence of wishes and instructions, addressed to the attorney, on the acceptance of the CPA by, eg banks. An example is the instruction, included in some CPAs, obliging the attorney to obtain the consent of a third-party regarding expenses that exceed a certain amount. In cases where banks lack the facility to check whether this consent has been obtained, they might be unwilling to accept the CPA in order to avoid potential liability claims in the future. The adult should consider the aforementioned aspects, preferably when the CPA is made, which once again makes the involvement of a professional advisable. A solution proposed in Germany and Belgium regarding the acceptance by organisations such as banks, is the distinction between an internal mandate and an external power of attorney. In the internal mandate between adult and attorney, the wishes and instructions of the adult can be recorded. The external power of attorney subsequently provides the attorney with the authority to act on behalf of the adult.[114] This opens up the possibility for the adult to provide the attorney with a detailed account of his wishes and preferences, which is preferable to a scenario where compromises have to be made to ensure the acceptance of the CPA. The alternative in cases where the CPA has already been made and where there is a risk of the CPA not being accepted, is damage control. In England and Wales, the court has the authority to sever provisions that are ineffective or illegal and in Switzerland where the protection of adults falls under the remit of cantonal adult protection authorities, these authorities may interpret the Vorsorgeauftrag and add clarifications or adjustments on minor, secondary points.[115] It goes without saying that with regard to practices like these, it is important that the will and preferences of the adult are respected as much as possible.

2 *Safeguards around the Entry into Force of the CPA*

Upon the entry into force of the CPA, it is important that attorneys are aware of their rights and responsibilities and are 'up to the task', meaning they at least have the necessary time, motivation, and capacity to act as attorney.

113. See, eg section 12(2) of the Mental Capacity Act 2005 (MCA 2005).
114. T. Wuyts, 'Een kritische doorlichting van (modellen inzake) zorgvolmachten' in G. Verschelden (ed.), *Rechtskroniek voor het Notariaat. Deel 37* (Knops Publishing, 2020) pp. 91-131; G. Müller and T. Renner, *Betreuungsrecht und Vorsorgeverfügungen in der Praxis* (Carl Heymanns Verlag, 2018) pp. 67-304.
115. Section 23(1) of the MCA 2005; Article 364 SCC.

A. States should provide for safeguards ensuring that attorneys are aware of their rights and responsibilities

Attorneys should, upon the entry into force of the CPA, be aware of their rights and responsibilities. Fassbind notes that prospective attorneys often agree to be nominated, without fully realising and understanding what the role entails.[116] In Switzerland, the adult protection agencies are therefore obliged to inform attorneys of their rights and responsibilities.[117] This is particularly important in cases where the attorney must consider restrictions and obligations imposed by law. Examples are the restrictions regarding gifts that can be made on behalf of the adult and the obligation for attorneys to keep accounts, applicable in England and Wales.[118] Attorneys should be made aware of these rights and obligations, preferably in an active manner as is the case in Switzerland.

B. States should ensure attorneys are 'up to the task'

An assessment of the skills of the attorney is preferably left to the discretion of the adult at the time the CPA is made. Most countries confine themselves to an exclusion of certain persons from the role of attorney. In England and Wales, eg a person who has recently been declared bankrupt, cannot act as attorney.[119] At first glance, this seems different in Switzerland, where the adult protection agencies, according to Article 363(2) of the Swiss Civil Code, are obliged to assess the suitability of the prospective attorney upon the entry into force of the CPA.[120] In practice, most authorities check whether the prospective attorney has a criminal record or appears in the insolvency register.[121] The process can be more extensive in situations where there seems to be a blatant mismatch between attorney and adult, eg a situation in which a billionaire with complex financial interests has appointed a person who has never dealt with such interests before.

3 *Safeguards When the CPA Has Become 'Active'*

There are several safeguards important when the CPA has become 'active' and the attorney, in other words, has assumed his responsibility.

A. Support of the first category (support enabling the adult to make a decision himself) should be ensured for adults who want to be involved in the execution of their CPA

A first direction that was mentioned in paragraph 2, is that there should be safeguards ensuring that adults who still want to be involved in the running of

116. https://www.aelterbasel.ch/finanzen-sicherheit/vorsorge/prima-bs-beratungsstelle-fuer-private-beistandspersonen-und-vorsorgebeauftragte/ (last accessed 25 October 2020).
117. Article 363(3) SCC.
118. Section 12 MCA 2005 and Section 7.58 MCA 2005 Code of Practice.
119. Section 10 MCA 2005.
120. Article 363(2) SCC.
121. This observation is based on enquiries I made at two adult protection authorities.

their affairs are given the opportunity to do so. This is clearly something with which in terms of safeguards more can be done in the various countries. A striking observation in this regard is that not all countries seem to be aware of the dynamic nature of capacity as being time- and decision-specific. In Switzerland, the CPA can only enter into force when the adult is 'no longer capable of judgement' (Article 360(1) SCC). This severely limits the possibilities of the CPA being used as an instrument for adults who, with support, are still able to make their own decision. In other countries, attorneys are legally obliged to consult and involve the adult in the execution of the CPA. In England and Wales, this follows from section 9(4) of the MCA 2005, where it states that attorneys should act in accordance with the principles of the MCA 2005. These principles include, among others, the principle that 'a person must be assumed to have capacity unless it is established that he lacks capacity' and the principle that 'a person is not to be treated as unable to make a decision unless all practicable steps to help him to do so have been taken without success.'[122] In Belgium, attorneys are according to Article 490/2 (2) of the Belgian Civil Code (BCC) obliged to involve the adult as much as possible in the execution of the CPA. In addition, the attorney needs to consult either the adult or a, by the adult, designated person at regular intervals and at least once a year. As has been noted, it is important that representatives are aware of such obligations and in addition receive support when needed.

B. States should ensure attorneys receive sufficient support

The need for adequate support is something that has been mentioned several times throughout this article. It is something, that is slowly getting more attention in all five countries. In Germany, support is provided by so-called 'Betreuungsvereine', associations focusing predominantly on the recruitment, training, and support of so-called 'ehrenamtliche Betreuer' (volunteers who can be appointed as guardian by the court). Pursuant to section 1908f of the German Civil Code, the activities of these associations must also include the provision of support for attorneys. A quick search of the web pages of several local 'Betreuungsvereine' shows that activities in this regard are often linked to already existing support initiatives open to voluntary guardians. Examples of the support provided are training, discussion groups focusing on the exchange of experiences and the possibility to consult a professional.[123] In Switzerland, the first initiatives to organise support for attorneys are also emerging. An example is the adult protection authority of Basel-Stadt, which has opened a helpdesk for attorneys.[124] It is, however, unknown whether

122. Section 1 of the MCA 2005.
123. See, eg the webpage of the Betreuungsverein Nordhessen-Kassel https://www.caritas-kassel.de/ichsuche-hilfe/allgemeine-hilfen/betreuungsverein/betreuungsverein (last accessed 25 October 2020).
124. https://www.aelterbasel.ch/finanzen-sicherheit/vorsorge/prima-bs-beratungsstelle-fuer-private-beistandspersonen-und-vorsorgebeauftragte/ (last accessed 25 October 2020).

these initiatives sufficiently meet the attorney's need for support and whether attorneys are at all able to find these organisations when they have questions or require assistance.

C. States should provide for safeguards ensuring there is some form of 'oversight' on the actions of the attorney

The attorney's need for support should not only be considered by states, but also by adult and attorney at the time the CPA is made. This can go hand in hand with creating some form of oversight on the actions of the attorney. All countries offer adults various possibilities to include their own safeguards in the CPA. Examples are the appointment of more than one attorney, the appointment of a 'supervisor', or the appointment of so-called 'trusted persons' with whom the attorney has to confer with regard to certain decisions. An interesting safeguard is the appointment of a so-called 'ad hoc attorney' in Belgium, a temporary attorney who is to act on behalf of the adult, instead of the 'regular' attorney, in cases where there is a conflict of interest.[125] Some authors note that counting on the adult to include these and other safeguards might be problematic as adults in most cases will not want to include safeguards as these might give the impression that the attorney is not trusted after all.[126] As noted earlier, however, safeguards are not only in the interest of the adult, but also in the interest of the attorney. In addition, safeguards do not only create some form of oversight, but may also provide the attorney with support. There are people in place with knowledge of affairs whom the attorney can turn to for assistance and advice.

D. General safeguards

In cases where there are suspicions of abuse or misuse of the CPA, it is important that it is clear where these suspicions can be reported. In Belgium, the 'alarmbelprocedure' (alert procedure) has been included in the law for this purpose.[127] Suspicions of misuse or abuse can be reported to the court and the court has according to Article 490/2(2) BCC the authority to replace the CPA partially or completely with an adult guardianship measure. Again, as noted throughout this article, it is important that the (previously recorded) wishes and instructions of the adult are respected as much as possible in these situations. In Belgium, the courts can also partially revoke the CPA, which means judges have room to conduct a tailor-made assessment of the responsibilities that should remain with the attorney and responsibilities that should be taken over. This seems appropriate, especially in cases where there has been unintentional misuse of the CPA by the attorney. Another example of a best practice in this regard is Germany,

125. 490/2 (1) BCC.
126. Autar (n 111); Zimmermann (n 108).
127. Wuyts (n 114).

where the court can appoint a so-called 'Kontrollbetreuer', a supervisor who has to monitor the actions of the attorney, meaning the attorney can remain in place.[128]

As noted, the directions as to appropriate safeguards formulated in paragraph 3 leave considerable room for implementation by means of a range of safeguards. This has become apparent in this paragraph where the development of safeguards is different from country to country and also differs from phase to phase. Safeguards are in some cases in the early stages of development. States can do, eg more to ensure that adults who want to be involved in the running of their affairs are given the opportunity to do so. Initiatives creating more awareness of the concept of capacity and the various ways in which adults can be provided with support in the exercise of their legal capacity, might help in this regard. In addition, states can do more to ensure attorneys are informed of rights and obligations in an active manner. Initiatives providing attorneys with support are slowly getting more attention. Steps could be taken to examine whether current initiatives meet the support needs of attorneys. Article 12(4) in the first instance creates an obligation for States Parties to provide for appropriate safeguards, but, as has become clear, adults and attorneys also have a responsibility in ensuring appropriate safeguards are in place to prevent situations of misuse. In that regard, states could, eg encourage adults and attorneys to think, at the time the CPA is made, about the inclusion of appropriate forms of oversight and other means to ensure the attorney is in the future adequately supported.

3.5 Conclusion

There is an increasing awareness of the risk of misuse or abuse associated with the use of CPAs. When contemplating which safeguards should be adopted to prevent this misuse or abuse, states must keep the need to strike a balance between protection on the one hand and trust and informality on the other hand in mind. In this regard, it is important to realise that the risk of misuse or abuse of CPAs can never be avoided completely. This has to do with the intrinsic nature of the CPA: it is based on a premise of trust, namely the assumption that the adult will choose an attorney who is trustworthy and has the necessary skills to take care of his affairs. This means there will always be situations in which this trust put in the attorney by the adult, turns out to be misplaced, and is abused by the attorney. This risk can at best be managed, it can never be avoided completely. In other words, efforts should be directed towards managing this risk of misuse or abuse as best as possible by adopting appropriate safeguards. As has become clear, designing such safeguards cannot be considered an easy task. Different levels and degrees of misuse and abuse can be distinguished, and various factors may play a role in

128. Zimmermann (n 108).

enabling the misuse and abuse of CPAs. Further research looking into the various factors and underlying dynamics remains important to ensure safeguards are as targeted as possible. Article 12(4) UNCRPD, nevertheless, requires States Parties to provide for appropriate safeguards preventing abuse. Based on the available information on the risk of misuse and abuse of CPAs, this article has provided directions as to how the three categories of safeguards, included in Article 12(4) UNCRPD, can be operationalised in the context of the CPA. These directions have subsequently been used to examine the safeguards implemented in five European countries with a view to providing insight into how these countries have tried to meet the requirement to ensure appropriate safeguards are in place. As has become clear, the development of safeguards differs from country to country and in some cases, safeguards are in the early stages of development. Steps can be taken by States to ensure that adults who want to be involved in the running of their affairs are given the opportunity to do so. In addition, States could do more to ensure that attorneys are aware of their rights and responsibilities upon the entry into force of the CPA and are provided with the support needed in the execution of the CPA. Future comparative research monitoring the development of these and other safeguards might be of value so that countries may continue to learn from one another. Assessing the appropriateness of safeguards has been the first step in ensuring compliance with Article 12(4) UNCRPD. However, Article 12(4) UNCRPD also requires safeguards to be 'effective' in preventing abuse. Further (empirical) research is, in other words, needed to assess whether safeguards that in the first instance seem appropriate, also work as intended and are effective in practice.

Acknowledgement
The author owes a huge debt of gratitude to Alzheimer Nederland for awarding her a Fellowship grant (WE.15-2018-08) which has enabled her to visit Belgium, Germany, England, and Switzerland as part of the comparative study featuring in the fourth paragraph of this article. In addition, the author would like to express her thanks and gratitude to prof. Volker Lipp (Georg-August-Universität Göttingen), prof. Regina Aebi-Müller (Universität Luzern), prof. Jens Scherpe (Cambridge Family Law Centre) and prof. Frederik Swennen (Universiteit Antwerpen) for hosting her at their universities, during the country visits. The author would finally like to thank prof. Masha Antokolskaia, Marit Buddenbaum, and Derek Monsuur and the two anonymous peer reviewers for their comments on (earlier drafts of) this article.

4 The legal basis and scope of the levenstestament in the Netherlands

The previous two chapters outlined the legal-normative context – in terms of human rights norms and principles – within which instruments such as the *levenstestament* operate. This chapter focuses on the legal basis and scope of the *levenstestament* in the Netherlands. The aim is twofold, namely firstly to discuss the regulatory framework of the *levenstestament* and secondly to address whether this regulatory framework complies with the international human rights norms and principles – in particular article 12 UNCRPD – outlined in the previous chapters. To discuss the regulatory framework of the *levenstestament*, it must first be clear what precisely a *levenstestament* is. As such, the *levenstestament* is not a statutory instrument. The instrument has been designed and conceptualised by the Dutch notariate within the framework of existing law. In practice, a *levenstestament* can include one or more of the following components: 1) the appointment of one or more attorneys for financial, medical and personal matters, 2) a medical treatment advance directive, and 3) and an advance directive addressed to the court in the context of an adult guardianship measure. In this book, I focus on the first component. Consequently, this chapter – after exploring the origins of the *levenstestament* in section 4.1 – focuses in section 4.2 on the regulatory framework for the appointment of an attorney through a *levenstestament* and whether this regulatory framework is in line with article 12 UNCRPD. This being so, there is a contentious issue that I felt could not remain undiscussed in this book. Already before the emergence of the *levenstestament*, article 7:450(3) of the Dutch Civil Code (CC) provided adults with the opportunity to make a medical treatment advance directive. This has raised the question of the added value of including such a treatment advance directive in a (notarised) *levenstestament*. Section 4.3 addresses this question.

4.1 Origin of the levenstestament in the Netherlands

The answer to where the origin of the Dutch *levenstestament* lies is mired with ambiguity. Since the 1970s, the term has been used by various organisations, referring to different instruments. The word '*levenstestament*' was first introduced by the Dutch Organisation for Voluntary Euthanasia (*Nederlandse Vereniging voor*

Vrijwillige Euthanasie – NVVE) in 1973 and used as the Dutch counterpart of what is in the United States known as a 'living will'.[1] According to Sutorius and Jansen, the NVVE aimed to introduce an instrument that could encompass both an advance directive for euthanasia (ADE) and a (non-)treatment directive. These directives were, at that time, not legally regulated in the Netherlands.[2] As becomes clear from a study of the parliamentary documents from the 1970s and 1980s, the use of the term *'levenstestament'* was adopted by Parliament in debates on whether these instruments should be statutorily regulated in the Netherlands. However, Parliament confined their use of the word *levenstestament* to (non-)treatment directives.[3] This directive was eventually statutorily regulated in 1995, followed by the advance directive for euthanasia in 2002.[4] The notariate was unhappy with the use of the term *'levenstestament'* for these purposes, as according to the board of the Dutch Notarial Association (*Koninklijke Nederlandse Beroepsorganisatie* – KNB) at the time, the Dutch term 'testament' (in English: last will) is generally understood to have meaning under inheritance law.[5] The KNB was afraid that using this term in a different context would lead to confusion and therefore kindly requested the NVVE to refrain from using the word *'levenstestament'*. However, the word was reintroduced by the notariate only a few decades later.

According to Engelbertink, judge Fikkers introduced the concept of what is now generally known as a *levenstestament*.[6] Fikkers presented the concept as a possible solution to the problem that judges could not grant the request of a financial guardian (bewindvoerder) to donate on behalf of an adult with impaired capacity placed under financial guardianship. In the Netherlands, financial guardians must obtain the court's consent for donations other than regular birthday gifts.[7] Courts frequently receive such requests as future heirs regularly search for ways in which

1. E.Ph.R. Sutorius & D.J. Jansen, 'De juridische status van het levenstestament', *Ars Aequi* 1991, pp. 990-997.
2. Ibid.
3. See for example House of Representatives, *Kamerstukken II* 1990/91, 21561, nr. 16 where, at the time, minister of Justice Hirsch-Ballin and the State Secretary of Welfare, Health and Culture Simons noted that a distinction should be made between a *levenstestament* (concerning wishes as to medical treatment in a life-threatening situation) and the advance directive for euthanasia (concerning a description of the circumstances in which an 'active' end of life is requested by the adult).
4. article 7:450(3) of the Dutch Civil Code (CC) and article 2(2) of the Law on Euthanasia. Section 4.3 will discuss both instruments in more detail.
5. C.G.C. Engelbertink, 'Ontwikkelingen van het levenstestament in de laatste tien jaren' in: F.W.J.M. Schols & B.C.M. Waaijer, *Het levenstestament. Nader verfijnd*, Den Haag: SDU 2017, pp. 195-213; *Notariële akte m.b.t. euthanasie*, WPNR 1974/5281, pp. 707-708.
6. Engelbertink 2017, p. 195; C.G.C. Engelbertink, 'Het levenstestament, een nieuwe ontwikkeling', *Kwartaalbericht Estateplanning* (*KWEP*) 2013/63.
7. Article 441(2) CC; Landelijk Overleg Vakinhoud Civiel en Kanton & Toezicht, *Aanbevelingen Meerderjarigenbewind 2018*, via: https://www.rechtspraak.nl/SiteCollectionDocuments/aanbevelingen-meerderjarigenbewind.pdf (last accessed: 02-06-2018).

assets can be transferred (to them) tax-efficiently. As a rule, courts only allow such donations when a so-called 'gifting tradition' can be shown.[8] Such a tradition may be inferred from proven repetitive actions conducted by the adult before the financial guardianship. Examples are annual donations to specific charities or recurring gifts to children exceeding the amount of a traditional birthday gift.[9] In other words, the court needs to establish whether the adult with impaired capacity would have wanted to donate would he be able to do so. If this can be sufficiently demonstrated in another way, the courts sometimes accept this alternative proof.[10] According to Van Mos, judges in practice frequently asked whether there was not a written document stating the wishes of the adult concerned regarding gifts.[11] Perhaps not surprisingly, judge Fikkers, therefore, gave the following advice: 'let every person with capacity express in a *levenstestament* his wishes regarding the allocation of assets in the context of estate planning'.[12]

The notariate has taken up the development of such an instrument in the Netherlands. Following judge Fikkers' recommendation, the Dutch Association for Notarial Estate Planners (*Vereniging van Estate Planners in het Notariaat* – EPN) set up a working group, and in 2010 this working group presented a model or format for the instrument that is known to date as the '*levenstestament*'. Although the instrument introduced by the EPN was modelled upon the ordinary power of attorney and included the conferral of authority to an attorney, in line with Fikkers' original suggestion, the possibility for adults to record their wishes and preferences was emphasised.[13] In addition to wishes regarding financial and personal matters, the *levenstestament* could, according to the working group, also contain the wishes and instructions of the adult about medical and health matters, as expressed in an advance directive for euthanasia, a (non-)treatment directive or a donor codicil.[14] However, not everyone has accepted this point of view, and – in the absence of a clear definition of the term '*levenstestament*' – different interpretations of what a *levenstestament* may entail have emerged. As discussed in

8. Ibid.
9. Ibid.
10. An exception was for example made by the Court of Appeal Arnhem-Leeuwarden in a case, where the financial guardian could show that the adult placed under guardianship – his mother –, had previously expressed the wish that her children should receive the proceeds of the sale of her house (Court of Appeal Arnhem-Leeuwarden 03-03-2016, ECLI:NL:GHARL:2016:1654, RN 2016/73).
11. S. Mos-van Gool, 'Het levenstestament in de praktijk', in: A.R. Autar, J.P.M. Stubbé & L.C.A. Verstappen, *Compendium Levenstestament*, Den Haag: SDU 2018, pp. 79-89.
12. Engelbertink 2013.
13. See e.g. A.H.N. Stollenwerck & R.C.E. van der Heide-van IJzinga Veenstra, 'Het levenstestament, een inleiding', *Fiscaal Tijdschrift Vermogen* 2010/10 where a list with wishes that can be recorded in the *levenstestament*, is provided (e.g. wishes with regard to assets, donations, non-treatment, euthanasia, the appointment of a guardian and practical affairs such as childcare, care of pets, funeral arrangements, etc.); See also Mos-van Gool 2018, pp. 82-87.
14. Ibid.

more detail in the next section, there are, on the one hand, notaries who consider the core of the *levenstestament* to be the appointment of one or more attorneys.[15] On the other hand, some notaries place emphasis on recording wishes, preferences and instructions in a *levenstestament*. Autar and Van Dijk, for example, define the *levenstestament* as a document in which the adult records one or more directives, prohibitions and/or wishes concerning financial matters, personal welfare, and end-of-life decisions to be acted upon accordingly in the event of his incapacity. According to Autar and Van Dijk, this instrument can include the appointment of one or more attorneys, but this does not necessarily have to be the case.[16] These different interpretations create the risk that an adult is unsure of what he is getting when approaching a notary with the wish to make a *levenstestament*.[17]

Besides the debate on the definition of the *levenstestament*, the question of whether the *levenstestament* should be statutorily regulated has also been the subject of debate. In 2011, a proposal to include the *levenstestament* in the Dutch Civil Code (CC) was presented by the Scientific Council of the EPN.[18] The EPN proposed to regulate the *levenstestament* within the framework of the existing law on ordinary powers of attorney. Although the majority opinion was that an ordinary power of attorney could remain in force upon the adult's incapacity, there was still some uncertainty at this point.[19] Therefore, the EPN's proposal included an amendment to article 3:72 CC to ensure that an ordinary power of attorney could remain in force after the principal's incapacity if the principal expressly so indicated. Furthermore, the amendment included the mandatory involvement of the notariate, as the EPN proposed that the principal could only grant a continuing power of attorney by notarial deed.[20] As section 3.3 of the Civil Code on ordinary powers of attorney is silent on an obligation to render an account, the EPN also proposed a new article 3:76a CC to allow the adult to include in the *levenstestament* a duty for the attorney to render an account. Finally, the EPN proposed the mandatory registration (including changes and terminations) of the *levenstestament*.[21]

15. A.R. Autar, 'Inleiding', in: A.R. Autar, J.P.M. Stubbé & L.C.A. Verstappen (eds.), *Compendium Levenstestament*, Den Haag: SDU 2018, pp. 19-27; See also K. Blankman & J. Kaljee, *Het levenstestament in de notariële rechtspraktijk*, Vrije Universiteit 2013, pp. 12 & 55.
16. A.R. Autar & H.C.E. van Dijk, 'Levenstestament', in: A.R. Autar, C.B. Baard, W.D. Kolkman & F. Sonneveldt (eds.), *Compendium Estate Planning*, Den Haag: Sdu 2017, pp. 681-682.
17. Autar 2018, p. 25. This also became apparent in the interviews conducted with adults who had recently made a *levenstestament*, as part of the study featured in chapter 6. In some cases, even the old definition of the *levenstestament* as entailing a euthanasia directive was adopted by the respondents.
18. EPN, *Toelichting Proeve van een Wetsvoorstel*, September 2012.
19. See for example M.J. van Mourik, 'Rechtsvragenrubriek', *WPNR*/6688, 2006, pp. 815-816.
20. EPN, *Toelichting Proeve van een wetsvoorstel*, September 2012.
21. Ibid.

Besides the EPN, scholars have highlighted the need for statutory regulation of the *levenstestament*. Blankman addressed the necessity of statutory regulation from a human rights law perspective, i.e. the United Nations Convention on the Rights of Persons with Disabilities (UNCRPD) and the Council of Europe Recommendation 2009(11) on principles concerning continuing powers of attorney and advance directives.[22] He distinguished three main points that require the attention of the Dutch legislator. First, Blankman argued that the legislator should introduce a so-called principle of subsidiarity, meaning that the *levenstestament* should take precedence over adult guardianship measures.[23] Second, Blankman argued that the requirement of article 12(4) UNCRPD to respect the rights, will, and preferences of the adult is of such importance that a legal standard for its implementation should be developed, not only for the attorney appointed through a *levenstestament*, but also for court-appointed and informal representatives.[24] Such a standard should ensure that the adult is involved in the decision-making process as much as possible, for example, through assistance in decision-making, co-decision-making or by informing and consulting the adult.[25] The third, and according to Blankman, the most crucial issue requiring the legislator's attention is to ensure that adults with impaired capacity are adequately protected against misuse or abuse by the attorney.[26] In addition to the points raised by Blankman, Van den Broeck has stressed the importance of mandatory registration of the *levenstestament* in a central register.[27] First, to ensure that, for example, judges in adult guardianship procedures are aware of the *levenstestament*. But also to prevent attorneys from using a *levenstestament* that has afterwards been changed or terminated by the adult.[28] Van den Broeck also recommended the adoption of a statutory rule obliging attorneys to inform the court when they are no longer able or willing to act as attorneys to avoid leaving the adult without support and protection.[29]

The necessity of statutory regulation of the *levenstestament* has been discussed several times in the Dutch Parliament. In 2012, several political parties raised

---

22. K. Blankman, 'Een wettelijke regeling voor het levenstestament', in: F.W.J.M. Schols & B.C.M. Waaijer, *Het levenstestament. Nader verfijnd*, Den Haag: SDU 2017, pp. 45-64.
23. Ibid, p. 53-54. See also R.E. Brinkman & J.M. van Anken, 'Het levenstestament en/in de notariële praktijk' in: F.W.J.M. Schols & B.C.M. Waaijer, *Het levenstestament. Nader verfijnd*, Den Haag: SDU 2017, pp. 65-82 (69).
24. Blankman 2017, p. 55.
25. Ibid, pp. 60-61.
26. Ibid, pp. 56-59.
27. A. Van den Broeck, 'Inspiratie uit het buitenland voor het Nederlandse levenstestament', in: F.W.J.M. Schols & B.C.M. Waaijer, *Het levenstestament. Nader verfijnd*, Den Haag: SDU 2017, pp. 17-44; See also: C.G.C. Engelbertink, 'Het levenstestament in de maatschappij', in: K. Blankman & C.G.C. Engelbertink, *Preadvies Notariële bescherming ouderen*, Den Haag: Sdu Uitgevers 2013, pp. 59-132 (70).
28. Ibid, pp. 24-26.
29. Ibid, pp. 42-43.

questions about the need for statutory regulation during the debate on the *Wet Wijziging Curatele, Bewind en Mentorschap* (Amendment Act on full guardianship, financial guardianship and personal guardianship). State Secretary Teeven of Justice and Security (J&S) confirmed at the time that an ordinary power of attorney remains in force upon the principal's incapacity and stated that legislation in this respect did not seem necessary.[30] According to the state secretary, an assessment of the need for further regulation required an inventory of practical problems and relevant gaps in the current legislation. Conducting such an inventory was considered beyond the scope of the Amendment Act and therefore deferred to the next cabinet.[31] In 2013, the question was raised again by Member of Parliament (MP) De Wit and Parliament was promised an inventory of problems and legislative gaps by State Secretary Teeven.[32]

The Minister of J&S Van der Steur eventually sent this inventory to Parliament in 2015.[33] The minister praised the efforts of the KNB. Through the development of a model – besides the model developed by the EPN – and conversations with the judiciary, banks, doctors and guardianship organisations, the KNB had tried to solve the practical problems with the *levenstestament*. In addition, the KNB had set up a register – the Centraal Levenstestamentenregister (CLTR) – to register notarised *levenstestamenten*. According to the minister, these efforts had already largely solved the problems with the *levenstestament* in practice. The inventory sent to Parliament discussed four issues. The minister stated that three of these issues had already been resolved, with the fourth issue soon to be resolved. The three allegedly solved problems concerned the following matters: the acceptance of the *levenstestament* by banks, the uncertainty among funeral directors about the possibility of recording funeral wishes in the *levenstestament* and judges' unfamiliarity with the *levenstestament*. Minister Van der Steur indicated that consultations between the KNB and the various organisations and – where necessary – adjustments to the model had led to a satisfactory solution of these issues.[34]

The fourth problem concerned the access of the courts to the CLTR. The minister noted that for the *levenstestament* to function properly, judges must be aware of its existence when considering an application for an adult guardianship measure. In this regard, the minister referred to ongoing conversations between the KNB

30. Dutch House of Representatives, *Kamerstukken II* 2011/12, 22054, nr. 6, pp. 2-4. See also Court of Appeal the Hague 14-03-2017, ECLI:NL:GHDHA:2017:801, §28. Although the Court of Appeal confirms that a power of attorney can remain in force upon the incapacity of the principal, the court also notes that legal regulation is desirable.
31. Ibid.
32. Dutch House of Representatives, *Handelingen II* 2012/13, nr. 60, item 25.
33. Dutch House of Representatives, *Kamerstukken II* 2014/15, 33054, nr. 20.
34. Ibid.

and the judiciary on access to the register and expressed his confidence that this fourth issue would soon be resolved.[35] Parliament has closely monitored the developments on this last point. In the process – besides whether the register could be made accessible to the judiciary – the question of whether the judiciary should be obliged to consult the register gradually emerged. In February 2017, following repeated questions, MP Van der Burg tabled a motion asking the government to re-engage in talks with both the KNB and the judiciary to provide the judiciary with access to the register.[36] In June 2017, the Minister of J&S Blok informed Parliament that talks with the KNB and the judiciary had not resulted in the judiciary having access to the register.[37] Although the KNB was prepared to provide access to the register, the judiciary was not convinced of the need to consult the CLTR. The CLTR only contains information on the existence of a *levenstestament*, not the content. The judiciary noted that during the adult guardianship procedure, there are sufficient opportunities for the adult, family members, the proposed guardian and other relevant parties to inform the court about the existence of the *levenstestament*.[38] The mandatory consultation of the CLTR in every adult guardianship procedure was considered a costly exercise. Instead, the judiciary proposed a procedure whereby the applicant for a measure would be explicitly asked about the existence of a *levenstestament* and, if applicable, to provide a copy of this document. The minister agreed with the judiciary and saw no need for an obligation to consult the register.[39]

In addition to the above issues, two other issues have attracted the attention of Parliament. First, in 2015, MP Krol expressed concern that the costs of a *levenstestament* might, in some cases, be a barrier for adults to make a *levenstestament*.[40] In this regard, the Minister of J&S indicated that while adults are advised to use the services of a notary, they can also make a *levenstestament* themselves without the involvement of a professional.[41] Second, Parliament has expressed interest in how notaries assess the mental capacity of adults. The minister of J&S referred to ongoing efforts of the notariate, such as the development of a guideline that notaries can use to assess their clients' capacity

35. Ibid.
36. Dutch House of Representatives, *Kamerstukken II* 2016/17, 28345, nr. 175. See also: Dutch House of Representatives, *Kamerstukken II* 2015/16, 28345, nr. 141.
37. Dutch House of Representatives, *Kamerstukken II* 2016/17, 28345, nr. 180.
38. Ibid, pp. 3-4. The proposal was to include such a question in the applicant form for an adult guardianship measure.
39. Ibid, p. 4.
40. Dutch House of Representatives, *Handelingen II* 2015/16, nr. 29, item 6.
41. Dutch House of Representatives, *Handelingen II* 2015/16, nr. 29, item 6, Appendix; Dutch House of Representatives, *Handelingen II* 2015/16, nr. 30, item 5.

and the development of a protocol regulating the involvement of independent doctors in the assessment process.[42]

The aforementioned shows that while Parliament has closely monitored the development of the *levenstestament*, the legislator has not deemed it necessary to enact specific legislation regulating the *levenstestament*. Regulation has, in practice, been left to the notariate and, to a lesser extent, to the judiciary. The following section focuses on the question of how – in the absence of a statutory framework – this regulation looks like, focusing in particular on the appointment of an attorney through a *levenstestament*.

4.2 Regulation in the absence of a statutory framework

This section explores the regulation of the *levenstestament* in the absence of a specific regulatory framework, focusing on the appointment of an attorney through a *levenstestament*. In addition, I explore whether this regulatory framework complies with article 12 UNCRPD. Before I can answer these questions, however, there is a contentious issue I need to address first. The lack of a clear legal definition of the term '*levenstestament*' has not only led to uncertainty about what a *levenstestament* can entail but has also sparked a debate about the legal basis of the *levenstestament*. In subsection 4.2.1, I address this debate and explore the various options for regulating the *levenstestament* within the framework of existing law. I then turn to whether – all options considered – compliance with article 12 UNCRPD is at all possible within the framework of existing law, given the setting of future incapacity of the adult, for which the *levenstestament* is intended to provide. In the absence of statutory regulation, the notariate has played a vital role in promoting the validity and acceptance of the *levenstestament* in practice and in developing safeguards to prevent abuse or misuse of the *levenstestament* by the attorney. In addition, the judiciary in the Netherlands has guided the development of the *levenstestament*. Sections 4.2.2 and 4.2.3. discuss the efforts of these (societal) actors and their role in ensuring compliance with article 12 UNCRPD.

4.2.1 An ambiguous legal basis

To date, there is no consensus on how the appointment of an attorney should be conceptualised within the framework of existing law. In this context, two different

42. Dutch House of Representatives, *Kamerstukken II* 2013/14, 29389, nr. 62; Dutch House of Representatives, *Kamerstukken II* 2014/15, 29389, nr. 90. In Dutch the guideline is known as the 'Stappenplan beoordeling wilsbekwaamheid ten behoeve van notariële dienstverlening'. In 2006 the KNB presented the first guideline, followed in 2013 by an updated version. The latest version of the guideline has been presented in 2021.

approaches can be distinguished.[43] Supporters of the first approach argue that the *levenstestament* is no more than an ordinary power of attorney (article 3:60 to 3:79 CC). A power of attorney (POA) concerns an act of representation. As article 3:60(1) CC makes clear, through a POA, a person – the principal – grants the authority to perform one or more legal acts on his behalf to another person – the attorney.[44] The POA creates a situation in which the acts performed by the attorney – within the scope of his authority – affect the principal's legal position in relation to a third party as if the principal had performed the act himself.[45] As such, the POA is an essential element of the *levenstestament*. Supporters of the second approach do not deny this. They argue, however, that the legal basis of the *levenstestament* should not be confined to a POA. First of all, because a *levenstestament* often encompasses more than a conferral of authority to perform *legal acts* on behalf of the adult (i.e. a POA). Kortmann notes that through a *levenstestament*, the attorney is frequently also authorised to perform other acts for or on behalf of the adult, such as managing the adult's bank account and taking care of the adult's financial administration, managing the adult's email account, etc.[46] Secondly, because – as I will explain in more detail below – a POA only applies to the so-called external relationships between the principal and a third party and the attorney and a third party. The POA does not provide a legal basis for the internal relationship between the principal and the attorney, which determines the rights and duties – such as an obligation to render account – that govern the use of the POA.[47] This internal relationship – according to supporters of the second approach – also requires a legal basis through an agreement between the principal and the attorney in which arrangements can be made concerning the tasks the attorney will perform for and on behalf of the principal and the rights and duties that govern the execution of the *levenstestament*. In this regard, the provisions on the service provision agreement (articles 7:400 to 413 CC) and the mandate agreement (articles 7:414 to 7:424 CC) are considered relevant and applicable.[48]

As the preceding makes clear, clarity – and perhaps more importantly, consensus – is needed on how the *levenstestament* should be conceptualised within the

43. R.E. Brinkman & J.M. van Anken, 'Levensexecuteur/volmacht', in: A.R. Autar, J.P.M. Stubbé & L.C.A. Verstappen (eds.), *Compendium Levenstestament*, Den Haag: SDU 2018, pp. 91-131.
44. Article 3:60 CC, translation via: dutchcivillaw.com (last accessed: 26-06-2021).
45. See also article II-6:105 of the Principles, Definitions and Model Rules of European Private Law Draft Common Frame of Reference (DCFR).
46. S.C.J.J. Kortmann, 'Rekening en verantwoording door de mantelzorger', in: F.W.J.M. Schols & B.C.M. Waaijer, *Het levenstestament. Nader verfijnd*, Den Haag: SDU 2017, pp. 139-151.
47. A.C. van Schaick, *Volmacht*, Deventer: Kluwer 2011, pp. 9-10.
48. L.C.A. Verstappen, 'Het levenstestament: een korte analyse van veel gebruikte modellen', in: F.W.J.M. Schols & B.C.M. Waaijer (eds.), *Het levenstestament. Nader verfijnd*, Sdu: The Hague 2017, pp. 153-167; Kortmann 2017, pp. 143-146; L.C.A. Verstappen, 'Het levenstestament: volmacht of toch opdracht/lastgeving?', *WPNR* 2013-6993, pp. 931-932.

framework of existing law. Therefore, in the remainder of this subsection, I will first elaborate on the abovementioned debate. In doing so, I will argue that while a POA is an essential part of the *levenstestament*, the *levenstestament* should not be confined to it. While it is important to address this contentious issue first, the quest for consensus should not distract attention from a more critical question, namely whether the *levenstestament* can be adequately regulated within the framework of existing law, given the specific setting of future incapacity of the adult, for which the *levenstestament* is intended to provide. Both the power of attorney, the service provision agreement and the mandate agreement have not been designed by the legislator for a setting where the adult's cognitive abilities are (gradually) declining. In other words, using these legal constructs as a legal basis for the *levenstestament* is not self-evident, especially from a human rights perspective. As I have argued in the previous chapter, from a human rights perspective, adequate safeguards must be in place to ensure respect for the adult's rights, will, and preferences, avoid undue influence and manage conflicts of interest.[49] These safeguards – included in article 12(4) UNCRPD – also concern the relationship between the principal and the attorney and should, to some extent, determine the rights and duties that underpin the attorney's actions. Examples of such safeguards have been mentioned in section 4.1 of this chapter. Blankman has advocated the adoption of a general standard requiring the attorney to involve the adult in the decision-making process as much as possible.[50] In addition, Blankman has stressed the importance of safeguards ensuring the adult is adequately protected against misuse or abuse by the attorney.[51] The regulatory framework on the ordinary power of attorney, the service provision agreement and the mandate agreement does provide certain general standards guiding the attorney's actions. An example is article 7:416 CC on conflicts of interest regarding mandate agreements, stipulating that a transaction with the attorney in a personal capacity may only be performed if the content of the legal act is so precisely determined that the possibility of a conflict of interest is excluded.[52] The question is whether general standards like these are sufficient to ensure compliance with article 12 UNCRPD. I will address this question in the second half of this subsection.

Why the legal basis of the levenstestament should not be confined to an ordinary power of attorney

As noted above, through a power of attorney, a principal authorises one or more attorneys to act on his behalf or, to put it differently, to represent him. Article 3:66

49. Article 12(4) UNCRPD. But see for example also the Council of Europe Recommendation CM/Rec(2009)11, titled Principles concerning continuing powers of attorney and advance directives for incapacity.
50. Blankman 2017, p. 55.
51. Ibid.
52. Article 7:416 CC; See also article II-6:109 DCFR.

CC clarifies that legal acts performed by the attorney – within the confines of his authority – produce a legal effect for the principal.[53] Without a POA, an attorney cannot act on behalf of the principal. There is, therefore, no question that the POA is an essential element of the *levenstestament*. As noted above, the debate focuses on whether the *levenstestament* can be confined to a POA. To understand why this question has risen, it is necessary to briefly look at the legal construct of the power of attorney and the doctrine of representation. Both Bloembergen and Van Schendel note that the law continues to evolve regarding the doctrine of representation. Moreover, in the Dutch legal community, there is no consensus on all points of this doctrine – something which has become visible in the context of the *levenstestament*.[54]

According to Van Schaick, the Dutch POA is based on the German model.[55] Within this model, two elements must be distinguished and considered separately. The first element is a unilateral act by which the principal establishes representation – in this case, the conferral of authority through a POA. The second element – some authors think that it does not always need to be present – is an underlying legal relationship between the principal and attorney, mostly a bilateral agreement, which falls outside the scope of the POA. In other words, the POA only pertains to the so-called external relationship between the principal and the attorney, on the one hand, and third parties, on the other hand. The rights and obligations between the principal and attorney are governed by another – internal – relationship.[56] That can be, for instance, an employment contract, a service provision agreement or a mandate agreement. With regard to the German system, Spalckhaver makes the following distinction: the POA defines the legal authority based on which the attorney *can* act, whereas the underlying agreement, which falls outside the scope of the POA, determines when the attorney *may* or *must* act.[57] This is logical, as the POA is a unilateral act, and its validity does not depend on the acceptance by the attorney. Thus, without his consent, no obligation to act can be imposed on the attorney. Such an obligation to act can only arise from an underlying bilateral agreement between the principal and the attorney. The advantage of this system is that third parties do not need to delve into all the details of the (contractual) relationship between the principal and the attorney. They can rely on the specification of the attorney's authority in the POA. In the Netherlands, the

53. A.R. Bloembergen & W.A.M. van Schendel, 'Vertegenwoordiging en volmacht', in: J. Hijma, C.C. van Dam, W.A.M. van Schendel & W.L. Valk, *Rechtshandeling en Overeenkomst*, Deventer: Kluwer 2010, pp. 78-134 (89-90)
54. Bloembergen & Van Schendel 2010, pp. 82-83.
55. Van Schaick 2011, pp. 1-2.
56. Ibid.
57. J. Spalckhaver, 'Die Vorsorgevollmacht und das ihr zugrunde liegende Rechtsverhältnis als umfassende Vorsorgeregelung', in: V. Lipp, *Handbuch der Vorsorgeverfügungen*, München: Verlag Franz Vahlen 2009, pp. 95-105 (98).

fact that the POA is legally separated from the underlying relationship between the principal and the attorney has sparked a discussion as to whether a PAO can also – de facto – exist without any underlying internal agreement between the principal and the attorney.[58] Bloembergen, Van Schendel, and Kortmann argue that a so-called 'isolated POA' is possible. In contrast, van Schaick argues that a POA is always based on an underlying agreement between the principal and the attorney.[59]

These two approaches to ordinary powers of attorney have led to two views on the *levenstestament*. On the one hand, some notaries consider the *levenstestament* an isolated POA. This allows for situations where the attorney is not aware of the contents of the *levenstestament* or – even worse – cases in which the designated attorney is not aware that he has been nominated as such.[60] On the other hand, some notaries argue that, although the POA is an essential element of the *levenstestament*, the *levenstestament* necessarily includes a more comprehensive internal legal relationship between the principal and attorney.[61] It is beyond the scope of this book to discuss the general theoretical question of whether an isolated POA is possible at all. Even if we assume that an isolated POA is possible, I would argue that an isolated POA is unsuitable as a legal basis for the *levenstestament*. The main argument I would like to put forward is that a POA, as such, merely authorises the attorney to act without imposing on him an obligation to act.[62] Any obligation to act follows not directly from the POA but rather from an internal agreement between the principal and the attorney.[63] This does not have to be a problem if the principal can still act and decide for himself. Granting a power of attorney does not preclude the principal from acting himself.[64] In other words, if the attorney does not use his authority when this is deemed necessary by the principal, the principal can – in theory – also act himself or appoint another attorney. However, the absence of an obligation to act becomes problematic if the principal (gradually) loses the ability to act and decide himself. Since the objective of the *levenstestament* is to ensure that the principal's interests in such a

58. Van Schaick 2011, pp. 9-10.
59. S.C.J.J. Kortmann, *Mr. C. Assers Handleiding tot de beoefening van het Nederlands Burgerlijk Recht. 3. Deel III. Vermogensrecht algemeen. Volmacht en vertegenwoordiging*, Deventer: Wolters Kluwer 2017, §22.
Bloembergen & Van Schendel 2010, pp. 94-96; Van Schaick 2011, pp. 9-10.
60. In the interviews conducted with adults who had recently made a *levenstestament* – featuring in the study in chapter 6 – there were several respondents who indicated that they intended to keep their *levenstestament* behind lock and key until the time, it would become relevant.
61. Brinkman & van Anken 2018, pp. 91-131.
62. Kortmann 2017, §101; Bloembergen & Van Schendel 2010, pp. 92-93.
63. Van Schaick 2011, pp. 20-21.
64. Kortmann 2017, §68.

situation are protected, an obligation for the attorney to use his authority seems indispensable.[65]

In addition to this main argument, two additional arguments can be presented. The first argument relates to how the attorney should use the authority conferred through the POA. The principal can include in the *levenstestament* wishes, preferences and instructions directed to the attorney on how the attorney should act. Considering the experiences with the *levenstestament* in practice, there are sound reasons to include these wishes, preferences and instructions in an internal agreement between the principal and attorney rather than in the POA.[66] The inclusion of instructions in the POA – which in principle only concerns the external relationship between principal/attorney and third parties – brings with it the risk that third parties may be reluctant to accept the *levenstestament* because they want to avoid the risk of being held accountable for a potential breach of the instruction by the attorney. As I will discuss in more detail in the following subsection, banks are, for example, unwilling to accept POAs that include an instruction stipulating that the attorney may only withdraw a certain amount of money from the principal's account to donate.

The second argument relates to whether the regulatory framework on the power of attorney – on its own – provides for sufficient safeguards considering the specific setting for which the *levenstestament* is intended to provide. Both Kortmann and Bloembergen and Van Schendel note that there are certain general standards with which the attorney must comply when he decides to exercise his authority.[67] Kortmann and Spierings note, for instance, that the attorney may not act contrary to the principal's instructions, should inform the principal about the use of the POA, and should return any documents confirming the POA when the authority to act on behalf of the principal has ended.[68] In short, the attorney must behave

65. See Blankman & Kaljee 2013, p. 17; Blankman and Kaljee note that the most predominant problem with the *levenstestament* is that there will never be any guarantee that the wishes and instructions recorded in the *levenstestament* will be fulfilled.
66. J. Kronenburg-de Jonge, 'Het ene levenstestament is het andere niet', *FTV* 2016-4. The POA and the internal agreement between principal and attorney can be included in one and the same document. In this case, it is important that the principal (and the attorney) clearly indicate in the document which provisions concern the power of attorney and which provisions concern the internal agreement between the principal and the attorney. Kronenburg-de Jonge notes that the distinction between the two components can also be made more explicit by including the principal's wishes, preferences and instructions directed to the attorney in an appendix, attached to the POA. A third option is to include the two components in two separate documents. This may also make it easier for the principal to update and revise his wishes, preferences and instructions, which may after all be subject to change.
67. Kortmann 2017, §101; Bloembergen & Van Schendel 2010, pp. 116-117; See also: C. Spierings, *De eenzijdigde rechtshandeling*, Nijmegen: Wolters Kluwer 2016, pp. 57-61.
68. Kortmann 2017, §101; Spierings 2016, pp. 57-61 (57).

in a manner befitting a 'prudent attorney'.[69] Although these standards are a first step in the right direction – especially with regard to the safeguards ensuring respect for the will and preferences of the adult – I would argue they do not go far enough. As outlined in the previous chapter, article 12 UNCRPD requires more profound tailor-made standards, ensuring, for example, that the adult – when he so desires – is involved in the execution of the *levenstestament* and is adequately protected against the misuse or abuse of the *levenstestament*.

Based on the preceding, I reiterate my conclusion that although the POA is an essential element of the *levenstestament*, the *levenstestament* should not be confined to it. Notaries still using the isolated POA as a legal basis for the *levenstestament* would be well advised to refrain from doing so any longer. This conclusion also finds support in the literature to date, where there seems to be a consensus that – in addition to a power of attorney – a *levenstestament* also encompasses an underlying internal agreement between the principal and the attorney.[70] As noted, in this regard, the provisions on the service provision agreement and the mandate agreement are considered relevant and applicable. I will now turn to a discussion of the relevance of these legal constructs in shaping the internal relationship between the principal and the attorney. In addition, I will consider whether these legal constructs can provide an adequate legal basis for the *levenstestament* ensuring compliance with article 12 UNCRPD.

Can an adequate legal basis for the levenstestament be provided within the framework of the existing law?

Two legal constructs have been proposed in the Dutch literature as a legal basis for the internal relationship between the principal and the attorney in the context

69. Ibid.
70. Brinkman & Van Anken 2018; B.M.E.M. Schols, 'Het levenstestament 'über den Tod hinaus'', in: F.W.J.M. Schols & B.C.M. Waaijer, *Het levenstestament. Nader verfijnd*, Den Haag: SDU 2017, pp. 121-137; Verstappen 2017, pp. 153-167. The legal basis of the *levenstestament* has in the literature also been discussed in relation to the question whether with a *levenstestament* there is an obligation for the attorney to render account. Such an obligation is in principle namely included in an internal agreement between principal and attorney. As subsection 3.3 CC on POAs does not contain any provisions on an obligation to render account, in practice the question arose whether – in the event the *levenstestament* is considered an isolated POA – an obligation to render account should also be assumed. Mellema-Kranenburg (2016) notes that although this with regard to POAs in general, is dependent on the circumstances of the case, such an obligation can – when it concerns the specific setting of the *levenstestament* – in the majority of cases be assumed. In this regard, Verstappen (2017) rightly observes that legal certainty would be enhanced if such an obligation is clearly set out in the *levenstestament* by means of an underlying agreement between principal and attorney. Providing yet another argument why the *levenstestament* should entail more than an isolated POA. See: H.J. Weijers, 'Het levenstestament en het afleggen van rekening en verantwoording', *FTV* 2019; T. Mellema-Kranenburg, 'Hoe ver gaat de verplichting tot rekening en verantwoording', JBN 2016-2; S.C.J.J. Kortmann 2017, pp. 139-151; J.M. Tempelaar, 'Volmacht en rekening en verantwoording', *WPNR* 2010-6838, pp. 278-283.

of the *levenstestament*. The first concerns the *opdracht* (service provision agreement), defined by article 7:400(1) CC as follows:

> 'A service provision agreement is the agreement under which one of the parties ('the service provider') has engaged himself towards the other party (' the client') to perform work on another basis than an employment agreement, which work consists of something else than the making of a tangible construction, the safekeeping of property, the publication of a work or the transportation of persons or goods'.[71]

The second concerns the *lastgeving* (mandate agreement), defined by article 7:414 CC as follows:

> 'A mandate agreement is a service provision agreement under which one of the parties, ('the mandatory') has engaged himself towards the other party ('the mandator') to perform one or more legal acts for account of the latter (the mandator).'[72]

As this definition shows, the mandate agreement is a species of the service provision agreement, which means the rules on the service provision agreement also apply to the mandate agreement unless explicitly stated otherwise.[73] To answer the question of which legal construct is appropriate as a legal basis for the internal relationship between the principal and the attorney, the objective of the *levenstestament* is decisive. In this regard, I concur with Kortmann that the *levenstestament* can – and perhaps should – encompass more than the arrangements concerning the representation of the adult.[74] In this context, I refer to the human rights framework – particularly the requirements of article 12 UNCRPD – discussed in the previous two chapters. As noted, with regard to article 12 UNCRPD, two categories of support can be distinguished. The first category concerns support enabling an adult to make a decision himself and providing the adult with the assistance to implement this decision so that it can produce a legal effect. The second category comes into play when the adult can no longer decide for himself, notwithstanding the support provided. In such a case, the attorney can support the adult by acting on his behalf based on his (previously expressed) wishes, preferences and instructions.[75] It should be emphasised that the first form

71. Article 7:400 CC, translation via: dutchcivillaw.com (last accessed: 26-06-2021).
72. Article 7:414 CC, translation via: dutchcivillaw.com (last accessed: 26-06-2021).
73. T.F.E. Tjong Tjin Tai, *Mr. C. Assers Handleiding tot de beoefening van het Nederlands Burgerlijk Recht. 7. Bijzondere overeenkomsten. Deel IV. Opdracht, incl. de geneeskundige behandelingsovereenkomst en de reisovereenkomst*, Deventer: Wolters Kluwer 2018, §43; A.H. Lamers, *Opdracht, lastgeving en bemiddeling*, Zutphen: Uitgeverij Paris 2012, p. 119.
74. Kortmann 2017, pp. 143-146.
75. H.N. Stelma-Roorda, C. Blankman & M.V. Antokolskaia, 'A changing paradigm of protection of vulnerable adults and its implications for the Netherlands', *Family & Law* 2019, pp. 1-18; W. Martin, S. Michalowski, J. Stavert, A. Ward, A. Ruck Keene, C. Caughey, A. Hempsey &

of support – support for the adult to make his own decision – is to be given preference over the second one.

Although the use of the *levenstestament* within the second category of support seems the most obvious, as discussed in the previous chapter, the *levenstestament* can also play an important role in enabling support of the first category.[76] The attorney can provide the adult with the support needed to make his own decisions and, when necessary, assist the adult in implementing this decision legally (support of the first category). As noted above, when the adult can no longer make his own decisions, the attorney can then step in and support the adult by acting based on his (previously expressed) wishes and preferences (support of the second category). In other words, both forms of support can go hand in hand. In this regard, it is essential to realise that capacity is a dynamic concept; it is time and decision specific. This means, for example, that although a person, at some stage, due to a decline of cognitive abilities, might no longer be able to decide on the sale of his house, he might still be able to determine what birthday gift his grandchildren should receive. The attorney can, in this respect, fulfil a double role, supporting the adult to make his own decisions when this is still possible, and acting on behalf of the adult, when this is no longer possible. In other words, I envisage a more significant role for the attorney than a mere representative.

Taking this objective as the starting point, both the service provision agreement and the mandate agreement seem relevant in shaping the internal legal relationship between the principal and attorney in the context of the *levenstestament*. Through a service provision agreement, the principal and the attorney can make arrangements about the support the attorney is going to provide, for example, accompanying the adult to hospital appointments, managing the adult's email account and bringing important emails to the attention of the adult and taking care of the adult's financial administration. The provisions on the mandate agreement come into play when the attorney is asked to perform legal acts on behalf of the principal, for example, selling the house when the principal has to move to a care home. In other words, through the mandate agreement, arrangements can be made about the legal acts the attorney is authorised to perform based on the POA. In contrast with the unilateral POA, both the service provision agreement and the mandate agreement are bilateral agreements and therefore create an obligation to act on behalf of the principal.[77] In addition, both the service provision agreement and the mandate agreement allow the principal to include his wishes, preferences and instructions addressed to the attorney in such

---

R. McGregor, *The Essex Autonomy Project. Three Jurisdictions Report. Towards Compliance with CRPD Art. 12 in Capacity/Incapacity legislation across the UK*, University of Essex 2016.

76. Chapter 3 section 3.

77. Article 7:400(1) CC; Article 7:414(1) CC.

a way as to avoid problems with the enforceability of the *levenstestament* by third parties, such as banks.

As the aforementioned makes clear, both the service provision agreement and the mandate agreement are essential elements of the *levenstestament* as they allow the adult and attorney to make arrangements about the tasks the attorney will perform for and on behalf of the adult. Both agreements also provide room for arrangements on the rights and duties of the attorney concerning the execution of the *levenstestament*.[78] However, a key question that remains is whether these legal constructs provide sufficient safeguards ensuring compliance with article 12 UNCRPD, given the specific setting of incapacity for which the *levenstestament* is intended to provide.

To answer this question, it is necessary to first briefly look at the legal construct of the service provision agreement. Article 7:400(1) CC makes clear that the scope of the service provision agreement is considerably broad, as it encompasses all arrangements for the provision of work except those excluded in the article.[79] That means, in other words, that various types of agreements fall under the scope of article 7:400(1) CC. Tjong Tjin Tai mentions the agreement with a doctor, lawyer, accountant or architect, but also the agreement with a physiotherapist, sports trainer, hairdresser and newspaper delivery boy.[80] An apt example in the context of this book is the agreement between a client and a notary whereby the latter agrees to assist the client in drafting the *levenstestament*. The legal framework of service provision agreements has been geared to accommodate this variety of agreements. A generic framework of broadly formulated statutory provisions has been created through articles 7:401 to 7:412 CC.[81] In drafting these statutory provisions, the legislator mainly envisaged a scenario in which the service provision agreement is used to make agreements on personal services, with the attorney acting in the principal's interest.[82] Looking at the provisions that guide the actions of the attorney, this is translated into an obligation for the attorney to exercise the care of a prudent attorney (article 7:401 CC), an obligation to follow the principal's instructions (article 7:402(1) CC), a duty to inform the principal about the work performed under the service provision agreement (article 7:403(1)

78. L.C.A. Verstappen, 'Het levenstestament: volmacht of toch opdracht/lastgeving?', *WPNR* 2013-6993, pp. 931-932.
79. Article 7:400(1) CC mentions in this regard 'the making of a tangible construction, the safekeeping of property, the publication of a work or the transportation of persons or goods' (translation via: dutchcivillaw.com – last accessed: 26-06-2021)
80. Tjong Tjin Tai 2018, §49.
81. Tjong Tjin Tai 2018, §46.
82. Tjong Tjin Tai 2018, §48.

CC) and an obligation to render account (article 7:403(2) CC).[83] These broadly formulated provisions – such as article 7:401 CC stipulating that the attorney must observe the care of a prudent attorney – provide room for customisation and further specification concerning specific types of the service provision agreement. Tjong Tjin Tai notes in this regard that the interpretation of these standards will depend on the circumstances of the case.[84] In addition, to the broadly formulated statutory provisions, the legislator has also provided the principal and the attorney with the possibility to ignore these provisions altogether. Article 7:400(2) CC makes clear that the principal and the attorney, through the service provision agreement, may derogate from the statutory requirements of article 7:401-7:412 CC.[85]

As indicated, the standards mentioned above on the service provision agreement also apply to the mandate agreement.[86] That being said, the regulatory framework on the mandate agreement includes three additional standards intended to manage conflicts of interest. I have already noted article 7:416 CC above, stipulating that an attorney may only perform a transaction in a personal capacity when the content of the legal act is so precisely determined that the possibility of a conflict of interests is excluded.[87] Article 7:417 CC makes clear that the same applies in the event the attorney, with regard to the same legal act, operates as the attorney of both the principal and the third party. Articles 7:416(3) CC and 7:417(2) CC make clear that the principal may permit the attorney to act in a personal capacity or as an attorney for both the adult and the third party. This permission must be given explicitly and in writing.[88] The principal may also give permission in advance for a sequel of relatively similar acts.[89] Article 7:418 CC covers the remaining situations, not falling under the scope of articles 7:416 and 7:417 CC. According to this article, the attorney must inform the principal if he has a direct or indirect interest in the realisation of the legal act, unless the content of the legal act is so precisely determined as to exclude the risk of a conflict of interest.[90]

83. Article 7:401-403 CC, translation via: dutchcivillaw.com (last accessed: 26-06-2021); Tjong Tjin Tai 2018, §92-114.
84. Tjong Tjin Tai 2018, §46.
85. See however article 7:413 CC; Tjong Tjin Tai 2018, §48 & §92.
86. Tjong Tjin Tai 2018, §43.
87. Article 7:416 CC, translation via: dutchcivillaw.com (last accessed: 26-06-2021); Lamers 2012, pp. 120-122.
88. A.G. Castermans & H.B. Krans, 'art. 7:416 BW' in: *Tekst en Commentaar Burgerlijk Wetboek*, Deventer: Wolters Kluwer 2021; Tjong Tjin Tai 2018, §234; Lamers 2012, p. 121; According to articles 7:416(2) CC and 7:417(2) CC this provision only applies in the event the mandator concerns an adult who did not enter the mandate agreement in the course of his professional practice or business (article 7:408(3) CC, translation via dutchcivillaw.com (last accessed: 26-06-2021). Adults who make a *levenstestament* will generally fall under the scope of this article.
89. Castermans & Krans 2021, art. 7:416 BW; Tjong Tjin Tai 2018, §234.
90. Article 7:418 CC, translation via: dutchcivillaw.com (last accessed: 26-06-2021); Lamers 2012, pp. 122-123.

Taking the aforementioned concerning both regulatory frameworks into account, the advantage of how the regulatory framework on the service provision agreement has been set up is that it offers significant leeway to design a specific type of agreement suited to the particular context of the *levenstestament*. Both principal and attorney may agree on a specification of the provisions mentioned in articles 7:401 till 7:412 CC, deviate from these provisions when they are considered not suited to the specific setting of the *levenstestament* and add to these provisions by including additional safeguards in the *levenstestament*. In other words, more profound and tailored safeguards in line with article 12 UNCRPD are possible. However, the downside is that the specification of the statutory requirements and the inclusion of (additional) safeguards in the *levenstestament* is ultimately left to the principal and the attorney. This is not without risks. Autar has noted, for example, that adults might find it difficult to include some form of supervision in their *levenstestament*, as this might give the impression that they do not trust their attorney completely.[91] Perhaps for the same reason, article 12(4) UNCRPD calls on *States* to provide appropriate and effective safeguards to prevent abuse by ensuring that the adult's rights, will and preferences are respected, undue influence is avoided and conflicts of interest are managed. This implies a task for the Dutch legislator to adopt certain (minimum) standards to prevent abuse in accordance with article 12 UNCRPD. By adopting such standards, the legislator also has the opportunity to tailor existing safeguards to the specific context of the *levenstestament*. A standard such as the requirement of article 7:418 CC to inform the adult in case of a conflict of interest could, for example, be adapted into a requirement to inform a trusted person or supervisor when the adult, due to a decline in cognitive abilities, is unable to supervise the attorney's actions himself.

Two questions that subsequently arise concern the question of which minimum standards should be adopted to ensure compliance with article 12 UNCRPD and the question of what a regulatory framework implementing such standards should look like. Concerning the first question, the previous chapter has provided guidance on how the safeguards of article 12(4) UNCRPD could be operationalised in the context of the *levenstestament*. One example is the recommendation that states should provide safeguards to ensure that support of the first category (support enabling the adult to make a decision himself and implement this decision with legal effect) is provided to adults who wish to be involved in the execution of their *levenstestament*. In line with this recommendation, Blankman has advocated the adoption of a standard requiring attorneys to involve the adult in the decision-making process as much as possible.[92] Another example is the recommendation that states should provide safeguards ensuring there is a form

91. Autar 2018, p. 26.
92. Blankman 2017, p. 55.

of 'oversight' on the attorney's actions. Using the above-mentioned article 7:418 CC as an example, this could be achieved, for instance, by a statutory provision requiring the involvement of a third person if there is a conflict of interest. In this regard, research on how other countries have regulated instruments similar to the *levenstestament* might help decide the best course of action to take. In chapter 7, I will explore what the Netherlands can learn from four jurisdictions (Belgium, Germany, England & Wales and Switzerland).

With regard to the second question, there are several possibilities concerning a regulatory framework for the *levenstestament*. Minimal standards and safeguards concerning the *levenstestament* could, for example, be included in Book 7 of the Dutch Civil Code, whereby the *levenstestament* would be made a species of the service provision agreement. Another option is to regulate the *levenstestament* in Book 1 of the Dutch Civil Code, which also contains legislation on adult guardianship measures. This would allow the legislator to include certain provisions addressing the interaction between the *levenstestament* and other adult protection measures.[93] An example concerns a provision stipulating that the *levenstestament* is given preference over the adult guardianship measures – the so-called principle of subsidiarity – or a provision stipulating to what extent a *levenstestament* can remain in force in the event the court orders an adult guardianship measure. Again, further comparative research could help determine the best course of action to take.

In determining the scope of legislation, it is also important to consider what – in the absence of statutory regulation – has been done in practice to regulate the *levenstestament* and to what extent these efforts have contributed towards compliance with article 12 UNCRPD. In this regard, the following subsection discusses the efforts of the notariate.

4.2.2 *The efforts of the notariate*

In the absence of a statutory framework, the notariate must be credited for several significant efforts in developing the *levenstestament*. This subsection discusses three of these efforts, namely the leading role played by the notariate in promoting the possibility of making a *levenstestament*, the efforts of the notariate to ensure that provisions included in the *levenstestament* are enforceable in practice, and, finally, the notarial profession's efforts to ensure that there is sufficient protection against undue influence and misuse or abuse of the *levenstestament* by the attorney.

---

93. The interaction between the *levenstestament* and the adult guardianship measures is discussed in more detail in section 4.2.3 of this chapter.

Creating awareness among the public

Not only has the notariate taken the initiative to develop an instrument that adults can use to make provisions for a future period of incapacity, but the notariate has also taken on the responsibility of informing and advising adults on the possibility of making a *levenstestament*.[94] Through several public campaigns, the *levenstestament* has been brought to the public's attention.[95] The notariate has also participated in online platforms such as dementie.nl, where information about the *levenstestament*, the adult guardianship measures and representation, in general, can be found and where adults can ask their questions to experts. Finally, the notariate has developed several information leaflets for adults and nominated attorneys. Examples are the *Checklist Levenstestament* containing information regarding what can be included in the *levenstestament*, and the information leaflet *Waar zeg ik JA tegen?* (To what do I say YES) with details for nominated attorneys about the tasks and responsibilities they are expected to take on.[96] Of course, one could argue that the notariate has an intrinsic motivation when providing this information as the *levenstestament* is also a product the notariate wants to sell. That would, however, not do justice to the efforts undertaken by the notariate. Most of the information is freely available online and can, therefore, be accessed and used by adults who consider making a *levenstestament* without the involvement of a notary.

Promoting the acceptance of the levenstestament in practice

From the onset, the notariate has tried to ensure that provisions included in the *levenstestament* are enforceable.[97] An important starting point is that third parties know the adult has made a *levenstestament*. In the absence of a statutory register, the KNB has therefore set up the Centraal Levenstestamentenregister (CLTR), in which notarised *levenstestamenten* can be registered.[98] However, as noted in section 4.1, this register has its limitations. Registration is voluntary, which means that the answer to whether or not the adult has made a *levenstestament* and whether the registered *levenstestament* is the most recent version cannot be given with 100% certainty. In addition, the register is only accessible to notaries, which means that judges and doctors have to consult a notary to obtain information from the register. Finally, the CLTR only contains information on whether the adult has

94. A responsibility that according to Blankman (2017, pp. 56-57) should have been taken up by the Dutch government.
95. An example is the public campaign *Wie van de drie?* (Who of these three?) in 2015, see: https://www.knb.nl/nieuwsberichten/publiekscampagne-levenstestament-positief-ontvangen (last accessed: 12-07-2021).
96. Both information leaflets can be found via the website https://www.notaris.nl/page/brochures-en-checklists (last accessed: 12-07-2021).
97. Mos-van Gool 2018, p. 80.
98. KNB, *KNB gaat levenstestamenten digitaal registreren*, 25-03-2013, via: https://www.knb.nl/nieuwsberichten/knb-gaat-levenstestamenten-digitaal-registreren (last accessed: 12-07-2021).

made a *levenstestament* and does not provide information on the content of the *levenstestament*. This significantly limits the value of the register in situations where consultation of the *levenstestament* is urgent, e.g. with medical treatment decisions.

Besides introducing the CLTR, the KNB has engaged in discussions with third parties such as banks and doctors to promote the acceptance of the *levenstestament* in practice. In 2015, talks with the Dutch Banking Association (*Nederlandse Vereniging van Banken* – NVB) resulted in an adaptation of the KNB model to ensure banks' acceptance of the *levenstestament*.[99] As noted in the previous subsection, the banks' reluctance to accept the *levenstestament* mainly concerns the inclusion of instructions to the attorney in the *levenstestament*.[100] Banks do not want to risk being sued for a breach of the adult's instructions by the attorney. The NVB indicated that banks do not have the means to check whether attorneys are acting within the limits of the authority granted to them. Provisions stipulating that an attorney is only authorised to donate up to a certain amount per year and provisions requiring two or more attorneys to act jointly are therefore problematic.[101] The NVB also noted that it should be clear when a *levenstestament* enters into force and when it terminates. This must be objectively determinable. In terms of the entry into force, for example, the mere notification of the attorney that the *levenstestament* has entered into force is insufficient.[102] Last but not least, the NVB noted that including in the *levenstestament* a list of specific powers granted to the attorney, instead of a single generic provision stating that the attorney can do anything, would improve the acceptance of the *levenstestament* in practice.[103]

Based on the aforementioned, the KNB changed their model.[104] The model to date includes a provision granting an unlimited POA to the attorney; restrictions have to be included in an internal agreement between the adult and the attorney. To ensure that these internal restrictions do not result in liability claims against banks, the model stipulates that the bank does not have to supervise the attorney's actions. Furthermore, to avoid the situation where two or more attorneys must act jointly concerning banking matters, the model includes a provision enabling

99. KNB, *Banken accepteren nieuw model levenstestament*, 23-03-2015, via: https://www.knb.nl/nieuwsberichten/banken-accepteren-nieuw-model-levenstestament (last accessed: 12-07-2021); J. aan de Stegge, 'Herziene model levenstestament. Zet niet de bank of notaris centraal, aar de cliënt', *Notariaat Magazine* 2015-4, pp. 10-11.

100. T. Denekamp, 'Het levenstestament en de bank', in: F.W.J.M. Schols & B.C.M. Waaijer, *Het levenstestament. Nader verfijnd*, Den Haag: SDU 2017, pp. 103-109; T. Denekamp, 'Wilsonbekwaamheid en de bank', in: A.R. Autar, J.P.M. Stubbé & L.C.A. Verstappen (eds.), *Compendium Levenstestament*, Den Haag: SDU 2018, pp. 187-197.

101. Denekamp 2017, pp. 104-107; Denekamp 2018, pp. 193-197.

102. Denekamp 2017, pp. 105-106 & 108; Denekamp 2018, pp. 193-197.

103. Denekamp 2017, p 107; Denekamp 2018, pp. 193-197.

104. The model presented in 2015 has been included as an appendix in: .W.J.M. Schols & B.C.M. Waaijer, *Het levenstestament. Nader verfijnd*, Den Haag: SDU 2017, pp. 215-232.

attorneys to grant an additional POA to each other. For example, attorney A may issue a subsequent POA to attorney B – giving B the authority to act in relation to bank matters – thus creating a situation where one attorney can act on behalf of the adult regarding banking matters.[105] The adjusted model also includes a section providing a detailed overview of the powers conferred to the attorney, with a generic provision stating that the attorney is authorised to do everything necessary. The readiness of the KNB to agree to what has been dubbed far-reaching concessions to the banks' wishes has not been welcomed by everyone.[106] Van Anken and Brinkman argue that by agreeing to include provisions tailored to the wishes of the banks, the KNB has created a 'dangerous precedent' since this has opened up the possibility for other third parties, such as municipalities and insurance companies, also to require provisions tailored to their wishes, as a condition for accepting the *levenstestament*.[107] Despite all these efforts, the KNB has not been able to secure the acceptance of the *levenstestament* by all banks in the Netherlands. There still seem to be a few (more minor) banks who do not accept the *levenstestament*.[108]

Besides engaging in talks with the banks, the KNB has also talked to several Dutch medical associations to promote the medical profession's acceptance of the *levenstestament* – specifically treatment advance directives. These talks led to changes to the KNB model in 2017 to resolve terminological and linguistic misunderstandings between doctors and notaries.[109] The revised model contains a guideline for notaries, developed with the assistance of medical professionals, including, among other, a list of the relevant medical terminology. In addition to a guideline developed for the notariate, a publication for doctors and patients on end-of-life conversations has been developed. The publication contains an example of a treatment advance directive and a euthanasia advance directive, explaining the potential role the notary can fulfil in drawing up these directives.[110] Finally, to promote a dialogue between doctors and notaries, the KNB and the

105. Aan de Stegge 2015, pp. 10-11.
106. Aan de Stegge 2015, pp. 10-11.
107. J.M. van Anken & R.E. Brinkman, 'Verrassende vragen over het levenstestament: is de opsomming van bevoegdheden (in het vermogens- en bestuursrecht) van de gevolmachtigde zinvol?', *JBN* 2018-6, pp. 11-14.
108. KNB, *Bij kleine banken soms problemen met levenstestament*, 05-12-2019, via: https://www.knb.nl/nieuwsberichten/bij-kleine-banken-soms-problemen-met-levenstestament (last accessed: 12-07-2021). This also becomes evident in two decisions taken by Kifid (Het Financiële Klachteninstituut) – a dispute committee for financial services – in which the Kifid also concludes there is no legal obligation for banks to accept the *levenstestament* (Kifid 13-01-2020, nr. 2020-324; Kifid 18-03-2020, nr. 2020-648).
109. J. aan de Stegge, 'Vernieuwde medische wilsverklaring. Lever maatwerk rondom iemands sterfbed', *Notariaat Magazine* 2017-8, pp. 20-21; E. Nyst, 'Artsen en notarissen stemmen werk rond levenseinde af', *Medisch Contact*, 2017-47, pp. 10-11. According to the article, concepts such as 'euthanasia', 'palliative care' and 'palliative sedation' were mixed up by notaries.
110. Ibid; http://levenseinde.knmg.nl/ (last accessed: 12-07-2021).

Royal Dutch Association of Physicians (KNMG) organised a series of meetings during which notaries and doctors could discuss their respective roles in providing clients/patients with assistance when making an advance directive.[111]

Ensuring protection against undue influence and misuse or abuse by the attorney

The notariate can be credited for various efforts to promote the protection of adults against misuse or abuse of the *levenstestament* by the attorney, both at the time the *levenstestament* is made and at the time the *levenstestament* is executed. Concerning the first, the notariate has tried to ensure there is a thorough procedure to assess whether clients, who want to make a *levenstestament*, have sufficient capacity to do so and are not unduly influenced by, for example, an aspiring attorney. Articles 3:33 and 3:34 CC clarify that a *levenstestament* can only be made by adults with sufficient capacity to do so. Notaries, therefore, are responsible for ensuring that clients who use their services to create a *levenstestament* have capacity. In the Netherlands, both the EPN and the KNB have contributed to the development of a guideline that notaries can use to assess their clients' capacity in relation to notarial services (a *levenstestament*, but also, e.g. a will).[112] In 2006, the KNB presented the first version of this guideline, followed in 2013 by an update. The latest version of the guideline was introduced in 2021.

Whereas previous versions of the guideline focused mainly on assessing the client's capacity, this latest version also explicitly mentions the risk of undue influence. The guideline includes several indicators notaries can use to assess whether undue influence occurs. Examples of indicators are situations in which a client does not want to speak with the notary without the presence of another person, situations in which instructions on what should be included in the *levenstestament* are (predominantly) given by someone other than the adult himself and situations in which the non-verbal communication of the client indicates that the client feels unable to speak freely.[113] When the notary gets the impression that there is a risk of undue influence, the guideline Financial Abuse – also developed by the KNB – can be followed. This guideline includes, for example, the directive that the notary can consult a colleague or can seek advice from *Veilig Thuis* – the advice and reporting agency for domestic violence, child abuse and elderly abuse

111. KNB, *Notarissen en artsen in gesprek over hun rol bij wilsverklaringen*, 01-11-2018, via: https://www.knb.nl/nieuwsberichten/notarissen-en-artsen-in-gesprek-over-hun-rol-bij-wilsverklaringen (last accessed: 12-07-2021).

112. In Dutch this guideline is known as the 'Stappenplan beoordeling wilsbekwaamheid ten behoeve van notariële dienstverlening'. This guideline is not only relevant in cases where a client requires the notary's assistance in making a *levenstestament*, but e.g. also in cases where a client wants to make a will.

113. KNB, *Stappenplan beoordeling wilsbekwaamheid ten behoeve van notariële dienstverlening*, april 2021.

in the Netherlands.[114] In cases where notaries are unsure about their assessment of the client's capacity to make a *levenstestament*, they can refer the client to a doctor. This doctor cannot be the client's family doctor. However, there is a register of medical experts that notaries can use to find a doctor near the client.[115]

In addition to promoting the protection of adults against misuse or abuse when the *levenstestament* is made, the notariate has also undertaken several initiatives to draw attention to the risk of misuse or abuse at the time the *levenstestament* is executed. From the outset, the starting point of the notariate has been that it is ultimately up to the client whether a form of supervision is included in the *levenstestament*.[116] That being said, the notariate does see a role for notaries in bringing supervision to the attention of their clients. In 2018, the KNB included a paragraph on supervision in their model, emphasising the importance of supervision and drawing attention to the possibility of appointing an (external) supervisor.[117] This supervisor can also be a professional. Examples included in the model are provisions on the rights and duties of supervisors and directions for situations in which there is a dispute between the attorney and supervisor. To gain more insight into the experiences and best practices with professional supervision in practice, in 2021, a pilot project together with professional supervisors was started.[118] The latter shows that developments in this area are still ongoing.

Ensuring compliance with article 12 UNCRPD

As the preceding shows, in the absence of statutory regulation, the notariate has played an instrumental role in developing and conceptualising the *levenstestament*. In doing so, the notariate has also contributed to compliance with article 12 UNCRPD. The notariate has implemented several directions presented in the previous chapter to operationalise the safeguards of article 12(4) UNCRPD in the context of the *levenstestament*. With the development of an information leaflet for nominated attorneys (To what do I say YES), the notariate has taken the first steps to make attorneys more aware of their rights and responsibilities. Through the development of a central register and talks with societal actors, the notariate has promoted the validity and acceptance of the *levenstestament*, ensuring respect for the adult's rights, will and preferences. Finally, and perhaps most importantly, through the development of a procedure notaries can use to assess their client's capacity and potential situations of undue influence, the

114. KNB, Beoordeling financieel misbruik, via: https://www.knb.nl/standpunten/financiele-bescherming-ouderen/beoordeling-financieel-misbruik (last accessed: 12-07-2021).
115. VIA Register Wilsbekwaamheid, VIA Register | Vereniging Artsen Volksgezondheid (vavolksgezondheid.nl) (last accessed: 12-07-2021).
116. R. Houwing, 'Rekening en verantwoording en de volmacht', *ftV* 2010/10.
117. J. aan de Stegge, 'Toezicht in het levenstestament. Transparantie haalt wantrouwen weg', *Notariaat Magazine* 2018-5, pp. 20-21.
118. W. van Hoeflaken, 'Voor het behoud van vertrouwen', *Notariaat Magazine* 2021-4.

notariate has contributed to the prevention of undue influence. Efforts like these demonstrate that compliance with article 12 UNCRPD cannot be achieved through legislation alone and thus remain essential. At the same time, notarial efforts such as these cannot completely fill the legislative gap. As discussed in the previous subsection, certain minimum, mandatory standards, such as requiring attorneys to involve the adult in the decision-making process as much as possible, remain important. Although notaries can promote the inclusion of such safeguards in the *levenstestament*, they cannot give these safeguards the mandatory character they need. In addition, as a societal actor, the notariate is mainly active at the beginning of the so-called life-span of the *levenstestament*, namely when the adult makes a *levenstestament*. However, safeguards to promote the adult's autonomy and prevent misuse and abuse are also important during the execution of the *levenstestament*. Examples include safeguards ensuring that suspicions of misuse or abuse are investigated and addressed if necessary. The notariate cannot provide such safeguards. The court can intervene and address abuse or misuse of the *levenstestament* by appointing a guardian to replace the attorney. However, this has raised certain questions in practice, such as whether a *levenstestament* can remain in force when the court deems an adult guardianship measure necessary. I address these and other questions in the following subsection, which focuses on the role of the judiciary in the development of the *levenstestament*.

4.2.3 *The judiciary*

In the absence of a specific regulatory framework, not only the notariate but also the judiciary has guided the development of the *levenstestament* by giving certain directions on, for example, the interaction between the *levenstestament* and the adult guardianship measures. As noted in the introduction, this book includes a study of all court cases published since the emergence of the *levenstestament*, in which the *levenstestament* plays a significant role.[119] These cases can be divided into two subcategories: 1) cases concerning the interaction between the *levenstestament* and adult guardianship measures; and 2) cases concerning the adult's capacity to draft a *levenstestament*.

The levenstestament vis-à-vis adult guardianship measures

Several questions are relevant concerning the position of the *levenstestament* in relation to the adult guardianship measures. The first question to be answered

119. The first court case included in this study was published on 14-08-2012 and the study was concluded in mid-July 2021. As to the criterion 'significant role', the search – using the term 'levenstestament' – on the website www.rechtspraak.nl also resulted in a list of cases in which the *levenstestament* only indirectly or minimally features. An example concerns a case before the Supreme Court in which the word 'levenstestament' is used only once (in a footnote) to indicate that in addition to financial guardianship, there are also other forms of protection, namely a *levenstestament* or personal guardianship.

is what happens if a request for an adult guardianship measure is made while the adult has already made a *levenstestament*. As noted in the previous section, Blankman argues that the courts should follow a so-called principle of subsidiarity whereby the *levenstestament* is given preference over adult guardianship measures.[120] Although, as yet, there is no such statutory principle, a recommendation to refrain from ordering an adult guardianship measure if the adult concerned has made arrangements through a *levenstestament* has been included in the *Aanbevelingen Meerderjarigenbewind 2018* – a policy document for all district courts in the Netherlands, containing recommendations on handling (in particular) financial guardianship cases.[121] Various court cases indicate that the courts follow this recommendation in practice.[122] Only in specific circumstances, such as the attorney's misuse or abuse of the *levenstestament*, the court deems an adult guardianship measure necessary. Chapter 5 discusses these circumstances in more detail.

A second question concerning cases where the court deems an adult guardianship measure necessary is whether the *levenstestament* can remain in force alongside an adult guardianship measure. Article 3:72(a) CC clarifies this is not the case with *curatele* (full guardianship). The attorney's authority conferred through a POA ends when the adult is placed under full guardianship.[123] As the law does not provide for a termination of the POA in the case of *bewind* (financial guardianship) or *mentorschap* (personal guardianship), it is unclear whether the POA should be considered terminated.[124] Indeed, several court cases show that it is not an uncommon occurrence that a *levenstestament* includes a provision stipulating that the POA remains in force when the adult is placed under financial or personal guardianship.[125] With regard to financial guardianship, Kortmann discusses three possibilities concerning the termination of the POA:

1) The powers conferred to the attorney through the POA are limited to the same extent as those of the adult placed under financial guardianship;

120. Blankman 2017, pp. 53-54.
121. Landelijk Overleg Vakinhoud Civiel en Kanton & Toezicht, *Aanbevelingen Meerderjarigenbewind 2018*, via: https://www.rechtspraak.nl/SiteCollectionDocuments/aanbevelingen-meerderjarigen bewind.pdf (last accessed: 02-06-2021).
122. See e.g. Court of Appeal Arnhem-Leeuwarden 13-12-2018, ECLI:NL:GHARL:2018:10856; District Court Zeeland-West-Brabant 13-12-2017, ECLI:NL:RBZWB:2017:8544.
123. This has been confirmed by the court in District Court Gelderland 26-02-2015, ECLI:NL:RBGEL:2015:1476, §16; and Court of Appeal Arnhem-Leeuwarden 03-02-2015, ECLI:NL:GHARL:2015:10171, §5.4. A guardian can subsequently ask the court – under article 3:75(2) CC – to determine how the publication of the termination of the *levenstestament* takes place, with the result that this termination can be invoked against any person (see e.g. District Court of Overijssel 30-12-2015, ECLI:NL:RBOVE:2015:5825).
124. Van Schaick 2011, pp. 87-91 argues that a POA can remain in force when the adult is placed under financial or personal guardianship.
125. E.g. Court of Appeal Amsterdam 17-12-2019, ECLI:NL:GHAMS:2019:4635.

2) An application by way of an analogy of article 3:63(2) CC, which states that when a POA has been granted by a principal who lacks the legal capacity to perform juridical acts himself, any acts performed by the attorney based on this POA, are to be considered valid, null and void, or voidable in the same way as when the principal himself would have performed this act.[126]
3) The POA remains in force but can be terminated by the court-appointed representative.[127]

In a case before the Court of Appeal in Amsterdam, the court adopted the first direction and argued that:

> 'The authority the applicant [attorney – RS] argues can be derived from the *levenstestament* cannot extend beyond the powers of the adult himself, which are in this case limited by the financial and personal guardianship. To that extent, the provision in the *levenstestament* that the applicant's [attorney's – RS] authority is to be maintained even after the establishment of guardianship is meaningless'.[128]

The court's direction provides room for an approach where a *levenstestament* can remain in force partly. For example, if the adult is placed under personal guardianship, the *levenstestament* can remain in force with regard to the financial affairs of the adult, and of course, vice versa.[129]

126. Article 3:62(2) CC, translation via: dutchcivillaw.com (last accessed: 14-07-2021)
127. Kortmann 2017, §57; See also: J.M. Tempelaar, 'Bewind en volmacht. Water en vuur?', *WPNR* 2013-6987, pp. 687-690; K. Blankman, 'Meerderjarigen- en voogdijbewind', in: F.W.J.M. Schols, K. Blankman & J.B. Vegter, *Bewind en aan bewind verwante vormen*, Den Haag: Koninklijke vermande 2004, pp. 73-103 (76-79).
128. E.g. Court of Appeal Amsterdam 17-12-2019, ECLI:NL:GHAMS:2019:4635, §5.9 (translated by RS). In a case before the Court of Appeal in The Hague, the court adopted a combination of the first and third approach (Court of Appeal the Hague 18-07-2012, ECLI:NL:GHSGR:2012:BX4175, §7). The court argued that although the law does not provide for a termination of the POA by default in the event of financial guardianship, the financial guardianship – and in particular the activities the financial guardian with the exclusion of others is authorised to perform (such as managing the adult's bank account) – in a practical sense mean that the POA, insofar as it concerns the affairs placed under financial guardianship, can no longer result in (legal) activities performed by the attorney. The court went on to say that an existing POA can be terminated by the financial guardian. Although the court did not specify whether this termination could concern the complete POA or only part of the POA, it seems logical that a termination of the POA by the financial guardian should only concern the affairs for which the guardian has been authorised by the court. Such an approach leaves room for a situation where the *levenstestament* can remain in force partly.
129. See e.g. District Court Noord-Holland 18-02-2020, ECLI:NL:RBNHO:2020:1161, where the adult was placed under personal guardianship because, while financial guardianship was not deemed necessary, since the affairs of the adult were satisfactorily taken care of by the attorney. In District Court Zeeland-West-Brabant 26-07-2018, ECLI:NL:RBZWB:2018:5036, §2.10 it was the other way around, the court ordered financial guardianship, but found that the *levenstestament* with regard to the medical affairs of the adult could be left in place.

A third question in practice concerns whether the emergence of the *levenstestament* should also result in changes to the list of persons and organisations that can apply for an adult guardianship measure. Articles 1:379 CC (full guardianship), 1:432 CC (financial guardianship) and 1:451 CC (personal guardianship) provide a list of persons and organisations that may request an adult guardianship measure. In general, a measure may be requested by the adult concerned, his partner (spouse, registered partner or other life companion), a close relative (not including the family-in-law), the public prosecutor or a (residential) care facility. As the preceding makes clear, a measure may, in principle, also be requested by the adult himself. In a case before the Court of Appeal in Amsterdam, the court was confronted with whether, by drawing up a *levenstestament*, the adult precludes the possibility of requesting an adult guardianship measure himself. The court ruled that this is not the case and stated that by making a *levenstestament*, the adult does not exclude the possibility of opting for 'another protection measure' at a later stage.[130] Although in principle, an application for an adult guardianship measure can only be made by the persons and organisations mentioned above, an exception was made in a case before the District Court of Zeeland-West Brabant.[131] In this case, an application for financial guardianship was submitted by the attorney (not falling under the list of persons mentioned in article 1:432 CC), who considered himself insufficiently qualified to look after the adult's financial interests and therefore requested the appointment of a professional to look after the adult's financial affairs.[132] The court noted that strictly speaking, the application should be declared inadmissible, and the applicant referred to the public prosecutor's office to lodge an application. This was, however, considered not to be in the interest of the adult concerned and given the importance of taking prompt action, the application was declared admissible.[133]

The adult's capacity to draft a levenstestament

As noted in subsection 4.2.2, under articles 3:33 and 3:34 CC, a *levenstestament* can only be made by adults with capacity. A question that subsequently arises is when the adult has the capacity to make a *levenstestament*. The court has addressed this question in two cases in which the annulment of a *levenstestament* under article 3:34 CC had been requested.[134] In both cases, the claimants argued that when the

130. Court of Appeal Amsterdam 07-07-2020, ECLI:NL:GHAMS:2020:1892, §5.4.3.
131. District Court of Zeeland-West Brabant 26-07-2018, ECLI:NL:RBZWB:2018:5036.
132. District Court of Zeeland-West Brabant 26-07-2018, ECLI:NL:RBZWB:2018:5036, §2.5.
133. District Court of Zeeland-West Brabant 26-07-2018, ECLI:NL:RBZWB:2018:5036, §2.6.
134. District Court of Limburg 13-01-2021, ECLI:NL:RBLIM:2021:381; District Court of Noord-Holland 28-04-2021, ECLI:NL:RBNHO:2021:3611. See also: Court of Appeal 18-07-2012, ECLI:NL:GHSGR:2012:BX4175, §8 where the court with regard to the renewal of a previously granted POA, notes that the fact that the adult concerned at the time the POA was renewed, resided in a residential care facility, not automatically means that she was unable to understand the consequences of the renewal of the POA. See however differently: District Court Midden-Nederland 14-03-2019, ECLI:NL:RBMNE:2019:1113, where the court in its decision to order an

levenstestament was made, the adult lacked the capacity needed to draw up the *levenstestament*. The consideration of the court is in both cases similar. In a case before the District Court in Limburg, the court notes:

> 'The court states first and foremost that great value must be attributed to the freedom of the adult concerned to draw up a *levenstestament*. This means the court must exercise caution in assuming too readily that the requirements of article 3:34 CC have been met. In this regard, the court notes that the mere presence of an intellectual impairment does not mean that the *levenstestament* has also been made under the influence of that impairment since an intellectual impairment does not have to prevent a clear appreciation of the interest involved by the adult. This will depend on the severity of the impairment and the simplicity or complexity of the *levenstestament* in question.'[135]

The court makes the aforementioned even clearer in a case before the District Court of Noord-Holland, where the court notes that a diagnosis of dementia not automatically means that a person is no longer able to make a *levenstestament*.[136] As discussed in the previous chapter, the court's approach aligns with the UNCRPD and the Council of Europe Recommendation 2009(11) on principles concerning continuing powers of attorney and advance directives. Both human rights instruments stress the importance of providing adults – even in the event of deteriorating cognitive abilities – with the opportunity to make a *levenstestament* for as long as the adult still has sufficient capacity to do so. This makes the notary's role as a gatekeeper in assessing whether the client has the capacity to make a *levenstestament* and is not unduly influenced by others to do so all the more important. Several cases show that the court assigns a certain weight to this assessment of capacity by the notary. In a case before the District Court of Noord-Holland, the court notes in this regard:

> 'There is no evidence that the adult concerned lacked capacity at the time the *levenstestament* was made. In this respect, the court considers that the *levenstestament* has been drawn up before a notary, which means that the adult's capacity has already been assessed by the notary'.[137]

The assessment of the client's capacity by the notary is, in other words, of importance and not without consequences. Through disciplinary proceedings, notaries can be held accountable when they fail to properly fulfil their role as

adult guardianship measure, takes into account that the *levenstestament* has been drafted after the adult has been diagnosed with dementia.

135. District Court of Limburg 13-01-2021, ECLI:NL:RBLIM:2021:381, §4.3 (translated by RS).
136. District Court of Noord-Holland 28-04-2021, ECLI:NL:RBNHO:2021:3611, §4.2.
137. District Court of Noord-Holland 18-02-2020, ECLI:NL:RBNHO:2020:1171 (translated by RS); See also: District Court Oost-Brabant 16-03-2015, ECLI:NL:RBOBR:2015:1548, §7; District Court of Gelderland 26-02-2015, ECLI:NL:RBGEL:2015:1476, §11-12.

gatekeepers.[138] The cases brought before the disciplinary court provide insight into the requirements set by the court on how the notary's assessment of the client's capacity should look like. In what seems by now established case law, the court has confirmed that a notary, in the first instance, may rely on his observations when assessing a client's capacity.[139] In this regard, the notary has a reasonable margin of appreciation. Only in case of reasonable doubt is further investigation indicated, in which case the notary can use the guideline mentioned in the previous subsection to assess the client's capacity. Although notaries have a margin of appreciation in assessing the client's capacity, this margin is not unlimited. There have been several cases in which the disciplinary court found that the notary in question had failed to adequately assess whether the client had sufficient capacity to make a *levenstestament* and was not unduly influenced by others to do so.[140] An example is a case before the disciplinary court of Arnhem-Leeuwarden, where the court found that, given the circumstances, the notary should have further investigated the client's capacity. Circumstances mentioned in this regard include the fact that the adult had not approached the notary for an appointment but the prospective attorney; that the notary had made a draft *levenstestament* based on information provided by the prospective attorney and had not sent this draft to the adult concerned beforehand; and that the notary did not speak to the adult in private but in the presence of the prospective attorney and another relative.[141]

Ensuring compliance with article 12 UNCRPD

As the preceding shows, in addition to the notariate, the judiciary has also played an instrumental role in guiding the development of the *levenstestament* and ensuring compliance with article 12 UNCRPD. As discussed in chapter 2, adult guardianship measures involving the appointment of a substitute decision-maker should be used as a last resort. In the absence of statutory regulation, courts have, in practice, adopted a principle of subsidiarity, which ensures that the *levenstestament* – drafted by the adult himself – takes precedence over adult guardianship measures. In addition, several court cases indicate that the *levenstestament* can remain partially in force if an adult guardianship measure is deemed necessary. This ensures that the adult's autonomy is respected as much as possible. Finally, the courts have given guidance on the capacity required to make a *levenstestament*, confirming – in line with international human rights norms and principles – that an intellectual impairment as such does not preclude

138. Article 93 of the Notarial Act (Wet op het Notarisambt).

139. Court of Appeal Amsterdam 17-09-2019, ECLI:NL:GHAMS:2019:3373, §2.8; Court of Appeal Amsterdam 22-01-2019, ECLI:NL:GHAMS:2019:117, §6.3-6.4; Court of Appeal Amsterdam 21-03-2017, ECLI:NL:GHAMS:2017:951, §6.4;

140. See e.g. Court of Appeal Amsterdam 12-01-2021, ECLI:NL:GHAMS:2021:3; Court of Appeal Amsterdam 07-10-2014; ECLI:NL:GHAMS:2014:4089; Disciplinary Court Arnhem-Leeuwarden, ECLI:NL:TNORARL:2018:49.

141. Disciplinary Court Arnhem-Leeuwarden, ECLI:NL:TNORARL:2018:11, §4.7.

the adult from making a *levenstestament*. That being so, further steps are also possible concerning the judiciary to improve compliance with article 12 UNCRPD. Although courts have, in practice, adopted a principle of subsidiarity, as discussed in section 4.1, they are not obliged to check in the central register whether or not the adult has made a *levenstestament*. Legislation could therefore give more weight to the principle of subsidiarity by requiring judges to check the central register and take steps to become aware of the contents of the *levenstestament*.

This section has focused on the regulatory framework for the appointment of one or more attorneys through a *levenstestament*. I have argued that – notwithstanding the efforts of the notariate and the judiciary – further steps can and should be taken to ensure compliance with article 12 UNCRPD. The following section discusses the regulatory framework of advance directives for medical treatment. These can be included in the *levenstestament*, but already before the emergence of the *levenstestament*, adults could draft treatment advance directives. The following section will therefore focus on the added value of including a treatment advance directive in a – notarised – *levenstestament*.

4.3 The levenstestament for health and medical affairs

Two provisions are generally distinguished with regard to provisions for a future period of incapacity in health and medical affairs. The first concerns the appointment of an attorney for health and medical matters, and the second concerns a so-called treatment advance directive (*hereafter:* treatment AD) containing the wishes and instructions of the adult regarding the type of medical treatment which under certain conditions is desired or refused.[142] In the Netherlands, both can be included in the *levenstestament*.[143] These provisions, however, also exist separately – 'in their own right'. Before the emergence of the *levenstestament*, article 7:465(3) CC provided adults with the opportunity to appoint an attorney for health and medical affairs and article 7:450(1) CC provided adults with the opportunity to draft a treatment AD.[144] This has raised the question of the added value of using the *levenstestament* – particularly a notarial *levenstestament* – to make provisions for health and medical matters. This question has been raised in particular in connection with the treatment AD.[145] In this subsection, I will address this question. I shall start with an overview of the Dutch legal framework on treatment ADs and will subsequently provide a synopsis of

142. De Boer 2011, p. 14.
143. A treatment AD can be included in the *levenstestament* or attached to the *levenstestament* as an appendix.
144. Based on article 7:454(2) CC the adult can ask the care provider to add this treatment AD to the adult's medical file.
145. J. Legemaate, 'Het levenstestament en zorgbeslissingen', in: F.W.J.M. Schols & B.C.M. Waaijer, *Het levenstestament. Nader verfijnd*, Den Haag: SDU 2017, pp. 83-95.

the research to date on treatment ADs in the Netherlands. Finally, based on the aforementioned, I will try to answer the question of the added value of including provisions for health and medical affairs in a – notarised – *levenstestament*.

4.3.1 *The legal status of treatment advance directives*

In the Netherlands, two types of treatment ADs are distinguished: the so-called 'negative treatment advance directive' in which specific medical treatment is refused, and the 'positive treatment advance directive' in which the adult requests specific medical treatment. Examples of a negative treatment AD are a do-not-resuscitate order and a refusal to receive, for example, chemotherapy, respiration treatment or antibiotics.[146] The negative treatment AD is closely linked to the principle of informed consent in the Netherlands. Article 7:450(1) CC stipulates that a care provider must obtain the patient's consent before medical treatment is performed. If a patient withholds his consent, a care provider is – in principle – not allowed to proceed with the treatment. Article 7:450(3) CC states that refusal of consent for specific treatment can also be provided, in written form, in advance:

> 'In the event that a patient of the age of sixteen years or older cannot be regarded as being capable to make a reasonable appreciation of his interests in the matter, the care provider and a person as referred to in Article 7:465, paragraph 2 or 3, shall comply with the apparent opinion of the patient expressed in writing while he was still capable of making a reasonable appreciation of his interests and containing a refusal to give his consent as referred to in paragraph 1. The care provider may nevertheless deviate from this statement if he thinks there are well-founded reasons for doing so.'[147]

The referral to article 7:465 (2) and (3) CC clarifies that in addition to the care provider, a guardian, attorney or informal representative is also obliged to act according to the treatment AD. The treatment AD only applies when the patient is no longer 'capable of making a reasonable appreciation of his interests in the matter'. As long as the patient can do so, the actual (verbal) expression of his will prevails. The aim of article 7:450(3) CC is to do justice to the patient's autonomy in situations where the patient can no longer express his wishes.[148] A care provider is, therefore, generally bound by the treatment AD. That being said, the legislator has indicated that the fact that the patient can no longer state whether – and if so, how – he would like to amend the statement he made in the past should also be considered.[149] With this in mind, an exception to the main rule has been

146. Legemaate 2017, p. 85.
147. Article 7:450(3) CC, translation via: dutchcivillaw.com (last accessed: 14-07-2021).
148. B. Sluijters & M.C.I.H. Biesaart, *De geneeskundige behandelingsovereenkomst*, Deventer: Kluwer 2005, p. 51.
149. Dutch House of Representatives, *Kamerstukken II* 1990/91, 21561, nr. 6, p. 36.

added to article 7:450(3) CC. This exception stipulates that the care provider may deviate from the treatment AD if there are well-founded reasons to do so. Leenen *et al.* mention as an example a treatment AD based on information that has over time become outdated or a treatment AD containing a refusal to receive treatment for an – at the time – incurable disease that can now be effectively treated.[150] The law gives the care provider room to deviate from the treatment AD in these situations since verifying the patient's wishes and intentions is no longer possible. This margin of appreciation should, however, not be pushed too far. Leenen *et al.* note that to justify a deviation from the treatment AD, there must be a significant difference between the statement and the actual situation.[151]

Whereas with a negative treatment AD the consent for specific medical treatment is withheld, with a positive treatment AD, the adult expresses the wish to receive specific medical treatment. An example is a statement in which the adult indicates that he wants resuscitation treatment in all events.[152] In contrast to the negative treatment AD, where the care provider is, in principle, obliged to comply with the adult's wishes and instructions, no such obligation exists for the positive treatment AD. In this instance, the patient's wish to (continue to) undergo specific treatment is not sufficient for the continuation or commencement of treatment. The care provider is not obliged to provide the care the patient wishes, and such treatment has to be indicated according to the relevant medical guidelines.[153] This follows from article 7:453 CC, according to which the care provider must act in accordance with the professional standard.[154]

A special positive treatment AD is the so-called advance directive for euthanasia (ADE). Article 2(2) of the Act on the Termination of life on request and assisted suicide (Wet toetsing levensbeëindiging op verzoek en hulp bij zelfdoding) – Euthanasia Law stipulates that:

---

150. H.J.J. Leenen, J. Legemaate, J. Dute, E.J.C. de Jong, M.E. Gelpke, J.K.M. Gevers en G.R.J. de Groot, *Handboek Gezondheidsrecht*, Den Haag: Boom Uitgevers 2020, pp. 133-135.
151. Ibid.
152. A.C. Hendriks, 'Het levenstestament in de gezondheidszorg', in: A.R. Autar, J.P.M. Stubbé & L.C.A. Verstappen (eds.), *Compendium Levenstestament*, Den Haag: SDU 2018, pp. 149-168 (155); Legemaate 2017, p. 85-86.
153. Leenen et al. 2014, p. 120; Legemaate 2017, p. 86.
154. According to the Dutch Royal Association of Physicians (KNMG), the phrase 'professional standard' is in the healthcare context used to refer to the body of medical norms that describe 'good practice' in a given situation. The professional standard is not a rule as such, but a guiding principle, which has been explained further by means of laws, guidelines, protocols, professional codes, the rulings of disciplinary courts, quality standards and codes of conduct. According to the KNMG the professional standard can therefore be seen as a set of shared values and norms within the professional group of healthcare providers (https://www.knmg.nl/advies-richtlijnen/ethische-toolkit/verdiepen/begrippen-2/professionele-standaard.htm (last accessed: 18-08-2021)).

> 'In the event that a patient of the age of sixteen years or older is no longer capable of expressing his will, but was considered capable of making a reasonable appreciation of his interests before he got into this state, and has made a written statement containing a request for termination of life, the physician may comply with this request. The requirements of due care referred to in the first paragraph apply mutatis mutandis.'[155]

The last sentence makes clear that in the case of an ADE, the requirements of due care that apply to all cases of euthanasia must be met. Article 2(1) of the Euthanasia law lists these six requirements, stating that the physician: 1) must be convinced that the patient's request is voluntary and well-considered, 2) must be convinced that the patient's suffering is unbearable and without a prospect of improvement, 3) must inform the patient about the situation and prospects (diagnosis and prognosis), 4) together with the patient has concluded that there is no reasonable alternative solution to the situation in which the patient finds himself, 5) has consulted at least one other, independent physician, who has seen the patient and has provided his judgement on the first four due care requirements in writing, and 6) has terminated the life of the patient or provided assistance with the patient's suicide with due medical care.[156]

4.3.2 *Research on treatment advance directives in the Netherlands*

Several studies in the Netherlands have examined how the regulatory framework discussed in the previous subsection is applied in practice. This subsection provides a synopsis of three of these studies. The first study concerns a study conducted by Vezzoni in 2005 focusing on the legal status and social practice of negative treatment ADs in the Netherlands.[157] Vezzoni's study consists of several sub-studies. However, the most significant study concerns a survey among family doctors and care home doctors looking at the frequency and effectiveness of negative treatment ADs.[158] Vezzoni concludes that only a small number of patients had drafted a negative treatment AD and that in cases where patients had made a negative treatment AD, the effect of this treatment AD was limited. The explanation for this limited effectiveness is primarily sought in the passive

155. Article 2(2) Euthanasia law, translated by RS.
156. Article 2(1) Euthanasia law; De Boer 2011, pp. 13-21 (15).
157. C. Vezzoni, *The legal status and social practice of treatment directives in the Netherlands*, dissertation RUG, 2005.
158. Other sub-studies included a comparative study looking at the legal status of treatment ADs in several – mostly Western – countries and a study of the international literature addressing the prevalence of advance directives. Another sub-study looked at the involvement of notaries in drafting treatment ADs. This sub study is, however, to a limited extent addressed in the conclusion of this study, as the KNB had at the time decided to discard the model for treatment ADs from its database and discouraged its members from providing clients with assistance in drawing up these directives.

approach and the negative attitude of doctors.[159] According to Vezzoni, his survey study shows that doctors are not prepared to accept the binding force of treatment ADs but instead regard the treatment AD as an additional source of information.[160] This negative attitude as to the binding force of treatment ADs, according to Vezzoni, not only influences the effectiveness of treatment ADs at the time of implementation, but also influences the behaviour of doctors in previous phases. He notes in this regard that doctors rarely take the initiative to inform patients about the possibility of drafting a treatment AD and are seldom involved in the drafting process.[161] In this context, Vezzoni also sees a connection with the low quality of treatment ADs, which he believes could be the result of the passive attitude of doctors in the drafting phase. It should be pointed out that the research method chosen by Vezzoni – a quantitative research study – offers only limited insight into the considerations of doctors not to consider the negative treatment AD binding. Vezzoni's reflections as to the underlying reasons for non-compliance are, in other words, to a large extent circumstantial, as is also acknowledged in the study.[162]

A study by Akerboom et al. provided more insight into the considerations of doctors not following a treatment AD.[163] In a comprehensive legal-normative, empirical and comparative study focusing on the regulatory framework concerning the position of adults with impaired capacity and representation in healthcare settings, Akerboom et al. also looked at the use of treatment ADs. Through interviews and focus groups with doctors and representatives, the role of treatment ADs in four sectors (care for adults with an intellectual impairment, nursing home care, psychiatry, and intensive care) was examined. Akerboom *et al.* conclude that treatment ADs do not play an important role in most sectors.[164] Moreover, even in cases where there is a treatment AD, this treatment AD is not in all cases followed. Factors that play a role in this regard concern the time that has elapsed since the drafting of the treatment AD and the conciseness and applicability of the treatment AD.[165] With regard to the latter, respondents in this study noted that in most cases, adults drafting a treatment AD do not know in advance what to expect, resulting in a lack of specificity of the treatment AD, rendering it not useful.[166] Another factor mentioned by respondents concerned the

159. Vezzoni 2005, pp. 176-181.
160. Ibid.
161. Ibid.
162. Vezzoni 2005, p. 183; A. Bood, 'Boekrecensie. Christiano Vezzoni, The legal status and social practice of treatment directives in the Netherlands', *Tijdschrift voor Gezondheidsrecht* 2006-7, pp. 559-562.
163. C.P.M. Akerboom, J.C.J. Dute, J.K.M. Gevers, H. Nys, H.B. Winter & N.O.M. Woestenburg, *Thematische wetsevaluatie. Wilsonbekwaamheid en vertegenwoordiging*, Den Haag: ZonMw 2011.
164. Akerboom *et al.* 2011, pp. 419-420.
165. Akerboom *et al.* 2011, pp. 348-350 (care home doctors) & 389-391 (intensive care doctors).
166. Ibid.

extent to which the patient's current behaviour indicates something different than what has been recorded in the treatment AD.[167]

With regard to the latter, Akerboom *et al.* – in the legal-normative part of their study – refer to the medical-ethical literature on treatment ADs, where it is argued that the patient's will frequently adapts to the specific circumstances of the case and that one cannot foresee what a future period of incapacity will mean.[168] Hertogh refers in this regard to the disability paradox: 'a life that was once despised before the advent of chronic disease is accepted and even embraced with advancing illness'.[169] Problematic in this regard is that when the adult has reached a stage of incapacity, the treatment AD can no longer be changed or revoked. According to Hertogh this is a key obstacle for compliance with treatment ADs.[170] The problems with the binding force of treatment ADs have also been underlined in the third study this subsection discusses. In this study, De Boer looked at the experiences of adults with early-stage dementia with their disease and their perspectives on future care and treatment.[171] De Boer notes in this regard:

> '[D]espite the great impact of dementia on the lives of those affected, people with dementia do not undergo their disease passively but try to deal with its effects and challenges by using different coping strategies. Dementia (especially Alzheimer's disease) allows people to adapt and adjust to their changing situation, as it is not a disease that appears overnight, but often involves a process of insidious onset and gradual progression. As a result of such adaptive processes, actual experiences of the disease can deviate from the ideas of the general public and people's own anticipatory beliefs about life with dementia. Such differences should be carefully considered in discussions on advance directives, because there is a reasonable chance that people with dementia ultimately will not act in accordance with their earlier values and anticipatory beliefs regarding a life with dementia. With this in mind, it becomes essential to communicate with people with dementia about future care and treatment on a continuing basis.'[172]

Linked to this, the notion of advance care planning is advocated, defined by Hertogh as a 'dialogical process of supporting patients and their proxies [representatives] to think ahead and formulate goals of care as they confront the challenge of a progressive illness trajectory'.[173]

167. Akerboom *et al.* 2011, pp. 369-370 & pp. 419-420.
168. Akerboom *et al.* 2011, pp. 42-43.
169. C.M.P.M. Hertogh, 'The misleading simplicity of advance directives', *International Psychogeriatrics* 2011 (23) 4, pp. 511-515.
170. Ibid.
171. De Boer 2011.
172. De Boer 2011, pp. 129-131 (130).
173. Hertogh 2011, p. 513.

In addition to describing the experiences of adults with early-stage dementia, De Boer's study also looked at compliance with advance directives for euthanasia (ADEs) in cases of dementia in Dutch nursing homes.[174] De Boer concluded that despite the solid legal status, ADEs are rarely complied with in Dutch nursing homes – and never in cases of advanced dementia – and, at best, result in limitations on life-sustaining treatment.[175] A crucial factor for non-compliance identified in this study concerned the fact that in cases of advanced dementia, it is often no longer possible for doctors to have a meaningful discussion about the patient's wish for euthanasia.[176] Communication with the patient is considered particularly important with regard to the second and fourth requirement of article 2(1) of the Euthanasia law, stipulating that doctors must be convinced that the patient's suffering is unbearable and, together with the patient, must have concluded that there is no other reasonable solution to the situation in which the patient finds himself.[177] De Boer found that doctors are reluctant to proceed with euthanasia when discussing the unbearableness and lack of alternatives with the patient is no longer possible. She noted in this regard: 'euthanasia in dementia seems to be reserved for patients in the early stages of the disease who are still able to actively communicate their wishes'.[178]

Although De Boer's study revealed no cases of performed euthanasia based on an ADE concerning patients with advanced dementia, this has changed since her study.[179] The most notable example concerns a case which was eventually brought before the Dutch Supreme Court 'in the interest of the law'.[180] The case involved criminal and disciplinary proceedings against a physician who had ended the life of her patient with advanced dementia and evolved around whether the physician had complied with the due care requirements of article 2 of the Euthanasia law. A detailed discussion of this case falls beyond the scope of this book.[181] In short, the Supreme Court confirmed that article 2 of the Euthanasia Law, even in cases of advanced dementia, provides room for doctors to perform euthanasia. The

174. De Boer 2011.
175. De Boer 2011, pp. 140-141.
176. De Boer 2011, pp. 131-134 (133) & 137-138.
177. Ibid.
178. De Boer 2011, pp. 140-141.
179. De Boer 2011, pp. 131-134 (133). See for example: J. Visser, 'Professionals leggen Euthanasiewet verschillend uit. Dement met een wilsverklaring, en dan?', *Medisch Contact* 2012 (67), no. 10, pp. 582-585.
180. Supreme Court of the Netherlands 21-04-2020, ECLI:NL:HR:2020:712; Supreme Court of the Netherlands 21-04-2020, ECLI:NL:HR:2020:713; Supreme Court of the Netherlands, Physician permitted to grant a written request for euthanasia from individuals suffering from advanced dementia, via: https://www.hogeraad.nl/actueel/nieuwsoverzicht/2020/april/physician-permitted/ (last accessed: 02-09-2021).
181. The reader is for more information referred to for example: A.C. Hendriks, 'Schriftelijk euthanasieverzoek bij vergevorderde dementie als basis. De Hoge Raad schept duidelijkheid, althans deels', *Themis* 2020-3, pp. 123-133.

court emphasised that in these situations, the statutory requirements of due care still have to be met but noted that these requirements have to be met in a way that does justice to the specific nature of cases involving advanced dementia.[182] The court noted in this regard that the request for euthanasia must specifically pertain to the situation in which the patient can no longer express his will due to advanced dementia. Contrary to the consideration of the disciplinary court in the first instance, that there is no room to interpret this request, the Supreme Court found that there is room for interpretation.[183] The request must not only be interpreted based on its wording, but interpretation can also be based on other circumstances from which the patient's intentions may be inferred.[184] The Supreme Court also addressed the requirement of unbearable suffering, acknowledging that the progression of dementia can cause unbearable suffering for patients. The court noted that there is ample reason to consult – as is already common practice – not only one but two independent doctors to determine whether the request can be met.[185] Based on these considerations, the Supreme Court reviewed the rulings in the first instance and found that the district court had not erred in its assessment that the physician had acted with due care. The decision of the disciplinary court that the physician had partly failed to comply with the requirements of due care was set aside.[186] The case received considerable attention, with not everyone agreeing with the Supreme Court's ruling.[187] Various doctors indicated that since the wishes and preferences of people frequently change over time, they continue to find the application of an ADE difficult in cases of advanced dementia.[188] The execution of ADEs in cases of advanced dementia remains, in other words, a contentious issue.

4.3.3 *Weighing the pros and cons*

The aforementioned shows that the adherence of advance directives by care providers is often complex. Against this backdrop, the question arises of the added value of including treatment advance directives and euthanasia advance

182. Supreme Court of the Netherlands 21-04-2020, ECLI:NL:HR:2020:712, §6.1.
183. Supreme Court of the Netherlands 21-04-2020, ECLI:NL:HR:2020:712, §6.3-§6.5.
184. Supreme Court of the Netherlands 21-04-2020, ECLI:NL:HR:2020:712, §4.5.2.
185. Supreme Court of the Netherlands 21-04-2020, ECLI:NL:HR:2020:712, §4.9.
186. Supreme Court of the Netherlands, Physician permitted to grant a written request for euthanasia from individuals suffering from advanced dementia, via: https://www.hogeraad.nl/actueel/nieuwsoverzicht/2020/april/physician-permitted/ (last accessed: 02-09-2021).
187. See e.g. N. Rozemond, 'Een mensenrechtelijke interpretatie van de uitspraken van de Hoge Raad over euthanasie bij mensen met dementie', *Themis* 2021-4, pp. 149-158; B. van Beers, 'Staat van verwarring. Over euthanasie, vergevorderde dementie en het recht op leven', Ars Aequi 2020-2, pp. 141-149.
188. See e.g. L. van der Meulen & J. Pennarts, 'Wat is de waarde van een wilsverklaring: kan je nog afzien van euthanasie', NOS 2019, via: https://nos.nl/nieuwsuur/artikel/2300995-wat-is-de-waarde-van-een-wilsverklaring-kan-je-nog-afzien-van-euthanasie (last accessed 02-0-2021).

directives in a *levenstestament*. Engelbertink and Hendriks note in this regard that the involvement of a notary ensures that the treatment AD genuinely contains the wishes of the adult concerned – and not the wishes of a third party – and guarantees that the adult had sufficient capacity to draft the treatment AD.[189] They also consider the registration of the treatment AD in a national register, an advantage of a notarial *levenstestament*.[190] Legemaate notes, in contrast, that the advantages mentioned by Engelbertink and Hendriks relate to issues with which doctors – with regard to ordinary treatment ADs – in practice do not seem to struggle. The main problem concerns, according to Legemaate, the lack of conciseness of treatment ADs, whereby wishes are formulated in too generic a manner.[191] Legemaate argues that to solve this problem, adults should draw up – in consultation with their relatives and family doctor – a treatment AD that is as clear and specific as possible.

The question is whether the notary's involvement in this process has added value. In a reaction to the contribution of Legemaate, Oomen notes that – referring to Vezzoni's conclusion that doctors rarely take the initiative to inform patients about the possibility of drafting a treatment AD and are seldom involved in the drafting process – notaries, when it comes to advising clients and recording treatment ADs, apparently fill a gap.[192] The question remains, however, whether a notary is the right person to fill this gap. This question has previously been answered negatively by the notariate. In 2002, a model for treatment ADs was removed from the KNB database because the terminology used in the model led to interpretation problems in practice. In addition, the KNB noted that due to a lack of medical knowledge, notaries do not seem ideally suited to guide clients in determining the content of the treatment AD.[193] This conclusion is underlined by Vezzoni, who noted:

> 'The added value of the involvement of a notary is particularly dubious as far as the medical quality of directives is concerned. Notaries produce exactly the sort of vague and general documents that have repeatedly been shown in the literature to be incapable of guiding medical decision-making'.[194]

189. C.G.C. Engelbertink & A. Hendriks, 'Meer duidelijkheid voor artsen over wensen van de patiënt. Met levenstestament houdt patiënt regie', *Medisch Contact* 2012 (67) no. 1, pp. 40-43. See also: J.H. Oomen, 'Reactie op 'Het levenstestament en zorgbeslissingen' van prof. mr. J. Legemaate', in: F.W.J.M. Schols & B.C.M. Waaijer, *Het levenstestament. Nader verfijnd*, Den Haag: SDU 2017, pp. 97-100.
190. Ibid.
191. Legemaate 2017, pp. 93-94.
192. Oomen 2017, p. 99.
193. Euthanasiemodel uit KNB-bestand, *Notariaat Magazine* 2002-2, p. 8.
194. Vezzoni 2005, pp. 111-114.

More recently, Hendriks has also noted specific disadvantages and risks attached to including medical wishes and preferences in a notarial *levenstestament*.[195] He notes in this respect that the (legal) texts drafted by notaries are often far removed from the language used by care providers. In some cases, wishes and preferences recorded in the *levenstestament* are incompatible with the professional standard of doctors.[196] Hendriks notes that close consultation between the various professional organisations will help mitigate these objections. However, more important is, according to Hendriks, that the notary emphasises the importance for the patient of having a timely conversation with the care provider. To ensure that wishes and preferences included in the treatment AD are realised as much as possible, both patient and physician should discuss these repeatedly, starting at an early stage.[197]

As discussed in section 4.2.2, the KNB – in cooperation with the KNMG – has undertaken several initiatives to mitigate the risks mentioned above as much as possible. It is unknown whether these initiatives have improved the content and acceptance of notarial *levenstestamenten*. However, given the preceding, the conclusion that making a treatment AD preferably takes place in close cooperation between physician and patient seems appropriate. Since the possible advantages of including a treatment AD in a notarial *levenstestament* do not seem to be of much importance in practice, the involvement of a notary in the drafting process is not evident. Doctors seem the most appropriate persons to support patients in determining their medical wishes and preferences. Even more so, since research indicates that a continuous dialogue between patient and physician in what is referred to as 'advance care planning' might be more beneficial to capture the (current) wishes and preferences of the patient – given the fact that these might change over time – than a 'static' treatment AD.[198] This observation not only points towards the preferable involvement of doctors in the drafting process of treatment ADs, but it also raises general questions regarding the weight to be attached to treatment ADs and the role they can fulfil in the process of advance care planning. Further research looking into these questions seems called for.

4.4 Conclusion

The *levenstestament* has, in the Netherlands, been designed and conceptualised by the notariate within the framework of existing law. Although Parliament has closely monitored the development of the *levenstestament*, it has yet to deem it necessary to enact specific legislation to regulate the *levenstestament*. Regulation has, in practice, been left to the notariate and, to a lesser extent, to the judiciary.

195. Hendriks 2018, pp. 164-166.
196. Hendriks, pp 164-166.
197. Hendriks 2018, pp. 166-167.
198. De Boer 2011; Hertogh 2011.

In the absence of a clear statutory definition of the term *'levenstestament'*, there are different interpretations as to what a *levenstestament* may entail. In practice, the term *'levenstestament'* is used to refer to enduring documents encompassing one or more of the following components: the appointment of one or more attorneys, a treatment advance directive; and/or a directive addressed to the court containing the adult's choice of guardian in the event an adult guardianship measure is deemed necessary. In other countries, the distinction between these components is made more explicit by employing different terms. In Germany, for example, adults can make a so-called *Vorsorgevollmacht* (entailing the appointment of an attorney), a *Betreuungsverfügung* (a directive addressed to the court and the future guardian) and a *Patientenverfügung* (a treatment advance directive).[199] Such a clear distinction between components would also be a welcome addition in the Netherlands. The various components could still be included in the same enduring document, but the distinction between them through terminology might help ensure that adults are aware of the multiple options they have to provide for a future period of incapacity. In this regard, the involvement of the right professional is essential. As I have argued in this chapter, the involvement of a notary in the process of drafting a treatment advance directive is not evident. Doctors seem more suited to the task of informing and advising adults about the drafting of a treatment AD.

Since this book focuses on the appointment of an attorney through a *levenstestament*, I have focused in section 4.2 of this chapter on the legal basis and scope of this component of the *levenstestament* and to what extent the regulatory framework complies with article 12 UNCRPD. Before I could do so, however, a contentious issue needed to be addressed. In the absence of a statutory framework, there is no consensus in practice on the legal basis for the appointment of an attorney through a *levenstestament*. In this regard, I have argued that a *levenstestament* should not be confined to an ordinary power of attorney (POA). A POA merely confers the authority to act on behalf of the adult and does not create an obligation to act. It determines when the attorney can act, not when he may or must act. However, a responsibility for the attorney to act seems paramount when the adult – due to a decline in cognitive abilities – can no longer act himself. In other words, the *levenstestament* should also include an agreement between the adult and the attorney, in which arrangements can be made about the tasks the attorney will perform for and on behalf of the adult. Such arrangements can be made through a service provision agreement or a mandate agreement.

I subsequently explored whether – considering all options – compliance with article 12 UNCRPD is at all possible within the framework of existing law, given

199. W. Zimmerman, *Vorsorgevollmacht, Betreuungsverfügung, Patientenverfügung für die Beratungspraxis*, Berlin: Erich Schmidt Verlag 2017, p. 26.

the setting of future incapacity of the adult, for which the *levenstestament* is intended to provide. In this regard, I have argued that while regulation within the framework of the existing law – through the service provision agreement and the mandate agreement – gives adults and attorneys ample opportunities to include safeguards in the *levenstestament*, the inclusion of safeguards should not be left entirely to the adult and the attorney. Article 12 UNCRPD requires *States* to provide safeguards to respect the adult's rights, will and preferences, avoid undue influence and manage conflicts of interest. Therefore, the Dutch legislator should introduce certain minimum safeguards to promote the adult's autonomy and prevent abuse of the *levenstestament* in accordance with article 12 UNCRPD. Although examples of safeguards have been provided in this chapter, further research is needed to determine which safeguards should be adopted. Research on the legislative framework in other countries could help determine the best course of action to take.

5 THE LEVENSTESTAMENT IN PRACTICE

5.1 INTRODUCTION

Although the *levenstestament* has become increasingly popular in the Netherlands, little is known about the use of and experiences with this instrument in practice. Empirical research data is scarce, and what is known about the application of the *levenstestament* in practice is primarily based on so-called 'anecdotal evidence'.[1] In the framework of this book, three exploratory studies have been conducted to gain more insight into how the *levenstestament* works in practice. The design of these studies had to consider that the *levenstestament* is an *enduring* instrument intended to make provisions for the future, a future in which the adult's cognitive abilities are likely to decline. This means it does not suffice to look at the experiences with the *levenstestament* at a single moment in time. To adequately capture the experiences with the *levenstestament*, it is essential to look at the application of the *levenstestament* at different stages in the 'lifespan' of the *levenstestament*. This can be done by looking at the experiences of various actors involved at different stages across the 'lifespan' of the *levenstestament*. This chapter presents the findings of two exploratory studies looking at the application of the *levenstestament* at the beginning and the end of the lifespan of the *levenstestament*. Section 5.2 presents the results of a survey study looking at the experiences with the *levenstestament* of the notariate, an actor in principle active at the beginning of the lifespan of the *levenstestament*. Section 5.3 contains the findings of a study looking at cases where the court, notwithstanding the presence of a *levenstestament*, deems an adult guardianship measure necessary. A measure that, in most cases, means the end of the lifespan of the *levenstestament*. An alternative approach to gain insight into the experiences with the *levenstestament* is to look at the expectations of the same actor at several moments in time. This approach has been adopted in the third and last exploratory study, presented in the next chapter. Chapter 6 presents the findings of a qualitative cohort study that attempted to chart the expectations and experiences

1. Prior to this book, only one survey study looking at the experiences of notaries with the *levenstestament* had been conducted – K. Blankman & J. Kaljee, *Het levenstestament in de notariële rechtspraktijk*, Vrije Universiteit 2013.

of the two most important actors – the adult and the attorney – at various stages across the lifespan of the *levenstestament*.

5.2 The application of the levenstestament by the notariate

In the absence of a specific regulatory framework, adults in the Netherlands do not require the involvement of a professional to make a *levenstestament*. Nonetheless, a significant number of adults use the services of a notary to make a *levenstestament*.[2] As discussed in detail in chapter 4, in the Netherlands, the notariate has designed and conceptualised the *levenstestament* within the framework of the existing law. This makes it interesting to learn more about this profession's application of the *levenstestament*. A first survey study, looking at the experiences with the *levenstestament* of the notariate, was conducted by Blankman and Kaljee in 2013, three years after the first model or format for the *levenstestament* was presented by the Dutch Association for Notarial Estate Planners (*Vereniging van Estate Planners in het Notariaat* – EPN) in 2010. With the support of the Dutch Notarial Association (*Koninklijke Notariële Beroepsorganisatie* – KNB), all 2895 members of the KNB were invited by Blankman and Kaljee to complete an online survey.[3] Eventually, 453 notaries completed the survey, resulting in a response rate of 15,7%. When relevant, the findings of this study have been included in the discussion below. The survey study conducted by Blankman and Kaljee was conducted quite soon after the emergence of the *levenstestament*. Developments concerning the *levenstestament* have not stood still since then. A lot has been done – predominantly the KNB – to promote the acceptance of the *levenstestament* by third parties. In addition, there have been several court cases after the study conducted by Blankman and Kaljee, confirming that the *levenstestament* can sometimes be associated with a risk of misuse or abuse.[4] It was therefore considered important to conduct a new survey study to capture the more recent experiences of the notariate with the *levenstestament* – this time, some eight years after the emergence of the first model developed by the EPN. Similar to the study conducted by Blankman and Kaljee, this second survey study looked at the models or formats used by notaries to make a *levenstestament*, the way the entry into force of the *levenstestament* is

2. In the first half of 2021, 93.136 *levenstestamenten* were registered in the Central Register of Levenstestamenten (CLTR). KNB, Factsheet Testamenten, July 2021, via: https://www.knb.nl/actueel/factsheets (last accessed: 05-10-2021).
3. Members of the KNB include both notaries and so-called 'candidate notaries'. A candidate notary is – similar to a notary – authorised to advise clients and draw up deeds. Unlike a notary, candidate notaries are however not authorised to execute deeds, unless they have been appointed as deputy to the notary. In the remainder of this chapter the phrase 'notaries' is used to refer to both notaries and candidate-notaries. Since all notaries and candidate-notaries in the Netherlands are required to become a member of the KNB, it was possible to approach the entire population of Dutch notaries and candidate-notaries with the invitation to participate.
4. District Court Overijssel 09-05-2017, ECLI:NL:RBOVE:2017:1932; District Court Noord-Nederland 08-04-2016, ECLI:NL:RBNNE:2016:1712.

regulated, how notaries perceive the need to include a form of supervision in the *levenstestament*, and how notaries perceive the acceptance of the *levenstestament* by third parties. In contrast with the study conducted by Blankman and Kaljee, this study also looked at the procedure notaries use to determine the client's capacity to make a *levenstestament*, the procedure notaries use to record medical wishes and preferences, and what notaries perceive to be the advantages and disadvantages of the *levenstestament*. This section discusses the findings of this study, conducted in 2018, focusing on the research questions, the methods, the results and finally, some conclusions that can be drawn.[5]

5.2.1 *Research questions*

This study aimed to answer the following research questions:

1. What are the characteristics of clients who make a *levenstestament*?
   a) In what age group do clients who make a *levenstestament* fall?
   b) What situation do clients want to make provisions for?
   c) What do clients include in their *levenstestament*?

2. Which model or format do notaries use for the *levenstestament*?

3. How do notaries determine whether the client has sufficient capacity to make a *levenstestament*?

4. How is the entry into force of the *levenstestament*, in most cases, regulated?

5. Supervision and monitoring
   a) How do notaries perceive the need to include a form of supervision in the *levenstestament*?
   b) Which type of supervision is generally included in the *levenstestament*?
   c) Do notaries register the *levenstestament*?

6. What procedure do notaries use to record medical wishes and preferences?

7. How do notaries perceive the acceptance of the *levenstestament* by third parties?

8. What are, according to notaries, the advantages and disadvantages of the *levenstestament*?

5. Because of the direct relevance of this study for the notariate in the Netherlands, parts of this study have been published in Dutch – R. Stelma-Roorda, 'Het levenstestament: gebruik en toepassing door het notariaat', Vrije Universiteit 2019. This section is partially based on a translation of this report.

5.2.2 *Methods*

With the support of the KNB, all 3239 members of the KNB received an email in May 2018 with the invitation to complete an online survey consisting of 25 questions.[6] A reminder was included in the online newsletter of the KNB six weeks later. Two hundred twenty respondents completed the survey, of which 164 respondents in full and 56 respondents partially. This means that the total response percentage is only 6,8%. This is relatively low, particularly when compared with the response rate of 15,7% in the first survey study conducted by Blankman and Kaljee.[7] It is not entirely clear why this response rate is so low. Perhaps for some notaries, the second survey followed too soon after the first survey. Several notaries indicated by email that they would not complete the survey as they were not working with the *levenstestament* in their practice. It is possible that more notaries did not complete the questionnaire for this reason. A question enquiring whether the office of the respondent provides clients with the possibility to make a *levenstestament* was included in the survey. 97,3% of all respondents indicated that clients could make a *levenstestament*, while 2,7% indicated that their office does not offer this possibility. In addition to the emails mentioned above, automatic reply emails showing that a notary was on leave or no longer working for the office were received. This may also explain a part, albeit an exceedingly small part, of the non-response.

Although the response rate is relatively low, table 1 indicates that the response rate seems evenly spread across the various regions compared to the number of notaries working in that region. The response rate is relatively low in the West region (Noord-Holland and Zuid-Holland) and the North region (Drenthe, Friesland and Groningen). A possible explanation for the relatively low response rate in the West region is that it is home to several large law firms that hardly work with the *levenstestament* in their practice.[8]

---

6. I would like to express my gratitude to the KNB for their assistance in bringing this study to the attention of their members. An overview of the questions can be found in Appendix 1. As indicated in footnote 3, all notaries and candidate notaries in the Netherlands are required to become a member of the KNB, which means that also in this second study, the entire population of notaries could be invited to complete the survey.
7. In this study 453 of all 2895 Dutch notaries had completed the questionnaire.
8. See http://www.advocatie.nl/notariaat-top-30-2018 for a list of the largest notarial law firms (last accessed: 15-04-2019). A subsequent check as to where these offices are based and whether these offices offer the *levenstestament* was undertaken.

Table 1. Response percentage per region

Regions	Notaries per region*	Respondents per region	Response percentage per region
Mid (Flevoland, Utrecht)	291	23	7,9
North (Drenthe, Friesland, Groningen)	285	13	4,6
East (Gelderland, Overijssel)	513	48	9,4
West (Noord-Holland, Zuid-Holland)	1475	82	5,6
South (Limburg, Noord-Brabant, Zeeland)	552	54	9,8

* As indicated in the KNB factsheet members and employees per Dutch province on 01-01-2018, via https://www.knb.nl/actueel/factsheets (last accessed: 02-04-2019).

A mixed methods approach has been used to analyse the data. Quantitative data were analysed with descriptive statistics using SPSS and Excel, while responses to open-ended questions were analysed through content analysis.

5.2.3 *Results*

1 *What are the characteristics of clients who make a levenstestament?*

In what age group do clients who make a levenstestament fall?
The survey contained several questions focusing on the so-called 'customer base' of notaries concerning the *levenstestament*.[9] First, notaries were asked in which age group most clients fall. One hundred sixty-four notaries answered this question. As table 2 shows, most notaries indicated that the majority of their clients are between 60 and 70 years old. However, 45 respondents indicated that most clients are older than 70. Only two notaries indicated that the majority of their clients are below the age of 50. This seems to suggest that in most cases, the *levenstestament* is drafted later in life.

9. Perhaps needless to say, the information presented here is based on the observations of notaries. Clients have not been asked directly.

Table 2. The average age of clients

Age	Frequency	Percent
Below 50	2	1,2
Between 50 and 60	22	13,4
Between 60 and 70	95	57,9
70 or older	45	27,4
Total	164	100

What situation do clients want to make provisions for?

International and national research shows that instruments such as the *levenstestament* are also used for purposes other than providing for a future period of incapacity. For example, the Council of Europe notes that instruments such as the *levenstestament* are increasingly made by people of all ages because incapacity may also occur suddenly, e.g. due to a car accident.[10] Engelbertink refers to situations where an adult appoints an attorney because the adult, due to physical impairments, cannot take care of his affairs or because the adult cannot keep up with the (technological) demands of modern society (e.g. online banking).[11] To get an idea of the type of situations for which a *levenstestament* is meant to provide, notaries were asked to indicate what motivates clients to make a *levenstestament*. Based on the literature, four situations – included in figure 1 – were distinguished. Using the option 'other', respondents had the opportunity to supplement the list of response options with other situations for which a *levenstestament* is also made in their practice.

Notaries were first asked to check all the options that apply in their practice (figure 1). One hundred sixty-four respondents answered this question. All but two respondents (98,8%) indicated that the objective of providing for a future period of incapacity due to a disease, such as dementia, occurs in their practice. 66,5% of the respondents indicated that the objective of providing for more sudden incapacity due to unexpected circumstances, such as a car accident, occurs in their practice. 53,7% of the respondents indicated they have clients who make a *levenstestament* because of physical impairments. 34,1 % of the respondents indicated that the *levenstestament* is in their practice also made because clients cannot keep up with the (technical) demands of modern society and therefore require the assistance of an attorney. Finally, 15 respondents (9,1%) used the option 'other' to supplement the list of response options with other objectives. Notaries mentioned objectives such as making provisions for a holiday or an

10. Council of Europe Recommendation CM/Rec (2009)11.
11. C.G.C. Engelbertink, 'Het levenstestament in de maatschappij', in: K. Blankman & C.G.C. Engelbertink, *Notariële bescherming ouderen*, Sdu Uitgevers: Den Haag 2013, p. 60 & p. 62-63.

extended stay abroad. Several respondents also referred to business objectives, such as a prolonged absence from the company or the 'presence of large assets'. Other objectives the respondents mentioned included preserving the client's autonomy and preventing adult guardianship measures.

Figure 1. **Type of situation for which clients aim to provide through a *levenstestament***

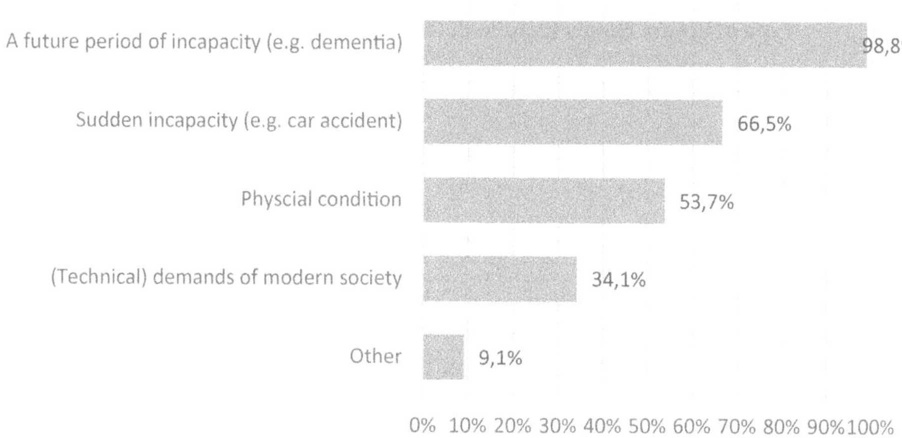

In addition to asking notaries to list all the options that apply in their practice, notaries were also asked to indicate which objective is most common in their practice. Table 3 shows that providing for a future period of incapacity due to a disease, such as dementia, is, by far, the most common objective for making a *levenstestament*.

Table 3. **Most common objective**

	Frequency	Percent
A future period of incapacity (e.g. dementia)	153	93,3
Sudden incapacity (e.g. car accident)	3	1,8
Physical condition	5	3,0
(Technical) demands of modern society	3	1,8
Total	164	100

What do clients include in their levenstestament?

Through a *levenstestament*, adults can appoint an attorney and record their wishes and instructions regarding their financial, medical, health and personal matters. Notaries were asked what provisions most clients include in their *levenstestament*. Do these provisions concern financial matters, medical and health matters, personal matters or a combination of all three? Figure 2 shows that almost 50% of the respondents indicated that most clients use the *levenstestament* to arrange financial matters. Approximately 46% of the respondents indicated that most clients use the *levenstestament* to arrange financial, medical and health, and personal matters. Only a few respondents indicated that most clients use the *levenstestament* to arrange medical and health matters (0,6%) or financial and personal matters (3,4%).

Figure 2. Type of affairs clients include in their *levenstestament*

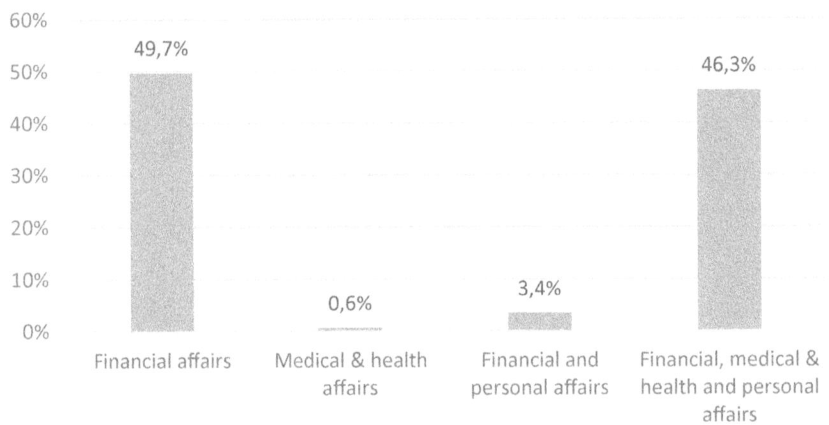

2 *Which model or format do notaries use for the levenstestament?*

Various notarial associations have developed a model or format for the *levenstestament*. In addition to the formats designed by the KNB and EPN, mentioned in chapter 4, another model has been developed by Netwerk Notarissen. Notaries do not have to use these models. Since no specific regulatory framework imposes requirements regarding the form of the *levenstestament*, notaries can design their own model. To gain more insight into the use of models in the Netherlands, notaries were asked whether they use a model developed by one of the notarial associations, an adjusted version of one of these models or their own model. One hundred seventy-five notaries answered this question. Most respondents use a tailored version of one of the models developed by the KNB, EPN and Netwerk Notarissen. Table 4 shows that with 36% of the respondents, a tailored version of the KNB model seems the most popular. A quarter of the respondents use a model developed by one of the notarial associations, with the KNB model being the most popular (18,9%). Finally, 21% of the respondents use their own model.

Table 4. The model used by notaries

	Frequency	Percent
Model KNB	33	18,9
Model Netwerk Notarissen	7	4,0
Model EPN	5	2,9
Adaptation model KNB	63	36,0
Adaptation model Netwerk Notarissen	11	6,3
Adaptation model EPN	19	10,9
Own model	37	21,1
Total	175	100

3 *How do notaries determine whether the client has sufficient capacity to make a levenstestament?*

Articles 3:33 and 3:34 of the Dutch Civil Code (DCC) clarify that a *levenstestament* can only be made by adults with sufficient capacity to do so. Notaries, therefore, are responsible for ensuring that clients who use their services to make a *levenstestament* have the capacity to do so. In the Netherlands, the KNB has developed a guideline notaries can use to assess their clients' capacity.[12] In addition, notaries can refer their clients to an independent physician when they are unsure about their assessment of the client's capacity. Notwithstanding these 'tools', there remain cases where the notary's assessment is contested by, for example, the relatives of the adult concerned. In some cases, this results in disciplinary proceedings against the notary. To better understand the procedure to assess the client's capacity in practice, notaries were asked how they determine whether the client has sufficient capacity to make a *levenstestament*.

One hundred fifty-four respondents answered this question. It concerned an open question, which means respondents could provide as many details as they wanted. The answers were subsequently coded and grouped into six categories.[13] Most respondents confined their response to a reference to the guideline mentioned above and the remark that they referred their clients to an independent physician in case of doubt. Several respondents mentioned elements included in the guideline, such as conducting various interviews with the client, involving one or more colleagues in assessing the client's capacity, having private conversations

12. See also chapter 4, section 2.2. In Dutch this guideline is known as the 'Stappenplan beoordeling wilsbekwaamheid ten behoeve van notariële dienstverlening'. In 2006 the KNB presented the first guideline, followed in 2013 by an updated version. The latest version of the guideline has been presented in 2021. However, at the time of this study, respondents had at their disposal the guideline presented in 2013.
13. Multiple categories could apply to one and the same answer.

with the client (without the presence of the prospective attorney) and visiting the client at home. From the responses emerged a picture of the following procedure:

> 'Capacity is assessed during the first interview. In case of doubt, the KNB guideline is followed. If necessary, a physician is consulted'.

In other words, a notary investigates whether there are reasons for a more in-depth assessment of the client's capacity during the first interview. If that is the case, notaries use the guideline. If the notary's doubts about the client's capacity persist, the client can be referred to an independent physician. This procedure, as apparent from the survey, is in line with the advice given in the guideline.

Table 5. Procedure to assess the client's capacity

Category	Frequency
First assessment by a notary	49
KNB guideline	93
Referral to an independent physician	96
Involving other colleagues	25
Private conversations / visiting people at home	12
Multiple conversations	18

From a few more detailed answers, it becomes clear that the setting in which a request to make a *levenstestament* is made can also influence how the procedure of assessing the client's capacity looks like:

> 'If the client indicates that he is worried that his 'environment' will act against his wishes, then we have [name of a care organisation for elderly with dementia] conduct an assessment beforehand.'

> 'During the intake, when the appointment is made, whether someone calls himself or via a third party is already checked. During the interview, we check in different ways if a client can follow the conversation, actively participate, ask questions, make wishes known, live independently, still take care of himself, go on holiday, etc. In case of doubt or when there are no direct family members and a third person is to be appointed as attorney, and this third person has phoned or is present during the first interviews, at least two more interviews will take place, where several colleagues will participate in turn and make a separate assessment. In cases of doubt or knowledge of family feuds or other unpleasant family situations, or cases of large assets and interests, [name expert] is called in and asked for advice. Especially when at the same time a request to make a will is made.'

4 *How is the entry into force of the levenstestament, in most cases, regulated?*
As noted in the previous chapter, a *levenstestament* can enter into force in various ways. A *levenstestament* can enter into force immediately after the adult's signature and remain in force upon the adult's incapacity. There are also *levenstestamenten* entering into force upon a specified moment in the future, most commonly when the adult becomes less able to act and decide himself. Finally, combining the two is possible; a *levenstestament* can enter into force immediately and partially upon the adult's incapacity. To get an idea of how the entry into force is regulated in the Netherlands, notaries were asked how, at their office, the entry into force of the *levenstestament*, in most cases, is regulated. Respondents could provide one of the three options mentioned above as a response. In addition, respondents could supplement the list of options by using the option 'other'.

One hundred seventy-four notaries answered this question. Most respondents (64,4%) indicated that for most of their clients, the *levenstestament* enters into force immediately. However, 22 respondents indicated that a *levenstestament*, in most cases, enters into force at a later stage after a physician – through a medical certificate – has confirmed the adult's incapacity. Only 12 respondents indicated that in most cases, a *levenstestament* enters into force partially, immediately after the adult's signature, and entirely after a physician has confirmed the adult's incapacity.

Table 6. Ways the *levenstestament* may enter into force

	Frequency	Percent
The *levenstestament* immediately enters into force	112	64,4
The *levenstestament* enters into force upon a medical certificate confirming incapacity	22	12,6
The *levenstestament* partially enters into force (e.g. concerning financial affairs) and enters into force entirely upon a medical certificate confirming incapacity	12	6,9
Other	28	16,1
Total	174	100

Twenty-eight notaries used the option 'other' to supplement the list of response options with alternative ways in which the *levenstestament* at their office enters into force. Most respondents used this option to provide a more nuanced answer indicating, for example, that a combination of the first and second option occurs in their practice. Several respondents indicated that the option chosen by their clients concerning the entry into force could depend on the person being appointed as an attorney:

> 'If the partner is appointed an attorney, the *levenstestament* usually enters into force immediately. If someone else is appointed as attorney, then the *levenstestament* usually enters into force after a declaration of incapacity.'

> 'The *levenstestament* takes effect immediately if the spouse is the attorney. If children are appointed attorneys, a medical certificate confirming incapacity is often required.'

Only one respondent mentioned an alternative not included in the list of response options, namely the entry into force of the *levenstestament* upon a joint decision of the attorneys.

5 *Supervision and monitoring*

How do notaries perceive the need to include a form of supervision in the levenstestament?

A declining ability to act and decide often goes hand in hand with a declining ability to supervise the attorney's actions. Interesting is in this regard how notaries perceive the need to include a form of supervision in the *levenstestament*. Respondents have therefore been asked when, in their opinion, a form of supervision needs to be included in the *levenstestament*. As table 7 shows, 33% of the 167 notaries who answered this question indicated that, in their opinion, a form of supervision should always be included in the *levenstestament*. Almost 40% of the respondents believed supervision should be included at the adult's request. Furthermore, 26,3% of the respondents indicated that supervision should be included in case there are particular sensitivities concerning the *levenstestament* (e.g. disturbed family relationships). Only two notaries did not consider a form of supervision in any situation necessary.

Table 7. Situations in which, according to notaries, supervision is indicated

	Frequency	Percent
In all cases	55	32,9
Upon request of the adult	66	39,5
In case of sensitivities	44	26,3
Never	2	1,2
Total	167	100

Which type of supervision is generally included in the levenstestament?

Notaries were subsequently asked which form of supervision is most frequently included in the *levenstestament*. Based on the literature, four types of supervision – included in figure 3 – were distinguished. Respondents could supplement the list of response options with other types of supervision used in their practice using the option' other'. Of the 167 notaries, who answered this question, 39,5% indicated that the appointment of multiple attorneys to act jointly is most common in their practice. For 25,7% of the respondents, the appointment of multiple attorneys is also the most common form of supervision included in the *levenstestament*, but here it involves the appointment of multiple attorneys to act only jointly in relation to important decisions. 13,2% of the respondents indicated that the attorney having to render account to an external supervisor was the most common form of supervision in their practice. Only a small number of notaries (1,8%) indicated that the obligation for the attorney to consult an expert concerning important decisions is the form of supervision chosen most often by the clients in their practice. The answer option 'other', used by 19,8% of the respondents, was used mainly to indicate that no particular form of supervision stands out and that a combination of several forms of supervision frequently occurs. An example is the appointment of multiple attorneys to render account to each other or an external supervisor. Another form of supervision mentioned concerns appointing one or more family members as supervisors.

Figure 3. Type of supervision included in the *levenstestament*

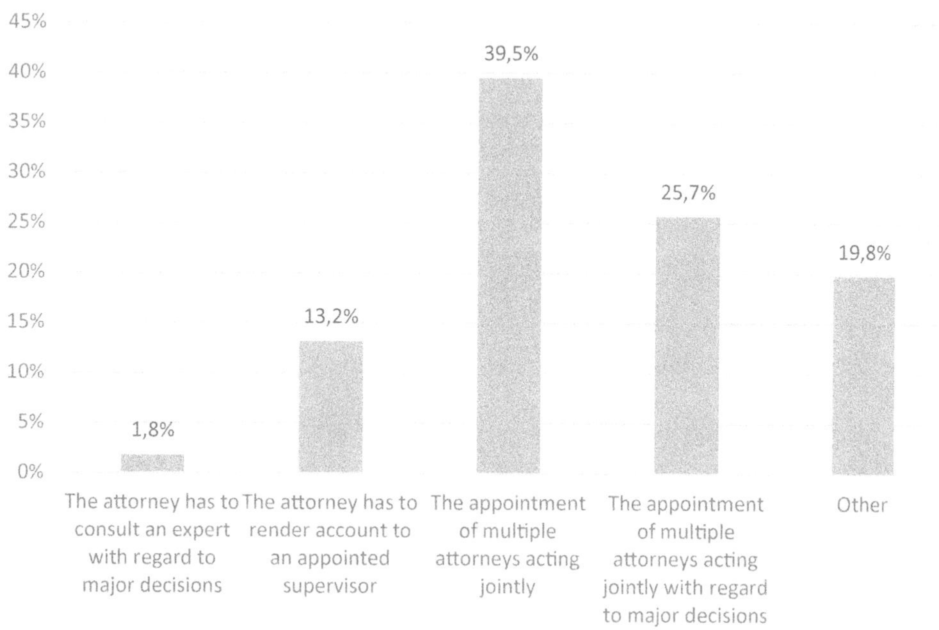

Do notaries register the levenstestament in the CLTR?

As discussed in chapter 4, a *levenstestament* can be registered in the Centraal Levenstestamentenregister (CLTR) in the Netherlands. Registration can fulfil several functions. First, it can play a role in ensuring that others, such as judges, are aware of the existence of the *levenstestament*. Second, registration can prevent the use of a *levenstestament* that has afterwards been changed or terminated by the adult. Finally, registration can provide an indication for notaries that something is not right in cases where a client, who has recently made or changed a *levenstestament*, comes to the notary to make a new *levenstestament*. Notaries were therefore asked whether, in their practice, the *levenstestament* is registered. As table 8 shows, of the 160 respondents who answered, the majority indicated that the *levenstestament* is always registered (90,6%) or in most cases (5,6%). Only in a limited number of cases, the *levenstestament* is not (1,3%) or in most cases not (2,5%) registered.

Table 8. Registration in the CLTR

	Frequency	Percent
Always	145	90,6
Mostly yes	9	5,6
Mostly not	4	2,5
Never	2	1,3
Total	160	100

6 *What procedure do notaries use to record medical wishes and preferences?*

As noted in chapter 4, the inclusion of so-called treatment advance directives – directives in which adults specify which type of treatment is under certain conditions desired or refused – in the *levenstestament* is not undisputed. Discussion between the KNB and the Royal Dutch Medical Association (KNMG) resulted in 2017 in a guideline notaries can use in end-of-life conversations with their clients. To gain more insight into how notaries deal with clients' requests to include medical wishes and preferences in the *levenstestament*, notaries were asked which procedure they use for this purpose.

One hundred fifty-one respondents answered this question. Again, it concerned an open question, meaning that respondents could provide as many details as they wanted. The answers were subsequently coded and grouped into six categories.[14] However, these six categories can be broken down into two broad categories. On the one hand, some respondents used the question to indicate which medical matters clients can include in the *levenstestament* in their practice. On the other hand, some respondents discussed the procedure they use for this purpose. Several respondents indicated that a *levenstestament* concerning health and medical affairs is in their practice confined to a medical power of attorney (POA). Some respondents referred in this regard to the dynamic character of medical wishes and

14. Multiple categories could apply to one and the same answer.

preferences or indicated they did not feel equipped to discuss medical matters with their clients:

> 'Personally, I am not so much in favour of treatment advance directives in *levenstestamenten* because *levenstestamenten* are more static than the subtle changes that are necessary with regard to treatment advance directives over time, if only because technology changes so quickly and people's wishes change when they become really ill. Moreover, I do not consider myself capable of discussing medical details.'

A few notaries also indicated that although clients could record medical wishes and preferences in the *levenstestament*, this possibility was confined to non-treatment directives. Clients wishing to make (more extensive) advance directives – e.g. a euthanasia advance directive – were referred to their family doctor.

Table 9. Procedure to record medical wishes and preferences

Category	Frequency
Levenstestament confined to a medical POA	37
Limited treatment directive	9
Referral to the family doctor	69
Informing/advising clients about the possibilities	88
Advice to discuss wishes and preferences with the attorney / other family members	7
Other*	22

* The category 'other' consists of responses indicating that clients can arrange both a medical POA, a (non-)treatment directive and a euthanasia directive in the *levenstestament*; responses confined to the remark that there is no specific procedure; and responses confined to a reference to the guideline developed by the KNB and the KNMG.

The scope and the procedure of notaries who do offer clients the possibility to include medical wishes and preferences in the *levenstestament* varies. Several respondents indicated that there is no specific procedure to record medical wishes and preferences; this is integrated into the ordinary course of affairs to make a *levenstestament*:

> 'The procedure for recording matters of a medical nature does not differ from that of a financial nature and runs as follows: potential clients call for an appointment; secretary sends them the KNB *levenstestament* checklist before the meeting; discussion follows during which the checklist and other choices mentioned in the KNB-model *levenstestament* are discussed; the draft deed is drawn up; the draft deed is sent to the client with an explanation of the content of the deed; an appointment is made with the client.'

Some respondents did indicate that they have a specific procedure to record the client's medical wishes and preferences:

> 'Extensive discussion with an explanation of the different options. Referral to the family doctor to also discuss/communicate wishes and preferences there. If I have doubts about whether something is medically possible/feasible, the client will contact his family doctor in advance. If necessary, the deed is adapted/supplemented based on this contact.'

As the quote above makes clear, this specific procedure generally involves the advice to discuss wishes and preferences with the family doctor or to, at least, inform the doctor about the wishes and preferences included in the *levenstestament*. Some respondents indicated they urge their clients to converse with the doctor before signing the *levenstestament*. Although it concerned only a few respondents, some notaries indicated they advise their clients to discuss medical wishes and preferences with the attorney and (other) family members.

7 How do notaries perceive the acceptance of the levenstestament by third parties?

The survey also addressed the issue of acceptance of the *levenstestament* by third parties. Notaries were asked whether, to their knowledge, clients experience problems with the acceptance of the *levenstestament* by third parties. Once again, it is emphasised that the responses concern observations by notaries. As notaries, in most cases, only have contact with their clients when the *levenstestament* is made, they will probably not, in all cases, be aware of problems with the acceptance of the *levenstestament*. These problems are, after all, more likely to occur at a later time when the *levenstestament* has entered into force. Of the 164 notaries who answered this question, 39 indicated that their clients had experienced problems with the acceptance of the *levenstestament*. These 39 respondents were then asked with which third party this was the case. Banks, doctors, and family members of the adult were mentioned most often.

8 What are, according to notaries, the advantages and disadvantages of the levenstestament?

Through two open questions, notaries were asked what they think are the advantages and disadvantages of the *levenstestament*. Since it concerned an open question, respondents could list multiple advantages or disadvantages. The responses were subsequently – using content analysis – coded into categories. One hundred fifty-seven respondents listed one or more advantages, compared to 152 notaries who listed one or more disadvantages of the *levenstestament*.

As table 10 shows, six categories were used to code the advantages. The category 'other' was used to code responses occurring less than ten times. Most respondents listed 'autonomy' as an advantage of the *levenstestament*. The term was, however, used in different ways. Some notaries used the word to indicate that adults can remain in control of their affairs and avoid the court's interference (e.g. an adult guardianship measure). Both the possibility of the adult appointing an attorney of his own choice and the opportunity of recording wishes, preferences and instructions were mentioned in this regard. Some notaries used the term to highlight the autonomy of the attorney or the family more broadly (the family including the adult, but also the adult's spouse and children). Again, the *levenstestament* was seen as a possibility to keep the management of affairs within the family and to exclude the 'interference' of others, such as the court:

> 'Control remains in one's own hands / within the family and the involvement/interference of the court or a financial guardian is prevented.'

> 'The possibility to resolve any consequences of, for example, ageing within the family.'

Table 10. Advantages of the *levenstestament*

Category	Frequency
Autonomy / no interference from third parties	110
Time gain/continuation	19
Affairs are put in order	13
Estate planning	18
Customisation	14
Other	32

Linked to the advantage of avoiding the involvement of the court, respondents noted that a *levenstestament* enables the attorney to act immediately without losing valuable time to await the court's decision. As court-appointed representatives in the Netherlands require the court's authorisation for certain acts (e.g. donating on behalf of the adult) and are subject to supervision by the court, several notaries also pointed out the advantages of the *levenstestament* in the context of estate planning. Respondents mentioned in this regard the attorney's leeway in acting without the involvement and supervision of the court. Notaries also indicated that with a *levenstestament*, there are more possibilities for customisation:

> 'That the next of kin of the principal (usually partner/children) can continue to dispose of the assets as they used to. Without the need to involve a judge, without the need to request authorisation for gifts etc. So that people can manage their assets (and transfer them to the next generation) as they see fit.'

> 'Customisation possible compared to financial guardianship. Being able to donate, also after legal incapacity, in the context of estate planning.'

Several respondents indicated that the *levenstestament* also gives clients a sense of security that all affairs are arranged. Linked to that, some notaries note advantages – coded in the category 'other' – such as 'awareness' and 'transparency within the family':

> 'Designating who is allowed to act and discussing this makes people aware of their choices!'

> 'Transparency in the family and thus preventing disagreements.'

Besides the advantages, notaries were also asked to list the disadvantages of the *levenstestament*. As table 11 shows, seven categories were used to code the responses. Again, the category 'other' was used to code responses occurring less than ten times. The two disadvantages mentioned most often concern the risk of abuse of the *levenstestament* by the attorney and the problems with the acceptance of the *levenstestament* by third parties. Regarding the risk of abuse, notaries mentioned situations where the adult is unduly influenced to make a *levenstestament* or to appoint a particular person and situations where the attorney abuses or misuses the authority conferred to him through the *levenstestament*. Several respondents noted that preventing or reacting to such abuse is not easy. In this regard, respondents mentioned the difficulties in uncovering undue influence, the challenges in convincing clients of the need to include a form of supervision in the *levenstestament* and the challenges in responding to abuse:

> 'The pressure that may be put on people, otherwise the children/those who receive a power of attorney will get angry. As notaries, we cannot always sense that; people are very good at hiding it.'

> 'Most difficult is a situation with multiple stakeholders where the 'chosen one' can do anything and an obligation to render account is not necessary according to the client, even after I have explained why it would be sensible to include such an obligation.'

> 'Abuse by the attorney. If the adult is no longer (fully) competent and stakeholders have doubts about the execution of the *levenstestament*. Setting up a financial guardianship through the court is difficult.'

Concerning the problems with the acceptance of the *levenstestament* by third parties, several respondents expressed their dissatisfaction with the difficulty of appointing more than one attorney for banking matters:

'Many banks cannot record multiple attorneys in their systems. So then you have to create a workable situation with additional POAs etc., while the problem can be solved by adjusting the computer system.'

Table 11. Disadvantages of the *levenstestament*

Category	Frequency
(Risk of) misuse/abuse	48
Clients approaching the notary too late	12
Acceptance	36
Disturbed family relationships	14
Treatment advance directive	15
None / yet to become visible	18
Other	37

In addition to the risk of misuse or abuse and the problems with the acceptance of the *levenstestament*, respondents mentioned the following disadvantages: clients who approach a notary too late – namely at a stage where the client is considered unable to make a *levenstestament* – and the limitations and uncertainties of treatment advance directives. Concerning the latter, several respondents noted that clients often expect what has been recorded in the levenstestament to be carried out. However, notaries cannot guarantee that this will be the case:

'It is important to be clear about what one can expect from medical powers of attorney and wishes. People think that it has been arranged at the notary's office and that the doctor has to carry out the wishes, but it is just not that simple for medical matters.'

Several notaries also mentioned troubled relationships within families or between attorneys as a disadvantage of the *levenstestament*. Conflicts can arise at the outset when one of the children is appointed as an attorney while the others are not. However, a dispute can also occur later and hinder the execution of the *levenstestament*:

'Children or other relatives disagree about who should receive a power of attorney and how this power of attorney should be used.'

Responses coded in the category 'other' include difficulties regarding the choice of attorney, concerning both situations where there is no one suitable and situations where there are too many appropriate persons; difficulties regarding the entry into force of the *levenstestament*; the non-compulsory character of registration; and the term '*levenstestament*' which some respondents find confusing. Finally, several respondents indicated that they saw no disadvantages to the *levenstestament*. In this context, respondents noted that disadvantages have yet to become apparent since many *levenstestamenten* have not yet entered into force.

5.2.4 *Discussion*

This survey study looked at the application of the *levenstestament* by the notariate. The findings provide insight into the customer base of notaries, the models or formats notaries use to make a *levenstestament*, how notaries assess the client's capacity, the entry into force of the *levenstestament*, supervision and the recording of medical wishes and preferences. Notaries were also asked whether they are aware of problems with the *levenstestament* and what they perceive as the advantages and disadvantages of the *levenstestament*. Although the low response rate means that findings cannot be considered representative, the study – particularly the open questions – provides insight into the diverse ways notaries work with the *levenstestament* in their practice. In this regard, there are a number of issues that draw attention.

Similar to the study conducted by Blankman and Kaljee in 2013, this study indicates that the risk of abuse or misuse of the *levenstestament* and the importance of supervision remain points of attention.[15] Respondents indicated that in most cases, the *levenstestament* is used to make provisions for a future period of incapacity – a time when the adult is generally less able to supervise the attorney's actions. Several respondents acknowledged this risk when asked about the disadvantages of the *levenstestament*. That being said, only 33% of the respondents indicated that a form of supervision should, in all cases, be included.[16] As noted in chapter 4, from the outset, the starting point of several notarial associations has been that it is ultimately up to the adult whether a form of supervision is included in the *levenstestament*, which is endorsed by 39,5% of the respondents in this study. Noteworthy is, however, that several respondents mentioned, as one of the disadvantages of the *levenstestament*, the difficulty in convincing clients to include a form of supervision in the *levenstestament*, even though supervision was considered appropriate by the notary in the case at hand. In other words, if the notariate continues to adhere to the view that it is ultimately up to the client whether a form of supervision is included, it seems crucial that the notarial associations continue to consider ways in which notaries can convince clients of the importance of doing so.

---

15. Blankman & Kaljee 2013, pp. 39-40.
16. In the study conducted by Blankman and Kaljee where a similar, although differently phrased, question was asked, 45% of the respondents indicated that in most cases no supervision is included in the *levenstestament*. In addition, 34,5% of the respondents in the study by Blankman and Kaljee, indicated that supervision is not included in cases where a spouse or one of the children is appointed as an attorney – Blankman & Kaljee 2013, pp. 28-30.

Another interesting observation is that several notaries considered the autonomy of the attorney – or the family more broadly – to keep the management of affairs within the family as one of the advantages of the *levenstestament*. In this regard, several respondents pointed out the possibility for the attorney to engage in estate planning without the prying eyes of the court. The risk of approaching the advantages of estate planning from the perspective of the attorney or the family is that the purpose of the instrument – protecting the interests of the adult – is overlooked. As discussed in chapter 3, there is a fine line between estate planning based on the wishes and preferences of the adult and estate planning based on the wishes and desires of the attorney. The first is generally accepted as a legitimate form of estate planning, whereas the second is not. It is therefore important that the adult's wishes and preferences regarding estate planning are carefully recorded in the *levenstestament*. In addition, notaries should ensure appropriate supervision is put in place to ensure that the attorney acts by the adult's wishes and preferences.

Concerning forms of supervision included in the *levenstestament*, 38,4% of the respondents indicated that the appointment of multiple attorneys to act jointly is most common in their practice. Furthermore, 25% of the respondents indicated that the appointment of multiple attorneys to act jointly concerning important decisions is most common in their practice. This is surprising since provisions stipulating that attorneys are to act jointly are considered problematic by banks, who do not have the means to check whether attorneys do so.[17] After consultation with the Dutch Banking Association (NVB), a provision has therefore been included in the KNB model stipulating that attorneys with regard to banking matters may grant each other a subsequent power of attorney. Thus, allowing attorneys to create a situation in which they can act separately from each other. The question that arises is whether this form of supervision has not lost much of its value with such a provision.

Respondents' comments regarding the risk of abuse indicate that efforts to prevent misuse or abuse should not be confined to the execution of the *levenstestament*. Several respondents pointed out the risk of undue influence of adults. Here lies a huge responsibility for notaries to act as gatekeepers to prevent situations where the content of the *levenstestament* and the choice of attorney do not reflect the adult's wishes. Mandatory registration could be helpful in this regard. As noted, registration of the *levenstestament* – in particular, changes and terminations of the *levenstestament* – could help notaries assess situations of undue influence. An example concerns cases where the notary is approached by an adult who has recently made or changed his *levenstestament*. As noted, only six respondents in this study indicated that in their practice, the *levenstestament* is not or in

17. Discussed more extensively in chapter 4 section 2 of this book.

most cases not registered. This is much less than the 25,9% in the study conducted by Blankman and Kaljee.[18] Registration seems, in other words, the norm in practice. That being said, a few respondents rightly pointed out that the *levenstestament* should be registered in all cases to have a watertight system. Although this study did not address the opinion of notaries on mandatory registration, most of the respondents in Blankman and Kaljee's study (72.7%) seemed to favour compulsory registration.[19] An assessment of whether the adult is unduly influenced can go hand in hand with assessing the adult's capacity to make a *levenstestament*. Several of the tools notaries can use to evaluate the adult's capacity – e.g. private conversations with the adult without the presence of the attorney – might also help assess signs of undue influence. In this regard, the update of the KNB guideline on assessing capacity in 2021 is a good step in the right direction. This new version includes directions that notaries can use to evaluate and prevent situations of undue influence.

This study also shows that further research on specific points is called for. Like the study conducted by Blankman and Kaljee, many respondents work either with an adapted version of the model developed by one of the notarial associations or their own model.[20] This is surprising since the notarial associations, over the past years, have put considerable time and effort into developing their models. These models have been made in consultation with third parties – such as banks – to ensure that provisions included in the *levenstestament* are enforceable in practice. It remains unclear why respondents adapt these models or use their own model, to what extent these models deviate from the models developed by the notarial associations and whether these amendments influence the acceptance of the *levenstestament* by third parties. Blankman and Kaljee note that a uniform model may be advisable to promote the acceptance of the *levenstestament*.[21] Further research on this point is needed. The same applies to the inclusion of treatment advance directives in the *levenstestament*. This study shows that the scope and thoroughness of the procedure used by notaries to record the client's medical wishes and preferences differs. In this regard, research examining whether these procedural differences influence how doctors in practice can fulfil the adult's wishes and preferences as expressed in the *levenstestament* seems called for. A final point of interest concerns the influence of conflicts within families or between attorneys about the execution of the *levenstestament*. Although mentioned by only a few respondents, this has not been substantially addressed in the research and literature on the *levenstestament*. With regard to these and other problems, further research examining the scope and impact of these problems and looking at ways

18. Blankman & Kaljee 2013, p. 30-39.
19. Ibid.
20. Blankman & Kaljee 2013, p. 20-23.
21. Ibid.

in which these problems can be solved seems important. As several respondents pointed out, most *levenstestamenten* have not yet entered into force, meaning that problems with the *levenstestament*, to an extent, remain to be seen.

5.3 An analysis of court cases featuring the levenstestament

Where notaries can be positioned at the beginning of the so-called lifespan of the *levenstestament*, judges can, in some cases, be positioned at the end. Namely in those cases where problems with the *levenstestament* occur, and the court's involvement becomes necessary. Examples are cases where an attorney is prosecuted for the abuse or misuse of the *levenstestament*.[22] But also cases where a request for an adult guardianship measure is made because – according to the applicant of the measure – the *levenstestament* insufficiently protects the adult's interests. Blankman distinguishes the following four situations on which, in practice, such requests are based, namely situations where: 1) the *levenstestament* is not accepted by third parties, 2) there is a troubled family relationship, 3) the *levenstestament* does not offer sufficient protection against 'unwise' decisions or actions by the adult himself, or 4) the *levenstestament* does not offer sufficient protection against misuse or abuse of the *levenstestament* by the attorney.[23] It is not necessarily the case that a request made on one of these grounds automatically results in an adult guardianship measure. As noted in chapter 4, the courts have adopted a principle of subsidiarity, meaning that an adult guardianship measure is not applied when a less restrictive alternative – e.g. a *levenstestament* – is in place. In other words, the court will, in each case, assess whether the *levenstestament* adequately protects the interests of the adult or whether an adult guardianship measure is necessary. This subsection presents the results of a study looking at cases in which the court – notwithstanding the existence of a *levenstestament* – was confronted with a request for an adult guardianship measure. More specifically, I will examine the court's considerations in deciding whether or not to impose an adult guardianship measure. After providing a brief outline of the legal framework, I will continue with a discussion of the methods, the results of the study and a succinct discussion addressing what these court cases tell us about the problems occurring with the *levenstestament* in practice.

22. District Court of Noord-Nederland 29-06-2021, ECLI:NL:RBNNE:2021:2845; District Court of Limburg 26-03-2021, ECLI:NL:RBLIM:2021:2690; District Court of Rotterdam 17-02-2021, ECLI:NL:RBROT:2021:1390; District court Midden-Nederland 02-10-2020, ECLI:NL:RBMNE:2020:4216; District Court Overijssel 09-05-2017, ECLI:NL:RBOVE:2017:1932; District Court Noord-Nederland 08-04-2016, ECLI:NL:RBNNE:2016:1712.
23. K. Blankman, 'Kroniek bescherming van meerderjarigen', *FJR* 2016 (11), pp. 274-279.

5.3.1 *A brief overview of the legal framework*

An adult guardianship measure can be requested by the adult concerned, his partner (spouse, registered partner or other life companion), a close relative (not including the family-in-law), the public prosecutor or a (residential) care facility.[24] The District Court, in the first instance, deals with a request for an adult guardianship measure.[25] An appeal can be lodged with the Court of Appeal and, after that, the Dutch Supreme Court (on matters of law only).[26] Upon receiving a request for an adult guardianship measure, the court has to determine whether the physical or mental condition of the adult is such that the adult is unable to look after his financial (financial guardianship), non-financial (personal guardianship) or both his financial and non-financial (full guardianship) interests.[27] The court will generally hear the applicant of the measure, the adult concerned and other interested parties to determine whether an adult guardianship measure is necessary.[28] In addition, the court can ask for a (medical) expert's opinion to verify whether the grounds for an adult guardianship measure have been met.[29] If the court finds this is the case, it subsequently considers whether the adult's interests cannot be protected through a less restrictive measure. This follows with regard to full guardianship from article 1:378(1) DCC, stipulating that an adult may only be placed under full guardianship when the adult's interests cannot be looked after properly through a more suitable and less far-reaching measure.[30] Although there is no such provision for financial and personal guardianship, in practice, the court has adopted a principle of subsidiarity. As discussed in chapter 4, according to this principle, preference should be given to less restrictive alternatives, such as the *levenstestament*. When the court deems an adult guardianship measure necessary, the court must appoint a guardian at the same time or as soon as possible

24. Article 1:379 DCC, article 1:432 DCC; article 1:451 DCC, translation via: dutchcivillaw.com (last accessed: 09-08-2021). This subsection provides a brief synopsis of the procedure regarding adult guardianship measures, more information on the scope and content of the adult guardianship measures can be found in chapter 2.
25. There are 11 District Courts in the Netherlands. An application for an adult guardianship measure must be submitted to the court of the area of residence of the adult concerned.
26. R. Frimston, C. Engelbertink & A. Vrenegoor, 'Netherlands', in: R. Frimston, A. Ruck Keene, C. van Overdijk & A.D. Ward (eds.), The International Protection of Adults, Oxford – New York: Oxford University Press 2015, pp. 568-574 (570).
27. Article 1:378 DCC: Article 1:431 DCC; Article 1:450 DCC, translation via: dutchcivillaw.com (last accessed: 09-08-2021).
28. Landelijk Overleg Vakinhoud Civiel en Kanton & Toezicht, *Aanbevelingen Meerderjarigenbewind 2018*, via: https://www.rechtspraak.nl/SiteCollectionDocuments/aanbevelingen-meerderjarigenbewind.pdf (last accessed: 02-06-2021); C. Blankman, 'Guardianship legislation in The Netherlands', in: K. Dayton, *Comparative Perspectives on Adult Guardianship*, Durham North Carolina: Carolina Academic Press 2014, pp. 181-190 (184-186).
29. Ibid.
30. Translation via dutchcivillaw.com (last accessed: 09-08-2021). Based on articles 1:432(3) DCC and 1:451(3) DCC, the court may, when confronted with a request for full guardianship, of its own motion, proceed with ordering financial and/or personal guardianship instead.

thereafter.[31] Articles 1:383(2) DCC, 1:453(3) DCC, and 1:452(3) DCC stipulate that the court shall follow the explicit preferences of the adult when appointing a guardian unless there are valid reasons not to do so.[32] It is generally accepted that the adult's wishes concerning the choice of a representative may also be expressed in advance in a *levenstestament*. If there are valid reasons not to follow the explicit preferences of the adult, or the adult has not expressed, and is currently unable to express, his preferences, articles 1:383(3) DCC, 1:453(4) DCC, and 1:452(4) stipulate that the court shall appoint the adult's partner or a close relative such as a parent, child, brother or sister as guardian.[33] The court may also appoint a professional as a guardian.[34]

5.3.2 Methods

The study of court cases featuring the *levenstestament* was undertaken in 2021. In March 2021, an initial search of judgements published on the website www.rechtspraak.nl was conducted.[35] Unfortunately, not all judgements are published on this website.[36] Several keywords were used to identify cases relevant to this study. The first keyword consisted of *'levenstestament'*, resulting in 106 hits. As the word 'volmacht' (English: power of attorney) is in practice also used to refer to instruments which show – as the court put it in a case before the District Court of Limburg – the 'characteristics' of a *levenstestament*, additional keywords consisted of the following combination of words: 'volmacht + bescherming-' (English: power of attorney + protection-) and 'volmacht + wils-' (English: power of attorney + [literally translated 'will', but part of several Dutch words such as 'wilsbekwaam' and 'wilsonbekwaam', translated in English as '(in)capacity']).[37] These keywords resulted in 45 additional hits (not including overlap). Upon a closer study, 12 cases were considered relevant and included in the study. An additional search – restricted to the keyword *'levenstestament'* – was conducted in mid-July 2021, resulting in an additional 18 hits. The strategies mentioned above resulted in a total number of 136 cases. Not all of these cases

31. articles 1:383 DCC, 1:435 DCC, and 1:452 DCC, translation via dutchcivillaw.com (last accessed: 09-08-2021).
32. Translation via dutchcivillaw.com (last accessed: 09-08-2021).
33. Blankman 2014, pp. 184-186.
34. Ibid.
35. Given the relatively small number of cases, the date of publication of the court's ruling did not play a role in the selection of cases. That means that all cases since the emergence of the instrument have been included in the study. The first court case included in this study was published on 14-08-2012.
36. In 2019 about 5% of all judgements were published – De Rechtspraak, *Kengetallen 2019*, via: https://www.rechtspraak.nl/SiteCollectionDocuments/kengetallen-2019.pdf (last accessed: 09-08-2021).
37. District Court of Limburg 26-03-2021, ECLI:NL:RBLIM:2021:2690.

were considered relevant for inclusion in the study.[38] In addition, as noted in chapter 4, a distinction between two types of court cases has been made. Cases where the court, in the absence of a statutory framework, has steered the development of the *levenstestament* have been discussed in chapter 4. This section focuses on cases that provide insight into the court's considerations to impose an adult guardianship measure, notwithstanding the existence of a *levenstestament*. Based on this distinction, 33 cases were selected for analysis as part of the study discussed in this section. Each case was carefully read, and a short synopsis was drafted to aid the analysis process.

5.3.3 *The deliberations of the court when issuing an adult guardianship measure*

As noted, Blankman distinguishes four situations in which the court – notwithstanding a *levenstestament* – can deem an adult guardianship measure necessary. As mentioned in chapter 4, an additional fifth situation was identified in this study, namely the situation in which the adult concerned requests an adult guardianship measure himself. In a case before the Court of Appeal in Amsterdam, the court ruled that a *levenstestament* does not mean that the adult concerned may no longer choose another measure of protection for himself.[39] The abovementioned categorisation was used as a starting point to categorise all cases as part of the analysis. Based on the content and number of cases in each category, a slightly different categorisation has, however, been adopted in the end, namely: situations in which there is a troubled family relationship, situations where the attorney is considered unsuitable for the task at hand and situations in which the *levenstestament* proves inadequate to protect and promote the adult's interests. As will become apparent, however, this categorisation is somewhat arbitrary, as in several cases, there were multiple grounds for the court to consider an adult guardianship measure necessary.

Disturbed family relationships

When it concerns situations where a troubled family relationship plays a role, a distinction can be made between cases where there is a disturbed relationship between the attorneys and cases where there is a disturbed relationship between the attorney(s) and one or more family members not appointed as attorneys. When there is a conflict between attorneys, a central consideration for the court

---

38. An example of a case that was not included in the study concerns a case before the District Court of Zeeland-West-Brabant 12-05-2021, ECLI:NL:RBZWB:2021:2528 where the court was asked to decide on the validity of a donation agreement. This case did not evolve around the *levenstestament*. The court in §3.31 only referred to the fact that the adult had made a *levenstestament* with the assistance of a notary, after the donation agreement had been made, in its reasoning that there was no evidence that the adult concerned lacked the capacity to make the donation agreement.
39. Court of Appeal Amsterdam 07-07-2020, ECLI:NL:GHAMS:2020:1892.

seems to be the extent to which the execution of the *levenstestament* is frustrated by the conflict. In three cases, the court ordered an adult guardianship measure because the execution of the *levenstestament* in practice proved 'unworkable'.[40] An example is a case before the District Court of Noord-Holland in which both financial and personal guardianship was requested by the daughter of the adult concerned.[41] In this case, a mother had appointed all three children as attorneys for health and medical matters and only her son as an attorney for financial matters. The court found that the *levenstestament* concerning the adult's health and medical matters had not proved workable due to the ongoing disagreements between the children and therefore ordered personal guardianship. However, the court did not deem financial guardianship necessary as there was no evidence that the son had not correctly looked after his mother's financial matters and therefore ruled that the *levenstestament* concerning the adult's financial matters could remain in force.[42] Although an 'unworkable' *levenstestament* due to constant disputes between attorneys can be a reason for the court to impose an adult guardianship measure, a case before the District Court of Noord-Holland showed that the court could be reluctant to assume an unworkable situation when the attorneys have barely started their task.[43] In a succinct judgement dealing with an application for financial guardianship filed because of a disturbed relationship between the two attorneys (two sisters), the court noted that in case one of the attorneys does not comply with the wishes of the mother stipulated in the *levenstestament*, there are other ways to solve this problem. The judgement notes that these ways have been discussed during the oral hearing, but these have unfortunately not been recorded in the decision itself. Considering the recent date the *levenstestament* had been made (a few months before the court case), the court was reluctant to act against the explicit wishes of the adult, and the request for financial guardianship was therefore denied.[44]

With regard to situations in which the relationship between the attorney(s) and one or more family members is disturbed, a subsequent distinction can be made. There are cases where the court considered the troubled family relationship insufficient ground to act against the adult's wishes as expressed in the *levenstestament*, and there are cases where the court, due to the disturbed family relationship, imposed an adult guardianship measure. A central consideration in this context seems to be whether the interests of the adult concerned can be sufficiently promoted and protected through the *levenstestament*. In a number of

40. District Court of 's-Hertogenbosch 08-04-2021, ECLI:NL:GHSHE:2021:1055; District Court of 's-Hertogenbosch 14-01-2021, ECLI:NL:GHSHE:2021:78; District Court of Noord-Holland 18-02-2020, ECLI:NL:RBNHO:2020:1161.
41. District Court of Noord-Holland 18-02-2020, ECLI:NL:RBNHO:2020:1161.
42. Ibid.
43. District Court Noord-Nederland 13-02-2017, ECLI:NL:RBNHO:2017:474.
44. Ibid.

cases, the request for an adult guardianship measure was made by one of the children of the adult concerned, not appointed as an attorney.[45] This request was, in two cases, accompanied by a request to be appointed as guardian instead of the attorney(s) appointed by the adult. [46] In other words, the legal proceedings in these instances were used as an attempt to circumvent the *levenstestament*. Such a request was denied in cases where the court found that the attorney(s) had acted satisfactorily thus far. In a case before the District Court of Zeeland West-Brabant, the court noted in this regard that not the interests of the parties concerned but the interests of the adult involved should be paramount.[47] In a case before the Court of Appeal in Amsterdam, the court made clear that the adult guardianship proceedings should also not be seen as a way to restore contact with the adult. In this case, the applicant (daughter of the adult concerned) had requested the appointment of a professional guardian in the hope that this guardian would be able to restore contact between her and her mother. The court referred to other means to improve the relationship, such as mediation.[48]

Another cause of action was taken in a number of cases where an adult guardianship measure was deemed necessary due to the context of the disturbed family relationship. Again, the central consideration of the court seems to be whether the interests of the adult concerned are sufficiently promoted and protected through the *levenstestament*. In some cases, a conjunction with the following category – the unsuitability of the attorney – becomes visible in this regard.[49] For this reason, in a number of cases, the court did not follow the adult's explicit preferences concerning the choice of representative.[50] In a case before the Court of Appeal Arnhem-Leeuwarden, for example, the court ruled that in an environment of mutual distrust between the husband of the adult concerned (the attorney) and the children, the attorney had failed to protect his wife from the

45. Court of Appeal Arnhem-Leeuwarden 13-12-2018, ECLI:NL:GHARL:2018:10856; District Court Zeeland-West-Brabant 13-12-2017, ECLI:NL:RBZWB:2017:8544; District Court Oost-Brabant 16-03-2015, ECLI:NL:RBOBR:2015:1548; District Court Gelderland 31-10-2014, ECLI:NL:RBGEL:2014:6918.
46. Court of Appeal Arnhem-Leeuwarden 13-12-2018, ECLI:NL:GHARL:2018:10856; District Court Oost-Brabant 16-03-2015, ECLI:NL:RBOBR:2015:1548;
47. District Court Zeeland-West-Brabant 13-12-2017, ECLI:NL:RBZWB:2017:8544, §7.
48. Court of Appeal Amsterdam 11-04-2017, ECLI:NL:GHAMS:2017:1252, §4.5.
49. Court of Appeal Arnhem-Leeuwarden 13-08-2020, ECLI:NL:GHARL:2020:6398; Court of Appeal Amsterdam 17-12-2019, ECLI:NL:GHAMS:2019:4635; Court of Appeal Arnhem-Leeuwarden 23-11-2017, ECLI:NL:GHARL:2017:10353; District Court of Noord-Holland 12-10-2017, ECLI:NL:RBNHO:2017:8481; District Court of Noord-Holland 12-10-2017, ECLI:NL:RBNHO:2017:8483; Court of Appeal Arnhem-Leeuwarden 19-04-2016, ECLI:NL:GHARL:2016:3283.
50. Court of Appeal Amsterdam 17-12-2019, ECLI:NL:GHAMS:2019:4635; Court of Appeal Arnhem-Leeuwarden 26-07-2018, ECLI:NL:GHARL:2018:6960; Court of Appeal Arnhem-Leeuwarden 23-11-2017, ECLI:NL:GHARL:2017:10353; Court of Appeal Amsterdam 26-04-2016, ECLI:NL:GHAMS:2016:1643.

consequences of these conflicts and had failed to put her interests first.[51] The court referred in this regard to the problems concerning the choice of a care home, the furnishing of the room and the care of the adult concerned. In addition, substantial sums of money had been withdrawn from the joint bank account, and it was unclear what had happened with these assets. Therefore, the court concluded that financial and personal guardianship was called for.[52] Although the adult concerned had expressed, in her *levenstestament*, the wish that her husband be appointed as guardian, the court ruled that there were sufficient grounds to consider the spouse's appointment unwise.[53]

The unsuitability of the attorney

As the preceding makes clear, there are situations in which the court deems an adult guardianship measure necessary and does not follow the explicit preferences of the adult, as expressed in the *levenstestament*, regarding the choice of attorney, because the court considers the attorney unsuited to the task at hand.[54] Such a ruling can be based on the observation that the attorney has, without justification, taken assets from the adult or has not sufficiently separated the adult's (financial) interests from his own.[55] The observation that the attorney is unwilling to act transparently and provide information to the court on how he fulfils his task can also be a reason for the court to consider the attorney unsuited.[56] The court can also find that the attorney's actions have negatively impacted the adult's interests. Examples are situations in which the attorney acts contrary to the adult's wishes and situations in which the attorney denies the adult the care or company of the (grand)children.[57] The opposite, leaving the care of the adult to others and being unable to respond promptly and adequately because the attorney lives abroad,

51. Court of Appeal Arnhem-Leeuwarden 23-11-2017, ECLI:NL:GHARL:2017:10353.
52. Court of Appeal Arnhem-Leeuwarden 23-11-2017, ECLI:NL:GHARL:2017:10353, §5.6.
53. Court of Appeal Arnhem-Leeuwarden 23-11-2017, ECLI:NL:GHARL:2017:10353, §5.7 & 5.8. The court in this regard also took into account that the spouse seemed physically and emotionally unable to act as attorney.
54. Court of Appeal 's-Hertogenbosch 02-07-2020, ECLI:NL:GHSHE:2020:2045; Court of Appeal 's-Hertogenbosch 10-10-2019, ECLI:NL:GHSHE:2019:3746; District Court of Midden-Nederland 14-03-2019, ECLI:NL:RBMNE:2019:1113; District Court of Noord-Holland 12-10-2017, ECLI:NL:RBNHO:2017:8483; District Court of Noord-Holland 12-10-2017, ECLI:NL:RBNHO:2017:8481; District Court of Midden-Nederland 14-09-2017, ECLI:NL:RBMNE:2017:4768; Court of Appeal Amsterdam 02-02-2016, ECLI:NL:GHAMS:2016:346; Court of Appeal Amsterdam 02-02-2016, ECLI:NL:GHAMS:2016:333; District Court of Gelderland 26-02-2015, ECLI:NL:RBGEL:2015:1476.
55. Court of Appeal 's-Hertogenbosch 02-07-2020, ECLI:NL:GHSHE:2020:2045, §3.6.2; District Court of Midden-Nederland 14-03-2019, ECLI:NL:RBMNE:2019:1113; Court of Appeal Amsterdam 02-02-2016, ECLI:NL:GHAMS:2016:346, §4.11.
56. District Court of Midden-Nederland 14-03-2019, ECLI:NL:RBMNE:2019:1113; District Court of Noord-Holland 12-10-2017, ECLI:NL:RBNHO:2017:8483, §2.3; District Court of Noord-Holland 12-10-2017, ECLI:NL:RBNHO:2017:8481, §2.3.
57. District Court of Midden-Nederland 14-03-2019, ECLI:NL:RBMNE:2019:1113; District Court of Noord-Holland 12-10-2017, ECLI:NL:RBNHO:2017:8483, §2.3; District Court of Noord-

can also be a reason for the court to consider the attorney unsuited to the task at hand.[58]

Levenstestament insufficiently protects the adult's interests

In only 3 of the 33 cases, the court deemed an adult guardianship measure necessary because the *levenstestament* proved inadequate to protect and promote the adult's interests. In a case before the District Court of Oost-Brabant, financial guardianship was ordered because the *levenstestament* was not accepted by the 'zorgkantoor', a Dutch institution responsible for providing long-term care.[59] In the two other cases, the court found an adult guardianship measure necessary because the *levenstestament* offered insufficient protection against unwise decisions taken by the adult himself.[60] Unfortunately, in both cases, the court is concise in outlining the underlying considerations for ordering financial guardianship. In a case before the District Court of Noord-Holland, the court ordered financial guardianship because the adult was regularly engaging in (financial) transactions, which subsequently had to be cancelled or withdrawn. The adult was also found to be susceptible to undue influence by one of her sons as large sums of money would be transferred after visits of this son. The court, in this regard, merely notes that the adult, due to her mental state, can no longer oversee these transactions.[61] Besides financial guardianship, the court ordered, in these cases, the registration of the financial guardianship in the Centraal Curatele en bewindregister (Register for full guardianships and financial guardianships) because of the protection this registration offers.[62]

5.3.4 Discussion

The small-scale study presented in this section looked at the court's considerations in imposing an adult guardianship measure notwithstanding the presence of a *levenstestament*. To a certain extent, these considerations provide insight into the problems that occur with the *levenstestament* in practice. Naturally, the picture painted in this regard is limited. Not only is the number of cases (33) included in this study small. In addition, not all instances where problems occur will be

Holland 12-10-2017, ECLI:NL:RBNHO:2017:8481, §2.3; Court of Appeal Amsterdam 02-02-2016, ECLI:NL:GHAMS:2016:346, §4.12.

58. District Court of Midden-Nederland 14-09-2017, ECLI:NL:RBMNE:2017:4768, §6.
59. District Court of Oost-Brabant 26-03-2015, ECLI:NL:RBOBR:2015:1997.
60. District Court of Noord-Holland 18-02-2020, ECLI:NL:RBNHO:2020:1171; District Court of Oost-Brabant 31-03-2015, ECLI:NL:RBOBR:2015:1998.
61. District Court of Noord-Holland 18-02-2020, ECLI:NL:RBNHO:2020:1171.
62. Based on article 1:439 DCC the invalidity of an act performed by the adult notwithstanding the financial guardianship can only be invoked against a third party if this third party was aware or should have been aware of the financial guardianship. Publication of the financial guardianship in the register generally ensures that the third party should have been aware of the financial guardianship.

brought to the court's attention. This holds true regarding problems with the *levenstestament* in general, but in particular with regard to problems brought to the court's attention in the context of adult guardianship proceedings. As noted, a request for an adult guardianship measure can only be made by certain persons in a close (family) relationship with the adult.[63] This means that persons not belonging to this group (e.g. neighbours or close friends) need to use other avenues, such as the police or the public prosecutor's office, to draw attention to suspicions of misuse or abuse. That being said, this study has identified various points of attention concerning the application of the *levenstestament* in practice. First, several court cases showed that a disturbed relationship between attorneys could hinder or prevent the execution of the adult's wishes and preferences to such an extent that the execution of the *levenstestament* becomes impossible. A second problem concerns the risk that the adult guardianship proceedings are used by dissatisfied family members – not appointed as an attorney – to circumvent the adult's wishes as expressed in the *levenstestament*. Although the court in these situations generally rejects the request for an adult guardianship measure, it is conceivable that the execution of the *levenstestament* in such a setting is not made any easier for the attorney. This brings me to the third problem: not everyone is suited to being an attorney. In several court cases, the court considered the attorney unsuitable for the task. This happened in cases where the attorney, in a context of family conflict and mistrust, lost sight of the adult's interests and failed to put these at the forefront. But the court also considered the attorney unsuitable in situations where the attorney had, without justification, taken assets from the adult or situations where the attorney had denied the adult the care and company of others.

Problems with the acceptance of the *levenstestament* by a third party and situations in which the adult was regularly engaging in transactions that subsequently had to be cancelled or withdrawn were other reasons for the court to order an adult guardianship measure. The court is, in these cases, concise in explaining why it deems an adult guardianship measure necessary. This means that little light is shed on the nature and scope of these problems and the court's rationale for ordering an adult guardianship measure. A more extensive explanation seems especially important in cases where the court deems an adult guardianship measure necessary because the *levenstestament* offers insufficient protection against unwise decisions taken by the adult himself. Blankman rightly points out that through a *levenstestament*, the adult has often tried to avoid the legal restrictions of a (financial) guardianship measure.[64] In addition, as noted in chapter 2, the Committee on the Rights of Persons with Disabilities has stated in General

63. Article 1:379 DCC, article 1:432 DCC; article 1:451 DCC.
64. Blankman 2016.

Comment No 1 that respect for the rights, will and preferences of the adult should include the right to take risks and make mistakes. Although, as discussed in chapter 2, this category of safeguards should be balanced with other safeguards (e.g. the prevention of undue influence and the management of conflicts of interest), it does seem important that the court in these cases more clearly explains and justifies why an adult guardianship measure in these instances is necessary.

As indicated, further research is needed to examine the nature, cause and prevalence of the abovementioned problems. This research should, also, focus on best practices to prevent and solve these problems. Although the courts are on this point once again succinct, a small number of cases show that the courts do see possibilities to prevent and resolve problems such as conflicts between attorneys and disputes in the family setting. Mediation is, in this regard, mentioned, and future research could examine to what extent such interventions are effective in preventing and resolving problems with the *levenstestament* in practice.

5.4 Overall conclusion

The aim of the two exploratory studies presented in this chapter has been to provide insight into the experiences with the *levenstestament* across different stages of the lifespan of the *levenstestament*. This has been done by looking at the experiences of two different professional actors, one active at the beginning (the notary) and the other active at the end (the court) of the lifespan of the *levenstestament*. Combining the findings of both studies, some final observations and conclusions can be drawn. First, both studies highlight the need to conduct further research on family disputes within the context of a *levenstestament*. Although only a few respondents in the survey study mentioned this problem, the study of court cases showed that conflicts between attorneys or between attorneys and other relatives could hinder the execution of the *levenstestament*. Further research should look at the nature, scope and prevalence of this problem and address how conflicts can be resolved or potentially be avoided. It is conceivable that notaries with regard to the latter also could play a role, for example, by advising their clients to be transparent about their motives for choosing a particular person as their attorney. Second, both studies highlight the need for more clarity on the attorney's role, rights and duties. The study of court cases showed that the court emphasises the character of the *levenstestament* as an instrument promoting and protecting the interests of the *adult*. The question that arises is how this relates to the advantage, mentioned by several notaries in the survey study, that the *levenstestament* enhances the autonomy of the family (including the adult and attorney) as a whole and offers room for estate planning. In several cases, the court considered situations in which the attorney, without clear justification, transferred assets from the adult to himself or situations in which the interests of the adult and the attorney became conflated, problematic. Clear guidelines regarding what attorneys may and may not do, seem called for in this regard. As both studies are exploratory and concern the study of an instrument still in development, future research looking at these and other issues remains important.

6 Decision-making by and for adults with impaired capacity: the potential of the Dutch levenstestament

This chapter was published as: H.N. Stelma-Roorda & V.I. Eichelsheim,' Decision-making by and for adults with impaired capacity: The potential of the Dutch levenstestament', International Journal of Law and Psychiatry 2023, vol. 86, pp. 1-11.

6.1 Introduction

There are various instances in which a person's ability to act and decide can be impaired. A progressive condition such as dementia may cause a gradual decline of decision-making capacity. This can also occur more suddenly, a recent example being adults suffering from Covid-19, who are so severely ill that they have to be put in an induced coma to receive ventilation treatment on the intensive care unit. In these situations, alternative mechanisms may become necessary to provide the adult with the support needed to make his own decisions and when this is not or no longer possible, to enable the involvement of someone else to act and decide on behalf of the adult, preferably based on the adult's wishes and preferences.[1] In many countries, adults have the possibility to set up and organise these alternative mechanisms themselves by means of anticipatory or advance decision-making instruments, otherwise known as enduring documents. Two such instruments are generally distinguished: the continuing, enduring or lasting power of attorney (CPA) and advance directives (ADs). In Recommendation 2009/11 the Council of Europe has defined the first as 'a mandate given by a capable adult with the purpose that it shall remain in force, or enter into force in the event of his incapacity' and the latter as 'instructions given or wishes made by a capable adult concerning issues that may arise in the event of his or her incapacity'. The two instruments can in the Netherlands be combined in one and the same instrument, known as a *levenstestament*. By means of a *levenstestament* adults may appoint an attorney who is to take care of their financial, medical and/or personal matters in the event of the adult's incapacity. In addition, adults may record their wishes and

1. Shepherd, V., Griffith, R., Hood, K., Sheehan, M., & Wood, F. (2021). There's more to life than money and health: family caregivers' views on the role of Power of Attorney in proxy decisions about research participation for people living with dementia. *Dementia*, 20, p. 308-325. doi: 10.1177/1471301219884426.

instructions addressed to either the attorney or a third party, such as a doctor. It is this instrument that provides the focus of this paper.

Although according to the Council of Europe, anticipatory decision-making instruments are increasingly viewed as something which should be considered by everyone in view of the fact that incapacity may occur suddenly, little is known about the experiences with anticipatory decision-making instruments, such as the *levenstestament*, in practice.[2] Research to date has predominantly focused on the validity and acceptance of health and social care ADs, barriers and facilitators in the uptake of anticipatory decision-making instruments and the risk of misuse and abuse of these arrangements by attorneys.[3] Research looking at the expectations adults have at the time they make an anticipatory decision-making instrument and research looking at the expectations and experiences of attorneys both at the time they are nominated by the adult to act as attorney in the future and at the time they start acting for or on behalf of the adult is scarce. Little is known about the role anticipatory decision-making instruments play in a process in which decision-making (gradually) transfers from the adult to the attorney. Such research seems important, first of all, because anticipatory decision-making instruments become active in a setting in which adults are probably increasingly less able to indicate whether they are satisfied with the execution of these alternative mechanisms. In addition, as Fetherstonhaugh *et al.* note, linked to the increasing number of adults who encounter diseases such as dementia, the number of people providing adults with impaired capacity with support, acting on their behalf when needed, is also expected to grow.[4] This makes it all the more important to understand

2. Recommendation 2009/11, Explanatory Memorandum.
3. De Boer, M. E. (2011). Advance directives in dementia care: perspectives of people with Alzheimer's disease, elderly care physicians and relatives. https://research.vumc.nl/en/publications/advance-directives-in-dementia-care-perspectives-of-people-with-a (accessed 9 February 2022); Vezzoni, C. (2005). The legal status and social practice of treatment directives in the Netherlands. https://research.rug.nl/en/publications/the-legal-status-and-social-practice-of-treatment-directives-in-t (accessed 9 February 2022); Beckett, A., Leary, K., Cumming, L., & Davies, G. (2014). The Future of Lasting Power of Attorney. A research report for the office of the public guardian. https://assets.publishing.service.gov.uk/government/uploads/system/uploads/attachment_data/file/368192/LPA_future_report_appendices.pdf (accessed 9 February 2022); Mitchell, L. K., Pachana, N. A., Wilson, J., Vearncombe, K., Massavelli, B., Byrne, G. J., & Tilse, C. (2014). Promoting the use of enduring powers of attorney in older adults: A literature review. *Australasian Journal on Ageing*, 33, p. 2-7. doi: 10.1111/ajag.12043; Tilse, C., Wilson, J., White, B., Willmott, L., & McCawley, A. (2014). Enduring Powers of Attorney: Promoting attorneys' accountability as substitute decision makers. *Australasian Journal on Ageing*, 33, p. 193-197. doi: 10.1111/ajag.12052; Setterlund, D., Tilse, C., & Wilson, J. (2002). Older people and substitute decision-making legislation: limits to informed choice. *Australasian Journal on Ageing*, 21, p. 128-133; Stelma-Roorda, R. (2021). The Misuse or Abuse of Continuing Powers of Attorney: What Are Appropriate Safeguards? *International Journal of Law, Policy and the Family*, 35-1, p. 1-25.
4. Fetherstonhaugh, D., McAuliffe, L., Shanley, C., Bauer, M., & Beattie, E. (2019) "Did I make the right decision?": The difficult and unpredictable journey of being a surrogate decision maker for a person living with dementia. *Dementia*, *18*, p. 1601-1614. doi: 10.1177/1471301217721862.

how alternative mechanisms such as anticipatory decision-making instruments can assist the attorney to support the adult. Lastly, and perhaps most importantly, as discussed in more detail in the next section, anticipatory decision-making instruments are presented as a promising way forward in protecting the adult's right to autonomy, by making the adult's voice an influential component of future decisions.[5] In this regard it is important to study whether instruments such as the *levenstestament*, live up to their expectations.

The aim of the current study is therefore to explore – by means of interviews – more broadly what the expectations and experiences of adults and attorneys with the Dutch *levenstestament* are. In addition, this study aims to explore the role the *levenstestament* plays in facilitating decision-making in a process in which decision-making gradually transfers from the adult to the attorney. Before turning to a detailed description of this study, the next section will first of all discuss the normative and social context in which anticipatory decision-making instruments, such as the Dutch *levenstestament* operate. Anticipatory decision-making instruments are meant to enable decision-making in a certain context, namely a setting in which the adult (gradually) loses the ability to act and/or decide. Decision-making in these situations is guided by legal norms and principles and may be influenced by practical difficulties both adult and attorney encounter. This context has in this paper been used as a sort to say 'lens' through which to look at the *levenstestament* and has provided the basis for the study to be discussed in the remainder of this paper.

6.2 Decision-making by and on behalf of adults with impaired capacity

6.2.1 *The Dutch levenstestament*

As noted above, adults in the Netherlands can provide for a future period of incapacity by means of a so-called *levenstestament*. The *levenstestament* is an instrument that has been designed and conceptualised by the Dutch notariate. It is not a statutory instrument as such; the word *levenstestament* does not appear in Dutch legislation. In the absence of clear – statutory – definition, the word *levenstestament* seems to function as an umbrella term for the various options adults have to make provisions for a future period of incapacity. In this regard, three elements are generally distinguished. A first element that can be included in the *levenstestament* is the appointment of an attorney for financial, medical and/or personal matters. This can be done for financial and personal matters through an

5. Gergel, T. (2020). The 'Mental Health and Justice Project': Using interdisciplinarity to move beyond impasse in disability rights. *International Journal of Law and Psychiatry, 71*, 101570. https://doi.org/10.1016/j.ijlp.2020.101570.

ordinary power of attorney (article 3:60 of the Dutch Civil Code) and for medical matters on the basis of article 7:465(3) of the Dutch Civil Code, which allows adults to appoint a representative for health and medical matters. While in some jurisdictions, such as England and Wales, there is an automatic revocation rule that causes an ordinary power of attorney to lapse upon the incapacity of the adult, the Dutch government has confirmed that in the Netherlands, an ordinary power of attorney can enter into force or remain in force upon the incapacity of the adult, giving it the character of a *continuing* power of attorney. This means that adults can choose whether the *levenstestament* enters into force immediately or upon a specified time in the future (e.g. the adult's incapacity). This is different for representation in medical matters, which is only possible if the adult is no longer deemed capable of a 'reasonable appreciation' of his interests (article 7:465(3) of the Dutch Civil Code). Besides appointing one or more attorneys, adults can also include their wishes, preferences and instructions addressed to these attorneys in their *levenstestament*. Article 7:465(5) of the Dutch Civil Code makes clear that an attorney for health and medical matters is obliged to act as a 'good attorney', which includes the duty to involve the adult in the decision-making process as much as possible. Article 7:450(3) of the Dutch Civil Code makes clear that the attorney also has the duty to respect the adult's wishes and preferences, as set out in a medical treatment advance directive (discussed below). A duty to behave as befits a 'good attorney' can also be assumed with regard to the ordinary power of attorney. It is however unclear what this duty in the context of the *levenstestament* entails. Stelma-Roorda has therefore argued that legislation clearly specifying the rights and duties of both adults and attorneys in the specific context of the *levenstestament* is called for.[6]

The second element that adults can include in the *levenstestament* is a treatment advance directive (article 7:450 of the Civil Code). In such an advance directive the adult specifies which medical treatment under certain conditions is desired or refused. A specific type of treatment directive in the Netherlands is the euthanasia directive (article 2(2) of the Termination of life on request and assisted suicide Act). Doctors cannot be bound by an advance directive containing a request for treatment. However, according to article 7:450 of the Dutch Civil Code, doctors are in principle obliged to follow so-called negative treatment advance directives (containing a refusal of treatment). A doctor may only deviate from such an AD if there are well-founded reasons for doing so. Leenen *et al.* refer to a situation where there is an 'outdated' treatment AD containing a refusal for an at the time incurable disease, that can now be effectively treated.[7] There is a special procedure

6. Stelma-Roorda, H. N. (forthcoming). *In anticipation of a future period of incapacity: the Dutch 'levenstestament' from a legal, empirical and comparative perspective.*
7. H.J.J. Leenen, J. Legemaate, J. Dute, E.J.C. de Jong, M.E. Gelpke, J.K.M. Gevers en G.R.J. de Groot, *Handboek Gezondheidsrecht*, Den Haag: Boom Uitgevers 2020, p. 133-135.

to be followed in case of a euthanasia directive.[8] A third element that can be included in the *levenstestament* is an advance directive addressed to the court containing the adult's preference as to who should be appointed as representative if an adult guardianship measure is deemed necessary. There is currently no legal basis for such a directive, but several court cases show that courts tend to accept such directives. Adults are not obliged to include all three elements in their *levenstestament*, they can confine their *levenstestament*, for instance, to the appointment of one or more attorneys.

6.2.2 The normative aspirations of the UNCRPD

The emergence and development of anticipatory decision-making instruments, such as the *levenstestament*, has resurfaced against the backdrop of an ongoing international discussion as to how the empowerment and protection of adults with impaired capacity should look like. This debate centres around article 12 of the United Nations Convention on the Rights of Persons with Disabilities (UNCRPD). Where for decades protection has been offered by means of a restriction or deprivation of legal capacity and the appointment of a substitute decision-maker, making decisions on behalf of the adult in his or her best interests, the UNCRPD, marked according to many the beginning of a new dawn. Premised on the principles of respect for the inherent dignity and individual autonomy, including the freedom to make one's own choice (article 3(1) UNCRPD), article 12 UNCRPD stipulates that persons with disabilities have the right to be recognized as persons before the law (article 12(1) UNCRPD) and the right to enjoy legal capacity on an equal basis with others in all aspects of life (article 12(2) UNCRPD). In order to ensure this, article 12(3) UNCRPD stipulates that states should provide persons with disabilities with the support they may require in the exercise of their legal capacity.

It is the question what this support should look like, which has been the subject of considerable debate. In its first General Comment, the Committee on the Rights of Persons with Disabilities (the Committee) made clear that article 12 UNCRPD must be understood as requiring a shift from regimes of substitute decision-making to supported decision-making alternatives enabling persons with disabilities to make decisions that have legal effect.[9] These aspirations of the Committee have on the one hand been credited as laudable. There seems to be

8. See e.g. De Boer 2011 for more information.
9. United Nations Committee on the Rights of Persons with Disabilities, General Comment No. 1. Article 12: Equal Recognition before the law, 2014. In this article, we have used the intuitive understanding of the expressions 'supported decision-making' and 'substitute decision-making' that are often used in the literature and research on this topic. In this context, the expression 'supported decision-making' is used to refer to support that enables adults to make their own decisions. The expression 'substitute decision-making is used to refer to support whereby

a general consensus that in situations where an adult is still able, with support, to make a decision himself, every support should be provided to enable the adult to do so. That being said, the debate seems to have reached an impasse with regard to the question whether measures of substitute decision-making, involving a decision being made on behalf of an adult, can be abandoned completely.[10] Gergel notes in this regard: 'even some of the most ardent human-rights advocates see removal of any provision for substitute decision-making on the basis of impaired mental capacity as potentially harmful, in cases where, for example, extreme risk to the individual may be at stake'.[11] A suggested way out of this impasse is to move beyond the question whether a decision can be made on behalf of someone else and instead focus on the question when, in which situations, substitute decision-making is required and subsequently the question how the process of decision-making in these situations should look like.[12] In other words, how are substitute decisions to be determined? Kim notes in this regard:

> '[T]he debate should not be over whether we sometimes should decide for others. The fact is that we inevitably do, whether we acknowledge this or not. Unfortunately, whether we make decisions for others with the respect and care they deserve is not inevitable. That is the true, and very demanding, challenge we should be debating.'[13]

This then draws attention to the role of the adult's wishes and preferences within the support provided to the adult. In the Committee's view, at the heart of the requirement of article 12(3) UNCRPD to support the adult in the exercise of his legal capacity, lies respect for the adult's rights, will and preferences.[14] In this sense, there seems to be room for substitute decision-making as long as the support that is provided is based on the adult's wishes and preferences. Anticipatory decision-making instruments are in this regard seen as a promising way forward. Gergel highlights the potential of these instruments in protecting the adult's rights in situations where substitute decision-making becomes necessary, by making the

someone else decides and acts on behalf of the adult. These interpretations do not (completely) correspond with the Committee's interpretation in GC 1.

10. Gergel 2020; Stelma-Roorda 2021; Martin, W., Michalowski, S., Stavert, J., Ward, A., Ruck Keene, A., Caughey, C., Hempsey, A., & McGregor, R. (2016). Three Jurisdictions Report. Towards compliance with CRPD Art. 12 in Capacity/Incapacity Legislation across the UK. https://autonomy.essex.ac.uk/resources/eap-three-jurisdictions-report/. (accessed 9 February 2022).
11. Gergel 2020, p. 1.
12. Gergel 2020; Craigie, J., Bach, M., Gurbai, S., Kanter, A., Kim, S. Y. H., Lewis, O., & Morgan, G. (2018). Legal capacity, mental capacity and supported decision-making: Report from a panel event. *International Journal of Law and Psychiatry*. https://doi.org/10.1016/j.ijlp.2018.09.006; Martin *et al.* 2016.
13. Craigie *et al.* 2019, p. 165.
14. United Nations Committee on the Rights of Persons with Disabilities, General Comment No. 1. Article 12: Equal Recognition before the law, 2014.

adult's voice 'an influential component of the 'substitute' decision'.[15] Anticipatory decision-making instruments such as the *levenstestament* provide a framework in which adults can express their wishes, preferences and instructions so that the attorney can take these into account. Stelma-Roorda highlights the potential of anticipatory decision-making instruments in allowing a flexible transition from supported decision-making, where the adult is supported to make his own decisions, to substitute decision-making where the attorney decides and acts on behalf of the adult when the adult is no longer able to do so himself.[16] As noted, a decline of a person's ability to act and decide may be gradual, meaning that although a person may at some stage be unable, even with support, to take certain major decisions such as the sale of a house, that person might be perfectly able, with support, to decide on a birthday present for a close friend or relative. In these situations the attorney can fulfil a double role, providing the adult with support to make his own decisions when this is still possible and taking over the handling of those affairs – based on the adult's previously expressed wishes, preferences and instructions – for which the adult is lacking the ability to act and decide.[17] With regard to the latter, the ability to *act* and decide, Martin *et al.* note that decision-making is but one aspect of article 12(3) UNCRPD's requirement to provide adults with the support needed to exercise their legal capacity.[18] The process of decision-making is often preceded by a process in which the decisions to be taken are identified and formulated.[19] In addition, a decision might require certain action to be taken in order to ensure the decision is executed or enforced. In this regard the legal authority granted to the attorney by means of the anticipatory decision-making instrument might be helpful. Attorneys can provide adults with the support they may need to make their own decisions and in addition enforce these decisions on behalf of the adult in situations where the adult's ability to act is impaired.

Although from a legal-normative perspective anticipatory decision-making instruments, such as the *levenstestament*, seem a promising way forward to enable decision-making for both the adult and the attorney, it is important to also understand how these instruments can be embedded in practice. More information is in other words needed about the context in which supported and eventually substitute decision-making becomes necessary in order to examine how anticipatory decision-making instruments such as the *levenstestament* can subsequently be positioned within this context.

15. Gergel 2020, p. 2.
16. Stelma-Roorda 2021.
17. Ibid.
18. Martin *et al.* 2016.
19. Ibid.

6.2.2 *Supported and substitute decision-making in practice*

As noted in the introduction, a *levenstestament* can become active in different settings. An inability to decide and act can be unilateral (e.g. with a person in a comatose state) or gradual.[20] The latter is often the case with dementia, as a diagnosis of dementia does not mean that the person immediately loses the ability to decide and act.[21] In such a setting, both supported and substitute decision-making are important, where the adult is supported to decide and act himself and when this is no longer possible an attorney starts acting on behalf of the adult based on the adult's wishes, preferences and instructions.

There is a growing body of research looking at supported and substitute decision-making focussing on health and social care decisions in the context of a dementia diagnosis. Within this body of research, support enabling adults to make their own decisions is emphasised. Not only because with the ability to make decisions the adult's autonomy is promoted, research shows that it also contributes to the adult's sense of self, well-being and quality of life.[22] Several studies focus in this regard on the interaction between adults, family carers, and sometimes also professional caregivers, in enabling decision-making. These studies show that decision-making entails far more than a dichotomy between supported and substitute decision-making. Instead, supported and substitute decision-making are frequently placed on either end of a continuum, reflecting a process in which the involvement of the adult in the decision-making process over time decreases, while the involvement of the family carer increases.[23] Several decisional styles are identified along this continuum.[24] For instance, Samsi and Manthorpe distinguish:

1) mutual decision-making (decisions are part of regular conversation);
2) reductive decision-making (decision-making is guided by cues and fewer options);
3) restrictive decision-making (decision-making is confined to significant decisions);
4) retrospective decision-making (decisions are made on behalf of the adult based on past knowledge, preferences and conversations); and

20. Samsi, K., & Manthorpe, J. (2013). Everyday decision-making in dementia: findings from a longitudinal interview study of people with dementia and family carers. *Int Psychogeriatr, 25*, p. 949-961. doi: 10.1017/S1041610213000306.
21. Smebye, K. L., Kirkevold, M., & Engedal, K. (2012). How do persons with dementia participate in decision making related to health and daily care? A multi-case study. *BMC Health Services Research, 12*. doi: 10.1186/1472-6963-12-241.
22. Smebye *et al.* 2012:2; Samsi & Manthorpe 2013:949; Fetherstonhaugh *et al.* 2019: 1220; Bhatt, J., Walton, H., Stoner, C. R., Scior, K., & Charlesworth, G. (2020). The nature of decision-making in people living with dementia: a systematic review. *Aging & Mental Health, 24*, p. 363-373 (363). doi: 10.1080/13607863.2018.1544212.
23. Samsi & Manthorpe 2013; Bhatt *et al.* 2020.
24. Samsi & Manthorpe 2013; Smebye *et al.* 2012; Bhatt *et al.* 2020.

5) best interest decision-making (decisions are made on behalf of the adult based on the adult's and the carer's best interests).[25]

As these decisional styles make clear, decision-making occurs within a process of close cooperation and negotiation between adult and family carer. Smebye et al. note in this regard:

> 'Autonomous decision making as an individual right is increasingly being questioned as people are dependent on each other and decisions are negotiated to ensure the interests of those involved. Decisions are made in the context of relationships and what meaning situations hold for the persons involved'.[26]

In other words, the emphasis shifts from a focus on autonomous decision-making to a focus on the participation of the adult in a process in which decisions are frequently taken together. Looking at the essence and meaning of decision-making for adults with dementia, Fetherstonhaugh *et al.* identified the feeling of 'still being here' as important for adults with dementia.[27] Adults felt marginalised and excluded when they were left out of the decision-making process, as was expressed by a research participant in their study: 'people talk about me, around me, but don't talk to me'.[28] Several studies indicate that adults want to be involved and consulted when decisions are made:

> 'I feel like I'm part of the decision, even though I know probably now I'm not contributing a great deal, at least I feel as if I'm part of the decision. And that's very, very important. So I feel enabled and empowered, even though each year goes by I'm less participating, at least I feel as if I am' (quote participant, Fetherstonhaugh *et al.* 2013: 148).[29]

Miller *et al.* highlight in this regard the ability of adults 'to communicate values and preferences long after their decision-making abilities are affected by cognitive changes'.[30] Family carers have a role in ensuring these values and preferences are translated into decisions, which are subsequently advocated on behalf of the adult.[31] The aforementioned shows that quite a lot is asked of family carers, namely by means of support strategies involving the adult in the decision-making

25. Samsi & Manthorpe 2013.
26. Smebye *et al.* 2012, p. 2.
27. Fetherstonhaugh, D., Tarzia, L., & Nay, R. (2013). Being central to decision making means I am still here!: the essence of decision making for people with dementia. *Journal of Aging Studies, 27,* p. 143-150. doi: 10.1016/j.jaging.2012.12.007.
28. Fetherstonhaugh *et al.* 2013, p. 148.
29. Fetherstonhaugh *et al.* 2019, p. 1227: Miller *et al.* 2016; Samsi & Manthorpe 2013.
30. Miller, L. M., Whitlatch, C. J., & Lyons, K. S. (2016). Shared decision-making in dementia: A review of patient and family carer involvement. *Dementia, 15,* p. 1141-1157 (1142). doi: 10.1177/1471301214555542. See also Smebye *et al.* 2012, p. 2.
31. Miller *et al.* 2016, p. 1142.

process and when this is no longer possible, making decisions based on the values and preferences of the adult. Research shows that this is not an easy role to take on.[32] Fetherstonhaugh *et al.* describe this role as a difficult and unpredictable journey, without a roadmap providing clear direction and certainty.[33] As the adult's cognitive abilities decline, family carers increasingly have to question whether the adult still – with support – has the capacity to make his own decisions.[34] This can cause conflict with the adult himself but also with family members who might believe nothing has changed.[35] Fetherstonhaugh *et al.* note that the journey will often become more and more complex as the cognitive abilities of the adult with dementia decline and the family carer increasingly has to advocate for the person with dementia.[36] Barriers described in this regard are a denial of the problem and the rejection of help by the adult with dementia, professionals not recognising problems, and a lack of access to information due to confidential and data protection issues and bureaucracy.[37] In addition several psychological factors are distinguished such as a change or reversal of long-time family roles, decision-making by the family carer in a context of family and professional mistrust and the difficulty family carers experience in taking certain decisions – sometimes contradicting the wishes of the adult – resulting in a sense of guilt and feelings of failure or betrayal.[38]

As the aforementioned shows enabling decision-making for both the adult and family carer in a process in which the cognitive abilities of the adult gradually decline, is far from being straightforward and clear-cut. A lot is asked from family carers who have to negotiate the complexities of the decision-making process in such a way as to ensure the adult's involvement and participation within this process.[39] In the literature several facilitators to promote decision-making have been distinguished in this regard. These include the provision of support by (healthcare) professionals, family cohesion by creating a setting in which decision-making can be shared, and information about the adult's previous wishes.[40] Linked

---

32. Livingston, G., Leavey, G., Manela, M., Livingston, D., Rait, G., Sampson, E., Bavishi, S., Shahriyarmolki, K., & Cooper, C. (2010). Making decisions for people with dementia who lack capacity: qualitative study of family carers in UK. *BMJ, 18*. doi: 10.1136/bmj.c4184; Lord, K., Livingston, G., & Cooper, C. (2015). A systematic review of barriers and facilitators to and interventions for proxy decision-making by family carers of people with dementia. *International Psychogeriatrics, 27*, p. 1301-1312. doi: 10.1017/S1041610215000411; Samsi & Manthorpe 2013.
33. Fetherstonhaugh *et al.* 2019, p. 1610.
34. Fetherstonhaugh, D., McAuliffe, L., Bauer, M., & Shanley, C. (2017) Decision-making on behalf of people living with dementia: how do surrogate decision-makers decide? *Journal of Medical Ethics, 43*, p. 35-40 (35). doi: 10.1136/medethics-2015-103301; Samsi & Manthorpe 2013.
35. Fetherstonhaugh *et al.* 2019, p. 1610; Livingston 2010, p. 4.
36. Fetherstonhaugh *et al.* 2019, p. 1611.
37. Livingston *et al.* 2010, p. 4.
38. Livingston *et al* 2010, p. 4-5; Lord *et al.* 2015.
39. Fetherstonhaugh *et al.* 2017, p. 35.
40. Lord *et al.* 2015; Fetherstonhaugh *et al.* 2019, p. 1611; Livingston *et al.* 2010, p. 5.

to this third facilitator, the value of anticipatory decision-making instruments is also within this body of research recognised.[41] Anticipatory decision-making instruments, such as the *levenstestament* are however placed in a broader context of advance care planning; defined as: 'discussions about one's values and wishes; discussing and planning future treatment and care; appointment of substitute decision-makers and development of written advance care directives'.[42] Fetherstonhaugh note in this regard:

> 'If seen as an ongoing process – rather than a one-off episode of form completion – ACP can provide a supportive structure to help family carers navigate their decision-making journey alongside their loved one living with dementia. It can facilitate open discussion about the trajectory of dementia, values and wishes, goals of care and possible treatment choices in the future. ACP can help family members understand and appreciate their role in supported decision-making by the person living with dementia. As the dementia progresses and the person progressively loses capacity, ACP can focus on the importance of substituted judgement and the need to make decisions based on what the person would have chosen themselves'.[43]

As the above makes clear, the use of anticipatory decision-making instruments, such as the *levenstestament*, is advocated in a setting in which the appointment of the attorney and the recording of wishes and preferences is followed by ongoing conversations between the adult and the attorney about what has been recorded and about the adult's (changing) values, wishes and preferences.[44]

6.3 Current study

As the previous section makes clear both from a legal-normative and a socio-medical perspective the value and potential of anticipatory decision-making instruments, such as the *levenstestament*, is recognised. From a legal-normative perspective, the *levenstestament* is seen as a promising way forward by making the adult's voice an influential component of future decision-making. From a socio-medical perspective, the potential of instruments such as the *levenstestament* – when placed within a broader context of advance care planning – as a supportive structure for attorneys to facilitate and navigate their decision-making journey is highlighted. An interesting question in this regard is how both perspectives relate to the expectations and experiences of both adults and attorneys with the *levenstestament*. This study aims to explore how – in addition to the legal

41. Livingston *et al.* 2010, p. 6; Fetherstonhaugh et al. 2017, p. 39, see however contrary Hertogh, C. M. P. M. (2011). The misleading simplicity of advance directives. *International Psychogeriatrics, 23*, 511-515. https://doi.org/10.1017/S1041610211000184.
42. Fetherstonhaugh *et al.* 2017, p. 39.
43. Fetherstonhaugh 2019, p. 39.
44. De Vries, K., & Drury-Ruddlesden, J. (2019). Advance care planning for people with dementia: Ordinary everyday conversations. *Dementia, 18*, 3023-3035. doi: 10.1177/1471301218764169.

and socio-medical perspective – the *levenstestament* is perceived by people who use the instrument in practice. In this regard, this study focuses on the use of the *levenstestament* as an instrument to appoint one or more attorneys (a 'continuing power of attorney') and on advance directives in terms of wishes and preferences addressed to these attorneys. It does so by exploring – by means of interviews – the expectations of both adults and their nominated attorneys at the time the levenstestament is made and the experiences of active attorneys with the *levenstestament* in practice. As noted in section 6.2.1, the *levenstestament* can also include other components, namely medical treatment advance directives or advance directives addressed to the court. Although the adult's expectations with regard to the *levenstestament* as a whole – including the two aforementioned components – have been explored, doctors and court officials were not included as participants in this study. An important reason for this decision is that, for instance, doctor's experiences with medical treatment advance directives in the Netherlands have already been explored in previous research.[45] In addition to exploring the adult's and the attorney's expectations and how these relate to the legal and socio-medical perspective, this study also aims to explore which role the *levenstestament* fulfils in a process in which decision-making gradually transfers from the adult to the attorney. Does the *levenstestament* indeed facilitate decision-making based on the adult's wishes, preferences and instructions and does it provide a supportive structure for attorneys enabling them to navigate through their decision-making journey? Based on the aforementioned objectives, we aim to address the following research questions:

1. What are the expectations of both adults and their nominated attorneys at the time the *levenstestament* is made? And what are the experiences of active attorneys with the *levenstestament* in practice?
2. To what extent are expectations realised in practice and what is the role of the *levenstestament* in facilitating decision-making in a process in which decision-making gradually transfers from the adult to the attorney?

6.4 Methods

6.4.1 *Research design*

In designing this study, it was important to take into account that the *levenstestament* is an instrument designed to make provisions for the future, and moreover a future in which the adult's cognitive abilities may decline. Bearing this in mind, the aim was to capture the expectations and experiences of adults and attorneys over time. To this end, a cohort design was adopted, enabling the research team to get an impression of the expectations and experiences at different

45. See e.g. De Boer 2011 and Vezzoni 2005.

stages of the so-called lifespan of the *levenstestament*. Initially three cohorts were distinguished, corresponding with three different stages in the lifespan of the *levenstestament*: 1) the stage where the adult has recently made a *levenstestament*, 2) the stage where the *levenstestament* has recently entered into force and/or the attorney has started to act, and 3) the stage where supported decision-making becomes increasingly difficult, and the attorney has fewer opportunities to involve the adult in the decision-making process. During the study cohorts 2 and 3 were merged together. In line with the findings of Fetherstonhaugh *et. al* and Samsi and Manthorpe, we found that attorneys take on the role of attorney gradually.[46] This made it difficult to pinpoint an exact time where attorneys start to act. In cohort 1 interviews were conducted with both adults and their nominated attorneys. In cohort 2 interviews were conducted with active attorneys. The method of interviewing was chosen to explore in-depth the expectations and experiences of both adults and attorneys. Adults and attorneys were interviewed separately as much as possible to also get an idea of the extent to which expectations and experiences correspond. As discussed in more detail in section 6.6.2, a limitation of this study is that no adults were interviewed in cohort 2. Although this was originally intended, due to the Covid-19 pandemic it was not possible to conduct face-to-face interviews with this group, which was considered a prerequisite. Before the start of the study, the advice and approval of the Ethical Committee of the Law Faculty of the Vrije Universiteit Amsterdam was obtained (22-05-2019).

6.4.2 *Procedure*

In order to study in-depth the expectations and experiences of both adults and attorneys with the *levenstestament*, a purposive sampling strategy was adopted.[47] This purposive sample provides insight into a range of expectations and experiences with the *levenstestament*, however no claims regarding the representativeness of the findings to a broader population are made. As in the Netherlands adults often make a *levenstestament* at a notary's office, the strategy for recruiting participants in the first cohort consisted in first instance of recruiting participants via notaries. A message calling on notaries to assist with the recruitment of participants by bringing the research study to the attention of their clients, was included in the newsletters of three professional notarial organisations (KNB, Netwerk Notarissen and EPN). In addition, professional contacts of the research team were asked to assist. Unfortunately, only a few notaries indicated they were able to provide assistance and to our knowledge this strategy has not resulted in the recruitment of any respondents. As a survey study conducted by Stelma-Roorda looking at the experiences of notaries with

46. Fetherstonhaugh *et. al* 2019; Samsi and Manthorpe 2013.
47. Bijleveld, C. C. J. H. (2018). *Methoden en Technieken van Onderzoek in de Criminologie* (7th ed.). Den Haag: Boom Criminologie.

the *levenstestament* showed that notaries classify the majority of their clients as 60 years or older, the second strategy focused on the recruitment of participants via elderly organisations.[48] A message drawing attention to the research study was included in newsletters distributed by Dutch elderly organisations (KBO-PCOB and Plusonline) and on the website alzheimernederland.nl and dementie.nl. In addition, the study was brought to the attention of patients visiting the Alzheimer's Centre in Amsterdam. Persons who were interested in participating in the study could contact the first author. These persons subsequently received an information leaflet and were approached by the first author to discuss participation and eventually to make an appointment for an interview. Participants were interviewed at a location of their choice (their own home, a public place such as café or library or at the university) and during the Covid-19 lockdown via telephone or skype. A semi-structured interview schedule was used. This schedule included open-ended questions such as: 'What do you expect from the *levenstestament*?', 'How did you involve your nominated attorney in the process of drafting your *levenstestament*?', 'What do you expect from your attorney?', and 'How is he/she supposed to take care of your affairs?'. All interviews were conducted by the first author and usually lasted between half an hour to one and a half hours. Respondents were mostly interviewed alone, in some cases the spouse or another family member was present. Informed consent was obtained prior to the interviews.

Nominated attorneys were recruited by means of a so-called snow-ball sampling strategy. Adults were asked if they were willing to ask their nominated attorney to also participate in the research study. In order to recruit participants for the second cohort, messages on the aforementioned websites and in addition the website goedvertegenwoordigd.nl were used to bring the research study to the attention of potential participants. Recruitment was stopped once it was felt that new information and perspectives were unlikely to be provided by additional respondents (Livingston *et al.* 2010).

6.4.3 *Analytic strategy*

Permission was asked to audio-record the interviews and these recordings were subsequently transcribed ad verbatim by two interns under the supervision of the first author. Transcripts were entered into ATLAS-TI qualitative data analysis software for coding. A thematic analysis approach was adopted to analyse

48. Stelma-Roorda, R. (2019). *Het levenstestament: gebruik en toepassing door het notariaat.* https://www.knb.nl/nieuwsberichten/regelen-financiele-kwesties-belangrijkste-reden-opstellen-levenstestament (accessed 9 February 2022).

the data.[49] In this regard, Braun and Clarke distinguish both a theoretical or deductive approach where analysis is driven by the researcher's theoretical or analytic interests, and an inductive approach where the identified themes are strongly linked to the data.[50] Although both approaches have been used, it was predominantly the deductive approach that has been used to analyse the data for this paper (a codebook can be shared by the first author upon request). As noted in section 6.1, the literature discussed in the previous sections has been used as a 'lens' through which to look at the *levenstestament* and to analyse the data pertaining to the research question. All transcripts were read and coded by the first author, while a subset was read and coded by the second author. Codes and themes were subsequently compared and discussed until consensus was reached. The interviews were conducted in Dutch, which means that the quotes used in this article had to be translated into English. The risk of such an undertaking is that the meaning of what was said by the respondents becomes distorted. In order to minimise this risk as much as possible, a so-called forward and backward translation strategy was employed.[51] A selection of quotes was translated from Dutch into English by the first author. The second author then translated the English quotes back into Dutch. Both versions were subsequently checked for accuracy and equivalence.[52]

6.5 Results

As noted in section 6.3, with the first research question we aim to explore how the *levenstestament* is perceived by people who use this instrument in practice. Therefore, after a brief discussion of the sample in section 6.5.1, section 6.5.2 focuses on the expectations of adults who have recently made a *levenstestament*. Section 6.5.3 zooms in on the expectations of nominated attorneys, while section 6.5.4 discusses the experiences of active attorneys. Taken together, these sections provide the information needed to address the question to what extend expectations and experiences correspond and the question which role the *levenstestament* plays in facilitating decision-making in a process in which decision-making gradually transfers from the adult to the attorney.

49. Braun, V., & Clarke, V. (2006). Using thematic analysis in psychology. *Qualitative Research in Psychology*, 3, 77-101. doi: http://dx.doi.org/10.1191/1478088706qp063oa.
50. Braun and Clarke 2006, p. 83-84.
51. Regmi, R., Naidoo, J., & Pilkington, P. (2010). Understanding the Processes of Translation and Transliteration in Qualitative Research. *International Journal of Qualitative Methods*, 9, p. 16-26.
52. Ibid.

6.5.1 *Sample*

In the first cohort a total of 23 adults who had 'recently' made a *levenstestament* were interviewed. The average age of these adults was 73,3 years. The time elapsed since the adult had made the *levenstestament* varied from about 5 months to 4 years. For the majority of the adults (all but three) no more than two years had elapsed. There was one adult who had not yet made a *levenstestament*, but was considering doing so. In addition to the adults interviewed in the first cohort, a total of 6 nominated attorneys were interviewed. These attorneys could all be linked to one of the adults who had recently made a *levenstestament*. Three of the nominated attorneys were a godchild of the adult concerned. The three remaining nominated attorneys were respectively the spouse, the child and a friend of the adult concerned. In the Netherlands, it is possible to appoint a so-called substitute or replacement attorney to cover situations where the first appointed attorney is unable or unwilling to act as attorney. Of the 6 attorneys, 4 attorneys where so-called first appointed attorneys, while the other 2 attorneys had been nominated as substitute attorneys. The sample in the second cohort consisted of interviews with 16 attorneys who had assumed their role as attorney. Seven of these attorneys were acting for and on behalf of a friend or acquaintance. The remaining nine attorneys were acting on behalf of a family member, such as a mother, father or sister. In two cases, the attorney in question was not the first appointed attorney, but a so-called substitute attorney. Although in most cases a decline of cognitive abilities due to dementia was the reason for the attorney to take on his role, in four cases there were other reasons, including old age or physical impairments of the adult concerned, that compelled the attorney to act.

6.5.2 *Expectations of adults who had recently made a levenstestament*

In the process of making a *levenstestament*, adults followed a more or less similar path in which several steps can be distinguished. Linked to these steps, three main themes emerged from the interviews. Participants first of all became motivated to make provisions for a future period of incapacity, they subsequently decided to use a *levenstestament* to do so and they to a more or lesser extent involved the prospective attorney in the process of making provisions for the future.

Rationale to make provisions for a future period of incapacity

Several factors for adults to make provisions for a future period of incapacity emerged from the interviews. Frequently it was a combination of these factors which ultimately led to the decision to make a *levenstestament*. Several participants indicated that negative experiences, they had witnessed with friends or relatives, had prompted them to think about making provisions for a future period of incapacity. Participants in this context frequently referred to a situation in which a friend or relative had made no provisions, thus leaving their spouse or children unable to make certain decisions – such as selling the family home – without asking the court for a financial guardianship measure. In this regard, several participants expressed a desire to alleviate the future burden of care for a partner or children designated to act on behalf of the participant:

> I want to make sure that it is properly arranged for when something happens to me... but also say... if I have a stroke, meaning that I can no longer decide about what should happen to my belongings, about what we should do with the house. I'm in a nursing home and my wife wants to sell the house to move to a flat or something like that, then they can't arrange that themselves. If it isn't arranged than there has to be a court ruling before they can take those steps on my behalf. So I want to get that sorted... that they don't run into obstacles like that if, um... something was to happen to me. (Participant A15)

Other examples of past experiences included situations in which a friend or relative had been placed in a care home, or situations in which a friend or relative had undergone certain medical treatment, in the participant's view against better judgement. This reason could frequently be linked to a desire to preserve autonomy, in a sense that the participant wanted to prevent the same thing from happening to him- or herself:

> So what I have seen in that caregiving period [participant had acted as family carer for a befriended couple], regarding nursing homes and all that comes with that. There I saw what I don't want. So no endless treatment and, well those kind of things. And when it comes to a nursing home, I am like 'Well I don't want to be there at all'. (Participant A18)

The role of the levenstestament in making provisions for a future period of incapacity

The role of the *levenstestament* in making provisions for a future period of incapacity in first instance depends on the perception participants have of the *levenstestament*. As noted, the *levenstestament* can encompass both a conferral of authority to act on behalf of the adult and the adult's wishes, preferences and instructions addressed to the attorney or to a third party, such as a doctor. In the absence of a clear legal definition, the meaning of the term *levenstestament* was not for all participants the same. One participant understood the *levenstestament* to be a medical treatment advance directive. This participant had also appointed an attorney to act on her behalf for financial matters, but according to the participant this conferral of authority was not a part of the *levenstestament* but rather included in a separate power of attorney. Several other participants indicated that their *levenstestament* only contained a conferral of authority to their attorney. Medical wishes and preferences were included in a separate advance directive, which in some cases was attached to the *levenstestament* as an appendix.

The role of the *levenstestament* in making provisions for a future period of incapacity, in second instance, depends on the participants' perception of what can and should be included in the *levenstestament*. In this context, the interviews revealed a picture in which notaries can shape or guide these perceptions. Several participants indicated that their notary had advised them to include a broad conferral of authority to the attorney, to cover all possible future scenarios. Other participants indicated that their notary had advised them not to include too detailed wishes and preferences in the *levenstestament*, because a change in the adult's wishes and preferences requires an alteration of the *levenstestament*:

> Um, that's one of the points that should be changed in the *levenstestament*. There's a lot in there that I just don't understand and doesn't apply to me. But according to the notary, that was all necessary because that was part of the protocol. (Participant A16)

> [A]t first I thought that more things would be arranged in the *levenstestament*, I also thought that, um... everything regarding how you want to divide your estate, everything regarding how you want your funeral... to include all that in the *levenstestament*, uhm... (..) that was advised against, um... both the advisor and the notary... they said that it's much better to arrange it privately, because it might be that your wishes change how you want your funeral to be... And then every time you have to change it [the *levenstestament*] or adjust it, it costs... that's just a costly exercise. So we didn't include that. I actually assumed that such things would be included in a *levenstestament*... That was my first expectation. .... But that didn't happen in the end, so now it's actually just the two powers of attorney both financial and um.... medical that are in there and all the things around that uhm.... we just arranged in private... (Participant A15)

A few participants had included wishes and preferences and practical information such as passwords in an additional document. However, there were also participants who did not feel the need to describe their wishes in detail because they relied on their attorney knowing their wishes and preferences. Other participants found it difficult to describe their wishes in detail or discuss these with the attorney, because 'you do not know what the future holds in store' (Participant A13):

> Well, it does not say much in that respect... I know that you can arrange, jokingly, where the canary must go, but I think that's all nonsense... I also know you can record your wishes as to whether you want a funeral or cremation, I'm not in favour of that, but that's up to everyone,... it's not even in there that... a choice between either has been made. Because they [the attorneys] just know what our wishes are. (Participant A5)

> Interviewer: What would you like [the attorney] to do for you?

> Whatever is necessary at the time. You can't say that in advance, but I know that he... uhm, in his way, wants what's good for you, and look, that's what it's about. Look what he decides at that moment, together with the GP, with his wife... I have every confidence in that. (Participant A11)

The choice and process of involving the attorney

As the quote above already illustrates this element of trust can make the choice of attorney particularly important. Several participants indicated that they had appointed someone as their attorney who knew them well or who would be able to carry out their wishes:

> You see, at a certain point, um... and I've seen it with my mother, you can have a... stroke and you have no.. you have no life, then I want my life to end. And he [the attorney] knows that and my daughter... couldn't do that and he can. (Participant A21).

Other participants gave a more practical reason for their choice of attorney, such as a child living nearby. One participant had appointed a professional to act as attorney. The participants involved their attorneys in different ways in the process of drafting the *levenstestament*. This involvement could range from the attorney merely receiving a copy of the *levenstestament* to the attorney accompanying the participant to the notary, discussing the *levenstestament* with the participant and providing feedback on drafts of the *levenstestament*. There were also participants who chose not to disclose the contents of the *levenstestament* to their attorney and confined themselves to asking the person in question if he/she would be willing to act as attorney, for instance, because they did not want to burden the attorney with future concerns:

> I have told one of my sons I have it. But I did not inform them how or what exactly... they will find out when the time comes. (Participant A2)

> In first instance, it is a conscious choice, because I don't want to burden them with this responsibility already. That they start thinking about it now like "Oh, what's that going to mean?" And I hope they won't have to take that responsibility..... So I don't want to burden them with that already. (Participant A14)

Although several participants to some extent involved their attorney in the process of making the *levenstestament*, not all participants, as noted, discussed their wishes and preferences in detail with the attorney. In addition to the reasons already mentioned above (trusting their attorney to know their wishes and not knowing what the future holds in store), one participant indicated that he did not think this was necessary, as he wanted to give the attorney a certain leeway to act on his behalf. Another participant indicated that, although wishes and preferences were not discussed in relation to the *levenstestament*, she did discuss her outlook on life with her attorneys. Based on these conversations and the fact that the attorneys know her, she assumed the attorneys would be able to act on her behalf:

> I have not discussed it in the context of the *levenstestament*. But I do share things like that with them and they know that, they know that, yes, those are the topics that I share with them on the basis of which I say, that's going to be fine if they take over. But not in the context of the *levenstestament*. Just, yeah, they just need to know what I'm like and what choices I make, I share that with them. (Participant A14)

Conversations with the attorney did not seem to focus on the participant's future involvement in the decision-making process, as not all participants seemed to be aware of the dynamic nature of the concept of 'capacity'. Several participants had a rather dichotomous understanding of the concept of capacity and linked to this the entry into force of the *levenstestament*, which in some cases was not helped by the fact that the *levenstestament* could only enter into force upon the incapacity of the participant:

> Interviewer: And what have you agreed with your [attorney] about when they will act on your behalf, should that be applicable?
>
> The moment I lack capacity, then they have to start acting, and before that... they can't act. (Participant A1)
>
> Interviewer: And how do they know when that point has been reached, so to speak?
>
> They have to have a doctor's certificate for that. You have to be in the nursing home and an independent doctor has to give a statement that you lack capacity. Then they... at least that's what the notary explained to us... only then can they start to act. (Participant A1)

6.5.3 *Expectations of nominated attorneys*

A theme that appeared throughout the interviews with the nominated attorneys is the potential future role of attorney as an unscripted task for which participants to a more or lesser extent feel prepared.

Feeling (un)prepared

Similar to the interviews with adults who had recently made a *levenstestament*, the interviews with the nominated attorneys revealed different levels of involvement in the process of drafting the *levenstestament*. Three attorneys – one first appointed and two substitute attorneys – had not yet seen the *levenstestament* and were largely unaware of its contents. Two participants indicated that although they had had an initial conversation with the adult, in which the adult had asked the participant to agree to the nomination, no (follow-up) conversation had taken place in which the content of the *levenstestament* had been discussed. This made the task of attorney for one participant a little daunting, as it was not clear what was expected from her:

> [I]t is still a bit vague, and for me that makes it... I really want to do it for them and I want to do it well. But I also find it quite um.. frightening, or the word 'fear' is perhaps a bit strong, but I feel like 'Oh I hope I am going to do it well', because I do not really know what exactly I am supposed to do, or how it will go. So I also find that a bit um... frightening, well frightening, how do I call it? Yes, frightening, like: will it be all right, will I do it right later on, if necessary? (Participant AT6)

For both participants who had not yet had a follow-up conversation with the adult, the interview had the unintended side effect of prompting the participants to make an appointment with the adult to discuss the content of the *levenstestament*, its entry into force and the wishes and preferences of the adult:

> I had absolutely no idea or expectations about what eh, what, what it substantively would mean. Um, in any case it makes it clear to me that I really do have to go there soon to, um, go over things and discuss them. Um, so I'll just put that on my schedule... (Participant AT2)

Participants who did express more confidence in their future role indicated that they have frequent and profound conversations with the adult concerned, albeit not necessarily linked to the *levenstestament*, but more generally on how they view life. In one case, a shared history of care for a relative, seemed to help the adult and attorney to talk about the adult's end-of-life wishes:

> Um well, first of all we talked about suffering. Well, of course we did, all the time, well, every day at some point because it [the care for the relative] was coming to an end and we had contact. And um, yes we often talked about "Is this it? Is this um..., what you want at the end of your, of your years? If you can't live on your own anymore, what, where is your limit then and what do you do?" .... And eh she [the adult] really wants it to be very clear as soon as she can no longer take care of herself or go shopping, then it's really finished for her. Also for instance now, this week we spoke to each other, once in a while she comes here and we have a chat. Then she said "I don't have to go to intensive care when I get Covid." Okay, well that was clear. And then I think, "That's pretty rigorous," because you might be able to come out of that quite well, of course that depends a bit on how serious it is and for how long. But that's her position, very clear, so that made me think "OK, that's what I need to know". So that's how we arrive at something every time. (Participant AT4)

6.5.4 *Experiences of active attorneys*

The interviews with active attorneys revealed a rich and detailed picture of how attorneys fulfil their role. Using the literature discussed in section 6.2 as a frame of reference, the analysis of these interviews focused on two aspects, namely how participants experience the task of being an attorney and how they involve the adult in the decision-making process.

An unscripted role

The general impression from the interviews is that the role of attorney is not an easy task to take on. Several participants indicated that their relationship with the adult had changed since the adult's decline of cognitive abilities. Some respondents used the phrase 'role reversal' to describe this change: 'my mother's house used to be the centre of all activities, especially at Christmas and New Year's, we moved it all this way a few years ago' (participant AT11). In this setting in which the relationship with the adult had changed, attorneys had to take on a new role, namely that of supporting the adult. However, this role did not in all cases seem straightforward or clear-cut:

> So that's also a role you have to grow into, if I look back now.... what I may and may not do as attorney, I didn't know that at first. I did sign it, but I didn't really know what it means. So I learned by doing it. (Participant AT9)

> At one point I thought of doing it myself a wiki page how to use the *levenstestament*. Most of the information you see... that you come across when you google is information from notaries and the information from notaries is focused on selling a product namely the *levenstestament* [to the adult] ... But the children are left with the execution- um... misery, well, misery, I'm now a month later but certainly the first week I was like... where on earth do I get an independent doctor, should I just start calling? Who? That's not at all obvious. (Participant AT17)

Adults can stipulate that the *levenstestament* enters into force immediately or upon a specified time in the future, often the incapacity of the adult. Several attorneys confronted with the second scenario indicated that they found it difficult to determine when the deterioration of the adult's cognitive abilities had reached the point where the *levenstestament* should be activated. Moreover, as the above quotation shows, the process of organising the entry into force of the *levenstestament* – for instance through an assessment of the adult's capacity by an independent doctor – is not perceived as simple in all cases either. When it comes to the execution of the *levenstestament*, a lack of support or even a conflict with friends or family members of the adult can make the role of attorney difficult or, in some cases, even impossible. Problems with the acceptance of the *levenstestament* by third parties such as banks, local authorities and health insurance companies, can also make the task of the attorney more complicated. Several participants indicated that it takes time and in some cases considerable effort to convince third parties of their authority to represent the adult. In this regard, participants mentioned that not all third parties are aware of the possibility to act on behalf of an adult with a *levenstestament*, that systems are not yet set up for this ('computer says no'), or that additional documentation is needed, such as a confirmation that the *levenstestament* is the latest version:

> Well, I mean, with the bank, for example... it's probably correct, but they are not easily satisfied with what you, um... and there's still this and that should be done and actually they'd prefer to have madam's [the adult's] signature. And ... [the adult] can't sign and doesn't want to sign, so she won't. But how often you have to make separate phone calls about the fact that the Mrs. doesn't sign herself and that I sign for her and that it's in the *levenstestament* and that it just has to be sorted out, so to speak. I have been a lot... really an awful lot on the phone. (Participant AT22)

Although several participants reported problems with the acceptance of the *levenstestament*, there were also participants who reported no problems with the acceptance by third parties at all. These participants indicated that the *levenstestament* was of great value to them in this respect:

> With the bank, that we were given access and a card, um, it was only then that I discovered the value of the *levenstestament*. I think, otherwise I just wouldn't have managed to do those things. Whereas before, it was actually not much more than a piece of paper to me. (Participant AT9)

In addition to third-party acceptance of the *levenstestament*, several participants indicated that the support of another attorney, family member or friend, was a great help to them in carrying out their task as attorney.

The adult's involvement

Attorneys involved the adult in various ways in the execution of the *levenstestament*. Several participants indicated that they acted based on the wishes and instructions of the adult. When the adult, due to a decline of cognitive abilities, took less initiative, several participants involved the adult by submitting certain decisions to the adult, such as whether or not to continue the membership of a specific magazine or whether or not to go forward with the customary annual donation to the (grand)children. In some cases, attorneys involved the adult afterwards, for example by showing receipts of purchases made by the attorney. Taking the adult's wishes and preferences into account is not always easy for attorneys. Several interviews revealed a balancing act between the interests of the adult and those of the attorney:

> My mother really wants to experience every step, um, and that's, um, well, and that's also sometimes, that's also nice because then we do it together. But sometimes it's also very tiring, because it goes faster when I can do it alone. Um.. so that's where the friction lies. (Participant AT21)

> But then again, at a certain point we decided for her to... even though we thought it was no longer possible.... to let her continue living at home. And that... I found it quite... difficult. I have no idea.... It fortunately has not happened.. I have no idea how I would have felt if she had been lying at the bottom of the stairs at some point. But we all noticed, and I noticed, what a relief it was... that it didn't happen. (Participant AT20)

The process of involving the adult in the execution of the *levenstestament* focuses on the here and now. Conversations with the adult rarely seem to focus on future events and such conversations seem to become difficult once there is a decline of cognitive abilities:

> So far I can discuss these kinds of decisions with him, but one by one... I can't discuss the whole financial package with him at once, but for each little thing separately, I discuss with him... I'm going to transfer the donations to [name brother] and me this weekend. Oh he says that's good. Then the following week I tell him that I have done it and every now and then I check it again... We are not talking about the sale of the house at all for the time being, because he still assumes that his admission is temporary. So that is not something I discuss with him (Participant AT17)

The absence of any prior conversations may in some cases mean that the adult is not involved in the decision-making process and that the attorney decides and acts in what is considered to be in the adult's best interests:

> We never really had an open conversation about it, so to speak. Like, how do we see the future, or what if this happens, or what if that happens, or whatever... We never really talked about it with my parents, and now we are also quite controlling in that, because they cannot do it anymore, so to speak... (Participant AT9)

> Interviewer: And what do you mean by controlling?

> Well, [name co-attorney] and I coordinate everything actually. Um, and, um, we um, yes, I trust him completely, he trusts me, and we both just want the best for our parents, and therefore... if I think "Well okay, if [name co-attorney] agrees too, well then we will do it like this. (Participant AT9)

6.6 Discussion and conclusion

6.6.1 Discussion

Although anticipatory decision-making instruments such as the *levenstestament* are from various perspectives seen as instruments with potential, little was known about the expectations and experiences the users of these instruments have in practice. By means of interviews conducted in a cohort design, our study looked at the expectations of both adults who had recently made a *levenstestament* and their nominated attorneys and the experiences of active attorneys who had assumed their role. This with the aim of exploring the extent to which expectations are realised in practice and with the aim of exploring the role of the *levenstestament* in facilitating decision-making in a process in which decision-making gradually transfers from the adult to the attorney. The adults who participated in this study seemed to be motivated to make a *levenstestament* for two reasons. First of all, to preserve a sense of autonomy, for example by trying to avoid certain events, such as the placement in a care home, from happening to the adult himself. Secondly, to alleviate a future burden of care for the attorney, for instance by making it easier to sell the family home without the necessity of a court order. These expectations of the adult seem to be in line with expectations expressed about the potential of the *levenstestament*, namely that it can make the adult's voice an influential component of future substitute decisions and that it – within a broader context of advance care planning – can provide a supportive structure for attorneys to navigate the decision-making journey.[53] The question is, however, to what extent these expectations are realised in practice.

Starting with the first expectation, the preservation of autonomy, this study shows that there is a danger that this expectation is not fully realised in practice. As it is a costly exercise in the Netherlands to draft a *levenstestament*, notaries advice against making an instrument that can easily become obsolete or in need of change when the adult's wishes and preferences change. This means that the inclusion of detailed wishes and preferences is discouraged. In addition, adults are advised to cover all possible future scenarios by means of a broad conferral of authority to the attorney. In the literature this broad conferral of authority has been linked to a risk of abuse of the *levenstestament* by the attorney.[54] However, a broad conferral of authority and a lack of detailed wishes and preferences also create the risk that the information included in the *levenstestament* as to the adult's voice – i.e. information concerning the adult's values, wishes and preferences – is limited. In other words, although there is a lot the attorney *can* do, the attorney knows

53. Gergel 2020; Fetherstonhaugh *et al.* 2019.
54. Tilse *et al.* 2014.

little about what the adult *wishes* him to do. This does not necessarily have to cause problems when the adult, to a certain extent, is still able to participate in the decision-making process. The majority of active attorneys in this study were committed to involve the adult as much as they considered possible in the decision-making process. Several of the decisional styles distinguished by Samsi and Manthorpe also emerged in this study, for example, reductive decision-making in which attorneys put certain decisions to the adult, such as whether to continue membership of a particular magazine.[55] The absence of information as to the adult's voice can, however, become problematic when the adult's cognitive abilities deteriorate and the adult becomes less able to participate in the decision-making process. Attorneys then have to adopt a retrospective decisional style, in which they rely on their knowledge of the adult's beliefs, habits, values, wishes and preferences.[56] Fetherstonhaugh *et al.* note in this regard that the 'veracity of such decisions in terms of how well they genuinely reflect what the person with dementia would have wanted is indeterminable'.[57] Indeed, research by Dening *et al.* confirms with regard to future treatment preferences, that family carers are not in all cases able to accurately predict what the adult would have wanted.[58]

Based on the above, the use of anticipatory decision-making instruments is in the predominantly socio-medical literature (as discussed in section 6.2.2) advocated within the broader context of advance care planning, where anticipatory decision-making instruments are embedded in and complemented by ongoing conversations about the adult's (changing) wishes and preferences. However, as the current study shows, not all adults and attorneys have such conversations. In this regard, adults in this study indicated that they trust their attorney to know their wishes and preferences, which, as discussed above, may be misplaced. Another reason was that adults did not want to burden the attorney with their future affairs already or found it difficult to discuss wishes and preferences because they did not know what the future holds in store. Both at the time the *levenstestament* is made and the time the *levenstestament* enters into force it seems difficult for the majority of participants to discuss future wishes and preferences. These conversations become even harder when there is a decline of the adult's cognitive abilities, which means that certain topics must be discussed in small steps or that certain topics cannot be discussed at all (such as the sale of the family home). The above underlines the importance of timely conversations. As not all adults and attorneys find it easy to have such conversations or are aware

55. Samsi and Manthorpe 2013.
56. Ibid.
57. Fetherstonhaugh *et al.* 2013:38.
58. Dening, K.H., King, M., Jones, L., Vickestaff, V. & Sampson, L. (2016). Advance Care Planning in Dementia: Do Family Carers Know the Treatment Preferences of People with Early Dementia? *PLoS ONE, 11*, p. 1-15.

of the necessity to do so, attention should be drawn to how both the adult and the attorney can be supported to have conversations about the future. This starts with creating awareness of the necessity to do so and, in this respect, notaries – at least in the Netherlands – can play an important role by acting as facilitators and making both the adult and the attorney aware of the need to have ongoing conversations.[59] In addition, tools such as conversations guides might help both adult and attorney to engage in conversations about the future. For one dyad (adult and nominated attorney) in this study, a shared history of care for a relative and, in other words, an awareness of the issues to be discussed, made it easier to discuss end-of-life wishes. Further research is needed to explore how support could best be provided and to establish what works in practice.

Conversations between the adult and the attorney could potentially also help to prepare attorneys for the task ahead, which brings us to the second expectation that the *levenstestament* alleviates a future burden of care and can provide a supportive structure to navigate the decision-making journey for attorneys.[60] The setting in this study in which the *levenstestament* becomes active, corresponds with the setting described in previous research. Fetherstonhaugh *et al.* characterise the role of attorney as a journey without roadmap.[61] This was also indicated by several active attorneys in this study. Besides a changing relationship with the adult, attorneys have to acquaint themselves with a new role. A role that not in all cases seems straightforward or clear-cut. Attorneys struggle with the dynamic nature of capacity and linked to that the question when the *levenstestament* should enter into force.[62] Several active attorneys indicated that decision-making in some cases includes a balancing act where a compromise between the adult's and the attorney's interests has to be found.[63] Problems with the acceptance of the *levenstestament* by third parties, such as banks, and a lack of support or conflicts with family members can also make the role of attorney more difficult. Naturally, timely conversations between the adult and the attorney cannot solve all these problems; attention must also be paid to how the acceptance of the *levenstestament* by third parties can be improved in practice. However, timely and ongoing conversations could play an important role in preparing attorneys for the task ahead, when both adult and attorney – in addition to the adult's wishes and preferences – discuss issues such as the entry into force of the *levenstestament*, the adult's expectations as to how the role of attorney should be carried out and the complexities of balancing both the adult's and attorney's interests. This study indicates that there is a lot to be gained here, as several nominated attorneys

59. Fetherstonhaugh *et al.* 2019.
60. Ibid.
61. Ibid.
62. Fetherstonhaugh *et al.* 2017; Samsi & Manthorpe 2013.
63. Fetherstonhaugh *et al.* 2017.

in this study were unaware of the content of the *levenstestament* and the adult's expectations concerning how the role of attorney should be fulfilled. Extending conversations about the future to relatives and/or friends who are close to the adult could potentially strengthen family cohesion and prevent disputes. Active attorneys in this study indicated that family support, together with third party acceptance of the *levenstestament*, were of great value in carrying out their task as attorney.

6.6.2 *Limitations and strengths*

A limitation of the study is that in the second cohort no adults were interviewed. As noted in section 6.2.1, the adult's right to autonomy and participation has in recent decades become more prominent. Kröber and Zomerplaag argue this also applies to the involvement of adults with disabilities as participants in research projects.[64] In first instance the intention was therefore to also interview adults in the second cohort. In order to assess the adult's capacity to participate in the study, a face-to-face setting was considered a prerequisite. Before interviews could be conducted, the world was struck by the Covid-19 pandemic, which meant this face-to-face setting was no longer possible. Unfortunately, the objective to interview adults in the second cohort subsequently had to be abandoned. Another limitation of this study is the cohort design, which in this study means that the interviewed attorneys consist of two different groups, each active at a different stage of the life-span of the *levenstestament*. As Ries notes ideally the expectations and experiences of adults and attorneys would be studied by means of a longitudinal design.[65] A longitudinal design would have enabled us to follow both adults and attorneys from the time the levenstestament is made across the different stages of the lifespan of the levenstestament. Such a design was however within the time available not possible. Important to realise in this regard is that when adults make a levenstestament to provide for an eventual period of incapacity, this incapacity might still be years away or never occur after all. Despite these limitations, this paper sheds light on the expectations and experiences of both adults and attorneys with the *levenstestament* in practice. It demonstrates the importance of research that not only looks at the potential of anticipatory decision-making instruments, but also at the actual experiences of people who use this instrument in practice.

64. Kröber, H. R. Th., & Zomerplaag, J. (2007). Mensen met een verstandelijke beperking betrekken bij onderzoek. Een kritisch emancipatoir perspectief. In J. Evers (ed.), *Kwalitatief interviewen: kunst én kunde*. (pp. 215-224) Den Haag: Uitgeverij Lemma.
65. Ries, N. M. (2019). Enduring Powers of Attorney and Financial Exploitation of Older People: A Conceptual Analysis and Strategies for Prevention. *Journal of Aging & Social Policy*, p. 1-18. doi: 10.1080/08959420.2019.1704143.

6.6.3 *Conclusion*

In conclusion, while anticipatory decision-making instruments such as the *levenstestament* have great potential in theory, there is work to be done to ensure this potential is realised in practice and, most importantly, to ensure that the adult's expectations are met. To realise this potential, anticipatory decision-making instruments must be embedded in robust, timely and ongoing conversations about both the adult's (changing) wishes and preferences and the role of the attorney. Both the adult and the attorney must be given the support they need to have these conversations and the support they need to navigate their decision-making journey.

Acknowledgements
The first author would like to thank interns Nadia van der Burg en Michelle Rijnen for their assistance with transcribing the interviews. In addition, both authors would like to thank prof. Masha Antokolskaia for proof-reading the final version of the article.

7 Continuing powers of attorney – different legal rules, similar problems and solutions: What can the Netherlands learn from Belgium, England and Wales, Germany and Switzerland?

This chapter was published as: R. Stelma-Roorda,' Continuing powers of attorney – different legal rules, similar problems and solutions: What can the Netherlands learn from Belgium, Germany, England and Wales and Switzerland?', Family & Law 2023, p. 1-49.

Abstract

The Dutch levenstestament allows adults in the Netherlands to make their own provisions for a future period of incapacity. Although this instrument is becoming increasingly popular, the current regulation and application of the levenstestament are not without problems. The levenstestament has been designed and conceptualised by the Dutch notariate within the framework of the existing law. This regulatory framework has not been designed with a setting of future incapacity in mind and compliance with international human rights norms and principles, such as Article 12 UNCRPD, is therefore not sufficiently guaranteed. Moreover, empirical research indicates that the application of the levenstestament, in practice, does not run smoothly in all cases. Across Europe there are countries where the possibility to make instruments, similar to the Dutch levenstestament, has already been in place for quite some time and where such instruments are regulated by law. This article presents the results of a comparative study of the legal regulation and practical application of enduring documents in four European jurisdictions (Belgium, Germany, England and Wales and Switzerland). Recommendation CM/Rec(2009)11 on Principles concerning continuing powers of attorney and advance directives for incapacity has been used as a frame of reference to look at the regulation on the form, content, entry into force, registration and/or certification of each enduring document as well as the appointment and role of attorneys, the preservation of legal capacity, conflicts of interests and supervision. The aim has also been to gain an impression of the law in action. Based on this information best practices have been identified which provide a solution to the problems with the regulation and application of the levenstestament in the Netherlands. The adoption of specific legislation incorporating these best practices in Book 1 of the Dutch Civil Code is recommended.

7.1 Introduction[1]

All over Europe, countries are searching for new measures and instruments allowing adults a greater role in the protection of their future interests when they are facing an impairment or insufficiency of their personal faculties. Among these instruments are so-called enduring documents: instruments enabling capable adults to make provisions for a future period of incapacity. Two instruments are generally distinguished: the continuing, enduring or lasting power of attorney (CPA) and the advance directive (AD). The CPA has been defined by the Council of Europe as 'a mandate given by a capable adult with the purpose that it shall remain in force or enter into force, in the event of the granter's incapacity'.[2] Advance directives, on the other hand, have been defined as 'instructions given or wishes made by a capable adult concerning issues that may arise in the event of his or her incapacity'.[3] As said, many European countries offer adults the opportunity to make one or both of these types of enduring documents. This is also the case in the Netherlands. Here, adults, since 1995, can make a so-called medical treatment advance directive, in which the adult specifies which medical treatment under certain conditions is desired or refused. Relatively new for the Netherlands is an instrument, which is called a *levenstestament*. As I will explain in more detail later on, a *levenstestament* can include a CPA, ADs or both of these instruments. The *levenstestament* is becoming increasingly popular as an alternative to the court-ordered adult guardianship measures and the number of adults who decide to make a *levenstestament* keeps increasing annually. However, despite its growing popularity, the *levenstestament* is currently not yet statutory regulated in the Netherlands. The instrument has been designed and conceptualised by the Dutch notariate within the framework of the existing law. Empirical research indicates that the application of the *levenstestament*, in practice, does not in all cases run smoothly and, in some cases, leads to problems.[4]

Across Europe, there are countries where the possibility to make enduring documents has already been in place for quite some time and where such instruments are regulated by law. The Netherlands may well learn something from the regulation and the experiences with the application of enduring documents

1. The author owes a huge debt of gratitude to Alzheimer Nederland for awarding her a Fellowshipgrant which has enabled her to visit all four countries as part of the comparative study central in this article. In addition, the author would like to express her thanks and gratitude to prof. Regina Aebi-Müller, prof. Volker Lipp, prof. Jens Scherpe and prof. Frederik Swennen.
2. Recommendation CM/Rec(2009)11, p. 9.
3. Recommendation CM/Rec(2009)11, p. 9.
4. H.N. Stelma-Roorda, *In anticipation of a future period of incapacity: the Dutch 'levenstestament' from a legal, empirical and comparative perspective*, forthcoming; H.N. Stelma-Roorda & V.E. Eichelsheim, 'Decision-making by and for adults with impaired capacity: the potential of the Dutch levenstestament', *International Journal of Law and Psychiatry* 2023, vol. 86, no. 1, p. 1-11.

in these countries. The central research question in this article, therefore, is: 'What can the Netherlands learn from the regulation and application of enduring documents in Belgium, England and Wales, Germany and Switzerland?' To answer this research question a comparative study of the legal regulation and practical application of enduring documents in these four jurisdictions has been conducted. The aim of this comparative study has been to find solutions and best practices in the aforementioned jurisdictions, that might provide solutions to the problems identified in the regulation and application of the *levenstestament* in the Netherlands.

In the next section of this article, I will continue with a description of the methods that have been employed in this comparative study (section 2). Then in section 3, I will focus on the problems associated with the way the *levenstestament* is currently regulated in the Netherlands and explore the problems related to the application of the *levenstestament* in practice. In sections 4, 5, 6 and 7, I will provide an outline of the instruments that can be used by adults to make provisions for a future period of incapacity, in each of the four jurisdictions in question. The four jurisdictions will be discussed successively, according to the same scheme. In each section, I will first describe the regulatory framework on the enduring document and then focus on what is known about the application of the instrument, looking at the problems and solutions as well as at the best practices. In section 8, I will provide a comparative synthesis and assess the suitability of legal solutions and best practices delineated in these jurisdictions, for resolving the problems identified in the Netherlands. The conclusion will comprise recommendations on how the foreign solutions and best practices – rendered suitable for resolving problems identified in the Netherlands – can best be implemented in the Dutch legal system. Although, as the title of this article indicates, the article focuses on solutions and best practices of interest to the Netherlands, this article might be equally relevant to other jurisdictions. First of all, because it provides a rather detailed comparative overview of the regulation of enduring instruments in Belgium, England and Wales, Germany, Switzerland, and the Netherlands. Secondly, because the identified solutions and best practices for problems experienced in the Netherlands can also be useful for other jurisdictions experiencing similar problems.

7.2 Methods

To identify jurisdictions that might contain best practices and workable solutions to the problems identified in the Netherlands, a quick scan was conducted. The report 'Enabling citizens to plan for incapacity', a review of the follow-up action undertaken by member states of the Council of Europe on Recommendation CM/Rec(2009)11 on Principles concerning continuing powers of attorney and advance directives for incapacity, conducted by Adrian Ward, formed the basis of this quick scan. This report provides information on the implementation of the aforementioned Recommendation in thirty jurisdictions. Based on this information, four jurisdictions were selected for in-depth comparative research: Belgium, England and Wales, Germany and Switzerland. Several criteria were used to select these jurisdictions. As it is possible to arrange both financial, medical and personal matters in a *levenstestament* in the Netherlands, I first of all selected jurisdictions where these matters can also be included in the enduring document. Secondly, I selected jurisdictions where, in contrast to the Netherlands, a specific regulatory framework for the enduring document has been adopted. In this regard, the timing of the regulation and, linked to this, the potential to identify best practices were considered. In both England and Wales and Germany, enduring documents are already regulated and applicated for quite some time.[5] The expectation was that these jurisdictions have gained a lot of experience with the regulation and application of enduring documents and, therefore, may have found solutions and developed best practices, that might be of interest to the Netherlands. In addition to the timing of regulation, the scope or extent of regulation – in terms of the involvement of the state – was considered. This led to the inclusion of Switzerland, where the state plays an important role in the execution of the enduring document. Finally, more practical considerations, such as access to legal sources, language barriers and the possibility to arrange a research visit, also played a role in the selection of jurisdictions. This resulted, for instance, in the inclusion of jurisdictions with legal sources available in the English, German and Dutch language.

The quick scan was followed by an in-depth study of the enduring documents in each of the four selected jurisdictions. A questionnaire consisting of 37 questions was used as a basis for this in-depth study. For the preparation of this questionnaire, I looked at previously conducted comparative studies – both in the field of adult capacity law and in the field of family law in general – to gain an impression of how an in-depth comparative study could best be designed.[6] For the design of the questionnaire in this comparative study, Recommendation CM/Rec(2009)11 on Principles concerning continuing powers of attorney and advance directives for incapacity was used as a frame of reference. This recommendation contains a list of principles that states are recommended to implement in their

5. The possibility to set up an enduring power of attorney was introduced in England and Wales by means of the Enduring Powers of Attorney Act 1985, which came into force on the 10 March 1986.
6. Examples of comparative studies in the field of adult capacity law include: A.D. Ward, *Enabling citizens to plan for incapacity. A review of follow-up action taken by member states of the Council of Europe to Recommendation CM/Rec(2009)11 on principles concerning continuing powers of attorney and advance directives for incapacity*, Strasbourg: Council of Europe 2018; A. van den Broeck, *Vermogensbescherming van kwetsbare meerderjarigen via lastgeving*, Antwerpen: Intersentia 2014; I. Doron, 'Elder Guardianship Kaleidoscope – A Comparative Perspective', *International Journal of Law, Policy and the Family* 2002, vol. 16, no. 3 p. 368-398.

country's legislation on enduring documents. Using these principles as a starting point, in this article I look at the regulation in each jurisdiction on the form, content, entry into force, registration and/or certification of enduring documents and the appointment and role of attorneys, the preservation of legal capacity, conflicts of interests and supervision.[7] The in-depth study of the situation in each jurisdiction commenced with a desk study of the relevant literature and case law. Each country was subsequently visited for a period of three weeks to finalise the study and to gain an impression of the law in action. During the research visits, I interviewed practitioners, including notaries, judges, government officials, lawyers and physicians. The aim of these interviews was to get an impression of the socio-legal context in which the relevant legal rules operate and to identify the strengths, weaknesses and best practices of the various systems.[8] As the above shows, in this comparative study I have adopted both a functional approach – looking at the functional equivalents in the four jurisdictions that allow adults to make their own provisions for a future period of incapacity – and a law-in-context approach – trying to get an impression of how these enduring documents function in practice.[9] Based on this research, country reports were made.[10] Sections 4, 5, 6 and 7 of this article provide a synopsis of these country reports, which means that a horizontal approach (by jurisdiction) has been chosen rather than an integrated, vertical approach (*e.g.* by principle included in Recommendation CM/Rec(2009)11). I chose this approach because I believe it provides more room to discuss the different particularities of each jurisdiction and possible interactions between the regulation and the application of the enduring document in practice.[11]

In presenting the findings of this study it is important to also address its limitations. This study has been conducted by one researcher in the timespan of one year as a part of her multidisciplinary PhD project on the Dutch *levenstestament*. This means that there were limitations regarding the amount of information that could be gathered, given the available time and the fact that the research was conducted by one person. As the Dutch say, the researcher had to

7. The scope of the questionnaire was slightly broader and included, for instance, also questions on the termination and revocation of enduring documents. However, given the already substantive scope of this article, I decided to focus on the abovementioned aspects in this article.
8. M. Adams & J. Griffiths, 'Against "Comparative Method": Explaining Similarities and Differences', in: M. Adams & J. Bomhoff, *Practice and Theory in Comparative Law*, Cambridge: Cambridge University Press 2012, p. 279-301 (293-296).
9. M. van Hoecke, 'Methodology of Comparative Legal Research', *Law and Method* 2015, pp. 1-35.
10. These country reports are included in the appendices to the dissertation of Stelma-Roorda, *In anticipation of a future period of incapacity: the Dutch 'levenstestament' from a legal, empirical and comparative perspective*.
11. Some problems that arise in practice may, for example, be related to how the enduring document is regulated (*e.g.* in Switzerland, the strict entry into force of the *Vorsorgeauftrag* on paper may cause problems with the entry into force in practice).

'row with the oars she had'.[12] This holds true in particular for the law in action aspect of the study. It is therefore fair to say that the findings in this regard provide an impression of the socio-legal context in which the enduring documents operate, but no more than that. The limitations on the amount of information that could be gathered also meant that a further delineation of the scope of the comparative study became necessary once the research had started. As noted in the introduction, internationally a distinction is made between two enduring documents: the continuing power of attorney (CPA) and advance directives (AD).[13] Some countries even make a subsequent distinction between various types of advance directives. In Germany, for example, a distinction is made between treatment advance directives (*Patientenverfügungen*) and directives addressed to the court in the event of an adult guardianship procedure (*Betreuungsverfügungen*). Although the initial objective was to include all enduring documents in this comparative study, answering all 37 questions of the questionnaire for each enduring document proved too big a task. In other words, a further delineation of the scope of the comparative study proved necessary. A clear demarcation was, however, not straightforward, as in practice there is frequently no clear distinction between the continuing power of attorney (the appointment of an attorney) and advance directives (a statement of the adult's wishes and instructions). In Belgium, for instance, a continuing power of attorney (*zorgvolmacht*) can also include the adult's wishes and instructions directed to the attorney. And in Switzerland, a treatment advance directive (*Patientenverfügung*) can also include the appointment of an attorney. In the end, I used the following interpretation, provided by Ward, to come to a clear delineation:

> 'The instructions and wishes in a CPA are directed to the attorney, who is responsible for implementing them. The instructions and wishes in an advance directive apply directly as "the voice of the granter", without being directed through another party such as an attorney.'

According to this interpretation, wishes and instructions directed to the attorney are part of the CPA, whereas wishes and instructions addressed to a third party – for example, a physician or the court – are considered an advance directive. Using this interpretation, I focus – after a brief exploration of all enduring documents – in the country reports, and consequently in this article, on what is internationally referred to as a continuing power of attorney, including both the appointment of an attorney and the adult's wishes and instructions addressed to this attorney.

12. Adams & Griffiths 2012, p. 301.
13. Recommendation CM/Rec(2009)11, p. 9.

7.3 The Netherlands: an exploration of the existing problems

As noted above, adults in the Netherlands can provide for a future period of incapacity through a *levenstestament*. This instrument is not statutory regulated in the Netherlands; it has been designed and conceptualised by the Dutch notariate within the framework of the existing law. This way of regulating – or rather not regulating – the *levenstestament*, has not been without problems in practice. In the absence of a clear (statutory) definition of the term *levenstestament*, there are different interpretations as to what a *levenstestament* entails. In practice, the term *levenstestament* is used to refer to an enduring document which may encompass one or more of three components for which, for instance, in Germany, three separate instruments (*Vorsorgevollmacht*, *Patientenverfügung* and *Betreuungsverfügung*) exist. The use of the same term for these three components raises the question of whether Dutch adults are sufficiently aware of the various options they have to make provisions for the future. In addition to the ambiguity concerning the content of the *levenstestament*, there is no consensus on the legal nature of the *levenstestament*. This applies, in particular, to the appointment of the attorney. There are, on the one hand, notaries who model the *levenstestament* predominantly on the statutory provisions of the ordinary power of attorney (Arts. 3:60-3:79 of the Dutch Civil Code). Since a power of attorney only grants an authority to act on behalf of the adult and does not create an obligation for the attorney to act, there are, on the other hand, notaries who argue that the *levenstestament* should also encompass an underlying agreement between the adult and the attorney. Through such an agreement, arrangements can be made about the tasks the attorney is going to perform for and on behalf of the adult and the rights and duties of both the adult and the attorney. In this regard, the provisions on the service provision agreement (Arts. 7:400-7:413 of the Dutch Civil Code) and the mandate agreement (Arts. 7:414-7:424 of the Dutch Civil Code) are considered applicable. According to Autar, both the absence of a generally accepted definition and the unclear nature of the *levenstestament*, mean that adults are not entirely sure what they 'get' when they ask the assistance of a notary to make a *levenstestament*.[14] In other words, clarity and uniformity are needed to ensure that adults are aware of the various options available to them while making provisions for a future period of incapacity, and to ensure that the *levenstestament* has a solid legal basis. Such clarity and uniformity can be achieved through statutory regulation of the *levenstestament*.

There is, however, another, more important, reason to consider statutory regulation of the *levenstestament*. This second reason relates to the question of

14. A.R. Autar, 'Inleiding' in A.R. Autar, J.P.M. Stubbé & L.C.A. Verstappen, *Compendium Levenstestament*, Den Haag; Sdu 2021, p. 19-28 (25).

whether the way the *levenstestament* is currently (not) regulated is compliant with international human rights norms and principles. In the context of the *levenstestament,* Article 12 of the United Nations Convention on the Rights of Persons with Disabilities (UNCRPD) and Recommendation CM/Rec(2009)11 are of particular importance. Based on Article 12(4) UNCRPD, states are obliged to provide for appropriate and effective safeguards to prevent the misuse and abuse of the *levenstestament* by the attorney.[15] Such safeguards must ensure that the adult's rights, will and preferences are respected, that undue influence is avoided and that conflicts of interest are managed. In addition to safeguards preventing the misuse and abuse of the *levenstestament,* Article 12 UNCRPD emphasises the need for support that enables the adult to decide and act himself and, when this is no longer possible, support provided by the attorney that is based on the adult's wishes, preferences and instructions.[16] This is, for example, reflected in Recommendation CM/Rec(2009)11 Principle 10, which stipulates that attorneys should be obliged to ascertain and take account of the adult's past and present wishes and feelings and, in addition, should be obliged to inform and consult the adult on an ongoing basis.[17] The Dutch government has, with regard to the implementation of these and other human rights norms and principles, taken a passive role. In practice, it is left to professional actors – most importantly the notariate – to ensure compliance with these human rights norms and principles and, in the end, to both the adult and the attorney who can include certain norms and principles guiding the actions of the attorney, in the *levenstestament.*

Stelma-Roorda *et al.* argue that this passive role of the Dutch state is not in line with the obligation of states to ensure that international human rights norms and principles are implemented.[18] The regulatory framework on the ordinary power of attorney, the service provision agreement and the mandate agreement has not been designed with a setting of future incapacity of the adult in mind and does not provide sufficient safeguards to ensure the prevention of misuse or abuse of the *levenstestament* and the active involvement of the adult.[19] The Dutch notariate has taken several steps to fill this gap, such as the development of a register in which notarised *levenstestamenten* can be registered and the development of a guideline notaries can use to assess whether clients have the capacity to make a *levenstestament* and are not unduly influenced by the

15. R. Stelma-Roorda, 'The Misuse or Abuse of Continuing Powers of Attorney: What Are Appropriate Safeguards?', *International Journal of Law, Policy and the Family,* 2021, vol. 35, no. 1, p. 1-25.
16. Stelma-Roorda 2021, p. 11-12.
17. Recommendation CM/Rec(2009)11, p. 9.
18. H.N. Stelma-Roorda, C. Blankman & M.V. Antokolskaia, 'A changing paradigm of protection of vulnerable adults and its implications for the Netherlands, *Family & Law* 2019, p. 1-18.
19. Stelma-Roorda (forthcoming).

prospective attorney.[20] However, it is important to realise that the notariate does not have the same authority and options to ensure compliance with, for instance, Article 12 UNCRPD as the Dutch legislature. A notary can, for instance, not oblige the adult to register the *levenstestament* as there is no statutory basis for mandatory registration. A notary can motivate his client to include additional safeguards in the *levenstestament*, such as a supervisory mechanism to prevent misuse or abuse, or to include an obligation for the attorney to involve the adult in the execution of the *levenstestament*. However, other than ceasing cooperation, notaries have limited means to oblige the adult to include such safeguards in the *levenstestament*. Taking the aforementioned into account, a more active approach by the Dutch state is needed to ensure that minimum safeguards are put in place to prevent the misuse and abuse of the *levenstestament* and to promote the involvement of the adult in the execution of the *levenstestament*.

In addition to these problems associated with the way the *levenstestament* is currently regulated in the Netherlands, several exploratory studies show that the application of the *levenstestament* in practice does not run smoothly in all cases. Both a survey study among notaries and a study of court cases show that safeguards to prevent the misuse and abuse of the *levenstestament* are not only a theoretical but also a practical necessity.[21] There have been several cases where an attorney has been prosecuted for financial abuse using a *levenstestament*.[22] In addition, the court has in several cases considered the attorney unsuited to the task at hand, for example, because the attorney had acted against the wishes of the adult or had denied the adult the care and company of others.[23] Notwithstanding the risk of misuse or abuse of the *levenstestament*, several notaries in the survey study pointed out the difficulty of convincing clients to include a form of supervision in the *levenstestament*.[24] Besides the risk of misuse and abuse, there is the problem of family disputes. Several court cases show that a disturbed relationship between either the attorneys or between the attorney(s) and other family members – not appointed as an attorney – can hinder the

20. In Dutch the guideline is known as the 'Stappenplan beoordeling wilsbekwaamheid ten behoeve van notariële dienstverlening'.
21. Stelma-Roorda (forthcoming).
22. District Court of Noord-Nederland 29 June 2021, ECLI:NL:RBNNE:2021:2845; District Court of Limburg 26 March 2021, ECLI:NL:RBLIM:2021:2690; District Court of Rotterdam 17 February 2021, ECLI:NL:RBROT:2021:1390; District court Midden-Nederland 2 October 2020, ECLI:NL:RBMNE:2020:4216; District Court Overijssel 9 May 2017, ECLI:NL:RBOVE:2017:1932; District Court Noord-Nederland 8 April 2016, ECLI:NL:RBNNE:2016:1712.
23. District Court of Midden-Nederland 14 March 2019, ECLI:NL:RBMNE:2019:1113; District Court of Noord-Holland 12 October 2017, ECLI:NL:RBNHO:2017:8483, §2.3; District Court of Noord-Holland 12 October 2017, ECLI:NL:RBNHO:2017:8481, §2.3; Court of Appeal Amsterdam 2 February 2016, ECLI:NL:GHAMS:2016:346, §4.12.
24. Stelma-Roorda (forthcoming).

execution of the *levenstestament* or even make it impossible.[25] In addition to family disputes, situations in which the *levenstestament* is not accepted by third parties, such as banks, can frustrate the execution of the *levenstestament* by the attorney.[26] As noted above, from a human rights perspective, the emphasis is put on support that enables the adult to decide and act himself and, when this is no longer possible, on support that takes into account the adult's wishes, preferences and instructions. Based on interviews with adults who had recently made a *levenstestament*, interviews with prospective attorneys and interviews with active attorneys, Stelma-Roorda and Eichelsheim observed that the *levenstestament* does not seem to fulfil its potential as an instrument providing this support. They observed, among other, that adults find it difficult to record their wishes and preferences as it is difficult to predict what the future holds in store. The authority of the attorney to act on behalf of the adult is, therefore, often considerably broad, resulting in situations where, although there is a lot the attorney *can* do, he knows very little about what the adult *wants* him to do. Based on these observations, Stelma-Roorda and Eichelsheim conclude that the value of the *levenstestament* can be enhanced, when the *levenstestament* is embedded in and accompanied by ongoing conversations between adults and attorneys about the adult's (changing) wishes, preferences and instructions. This recommendation could, however, be extended in the context of this article by examining how other countries promote the involvement of the adult in the execution of enduring documents.

7.4 Belgium: the *zorgvolmacht*

7.4.1 *Regulatory framework*

With the Act 17 March 2013, which entered into force on 1 September 2013, adults in Belgium were given the opportunity to provide for a future period of incapacity through a specific mandate agreement, in practice better known as a *zorgvolmacht*.[27] Although before that time it was already possible to make provisions for the future using an ordinary mandate agreement (Art. 1984-2010 of the Belgian Civil Code (BCC)), the Belgian legislator deemed it necessary to adopt a specific regulatory framework. With this regulatory framework the Belgian legislator sought to achieve various objectives, such as: creating legal certainty (there was at the time uncertainty regarding the legal status of ordinary mandate

25. *Ibid.*
26. *Ibid.*
27. T. Wuyts, 'Buitengerechtelijke bescherming', in: J.P. Bogaert, K. Rotthier, E. van den Eenden & T. Wuyts, *Handboek bescherming wilsonbekwamen. Zorgvolmacht en bewind na de wet van 21 december 2018*, Mechelen: Wolters Kluwer 2020a, §70. Adults, in addition, have the possibility to draw up an advance directive addressed to the court and a future court-appointed representative (Art. 496 BCC) and the possibility to draw up an advance directive for euthanasia (Art. 4 of the Belgian Law on Euthanasia).

agreements as instruments to provide for a future period of incapacity), creating awareness of the possibility to make a *zorgvolmacht*, preventing the misuse and abuse of *zorgvolmachten*, assigning a more significant role to the social network of the adult concerned and reducing the workload of the courts.[28] Provisions on the *zorgvolmacht* (Arts. 489-490/2 BCC) were included in Title IX, on the protection of adults, in the Belgian Civil Code. Article 490/2 §1 BCC makes clear that, unless otherwise stipulated by law, the provisions on the ordinary mandate agreement also apply. Adults can include provisions on their property and financial matters in the *zorgvolmacht* and – since March 2019 – also provisions on their personal affairs.[29] Article 14 of the Belgian Act on Patient's Rights makes clear that adults may also appoint an attorney for health and medical affairs. Wuyts notes that the appointment of such an attorney can be included in the *zorgvolmacht*. In this case, attention should, however, be paid to the requirements of the Act on Patient's Rights, which – as a *lex specialis* – takes precedence over the generic provisions of Arts. 489-490/2 BCC.[30] A *zorgvolmacht* must have the specific aim to provide for a future period of incapacity and must be registered.[31] Mandate agreements which do not fulfil these requirements terminate upon the incapacity of the adult.[32]

7.4.2 *Form and registration*

Adults can make the *zorgvolmacht* in the form of a private document or through a notarial deed. The second form is required when the adult authorises the attorney to perform acts – such as the sale of the house – for which, in principle, a notarial deed is required.[33] Both private and notarial *zorgvolmachten* must be registered.[34] The adult may request the clerk's office of the court in the district where the adult resides to register the *zorgvolmacht*. Alternatively, the adult may ask a notary

28. Belgian House of Representatives, Parl. St. Kamer 2011-12, nr. 53-1009/10, p. 29-31; T. Wuyts, 'Zorgvolmachten: een zegen of een vloek?', in: W. Pintens & C. Declerck (eds.), *Patrimonium 2020*, Brugge: Die Keure 2020b, p. 235-323 (235).
29. The scope of affairs that can be included in the *zorgvolmacht* was extended with the Act 21 December 2018, which entered into force on the 1 March 2019.
30. Wuyts 2020a, §72.
31. Art. 490 BCC.
32. Both Wylleman (p. 28-33) and Swennen (p. 622-623) note, however, that this does not apply to mandate agreements made before September 2014 with regard to financial affairs and mandate agreements made before March 2019 concerning personal affairs. A. Wylleman, 'Buitengerechtelijke bescherming', in: P. Senaeve, F. Swennen & G. Verschelden (eds.), *Meerderjarige beschermde personen*, Brugge: Die Keure 2014, p. 23-48; F. Swennen, 'De meerderjarige beschermde personen (Deel II)', *Rechtskundig Weekblad* 2013, no. 15, p. 602-623.
33. Wuyts 2020a, §84; A. van Moerkercke, 'De zorgvolmacht: hoe gedetailleerd moet dat zijn?', *Vermogensplanning in de praktijk* 2019, no. 3, p. 14-19 (16); L. de Feyter & E. de Nolf, 'Enkele praktische aandachtspunten bij de redactie van een zorgvolmacht, in het bijzonder in relatie met een Belgische bancaire instelling', *Vermogensplanning in de praktijk* 2017, no. 3, p. 4-11 (6).
34. Wuys 2020a, §85; J. Verstraete, 'Krijtlijnen voor de zorgvolmacht', in: C. de Wulf, M. op de Beeck & J. Verstraete (eds.), *Liber Amicorum Aloïs Van den Bossche*, Brugge: die Keure 2019, p. 163-193 (182-183).

to register the *zorgvolmacht*. Both the clerk's office and the notary are obliged to ensure that the *zorgvolmacht* is registered within fifteen days in the Central Register kept by the Royal Association of Belgian Notaries.[35] This register contains information such as the adult's name, domicile, date and place of birth, but does not provide access to the content of the *zorgvolmacht*. A request to consult the register may be submitted by notaries, courts, public prosecutors, the attorney and the adult. According to Article 1242 of the Belgian Judicial Code, the clerk's office is obliged to verify whether the adult has made a *zorgvolmacht* when the court is confronted with an application for an adult guardianship measure. If the clerk's office finds that a *zorgvolmacht* has been made, it subsequently asks the notary or the clerk's office of the court where the *zorgvolmacht* has been deposited, to forward a certified copy of the document.[36] Article 490 BCC makes clear that terminations of the *zorgvolmacht* must also be registered. With this obligation, the legislator wanted to enable the courts to check whether the *zorgvolmacht* presented by the attorney, concerns a valid *zorgvolmacht*.[37]

7.4.3 Entry into force and appointment of the attorney

The *zorgvolmacht* can enter into force immediately or upon the incapacity of the adult. The adult can also combine these two options and determine, for instance, that the spouse – appointed as primary attorney – may act immediately, while the children – appointed as substitute attorneys – may only act after a formal assessment establishing the incapacity of the adult.[38] Such an assessment can be conducted by a physician. However, the adult can also require the attorney to ask the court to determine the moment of entry into force of the *zorgvolmacht*.[39] A person who has been placed under an adult guardianship measure cannot be appointed as an attorney.[40] In addition, the adult cannot appoint as attorney, persons or legal entities who, according to Article 496/6 BCC, may not be appointed by the court as guardians. This includes, for instance, the management or staff members of an institution, where the adult resides.[41] In line with Principle 4(2) of Council of Europe Recommendation CM/Rec(2009)11, the adult may appoint more than one attorney. The adult can require these attorneys to act jointly, concurrently, separately or as substitutes.[42] The risk of a conflict between

35. Wuyts 2020a, §86; Verstraete 2019, p. 182-183.
36. Wuyts 2020a, §116.
37. Belgian House of Representative, Parl. St. Kamer 2018-19, nr. 54-3303/001, p. 22; Wuyts 2020a, §112.
38. De Feyter & De Nolf 2017, p. 6.
39. 490/1 §2 BCC; Belgian House of Representatives, Parl. St. Kamer 2018-19, nr. 54-3303/11, p. 6; Wuyts 2020a, §82.
40. Art. 490/1 §1 BCC.
41. Wuyts 2020a, §96; Wylleman 2014, p. 34-37.
42. Wuyts 2020a, §96; Belgian House of Representatives, Parl. St. Kamer 2011-12, nr. 53-1009/10, p. 31. The explanatory memorandum attached to Recommendation CM/Rec(2009)11 makes clear that

attorneys has been addressed by the Belgian legislator in Article 490/2 §1 BCC, stipulating that the court shall settle disputes between attorneys based on what is considered in the adult's interests. Before taking a decision, the court must attempt to reconcile both parties.[43] Instead of leaving it to the court to reconcile both parties, the adult can also include in the *zorgvolmacht* provisions on a decision-making procedure, specifically aimed at dealing with a difference of opinion between the attorneys.[44] The adult cannot authorise the attorney to perform certain 'highly personal acts', such as making a will or getting married.[45] The adult may authorise the attorney to donate on his behalf. To do so, the adult must stipulate the object, the beneficiary and the terms and conditions of the donations.[46]

7.4.4 Rights and duties of the attorney

The adult retains legal capacity upon the entry into force of the *zorgvolmacht*.[47] According to Article 490 BCC, the adult can include his wishes and preferences in the *zorgvolmacht*. Article 490/2 §1 BCC makes clear that the attorney must observe these wishes and preferences as much as possible.[48] Wuyts argues that the attorney can ask the court – when necessary – to deviate from the stipulated wishes and preferences in the event the adult is no longer able to indicate his current wishes and preferences due to incapacity.[49] In addition to observing the adult's wishes and preferences, the attorney is obliged to involve the adult as much as possible in the execution of the *zorgvolmacht*. In this regard, the attorney must consult the adult – and if applicable, a so-called 'trusted person' or supervisory attorney appointed by the adult – at regular intervals, but at least once a year.[50] The adult's assets must be separated from the attorney's assets and the adult's

the adult may require the attorneys to act and decide together (jointly); may appoint attorneys for different affairs, *e.g.* an attorney for financial affairs and an attorney for health and medical affairs (concurrently); may authorise attorneys to act and decide independently (separately); and, may appoint one or more substitute attorneys who are to replace the first-mentioned attorney in case this person is unable or unwilling to take up the task of attorney (substitutes).

43. Verstraete 2019, p. 189.
44. Wuyts 2020a, §98.
45. Wuyts 2020a, §73 & §94; Verstraete 2019, p. 174-175.
46. Verstraete 2019, p. 175; Wylleman 2014, p. 35.
47. Wuyts 2020a, §77.
48. Art. 490 BCC uses the term 'principles', but discussion in Parliament has made clear that this term is to be understood as encompassing the adult's wishes and preferences concerning the execution of the *zorgvolmacht* – Belgian House of Representatives, Parl. St. Kamer 2011-12, nr. 53-1009/10, p. 39; see also T. Wuyts, 'Een kritische doorlichting van (modellen inzake) zorgvolmachten', in: G. Verschelden (ed.), *Rechtskroniek van het Notariaat*, Herentals: Knops Publishing 2020c, p. 91-131 (124).
49. There is no legal provision stipulating as such, Wuyts (2020c, p. 126-127) seems to indicate that the courts can apply Art. 499/1 §3 BCC by way of analogy. This legal provision concerns the wishes and preferences of the adult included in an advance directive addressed to the court and the court-appointed representative.
50. Wuyts 2020a, §98.

bank account must be registered in his own name.[51] Article 1993 BCC makes clear that the attorney is obliged to render account.[52] The attorney cannot act as the counterparty of the adult. In the event there is a conflict of interests, the court appoints a so-called 'attorney ad hoc'.[53] This attorney ad hoc temporarily acts instead of the attorney concerning those matters, involving a conflict of interests. The appointment of an attorney ad hoc can be left to the discretion of the court. The adult can, however, also include provisions on the appointment of an attorney ad hoc in the *zorgvolmacht*.[54]

7.4.5 *Supervision*

The adult may include supervisory mechanisms in the *zorgvolmacht*, such as the appointment of a supervisory attorney or 'trusted person', who supervises the actions of the attorney and initiates a so-called 'alarm bell procedure' upon signs that something is going wrong.[55] This 'alarm bell procedure' can be used by any person having an interest (family, neighbours, friends, etc.) to bring (potential) situations of misuse or abuse to the attention of the court.[56] When the court finds that the execution of the *zorgvolmacht* by the attorney adversely affects the interests of the adult concerned, the court may partially or completely terminate the *zorgvolmacht* and order an adult guardianship measure instead. The court can also subject the execution of the *zorgvolmacht* to the same procedural requirements that apply when an adult guardianship measure is ordered. Examples are an obligation for the attorney to obtain the authorisation of the court for certain actions (Art. 499/7 BCC) or an obligation to periodically render account to the court (Art. 499/14 BCC).[57]

7.4.6 *Law in action*

An evaluation of the Act 17 March 2013, including the provisions on the *zorgvolmacht*, is scheduled to take place in 2023. In anticipation of this evaluation, Wuyts conducted an exploratory study to examine whether the objectives of the legislator have been achieved in practice.[58] This study, conducted in 2020, consists of an analysis of published case law, an analysis of the information on

51. Art. 490/2 §1 BCC.
52. Wuyts 2020a, § 102; Verstraete 2019, p. 169.
53. Art. 490/2 §1 BCC.
54. Wuyts 2020a, §98.
55. See also Verstraete 2019, p. 173.
56. Wuyts 2020a, §107; Verstraete 2019, p. 191.
57. Wuyts 2020a, §107; D. Scheers, 'Rechtsplegingen', in: P. Senaeve, F. Swennen & G. Verschelden (eds.), *Meerderjarige beschermde personen*, Brugge: Die Keure 2014, p. 213-276 (214-216).
58. The results of this study were presented at a conference in December 2020 and in written form by means of the publication *Zorgvolmachten: een zegen of een vloek?*.

zorgvolmachten registered in the Central Register and interviews with relevant stakeholders (lawyers, judges, notaries, financial institutions, social services) in the Belgian district of Limburg.[59] The study provides insight into the problems encountered with the *zorgvolmacht* in practice. Wuyts also presents recommendations to address the detected problems. An extensive discussion of this study falls beyond the scope of this article; I will confine myself to presenting what I consider the most significant observations and recommendations.[60] The study, first of all, indicates that mere statutory regulation of the *zorgvolmacht* has not automatically resulted in more general awareness of the possibility to make a *zorgvolmacht*. Although in Belgium the number of registered *zorgvolmachten* is still increasing annually, Wuyts argues that more can be done to make the general public aware of the possibility to make a *zorgvolmacht*, and, more specifically, to provide both the public and professionals with correct information about the benefits and consequences of making a *zorgvolmacht*.[61] Wuyts' study also signals the phenomenon of family disputes as a problem that can occur in the execution of the *zorgvolmacht*. Such disputes can arise, when the adult to the dismay of the other children, singles out one of the children as attorney. In some cases, this results in an application for an adult guardianship measure by family members who have not been appointed as attorneys.[62] However, the appointment of all children as attorneys can also lead to family disputes. For example, when the adult has authorised all children to act separately and one of the children starts to act – independently – without informing and consulting the other attorneys.[63] According to Wutys, the proposed solution to these problems is to oblige the attorney to execute his charge clearly and transparently, thus preventing suspicions of other attorneys and/or family members.[64] Should a family dispute reach the court, the court may, as indicated, mediate in a conflict. In practice, in some cases the court also imposes an evaluation period during which the court monitors the actions of the attorney.[65]

As noted above, the Belgian legislator has through various provisions – such as the obligation for the attorney to involve the adult in the execution of the *zorgvolmacht* – tried to promote the adult's autonomy. Wuyts concludes, however, that in practice there is little attention to the execution of these provisions.[66] He

59. Wuyts 2020b, p. 240-244. These interviews were conducted by students at Hasselt University.
60. A more detailed discussion is included in the country report on Belgium, which can be found in the appendix section of the dissertation by Stelma-Roorda (forthcoming).
61. Wuyts 2020b, p. 244-265 & pp. 316-318; in 2017, 28.644 *zorgvolmachten* were registered; in 2018, 37.312 *zorgvolmachten* and in 2019, 54.955 *zorgvolmachten*.
62. Wuyts 2020b, p. 265-267 and p. 318-319.
63. *Ibid.*
64. *Ibid.*
65. Wuyts 2020b, p. 281-291 and p. 321-322.
66. Wuyts 2020b, p. 276-281 and p. 319-320.

notes in this respect that the belief in tailor-made protection and the workload it entails seems to play an important role in the promotion of the adult's autonomy when it comes to the execution of the *zorgvolmacht*.[67] Concerning the latter aspect (the workload), the task of providing adults with the assistance to formulate and include tailor-made wishes and instructions in the *zorgvolmacht* has in practice appeared a task too time-consuming for notaries. Several ideas are presented to mitigate this problem. Wuyts suggests, for instance, that adults can be encouraged to think about their wishes and instructions in advance – before the meeting with the notary – using a checklist or questionnaire which also contains examples of wishes and instructions that can be included in the *zorgvolmacht*.[68] New developments such as 'legal tech' and 'legal design' might, in addition, according to Wuyts, offer possibilities for clients to draft their own *zorgvolmacht* in advance. This *zorgvolmacht* can subsequently be sent to and discussed with the notary, enabling, according to Wuyts, a more targeted contribution by the notary to the process of making a *zorgvolmacht*.[69] Wuyts also addresses the impact of time, meaning that the adult's wishes and preferences might be subject to change. In this regard, Wuyts observes that adults do not always seem to be aware of the possibility to appoint another attorney or to amend their *zorgvolmacht*. In some cases, adults are afraid to oppose the decisions or actions of their attorney and therefore leave the *zorgvolmacht* unchanged.[70] In this respect, Wuyts recommends informing adults about the impact of time in terms of changing wishes and preferences and about the possibilities to amend or terminate the *zorgvolmacht*. He further recommends that adults include provisions in the *zorgvolmacht* that anticipate the scenario in which the adult's wishes and preferences change.[71] This can be done, for example, by stipulating in which circumstances the attorney may deviate from the adult's recorded wishes and preferences. Another possibility, according to Wuyts, is to appoint one or more 'trusted persons', who can assess whether circumstances indeed have changed and can assess the impact of these changes on the recorded wishes and preferences of the adult.[72]

Wuyts observes that in practice there seem to be few difficulties with the enforceability of the *zorgvolmacht*. That being said, according to Wuyts the privacy of the adult deserves special attention. Financial institutions, for example, require a copy of the entire *zorgvolmacht* and proof of its registration. However, these institutions do not have any interest in becoming acquainted with the adult's personal and medical preferences, which the adult may also have included in the

67. Wuyts 2020b, p. 319-320.
68. Wuyts 2020c, p. 96-97. Wuyts refers in this regard to the checklists and information materials which have been made publicly available in the Netherlands by the Dutch notariate.
69. *Ibid.*
70. *Ibid.*
71. Wuyts 2020b, p. 323-324.
72. Wuyts 2020c, p. 126-127.

zorgvolmacht. In this context, Wuyts proposes to introduce so-called 'certificates', which only include the information that is relevant for the third party in question.[73] To address (potential) situations of misuse or abuse, more attention is, according to Wuyts, needed for the 'alarm bell procedure'.[74] In addition, Wuyts recommends adopting an obligation for banks to report suspicious transactions; and to adopt an obligation for the adult to include at least one supervisory mechanism in the *zorgvolmacht*. The obligation for the attorney to keep the assets of the adult separate from his own assets should, according to Wuyts, be explicitly included in the *zorgvolmacht*, to ensure the attorney is aware of this obligation.[75]

7.5 England and Wales: the lasting power of attorney

7.5.1 *Regulatory framework*

In England and Wales, the opportunity for adults to make their own provisions for a future period of incapacity was introduced with the Enduring Powers of Attorney Act 1985. Until this act came into force in 1986, the only way to empower another person to act on behalf of the adult was to apply to what is referred to as the Court of Protection to be appointed as what is nowadays called a 'deputy'.[76] Ordinary powers of attorney could not be used to provide for a future period of incapacity as these are automatically revoked when the adult loses capacity.[77] The Enduring Powers of Attorney Act 1985, which introduced the *enduring power of attorney* (EPA), was replaced by the Mental Capacity Act 2005 (MCA 2005). This act, which entered into force on 1 October 2007, introduced the so-called *lasting power of attorney*. The difference between the EPA and the LPA is that EPAs became effective as soon as they were granted by the adult unless the EPA specifically stated that the instrument would enter into force upon the incapacity of the adult.[78] The requirement to register the EPA arose upon the incapacity of the adult and the EPA could function as an ordinary power of attorney in the meantime. As I will discuss in more detail below, the LPA must be registered before it can enter into force. Ward notes that problems with the registration of the EPA (registration in practice frequently did not take place) and the widespread belief that EPAs

73. Wuyts 2020b, p. 291-294 and p. 322-323; Wuyts 2020, p. 281-291 and p. 321-322.
74. Wuyts 2020b, p. 324-326.
75. *Ibid*.
76. D. Lush, 'Adult Guardianship and Powers of Attorney in England and Wales', in: L. Ho & R. Lee, *Special Needs Financial Planning. A Comparative Perspective*, Cambridge: Cambridge University Press 2019, p. 117-148 (133); C. Ward, *Lasting Powers of Attorney. A Practical Guide*, London: The Law Society 2016, p. 3-4.
77. D. Lush & C. Bielanska, *Cretney & Lush on Lasting and Enduring Powers of Attorney*, London: LexisNexis 2017, p. 3 referring to the case of *Drew v. Nunn* (1878) 4 QBD 661; Ward 2016, p. 3-4.
78. J. Thurston, *A Practitioner's Guide to Powers of Attorney*, London: Bloomsbury 2015, p. 4 and p. 33.

were misused, were among the reasons for the introduction of the LPA.[79] With the introduction of the LPA, the scope of affairs that can be included in the LPA was expanded. According to section 9(1) of the MCA 2005, the adult can authorise the attorney to make decisions about property and financial affairs, personal welfare or both. Section 11(7) of the MCA 2005 makes clear that the authority to make decisions about the adult's personal welfare extends to decisions about the adult's health and medical affairs, unless otherwise stated by the adult in the LPA. If the adult wishes to authorise the attorney to make decisions on life-sustaining treatment, this must be explicitly stated in the LPA.[80]

7.5.2 *Form and registration*

Adults must use a prescribed form to create an LPA. Two different forms can be distinguished. The so-called LP1H form can be used for an LPA for health and care affairs and the LP1F form for an LPA for property and financial affairs.[81] Both forms can be completed online or downloaded from the website of the Office of the Public Guardian and completed on paper.[82] In England and Wales the Office of the Public Guardian (OPG) is responsible for maintaining a register of LPAs and EPAs and for investigating complaints about the manner in which an attorney is exercising his powers.[83] The LPA must be signed by both the adult, the attorney(s) and a so-called certificate provider. With his signature, the certificate provider confirms that the adult understands the purpose of the LPA, that no fraud or undue pressure has been used to induce the adult to make the LPA, and that the adult understands the scope of the authority conferred to the attorney.[84] The certificate provider can either be a person who has known the adult personally for the last two years or a professional, such as a care worker, a barrister, a lawyer or a social worker.[85] The attorney, family members of the adult or the attorney and, for instance, the staff of the care home where the adult is residing, cannot act as certificate providers.[86] The LPA may not be used until it has been registered

79. Ward 2016, p. 9-10; See for a more detailed discussion of the reasons to introduce the LPA, Lush & Bielanska 2017, p. 10-15.
80. Section 11(8) of the MCA 2005.
81. Ward 2016, p. 212.
82. www.gov.uk/government/publications/make-a-lasting-power-of-attorney (last accessed: 1 April 2022).
83. A. Stanyer, *Financial abuse of older clients: law, practice and prevention*, London: Bloomsbury 2017, p. 96.
84. See section 10 of the LP1H and LP1F forms, www.gov.uk/government/publications/make-a-lasting-power-of-attorney (last accessed: 1 April 2022); Schedule 1, section 2(1) under e of the MCA 2005; Lush & Bielanska 2017, p. 90-91 and p. 116-118; Ward 2016, p. 11-12.
85. Regulation 8 of the Lasting Powers of Attorney, Enduring Powers of Attorney and Public Guardian Regulations 2007; Lush & Bielanska 2017, p. 93-97.
86. Regulation 8(3) of the Lasting Powers of Attorney, Enduring Powers of Attorney and Public Guardian Regulations 2007; Lush & Bielanska 2017, p. 97-98.

with the OPG.[87] Both the adult and the attorney(s) may apply to register the LPA. When the adult has appointed two or more attorneys to act jointly, the application must be made by all attorneys.[88] The register provides access to the content of the LPA. A request to search the register can, in principle, be made by anyone as long as the person in question can provide the name of the adult, the date of birth and the address. Two different types of searches are distinguished, a so-called 'first tier' and 'second tier' search.[89] Information received after a 'first tier' search includes, among other, the name of the attorney(s), whether the LPA concerns property and financial affairs and/or personal welfare affairs, the date the LPA was made and, if applicable, the date the LPA was revoked. The information revealed in a 'second tier' search, varies according to the individual circumstances of the case. The OPG carefully considers each application before deciding on whether additional information is released.[90] Although nowhere stipulated as such, an obligation for the Court of Protection to check whether an LPA is in place can be inferred from section 1(6) of the MCA 2005 stipulating that the interests of the adult must be protected in a way that restricts the rights and freedom of action of the adult as little as possible. In addition to first-time registrations, the OPG is obliged to register changes and revocations of the LPA.[91]

7.5.3 *Entry into force and appointment of the attorney*

As noted above, the LPA may not be used until it has been registered with the OPG. The adult may name up to five persons who are to be notified when a request to register the LPA is made. These named persons may object to the registration and consequently the entry into force of the LPA. In this regard, a distinction is made between factual objections, such as the death of the adult or the attorney, and prescribed objections, such as an allegation that the adult lacked the capacity to make an LPA.[92] Enquiries made at the OPG revealed that, in practice, the majority of adults do not make use of the possibility to name persons.[93] In other words, this safeguard seems of little importance in practice. Once registered, the LPA for property and financial affairs can enter into force immediately or upon the incapacity of the adult. This is different from an LPA for health and care affairs. The attorney can only act on behalf of the adult regarding health and care affairs if

87. Lush & Bielanska 2017, p. 125; Ward 2016, p. 232.
88. Lush & Bielanska 2017, p, 126.
89. Stanyer 2017, p. 99.
90. Stanyer 2017, p. 100.
91. Schedule 1, part 4, section 21-25 of the MCA 2005; Regulation 21 of the Lasting Powers of Attorney, Enduring Powers of Attorney and Public Guardian Regulations 2007; Lush & Bielanska 2017, p. 171-172.
92. www.gov.uk/object-registration-power-attorney (last accessed: 1 April 2022).
93. According to internal research of the Office of the Public Guardian in 2017, 83% of the adults in the sample did not choose to name any persons, 13% of the adults only named one person and 4% of the adults named two persons.

the adult lacks the capacity to make a decision himself.[94] A person who is bankrupt or subject to a debt relief order cannot be appointed as an attorney for property and financial affairs.[95] The MCA 2005 Code of Practice – a further guide for people with duties and functions under the MCA 2005 – stipulates that a paid care worker, in principle, should not agree to act as an attorney.[96] Section 10(3) of the MCA 2005 makes clear that the adult may appoint more than one attorney. The adult can appoint the attorneys to act jointly, jointly and severally, or a combination of the two aforementioned. Jointly means that the attorneys are obliged to make all decisions together. If the attorneys are to act jointly and severally, decisions may be taken both together and independently of each other. The adult can also appoint a replacement attorney. The attorneys cannot be authorised to perform 'highly personal acts', such as consenting to a marriage or civil partnership or voting on behalf of the adult.[97] The adult may authorise the attorney to donate on his behalf subject to the conditions of section 12(2) of the MCA 2005. This provision makes clear that donations may only be made on customary occasions – such as a birthday – to persons related to or connected to the adult or to any charity to which the adult would be expected to donate.[98] Section 12(2) of the MCA 2005, in addition, stipulates that the value of such a donation may not be unreasonable considering all circumstances and, in particular, the size of the adult's estate.

7.5.4 *Rights and duties of the attorney*

The adult retains legal capacity upon the entry into force of the LPA.[99] Section 9(4) of the MCA 2005 requires the attorney to act in accordance with the adult's preferences and instructions as recorded in the LPA. The attorney must, in addition, act in accordance with the provisions of the MCA 2005, in particular section 1 – which lists the foundational principles of the act – and section 4 on best interests.[100] Section 1(3) of the MCA 2005 stipulates that 'a person is not to be treated as unable to make a decision unless all practical steps to help him do so have been taken without success'. The attorney is, in other words, obliged to provide the adult with the support to make his own decisions.[101] Chapter 3 of the MCA 2005 Code of Practice provides information on the steps the attorney can take in this respect. Lush and Bielanska note that the attorney should, for

94. Lush & Bielanska 2017, p. 61.
95. Section 10(2) of the MCA 2005; Lush & Bielanska 2017, p. 48.
96. Section 7.10 of the MCA 2005 Code of Practice.
97. Section 27(1) and section 29(1) of the MCA 2005; Lush & Bielanska 2017, p. 223-224.
98. Section 12(3) of the MCA 2005.
99. This follows from section 1 of the MCA 2005 which sets out five principles upon which the act is built. According to the first principle 'a person must be assumed to have capacity unless it is established that he lacks capacity'.
100. Lush & Bielanska 2017, p. 233.
101. Lush & Bielanska 2017, p. 236-237.

instance, consider whether the adult has received the relevant information to make a decision, whether the information has been presented in such a way as to make it easier for the adult to understand it and whether the aspects of time and place have been considered in enabling the adult to make a decision.[102] If the adult lacks the capacity to decide himself, the attorney may decide on behalf of the adult.[103] Section 1(5) of the MCA 2005 makes clear that the attorney must act in the best interests of the adult. Section 4 of the MCA 2005 sets out how the attorney can determine what is in the adult's best interests. The attorney is, for instance, obliged to consider the adult's past and present wishes and feelings and the beliefs and values that would likely influence the adult's decision if the adult would have had capacity.[104] In addition to adhering to the provisions of the MCA 2005, the attorney is obliged to take into account the provisions of the MCA 2005 Code of Practice.[105] Section 7.58 of the MCA 2005 Code of Practice outlines the duties that the attorney has under the law of agency. These include the fiduciary duty of the attorney not to take advantage of his position and benefit himself, but to benefit the adult; the duty not to give up the position of attorney without informing the adult and the court, the duty to keep accounts and the duty to keep the adult's money and property separate from his own.

7.5.5 *Supervision*

The adult may include supervisory mechanisms in the LPA, such as the appointment of more than one attorney or the appointment of a person to periodically audit the accounts of the adult.[106] Passive supervision – supervision upon grounds for concern – is carried out by the Office of the Public Guardian and the Court of Protection. Any party of interest can report concerns with the OPG. The OPG may require the attorney to provide information or produce specified documents when it suspects that the attorney has behaved or may be having in a way that contravenes with the attorney's mandate or is not in the best interests of the adult.[107] The OPG can also direct a so-called Court of Protection Visitor to visit the attorney and subsequently report to the OPG.[108] If the Office of the Public Guardian finds that there are grounds for concern, it may apply to the Court

102. Lush & Bielanska 2017, p. 237; see also the MCA 2005 Code of Practice, chapter 3.
103. *Ibid.*
104. Section 4(6) of the MCA 2005. Chapter 5 of the MCA 2005 Code of Practice provides further guidance on best interests decision-making.
105. Lush & Bielanska 2017, p. 241.
106. Thurston 2015, p. 277 referring to section 7.39 of the MCA 2005 Code of Practice.
107. Regulation 46 of the Lasting Powers of Attorney, Enduring Powers of Attorney and Public Guardian Regulations 2007; Stanyer 2017, p. 277.
108. Regulation 44 of the Lasting Powers of Attorney, Enduring Powers of Attorney and Public Guardian Regulations 2007; Lush & Bielanska 2017, p. 174-175.

of Protection and require the revocation of the LPA and the appointment of a court-appointed deputy instead of the attorney.[109]

7.5.6 *Law in action*

Several studies have been conducted in England and Wales, looking at how the LPA operates in practice. In 2014 a study exploring the potential customer base of the LPA was conducted by Beckett *et al.* at the behest of the Office of the Public Guardian. Beckett *et al.* found a lack of awareness of the LPA among potential customers; 45% of the respondents in their survey had never heard of the LPA or knew nothing about it.[110] Upon being informed of the possibility to make an LPA, only 34% of the respondents were interested in making an LPA at some stage in the future.[111] Several reasons for adults not to make an LPA were distinguished, including so-called 'attitudinal and emotional barriers', such as the adult's belief that they would not lose capacity, and so-called 'relevance barriers', such as the belief that their relatives would be able to manage without an LPA.[112] Other barriers included 'practical barriers' such as not having someone to appoint as an attorney; 'information barriers,' reflecting a lack of awareness of the LPA; and, 'process barriers' such as the costs of registering an LPA.[113]

In 2013, a committee of the House of Lords conducted a so-called post-legislative scrutiny of the Mental Capacity Act 2005 to examine whether the act was working as parliament intended.[114] In March 2014, the final report was presented based on fifteen public evidence hearings and 216 written submissions from both organisations and individuals with experience with the MCA 2005.[115] Concerning LPAs, the Committee, among other, expressed its concern that LPAs are in practice not always recognised or understood.[116] In this context problems with the acceptance of the LPA by banks were mentioned, but also a lack of knowledge and awareness of LPAs in the medical and care sector. Several experts heard by the committee also expressed their concern about attorneys' lack of awareness and knowledge of their rights and duties.[117] The committee recommended, among other, that the government – together with the OPG – should address the poor understanding of LPAs among professional groups and consider how attorneys,

109. Stanyer 2017, p. 106; Section 22 of the MCA 2005.
110. A. Beckett, K. Leary, L. Cumming & G. Davies, *The Future of Lasting Power of Attorney. A research report for the Office of the Public Guardian*, London: Ipsos MORI2014, p. 5.
111. *Ibid.*
112. Ibid., p. 6-7.
113. *Ibid.*
114. House of Lords, Select Committee on the Mental Capacity Act 2005, *Mental Capacity Act 2005: post legislative scrutiny*, 2014, p. 22.
115. *Ibid.*
116. House of Lords, Select Committee on the Mental Capacity Act 2005 2014, p. 72.
117. *Ibid.*, p. 73.

faced with non-compliance by public authorities or private companies, such as banks, could be supported in the absence of specific remedies.[118]

In a study on the financial abuse of adults lacking capacity, Daley *et al.* looked at a sample of 34 cases heard in the Court of Protection between 1 January and 9 November 2015, to study the characteristics of financial abuse by both attorneys and deputies.[119] In eighteen of these 34 cases, the court was confronted with a situation in which the attorney allegedly had breached his authority or had failed to act in the bests interests of the adult concerned.[120] Examples of situations raising suspicions or indicating misbehaviour by the attorney included: co-mingling of the adult's and attorney's assets; a failure to pay the adult's care home fees; donations exceeding the permissible amount and chaotic management of the adult's assets.[121] In addition, to situations of abuse or misuse of the LPA, Daley *et al.* found indications of family disputes in 23 cases, such as disputes about who should act as attorney or disputes about the way the attorney had handled the affairs of the adult.[122] Daley *et al.* note in this regard that the role of attorney can have a negative side-effect, namely that it further exacerbates a bad relationship or that it creates suspicions or conflicts where none existed in the past.[123] In addition to the phenomenon of family disputes, Daley *et al.* also found that in some cases attorneys are insufficiently aware of their rights and duties. In this regard, they note:

> 'Individuals do not always remember the information that has been provided to them, but there seems to be too little information provided to them about their role as attorneys when LPAs are first registered. Better information – including warnings about the implications of failing to exercise their duties properly – might head off difficulties that crop up when LPAs are put into effect.'

7.6 Germany: the *Vorsorgevollmacht*

7.6.1 *Regulatory framework*

In Germany, the opportunity for adults to make their own provisions for a future period of incapacity using a *Vorsorgevollmacht* already exists for quite some time.

118. *Ibid.*, p. 74-75; see also Lush & Bielanska 2017, p. 21-22.
119. G. Daley, M. Gilhooly, K. Gilhooly, P. Harries & M. Levi, *Financial Abuse of People Lacking Mental Capacity. A Report to the Dawes Trust*, London: Brunel University London 2017, p. 70. Important to note here, is that the 32 of the 34 cases had been dealt with by the same judge (Daley *et al.* 2017, p. 73).
120. Daley *et al.* 2017, p. 72.
121. *Ibid*, p. 73.
122. *Ibid*, p. 82.
123. *Ibid*, p. 85.

The *Vorsorgevollmacht* is rooted in the ordinary power of attorney (*Vollmacht*) and the mandate or agency agreement (*Auftrag* or *Geschäftsbesorgungsvertrag*), which means that adults in Germany have been able to make their own provisions for the future since the introduction of the German Civil Code (GCC) in 1900.[124] In 1990, the German legislator with the *Betreuungsgesetz* – a law fundamentally reshaping the system of adult protection in Germany – acknowledged that instruments such as the *Vorsorgevollmacht* take precedence over the appointment of a *Betreuer* or representative by the court.[125] The *Betreuungsgesetz* has been amended and complemented four times (1999, 2005, 2009 and 2013). Important changes and additions concerning the *Vorsorgevollmacht* were the adoption of §1904 and §1906 GCC in 1999, which will be discussed in more detail below. Another major reform act – the *Gesetz zur Reform des Vormundschafts- und Betreuungsrechts* – will enter into force on 1 January 2023. However, this act changes the regulation of the *Vorsorgevollmacht* only on minor points.[126] With a *Vorsorgevollmacht*, adults can make provisions for financial, medical and personal matters. Although the term at first glance seems to indicate otherwise, the *Vorsorgevollmacht* consists of two legally separate components. A distinction is made between the *Vollmacht* or ordinary power of attorney, *i.e.* a conferral of authority to the attorney to act on behalf of the adult, and the so-called *Vorsorgeverhältnis*, a basic agreement between the adult and the attorney stipulating how the *Vollmacht* should be used.[127] Lipp notes that the basic agreement or *Vorsorgeverhältnis* will in most cases be based on the legal construct of the non-remunerated mandate (*Auftrag*) or the remunerated agency agreement (*Geschäftsbesorgungsvertrag*).[128] The foregoing means that to determine the provisions applicable to the *Vorsorgevollmacht*, it is necessary to look at various sections of the German Civil Code. These include the legal provisions on the ordinary power of attorney (§164-181 GCC) and the mandate and agency agreement (§662-675b GCC). In addition, section 3, title 2 of the GCC, titled 'Legal Custodianship' (*Rechtliche Betreuung*) contains several provisions which apply to the *Vorsorgevollmacht*.

---

124. V. Lipp, *Going Private: "Vorsorgevollmacht" as an Alternative to Legal Guardianship for Adults*, revised version (11 January 2016) of a lecture held at the University of Leuven on 10 February 2015, p. 2, via: www.bgt-ev.de/fileadmin/Mediendatenbank/Themen/Einzelbeitraege/Lipp/Lipp_Vorsolgevollmacht_as_an_Alternative.pdf (last accessed: 1 May 2022); V. Lipp, 'Germany', in: R. Frimston, A. Ruck Keene, C. van Overdijk & A. Ward, *The international protection of adults*, Oxford: Oxford University Press 2015, p. 375-385 (379). This holds true in particular for *Vorsorgevollmachten* for financial and property matters. Until 1999, it was unclear and debated whether personal matters could also be included in the *Vorsorgevollmacht*.
125. *Ibid*.
126. Where relevant changes will be noted in this article.
127. V. Lipp, 'Instrumente privater Vorsorge', in: V. Lipp, *Handbuch der Vorsorgeverfügungen*, München: Verlag Franz Vahlen 2009, p. 51-60 (56); J. Spalckhaver, 'Die Vorsorgevollmacht und das ihr zugrunde liegende Rechtsverhältnis als umfassende Vorsorgeregelung', in: V. Lipp, *Handbuch der Vorsorgeverfügungen*, München: Verlag Franz Vahlen 2009, p. 95-105 (96-97).
128. Lipp 2016, p. 3; Lipp 2009, p. 56; see also W. Zimmerman, *Vorsorgevollmacht, Betreuungsverfügung, Patientenverfügung für die Beratungspraxis*, Berlin: Erich Schmidt Verlag 2017, p. 108-109.

7.6.2 *Form and registration*

Based on Article 167 GCC on the *Vollmacht*, there are, in general, no specific requirements concerning the form of the *Vorsorgevollmacht*. This means that the *Vorsorgevollmacht* can, in theory, be granted orally. However, Zimmerman notes that this is not advisable because in practice such a *Vorsorgevollmacht* will generally not be accepted by third parties.[129] In other words, the written form is recommended. In some cases, the written form is also required. Article 1904 GCC, for instance, makes clear that when the adult wants to authorise the attorney to take medical decisions on his behalf, this authority must be granted explicitly and in writing. In addition to the written form, in some cases, an authentication or *Beglaubigung* of the *Vorsorgevollmacht* is required. This is for example the case when the adult wants to authorise the attorney to sell the family home. With a *Beglaubigung*, a notary or *Betreuungsbehörde* – an authority responsible at the local level for certain matters regarding the protection of adults – verifies the identity of the adult and confirms that the signature on the *Vorsorgevollmacht* is that of the adult concerned.[130] The adult can register the *Vorsorgevollmacht* in a register kept by the Federal Chamber of Notaries (the *Bundesnotarkammer*).[131] This register contains information such as the name of the adult and the attorney(s) but does not provide access to the content of the *Vorsorgevollmacht*. Registration is voluntary, the adult is not obliged to register the *Vorsorgevollmacht*, nor any changes or terminations thereof.[132] Currently, only the court (*Betreuungsgericht*) has access to the information included in the register.[133] An obligation for the court to check whether a *Vorsorgevollmacht* is in place can be inferred from Article 1896(2) GCC stipulating that legal representation by a court-appointed representative (*Betreuung*) may only be ordered when necessary.

7.6.3 *Entry into force and appointment of the attorney*

It is for the adult to decide when the *Vorsorgevollmacht* enters into force. The adult can decide that the *Vorsorgevollmacht* enters into force immediately or at a specified time in the future (*e.g.* the incapacity of the adult). Both Zimmerman and Müller and Renner note that adults who choose the second option are well advised to include a provision stipulating when the attorney may make use of the authority granted to him, in the basic agreement between the adult and the

129. Zimmerman 2017, p. 50-51. See also D. Kurze, *Vorsorgerecht. Vollmacht, Patientenverfügung, lebzeitige Verfügungen*, München: C.H. Beck 2017, p. 91 and p. 96-97.
130. Kurze 2017, p. 92-93.
131. §78a of the Federal Code for Notaries.
132. Zimmerman 2017, p. 143.
133. *Ibid*.

attorney.[134] Including such a provision in the *Vollmacht* – using a conditional power of attorney – may cause problems with the acceptance of the *Vorsorgevollmacht* by third parties such as banks, as these could require proof that the condition for the entry into force of the *Vollmacht* has been met.[135] Although the adult is free to decide whom to appoint as an attorney, the German legislator has tried to discourage the appointment of certain persons as attorney. According to §1896(2) in conjunction with §1897(3) GCC, the principle of subsidiarity – according to which the *Vorsorgevollmacht* should take precedence over the *Betreuung* – does not apply when the adult has appointed as attorney the management or staff of the institution in which he resides.[136] In addition to this discouragement, there is a restriction with regard to the appointment of so-called professional attorneys. Under the German Legal Services Act (*Rechtsdienstleistungsgesetz*), only a solicitor (*Rechtsanwalt*) may act as a professional attorney.[137] The adult may appoint more than one person to act as attorney and may direct these attorneys to act jointly, concurrently, separately or as substitutes. Although in theory possible, not all these options seem feasible in practice. Both Zimmerman and Müller and Renner note that practical difficulties can, for instance, arise when attorneys have to act jointly, meaning that all decisions must be taken together.[138] The attorney's task can then quickly become cumbersome, as every bank transfer – even for a small amount – requires the signature of both attorneys. Problems may also arise in the event of a conflict between the attorneys, in which case the attorneys might block each other's actions.[139] The German notariate, therefore, recommends adults to grant an unlimited *Vollmacht* (power of attorney) to each attorney and to include restrictions – for instance, that certain important, clearly defined decisions must be taken together – in the basic agreement between the adult and the attorney.[140] The adult cannot authorise the attorney to perform certain 'highly personal acts', such as making a will or entering into a marriage or a divorce.[141] A power of attorney (*Vollmacht*), in principle, includes the power to donate on behalf of the adult,

134. G. Müller & T. Renner, *Betreuungsrecht und Vorsorgeverfügungen in der Praxis*, München: Carl Heymanns Verlag 2018, p. 94-97 and p. 100-101; Zimmerman 2017, p. 56-57.
135. *Ibid.*
136. By means of a new section 1816(6) of the German Civil Code which will enter into force on 1 January 2023, the German legislator has widened the range of persons who are considered unsuited to act as attorney. Section 1816(6) GCC-new stipulates that 'a person who is in a relationship of dependency or in another close relationship with an institution or service provider involved in the care of the adult cannot be appointed as *Betreuer* [court-appointed support person]'. Such a person can consequently also not be appointed as attorney. This includes, for example, persons employed by organisations that provide outpatient care.
137. Kurze 2017, p. 239-241; Lipp 2016, p. 4. See, however, also Müller & Renner 2018, p. 91-93 who provide a more nuanced view.
138. Müller & Renner 2018, p. 227; Zimmerman 2017, p. 87-88.
139. Zimmerman 2017, p. 87-88.
140. Müller & Renner 2018, p. 227; Zimmerman 2017, p. 87-88.
141. Müller & Renner 2018, p. 127 & pp. 143-144; Zimmerman 2017, p. 75.

unless this is expressly excluded by the adult.[142] Once again, adults are advised to include more detailed arrangements and restrictions concerning, for example, the extent to which the attorney can donate in the basic agreement between the adult and the attorney.[143]

7.6.4 *Rights and duties of the attorney*

The adult retains legal capacity upon the entry into force of the *Vorsorgevollmacht*.[144] According to Lipp, the duties and obligations of the attorney are modelled upon the duties and obligations of the court-appointed *Betreuer*. Lipp seems to deduce this from §1896(2) GCC – the principle of subsidiarity discussed above – according to which the appointment of a *Betreuer* is unnecessary when an attorney can take the place of the *Betreuer*.[145] Consequently, the task of the attorney is, according to Lipp, 'to assist and represent the grantor [adult] on the one hand and to protect him from inflicting harm onto himself or his property on the other'.[146] The adult can make this general duty more concrete by including specific provisions in the basic agreement between the adult and the attorney. In addition, the general provisions on the *Auftrag* (mandate) apply.[147] The adult can, for example, stipulate in the basic agreement that the attorney is obliged to consult the adult or another person before making certain important decisions, such as the sale of the house.[148] In addition, the adult can include wishes and instructions in the *Vorsorgevollmacht*. The attorney is, according to §665 GCC, obliged to follow these instructions. Under §666 GCC the attorney is – upon request – also obliged to keep the adult informed about the management of his affairs and to render account. However, the adult and the attorney can derogate from this statutory provision through the basic agreement and organise the duties included in §666 GCC differently or waive these altogether.[149] According to §181 GCC, the legal starting point is that the attorney cannot act as a counterparty of the adult. Kurze notes that this statutory provision is intended to prevent conflicts of interest.[150] However, here too, the adult and the attorney can derogate from this statutory provision and the adult can exempt the attorney from the prohibition to self-contract.

142. Kurze 2017, p. 65; Müller & Renner 2018, p. 125-126.
143. Kurze 2017, p. 65.
144. Zimmerman 2017, p. 109; Lipp 2016, p. 8.
145. Lipp 2016, p. 7-8.
146. *Ibid.*
147. Müller & Renner 2018, p. 215-219; Lipp 2016, p. 7. See for an extensive overview of the provisions that can be included in the basic agreement, Spalckhaver 2009, p. 267-313.
148. Müller & Renner 2018, p. 216; Spalckhaver 2009, p. 275-276.
149. Spalckhaver 2009, p. 287-290.
150. Kurze 2017, p. 130.

7.6.5 *Supervision*

Adults can include a form of supervision in the *Vorsorgevollmacht*. Examples are the appointment of multiple attorneys to act jointly in important matters or an obligation for the attorney to obtain the consent of others who have not been appointed attorney – for example, the attorney's siblings – for important decisions, such as the sale of the house.[151] Adults can also appoint a supervisory attorney to supervise the actions of the attorney. According to §1896(3) GCC – as of 1 January 2023 §1820 GCC-new – the court can also appoint a supervisor or so-called *Kontrollbetreuer*. A *Kontrollbetreuer* is assigned the task of supervising the attorney and enforcing the adult's rights as agreed in the basic agreement.[152] The court appoints a *Kontrollbetreuer* when it finds that the adult is no longer capable of supervising the attorney himself and when it establishes that there is a concrete need to monitor the attorney's actions.[153] Furthermore, the appointment of the *Kontrollbetreuer* must be a sufficient and appropriate intervention. If this is not the case, the court may also appoint an ordinary *Betreuer* to take over the handling of the adult's affairs from the attorney.[154]

7.6.6 *Law in action*

Little empirical information is available on how the *Vorsorgevollmacht* functions in practice. Indeed in their opinion on the bill of the new act entering into force on 1 January 2023, the organisation *VorsorgeAnwalt* noted that the government's strong focus on the *Betreuung* had led to a neglect of the problems with the *Vorsorgevollmacht*. The organisation, therefore, recommended the government to further address the problems with the *Vorsorgevollmacht*, for instance, by promoting (empirical) research into the misuse and abuse and the acceptance of *Vorsorgevollmachten*.[155] Annually, the *Bundesnotarkammer* publishes reports containing information on, for example, the number of registered *Vorsorgevollmachten* and the number of cases in which a request to consult the register has been received from the courts.[156] Apart from these annual reports, the most recent empirical study seems to be an evaluation study carried out by Köller and Engels in 2009 on the effects of a law amending the *Betreuungsgesetz*

151. Zimmerman 2017, p. 170-172.
152. Zimmerman 2017, p. 173-174; Lipp 2016, p. 9.
153. §1820 GCC-new; Müller & Renner 2018, p. 229-232; Zimmerman 2017, p. 174-175.
154. Müller & Renner 2018, p. 229-232.
155. VorsorgeAnwalt e.V., *Stellungnahme des VorsorgeAnwalt e.V. zum Entwurf eines Gesetzes zur Reform des Vormundschafts- und Betreuungsrechts*, 10 August 2020, via www.bmj.de/SharedDocs/Gesetzgebungsverfahren/DE/Reform_Betreuungsrecht_Vormundschaft.html (last accessed: 1 May 2022).
156. See *e.g.* Bundesnotarkammer Zentrales Vorsorgeregister, *Jahresbericht 2020*, via www.vorsorgeregister.de/footer/jahresbericht-und-statistik (last accessed: 8 April 2022).

of 1990. One of the aims of this amendment act – which entered into force in 2005 – was to strengthen the *Vorsorgevollmacht* to avoid the necessity of a *Betreuung*.[157] Most of the information presented by Köller and Engels, concerning for instance information on the number of registered *Vorsorgevollmachten*, seems outdated. This seems different for the part of the study that looks at the reasons for the court to appoint a *Kontrollbetreuer*, an ordinary *Betreuer* or a replacement of the attorney, notwithstanding the presence of a *Vorsorgevollmacht*. When asked how often problems with asset management or problems within the family are the reason to appoint a *Kontrollbetreuer*, 56% of the courts (N=170) in a survey study conducted by Köller and Engels, indicated that problems with asset management are often a reason to order a *Kontrollbetreuung*. Thirty-two per cent of the courts indicated that problems within the family are often a reason to order a *Kontrollbetreuung*.[158] The courts were also asked about the reasons to order a *Betreuung* despite the adult's *Vorsorgevollmacht*. Reasons mentioned in this regard included: the *Vorsorgevollmacht* not covering all affairs for which assistance was considered necessary, problems with the acceptance of the *Vorsorgevollmacht*, the factual or legal inability of the attorney to act on behalf of the adult or the court not being aware of the *Vorsorgevollmacht* in the context of the proceedings.[159] Finally, Köller and Engels also inquired about the reasons for replacing an attorney with a *Betreuer*. In this respect, the courts indicated that problems with the asset management of the adult, the attorney being overburdened, the factual or legal inability of the attorney to act for the adult and problems within the family were reasons to replace an attorney.[160]

Apart from this one empirical study, observations by practitioners – both in the literature on the *Vorsorgevollmacht* and in the interviews conducted as part of the law in action components of this comparative study – can shed some light on how the *Vorsorgevollmacht* functions in practice. Kurze discusses the risk of abuse or misuse of *Vorsorgevollmachten* and possible solutions to address this problem, from a solicitor's perspective. Misuse or abuse occurs, according to Kurze, frequently within a setting of familial conflicts.[161] As possible factors causing conflict and abuse, he points to attorneys underestimating their task (resulting in non-transparent actions by the attorney causing distrust among other family members) and poorly drafted *Vorsorgevollmachten*, which fail to include a basic agreement between the adult and the attorney.[162] The latter can, for instance,

157. R. Köller & D. Engels, *Rechtlichen Betreuung in Deutschland. Evaluation des Zweiten Betreuungsrechtsänderungsgesetzes*, Köln: Bundesanzeiger Verlag 2009, p. 42-43.
158. *Ibid.*, p. 233-235.
159. *Ibid.*, p. 235-236.
160. *Ibid.*, p. 236-237.
161. D. Kurze, 'Tätigkeit des Vorsorgebevollmächtigten aus anwaltlicher Sicht', *BtPrax* 2018, no. 2, p. 47-53 (48-49).
162. Kurze 2018, p. 50.

result in a situation in which the (extensive) statutory provisions on rendering account apply, while the attorney is unaware of these obligations. Kurze notes that the lack of clear provisions on donations and reimbursement for the attorney in a basic agreement can also lead to conflicts and may advance the misuse or abuse of the *Vorsorgevollmacht*.[163] The avoidance of (extensive) basic agreements was also confirmed by the experts interviewed in the framework of this comparative study, although not all experts agreed on the need to include such basic agreements in the *Vorsorgevollmacht*. Kurze also notes that current actions and instruments – such as the intervention of the court – seem insufficient and inadequate to resolve conflicts.[164] In this regard, he notes that it is not easy for the adult, a new representative – such as a *Betreuer* or new attorney – or the adult's heirs to ensure that justice is done when misuse or abuse occurs. It is, for instance, difficult for the adult or his heirs to obtain the necessary information (*e.g.* bank statements) to build a case against the (former) attorney.[165]

Several directions are suggested by Kurze as possible solutions to the above-mentioned problems. First of all, he notes that attorneys should be advised by professionals to act transparently. This can be done, for example, by allowing others (*e.g.* siblings) who have not been appointed as attorney to view the online banking environment to check the attorney's transactions. This can prevent distrust.[166] Secondly, attention should be paid to a better design of *Vorsorgevollmachten*.[167] In this regard, Kurze notes that the involvement of a legal professional ensures that the *Vorsorgevollmacht* is tailored to the specific situation of the adult and includes details on the rights and obligations of the attorney. Such a *Vorsorgevollmacht* should also include clear instructions on the appointment of multiple attorneys, of which one supports and supervises the actions of the other. Kurze also highlights the importance of notaries keeping an eye on the adult's capacity to make a *Vorsorgevollmacht*, particularly in certain situations in which there is a risk the adult might be unduly influenced (*e.g.* when the attorney approaches the notary with a request to make a *Vorsorgevollmacht*).[168] Thirdly, Kurze notes that mediation – so-called *Vorsorgemediation* – might be a potential way forward to solve conflicts between the attorney and other family members.[169]

163. *Ibid.*
164. *Ibid.*, pp. 50-51.
165. *Ibid.*, p. 49.
166. *Ibid.*, p. 51.
167. *Ibid.*, p. 52.
168. *Ibid.*
169. *Ibid.*

7.7 Switzerland: the *Vorsorgeauftrag*

7.7.1 *Regulatory framework*

With the entry into force of a new adult protection law in 2013, adults in Switzerland were given the opportunity to provide for a future period of incapacity using the *Vorsorgeauftrag* and the *Patientenverfügung*. The former allows adults to appoint an attorney for financial and personal matters, while the latter allows adults to appoint an attorney for health and medical matters.[170] Both instruments can be combined in the same document when the adult appoints a 'natural person' to act as attorney.[171] Although before the entry into force of the new act, it was already possible to make provisions for the future using an ordinary power of attorney (*Vollmacht*), an agency contract (*Auftrag*) and using *Patientenverfügungen* subject to regional (cantonal) legislation, the Swiss legislator deemed it necessary to adopt a specific regulatory framework. First, to create legal certainty since there was no consensus regarding the validity of the *Vollmacht* and *Auftrag* as instruments to provide for a future period of incapacity. Second, to create uniformity concerning the status of *Patientenverfügungen*, since the range and scope of this instrument were judged differently because of differences in regional (cantonal) legislation.[172] Provisions on the *Vorsorgeauftrag* (Art. 360-369) and the *Patientenverfügung* (Art. 370-373) were included in Title X of the Swiss Civil Code (SCC), titled 'Own Arrangements for Care'. Article 365 SCC makes clear that, unless otherwise stipulated by law, the provisions on the *Auftrag* also apply. Notwithstanding the introduction of the *Vorsorgeauftrag*, the *Vollmacht* and the *Auftrag* can still be used to some extent to make provisions for the future. This is the case when the adult uses the *Vollmacht* and the *Auftrag* to make an enduring document that *remains* in force upon the incapacity of the adult. Enduring documents that *enter* into force upon the incapacity of the adult are subject to the new legal regime of the *Vorsorgeauftrag*.[173]

170. Art. 360(1) of the Swiss Civil Code; Art. 370(1) and (2) of the Swiss Civil Code.
171. A. Jungo, 'Art. 360', in: T. Geiser & C. Fountoulakis (eds.), *Basler Kommentar. Zivilgesetzbuch I*, Basel: Helbing Lichtenhahn Verlag 2018a, p. 2109-2129 (2127); E. Langenegger, 'Art. 360', in: D. Rosch, A. Büchler & D. Jakob (eds.), *Erwachsenenschutzrecht. Einführung und Kommentar zu Art. 360ff. ZGB und VBVV*, Basel: Helbing Lichtenhahn Verlag 2015, p. 43-58 (57). The adult can by means of a *Patientenverfügung* only appoint a 'natural person' to act on his behalf for health and medical matters.
172. *Botschaft zur Änderung des Schweizerischen Zivilgesetzbuches* (*Erwachsenschutz, Personenrecht und Kindesrecht*) 2006, p. 7012; Jungo 2018a, p. 2111.
173. Y. Biderbost, 'Erwachsenenschutz: Subsidiarität über alles?!', in: R. Arnet, P. Eitel, A. Jungo & H.R. Künzle (eds.), *Der Mensch als Mass. Festschrift für Peter Breitschmid*, Zürich: Schulthess Juristische Medien 2019, p. 91-111 (106-107); Jungo 2018a, p. 2115-2116; Langenegger 2015, p. 49.

7.7.2 *Form and registration*

Adults have two options when it comes to the form of the *Vorsorgeauftrag*. The adult can make the *Vorsorgeauftrag* in the form of a private document, in which case it must be handwritten from beginning to end.[174] With this requirement, the Swiss legislator hoped to avoid situations where the adult would simply sign a document drafted by a third person, without being aware of the content.[175] The adult can also choose to make a *Vorsorgeauftrag*, which is publicly authenticated by a so-called *Urkundsperson*. Who may act as *Urkundsperson* is determined by cantonal law, in most cases this person will be a notary.[176] The *Urkundsperson* has to advise the adult, establish the identity of the adult and assess whether the content of the *Vorsorgeauftrag* truly reflects the wishes of the adult.[177] The adult can register both the fact that a *Vorsorgeauftrag* has been made and the place where it is kept, in a register kept by the Swiss Civil Register Office.[178] Registration is, however, voluntary. Changes and terminations of the *Vorsorgeaufrag* can also be registered, but, once again, the adult is not obliged to do so.[179] The register can be checked by the Swiss adult protection authorities. Adult protection authorities play a key role in Switzerland when it comes to the protection of adults. As discussed in more detail later on, they are with respect to the *Vorsorgeauftrag*, for instance, responsible for the entry into force of the *Vorsorgeauftrag*. Upon receiving a notification that the adult is no longer capable of judgement, the adult protection authority must initiate proceedings to examine the necessity of an adult protection measure. In the context of these proceedings, the adult protection authority is obliged to check whether the adult has made a *Vorsorgeauftrag* according to Article 363(1) SCC.

7.7.3 *Entry into force and appointment of the attorney*

As noted above, the adult protection authorities in Switzerland play an important role when it comes to the entry into force of the *Vorsorgeauftrag*. Through a so-called validation process the adult protection authority must confirm that the *Vorsorgeauftrag* can enter into force. This validation process consists of four steps.[180]

174. Art. 361 SCC.
175. *Botschaft zur Änderung des Schweizerischen Zivilgesetzbuches (Erwachsenschutz, Personenrecht und Kindesrecht)* 2006, p. 7026.
176. H. Hausheer, T. Geiser & R.E. Aebi-Müller, *Das Familienrecht des Schweizerischen Zivilgesetzbuches*, Bern: Stämpfli Verlag 2018, p. 494-495; *Botschaft zur Änderung des Schweizerischen Zivilgesetzbuches (Erwachsenschutz, Personenrecht und Kindesrecht)* 2006, p. 7026.
177. Hausheer, Geiser & Aebi-Müller 2018, p. 494-495; J. Schmid, *'Vollmachten und Vorsorgeauftrag'*, in: *Stiftung Schweizerisches Notariat, Nachlassplanung und Nachlassteilung*, Zürich: Schultess Juristische Medien 2014, p. 259-300 (285-287).
178. Art. 361(2) SCC.
179. Art. 23a of the Civil Status Decree (*Zivilstandsverordnung*).
180. Art. 363(2) SCC.

The adult protection authority must, first of all, verify whether the *Vorsorgeauftrag* has been validly drawn up, *i.e.* whether the requirements concerning the form of the *Vorsorgeauftrag* have been met, whether the adult had the capacity to make the *Vorsorgeauftrag* and whether the content of the *Vorsorgeauftrag* is not contrary to the law.[181] Secondly, the adult protection authority must assess whether the conditions for the entry into force of the *Vorsorgeauftrag* are met. In Switzerland, the *Vorsorgeauftrag* can only enter into force when the adult concerned is no longer capable of judgement (*Urteilsunfähig*) concerning the matters included in the *Vorsorgeauftrag*.[182] There is no prescribed course of action to assess the adult's capacity. Büttner and Fountoulakis note that in practice an assessment by a physician is often requested.[183] Thirdly, the adult protection authority must assess whether the attorney is suited to the task at hand. The attorney must have the capacity to act on behalf of the adult and must be willing and able (in terms of time and place) to act on behalf of the adult.[184] The attorney must also be a reliable and honest person. To assess this, in practice, the adult protection authority checks whether the attorney has any criminal records and whether the attorney appears in the bankruptcy and insolvency register.[185] The adult protection authority is also obliged to inform the attorney about his rights and obligations. The fourth and final step of the validation proves concerns an assessment by the adult protection authority whether an (additional) protection measure is necessary. This can, for example, be the case when the attorney only accepts part of the responsibility conferred to him by the adult.[186] The adult can appoint both a natural person or a legal entity to act as an attorney for financial and personal matters. However, only a natural person can be appointed for medical matters.[187] The adult may appoint multiple attorneys to act either jointly or concurrently. Article 360(3) SCC makes clear that the adult can also appoint a substitute attorney. The adult cannot authorise the attorney to perform highly personal acts on his behalf. [188] Opinions differ in the literature as to the extent to which the adult can authorise the attorney to donate on his behalf. Hopf argues that the adult must explicitly authorise the attorney to donate on his behalf by clearly specifying the amount and the

181. A. Jungo, 'Art. 363', in: T. Geiser & C. Fountoulakis (eds.), *Basler Kommentar. Zivilgesetzbuch I*, Basel: Helbing Lichtenhahn Verlag 2018b, p. 2137-2150 (2141-2142).
182. Hausheer, Geiser & Aebi-Müller 2018, p. 497; Jungo 2018b, p. 2143.
183. J. Büttner & C. Fountoulakis, 'Der *Vorsorgeauftrag*: erste Erfahrungen aus der Praxis – Zahlen und Fallbeispiele von den Berner Erwachsenenschutzbehörden', *FamPra* 2015, no. 2, p. 507-535 (517); see also Jungo 2018b, p. 2144.
184. Jungo 2018b, p. 2145; Büttner & Fountoulakis 2015, p. 514-515.
185. Büttner & Fountoulakis 2015, p. 515.
186. Jungo 2018b, p. 2146.
187. Jungo 2018a, p. 2123; *Botschaft zur Änderung des Schweizerischen Zivilgesetzbuches* (*Erwachsenenschutz, Personenrecht und Kindesrecht*) 2006, p. 7025-7026.
188. Jungo 2018a, p. 2128; Langenegger 2015, p. 59.

beneficiary of the donation.[189] Millauer and Jaussi note that under Article 240(2) of the Swiss Code of Obligations, the attorney may only make customary occasional donations on behalf of the adult.[190]

7.7.4 *Rights and duties of the attorney*

Although full deprivation of legal capacity cannot be assumed, the entry into force of the *Vorsorgeauftrag* does have certain consequences for the adult. If the adult is no longer capable of judgement (*Urteilsunfähig*), the adult cannot revoke the *Vorsorgeauftrag*. Under Article 2 of the Federal Act on Political Rights, the adult is – when *Urteilsunfähig* – also considered ineligible to vote.[191] Article 365(1) SCC makes clear that the attorney must represent the adult in accordance with the adult's wishes, preferences and instructions as recorded in the *Vorsorgeauftrag*.[192] According to Hrubesch-Millauer and Jaussi, the attorney is obliged to contact the adult protection authority in the event of ambiguities or uncertainties concerning the content of the *Vorsorgeauftrag*.[193] The adult protection authority can in these instances interpret the *Vorsorgeauftrag* and add clarifications on minor points.[194] Article 365(1) SCC stipulates that, in addition to the provisions on the *Vorsorgeauftrag* included in Title X of the Swiss Civil Code, the attorney is obliged to act in accordance with the provisions on the *Auftrag* included in the Swiss Code of Obligations. Article 397 of the Code of Obligations reaffirms that the attorney must act in accordance with the adult's instructions.[195] The attorney has a duty of care and must put the interests of the adult first and refrain from doing anything that might harm the adult.[196] According to Hrubesch-Millauer and Jaussi, higher standards apply to professional attorneys, such as notaries and lawyers, when it comes to their duty of care.[197] According to Article 398(3) of the Code of Obligations, the attorney is, in principle, obliged to act himself. Article 400 of the Code of Obligations stipulates that the attorney must render account. Article 365(2) and (3) SCC make clear that the authority of the attorney is restricted when there is a conflict of interests unless the adult has explicitly

---

189. M. Hopf, 'Neues Erwachsenenschutzrecht und *Vorsorgeauftrag*. Regelungsmöglichkeiten und Wirkungen für die Vorsorgebeauftragten', *Der Schweizer Treuhänder* 2013, no. 3, p. 145-150 (146).
190. S. Hrubesch-Millauer & M. Jaussi, 'Vorsorgeauftrag – Pflichten und Haftung des Beauftragten', *Plädoyer* 2013, no. 1, p. 33-39 (35).
191. *Botschaft zur Änderung des Schweizerischen Zivilgesetzbuches (Erwachsenenschutz, Personenrecht und Kindesrecht)* 2006, p. 7082.
192. Hausheer, Geiser & Aebi-Müller 2018, p. 498-450.
193. Hrubesch-Millauer & Jaussi 2013, p. 34.
194. Art. 364 SCC.
195. Hrubesch-Millauer & Jaussi 2013, p. 35.
196. Art. 398(1) and (2) of the Code of Obligations – English translation of the Swiss Code of Obligations via: www.fedlex.admin.ch/eli/cc/27/317_321_377/en (last accessed: 23 March 2022); Hausheer, Geiser & Aebi-Müller 2018, p. 499; Hrubesch-Millauer & Jaussi 2013, p. 35.
197. Hrubesch-Millauer & Jaussi 2013, p. 35.

authorised the attorney to perform the transaction concerned.[198] If the latter is not the case, the attorney is obliged to inform the adult protection authority, which will then order an adult protection measure – a so-called *Beistandschaft* – for the affair in question.[199]

7.7.5 Supervision

The adult may include supervisory mechanisms in the *Vorsorgeauftrag*, such as the appointment of a supervisory attorney.[200] The adult may also require the attorney to submit periodic reports to an auditor – a so-called *Revisionsstelle* – who must inform the adult protection authority in the event of abuse by the attorney.[201] Passive supervision is carried out by the adult protection authority, which is obliged to intervene when the adult's interests are endangered in accordance with Article 368 SCC.[202] This is the case when the attorney abuses the authority vested in him, but also when the interests of the adult are no longer adequately safeguarded because the attorney remains passive, negligent or inattentive.[203] The adult protection authority has several options when it finds the conditions of Article 368(1) SCC are met. Under Article 368(2) SCC, the adult protection authority can oblige the attorney to submit an inventory and periodical (financial) reports. The adult protection authority can also give certain instructions regarding the execution of the *Vorsorgeauftrag*. If the interests of the adult are no longer (sufficiently) protected through the *Vorsorgeauftrag*, the adult protection authority can order an (additional) adult protection measure.[204] Finally, the adult protection authority can – wholly or partially – terminate the *Vorsorgeauftrag*.[205] Although not included in Article 368(2) SCC, both Hausheer *et al.* and Jungo note that the adult protection authority can also oblige the attorney to ask for the consent of the adult protection authority for certain acts.[206]

198. *Ibid.*
199. Hausheer, Geiser & Aebi-Müller 2018, p. 498; *Botschaft zur Änderung des Schweizerischen Zivilgesetzbuches (Erwachsenenschutz, Personenrecht und Kindesrecht)* 2006, p. 7028.
200. Langenegger 2015, p. 54; Schmid 2014, p. 285. See also Hrubesch-Millauer & Jaussi 2013, p. 37.
201. Langenegger 2015, p. 54.
202. A. Jungo, 'Art. 368', in: T. Geiser & C. Fountoulakis (eds.), *Basler Kommentar. Zivilgesetzbuch I*, Basel: Helbing Lichtenhahn Verlag 2018c, pp. 2170-2173 (2170); Hrubesch-Millauer & Jaussi 2013, p. 36.
203. Jungo 2018c, p. 2170-2171; S. Hotz, 'Zum Selbstbestimmungsrecht des Vorsorgenden de lege lata und de lege ferenda – Die Vorsorgevollmacht de lege ferenda', *Zeitschrift für Kindes- und Erwachsenenschutz* 2011, vol. 66, no. 2, p. 102-115 (112).
204. Hausheer, Geiser & Aebi-Müller 2018, p. 502; Jungo 2018c, p. 2172.
205. Jungo 2018c, p. 2172-2173; Hrubesch-Millauer & Jaussi 2013, p. 36.
206. Hausheer, Geiser & Aebi-Müller 2018, p. 502 referring to Art. 416 SCC; Jungo 2018c, p. 2173.

7.7.6 *Law in action*

At the behest of the Swiss organisation Pro Senectute, a survey study was conducted by the GFS-Zürich research institute in 2017.[207] The survey focused on the awareness of the *Vorsorgeauftrag* and the *Patientenverfügung* among the Swiss population and the number of people who had made a *Vorsorgeauftrag* or *Patientenverfügung*. The survey was completed by 1,200 people through computer-assisted telephone interviewing (CATI) and the study was considered representative for the Swiss population. Only half (48%) of the respondents were familiar with the possibility to make a *Vorsorgeauftrag*; 65% of the respondents were aware of the possibility to make a *Patientenverfügung*. Twelve per cent of the respondents indicated they had made a *Vorsorgeauftrag*, compared to 22% who had made a *Patientenverfügung*.[208] The study was repeated in 2021 and a significant increase in awareness of enduring documents was found; 65% of the respondents were familiar with the possibility to make a *Vorsorgeauftrag*, compared to 82% of the respondents who were aware of the possibility to make a *Patientenverfügung*.[209] The COVID-19 pandemic was presented as a potential reason for this increased awareness. However, respondents indicated that they did not feel increased pressure to make a *Vorsorgeauftrag* or a *Patientenverfügung* because of the pandemic. The reasons given by respondents for making a *Vorsorgeauftrag* or *Patientenverfügung* included maintaining a sense of autonomy and easing the burden of care for family members.[210] Besides these two survey studies, few empirical studies have dealt with the question of how the *Vorsorgeauftrag* functions in practice. In a study looking at the experiences of the adult protection authority Bern Mittelland Süd with the *Vorsorgeauftrag*, Büttner and Fountoulakis present examples of cases this adult protection authority had encountered.[211] These examples have in this comparative study been used – together with the experiences of the experts interviewed as part of the law in action component of this comparative study and the observations presented by both scholars and practitioners in the literature on the *Vorsorgeauftrag* – to get an impression of the experiences with the *Vorsorgeauftrag* in practice.

207. Pro Senectute, *Selbstbestimmen bei Urteilsunfähigkeit – Zahlen und Fakten*, 2017; Pro Senectute, *Medienmitteilung 'Nur jede zehnte Person in der Schweiz hat bei Urteilsunfähigkeit vorgesorgt'*, 2017; A. Umbricht (GFS-Zürich, Markt- & Sozialforschung), *Telefonische Omnibus-Befragung zur persönliche Vorsorge*, 2017, accessible via: https://gfs-zh.ch/nur-jede-zehnte-person-in-der-schweiz-hat-bei-urteilsunfaehigkeit-vorgesorgt/ (last accessed: 23 March 2022).

208. *Ibid.*

209. Pro Senectute, *Medienmitteilung 'Wunsch nach Selbstbestimmung ist stärker als Druck durch Corona'*, 2021; A. Umbricht & J. Yin (GFS-Zürich, Markt- & Sozialforschung), *Telefonische Omnibus-Befragung zur persönliche Vorsorge*, 2021, accessible via: https://gfs-zh.ch/bekanntheitszunahme-bei-vorsorgedokumenten/ (last accessed: 23 March 2022).

210. *Ibid.*

211. Büttner & Fountoulakis 2015.

A first problem concerns *Vorsorgeaufträge* which have been made by adults, who at the time, lacked the capacity – *Urteilsfähigkeit* – to do so. Fassbind notes that it is not uncommon for adult protection authorities to be confronted with a request for validation quite soon after the adult has made the *Vorsorgeauftrag*.[212] Rather than abuse, a lack of information lies, according to Fassbind, at the root of this problem. He refers, in this regard, to situations in which relatives of the adult are concerned that without a *Vorsorgeauftrag* they will not be able to continue their care of the adult and subsequently urge the adult to make a *Vorsorgeauftrag* although the adult lacks the capacity to do so. These situations can be avoided by ensuring that both adults and relatives are informed in good time about how and when the *Vorsorgeauftrag* can be used to make provisions for the future.[213] A second problem concerns the adult's capacity – *Urteilsfähigkeit* – at the time the *Vorsorgeauftrag* enters into force. Several of the interviewed experts noted that the requirement that the adult must be *Urteilsunfähig* – or no longer capable of judgement – before the *Vorsorgeauftrag* can enter into force, is not always practicable. In this respect, it is pointed out that *Urteilsunfähigkeit* is often preceded by *Hilfsbedürftigkeit*, a phase whereby the adult is still able to act and decide, but requires the assistance of others to do so.[214] In practice, the adult protection authorities, therefore, adopt a pragmatic approach concerning the requirement that the adult must be *Urteilsunfähig* before the *Vorsorgeauftrag* may enter into force. Fassbind notes that the adult protection authority might, for instance, decide to validate the *Vorsorgeauftrag* somewhat prematurely, in a situation in which the adult – although still being *Urteilsfähig* to a certain extent – is no longer in a state of health that enables him to cope with day-to-day administrative and legal matters.[215] The alternative would be a partial entry into force of the *Vorsorgeauftrag*. Within the framework of this country report, three experts from different adult protection authorities have been interviewed. All three experts indicated that in their experience, the *Vorsorgeauftrag* never partially enters into force. In some instances, adults are advised to use an ordinary power of attorney (*Vollmacht*) or agency contract (*Auftrag*) to make provisions for the phase preceding *Urteilsunfähigkeit*. Fassbind notes, however, that a *Vollmacht*/*Vorsorgeauftrag*-construction is not without problems because such constructions in some cases cause confusion in practice and meet with resistance from for

212. P. Fassbind, '*Vorsorgeauftrag* in der Praxis. Risiken und Nebenwirkungen', in: R. Fankhauser, R.E. Reusser & I. Schwander (eds.), *Brennpunkt Familienrecht, Festschrift für Thomas Geiser zum 65. Geburtstag*, Zürich/St. Gallen: Dike Verlag 2017, p. 217-241 (224).
213. Fassbind 2017, p. 224-225; See also Büttner & Fountoulakis (2015, p. 525-527) who also address this problem but zoom in on the question whether there is merit in the argument that a person, on the one hand, no longer has the capacity to carry out certain affairs, but, on the other hand, does have the capacity to entrust the handling of these affairs to another person by means of the *Vorsorgeauftrag*.
214. Biderbost 2019, p. 101-102.
215. Fassbind 2017, p. 223.

example banks.[216] To avoid the aforementioned problems, the Swiss legislator could change the law to allow the entry into force of the *Vorsorgeauftrag* when the adult protection authority establishes that the adult is *Hilfsbedürftig*.[217]

A third area of interest to which several problems can be linked concerns the role and position of the attorney. A first problem, in this regard, concerns the absence of a suitable person to be appointed as attorney, which could prevent the adult from making a *Vorsorgeauftrag*.[218] A second problem concerns situations in which the adult's choice of attorney or attorneys in practice proves problematic. This can, for instance, occur when the adult appoints an older person as attorney – such as a brother or sister – who, when the *Vorsorgeauftrag* enters into force, is physically unable to take care of the adult's affairs.[219] The execution of the *Vorsorgeauftrag* can also become problematic when the adult appoints more than one attorney, but fails to clearly delineate the tasks of these attorneys resulting, for instance, in conflicts between the attorneys.[220] Fear of conflicts can also result in the attorney taking on only part of the authority conferred through the *Vorsorgeauftrag*.[221] A fourth point of interest concerns the involvement of the adult protection authority through, among other, the validation process. This involvement has both advantages and disadvantages. An advantage is that the adult protection authority has the authority to interpret the provisions of the *Vorsorgeauftrag* and add clarification or adjustments on minor points.[222] One of the interviewed experts, who works at an adult protection authority, noted that interpretation and clarification of the *Vorsorgeauftrag* often take place with the acceptance of the *Vorsorgeauftrag* with third parties in mind. The adult protection authority can, in other words, promote the acceptance of the *Vorsorgeauftrag* in practice. At the same time, the adult protection authority seems to have made itself indispensable in ensuring the acceptance of the *Vorsorgeauftrag* in practice. Fassbind notes in this regard:

> 'Enduring documents are not accepted, nor are representatives, without the state's approval in the form of an official stamp on a piece of paper – purely because of the existing liability risks. Not only the liability risks of the banks but also the tendency of the courts to interpret the banks' duty of care broadly (in dubio pro small savers) contributes to the necessary involvement of the state. Experience has shown that nothing works in practice without official documents. Banks cover their risks, no matter what the law says.'

216. Fassbind 2017, p. 223-224; see also Biderbost 2019, p. 97 and p. 108-109.
217. Fassbind 2017, p. 223-224.
218. C. Walser Kessel, 'Der Vorsorgeauftrag. Einige praktische Überlegungen', *Der Schweizer Treuhänder* 2015, no. 5, p. 355-358 (357); see also Büttner & Fountoulakis 2015, p. 521.
219. Büttner & Fountoulakis 2015, p. 527-529; Walser Kessel 2015, p. 357.
220. Fassbind 2017, p. 229.
221. Büttner & Fountoulakis 2015, p. 529-530.
222. Fassbind 2017, p. 227; Büttner & Fountolakis 2015, p. 530-531.

Fassbind goes on to note that a tendency to pass risks – in particular liability risks – to the state has emerged, which, in his opinion, cannot be considered the objective of an instrument that is intended to promote self-determination.[223] Another disadvantage of the involvement of the adult protection authority is that the process of validation takes time.[224] Jungo notes that this may result in a 'competency gap' between the onset of incapacity (*Urteilsunfähigkeit*) and the entry into force of the *Vorsorgeauftrag*.[225] The adult can prevent such a 'competency gap' using an ordinary *Vollmacht* or *Auftrag*. However, as discussed above, the acceptance of these instruments can in practice prove problematic.

7.8 Comparative synthesis and best practices for the Netherlands

In the preceding sections an overview of the regulatory framework and the application of the *zorgvolmacht*, the *lasting power of attorney*, the *Vorsorgevollmacht* and the *Vorsorgeauftrag* has been presented. In this section, I will use this information to identify best practices that could provide a solution to the problems identified in the regulation and application of the *levenstestament*. Section 3 has outlined these problems. With regard to the regulation of the *levenstestament*, I have argued that a clear, solid legal basis that ensures compliance with international human rights norms and principles – such as Article 12 UNCRPD and the principles of Recommendation CM/Rec 2009(11) – is currently lacking. With respect to the application of the *levenstestament*, the following problems have been identified: a risk of misuse or abuse by the attorney, family disputes between attorneys or between the attorney and other family members, and third parties not accepting the *levenstestament*. In addition, a qualitative study involving interviews with both adults and nominated and active attorneys showed that more can be done to promote the active involvement of adults in the execution of the *levenstestament*. However, before turning to a discussion of best practices which could provide a solution to the aforementioned problems, it is important to first briefly outline the lens through which to look at the information presented in the previous sections. Scherpe notes with regard to comparative law research:

> 'A comparative lawyer, and particularly a comparative family lawyer, must never forget that all legal rules are embedded in their own unique cultural, social and traditional legal context. Whether or not we believe that societies and laws are converging, a solution or concept from one social, cultural and legal context cannot necessarily be transplanted into another and achieve the same results.'

223. Fassbind 2017, p. 235-236.
224. Büttner & Fountoulakis 2015, p. 513.
225. Jungo 2018, p. 2144.

In terms of the legal context, there are, for example, differences between the broader legal constructs – such as the ordinary power of attorney or the mandate agreement – that underlie each enduring document.[226] For instance, the German *Auftrag* (mandate agreement) only partly corresponds to the Dutch *opdracht* (service provision agreement), although both words literally mean the same in the original languages.[227] Another example concerns the differences in each jurisdiction's organisational structure. In England and Wales and Switzerland, important tasks are carried out by administrative authorities, namely the Office of the Public Guardian and the adult protection authority. As the Netherlands currently has no equivalent of such an administrative authority, certain solutions may be less suitable for implementation here.

Notwithstanding these and other differences in the cultural, social and legal context, all four jurisdictions have to a more or lesser extent tried to implement the principles of Recommendation CM/Rec(2009)11. As noted in section 2, these principles have been used as a framework to compare the legislation of the four jurisdictions, looking at the form, content, entry into force, registration and/or certification of each enduring document and the appointment and role of attorneys, the preservation of legal capacity, conflicts of interests and supervision. In implementing the principles of Recommendation CM/Rec(2009)11 each jurisdiction has tried to balance the adult's right to autonomy with the need for adequate safeguards to prevent misuse or abuse by the attorney. With respect to the right to autonomy, a distinction can be made between the adult's right to autonomy at the time the enduring document is drafted and at the time it is executed. In this regard, jurisdictions seek to minimise administrative and financial barriers for adults to make an enduring document, while also ensuring that, at the time the enduring document is executed, support is based as much as possible on the adult's wishes, preferences and instructions. As Table 1 shows, there are differences in the way the four jurisdictions have implemented the principles of Recommendation CM/Rec(2009)11, which means that the balance between the aforementioned rights has been struck in different ways. In identifying best practices for the regulation of the *levenstestament*, the need to strike an appropriate balance between the above rights in the Netherlands has been kept in mind.

---

226. In all five jurisdictions enduring documents can be linked to broader legal constructs either because they are based on such constructs (Germany and the Netherlands), or because the legislation on these legal constructs is also (partly) applicable to the enduring document (Belgium, England and Wales and Switzerland).

227. T.F.E. Tjong Tjin Tai, *Mr. C. Assers Handleiding tot de beoefening van het Nederlands Burgerlijk Recht. 7. Bijzondere overeenkomsten. Deel IV. Opdracht, incl. de geneeskundige behandelingsovereenkomst en de reisovereenkomst*, Deventer: Wolters Kluwer 2012, §9.

Table 1 Comparative synthesis

		Belgium	England & Wales	Germany	Switzerland
1. Adult makes the enduring document	**Form**	Private document or notarial deed	Prescribed form + assessment by certificate provider	Private document or certified document[1]	Private (handwritten) document or certified document
	Restrictions appointment attorney	Persons placed under a guardianship measure; persons who according to the law cannot be appointed as guardian	Persons who are bankrupt or subject to a debt relief order; paid care workers	Management or staff of an institution in which the adult resides	Assessment of suitability by the adult protection authority
	Restrictions content	No highly personal acts. Donations are possible when the object, the beneficiary and the terms and conditions of the donation are clearly stipulated.	No highly personal acts. Donations are possible, but only on customary occasions to persons or charities connected to the adult.	No highly personal acts. Donations are possible. The adult should explicitly exclude the possibility of donation when it is not wanted.	No highly personal acts. Donations are possible but only on customary occasions.
	Registration	Mandatory	Mandatory	Voluntary	Voluntary
2. Entry into force enduring document	**Entry into force**	For the adult to determine in the *zorgvolmacht*	For the adult to determine in the *LPA*, except for health and care affairs where the attorney can only act upon the incapacity of the adult	For the adult to determine in the *Vorsorgevollmacht*.	Upon the incapacity of the adult, subject to a validation procedure
	Legal capacity	Yes	Yes	Yes	No, limitation regarding termination *Vorsorgeauftrag* and right to vote

		Belgium	England & Wales	Germany	Switzerland
3. Active enduring document	**Rights and duties attorney**	- Duty to follow the adult's wishes and preferences; - duty to involve the adult; - duty to keep the adult's and the attorney's assets separate; - duty to render account;	- Duty to follow the adult's wishes and preferences; - duty to provide the adult with the support to make his own decisions; - duty to render account; - duty to keep the adult's and the attorney's assets separate	- General duty to assist and represent the adult and to protect the adult against self-inflicted harm; - tailored provisions can be included in the *Vorsorgevollmacht*	- Duty to follow the adult's wishes and preferences; - duty to put the interests of the adult first; - duty to render account
	Conflicts of interest	The attorney cannot act as a counterparty of the adult. An attorney ad hoc can be named by the adult or appointed by the court	The attorney has a fiduciary duty not to take advantage of his position and benefit himself, but benefit the adult	The adult can exempt the attorney from the legal prohibition act as a counterparty of the adult	The attorney may not act when there is a conflict of interest and must notify the adult protection authority, unless the adult has expressly agreed to the conflict of interest in the *Vorsorgeauftrag*
	Supervision	Passive supervision by the court by means of an alarm bell procedure	Passive supervision by the Office of the Public Guardian and the Court of Protection	Passive supervision by the court	Passive supervision by the adult protection authority

* Second form in certain cases required.

As Table 1 shows, all elements can be placed in one of three phases: 1) when the adult makes an enduring document, 2) when the enduring document enters into force, and 3) when one or more attorneys act on behalf of the adult.[228] In phase 1, four elements can be distinguished: requirements on the form of the enduring document; restrictions on the choice of attorney; restrictions on the content of the enduring document and requirements concerning the registration or certification of the enduring document. It is of course in this phase that the adult's right to autonomy, in the sense of minimising administrative and financial barriers to make an enduring document, is particularly relevant. As to the form of the enduring document, this means that the possibility to make an enduring document must be easily accessible for all adults. At the same time, there must be sufficient safeguards to ensure that adults who consciously choose to make an enduring document are aware of its content and are not subject to undue influence.[229] In this respect, I have stressed the importance of the involvement of a third party, who has to verify that the adult understands the significance of the enduring document, has the capacity to make it and is not unduly influenced.[230] In the Netherlands, this position is currently fulfilled by notaries. In theory, Dutch adults also have the option of making an enduring document by way of a private document. However, in practice, this is not recommended as such a *levenstestament,* not authenticated by a notary, may not be accepted, for example, by banks. One aspect not yet covered in this article is the costs of making an enduring document. In the Netherlands, the cost of engaging a notary to make a *levenstestament* can range from €278-€1,258.[231] Not everyone can afford this, meaning that not everyone can make a *levenstestament* that is also accepted by third parties. In England and Wales the involvement of a professional – although recommended – is not required. Adults must use a prescribed form to make a lasting power of attorney. A so-called certificate provider – who can be a person who has known the adult personally for at least two years – confirms that the adult understands the purpose of the LPA and has not been unduly influenced to make it. Not taking into account the cost of engaging a professional, the cost of making an LPA in England and Wales at £82 (registration fee) is significantly lower than in the Netherlands. However, as noted above, any best practice must be evaluated within the organisational structure of the jurisdiction. In England and Wales, the Office of the Public Guardian checks upon registration whether the LPA has been made in the prescribed form and whether a certificate provider has been

228. Stelma-Roorda 2021, p. 18.
229. Recommendation CM/Rec(2009)11, p. 42.
230. Stelma-Roorda 2021, p. 19.
231. www.degoedkoopstenotaris.nl/informatie/kosten-levenstestament?ref=adwords&gclid=EAIaIQobChMIzaWBssTI-gIVxQOLCh2gwgQLEAAYAiAAEgIVBfD_BwE# (last accessed 5 October 2022).

involved.[232] In the Netherlands, there is no equivalent authority that could carry out such an assessment. As I will discuss below, it might be worth considering the introduction of such an authority in the Netherlands. Such an authority would not only be responsible for the homologation of the *levenstestament* and the assessment of the adult's capacity when making a *levenstestament* but could also be responsible for the supervision of attorneys.

However, in the absence of such an authority, other best practices could be explored as a 'second best' option to promote the possibility for all adults to make a *levenstestament*. Legislation regarding the form of the *levenstestament* – including both the possibility of a notarial deed and a private document – might help to promote the acceptance of privately drafted *levenstestamenten* by third parties. Like the German government, the Dutch government could make available a form adults can use to make a *levenstestament*.[233] To ensure that adults have the capacity to make a levenstestament and are not unduly influenced, the possibility of asking adults to sign a privately drafted *levenstestament* at the local authority could be explored.[234] In Germany, the so-called *Betreuungsbehörde* – authorities responsible at the local level for certain adult protection matters – can verify the identity of the adult and confirm that the signature on the enduring document is that of the adult concerned. Again, there is no equivalent authority in the Netherlands, but perhaps other options could be explored to entrust this task to the local authorities. For example, consideration could be given to extending and strengthening the position of what in Dutch is called the 'ambtenaar van de burgerlijke stand' (civil registry officer). In the Netherlands, the *ambtenaar van de burgerlijke stand* (hereafter: *ambtenaar*) is authorised to draw up certificates of births, marriages, registered partnerships and deaths. In the context of marriages and registered partnerships, the *ambtenaar* is obliged to verify that there is no impediment to marry or enter into a registered partnership (Art. 1: 57 of the Dutch Civil Code). This includes an assessment of the impediment to enter into a marriage or registered partnership when the capacity of one of the parties is impaired (Art. 1:32 of the Dutch Civil Code). In other words, one could say that there is already a situation in which the *ambtenaar* has to carry out a (basic) assessment of the adult's capacity, namely the adult's capacity to marry or enter into a registered partnership. The duties of the *ambtenaar* could be extended to include an assessment of the adult's capacity to make a *levenstestament*. The position of the *ambtenaar* in this regard could be strengthened by providing him with the tools to make such an assessment. Like

232. Lush & Bielanska 2017, p. 170. The OPG is also obliged to apply to the Court of Protection to determine the meaning of provisions which seem ineffective or which could prevent the instrument from operating as a valid LPA.

233. www.bmj.de/SharedDocs/Downloads/DE/Service/Formulare/Vorsorgevollmacht.html (last accessed: 5 October 2022).

234. In Germany, so-called *Betreuungsbehörde* verify the identity of the adult and confirm that the signature on the *Vorsorgevollmacht* is that of the adult concerned.

the notary, the *ambtenaar* is not a medical expert and is therefore expected to infer the presence of an impediment based on the information known to him.[235] This will be sufficient in most cases, but in cases of doubt, a guideline similar to the guideline for notaries could be developed for the *ambtenaar* to assess the capacity of his clients.[236]

Besides the form of the enduring document, all four jurisdictions have legislation that regulates the content of the enduring document. Adults are limited in the matters they can include in the enduring document and in their choice of attorney. Representation for certain highly personal acts, such as marriage, divorce, and making a will, is excluded in all four jurisdictions. In all four jurisdictions, the attorney can be authorised to donate on behalf of the adult, but such donations are confined to customary occasions in England and Wales and Switzerland. In Belgium, the adult must clearly stipulate the object, beneficiary and the terms and conditions of the donation. The aforementioned restrictions limit adults in their right to shape the enduring document as they see fit. Such restrictions, especially regarding donations, seem however justified from the point of view of protecting the adult against potential misuse or abuse of the enduring document. Specific legislation on highly personal acts is not necessary in the Netherlands, because representation in such cases is already not possible under current legislation. When it comes to donations, I do recommend adopting specific legislation restricting the possibility to donate. In this context, a combination of the above options seems appropriate, allowing attorneys to continue customary donations that fit the adult's gifting pattern, such as birthday presents and annual donations to charities. 'Exceptional' donations should be allowed up to a certain amount when the adult clearly defines the object, beneficiary and the terms and conditions of the donation. As in England and Wales, I recommend that donations above the set amount should be subject to court approval.

Various motives underlie the exclusion of certain persons as an attorney. With regard to the exclusion in Germany of the management or staff of the institution where the adult resides, Zimmerman notes that the aim is to avoid potential conflicts of interest between the interests of the institution and those of the adult.[237] Another motive is that the attorney's task is not an easy one. Much is demanded of attorneys, such as promoting the active involvement of the adult and, if necessary, managing the adult's affairs and acting on the adult's behalf. Thus, in Belgium, persons deemed unfit to act as court-appointed representative, are also barred

235. See *e.g.* the conclusion of the Attorney General of the Dutch Supreme Court, ECLI:NL:PHR:2013:BZ8782.
236. See section 3. In Dutch the guideline for notaries is known as the 'Stappenplan beoordeling wilsbekwaamheid ten behoeve van notariële dienstverlening'.
237. Zimmerman 2017, p. 92.

from acting as attorney. I recommend the adoption of similar legislation in the Netherlands, so that at least persons, who cannot act as court-appointed guardian, can also not act as an attorney. In addition, it seems sensible to exclude persons who are bankrupt or subject to a debt relief order from acting as financial attorney. A final element in phase 1 is the registration of the enduring document. This element has two sides. First, registration ensures that others, for example, the court, can take note of the adult's wishes and preferences and choice of attorney, thus respecting and promoting the adult's right to autonomy. Second, registration constitutes a safeguard against abuse of the enduring document by the attorney, as it allows for verification that the presented enduring document is the most recent version. To achieve the latter, registration – including amendments and terminations – of the enduring document must be made mandatory. Given the benefits of such a safeguard and its minor impact on the adult's right to autonomy, it seems sensible to make registration mandatory. Legislation in this regard should also include an obligation for the court to check the register when confronted with a request for an adult guardianship measure. As in Germany, the register could still be maintained by the notariate, but it should be opened for registration of privately drafted *levenstestamenten*.

In the second phase – the entry into force of the *levenstestament* – two elements can be distinguished, namely the time and manner in which the *levenstestament* enters into force and whether or not the adult retains legal capacity when the *levenstestament* enters into force. These matters seem already well-regulated in the Netherlands. Adults can choose whether the *levenstestament* enters into force immediately or whether it takes effect at a specified time in the future, often upon the incapacity of the adult. With regard to the second option, adults can, for example, include a provision in the *levenstestament* stipulating that a physician should assess the capacity of the adult. Adopting legislation that involves an assessment by a government authority, as is the case in Switzerland, is, in my view, not advisable. As noted above, the Swiss requirement that the *Vorsorgeauftrag* can only take effect upon the incapacity of the adult is not always practicable. Before the actual period of incapacity, there is often a phase in which the adult is still able to act and decide, but requires the assistance of others to do so. Because of this, an informal entry into force of the *levenstestament* seems preferable. This allows the attorney to gradually step in and fulfil a double role, initially providing the adult with the support needed to make his own decisions and taking over the handling of the matters for which the adult is no longer able to decide and act.[238] In this context, it is also important that the adult retains his legal capacity when the enduring document enters into force so that the adult remains (legally) able to also act himself. Naturally, there may be circumstances where adults, although

238. Stelma-Roorda 2021, p. 12.

perfectly capable of managing their own affairs, would prefer someone else to manage their affairs for them. In these cases, the enduring document can function as an ordinary power of attorney as long as the adult can still supervise the actions of the attorney himself. However, as in England and Wales, this should only be made possible for financial matters and not for health and care matters. These are very personal matters and a decision in this regard should be taken by the adult when possible. Specific legislation on the aforementioned points is not necessary in the Netherlands, as current legislation already provides for this.

Specific legislation is important concerning the third and final phase when the attorney acts on behalf of the adult. In all four jurisdictions, the legislative framework provides for various rights and duties of the attorney. These include, for example, a duty to follow the adult's wishes and preferences, a duty to render account and a duty to keep the assets of the adult and the attorney separate. These rights and duties seem clearly defined in Belgium, England and Wales and Switzerland and less clearly defined in Germany. In Germany, there is a general duty to assist and represent the adult. However, the inclusion of specifically tailored provisions in the *Vorsorgevollmacht* is left to the adult. As in Germany, in the Netherlands adults also have the opportunity of including tailored provisions on the rights and duties of the attorney in the *levenstestament*. Nevertheless, I would argue that clear rights and duties guiding the actions of the attorney are of such importance that it should not be left (completely) to the discretion of the adult to include these in the enduring document. The most important rights and duties should also be enshrined in legislation. While this may be seen by some as infringing the adult's right to draft the enduring document as he sees fit, it is important to realise that the right to autonomy of the adult must be respected not only when the enduring document is drafted, but also when the enduring document is applied. This means, first, that a duty for the attorney to actively involve the adult in the execution of the enduring document when the adult wants to be involved and a duty to follow the adult's wishes and preferences are of such importance that they should be included in legislation. Second, it means that safeguards in the form of, for example, a duty for the attorney to render account are important to prevent the misuse or abuse of the enduring document by the attorney. In this regard, it should be noted that in a situation where the attorney misuses or abuses the authority granted, he will often also act against the adult's wishes and preferences, thus violating the adult's autonomy. Clear provisions on the attorney's duties are particularly important in situations of conflict of interest. In this context, a best practice seems to be the appointment of an attorney ad hoc in Belgium, who temporarily acts instead of the attorney for those matters where there is a conflict of interests.

A final element for which legislation is important concerns the supervision of the *levenstestament*. It is in line with the nature of enduring documents as privately organised instruments of support and protection that the responsibility for ensuring supervision is left initially to the adult. The adult can include modes of supervision (*e.g.* the appointment of a supervisory attorney) in the enduring document. However, according to Principle 12 states should also consider introducing a system of supervision whereby a competent authority has the power both to investigate suspicions of misuse or abuse and to intervene if necessary. In this regard, it should, first of all, be clear where suspicions of misuse or abuse can be reported.[239] In the Netherlands, suspicions of misuse or abuse by the attorney can be reported to *Veilig Thuis*. This is an organisation responsible for the investigation of concerns about domestic violence or child abuse at the local level. *Veilig Thuis* does not have the power to intervene when it finds that a concern is founded and must inform other authorities (*e.g.* the police or the Child Care and Protection Board) so that appropriate action can be taken (Art. 4.1.1 of the Social Support Act 2015). In addition, *Veilig Thuis* appears to have limited powers to investigate concerns in the specific context of the *levenstestament*. While *Veilig Thuis* can ask third parties, such as doctors, for information in some instances, it cannot, for example, require an attorney to provide information or submit documents such as financial statements. Suspicions of misuse or abuse of the *levenstestament* can also be reported to the court in the context of an adult guardianship procedure. The court does have the power to intervene, but will generally have limited possibilities in terms of time and resources to investigate complaints. In addition, only a certain group of persons – the adult, his partner, a close relative (not including the family-in-law), the public prosecutor or a (residential) care facility – can apply for an adult guardianship measure, which means that this procedure cannot be used by other interested parties, such as neighbours or friends of the adult, to report concerns of misuse or abuse to the court. Even *Veilig Thuis* cannot report directly to the court but must do so through the Public Prosecutor's office.

In other jurisdictions, the procedure seems less cumbersome either because there is a direct link between the authority responsible for investigating signs of abuse and the authority responsible for intervention (the Office of the Public Guardian and the Court of Protection in England and Wales) or because the responsibility for the investigation of complaints and intervention lies in the hands of the same authority (the adult protection authority in Switzerland). As noted above, it might be worth considering the introduction of an equivalent authority in the Netherlands. Such an organisation could be responsible – in addition to the homologation of the *levenstestament* mentioned above – for the investigation of suspicions of misuse and abuse and could be given specific powers to do so. This

239. Stelma-Roorda 2021, p. 17.

would include, at a minimum, the power to demand information and documents such as financial statements from the attorney. However, I recognise that it does not seem feasible to establish such an authority solely for the regulation of the *levenstestament*. In England and Wales and Switzerland, the Office of the Public Guardian and the adult protection authorities also have other responsibilities, such as the supervision of court-appointed representatives. The necessity of an authority to also assume such tasks in the Netherlands cannot automatically be assumed and is something that must be examined further.[240] In the meantime, it seems sensible that legislation is amended to give *Veilig Thuis* the power to bring founded suspicions of misuse or abuse to the attention of the court. The court must subsequently have the power to intervene. In the Netherlands, the court currently only has the power to terminate the *levenstestament* partly or completely. The competent authorities in the four jurisdictions have more options to intervene. In Belgium, the court can subject the execution of the *zorgvolmacht* to the same procedural requirements that apply to the adult guardianship measures, such as the obligation to obtain court approval for certain actions or the obligation to periodically render account. In Germany, the court can appoint a *Kontrollbetreuer* – a supervisory court-appointed representative – whose role is to supervise the attorney. In Switzerland, the adult protection authority may require the attorney to submit an inventory and subsequent periodical financial report or give the attorney certain instructions regarding the execution of the *Vorsorgeauftrag*. Such interventions allow the enduring document to remain in force, which means the autonomy of the adult is respected as much as possible. Legislation extending the powers of the court seems therefore also appropriate in the Netherlands.

Turning to a discussion of the problems that arise in the application of the *levenstestament*, several of the problems that occur in the Netherlands also occur abroad. The risk of misuse or abuse of the enduring document by the attorney is something all four jurisdictions struggle with. It is a problem that is inherent to the intrinsic nature of enduring documents as instruments based on trust. When adults are given the possibility to appoint an attorney of their own choice in whom they place their trust, there will inevitably be situations where this trust proves to be misplaced.[241] I have argued elsewhere that this risk can at best be managed through legislation, including safeguards, but it can never be completely eliminated.[242] The adoption of legislation that can help to tackle this risk has been already discussed above. However, this risk can also be managed by taking certain steps in practice. Experts from several jurisdictions indicated that attorneys seem to be insufficiently aware of their rights and obligations, which may contribute to the

240. A large-scale, multidisciplinary research project on a new system for the empowerment and protection of older adults is currently underway in the Netherlands.
241. Stelma-Roorda 2021, p. 24.
242. *Ibid.*

misuse of the enduring document by the attorney.[243] As noted, a first step towards improving this situation seems to be the inclusion of the most important rights and duties of the attorney in legislation. The second step towards improvement is to make sure that attorneys are aware of their rights and obligations.[244] This can, for instance, be done by attaching or including information about the attorney's rights and obligations in the enduring document, which is recommended in Belgium and Germany, or by actively informing the attorney when the enduring document enters into force (Switzerland).[245] The first option seems the most feasible for the Netherlands, as the time of entry into force of the *levenstestament* is flexible and the Netherlands does not have a similar authority like the Swiss adult protection authority, actively monitoring the entry into force of the *levenstestament*. Another best practice is the Code of Practice of England and Wales, where the attorney's rights and duties are explained – using examples – in a clear and illuminating manner.[246]

Family disputes in the form of disputes between multiple attorneys or disputes between attorneys and other family members also occur in all four jurisdictions. Various recommendations and best practices are put forward to prevent or resolve such disputes. Both Kurze (Germany) and Fassbind (Switzerland) recommend that adults and professionals pay more attention to the drafting of the enduring document. For example, in cases where the adult appoints multiple attorneys, the tasks of these attorneys should be clearly delineated.[247] In addition, Wuyts (Belgium) and Kurze (Germany) recommend that attorneys should be asked to act clearly and transparently, for instance, by allowing family members to view the adult's online banking environment to check the attorney's transactions.[248] When conflicts do occur, the court or the administrative authority in several jurisdictions can intervene. In Belgium, the court can try to reconcile the conflicting parties through mediation. However, mediation does not necessarily have to be offered in the context of court proceedings; in Germany, so-called *Vorsorgemediation* is offered by solicitors.[249] In addition to mediation, the Belgian court has the option of ordering an evaluation period, during which the attorney's actions are monitored by the court, to eliminate a sense of distrust among family members. Something similar can be achieved through the appointment of the *Kontrollbetreuer*

243. Kurze 2018, p. 50 (Germany); Daley *et al.* 2017, p. 97 (England and Wales). See for other recommendations concerning steps to be taken to prevent the misuse or abuse of enduring documents, Stelma-Roorda 2021.
244. For other recommendations concerning steps to be taken to prevent the misuse or abuse of enduring documents see Stelma-Roorda 2021.
245. Wuyts 2020b, p. 324-326 (Belgium); Kurze 2018, p. 50 (Germany); Art. 363(3) SCC (Switzerland).
246. MCA 2005 Code of Practice.
247. Kurze 2018, p. 50; Fassbind 2017, p. 229.
248. Wuyts 2020b, p. 265-267 and p. 318-319; Kurze 2018, p. 51.
249. See *e.g.* https://vorsorgevollmacht-anwalt.de/mediation-betreuung-vorsorgevollmacht (last accessed: 1 August 2022).

by the court in Germany. All the above recommendations and best practices seem to be relevant for the Netherlands. As noted above, currently the only intervention possibility in the Netherlands in cases of family conflicts seems to be the appointment of a guardian by the court. However, given the already considerable overburdening of the Dutch courts and the role of the court in the supervision of enduring documents, best practices that increase the workload of the courts as little as possible seem best suited for the Netherlands.[250] So-called inheritance mediation is already offered by several solicitors in the Netherlands and perhaps these solicitors could be persuaded to also offer mediation in case of disputes with the *levenstestament* as well. Instead of granting the court the power to order an evaluation period, the possibility for the court to appoint a supervisory guardian who supervises the actions of the attorney seems preferable.

Problems with the enforceability of the enduring document are also encountered in several jurisdictions. Various sectors are mentioned in this regard, including banks and the medical and care sector. Best practices to solve this problem are unfortunately less evident. In Germany, a distinction is made between the *Vollmacht* (power of attorney), *i.e.* the conferral of authority to act on behalf of the adult, and the basic agreement, *i.e.* the agreement between the adult and the attorney on how the conferred authority should be used. By including certain items in the basic agreement – such as the time of entry into force, restrictions and directions on how attorneys are to take decisions together and instructions regarding donations – the assumption is that problems with the acceptance by for example banks can be avoided. As noted, in practice the impression is that adults frequently fail to include a basic agreement in the *Vorsorgevollmacht*. This then creates the risk of an unlimited *Vollmacht* for the purpose of acceptance, which does not offer sufficient safeguards to counterbalance the risk of misuse or abuse. In Switzerland, the adult protection authority has the authority to interpret the *Vorsorgeauftrag* and add clarifications on minor points, which can promote the acceptance of the *Vorsorgeauftrag*. However, the downside of this provision is that the adult protection authority has seemed to have made itself indispensable as in practice a tendency to pass any liability risks to the state seems to have emerged. According to Wuyts, there seem to be few problems with the enforceability of the *zorgvolmacht* in Belgium. However, clear reasons why this is the case are not given.[251] Further research exploring this problem and potential solutions is in other words called for. However, there is a best practice that safeguards the adult's privacy. To avoid situations where third parties become privy to information they do not need to know, Wutys advocates the introduction of so-called 'certificates'.

250. See *e.g.* NOS, 'Rechtspraak krijgt meer geld, 155 miljoen om overbelasting op te lossen', via https://nos.nl/artikel/2436315-rechtspraak-krijgt-meer-geld-155-miljoen-om-overbelasting-op-te-lossen (last accessed: 1 August 2022).
251. Wuyts 2020b, p. 324-326.

These certificates contain information relevant to the third party but exclude non-relevant information, thus ensuring that the adult's privacy is respected concerning the information the third party in question does not need to know.[252]

While this is not an indication of a problem but merely an observation, as noted above, a qualitative study with both adults and nominated and active attorneys showed that more could be done in the Netherlands to promote the adult's autonomy in terms of the active involvement of adults in the execution of the *levenstestament*. Research in the four jurisdictions on this issue is limited. In relation to Belgium, Wutys examined the extent to which various legal provisions to promote the adult's autonomy have been successful. What Wuyts' study shows is that legislation on adult involvement alone is not enough to bring about a change in attitudes. There are practicable obstacles – such as time constraints – that hinder the implementation of legal provisions. While legislation creates a legal obligation for professionals and attorneys, among other, to consider ways in which the adult's autonomy can be promoted, finding ways to do so should not be left entirely to practice. Wuyts mentions developments such as 'legal tech' and 'legal design', which could be further explored as a means to support a process in which the adult considers his wishes and preferences to be included in the enduring document in advance. More research into these and other developments is needed to explore how best to promote the adult's right to autonomy in practice.

7.9 Conclusion

The aim of this article has been to find solutions and best practices in the regulation and application of enduring documents in four jurisdictions that might provide a solution to the problems identified with the *levenstestament* in the Netherlands. With regard to the regulation of the *levenstestament*, this concerns the absence of a clear, solid legal basis that ensures compliance with international human rights norms and principles. Although the *levenstestament* is currently regulated within the framework of the existing law on ordinary powers of attorney, service provision agreements and mandate agreements, I concluded that the adoption of specific legislation on the Dutch *levenstestament* is called for. Looking at the legislation of enduring documents in the four jurisdictions, several best practices could serve as an inspiration for the legal framework in the Netherlands. These concern – at the stage when the adult makes the *levenstestament* – clear regulation of the form of the *levenstestament* (both private and notarial) and the formal requirements that must be met when making a *levenstestament*, such as signing a *levenstestament* either before a notary or a civil registry officer (*ambtenaar van de burgerlijke stand*), who verifies that the adult has capacity and has not been

252. *Ibid.*

unduly influenced. Furthermore, I recommend legislation on the content of the *levenstestament* – especially concerning donations – and the suitability of attorneys (*e.g.* the exclusion of, for example, persons deemed unfit to act as court-appointed representative). I have also argued that the Dutch government should through legislation provide for mandatory registration of the *levenstestament*, including an obligation for the court to check the register, thus ensuring that the adult's rights to autonomy is respected.

Legislation is also important at the stage when the *levenstestament* is active. In this regard, I have argued that it should not be left completely to the adult whether or not to specify certain main rights and duties of the attorney in the *levenstestament*. Legislation should provide for certain minimum rights and duties to be observed by the attorney. These include a duty for the attorney to involve the adult in the execution of the *levenstestament* by informing and consulting him, a duty for the attorney to respect the adult's wishes and preferences, a duty for the attorney to render account and a duty to keep the adult's assets separate from his own. Legislation should, in addition, ensure that conflicts of interest are managed by prescribing the appointment of an attorney ad hoc, who temporarily acts when a conflict of interest arises. Finally, legislation is important to ensure that there is passive supervision by the state. In this regard, I have argued that the introduction of an adult protection authority is something that should be explored further. In the meantime, it seems important that there is at least a direct link between the organisation responsible for the investigation of complaints (*Veilig Thuis*) and the authority responsible for intervention (the court). When faced with a situation of misuse or abuse of the *levenstestament*, the court should have more options to intervene than is currently the case. Best practices in this respect seem an obligation for the attorney to obtain court approval for certain actions, the appointment of a supervisory court-appointed representative to whom the attorney must render account and the possibility of giving the attorney certain instructions regarding the execution of the *levenstestament*. These powers to intervene can also be used by the court in situations where there are family disputes.

I recommend that this legal framework be included in Book 1 of the Dutch Civil Code, more specifically in a subsection before the legislation on the Dutch adult guardianship measures. This would allow the Dutch legislator to simultaneously enact legislation regulating the relationship between the *levenstestament* and the adult guardianship measures. The enactment of legislation should be accompanied by efforts to address the problems with the *levenstestament* in practice. In this context, greater awareness of the attorney's rights and duties could be raised to prevent situations of misuse. Furthermore, alternatives to court intervention, such as mediation offered by solicitors, should be explored to resolve family disputes. In addition, ways to prevent or resolve problems with third-party acceptance of the *levenstestament* should be explored. Finally, further research is needed to explore how professionals and attorneys can be supported in their task of promoting the adult's autonomy by involving the adult in the execution of the *levenstestament* and respecting the adult's wishes and preferences.

8 Conclusion

8.1 Introduction

The *levenstestament* has become increasingly popular in the Netherlands as an instrument enabling adults to exercise their right to autonomy in advance by making their own tailor-made provisions for a future period of incapacity. Adults can appoint an attorney of their choosing and record their wishes, preferences and instructions. Moreover, adults do not face a limitation or deprivation of their legal capacity when the *levenstestament* enters into force. At the same time, there are concerns about the protective value of the *levenstestament* and the lack of safeguards when the adult's trust in the attorney turns out to be misplaced. In addition, it is essential from a human rights perspective that the *levenstestament* not only promotes the adult's right to autonomy when the *levenstestament* is made but also when there is a decline in the adult's cognitive abilities and the *levenstestament* is executed. In doing justice to both the adult's right to autonomy and the adult's right to protection, a balance between the two rights needs to be found. This book aimed to explore how both the adult's right to autonomy and the adult's right to protection can be balanced in the context of the *levenstestament*. The main research question formulated at the outset of the study was:

Is the Dutch levenstestament, both in theory and in practice, suited to the task of empowering adults with impaired capacity in the exercise of their legal capacity by ensuring that both their right to autonomy and self-determination and their right to protection are balanced and, if not, how it can be improved?

This question has been approached from a legal-normative, empirical and comparative perspective. Through this triptych design, a perspective of both the *law in the books* and the *law in action* has been gained. Comparative research was then employed to make sure that the wheel regarding the *levenstestament* is not reinvented but that lessons and best practices from abroad can be taken on board. Six sub-questions have been formulated at the outset. These questions have been addressed in the previous chapters and form the building blocks for answering the main research question. In part I of this book, legal-normative research has been used to answer the first three sub-questions, setting the stage by exploring the legal-normative context – in terms of applicable human rights norms and principles – within which instruments such as the *levenstestament* operate (chapters 2 and 3). In addition, legal-normative research was used to determine whether the *levenstestament* is, in theory – considering the current regulatory framework – suited to the task of empowering adults with impaired capacity in the exercise of their legal capacity (chapter 4). In part II of this book (chapters 5 and 6), empirical research has been used to explore whether the *levenstestament* is in practice fit to empower adults with impaired capacity in the exercise of their legal capacity. Finally, focusing on the problems identified in parts I and II and the need for improvements, comparative research has been used in part III of this book (chapter 7) to identify best practices abroad that could help to resolve the problems in the regulation and application of the *levenstestament* in the Netherlands.

The remainder of this chapter will summarise the main findings of parts I, II and III (sections 8.2-8.4). Next, these findings will be interpreted in a general conclusion (section 8.5). I then discuss the strengths and limitations of the methods used in this book (section 8.6). Finally, the implications for policy and practice will be discussed, along with suggestions for future research (section 8.7).

8.2 Part I: a legal-normative perspective

How does the levenstestament fit within the changed and still changing international landscape concerning the empowerment and protection of adults with impaired capacity?

An important starting point to answer the main research question was first to explore how adults can be empowered in the exercise of their legal capacity by ensuring that both their right to autonomy and self-determination and their right to protection are properly balanced. Chapter 2, therefore, addressed how the *levenstestament* fits within a changed and still changing international landscape concerning the empowerment and protection of adults with impaired capacity. In recent decades, the perception of how adults with impaired capacity should be empowered and protected has changed. Traditionally, the emphasis was on the protection of the adult's interests. This protection often involved a deprivation or restriction of the adult's legal capacity, i.e. his ability to hold rights and duties (legal standing) and his ability to exercise those rights and duties (legal agency).[1] A status-based or binary approach was used to determine whether a person had

1. United Nations Committee on the Rights of Persons with Disabilities, *General Comment No. 1. Article 12: Equal Recognition before the law*, 2014, p. 3.

capacity, meaning that if an intellectual impairment was established, a lack of legal capacity was presumed. A proxy or guardian was then appointed to act on the adult's behalf in the adult's best interests. In the 1960s, the status-based approach was gradually replaced by a functional approach, with the focus shifting from the adult's status (i.e. having an intellectual impairment) to the adult's decision-making abilities. The assessment of the adult's decision-making capacity became time- and decision-specific, meaning that an adult could be found to have capacity for one decision and not for another. Guardians were no longer supposed to act only in the adult's best interests but to consider the adult's wishes and preferences.

The United Nations Convention on the Rights of Persons with Disabilities, particularly article 12 UNCRPD, marked another significant change; sometimes even referred to as a 'paradigm shift'. With the emphasis on the adult's right to autonomy and self-determination, the focus has shifted from protection through a restriction of legal capacity to empowerment through support, or as Flynn and Arstein-Kerslake put it: '[I]f an individual is having difficulty making a decision or communicating a decision, the answer is not to deny legal capacity to the individual, it is instead to provide access to support for the exercise of legal capacity'.[2] However, the question of what this support should look like has been the subject of considerable debate. The Committee on the Rights of Persons with Disabilities has stated that article 12 UNCRPD calls for a total abolition of substitute decision-making, implying a restriction of the adult's legal capacity and the appointment of a substitute decision-maker, and instead requires the development of supported decision-making alternatives that allow respect for the adult's will and preferences. Not everyone agrees with this extreme stance. The debate seems to have reached an impasse as to whether measures involving substitute decision-making should be abandoned completely, even when adults, for example, due to a severe intellectual impairment or a coma, cannot make a decision themselves.

To move beyond this impasse, an alternate framework has been proposed by Martin *et al.*[3] Using the term 'support' from article 12(3) UNCRPD as the starting point, two categories of support have been distinguished. The first category concerns support that enables an adult to make a decision himself and to implement this decision with legal effect. The second category comes into play when the adult – notwithstanding the support provided – can no longer make his

2. A. Arstein-Kerslake & E. Flynn, 'The General Comment on Article 12 of the Convention on the Rights of Persons with Disabilities: a roadmap for equality before the law', *The International Journal of Human Rights* 2016 vol 20, no. 4, pp. 471-491 (p. 475).
3. W. Martin, S. Michalowski, J. Stavert, A. Ward, A. Ruck Keene, C. Caughey, A. Hempsey & R. McGregor, *The Essex Autonomy Project. Three Jurisdictions Report. Towards Compliance with CRPD Art. 12 in Capacity/Incapacity legislation across the UK*, Essex: University of Essex 2016.

own decisions and involves support to help the adult in the exercise of his legal agency. As noted above, legal agency concerns the ability to exercise rights and duties. The Committee has also defined it as 'the power to engage in transactions and create, modify or end legal relationships'.[4] According to Martin *et al.*, the challenge concerning the second category of support is finding ways to support the adult in the exercise of his legal agency, even in the absence of decision-making capacity.[5] The *levenstestament* or continuing power of attorney can be such an instrument. Adults can authorise an attorney to act on their behalf on this basis of their (previously expressed) wishes and instructions, thus supporting their legal agency. Only when this is not or no longer possible, as a last resort in so-called 'hard cases' when the adult is, for example, in a comatose state or an advanced stage of dementia and his wishes have not been expressed and cannot now be expressed, the law can provide for the appointment of someone else to make the decisions that the adult can no longer make.[6]

Regardless of the mode of support, all measures relating to the exercise of legal capacity must, according to article 12(4) UNCRPD, provide appropriate and effective safeguards to prevent abuse. Three categories of safeguards can be distinguished, namely 1) safeguards to ensure that the adult's rights, will and preferences are respected, 2) safeguards to manage conflicts of interests, and 3) safeguards to prevent undue influence. The interpretation of the first category of safeguards has again provoked much debate. In this regard, the Committee has argued that support should be based on the adult's will and preferences rather than what is deemed in the adult's best interests.[7] Again, a middle ground has been proposed by Martin *et al.*, who strike a balance between merely considering the adult's will and preferences and unconditionally respecting the adult's will and preferences. They propose a so-called 'rebuttable presumption approach', according to which a support person such as an attorney should 'operate with the rebuttable presumption that the reasonably ascertainable will and preferences of [the adult] should be given effect in the matter'.[8]

Using the alternate framework of Martin *et al.* as a starting point, chapter 2 provided an initial exploration of the state of the art in the Netherlands in terms of compliance with the new human rights-based paradigm of article 12 UNCRPD. I concluded that more must be done to ensure the Netherlands complies with this new human rights-based paradigm. Dutch law provides three

4. United Nations Committee on the Rights of Persons with Disabilities, *General Comment No. 1. Article 12: Equal Recognition before the law*, 2014, p. 3.
5. Martin *et al.* 2016, pp. 37 & 24-25.
6. Martin *et al.* 2016, pp. 37.
7. United Nations Committee on the Rights of Persons with Disabilities, *General Comment No. 1. Article 12: Equal Recognition before the law*, 2014, p. 5 & 7.
8. Martin *et al.* 2016, pp. 40-41.

adult guardianship measures: *curatele, bewind* and *mentorschap.* All three measures involve the appointment of a guardian by the court and a restriction of the adult's legal capacity and are, therefore, a form of substitute decision-making. Within the human rights-based paradigm of article 12 UNCRPD, such measures should only be used as a last resort. However, that does not appear to be the case in the Netherlands. In addition to the three adult guardianship measures, there is the *levenstestament.* This instrument has been designed and conceptualised by the Dutch notariate within the framework of existing law. While the *levenstestament* has the potential to play an important role as a tool to support adults in the exercise of their legal agency, there is a justifiable concern that, in the absence of specific statutory regulation, there are insufficient safeguards to prevent the misuse and abuse of the *levenstestament* by the attorney.

What is known from international and national research about the risk of misuse or abuse of continuing powers of attorney, such as the levenstestament? What do appropriate safeguards in this respect look like?

Chapter 3 subsequently explored appropriate safeguards to prevent the attorney's misuse and abuse of enduring documents, such as the levenstestament. As noted repeatedly in this concluding chapter, article 12(4) UNCRPD requires states to provide appropriate and effective safeguards that ensure respect for the adult's rights, will and preferences, prevent undue influence and manage conflicts of interest. However, as these three categories of safeguards are considerably broad, the operationalisation of these safeguards in the context of enduring documents, such as the *levenstestament,* was required. Since chapter 3 did not focus specifically on the *levenstestament* but on enduring documents involving the appointment of an attorney to provide for a future period of incapacity in general, the expression continuing power of attorney (CPA) was used throughout this chapter.

An important aspect to consider when operationalising article 12(4) UNCRPD in the context of CPAs is that the need to create safeguards should be balanced with keeping the CPA a simple and easy-to-use instrument. Failure to do so creates the risk that adults and attorneys bypass the CPA and instead seek less restrictive alternatives, such as simply handing over bank account details. In other words, safeguards should not impose more restrictions on the adult and the attorney than is necessary to adequately protect the adult from misuse or abuse by the attorney. To achieve this balance between protection and informality, chapter 3 commenced with a review of the available normative and empirical literature on the risk of misuse and abuse of CPAs, exploring: 1) the profile of adults at risk of abuse, 2) the nature of the abuse, 3) the profile of 'wrongdoers', and 4) the response to abuse. Interesting observations in this regard include the tendency of adults to wait until the 11th hour to make a CPA, which creates a sense of urgency and creates the risk that adults find it difficult to make well-informed decisions. Another observation is that abuse by the attorney need not be intentional and can also occur because the attorney is ill-informed or unaware of specific responsibilities or lacks the time, skills and motivation or capacity to act as an attorney, which explains the use of the term 'misuse'.

These and other observations were subsequently used to operationalise the three categories of safeguards of article 12(4) UNCRPD and to provide directions and recommendations on what appropriate safeguards look like in the context of CPAs. The observation that misuse by the attorney could occur because the attorney lacks the time, skills, motivation or capacity to act as an attorney was used as part of the operationalisation of the first category of safeguards (respect for the rights, will and preferences), resulting in the recommendation that states should ensure that attorneys are 'up to the task' and receive adequate support in performing their task. Other recommendations related to this first category included the recommendation that the adult's wishes, preferences and instructions should be clearly documented, for example, concerning donations and the recommendation that support enabling adults to make a decision themselves should be ensured for adults who want to be involved in the execution of their CPA. The observation that adults might wait until the 11th hour to make a CPA was used to operationalise the second category of safeguards (prevention of undue influence), resulting in the recommendation that states would do well to consider strategies to promote the timely drafting of CPAs. Another recommendation in this regard was that states should provide safeguards ensuring that CPAs are made by adults with capacity who are not unduly influenced by the attorney. Two recommendations were also given concerning the third category of safeguards (managing conflicts of interests), namely that states should ensure that attorneys are aware of their rights and responsibilities and that states should provide safeguards ensuring that a form of 'oversight' on the actions of the attorney is in place.

As these directions and recommendations remain rather abstract, chapter 4 explored the safeguards put in place in five European jurisdictions (Belgium, England & Wales, Germany, the Netherlands and Switzerland) to implement these recommendations. Here, I confine myself to giving a few examples. Concerning the recommendation to adopt safeguards ensuring that the adult has capacity and is not unduly influenced and the direction that the adult's wishes, preferences and instructions are clearly documented, the involvement of a professional is, in several jurisdictions, considered advisable. This professional can check whether the adult has capacity and is not unduly influenced and, at the same time, assist the adult in clearly documenting his wishes, preferences and instructions. The recommendation that attorneys should be 'up to the task' has been implemented in several jurisdictions by excluding certain persons from acting as attorneys (e.g. Belgium) and in other jurisdictions through an assessment of the attorney's suitability by an administrative authority (e.g. Switzerland). Chapter 3 concluded that with regard to some recommendations, there is still work to be done. For example, in all five jurisdictions, steps can be taken to ensure that adults who want to be involved in their affairs can do so. In addition, states could do more to ensure that attorneys are aware of their rights and responsibilities when the CPA enters into force and receive the support needed to exercise their task.

What is the regulatory framework in the Netherlands on which the levenstestament is based? And is this regulatory framework compliant with article 12 UNCRPD?

The aim of chapter 4 was twofold: firstly, to discuss the current regulatory framework of the *levenstestament* in the Netherlands and secondly, to examine whether this regulatory framework is in line with article 12 UNCRPD. In answering these questions, I addressed two contentious issues in the Netherlands. The first concerned the legal basis of the *levenstestament* and the applicable legislation in this regard. The second involved the added value of including a medical treatment advance directive in the *levenstestament*.

Starting with the latter, as noted above, the *levenstestament* is an instrument designed and conceptualised by the Dutch notariate within the framework of existing law. As such, the word *levenstestament* does not appear anywhere in the statutory law. In other words, the *levenstestament* is not a statutory instrument but a term used in practice as an umbrella term for the various options that adults have to make their own provisions for a future period of incapacity. A *levenstestament* usually includes the appointment of an attorney for financial, medical and personal matters. In addition, a *levenstestament* may include a medical treatment advance directive (article 7:450(3) of the Dutch Civil Code (CC) and article 2(2) of the Euthanasia Act) and an advance directive addressed to the court in the context of an adult guardianship procedure. This book focuses on what is internationally referred to as a CPA, i.e. the appointment of an attorney, including the wishes and instructions addressed to this attorney. Chapter 4, therefore, focused on the regulatory framework concerning the appointment of an attorney. But while medical treatment advance directives (AD) were not the focal point of this book, a discussion had arisen in practice concerning whether a medical treatment AD should be included in a notarised *levenstestament*. This could not be left unaddressed in this book. Chapter 4, therefore, briefly discussed the regulatory framework on medical treatment ADs and explored the added value of including medical treatment ADs in a notarised *levenstestament*. I concluded that medical treatment ADs are preferably drawn up by patients in close consultation with their doctor. The potential benefits of including a notary in this process (registration of the medical treatment AD and confirmation of the adult's identity and capacity to draft a medical treatment AD by the notary) do not outweigh the risk of adults drafting a notarised medical treatment AD without the involvement of and consultation with a medical professional. Thus, the inclusion of medical treatment ADs in the *levenstestament* should not be recommended.

Before I could turn to a discussion of the regulatory framework concerning the appointment of an attorney through a *levenstestament* and an assessment of compliance with article 12 UNCRPD, another contentious issue needed to be addressed first. In the absence of statutory regulation of the *levenstestament*, there is, in practice, no consensus on how the appointment of the attorney should be conceptualised within the framework of the existing law. Two approaches can be distinguished. Supporters of the first approach model the *levenstestament* predominantly on the ordinary power of attorney (article 3:60-3:79 of the Dutch Civil Code). Through a power of attorney, the adult authorises the attorney to act on his behalf. Therefore, a power of attorney is an essential element of the *levenstestament*. Supporters of the second approach do not deny this. However, they argue that a *levenstestament* should also include an agreement on the tasks the attorney will perform for and on behalf of the adult as well as arrangements about the rights and duties of both the adult and the attorney. In this regard, the rules on the service provision agreement (articles 7:400-7:413 of the Dutch Civil Code) and the mandate agreement (articles 7:414-7:424 of the Dutch Civil Code) are considered applicable. This discussion can be traced back to a more general Dutch theoretical debate on the doctrine of representation and, more specifically, whether an 'isolated power of attorney' – a power of attorney without any underlying agreement between the adult and the attorney – is possible in the Netherlands. Chapter 3 did not address this general theoretical question (which in itself could be the subject of a new study). I confined myself to arguing that an isolated power of attorney is unsuitable as a legal basis for the *levenstestament* because the specific situation in which the adult eventually becomes unable to act, requires not only the authority for the attorney to act but also a duty to exercise this authority.

Having discussed the applicable legal basis and regulatory framework for the appointment of an attorney through a levenstestament, I then examined whether this regulatory framework is compliant with article 12 UNCRPD. After all, the regulatory framework on the ordinary power of attorney, the service provision agreement and the mandate agreement was not designed with the future incapacity of the adult in mind. Article 12(4) UNCRPD requires states to provide safeguards that ensure that the adult's rights, will and preferences are respected, that undue influence is avoided and that conflicts of interests are managed. Furthermore, article 12(3) UNCRPD emphasises the need for support enabling the adult to decide and act himself. When this is no longer possible, support should be provided based on the adult's wishes, preferences and instructions. While the legislation on the aforementioned legal constructs provides for certain standards – such as an obligation to exercise the care of a prudent attorney – these are insufficiently tailored to a setting in which the adult gradually loses the ability to decide and act and the ability to supervise the execution of the *levenstestament*. More profound, tailored safeguards are required, such as an obligation for the attorney to involve the adult as much as possible in the decision-making process. Currently, the inclusion of such safeguards is left to adults, who can include safeguards in their *levenstestament*. However, article 12(4) UNCRPD calls on *states* to ensure that measures that relate to the exercise of legal capacity provide appropriate and effective safeguards. In other words, the inclusion of safeguards should not be left entirely to the volition of the adult and the attorney. The Dutch legislator should introduce certain mandatory minimum safeguards to prevent the abuse and misuse of the *levenstestament* by the attorney and to promote the adult's autonomy not only when the *levenstestament* is drafted but also when it is executed. Comparative research could help identify best practices in this regard.

8.3 Part II: an empirical perspective

How is the levenstestament applied in practice?

Part II of this book explored the practical suitability of the *levenstestament* to empower adults with impaired capacity in the exercise of their legal capacity. Three exploratory studies were conducted to explore this question. The design of these studies had to take into account that the *levenstestament* is an *enduring* instrument designed to make provisions for a future period of incapacity, a period when the adult's cognitive abilities are likely to decline. It was therefore important to obtain a picture of the use and experiences with the *levenstestament* over time. Thus, chapter 5 looked at the experiences with the *levenstestament* at the beginning and the end of the lifespan of the *levenstestament*. Through a survey study, the experiences with the *levenstestament* of the notariate – an actor active at the beginning of the lifespan of the *levenstestament* – were explored. Problems that may occur at the end of the lifespan of the *levenstestament* were explored through an analysis of court cases in which the court found an adult guardianship measure necessary despite the presence of a *levenstestament*. As discussed in more detail below, chapter 6 sought to explore the experiences with the *levenstestament* over time by looking at the experiences of both adults and attorneys at various stages across the lifespan of the *levenstestament*.

The survey study on the application of the *levenstestament* by the notariate provided insight into the characteristics of clients, the models or formats notaries use to make a *levenstestament*, the way notaries deal with the assessment of their client's capacity, the entry into force of the *levenstestament*, supervision and the recording of medical wishes and preferences. In addition, notaries were asked what they considered the advantages and disadvantages of the *levenstestament*. Due to the low response rate (6,8% or 164 out of all 3239 notaries in the Netherlands), the findings of the survey study cannot be considered representative. However, the survey study (especially the answers to the open questions) provides insight into the varying ways in which notaries in the Netherlands work with the *levenstestament*. Here, I will not repeat all findings but highlight two issues that drew attention. The first concerns the risk of misuse and abuse by the attorney. Although this risk was recognised as one of the disadvantages of the *levenstestament*, only 33% of the respondents indicated that a form of supervision should be included in all cases. According to 39,5% of the respondents, supervision should be included upon the adult's request. This seems to align with the views of several notarial associations that it is ultimately up to the adult whether a form of supervision is included in the *levenstestament*.[9] Interestingly, several respondents also noted that it could be challenging to convince clients to include a form of supervision in their *levenstestament*. Therefore, if the notariate remains committed to the view that it is ultimately up to the adult to include a form of supervision in the *levenstestament*, it seems essential that the notariate at the same time continues to consider ways in which notaries can convince their clients of the importance of doing so.

Another interesting observation was that several respondents considered the autonomy of the attorney – or the family more broadly – to engage in estate planning without the 'prying eyes' of the court, to be an advantage of the *levenstestament*. However, perceiving the benefits of estate planning from the attorney's perspective creates the risk that the purpose of the *levenstestament* – protecting the adult's interests – is overlooked. Therefore, the adult's wishes and preferences regarding estate planning must be carefully recorded in the *levenstestament*. The purpose of the *levenstestament* as an instrument protecting the adult's interests was also confirmed in the study of court cases. In several court cases, the court deemed an adult guardianship measure necessary because the attorney had, without justification, taken assets from the adult or failed to put the adult's interest first, for instance, by denying the adult the care and company of others. The study of court cases also revealed several other problems that occur in the execution of the *levenstestament*, such as a disturbed relationship between attorneys, which can hinder the execution of the *levenstestament* or even make it impossible. Another problem is the risk that dissatisfied family members (who have not been appointed as an attorney) may use the adult guardianship proceedings to circumvent the adult's wishes as expressed in the *levenstestament*.

9. Section 3.2.2.

Finally, problems with the acceptance of the *levenstestament* by a third party and situations in which the adult was regularly engaging in unwise transactions that subsequently had to be cancelled or withdrawn were also reasons for the court to deem an adult guardianship measure necessary. As the number of studied court cases was relatively small, further research is needed to explore the nature, scope and prevalence of these problems.

What are the expectations adults have when they decide to make a levenstestament? What are the expectations of nominated attorneys regarding their (future) role? And what are the experiences of active attorneys with the levenstestament in practice?

In chapter 6, I sought to explore the experiences of two actors – adults and attorneys – over time. Through interviews in a cohort design, the expectations of both adults and nominated attorneys at the time of drafting the *levenstestament* and the experiences of active attorneys with the *levenstestament* in practice were explored. This study aimed to find out the extent to which expectations are realised in practice and the role of the *levenstestament* in facilitating decision-making in a process in which decision-making gradually transfers from the adult to the attorney. The adults who participated in the interview study seemed motivated to make a *levenstestament* for two reasons. First, to maintain a sense of autonomy by trying to avoid certain future events from happening, such as being placed in a care home. Second, to ease a future burden of care on the attorney, such as having to go the court to obtain permission to sell the family home. These expectations of the adult are consistent with those discussed in the literature on the potential of enduring documents, namely that such instruments can make the adult's voice an influential component of future decisions and that – within a broader structure of advance care planning – they can provide a supportive structure for attorneys to navigate their decision-making journey.

However, the interview study in chapter 6 showed that there is a risk that the adult's expectations are not realised in practice. Because drafting a notarial *levenstestament* is costly in the Netherlands, notaries warn adults against making an instrument that is quickly outdated or in need of change when the adult's wishes and preferences change over time. This means that adults are advised not to include too detailed wishes and preferences in their *levenstestament*. Moreover, adults are advised to give the attorney broad authority to cover all possible future scenarios. However, both carry the risk that the information about the adult's values, wishes and preferences included in the *levenstestament* is limited. In other words, although there is a lot the attorney *can* do, he knows little about what the adult *wishes* him to do. This need not be a problem if the adult can still participate in the decision-making process, at least to some extent. Interviews with active attorneys showed that most of these attorneys were committed to involving the adult in the decision-making process as much as they considered possible. However, the lack of information about the adult's values, wishes and preferences can become problematic when the adult's cognitive abilities decline and the adult is less able to participate in the decision-making process. Attorneys must then adopt a retrospective decisional style, relying on their knowledge of the adult's values, wishes and preferences.

A solution to the lack of detailed information on wishes and preferences in the *levenstestament* could be ongoing conversations between the adult and the attorney about the adult's (changing) wishes and preferences. This has been advocated in the socio-medical literature within the broader context of advance care planning. The interview study in chapter 6, therefore, explored whether adults and attorneys have such conversations and found that this is frequently not the case. Barriers in this regard include not wanting to burden the attorney with future affairs in advance or finding it challenging to discuss wishes and preferences regarding future matters because adults do not know what that future holds. Some adults did not have conversations about wishes and preferences in the mistaken belief that their attorney already knew their wishes and preferences. Both when the *levenstestament* is made and when it enters into force, participants seemed to find it difficult to discuss future wishes and preferences. However, such conversations become even more complex when the adult's cognitive abilities decline, highlighting the importance of timely conversations. Attention is therefore needed to consider how both adults and attorneys could be supported to have timely conversations. In this regard, the notariate could play a vital role by making both adults and attorneys aware of the importance of such conversations.

Timely conversations could also help attorneys to prepare beforehand for the task ahead. Interviews with active attorneys showed that the role of an attorney could be challenging. The relationship with the adult frequently changes, and attorneys must acquaint themselves with a new role. A role that does not, in all cases, seem straightforward or clear-cut. Some attorneys struggled with the dynamic nature of capacity and linked to that the question of when the *levenstestament* should enter into force. The task of attorney in some cases also required a balancing act where attorneys had to find a compromise between the adult's interests and their own. A lack of support or even conflicts with family members and problems with the acceptance of the *levenstestament* were also factors which made the role of attorney more difficult. Of course, timely conversations between the adult and the attorney cannot solve all these problems. Further attention is needed to address, for example, the problem of family conflicts and the acceptance by banks. However, when adults and attorneys discuss issues such as the entry into force of the *levenstestament*, the adult's expectations as to how the attorney should fulfil his role and the complexities of balancing the interests of both the adult and the attorney, this could potentially help the attorney prepare for his future role. The interview study in chapter 6 revealed that several nominated attorneys were unaware of the content of the *levenstestament* and the adult's expectations of how the role of attorney should be fulfilled. Thus, there is much ground to be gained here.

8.4 Part III: a comparative perspective

What are the experiences of other jurisdictions with enduring documents? Which problems are experienced in other jurisdictions? Which solutions have been found? And what are best practices that might be adopted as a solution to similar problems experienced in the Netherlands?

Part III of this book examined the legal regulation and practical application of enduring documents abroad. This study aimed to identify best practices abroad that can be used to solve the problems experienced with the regulation and application of the *levenstestament* in the Netherlands. These problems have been discussed above and, with regard to the regulation of the *levenstestament*, mainly concern the absence of a clear, solid legal basis that ensures compliance with human rights norms and principles. In addition, the application of the *levenstestament* can be hindered by misuse or abuse by the attorney, conflicts between attorneys or other family members and problems with the acceptance of the *levenstestament* by third parties. The report 'Enabling citizens to plan for incapacity', a review of the follow-up action undertaken by member states of the Council of Europe on Recommendation CM/Rec(2009)11, conducted by Adrian Ward, was used as the basis for a quickscan. This report provides information on the implementation of Recommendation CM/Rec(2009)11 titled 'Principles concerning continuing powers of attorney and advance directives for incapacity' in 30 jurisdictions. As throughout this book, the focus was on instruments that enable adults to appoint one or more attorneys and allow adults to communicate their instructions, wishes and preferences to these attorneys. Based on this quickscan, four jurisdictions were selected for in-depth comparative research: Belgium, Germany, England and Wales, and Switzerland. First, jurisdictions were selected where adults can include financial, medical and personal matters in the enduring document. Second, it was considered important that specific legislation on enduring documents had been adopted. In this regard, the time of entry into force and the scope or extent of regulation were considered. Third, practical considerations, such as access to legal sources and language barriers, guided the selection of jurisdictions.

The quickscan was followed by an in-depth study of the *zorgvolmacht* (Belgium), the lasting power of attorney (England and Wales), the *Vorsorgevollmacht* (Germany) and the *Vorsorgeauftrag* and the *Patientenverfügung* (Switzerland). Recommendation CM/Rec(2009)11 was used as a frame of reference for developing a questionnaire used as the basis for this in-depth study. Using the principles of the Recommendation as the starting point, I looked at the regulation in each jurisdiction on the form, content, entry into force, registration and certification of the enduring documents and the appointment and role of attorneys, the preservation of legal capacity, conflicts of interests and supervision. The in-depth study of each jurisdiction began with a desk study of the relevant literature and case law. Each country was subsequently visited for three weeks to complete the study and get an impression of the law in action. During these research visits, practitioners such as notaries, judges, government officials, solicitors and physicians were interviewed. Based on the desk study and research visits, country reports were produced. These can be found in the appendix of this book. In addition, a synopsis of all reports was included in chapter 7.

As indicated, the comparative study aimed to identify best foreign practices that could be used to address the problems encountered in the regulation and application of the *levenstestament* in the Netherlands. Although the principles of Recommendation 2009(11) provide a framework for the regulation of enduring documents, these principles are broadly formulated, leaving much room for implementation. Therefore, the comparative study examined how the four jurisdictions have implemented the Recommendation, thus providing detailed material for the selection of best practices for the regulation of the *levenstestament* in the Netherlands. In addition, the comparative study explored the problems the four jurisdictions face in the application of enduring documents and how they address these problems. The selection of best practices resulted in several recommendations regarding steps that could be taken in the Netherlands to improve the regulation and the application of the *levenstestament*. Section 8.7 addresses these recommendations in detail.

8.5 Main conclusion

Based on the legal-normative, empirical and comparative research discussed in the preceding sections, the main research question can be answered as follows: while the *levenstestament*, in principle, has great potential as an instrument empowering adults with impaired capacity in the exercise of their legal capacity, further steps need to be taken concerning both the regulation and the application of the *levenstestament* to ensure the *levenstestament* lives up to this potential.

With regard to the regulation of the *levenstestament*, I would argue that article 12 UNCRPD requires more profound and tailored safeguards than is presently the case. The current regulatory framework gives adults considerable leeway to draft the *levenstestament* as they see fit and, in other words, promotes the adult's autonomy while drafting the *levenstestament*. However, as article 12 UNCRPD makes clear, the adult's autonomy should be promoted not only when the *levenstestament* is made but also when it is executed. Adults can be empowered in the exercise of their legal capacity by support that enables them to make their own decisions and execute these decisions with legal effect, and by support whereby the attorney acts for and on behalf of the adult in accordance with the adult's (previously expressed) wishes, preferences and instructions. In this context, a general legal standard, requiring attorneys to involve the adult in the decision-making process as much as possible, would be a first step in the right direction. In addition to safeguards that promote the adult's autonomy, safeguards are also needed to prevent misuse or abuse of the *levenstestament* by the attorney. The following section provides recommendations for such safeguards.

With regard to the application of the *levenstestament*, there is a need to further identify and address problems that may hinder the execution of the *levenstestament* in practice. This study has identified several problems that can occur in practice, including the risk of misuse or abuse of the *levenstestament*, problems with the acceptance of the *levenstestament* and conflicts between attorneys or between attorneys and other family members of the adult. Through comparative research, ways have been found to address these problems. However, as the number of *levenstestamenten* entering into force is likely to increase in the future, further empirical research exploring problems occurring in practice and ways to address these problems remains essential.

Last but not least, and probably the most important conclusion of this book, is that more attention needs to be paid to the enduring and dynamic nature of the *levenstestament*. The *levenstestament* is a static document reflecting the adult's wishes and preferences at a given time. But life itself is, of course, dynamic. Values, wishes and preferences that were once important to the adult may change over time. Therefore, to empower adults in the exercise of their legal capacity, the *levenstestament* needs to be more than a one-off episode of making the *levenstestament*. It is essential that the *levenstestament* is seen as the beginning of a process in which the adult makes provisions for a future period of incapacity, rather than the end of it! The drafting of a *levenstestament* should be embedded in and followed by ongoing conversations between the adult and the attorney about the adult's (changing) values, wishes and preferences. The interview study featured in chapter 6 of this book indicates that not all adults and attorneys are aware of the importance of having such conversations or find it difficult to engage in such conversations. Ways in which adults and attorneys can be encouraged to have such conversations therefore need to be explored further and embedded into practice.

8.6 Methodological reflection: strengths and limitations

Like every study, the research featuring in this book has its methodological strengths and limitations. The main strength of this book is the combination of legal-normative, empirical and comparative research. Legal-normative research has been used 1) to examine the human rights framework in which instruments such as the *levenstestament* operate, 2) to examine the current regulatory framework of the *levenstestament,* and 3) to assess the extent to which this regulatory framework is consistent with the human rights framework. The empirical research explored the problems that can occur with the *levenstestament* in practice and examined the expectations and experiences of the two main actors – adults and attorneys – who use the *levenstestament* in practice. An important insight – underscoring the added value of empirical research on this topic – is that to empower adults in the exercise of their legal capacity, there is a need to look beyond the static nature of the *levenstestament* and promote a more enduring process in which both the adult and the attorney discuss the adult's (changing) wishes and preferences. Finally, comparative research on the regulation and application of instruments similar to the levenstestament abroad has been used to draw lessons and best practices from abroad so that the Netherlands does not have to reinvent the wheel when it comes to the *levenstestament.* A further strength of the comparative study is that, besides getting an impression of the *law in the books,* I have also tried to get an impression of the *law in action* in the countries visited through interviews with practitioners. Together, the three strands of research provide a multifaceted answer to the main research question, resulting in recommendations – presented in the next section – on steps the Netherlands can take to comply with international human rights norms and principles and address problems occurring with the *levenstestament* in practice.

In addition to these strengths, there are, of course, also limitations, which are of particular importance when interpreting the empirical findings discussed in this book. These have already been discussed to some extent in the previous chapters. First, as discussed in chapter 5, the findings of the survey study on notaries' experiences with the levenstestament cannot be considered representative, although they do provide insights – particularly the responses to the open-ended questions – into the diverse ways in which notaries work with this instrument in practice. Second, as discussed in chapter 6, while I looked at the expectations of adults who had recently made a *levenstestament,* I could not explore the experiences of adults whose *levenstestament* had recently entered into force. This is especially unfortunate given the focus of this book on how the adult's right to autonomy can be promoted, which of course, also pertains to the adult's participation in research. Finally, a more general reflection not discussed in the previous chapters concerns the methods used to review the available normative and empirical literature in chapters 3, 4 and 6 and the analysis of court cases in chapters 4 and 5. As discussed in the introduction of this book, I used several national and international search engines to locate relevant literature and supplemented this literature using the snowball method. These methods are perfectly acceptable within legal scholarship to identify relevant publications. However, as Laarman notes, legal scholarship is in a transition period.[10] The expectation is that more robust methods, such as a systematic or scoping review of literature and a systematic case-law analysis, will increasingly become the new norm. That the research discussed in this book falls within this transition period becomes apparent not only when looking at the methods used to identify relevant literature but also when looking at the analysis of court cases. Although the search terms and search period were clearly described, the subsequent analysis of court cases could have been approached more systematically, which would have allowed for better replicability of the study.

8.7 Recommendations

This study aimed to examine whether the *levenstestament* is, in theory and practice, suited to the task of empowering adults in the exercise of their legal capacity. Through comparative research, best practices were subsequently sought as solutions to the identified problems in the regulation and application of the Dutch *levenstestament*. Based on the results of this research, in this final section, I shall make a number of recommendations for future legislation and steps that need to be taken by both the Dutch government and professional actors. I will also make suggestions for further research.

8.7.1 Implications for policy and practice

1 A clear distinction between the various options adults have to make provisions for a future period of incapacity

In the absence of a clear, statutory definition of the term *levenstestament*, there are different interpretations in practice as to what this instrument can entail. Although the term *levenstestament* is generally used for a deed in which the adult authorises an attorney to act on his behalf in financial, medical and/or personal matters, the term *levenstestament* is also used to refer to an instrument in which

10. B. Laarman, *Het recht als er iets misgaat in de gezondheidszorg*, The Hague: Boom Juridisch 2022, pp. 296-298.

the adult directs his wishes and preferences to a healthcare provider or the court. Using the same term for these three instruments raises the question of whether adults are sufficiently aware of the options to make provisions for a future period of incapacity. The first recommendation is, therefore, to ensure there is a clear distinction between the various advance decision-making instruments, namely 1) the appointment of an attorney and the wishes, preferences and instructions addressed to this attorney, for which the term *levenstestament* could remain in use; 2) a medical treatment advance directive and 3) an advance directive addressed to the court.

Such a distinction could, for instance, be achieved through legislation. Legislation on medical treatment advance directives is already in place (article 7:450 of the Dutch Civil Code). A clear distinction between medical treatment advance directives and the *levenstestament* – i.e. the appointment of an attorney – could potentially help to reinforce the message that medical treatment advance directives should preferably be drafted in close consultation with healthcare providers (in the context of advance care planning), rather than with notaries. There is currently no specific legislation regulating the appointment of an attorney, but the necessity of such legislation will be addressed in subsequent recommendations. There is currently also no legislation on advance directives addressed to the court in the context of a possible future adult guardianship procedure. As this instrument has not been the primary focus of this book and has only been dealt with in the margins, recommendations on the scope and extent of legislation on this instrument are beyond the scope of this book. Further research is needed to explore the potential of and the need for specific legislation of such advance directives. In this regard, similar instruments abroad can provide a source of inspiration. In Belgium, for example, an advance directive addressed to the court allows adults to specify both their choice of representative if a guardianship measure is deemed necessary and certain wishes, preferences and instructions to be observed by the representative in performing his duties.[11] While in the Netherlands, there are several examples of courts accepting advance directives containing the adult's choice of representative, I have not encountered any examples of advance directives containing wishes, preferences and instructions directed to the court-appointed representative.[12] This is worth exploring, as the recording of wishes and preferences (for example, regarding donations) for the court to take into account

11. Article 496 of the Belgian Civil Code; T. Wuyts, 'Buitengerechtelijke bescherming', in: J.P. Bogaert, K. Rotthier, E. van den Eenden & T. Wuyts, *Handboek bescherming wilsonbekwamen. Zorgvolmacht en bewind na de wet van 21 december 2018*, Mechelen: Wolters Kluwer 2020, §119; See also Germany where adults have the possibility to make a so-called *Betreuungsverfügung* (§1901c of the German Civil Code).

12. See e.g. Court of Appeal Arnhem Leeuwarden 23-11-2017, ECLI:NL:GHARL:2017:10353, §5.7. However, in this case the court found that it could not follow the adult's choice, as set out in the advance directive.

was at the heart of where the idea of the *levenstestament* came from in the first place.[13]

2 *The adoption of a specific legislative framework on the levenstestament in Book 1 of the Dutch Civil Code*

As this study has made clear, the current regulation of the *levenstestament* within the general framework of the existing law on ordinary powers of attorney, service provision agreements and mandate agreements has its limitations. Most importantly, the legislative framework on these legal constructs has not been designed for a setting of future incapacity of the granter and thus does not provide sufficient safeguards that ensure that both the adult's right to autonomy and the right to protection are respected. Consequently, I recommend the introduction of a specific legislative framework for the *levenstestament* that can provide the safeguards that are currently lacking. A positive side-effect of such legislation could be that it would settle the debate in the Netherlands as to the legal basis of the *levenstestament*, confirming that a *levenstestament* cannot be based solely on an ordinary power of attorney, highlighting the importance of an agreement between the adult and the attorney on the tasks the attorney is going to perform for and on behalf of the adult.

As in other countries (e.g. Belgium, Germany and Switzerland), this legislative framework can still take the instruments of the ordinary power of attorney, the service provision agreement and the mandate agreement as the starting point. An ordinary power of attorney, for instance, is an essential element of the *levenstestament* as it grants the attorney the authority to act on behalf of the adult. In other words, I am not in favour of creating an entirely new instrument *sui generis* but rather suggest the regulation of a setting where the instruments mentioned above are used to make provisions for a future period of incapacity. The various elements this legislative framework should include will be addressed in subsequent recommendations. Such legislation should ensure compliance with international human rights norms and principles and address the problems that occur in practice with the application of the *levenstestament*. Moreover, it is important to consider the efforts to regulate the *levenstestament* made by the notariate and by the courts.

Legislation regulating the *levenstestament* should preferably be included in Book 1 of the Dutch Civil Code, which also includes the legislation on the adult guardianship measures. As discussed further under recommendation 3, this would allow the legislator to include specific key provisions relating to the interaction between the *levenstestament* and the adult guardianship measures. In establishing

13. See chapter 3 section 1.

such a legislative framework, it is important that the legislator simultaneously rules out the possibility that adults use the ordinary power of attorney, service provision agreement and mandate agreement to make provision for a future period of incapacity without the newly adopted safeguards. This prohibition should cover both situations where these instruments enter into force upon the incapacity of the adult and situations where these instruments remain in force upon the adult's incapacity.[14] This could be done by including in the new legislation a statutory prohibition for governmental bodies, local authorities, banks and other third parties to accept an enduring document lacking the statutory safeguards.

3 *Legislation adopting a principle of subsidiarity and a duty of care for the court to become aware of the levenstestament*

As this study has made clear, from a human rights perspective, it is important that instruments such as the *levenstestament*, drawn up by adults themselves, are preferred to adult guardianship measures, which should be used as a last resort. Through a so-called principle of subsidiarity, the legislator could oblige the court to refrain from ordering an adult guardianship measure when a well-functioning *levenstestament* is in place. Although a recommendation to this effect has already been included in the so-called *Aanbevelingen Meerderjarigenbewind* (Recommendation Financial Guardianship), a policy document for all courts in the Netherlands, legislation giving more weight to what is now a mere recommendation is important.[15] Such legislation should include an obligation for the court to check in the central register whether the adult has made a *levenstestament* and a duty of care for the court to take steps to become aware of the content of this *levenstestament*.

4 *Legislation on the form of the levenstestament, the suitability of attorneys, donations and mandatory registration*

Legislation providing for safeguards ensuring compliance with international human rights norms and principles is important at different stages of the lifespan of the *levenstestament*. It starts with the phase when adults draft the *levenstestament*. At this point, it is important that legislation ensures a balance between the adult's right to autonomy – both at the time the levenstestament is made and the time it enters into force – and the adult's right to protection against misuse or abuse by the attorney. Balancing the two rights requires legislation on the

14. In Switzerland, for example, adults can stipulate that a so-called *Vollmacht* or *Auftrag* remain in force upon their incapacity, which means that the legal regime on the *Vorsorgeauftrag* can be circumvented.
15. Landelijk Overleg Vakinhoud Civiel en Kanton & Toezicht, *Aanbevelingen Meerderjarigenbewind 2018*, via: https://www.rechtspraak.nl/SiteCollectionDocuments/aanbevelingen-meerderjarigen bewind.pdf (last accessed: 02-06-2021).

form of the *levenstestament*, the suitability of attorneys, donations and mandatory registration. Starting with the legislation on the form of the *levenstestament*, there must be sufficient safeguards ensuring that adults consciously choose to make a *levenstestament*, are aware of its content and are not subject to undue influence. To verify this, the involvement of a third party, such as a notary, is essential. At the same time, however, it is important that the financial barriers for adults to make a *levenstestament* are not too high and that the possibility of making a *levenstestament* is available to everyone. Although adults can currently make a levenstestament in the form of a notarial deed and a private document, the latter form is generally not accepted in practice and, as argued above, not accompanied by sufficient safeguards. Since it can be costly to involve a notary to make a levenstestament, other ways must be considered to ensure that all adults can make a *levenstestament* surrounded by sufficient safeguards. Recommendation 5 will discuss the options in this regard in more detail.

Articles 1:383(5), 1:435(6) and 1:452 of the Dutch Civil Code contain certain restrictions regarding the persons, who can be appointed as full, financial, and personal guardians. For instance, all articles exclude the appointment as guardian of management or staff of an institution where the adult resides. Furthermore, persons who are bankrupt or subject to a debt relief order cannot be appointed financial guardians. As the comparative study in chapter 7 showed, there is a good reason behind such restrictions. For example, the appointment of an institution's management or staff is discouraged in Germany to avoid potential conflicts of interest between the institution and the adult. In addition, much can be said for precluding individuals, who have problems with managing their own financial affairs, from managing someone else's financial affairs. Currently, there are no restrictions in the Netherlands regarding the appointment of such persons as attorneys through a *levenstestament*. Such restrictions are obviously as important for the adult guardianship measures as for the *levenstestament*. I, therefore, recommend the adoption of similar restrictions concerning the appointment of attorneys.

Although restrictions on the choice of attorney and the content of the *levenstestament* are controversial because they limit the adult's right to shape the *levenstestament* as he sees fit, these restrictions can, to a certain extent, be justified from the point of view of protecting the adult's interests. This applies, for example, to the restrictions on performing highly personal acts, such as making a will, for which representation is impossible in the Netherlands. However, this should also apply to donations made by the attorney on behalf of the adult. Safeguards regulating the power to donate on behalf of the adult are necessary to protect the adult against the attorney's potential misuse or abuse of the levenstestament. Based on the comparative study, I recommend a combination of the safeguards adopted abroad, allowing the attorney to continue to make customary donations that fit the adult's gifting patterns, such as birthday presents and annual donations to charities. 'Exceptional' donations should be allowed up to a certain amount when the adult has clearly defined the object, beneficiary and the terms and conditions of the donation. Donations above the set amount should be subject to court approval.

Another safeguard related to the stage in which adults make a *levenstestament* concerns the mandatory registration of the *levenstestament*. A statutory provision obliging adults to register the *levenstestament* and subsequent amendments or terminations is important for two reasons. First, such registration would enable others, primarily the courts, to become aware of the existence of the *levenstestament*, thus ensuring respect for the adult's autonomy. Second, mandatory registration – when it includes the registration of amendments and terminations – provides an important safeguard against abuse, as it allows for verification that the presented *levenstestament* is the most recent version. Of course, this requires more comprehensive access to the register than is currently the case, a problem that is addressed in recommendation 6.

5 *The possibility of making a levenstestament should be promoted for all adults*

As noted in chapter 7, the cost of engaging a notary to make a *levenstestament* can be high.[16] Not everyone will be able to afford this. While adults theoretically have the option of making a privately drafted *levenstestament*, as discussed above, such a *levenstestament* is unlikely to be accepted by third parties and is not surrounded by sufficient safeguards. Therefore, I recommend that the Dutch government considers ways in which all adults are given the opportunity to make a *levenstestament*. In this regard, the Dutch government could start by making available a general form that adults can use to make a *levenstestament*. Such a form – accompanied by legislation allowing for the possibility of making a *levenstestament* in the form of a notarial deed and a private document – would promote the acceptance of the *levenstestament*. Ensuring acceptance is one side of the coin; safeguards are the other. As discussed above, I consider the involvement of a third party essential to verify that the adult consciously chooses to make a *levenstestament*, is aware of its contents and is not subject to undue influence. In chapter 7, I discussed the possibility of entrusting local authorities with the task of verifying these matters. In this regard, I have touched upon the option to extend and strengthen the position of what in the Netherlands is called an 'ambtenaar

16. According to the website degoedkoopstenotaris.nl, the cost of making a *levenstestament* can range from €278-€1250, with an average of €750 in 2022 – https:/www.degoedkoopstenotaris.nl/informatie/kosten-levenstestament?ref=adwords&gclid=EAIaIQobChMIzaWBssTI-gIVxQOLCh2gwgQLEAAYAiAAEgIVBfD_BwE# (last accessed: 13-12-2022).

van de burgerlijke stand' (a civil registry officer).[17] However, at the time of the completion of this book, there is another interesting development. Several political parties are discussing ways of making the services of notaries more accessible, among other, by creating a form of legal aid for adults who cannot afford the services of a notary.[18] A bill titled 'Towards a Social Notariate' has been tabled in Parliament. Although it is currently unknown how these plans will develop further, it seems an appealing initiative in relation to the levenstestament.[19] Not only would this ensure the involvement of a professional who can verify that the adult is consciously making a *levenstestament* and is not unduly influenced, but it would also enable adults to seek the advice of a professional when making their *levenstestament*.

6 *The register should be made more accessible, contain more information and be opened to privately drafted levenstestamenten*

As discussed under recommendation 4, mandatory registration of the *levenstestament* is important for two reasons: to ensure that relevant authorities, such as the court, can take note of the *levenstestament* and to enable verification of the *levenstestament* as a safeguard against abuse. To achieve these two objectives, three additional aspects are important. First, all *levenstestamenten* must be registered. The Dutch Notarial Association (Koninklijke Nederlandse Beroepsorganisatie – KNB) keeps the current register and only provides for the voluntary registration of notarised *levenstestamenten*. This means that, depending on the action taken based on recommendation 5, this register should also be opened for the registration of privately drafted *levenstestamenten*. Second, access to the register by competent authorities and organisations is required. Currently, only notaries have access to the register, but it seems evident that at least courts should also have access to the register. In addition, there is a strong case for allowing banks to access the register so that a power of attorney to act on behalf of the adult in financial matters can be verified. In this regard, organisations such as banks need not be given unrestricted access to the register. To respect the privacy of adults as much as possible, a system similar to that of England and Wales could be set up, whereby banks could obtain basic information from the register after providing the adult's name, date of birth and address. This basic information would include the name of the attorney(s), whether the *levenstestament* concerns financial, medical and/or personal matters, the date the *levenstestament* has been made and whether or not the *levenstestament* has been altered or revoked. The latter requires that such information is also recorded in the register. Currently, only the adult's name, the fact that a *levenstestament* has been made, and the name

17. Section 7.8.
18. https://www.knb.nl/nieuwsberichten/michiel-van-nispen-sp-komt-met-initiatiefnota-voor-sociaal-notariaat (last accessed: 13-12-2022).
19. House of Representatives, *Kamerstukken II* 2022/23, 36248, nr. 2.

of the notary where the *levenstestament* has been made are registered. A third aspect is, therefore, that the scope of information recorded in the register has to be expanded.

7 *Legislation on the rights and duties of attorneys*

Legislation providing for safeguards to ensure compliance with the international human rights norms and principles is important not only when adults draft the levenstestament but also when the attorney acts on behalf of the adult. To ensure that the adult's right to autonomy is respected not only at the time the *levenstestament* is made but also when it is executed and that the adult is adequately protected against misuse and abuse, I recommend the adoption of legalisation providing for certain (minimum) rights and duties for the attorney. Such legislation should include a duty to actively involve the adult in the execution of the *levenstestament* when the adult so wishes and a duty to respect the adult's wishes, preferences and instructions. As in Belgium, such obligations could be made more concrete, for example, by requiring the attorney to consult the adult at regular intervals but at least once a year. Other important rights and duties include a duty for the attorney to keep the adult's assets separate from his own and a duty to render account. Although, as noted under recommendation 4, adults should be able to grant attorneys the authority to donate, I consider additional safeguards necessary when an attorney donates to himself on behalf of the adult. In this and other similar situations where there is a conflict of interests, as in Belgium, a so-called attorney ad hoc could temporarily act instead of the attorney. The adult can appoint the attorney ad hoc in the *levenstestament*, but it seems sensible to also give the court the power to appoint an attorney ad hoc in situations where the adult has not done so himself.

8 *Attorneys should be supported in the exercise of their task*

Regarding the obligation under article 12(3) UNCRPD to support adults in the exercise of their legal capacity, the focus is on support for the adult. However, support for attorneys in the exercise of their task must not be forgotten either. The role of an attorney is not always an easy task to take on, and not all attorneys realise what they agree to when they are asked as an attorney by the adult. Therefore, I recommend that both the Dutch government and the notariate, as the societal actor involved when adults make a levenstestament, consider ways in which attorneys can be supported in the exercise of their task. This begins with creating awareness of the rights and duties of the attorney. As discussed under recommendation 7, the first step is to provide for regulation of the most important rights and duties of the attorney through legislation. The second step is ensuring that attorneys are aware of these rights and duties. This can be done, for instance, by attaching or including information about the attorney's rights and duties in the *levenstestament*. In addition, a Dutch equivalent of the Code of

Practice adopted in England and Wales, which explains the attorney's rights and duties clearly and illuminatingly, is a welcome addition. Finally, notaries have a vital role in encouraging both adults and attorneys to have frequent conversations about the adult's (changing) wishes and preferences and the expectations that both parties have about how the attorney's role should be fulfilled. The latter may help attorneys to prepare beforehand for the task that lies ahead.

9 Legislation introducing a system of supervision with adequate powers to investigate complaints of misuse or abuse of the levenstestament and establishing a direct link between the authority in charge of investigating complaints and the competent authority with the power to intervene

In line with the nature of the levenstestament as an instrument enabling adults to make their own provisions for a future period of incapacity, the responsibility for ensuring supervision is left initially to the adult. The adult can include a form of supervision, such as appointing a supervisory attorney, in the *levenstestament* and would be well advised to do so. However, to address the risks of misuse or abuse of the *levenstestament*, the Dutch government should provide for a system of supervision whereby suspicions of misuse and abuse can be investigated, and a competent authority can intervene when necessary. In this regard, the current Dutch legislation does not appear to be sufficiently tailored to the task of detecting and addressing concerns of abuse or misuse in the context of a *levenstestament*. Veilig Thuis, the organisation responsible in the Netherlands for investigating concerns about domestic violence or child abuse, has limited powers to investigate complaints of misuse or abuse in connection with the *levenstestament*. It cannot, for example, request the attorney to provide information or submit documents such as financial statements. Moreover, there is no direct link between the organisation responsible for investigating complaints, Veilig Thuis, and the authority that is competent to intervene in the Netherlands, the court. Articles 1:379, 1:432 and 1:451 of the Dutch Civil Code do not list Veilig Thuis as one of the applicants that can request an adult guardianship measure. In other words, if Veilig Thuis detects misuse or abuse by the attorney and renders the dismissal of this attorney and a subsequent adult guardianship measure necessary, it can only request such a measure through the public prosecutor's office. This entails a risk of delay in the process of addressing the abuse or misuse by the court. Therefore, it seems prudent to enact legislation giving Veilig Thuis adequate powers to investigate suspicions of misuse and abuse and to include Veilig Thuis in the group of applicants that can request an adult guardianship measure.

10 *Legislation enhancing the powers of the court to intervene in cases of misuse or abuse of the levenstestament and conflicts between attorneys or family members*

In cases where the court finds misuse or abuse of the *levenstestament* by the attorney or where there is a conflict between the attorneys or between the attorneys and other family members, the court currently only has the power to terminate the *levenstestament* partly or entirely and order an adult guardianship measure. However, such termination may not be necessary in all cases. Temporary supervision of the attorney could, for example, eliminate distrust from family members. It is in keeping with the adult's right to autonomy to ensure that the *levenstestament* remains in force as far as possible. I, therefore, recommend adopting legislation enhancing the court's power to intervene. As in Germany, such powers could include appointing a court-appointed supervisor to supervise the attorney's actions. Where possible, alternatives that affect the court's workload as little as possible should be considered. While in Belgium, for example, in family conflicts, the court may try to reconcile both parties through mediation, the Dutch government could also consider ways to promote the development of mediation alternatives by professional actors. In Germany, for example, so-called *Vorsorgemediation* is offered by solicitors. In the Netherlands, inheritance mediation is already offered in practice by notaries and solicitors. So-called *levenstestament* mediation seems an excellent addition to the services of these professionals.

11 *Greater awareness of the dynamic and enduring nature of the levenstestament is needed*

An important, last but certainly not least, recommendation is that more awareness of the dynamic and enduring nature of the *levenstestament* is needed. As discussed in section 8.5, to empower adults in the exercise of their legal capacity, the *levenstestament* needs to be more than a one-off episode. Ongoing conversations between the adult and the attorney about the adult's (changing) values, wishes and preferences are important. Not all adults and attorneys are aware of the importance of having such conversations or find it difficult to engage in such conversations. In other words, initiatives and efforts are needed to raise awareness and encourage conversations about the future. As noted under recommendation 8, notaries can play a vital role in encouraging both adults and attorneys to have frequent conversations about the adult's (changing) values, wishes and preferences, as they are the societal actor involved in the process of drafting a *levenstestament*. Alternatively and in addition, there are several organisations for older persons in the Netherlands that can raise awareness and consider ways to support adults to engage in conversations about the future. Finally, and to end this last recommendation on a personal note, I would argue that there is also a task for us as individuals within society to think about ways in which we can support each other to face the different stages of life.

8.7.2 *Suggestions for future research*

Suggestions for future research can be made at different levels. First, linked to the context in which the *levenstestament* becomes active, certain existential questions require further research. These concern questions such as how the adult's current wishes and preferences should be balanced with the adult's past wishes and preferences as recorded in the *levenstestament*. This is a particularly poignant question when there is a conflict between past and present wishes and preferences. Another existential question concerns the extent to which adults with impaired capacity should be allowed to make so-called 'unwise decisions'. A third and final example concerns the question of when influence by, for example, the attorney should be considered 'undue'. In this research, I could only touch upon these questions; further research is needed to explore these questions more in-depth.

Second, directions for future research can also be identified at the systemic level in the Netherlands. While the debate on the full scope of article 12 UNCRPD is still ongoing; it is clear that article 12 UNCRPD has brought a change of perspective in the sense that the starting point has changed. Instead of an emphasis on the protection of adults with impaired capacity through a restriction of their legal capacity, article 12 UNCRPD makes clear that the focus should be put on measures and instruments that enable adults – through support – to exercise their legal capacity. The Dutch government has acknowledged this change of perspective through its interpretative statement to article 12 UNCRPD, in which it declares that substitute decision-making arrangements – which include a restriction of legal capacity – should only be used when necessary and as a last resort. However, it is unclear whether and to what extent this interpretative statement by the Dutch government is adhered to in practice. As discussed in chapter 2, the impression is that the adult guardianship measures still seem to be the norm rather than the exception. However, further research is needed to assess the extent to which the current Dutch system of adult protection measures and instruments as a whole is in line with international human rights instruments – most notably the UNCRPD – and, in case of non-compliance, to explore ways in which compliance can be ensured. As the above makes clear, such research should look not only at one instrument in particular (as in this study, the *levenstestament*) but also at the system as a whole. At the same time, it is important to focus not only on already existing measures and instruments. In its General Comment on article 12, the Committee on the Rights of Persons with Disabilities has purposely refrained from providing a description of support. Instead, it has confined itself to remarking that support is 'a broad term that encompasses both informal and formal support arrangements, of varying types and intensity'.[20] Here lies a challenge to explore new ways in which adults can be empowered in the exercise of their legal capacity, which are tailored to the adult's (individual) needs.

Third, some suggestions for future research can be identified at the instrumental level. As noted several times, the *levenstestament* is an instrument in development. The number of *levenstestamenten* entering into force is expected to increase in the coming years. In other words, problems with the *levenstestament* to some extent still remain to be seen. This means that research further exploring the prevalence, nature, consequences and response to misuse and abuse of the *levenstestament* will remain important. The same applies to further research on problems with the acceptance of the *levenstestament*, problems resulting from family conflicts and any other issues that might occur in the execution of the *levenstestament*. In addition to research focusing on problems that might arise in the execution of the levenstestament, research on ways to address these problems and research to assess the effectiveness of safeguards and interventions implemented to address these problems will also remain important.

20. United Nations Committee on the Rights of Persons with Disabilities, General Comment No. 1. Article 12: Equal Recognition before the law, 2014, p. 4.

References

M. Adams & J. Griffiths, 'Against "Comparative Method": Explaining Similarities and Differences', in: M. Adams & J. Bomhoff, *Practice and Theory in Comparative Law*, Cambridge: Cambridge University Press 2012, p. 279-301.

C.P.M. Akerboom, J.C.J. Dute, J.K.M. Gevers, H. Nys, H.B. Winter & N.O.M. Woestenburg, *Thematische wetsevaluatie. Wilsonbekwaamheid en vertegenwoordiging*, Den Haag: ZonMw 2011.

J.M. van Anken & R.E. Brinkman, 'Verrassende vragen over het levenstestament: is de opsomming van bevoegdheden (in het vermogens- en bestuursrecht) van de gevolmachtigde zinvol?', *JBN* 2018, no. 6, p. 11-14.

A. Arstein-Kerslake & E. Flynn, 'The General Comment on Article 12 of the Convention on the Rights of Persons with Disabilities: a roadmap for equality before the law', *The International Journal of Human Rights* 2016 vol. 20, no. 4, p. 471-491

A.R. Autar, 'Inleiding' in A.R. Autar, J.P.M. Stubbe and L.C.A. Verstappen (eds.), *Compendium Levenstestament*, The Hague: Sdu uitgevers 2018, p. 19-27.

A.R. Autar & H.C.E. van Dijk, 'Levenstestament', in: A.R. Autar, C.B. Baard, W.D. Kolkman & F. Sonneveldt (eds.), *Compendium Estate Planning*, Den Haag: Sdu 2017.

D. Bagshaw, S. Wendt, L. Zannettino, and V. Adams, 'Financial Abuse of Older People by Family Members: Views and Experiences of Older Australians and their Family Members', *Australian Social Work* 2013 vol. 66, no. 1, p. 86-103.

A. Beckett, K. Leary, L. Cumming & G. Davies, *The Future of Lasting Power of Attorney. A research report for the Office of the Public Guardian*, Beckett et al. 2014.

B. van Beers, 'Staat van verwarring. Over euthanasie, vergevorderde dementie en het recht op leven', Ars Aequi 2020 no. 2, p. 141-149.

C. de Bhailís & E. Flynn, 'Recognising legal capacity: commentary and analysis of Article 12 CRPD', *International Journal of Law in Context* 2017 vol. 13, no. 1, p. 6-21.

J. Bhatt, H. Walton, C.R. Stoner, K. Scior & G. Charlesworth, 'The nature of decision-making in people living with dementia: a systematic review', *Aging & Mental Health* 2020 vol. 24, p. 363-373.

Y. Biderbost, 'Erwachsenenschutz: Subsidiarität über alles?!', in: R. Arnet, P. Eitel, A. Jungo & H.R. Künzle (eds.), *Der Mensch als Mass. Festschrift für Peter Breitschmid*, Zürich: Schulthess Juristische Medien 2019, p. 91-111.

C.C.J.H. Bijleveld, *Research Methods for Empirical Legal Studies: An Introduction*, Den Haag: Eleven International Publishers 2019.

C.C.J.H. Bijleveld, *Methoden en Technieken van Onderzoek in de Criminologie*, Den Haag: Boom Criminologie 2018.

K. Blankman & K. Vermariën, *Conformiteit van het VN-Verdrag inzake de rechten van personen met een handicap en het EVRM met de huidige voorgestelde wetgeving inzake vertegenwoordiging van wilsonbekwame personen in Nederland*, Amsterdam: Vrije Universiteit 2015.

K. Blankman & J. Kaljee, *Het levenstestament in de notariële rechtspraktijk*, Amsterdam: Vrije Universiteit 2013.

K. Blankman, 'Een wettelijke regeling voor het levenstestament?', in: F.W.J.M. Schols & B.C.M. Waaijer, *Het levenstestament. Nader verfijnd*, The Hague: Sdu 2017, p. 45-64

K. Blankman, 'Kroniek bescherming van meerderjarigen', *FJR* 2016 no. 11, p. 274-279.

C. Blankman, 'Guardianship legislation in The Netherlands', in: K. Dayton (ed.), *Comparative Perspectives on Adult Guardianship*, Durham North Carolina: Carolina Academic Press 2014, p. 181-190.

K. Blankman, 'Meerderjarigen- en voogdijbewind', in: F.W.J.M. Schols, K. Blankman & J.B. Vegter, *Bewind en aan bewind verwante vormen*, Den Haag: Koninklijke vermande 2004, p. 73-103.

K. Blankman, 'Guardianship Models in the Netherlands and Western Europe', *International Journal of Law and Psychiatry* 1997 vol. 20, no. 1, p. 47-57.

K. Blankman, *Curatele voor personen met een geestelijke stoornis en bescherming op maat*, Zwolle: Tjeenk Willink 1994.

A.R. Bloembergen & W.A.M. van Schendel, 'Vertegenwoordiging en volmacht', in: J. Hijma, C.C. van Dam, W.A.M. van Schendel & W.L. Valk, *Rechtshandeling en Overeenkomst*, Deventer: Kluwer 2010, p. 78-134.

M.E. de Boer, *Advance directives in dementia care. Perspectives of people with Alzheimer's disease, elderly care physicians and relatives*, 2011.

J.B. Bond, R. Cuddy, G.L. Dixon, K.A. Duncan, and D.L. Smith, 'The Financial Abuse of Mentally Incompetent Older Adults: A Canadian Study', *Journal of Elder Abuse & Neglect* 2000 vol. 11, no. 4, p. 23-38.

A. Bood, 'Boekrecensie. Christiano Vezzoni, The legal status and social practice of treatment directives in the Netherlands', *Tijdschrift voor Gezondheidsrecht* 2006 no. 7, p. 559-562.

K. Booth-Glen, 'Changing Paradigms: Mental Capacity, Legal Capacity, Guardianship, and Beyond', *Columbia Human Rights Law Review* 2012 vol. 44, p.93-169.

H. Bows and B. Penhale, 'Editorial: Elder Abuse and Social Work: Research, Theory and Practice', *British Journal of Social Work* 2018 vol. 48, p. 873-886.

V. Braun & V. Clarke, 'Using thematic analysis in psychology', *Qualitative Research in Psychology* 2006, vol. 3, p. 77-101.

R.E. Brinkman & J.M. van Anken, 'Levensexecuteur/volmacht', in: A.R. Autar, J.P.M. Stubbé & L.C.A. Verstappen (eds.), *Compendium Levenstestament*, Den Haag: SDU 2018, p. 91-131.

A. van den Broeck, 'Inspiratie uit het buitenland voor het Nederlandse levenstestament', in: *Het levenstestament. Nader verfijnd*, Den Haag: Sdu uitgevers 2017, p. 17-43.

A. van den Broeck, *Vermogensbescherming van kwetsbare meerderjarigen via lastgeving*, Antwerpen: Intersentia 2014.

J. Büttner & C. Fountoulakis, 'Der Vorsorgeauftrag: erste Erfahrungen aus der Praxis – Zahlen und Fallbeispiele von den Berner Erwachsenenschutzbehörden', *FamPra* 2015-2, p. 507-535.

A.G. Castermans & H.B. Krans, 'art. 7:416 BW' in: *Tekst en Commentaar Burgerlijk Wetboek*, Deventer: Wolters Kluwer 2021.

J. Chesterman, 'Taking: Control: Putting Older People at the Centre of Elder Abuse Response Strategies', *Australian Social Work* 2016 vol. 69, no. 1, p. 115-124.

K.J. Conrad, M. Iris, J.W. Ridings, K.P. Fairman, A. Rosen, and K.H. Wilber, 'Conceptual Model and Map of Financial Exploitation of Older Adults', *Journal of Elder Abuse and Neglect* 2011 vol. 23, no. 4, p. 304-325.

J. Craigie, M. Bach, S. Gurbai, A. Kanter, S.Y.H. Kim, O. Lewis & G. Morgan, 'Legal capacity, mental capacity and supported decision-making: Report from a panel event', *International Journal of Law and Psychiatry* 2019 vol. 62, p. 160-168.

C. Cross, K. Purser, and T. Cockburn, *Examining Access to Justice for Those with an Enduring Power of Attorney (EPA) Who Are Suffering Financial Abuse*, Crime and Justice Research Centre, Queensland University of Technology 2017, p. 1-61.

G. Daley, M. Gilhooly, K. Gilhooly, P. Harries & M. Levi, *Financial Abuse of People Lacking Mental Capacity. A Report to the Dawes Trust*, Brunel University London 2017.

S. Davidson, P. Rossall, and S. Hart, *Financial Abuse Evidence Review*, Age UK 2015.

T. Denekamp, 'Wilsonbekwaamheid en de bank', in: A.R. Autar, J.P.M. Stubbé & L.C.A. Verstappen (eds.), *Compendium Levenstestament*, Den Haag: SDU 2018, p. 187-197.

T. Denekamp, 'Het levenstestament en de bank', in: F.W.J.M. Schols & B.C.M. Waaijer, *Het levenstestament. Nader verfijnd*, Den Haag: SDU 2017, p. 103-109.

K.H. Dening, M. King, L. Jones, V. Vickestaff & L. Sampson, 'Advance Care Planning in Dementia: Do Family Carers Know the Treatment Preferences of People with Early Dementia?', *PLoS ONE* 2016, vol. 11, no. 7, p. 1-15.

A. Dhanda, 'Legal Capacity in the Disability Rights Convention: Stranglehold of the Past or Lodestar for the Future', *Syracuse Journal of International Law and Commerce* 2007 vol. 34, p. 429-462.

M. Donnelly, 'Deciding in dementia: The possibilities and limits of supported decision-making', *International Journal of Law and Psychiatry*, 2019, vol. 66, p. 1-7.

I. Doron, 'Mental incapacity, guardianship, and the elderly: An exploratory study of Ontario's consent and capacity board', *Canadian Journal of Law and Society* 2003 vol. 18, no. 1, p. 131-145.

I. Doron, 'Elder Guardianship Kaleidoscope – A Comparative Perspective', *International Journal of Law, Policy and the Family* 2002, p. 368-398.

C.G.C. Engelbertink, 'Ontwikkelingen van het levenstestament in de laatste tien jaren' in: F.W.J.M. Schols & B.C.M. Waaijer, *Het levenstestament. Nader verfijnd*, Den Haag: SDU 2017, p. 195-213.

C.G.C. Engelbertink, 'Het levenstestament in de maatschappij', in: K. Blankman & C.G.C. Engelbertink, *Preadvies Notariële bescherming ouderen*, Sdu Uitgevers: Den Haag 2013, p. 59-110.

C.G.C. Engelbertink, 'Het levenstestament, een nieuwe ontwikkeling', *Kwartaalbericht Estateplanning* (*KWEP*) 2013, no. 63.

C.G.C. Engelbertink & A. Hendriks, 'Meer duidelijkheid voor artsen over wensen van de patiënt. Met levenstestament houdt patiënt regie', *Medisch Contact* 2012 vol. 67, no. 1, p. 40-43.

P. Fassbind, 'Vorsorgeauftrag in der Praxis. Risiken und Nebenwirkungen', in: R. Fankhauser, R.E. Reusser & I. Schwander (eds.), *Brennpunkt Familienrecht, Festschrift für Thomas Geiser zum 65. Geburtstag*, Zürich/St. Gallen: Dike Verlag 2017, p. 217-241.

D. Fetherstonhaugh, L. McAuliffe, C. Shanley, M. Bauer & E. Beattie, '"Did I make the right decision?": The difficult and unpredictable journey of being a surrogate decision maker for a person living with dementia', *Dementia* 2019 vol. 18, p. 1601-1614.

D. Fetherstonhaugh, L. McAuliffe, M. Bauer & C. Shanley, 'Decision-making on behalf of people living with dementia: how do surrogate decision-makers decide?', *Journal of Medical Ethics* 2017 vol. 43, p. 35-40.

D. Fetherstonhaugh, L. Tarzia & R. Nay, 'Being central to decision making means I am still here!: the essence of decision making for people with dementia', *Journal of Aging Studies* 2013 vol. 27, p. 143-150.

L. de Feyter & E. de Nolf, 'Enkele praktische aandachtspunten bij de redactie van een zorgvolmacht, in het bijzonder in relatie met een Belgische bancaire instelling', *Vermogensplanning in de praktijk* 2017, no. 3, p. 4-11.

E. Flynn & A. Arstein-Kerslake, 'The Support Model of Legal Capacity: Fact, Fiction, or Fantasy?', *Berkeley Journal of International Law* 2014 vol. 32, no. 1, p. 124-143.

R. Frimston, A. Ruck Keene, C. van Overdijk & A.D. Ward, *The International Protection of Adults*, Oxford: Oxford University Press 2015.

R. Frimston, C. Engelbertink & A. Vrenegoor, 'Netherlands', in: R. Frimston, A. Ruck Keene, C. van Overdijk & A.D. Ward (eds.), *The International Protection of Adults*, Oxford – New York: Oxford University Press 2015, p. 568-574.

W. Fuchs, *Systems of advocacies for the elderly in a comparative perspective*, Presentation at the Advocacies for frail and incompetent elderly in Europe (ADEL) project final conference on 24 September 2010 in Berlin.

T. Gergel, 'The 'Mental Health and Justice Project': Using interdisciplinarity to move beyond impasse in disability rights' *International Journal of Law and Psychiatry* 2020 vol. 71, p. 1-4.

P. Gooding, 'Navigating the 'Flashing Amber Lights' of the Right to Legal Capacity in the United Nations Convention on the Rights of Persons with Disabilities: Responding to Major Concerns', *Human Rights Law Review* 2015, vol. 15, p. 45-71.

R.M. Gordon, 'Material Abuse and Powers of Attorney in Canada: A Preliminary Examination', *Journal of Elder Abuse and Neglect* 1993 vol. 4, no. 1-2, p. 173-193.

T.L. Hafemeister, 'Financial Abuse of the Elderly in Domestic Settings', in: R.J. Bonnie and R.B. Wallace (eds.), *Elder Mistreatment: Abuse, Neglect, and Exploitation in Aging America*, National Academies Press 2003, p. 382-445.

H. Hausheer, T. Geiser & R.E. Aebi-Müller, *Das Familienrecht des Schweizerischen Zivilgesetzbuches*, Bern: Stämpfli Verlag 2018.

A.C. Hendriks, 'Schriftelijk euthanasieverzoek bij vergevorderde dementie als basis. De Hoge Raad schept duidelijkheid, althans deels', *Themis* 2020 no. 3, p. 123-133.

A.C. Hendriks, 'Het levenstestament in de gezondheidszorg', in: A.R. Autar, J.P.M. Stubbé & L.C.A. Verstappen (eds.), *Compendium Levenstestament*, Den Haag: SDU 2018, pp. 149-168.

C.M.P.M. Hertogh, 'The misleading simplicity of advance directives', *International Psychogeriatrics* 2011 vol. 23, no. 4, p. 511-515.

M. van Hoecke, 'Methodology of Comparative Legal Research', *Law and Method* 2015, p. 1-35.

W. van Hoeflaken, 'Voor het behoud van vertrouwen', *Notariaat Magazine* 2021 no. 4.

M. Hopf, 'Neues Erwachsenenschutzrecht und Vorsorgeauftrag. Regelungsmöglichkeiten und Wirkungen für die Vorsorgebeauftragten', *Der Schweizer Treuhänder* 2013 no. 3, p. 145-150.

S. Hotz, 'Zum Selbstbestimmungsrecht des Vorsorgenden de lege lata und de lege ferenda – Die Vorsorgevollmacht de lege ferenda', *Zeitschrift für Kindes- und Erwachsenenschutz* 2011, p. 102-115.

House of Lords, Select Committee on the Mental Capacity Act 2005, *Mental Capacity Act 2005: post-legislative scrutiny*, 2014.

R. Houwing, 'Rekening en verantwoording en de volmacht', *ftV* 2010 no. 10.

S. Hrubesch-Millauer & M. Jaussi, 'Vorsorgeauftrag – Pflichten und Haftung des Beauftragten', *Plädoyer* 2013, no. 1, p. 33-39.

A. Jungo, 'Art. 360', in: in: T. Geiser & C. Fountoulakis (eds.), *Basler Kommentar. Zivilgesetzbuch I*, Basel: Helbing Lichtenhahn Verlag 2018, p. 2109-2129.

A. Jungo, 'Art. 363', in: in: T. Geiser & C. Fountoulakis (eds.), *Basler Kommentar. Zivilgesetzbuch I*, Basel: Helbing Lichtenhahn Verlag 2018, p. 2137-2150.

A. Jungo, 'Art. 368', in: in: T. Geiser & C. Fountoulakis (eds.), *Basler Kommentar. Zivilgesetzbuch I*, Basel: Helbing Lichtenhahn Verlag 2018, p. 2170-2173.

M. Kaser, *Römisches Privatrecht. Ein Studienbuch*. 15 Auflage, München: C.H. Beck'sche Verlagsbuchhandlung 1989.

R. Köller & D. Engels, *Rechtlichen Betreuung in Deutschland. Evaluation des Zweiten Betreuungsrechtsänderungsgesetzes*, Köln: Bundesanzeiger Verlag 2009.

S.C.J.J. Kortmann, *Mr. C. Assers Handleiding tot de beoefening van het Nederlands Burgerlijk Recht. 3. Deel III. Vermogensrecht algemeen. Volmacht en vertegenwoordiging*, Deventer: Wolters Kluwer 2017.

S.C.J.J. Kortmann, 'Rekening en verantwoording door de mantelzorger', in: F.W.J.M. Schols & B.C.M. Waaijer, *Het levenstestament. Nader verfijnd*, Den Haag: SDU 2017, p. 139-151.

H.R.Th. Kröber & J. Zomerlaag, 'Mensen met een verstandelijke beperking betrekken bij onderzoek. Een kritisch emancipatoir perspectief', in: J. Evers (ed.), *Kwalitatief interviewen: kunst én kunde*, Den Haag: Uitgeverij Lemma 2007, p. 215-224.

J. Kronenburg-de Jonge, 'Het ene levenstestament is het andere niet', *FTV* 2016 no. 4.

D. Kurze, 'Tätigkeit des Vorsorgebevollmächtigten aus anwaltlicher Sicht', *BtPrax* 2018, no. 2, p. 47-53.

D. Kurze, *Vorsorgerecht. Vollmacht, Patientenverfügung, lebzeitige Verfügungen*, München: C.H. Beck 2017.

B. Laarman, *Het recht als er iets misgaat in de gezondheidszorg*, The Hague: Boom Juridisch 2022.

A.H. Lamers, *Opdracht, lastgeving en bemiddeling*, Zutphen: Uitgeverij Paris 2012.

J. Langan and R. Means, 'Financial Management and Elderly People with Dementia in the UK: As Much a Question of Confusion as Abuse?', *Ageing and Society* 1996 vol. 16, p. 287-314.

E. Langenegger, 'Art. 360', in: D. Rosch, A. Büchler & D. Jakob (eds.), *Erwachsenenschutzrecht. Einführung und Kommentar zu Art. 360ff. ZGB und VBVV*, Basel: Helbing Lichtenhahn Verlag 2015, p. 43-58.

The Law Commission of England and Wales, *The Incapacitated Principal* (Law Com. No. 122, 1983).

The Law Commission of New Zealand, *Misuse of Enduring Powers of Attorney* (Law Com. No. 40, 2000).

H.J.J. Leenen, J. Legemaate, J. Dute, E.J.C. de Jong, M.E. Gelpke, J.K.M. Gevers en G.R.J. de Groot, *Handboek Gezondheidsrecht*, Den Haag: Boom Uitgevers 2020,

J. Legemaate, 'Het levenstestament en zorgbeslissingen', in: F.W.J.M. Schols & B.C.M. Waaijer, *Het levenstestament. Nader verfijnd*, Den Haag: SDU 2017, p. 83-95.

V. Lipp, *Going Private: "Vorsorgevollmacht" as an Alternative to Legal Guardianship for Adults*, revised version (11 January 2016) of a lecture held at the University of Leuven on 10. February 2015, via: https://www.bgtev.de/fileadmin/Mediendatenbank/Themen/Einzelbeitraege/Lipp/Lipp_Vorsolgevollmacht_as_an_Alternative.pdf (last accessed: 01-05-2022).

V. Lipp, 'Germany', in: R. Frimston, A. Ruck Keene, C. van Overdijk & A. Ward, *The international protection of adults*, Oxford: Oxford University Press 2015, p. 375-385.

V. Lipp, 'Instrumente privater Vorsorge', in: V. Lipp, *Handbuch der Vorsorgeverfügungen*, München: Verlag Franz Vahlen 2009, p. 51-60.

G. Livingston, G. Leavey, M. Manela, D. Livingston, G. Rait, E. Sampson, S. Bavishi, K. Shahriyarmolki & C. Cooper, 'Making decisions for people with dementia who lack capacity: a qualitative study of family carers in UK', *BMJ* 2010, vol. 18.

K. Lord, G. Livingston & C. Cooper, 'A systematic review of barriers and facilitators to and interventions for proxy decision-making by family carers of people with dementia', *International Psychogeriatrics* 2015 vol. 27, p. 1301-1312.

D. Lush, 'Adult Guardianship and Powers of Attorney in England and Wales', in: L. Ho & R. Lee, *Special Needs Financial Planning. A Comparative Perspective*, Cambridge University Press 2019, p. 117-148.

D. Lush & C. Bielanska, Cretney & Lush on Lasting and Enduring Powers of Attorney, London: LexisNexis 2017.

D. Lush, 'The civil law and the common law' in: R. Frimston, A. Ruck Keene, C. van Overdijk & A.D. Ward, *The International Protection of Adults*, Oxford: Oxford University Press 2015, p. 37-52.

J. Manthorpe, K. Samsi, and J. Rapaport, 'Responding to the Financial Abuse of People with Dementia: A Qualitative Study of Safeguarding Experiences in England', *International Psychogeriatrics* 2012 vol. 24, no. 9, p. 1454-1464.

W. Martin, S. Michalowski, J. Stavert, A. Ward, A. Ruck Keene, C. Caughey, A. Hempsey & R. McGregor, *The Essex Autonomy Project. Three Jurisdictions Report. Towards Compliance with CRPD Art. 12 in Capacity/Incapacity legislation across the UK*, Essex: University of Essex 2016.

F. Matthews, 'Doctors, Elder Abuse, and Enduring Powers of Attorney', *The New Zealand Medical Journal* 2004 vol. 117, p. 1-8.

A. McCawley, C. Tilse, J. Wilson, L. Rosenman, and D. Setterlund 'Access to Assets: Older People with Impaired Capacity and Financial Abuse', *The Journal of Adult Protection* 2006 vol. 8, no. 1, p. 20-32.

T. Mellema-Kranenburg, 'Hoe ver gaat de verplichting tot rekening en verantwoording', *JBN* 2016 no. 2.

L.M. Miller, C.J. Whitlatch & K.S. Lyons, 'Shared decision-making in dementia: A review of patient and family carer involvement', *Dementia* 2016 vol. 15, p. 1141-1157.

L.K. Mitchell, N.A. Pachana, J. Wilson, K. Vearncombe, B. Massavelli, G.J. Byrne, and C. Tilse, 'Promoting the Use of Enduring Powers of Attorney in Older Adults: A Literature Review', *Australasian Journal on Ageing* 2014 vol. 33, no. 1, p. 2-7.

A. van Moerkercke, 'De zorgvolmacht: hoe gedetailleerd moet dat zijn?', *Vermogensplanning in de praktijk* 2019, no. 3, p. 14-19.

S. Mos-Van Gool, 'Het levenstestament in de praktijk', in: A.R. Autar, J.P.M. Stubbé & L.C.A. Verstappen, *Compendium Levenstestament*, Sdu Uitgevers: Den Haag 2021, p. 79-92.

M.J. van Mourik, 'Rechtsvragenrubriek', *WPNR* 2006 no. 6688, p. 815-816.

G. Müller & T. Renner, *Betreuungsrecht und Vorsorgeverfügungen in der Praxis*, München: Carl Heymanns Verlag 2018.

E. Nyst, 'Artsen en notarissen stemmen werk rond levenseinde af', *Medisch Contact* 2017 no. 47, p. 10-11.

J.H. Oomen, 'Reactie op 'Het levenstestament en zorgbeslissingen' van prof. mr. J. Legemaate', in: F.W.J.M. Schols & B.C.M. Waaijer, *Het levenstestament. Nader verfijnd*, Den Haag: SDU 2017, p. 97-100.

K. Purser, T. Cockburn, and E. Ulrick, 'Examining Access to Formal Justice Mechanisms for Vulnerable People in the Context of Enduring Powers of Attorney', *Elder Law Review* 2019 vol. 12, no. 1, p. 1-32.

K. Purser, T. Cockburn, C. Cross, and H. Jacmon, 'Alleged Financial Abuse of Those under an Enduring Power of Attorney: An Exploratory Study', *British Journal of Social Work* 2018 vol. 48, p. 887-905.

D.J. Rabiner, J. O'Keeffe, and D. Brown, 'A Conceptual Framework of Financial Exploitation of Older Persons', *Journal of Elder Abuse and Neglect* 2005 vol. 16, no. 2, p. 53-73.

R. Regmi, J. Naidoo & P. Pilkington, 'Understanding the Processes of Translation and Transliteration in Qualitative Research', *International Journal of Qualitative Methods* 2010 vol. 9, p. 16-26.

N.M. Ries, 'Enduring Powers of Attorney and Financial Exploitation of Older People: A Conceptual Analysis and Strategies for Prevention', *Journal of Aging & Social Policy* 2019, p. 1-18.

N. Rozemond, 'Een mensenrechtelijke interpretatie van de uitspraken van de Hoge Raad over euthanasie bij mensen met dementie', *Themis* 2021 no. 4, p. 149-158.

A. Ruck Keene & A.D. Ward, 'With and Without "Best Interests": the Mental Capacity Act 2005, the Adults with Incapacity (Scotland) Act 2000 and Constructing Decisions', *International Journal of Mental health and Capacity Law* 2016, p. 17-37.

A. Ruck Keene, 'Fundamental Definitions' in: R. Frimston, A. Ruck Keene, C. van Overdijk & A.D. Ward, *The International Protection of Adults*, Oxford: Oxford University Press 2015, p. 3-7.

E. Ryrstedt, 'Dementia and autonomy' in E. Numhauser-Henning, *Elder Law. Evolving European Perspectives*, Cheltenham: Edward Elgar Publishing 2017, p. 358-378.

K. Samsi & J. Manthorpe, 'Everyday decision-making in dementia: findings from a longitudinal interview study of people with dementia and family carers', *Int Psychogeriatr* 2013 vol. 25, p. 949-961.

K. Samsi and J. Manthorpe, ''I Live for Today': A Qualitative Study Investigating Older People's Attitudes to Advance Planning', *Health and Social Care in the Community* 2011 vol 19, no. 1, p. 52-59.

A.C. van Schaick, *Volmacht*, Deventer: Kluwer 2011.

D. Scheers, 'Rechtsplegingen', in: P. Senaeve, F. Swennen & G. Verschelden (eds.), *Meerderjarige beschermde personen*, Brugge: Die Keure 2014, p. 213-276.

J.M. Scherpe, 'A Comparative Overview of the Treatment of Non-Matrimonial Assets, Indexation and Value Increases', *Child & Family Law Quarterly* 2013 vol. 25, no. 1, p. 61-79.

J. Schmid, 'Vollmachten und Vorsorgeauftrag', in: *Stiftung Schweizerisches Notariat, Nachlassplanung und Nachlassteilung*, Zürich: Schultess Juristische Medien 2014, p. 259-300.

B.M.E.M. Schols, 'Het levenstestament 'über den Tod hinaus'', in: F.W.J.M. Schols & B.C.M. Waaijer, *Het levenstestament. Nader verfijnd*, Den Haag: SDU 2017, p. 121-137.

L. Series, 'Relationships, autonomy and legal capacity: Mental capacity and support paradigms', *International Journal of Law and Psychiatry* 2015 vol. 40, p. 80-91.

D. Setterlund, C. Tilse, J. Wilson, A. McCawley, and L. Rosenman, 'Understanding Financial Elder Abuse in Families: The Potential of Routine Activities Theory', *Ageing and Society* 2007 vol. 27, no. 4, p 599-614.

D. Setterlund, C. Tilse, and J. Wilson, 'Older People and Substitute Decision-Making Legislation: Limits to Informed Choice', *Australasian Journal on Ageing* 2002 vol. 21, no. 3, p. 128-133.

V. Shepherd, R. Griffith, K. Hood, M. Sheehan & F. Wood, 'There's more to life than money and health: family caregivers' views on the role of Power of Attorney in proxy decisions about research participation for people living with dementia', *Dementia* 2021 vol. 20, p. 308-325.

B. Sluijters & M.C.I.H. Biesaart, *De geneeskundige behandelingsovereenkomst*, Deventer: Kluwer 2005.

K.L. Smebye, M. Kirkevold & K. Engedal, 'How do persons with dementia participate in decision making related to health and daily care? A multi-case study', *BMC Health Services Research* 2012 vol. 12.

J. Spalckhaver, 'Die Vorsorgevollmacht und das ihr zugrunde liegende Rechtsverhältnis als umfassende Vorsorgeregelung', in: V. Lipp, *Handbuch der Vorsorgeverfügungen*, München: Verlag Franz Vahlen 2009, p. 95-105.

C. Spierings, *De eenzijdigde rechtshandeling*, Nijmegen: Wolters Kluwer 2016.

J. aan de Stegge, 'Toezicht in het levenstestament. Transparantie haalt wantrouwen weg', *Notariaat Magazine* 2018 no. 5, p. 20-21.

J. aan de Stegge, 'Vernieuwde medische wilsverklaring. Lever maatwerk rondom iemands sterfbed', *Notariaat Magazine* 2017 no. 8, p. 20-21.

J. aan de Stegge, 'Herziene model levenstestament. Zet niet de bank of notaris centraal, aar de cliënt', *Notariaat Magazine* 2015 no. 4, p. 10-11.

A. Stanyer, *Financial abuse of older clients: law, practice and prevention*, London: Bloomsbury 2017.

A.H.N. Stollenwerck & R.C.E. van der Heide-van IJzinga Veenstra, 'Het levenstestament, een inleiding', *Fiscaal Tijdschrift Vermogen* 2010, no. 10.

E.Ph.R. Sutorius & D.J. Jansen, 'De juridische status van het levenstestament', *Ars Aequi* 1991, p. 990-997.

F. Swennen, 'De meerderjarige beschermde personen (Deel II), *Rechtskundig Weekblad* 2013 vol. 15, p. 602-623.

J.M. Tempelaar, 'Bewind en volmacht. Water en vuur?', *WPNR* 2013 no. 6987, p. 687-690.

J.M. Tempelaar, 'Volmacht en rekening en verantwoording', *WPNR* 2010 no. 6838, p. 278-283.

J. Thurston, *A Practitioner's Guide to Powers of Attorney*, London: Bloomsbury 2015.

C. Tilse, J. Wilson, B. White, L. Wilmott, and A. McCawley, 'Enduring Powers of Attorney: Promoting Attorneys' Accountability as Substitute Decision Makers', *Australasian Journal on Ageing* 2014 vol. 33, no. 3, p. 193-197.

C. Tilse, D. Setterlund, J. Wilson, and L. Rosenman, 'Managing the Financial Assets of Older People: Balancing Independence and Protection', *The British Journal of Social Work* 2007 vol. 37, no. 3, p. 565-572.

C. Tilse, D. Setterlund, J. Wilson, and L. Rosenman, 'Minding the Money: A Growing Responsibility for Informal Carers', *Ageing and Society* 2005 vol. 25, p. 215-227.

C. Tilse, J. Wilson, D. Setterlund, and L. Rosenman, 'Older People's Assets: A Contested Site', *Australasian Journal on Ageing* 2005 vol. 24, p. 51-56.

T.F.E. Tjong Tjin Tai, *Mr. C. Assers Handleiding tot de beoefening van het Nederlands Burgerlijk Recht. 7. Bijzondere overeenkomsten. Deel IV. Opdracht, incl. de geneeskundige behandelingsovereenkomst en de reisovereenkomst*, Deventer: Wolters Kluwer 2018.

L.C.A. Verstappen, 'Het levenstestament: een korte analyse van veel gebruikte modellen', in: F.W.J.M. Schols & B.C.M. Waaijer (eds.), *Het levenstestament. Nader verfijnd*, Sdu: The Hague 2017, p. 153-167.

L.C.A. Verstappen, 'Het levenstestament: volmacht of toch opdracht/lastgeving?', *WPNR* 2013 no. 6993, p. 931-932.

J. Verstraete, 'Krijtlijnen voor de zorgvolmacht', in: C. de Wulf, M. op de Beeck & J. Verstraete (eds.), *Liber Amicorum Aloïs Van den Bossche*, Brugge: die Keure 2019, p. 163-193.

C. Vezzoni, *The legal status and social practice of treatment directives in the Netherlands*, dissertation RUG, 2005.

J. Visser, 'Professionals leggen Euthanasiewet verschillend uit. Dement met een wilsverklaring, en dan?', *Medisch Contact* 2012 vol 67, no. 10, p. 582-58.

P. Vlaardingerbroek, K. Blankman, A.P. van der Linden, E.C.C. Punselie & W.M. Schrama, *Het hedendaagse personen- en familierecht*, Deventer: Wolters Kluwer 2017.

K. De Vries & J. Drury-Ruddlesden, 'Advance care planning for people with dementia: Ordinary everyday conversations', *Dementia* 2019 vol. 18, p. 3023-3035.

C. Walser Kessel, 'Der Vorsorgeauftrag. Einige praktische Überlegungen', *Der Schweizer Treuhänder* 2015 no. 5, p. 355-358.

A.D. Ward, *Enabling citizens to plan for incapacity. A review of follow-up action taken by member states of the Council of Europe to Recommendation CM/Rec(2009)11 on principles concerning continuing powers of attorney and advance directives for incapacity*, Strasbourg: Council of Europe 2018.

C. Ward, *Lasting Powers of Attorney. A Practical Guide*, London: The Law Society 2016.

P. Webb, G. Davidson, R. Edge, D. Falls, F. Keenan, B. Kelly, A. McLaughlin, L. Montgomery, C. Mulvenna, B. Norris, A. Owens, and R.S. Irvine, 'Key Components of Supporting and Assessing Decision Making Ability', *International Journal of Law and Psychiatry* 2020 vol. 72, p. 1-9.

H.J. Weijers, 'Het levenstestament en het afleggen van rekening en verantwoording', *FTV* 2019.

J. Wilson, C. Tilse, D. Setterlund, and L. Rosenman, 'Older People and Their Assets: A Range of Roles and Issues for Social Workers', *Australian Social Work* 2009 vol. 62, no. 2, p. 155-167.

T. Wuyts, 'Buitengerechtelijke bescherming', in: J.P. Bogaert, K. Rotthier, E. van den Eenden & T. Wuyts, *Handboek bescherming wilsonbekwamen. Zorgvolmacht en bewind na de wet van 21 december 2018*, Mechelen: Wolters Kluwer 2020.

T. Wuyts, 'Zorgvolmachten: een zegen of een vloek?', in: W. Pintens & C. Declerck (eds.), *Patrimonium 2020*, Brugge: Die Keure 2020, p. 235-323.

T. Wuyts (c), 'Een kritische doorlichting van (modellen inzake) zorgvolmachten', in: G. Verschelden (ed.), *Rechtskroniek van het Notariaat*, Herentals: Knops Publishing 2020, p. 91-131.

A. Wylleman, 'Buitengerechtelijke bescherming', in: P. Senaeve, F. Swennen & G. Verschelden (eds.), *Meerderjarige beschermde personen*, Brugge: Die Keure 2014, p. 23-48.

W. Zimmerman, *Vorsorgevollmacht, Betreuungsverfügung, Patientenverfügung für die Beratungspraxis*, Berlin: Erich Schmidt Verlag 2017.

Appendix 1: Questionnaire 'Experiences of notaries with the levenstestament'

Survey study 'Experiences of notaries with the levenstestament'

Questionnaire

In May 2018, all members of the Dutch Notarial Association (KNB) received an email with the invitation to participate in the survey study 'Experiences of notaries with the levenstestament'. The questionnaire (in Dutch) with a translation into English is included in this appendix.

Algemene vragen / *General questions:*

1. Wat is het inwonertal van de gemeente waar u werkzaam bent?
a) Minder dan 10.000
b) 10.000 tot 40.000
c) 40.000 tot 80.000
d) 80.000 tot en met 125.000
e) Meer dan 125.000

What is the population of the municipality where you work?
a) *Less than 10.000*
b) *10.000 to 40.000*
c) *40.000 to 80.000*
d) *80.000 to 125.000*
e) *More than 125.000*

2. In welke regio bevindt zich het kantoor waar u werkzaam bent?
a) West (Noord-Holland, Zuid-Holland)
b) Noord (Groningen, Friesland, Drenthe)
c) Zuid (Zeeland, Noord-Brabant, Limburg)
d) Oost (Overijssel, Gelderland)
e) Midden (Flevoland, Utrecht)

In which region is the office where you work located?
a) *West (North Holland, South Holland)*
b) *North (Groningen, Friesland, Drenthe)*
c) *South (Zeeland, North Brabant, Limburg)*
d) *East (Overijssel, Gelderland)*
e) *Central (Flevoland, Utrecht)*

3. Hoeveel (kandidaat-)notarissen zijn er werkzaam op uw kantoor? [1]
a) Eenmanskantoor
b) 2 tot 5 (kandidaat-)notarissen
c) 6 tot 20 (kandidaat-)notarissen
d) 21 of meer (kandidaat-)notarissen

How many (candidate) notaries work at your firm?
a) *One-man office*
b) *2 to 5 (candidate) notaries*
c) *6 to 20 (candidate) notaries*
d) *21 or more (candidate) notaries*

4. Welke rol vervult u op kantoor?
a) Notaris
b) Kandidaat-notaris
c) Notarisklerk, notarieel medewerker
d) Secretaresse

What role do you perform in the office?
a) *Notary*
b) *Candidate notary*
c) *Notary clerk, notarial assistant*
d) *Secretary*

5. Biedt uw kantoor het product levenstestament aan?
a) Ja
b) Nee, want ....

Does your firm offer clients the possibility of drawing up a levenstestament?
a) *Yes*
b) *No, because ....*

1. Explanation of the term candidate notary: A candidate notary – similar to a notary – is authorised to advise clients and draw up deeds. Unlike a notary, however, a candidate notaries is not authorised to execute deeds unless he is appointed as deputy to the notary.

6. Wat kan op uw kantoor in een levenstestament worden vastgelegd?

a) Zaken van vermogensrechtelijke en persoonlijke aard (voorbeelden zaken van persoonlijke aard: wensen m.b.t. huisdieren of de inrichting van de kamer in het verzorgingstehuis)
b) Zaken van medische aard
c) Beide

What can be recorded in a levenstestament at your office?

a) *Financial and personal matters (examples of personal matters: wishes regarding pets or the layout of the room in the nursing home)*
b) *Medical matters*
c) *Both*

7. Hoeveel akten worden er bij benadering jaarlijks op uw kantoor gepasseerd?

Open veld

Toelichting vraag: Uw schatting mag bij benadering zijn. Graag in uw antwoord aangeven hoe zeker u bent van deze schatting.

Approximately how many deeds are executed at your office each year?

Open field

Clarification: Your estimate may be approximate. Please indicate in your answer how confident you are of this estimate.

8. Hoeveel akten op het rechtsgebied *familierecht* worden er bij benadering jaarlijks op uw kantoor gepasseerd?

Open veld

Toelichting vraag: Uw schatting mag bij benadering zijn. Graag in uw antwoord aangeven hoe zeker u bent van deze schatting.

Approximately how many deeds in the field of family law are executed at your office each year?

Open field

Clarification: Your estimate may be approximate. Please indicate in your answer how certain you are of this estimate.

9. Welk deel beslaan de levenstestamentakten ten opzichte van het totale aantal gepasseerde akten *familierecht*?
a) Minder dan 10%
b) 10 tot 25%
c) 25 tot 50%
d) 50% of meer
e) Weet ik niet

What proportion do levenstestamenten account for compared to the total number of family law deeds executed?
a) *Less than 10%*
b) *10 to 25%*
c) *25 to 50%*
d) *50% or more*
e) *I do not know*

Model en inhoud levenstestament / *Model and contents of the levenstestament*

10. Met welk model levenstestament werkt u?
a) KNB-model levenstestament
b) Model Netwerknotarissen
c) EPN-model levenstestament
d) Aanpassing van het model KNB-levenstestament
e) Aanpassing van het model Netwerknotarissen
f) Aanpassing van het model EPN-levenstestament
g) Eigen model

Which model/template of the levenstestament do you work with?
a) *KNB template levenstestament*
b) *Netwerk Notarissen template*
c) *EPN template levenstestament*
d) *Adaptation of the KNB template levenstestament*
e) *Adaptation of the Netwerk Notarissen template*
f) *Adaptation of the EPN template levenstestament*
g) *I use my own template*

11. Voor zover u kunt nagaan, wat is voor uw cliënten de belangrijkste reden om een levenstestament af te sluiten?
a) Het regelen van zaken van vermogensrechtelijke aard
b) Het regelen van zaken van persoonlijke aard (bijv. wensen m.b.t. huisdieren of de inrichting van de kamer in het verzorgingstehuis)

c) Het regelen van zaken van medische aard (bijv. euthanasieverklaring of behandelverbod)
d) Het regelen van zaken van zowel vermogensrechtelijke als van persoonlijke aard
e) Het regelen van zaken van zowel vermogensrechtelijke, als van persoonlijke en medische aard

As far as you can tell, what is the main reason for your clients to make a levenstestament?
a) *To arrange financial matters*
b) *To arrange personal matters (e.g. wishes concerning pets or the layout of a room in a nursing home)*
c) *To arrange medical matters (e.g. euthanasia or non-treatment directive)*
d) *To arrange both financial and personal matters*
e) *To arrange financial, personal and medical matters*

12. Wat is bij uw kantoor de gangbare procedure voor het vastleggen van zaken van medische aard? Beschrijf zo nauwkeurig mogelijk, geef evt. een voorbeeld.

Open veld

Toelichting bij de vraag: Als op uw kantoor de mogelijkheid om zaken van medische aard in het levenstestament te regelen **niet** wordt geboden, wat doet u dan?

What is the usual procedure at your firm for recording medical matters? Please describe as accurately as possible, giving an example if necessary.

Open field

*Clarification: At your firm, if the possibility of recording matters of a medical nature in the levenstestament is **not** offered, what do you do?*

13a. Biedt uw kantoor cliënten de mogelijkheid om u of een van uw medewerkers als gevolmachtigde te benoemen?
a) Ja
b) Nee

b. Zo ja, in hoeveel procent van de gevallen gebeurt dit?
a) Minder dan 10%
b) 10 tot 25%
c) 25 tot 50%
d) 50% of meer

a. Does your firm offer clients the option of appointing you or one of your employees as a proxy?

a) *Yes*
b) *No*

b. If yes, in what percentage of cases does this happen?

a) *Less than 10%*
b) *10 to 25%*
c) *25 to 50%*
d) *50% or more*

14. Hoe is in de meeste gevallen de inwerkingtreding van de volmacht in het levenstestament geregeld?

a) De volmacht treedt direct in werking
b) De volmacht treedt in werking na een medische verklaring waarin wilsonbekwaamheid wordt vastgesteld
c) De volmacht treedt gedeeltelijk direct in werking (bijv. voor alledaagse financiële beslissingen) en treedt volledig in werking na een medische verklaring waarin wilsonbekwaamheid wordt vastgesteld
d) Anders, namelijk...

In most cases, how is entry into force of the levenstestament regulated?

(a) *The power of attorney takes effect immediately*
(b) *The power of attorney takes effect following a medical certificate confirming the adult's incapacity*
(c) *The power of attorney takes effect partially immediately (e.g. for day-to-day financial decisions) and takes effect fully after a medical certificate confirming the adult's incapacity*
(d) *Other, namely ....*

15. Kunt u uitleggen wat de procedure is die uw kantoor hanteert om eventuele wilsonbekwaamheid vast te stellen?

Open veld

Can you explain the procedure used by your office to determine the adult's capacity to make a levenstestament?

Open field

Toezicht en controle / *Supervision and monitoring*

16. Wanneer is volgens u een vorm van toezicht geïndiceerd?
a) Standaard
b) Als de volmachtgever erom vraagt
c) Als de familie erom vraagt
d) Als er gevoeligheden zijn
e) Nooit

In your opinion, when is a form of supervision indicated?
a) *By default*
b) *When the adult requests it*
c) *If the family requests it*
d) *If there are certain sensitivities*
e) *Never*

17. Welke vorm van toezicht of controle wordt bij uw kantoor het meeste ingebouwd?
a) Verplichte adviesaanvraag bij belangrijke handelingen
b) Rekening/verantwoording aan een externe toezichthouder
c) Meerdere gevolmachtigden, die bij alle handelingen samen bevoegd zijn
d) Meerdere gevolmachtigden, die alleen bij belangrijke handelingen samen bevoegd zijn
e) Anders, namelijk...

Which form of supervision or monitoring is most commonly incorporated in the levenstestament at your firm?
(a) *Mandatory request for advice on significant actions*
(b) *Rendering account to an external supervisor*
c) *Multiple attorneys, with joint authority in all acts*
d) *Multiple attorneys, authorised together only for important acts*
e) *Other, namely....*

18a. Biedt uw kantoor cliënten de mogelijkheid om u of een van uw medewerkers als toezichthouder te benoemen?
a) Ja
b) Nee

b. Zo ja, in hoeveel procent van de gevallen gebeurt dit?
a) Minder dan 10%
b) 10 tot 25%
c) 25 tot 50%

d) 50% of meer

a. Does your firm offer clients the option of appointing you or one of your staff as a supervisor?

a) *Yes*

b) *No*

b. If yes, in what percentage of cases does this happen?

a) *Less than 10%*

b) *10 to 25%*

c) *25 to 50%*

d) *50% or more*

<u>**Cliënt** / *Clients*</u>

19. In welke leeftijdscategorie bevindt het merendeel van de cliënten die een levenstestament komt opstellen zich?

a) Jonger dan 50 jaar

b) Tussen de 50-60 jaar

c) Tussen de 60-70 jaar

d) 70 jaar of ouder

In which age group do most client who come to make a levenstestament fall?

a) *Younger than 50 years*

b) *Between 50-60 years old*

c) *Between 60-70 years old*

d) *70 years or older*

20a. Met welk oogmerk(en) stellen cliënten een levenstestament op? (Graag <u>alle</u> antwoordmogelijkheden aanvinken die u in uw praktijk tegenkomt)

o Een toekomstige situatie van wilsonbekwaamheid door ziektes als dementie en Alzheimer

o Een toekomstige situatie van wilsonbekwaamheid door bijv. een ernstig auto-ongeluk

o Een (toekomstige) situatie waarin de cliënt door mobiliteitsproblemen niet meer alles zelf kan regelen.

o Een (toekomstige) situatie waarin de cliënt door de digitalisering en de modernisering van de samenleving niet meer alles zelf kan regelen.

o Anders, namelijk ....

For what purpose(s) do clients draw up a levenstestament? (Please tick all response options you encounter in your practice)

- o *A future situation of incapacity due to dementia or Alzheimer*
- o *A future situation of incapacity due to, for example, a serious car accident*
- o *A (future) situation in which the client can no longer manage everything himself due to mobility problems.*
- o *A (future) situation in which, due to digitalisation and modernisation of society, the client can no longer manage everything himself.*
- o *Other, namely ....*

b. Welk van de in de vorige vraag genoemde oogmerken komt in uw praktijk het meeste voor?

a) Een toekomstige situatie van wilsonbekwaamheid door ziektes als dementie en Alzheimer
b) Een toekomstige situatie van wilsonbekwaamheid door bijv. een ernstig auto-ongeluk
c) Een (toekomstige) situatie waarin de cliënt door mobiliteitsproblemen niet meer alles zelf kan regelen.
d) Een (toekomstige) situatie waarin de cliënt door de digitalisering en de modernisering van de samenleving niet meer alles zelf kan regelen.

Which of the purposes mentioned in the previous question is most common in your practice?

a) *A future situation of incapacity due to dementia or Alzheimer*
b) *A future situation of incapacity due to, for example, a serious car accident*
c) *A (future) situation in which the client can no longer manage everything himself due to mobility problems.*
d) *A (future) situation in which, due to digitalisation and modernisation of society, the client can no longer manage everything himself.*

21. Hoe zijn uw cliënten overwegend bekend geworden met het levenstestament? Zet de volgende vijf antwoorden in volgorde van belangrijkheid, waarbij het meest voorkomende antwoord bovenaan komt en het minst voorkomende antwoord onderaan.

a) Via de notaris
b) Via de media (krant, tv, radio, internet, etc.)
c) Via de bank
d) Via de partner, familieleden, kennissen
e) Anders

How did your clients become familiar with the possibility to make a levenstestament? Put the following five answers in order of importance, with the most common answer at the top and the least common at the bottom.

a) *Through the notary*

b) *Through the media (newspaper, TV, radio, internet, etc.)*
c) *Through the bank*
d) *Through the partner, relatives, acquaintances*
e) *Other*

22a. Heeft u het idee dat cliënten weleens problemen ervaren waar het gaat om de acceptatie van het levenstestament door derden?
a) Ja
b) Nee

b. Zo ja, bij welke instanties/personen? (Meerdere antwoorden mogelijk)
o Banken
o Verzekeraars
o Zorgkantoren
o Zorginstellingen (bijv. verzorgingstehuis)
o Artsen
o Rechters
o Familieleden

22a. Are you aware of signs that clients in some cases experience problems with the acceptance of the levenstestament by third parties?
a) *Yes*
b) *No*

b. If yes, with which parties/persons? (Multiple answers possible)
o *Banks*
o *Insurance companies*
o *Care administration offices*
o *Care home institutions (e.g. nursing home)*
o *Doctors*
o *Judges*
o *Family members*

Overig / *Remaining questions*

23. Schrijft uw kantoor het levenstestament bij het Centraal Levenstestamentenregister in Den Haag in?
a) Altijd
b) Meestal wel
c) Meestal niet
d) Nooit

Does your office register the levenstestament in the Central Register of Levenstestamenten in The Hague?
a) *Always*
b) *Usually yes*
c) *Usually not*
d) *Never*

24. Wat zijn volgens u de grootste voordelen van het levenstestament?

Open veld

What do you think are the main advantages of the levenstestament?

Open field

25. Wat zijn volgens u de grootste knelpunten rondom de praktijk van het levenstestament?

Open veld

What do you think are the main bottlenecks regarding the levenstestament?

Open field

Appendix 2: Interview schedule Adult cohort 1 – interview study 'The levenstestament in practice'

Dutch interview schedule Adult cohort 1
English translation interview schedule Adult cohort 1

Interviewschema meerderjarige – cohort 1

Aanwijzingen voor de interviewer

De interviewer neemt naar elk interview het volgende mee:
- Topiclijst interview
- Adres- en contactgegevens, respondentnummer (niet laten slingeren en los van elkaar bewaren)
- Een voice recorder
- Extra kopie informatiefolder
- Informed consentformulier (4x)
- Notitieblok en pennen
- Twee enveloppen
- Bedankje

Instructie

De respondent heeft voorafgaand aan het interview een informatiefolder per post of e-mail ontvangen met als inhoud (samengevat):
- Doel van het onderzoek: studie naar de verwachtingen en ervaringen van gebruikers van het levenstestament en de verschillende partijen die bij de uitvoering van het levenstestament zijn betrokken
- Duur: 3 kwartier
- Toestemming respondent: het is aan de respondent om te beslissen over deelname, toestemming kan te allen tijde zonder opgaaf van redenen worden ingetrokken
- Opslag en bewaartermijn data: opslag op een beveiligde computer
- Gebruik geluidsopname
- Uitkomsten onderzoek: publicatie in open access tijdschriften

Bovengenoemde punten worden voorafgaand aan het interview kort doorgenomen met de respondent. Daarnaast leg je uit aan de respondent dat je geïnteresseerd bent in de ervaringen en verwachtingen van de respondent. Je hebt als onderzoeker geen opinie over de inhoud van het levenstestament en kunt de respondent daarover ook niet adviseren. Mocht het interview vragen bij de respondent oproepen, dan verwijs je de respondent allereerst door naar de eigen notaris en vervolgens naar de onafhankelijke adviseur. Na beantwoording van eventuele vragen en bij akkoord vraag je de respondent om het informed consentformulier te ondertekenen. Een exemplaar gaat meteen in de envelop die je daarna direct dichtplakt. Het tweede exemplaar is voor de respondent.

Na afloop checkt de interviewer het volgende:
- Is het respondentnummer ingesproken voorafgaand aan het interview?
- Is het informed consent formulier ondertekend? (1 voor respondent, 1 mee terug)
- Bedankje overhandigt?
- Zijn de informed consentformulieren in een gesloten envelop gedaan?

Algemene gegevens respondent

1. Wat is uw leeftijd?
2. Weet u nog op welke datum het levenstestament is opgesteld? Hoe ging dat destijds bij de notaris?

Motivatie en algemene verwachtingen

3. Wanneer heeft u voor het eerst gehoord van het bestaan van het levenstestament?

4. Wat was voor u de reden om een levenstestament op te stellen?
   o Wat was de directe aanleiding?
   o Kunt u zich nog herinneren wat hieraan voorafging?
   o Wat heeft u doen besluiten om het levenstestament op te stellen?

5. Welke verwachtingen heeft u bij het levenstestament?
   o *N.B. sluit aan bij de reden die bij vraag 2 is genoemd en vraag door*: U zegt net, dat de belangrijkste reden voor het opstellen van het levenstestament was dat ... Wat verwacht u precies van het levenstestament? Hoe gaat u dat hierbij helpen?

Inhoud en type levenstestament

Achtergrondinformatie voor de interviewer: het doel is hier om een beeld te krijgen van hetgeen door de respondent in het levenstestament is geregeld. Hierbij gaat het om de verschillende zaken/onderwerpen die in het levenstestament zijn opgenomen, niet om specifieke informatie over deze zaken. Deze inventarisatie doen we door middel van open, algemeen geformuleerde vragen, waarvoor onderstaande vragen gebruikt kunnen worden. Probeer zoveel mogelijk te voorkomen dat je specifiek naar een bepaald onderwerp vraagt, maar verwijs in dergelijke gevallen bijvoorbeeld naar hetgeen in algemene termen op internet te vinden is, dus bijvoorbeeld: 'Ik heb gezien op internet dat sommige mensen ook iets opnemen over ... Heeft u dit ook gedaan?' In de kaders hieronder staan voorbeelden uit de checklist van de Koninklijke Notariële Beroepsorganisatie, die je tijdens het interview kunt gebruiken om de respondent op weg te helpen als de vraag voor de respondent onduidelijk is.

Doel is om in het gesprek de volgende onderwerpen voorbij te laten komen:
- Onderwerpen waarover bepalingen zijn opgenomen: financiële zaken, medische zaken en/of persoonlijke zaken.
- Bevoegdheden vertegenwoordiger
- Medische wilsverklaring
- Wensen en voorkeuren m.b.t. persoonlijke zaken: e.g. huisdieren, verzorgings-/verpleegtehuis
- Moment inwerkingtreding levenstestament
- Toezicht/controle (e.g. toezichthouder)

6. Kunt u mij wat meer vertellen over welke onderwerpen voor u van belang waren om op te nemen in levenstestament? U vertelde al dat u om ... en .... reden dit levenstestament afsloot.

7. Sommige mensen nemen ook iets op over ... (zie lijst onderwerpen hierboven) Heeft u dit ook gedaan?

Iets minder abstracte voorbeelden die in de checklist van de KNB genoemd worden, zijn:
- *regelen van belastingzaken*
- *persoonlijke verzorging*
- *wensen in het geval persoon naar een verzorgingstehuis of verpleeghuis gaat*
- *huisdieren*

8. Kunt u me wat meer vertellen over de medische zaken die u hebt vastgelegd? Sommige mensen, bijvoorbeeld, wijzen hier niet alleen een vertegenwoordiger aan, maar nemen ook een wilsverklaring op waarin zij aangeven welke medische behandelingen ze wel of niet willen. Hoe is dit bij u?

Relatie met de vertegenwoordiger

Doel is om in het gesprek de volgende onderwerpen voorbij te laten komen:
- Relatie met de vertegenwoordiger
- Verwachtingen t.a.v. de vertegenwoordiger
- Instructies m.b.t. de vertegenwoordiger in het levenstestament
- Communicatie met de vertegenwoordiger
- Beloning/vergoeding vertegenwoordiger
- Toezicht op en controle van de vertegenwoordiger?

9. Heeft u ook een vertegenwoordiger of vertegenwoordigers aangewezen in uw levenstestament? Zou u mij daar iets meer over willen vertellen?
   - o Kunt u mij vertellen wat uw relatie is tot ... (*liefst bij naam*)?

10. Hoe ziet u het voor zich als het levenstestament straks in werking treedt, wat gaat persoon x (liefst met naam) voor u regelen? Wat wilt u dat hij/zij van u overneemt?

11. Heeft u in het levenstestament ook instructies opgenomen voor de vertegenwoordiger of daar op een andere manier met de vertegenwoordiger over gesproken?

12. Sommige mensen nemen ook iets op over toezicht en controle op het handelen van de vertegenwoordiger. Heeft u dit ook gedaan? Kunt u me vertellen hoe u dit heeft gedaan?

Voorbeelden die in de checklist van de KNB worden genoemd zijn:
- *rekening en verantwoording afleggen (een overzicht van inkomsten en uitgaven) aan toezichthouder*
- *overleg met een familielid bij belangrijke beslissingen, zoals de verkoop van een huis*

Bekendheid van het levenstestament bij derden

13. Heeft u andere mensen verteld dat u een levenstestament heeft gemaakt? Kunt u daar iets meer over vertellen?
    - o Heeft u ook met mensen in uw directe omgeving gesproken over wat u in uw levenstestament heeft vastgelegd?

> *Voorbeelden van 'andere mensen' die in de checklist van de KNB worden genoemd zijn:*
> - *de bank*
> - *de huisarts*
> - *specialist in het ziekenhuis*
> - *familieleden*

Afsluiting/slotvraag

14. Is er nog iets dat niet in het interview aan de orde is gekomen, dat u nog graag aan mij/ons wilt vertellen?

> Als de setting daar geschikt voor is, respondent vragen of hij/zij het goed zou vinden als we ook met de vertegenwoordiger(s) praten en zo ja, of de respondent zijn/haar vertegenwoordiger wil vragen of deze mee wil werken aan een interview. Vragen of je nog een keer contact mag opnemen met de respondent hierover.

Interview schedule adult – cohort 1[1]

Directions for the interviewer

The interviewer brings the following to each interview
- Interview topic list
- Address and contact details respondent, respondent number (keep this stored separately!)
- A voice recorder and extra batteries
- An extra copy of the respondent information leaflet
- Informed consent form (4x)

1. This is an English translation of the original interview topic list, which was in Dutch. The free version of DeepL was used to translate this document.

- Notepad and pens
- Two envelopes
- Chocolate bar for the respondent

Instruction interviewer

Before the interview, the respondent received an information leaflet by post or email with the following content (summarised):
- Purpose of the survey: this study explores the expectations and experiences of both adults and attorneys with the *levenstestament*
- Duration of the interview: approximately 45 minutes
- Informed consent: it is up to the respondent to decide whether to participate; consent can be withdrawn at any time without the respondent having to explain the reasons for withdrawal
- Storage and data retention period: storage on a secure computer
- Use of a recording device
- Research results: publication in open-access journals

The above points are briefly discussed with the respondent before the interview. In addition, you explain to the respondent that you are interested in the respondent's experiences and expectations. As a researcher, you do not have an opinion on the content of the *levenstestament* and cannot advise the respondent. Should the interview raise any questions about the content of the *levenstestament*, you refer the respondent first to their notary and then to the independent adviser. After answering questions and upon agreement, the interviewer asks the respondent to sign the informed consent form. One copy goes directly into the envelope, which the interviewer immediately seals. The second copy is for the respondent.

After the interview, the interviewer checks the following:
- Was the respondent number recorded at the beginning of the interview?
- Was the informed consent form signed? (1 for respondent, 1 for the research team)
- Thank you present handed over?
- Were the informed consent forms placed in a sealed envelope?

General information respondent

1. What is your age?
2. Do you remember when the *levenstestament* was drawn up? How did that go at the notary's office at the time?

Motivation and general expectations

3. When did you first hear about the possibility of making a *levenstestament*?

4. What was the reason for you to make a *levenstestament*?
   - o What was the immediate reason?
   - o Can you remember what preceded this?
   - o What made you decide to draw up a *levenstestament*?

5. What expectations do you have concerning the *levenstestament*?
   - o *Note: refer to the reasons mentioned under question 4 and enquire further*:
   - 2 You just mentioned that the main reason for making the *levenstestament* was that ... What exactly do you expect from the *levenstestament*? How will the *levenstestament* help in this regard?

Content and type levenstestament

Background information for the interviewer: the aim is to explore what matters the adult has included in the levenstestament. This involves general information about the various matters included in the levenstestament rather than specific information about them. This is explored through open, generally formulated questions, for which the questions below can be used. As far as possible, try to avoid asking specifically about a particular subject, but in such cases, refer, for example, to what can be found in general terms on the internet, so for example: 'I have seen on the internet that some people also include something about ... Have you done this too?' The boxes below give examples from the Royal Notarial Association's checklist, which you can use during the interview to get the respondent started if the question is unclear to the respondent.

The aim is to include the following topics in the interview:
- Subjects on which provisions are included: financial, medical, and/or personal matters.
- The attorney's powers
- Medical advance directives
- Wishes and preferences regarding personal matters: e.g. pets, care/nursing home
- Moment of entry into force of the *levenstestament*
- Supervision/control (e.g. appointment supervisor)

6. Can you tell me more about what matters were important for you to include in the *levenstestament*? You already mentioned that you made the *levenstestament* for .... and .... reason.

7. Some people also include something about .... (see list of topics above). Have you done so?

> *Less abstract examples mentioned in the KNB checklist are:*
> - *arranging tax matters*
> - *personal care*
> - *wishes in case the person goes to a care home or a nursing home*
> - *pets*

8. Can you tell me more about the medical matters you recorded? Some people, for example, not only appoint an attorney but also include advance directives stating which medical treatments they do or do not want. Have you done so?

Relationship with the attorney

Try to address the following topics during the interview:
- Relationship with the attorney
- Expectations regarding the attorney
- Instructions for the attorney in the *levenstestament*
- Communication with the attorney
- Remuneration/expenses of the attorney
- Supervision and control of the attorney

9. Have you also appointed one or more attorneys through your *levenstestament*? Could you tell me more about this?
    - o Can you tell me what your relationship is to .... (name attorney)?

10. How do you envisage it when the *levenstestament* enters into force? What will .... (name attorney) arrange for you? What would you like him/her to take over from you?

11. Have you included instructions for the attorney in the *levenstestament* or discussed this with the attorney in any other way?

12. Some people also include a form of supervision or control on the attorney's actions in their *levenstestament*. Have you done this as well? Could you tell me how you have done this?

Examples mentioned in the KNB checklist include the following:
- *submitting accounts (a statement of income and expenditure) to a supervisor*
- *consulting family members on important decisions, such as the sale of the family home*

Awareness of the levenstestament among third parties

13. Have you told other people that you have made a *levenstestament*? Could you tell me a bit more about this?
    - Have you also talked to people in your immediate surroundings about what you have recorded in your *levenstestament*?

Examples of 'other people' mentioned in the KNB checklist are:
- *the bank*
- *the family doctor*
- *hospital specialist*
- *family members*

Closing question

14. Is there anything else you would like to share that was not discussed during this interview?

If appropriate, ask the respondent whether they agree to their nominated attorney(s) being interviewed and, if so, whether the respondent is willing to ask the attorney(s) if they would like to participate in the study or share their contact details.

Appendix 3: Interview schedule Attorney cohort 1 – interview study 'The levenstestament in practice'

Dutch interview schedule Attorney cohort 1
English translation interview schedule Attorney cohort 1

Interviewschema vertegenwoordiger – cohort 1

Aanwijzingen voor de interviewer

De interviewer neemt naar elk interview het volgende mee:
- Topiclijst interview
- Adres- en contactgegevens, respondentnummer (niet laten slingeren en los van elkaar bewaren)
- Een voice recorder, extra batterijen
- Extra kopie informatiefolder
- Informed consent formulier (4x)
- Notitieblok en pennen
- Twee enveloppen
- Bedankje

Instructie

De respondent heeft voorafgaand aan het interview een informatiefolder per post of e-mail ontvangen met als inhoud (samengevat):
- Doel van het onderzoek: studie naar de verwachtingen en ervaringen van gebruikers van het levenstestament en de verschillende partijen die bij de uitvoering van het levenstestament zijn betrokken
- Duur: ongeveer 3 kwartier
- Toestemming respondent: het is aan de respondent om te beslissen over deelname, toestemming kan te allen tijde zonder opgaaf van redenen worden ingetrokken
- Opslag en bewaartermijn data: opslag op een beveiligde computer
- Gebruik geluidsopname
- Uitkomsten onderzoek: publicatie in open access tijdschriften

Bovengenoemde punten worden voorafgaand aan het interview kort doorgenomen met de respondent. Na beantwoording van eventuele vragen en bij akkoord vraag je de respondent om het informed consentformulier te ondertekenen. Een exemplaar gaat meteen in de envelop die je daarna direct dichtplakt. Het tweede exemplaar is voor de respondent.

N.B. In de praktijk wordt de persoon die als 'vertegenwoordiger' is aangewezen met verschillende termen aangeduid, zoals 'vertrouwenspersoon', 'gevolmachtigde', 'vertegenwoordiger'. Neem in het interview de term over die de respondent zelf gebruikt.

Na afloop checkt de interviewer het volgende:
- Is het respondentnummer ingesproken voorafgaand aan het interview?
- Informed consent ondertekend? (1 voor respondent, 1 mee terug)
- Bedankje overhandigd?
- Zijn de informed consent formulieren in een gesloten envelop gedaan?

Doel van dit interview is om een beeld te krijgen van de verwachtingen van de gevolmachtigde met betrekking tot hetgeen er van hem verwacht wordt bij de uitvoering van het levenstestament. Heeft de gevolmachtigde een goed beeld van de wensen, voorkeuren en instructies van de volmachtgever? Is hij betrokken geweest bij de totstandkoming van het levenstestament? Weet hij/zij wat hem/haar te doen staat op het moment dat de uitvoering van het levenstestament in beeld komt? En hoe wordt hier vorm aan gegeven bij meerdere gevolmachtigden?

In dat kader wordt ingegaan op de volgende topics:
- **Relatie volmachtgever-gevolmachtigde**
- **Betrokkenheid bij de totstandkoming van het levenstestament**
- **Instructies, wensen en voorkeuren van de volmachtgever**
- **Verwachtingen gevolmachtigde**

Relatie volmachtgever-gevolmachtigde

Onderzoeksvragen: Wat is de relatie tussen de volmachtgever en gevolmachtigde? Waarom is voor deze gevolmachtigde gekozen?

1. Kunt u mij vertellen wat uw relatie is tot ... (*naam volmachtgever*)?

2. Weet u nog (ongeveer) wanneer het levenstestament is opgesteld?

Betrokkenheid bij de totstandkoming van het levenstestament

Onderzoeksvraag: Is de gevolmachtigde betrokken geweest bij de totstandkoming van het levenstestament? Hoe zag deze betrokkenheid eruit?

Doorvragen op de vorige vraag:

3. Wat kunt u mij vertellen over hoe dat is gegaan....?

4. Wat hebben jullie over de inhoud van het levenstestament besproken met elkaar?

Instructies, wensen en voorkeuren volmachtgever

Onderzoeksvragen:
- ***Op welke wijze wordt instructie gegeven aan de gevolmachtigde omtrent de wensen en voorkeuren van de volmachtgever?***
- ***Welke bevoegdheden zijn aan de gevolmachtigde toegekend?***
- ***Zijn er in het levenstestament toezicht- en/of controlemaatregelen opgenomen?***

5. Hoe hebben jullie met elkaar afgesproken dat de rol van vertegenwoordiger zal zijn?
   - o Wat heeft u met ... (*naam volmachtgever*) afgesproken over het moment waarop u namens hem/haar gaat handelen?
   - o Wat gaat u vanaf dat moment voor ... (*naam volmachtgever*) als het nodig is regelen?

Doel is om in het gesprek de onderwerpen waarover bepalingen zijn opgenomen voorbij te laten komen: financiële zaken, medische zaken en/of persoonlijke zaken; medische wilsverklaring en waar mogelijk de manier waarop de gevolmachtigde hier uitvoering aan gaat geven.

Voorbeelden die in de checklist van de KNB genoemd worden, zijn:
- *regelen van belastingzaken*
- *persoonlijke verzorging*
- *wensen in het geval persoon naar een verzorgingstehuis of verpleeghuis gaat*
- *huisdieren.*

Een tweede doel bij deze vraag is om in het gesprek de instructies, voorkeuren en wensen van de volmachtgever voorbij te laten komen. Is hier iets over opgenomen in het levenstestament? Of heeft de volmachtgever hier met de vertegenwoordiger over gesproken?

Verwachtingen gevolmachtigde

Onderzoeksvragen: Wat zijn de verwachtingen en aannames van de gevolmachtigde ten aanzien van hetgeen er van hem verwacht wordt met betrekking tot de uitvoering van het levenstestament?

6. Hoe ziet u, uw (toekomstige) rol als vertegenwoordiger?
   - o Hoe ziet u dat voor u, als u straks namens ... (*naam volmachtgever*) gaat handelen?

Iemand vertegenwoordigen kan natuurlijk soms best moeilijk zijn.

7. Kunt u me vertellen wat jullie hierover hebben afgesproken?
   - o Hoe hebben jullie het geregeld in situaties waarin u bijvoorbeeld zou twijfelen aan een beslissing?
   - o En in situaties waarin u misschien wel een moeilijke beslissing moet nemen (teruggrijpen op zaken die hierboven zijn genoemd, bijv. verkoop van het huis)?

8. Is er naast u ook nog iemand anders als vertegenwoordiger aangewezen? Zo ja, kunt u mij hier iets meer over vertellen?
   - o Hoe gaat u samen de belangen van ... (*naam volmachtgever*) behartigen?

Afsluiting/slotvraag

9. Is er nog iets dat niet in het interview aan de orde is gekomen, dat u nog graag aan mij/ons wilt vertellen?

INTERVIEW SCHEDULE (NOMINATED) ATTORNEY – COHORT 1[1]

Directions for the interviewer

The interviewer brings the following to each interview
- Interview topic list
- Address and contact details respondent, respondent number (keep this stored separately!)

1. This is an English translation of the original interview topic list, which was in Dutch. The free version of DeepL was used to translate this document.

- A voice recorder and extra batteries
- An extra copy of the respondent information leaflet
- Informed consent form (4x)
- Notepad and pens
- Two envelopes
- Chocolate bar for the respondent

Instruction interviewer

Before the interview, the respondent received an information leaflet by post or email with the following content (summarised):
- Purpose of the survey: this study explores the expectations and experiences of both adults and attorneys with the *levenstestament*
- Duration of the interview: approximately 45 minutes
- Informed consent: it is up to the respondent to decide whether to participate; consent can be withdrawn at any time without the respondent having to explain the reasons for withdrawal
- Storage and data retention period: storage on a secure computer
- Use of a recording device
- Research results: publication in open-access journals

The above points are briefly discussed with the respondent before the interview. Then, after answering questions and upon agreement, the interviewer asks the respondent to sign the informed consent form. One copy goes directly into the envelope, which the interviewer immediately seals. The second copy is for the respondent.

Note: In practice, the person designated as "attorney" is referred to by different terms, such as "trusted person", "attorney", or "representative". During the interview, please adopt the term used by the respondent.

Afterwards, the interviewer checks the following:
- Was the respondent number recorded at the beginning of the interview?
- Was the Informed consent form signed? (1 for respondent, 1 for the research team)
- Thank you present handed over?
- Were the informed consent forms placed in a sealed envelope?

This interview explores the attorney's expectations of what is expected of him when executing the *levenstestament*.Does the attorney understand the adult's wishes, preferences and instructions well? Has he/she been involved in the drafting of the *levenstestament*? Does he/she know what to do when the

execution of the *levenstestament* commences? And what are the arrangements in case there are multiple attorneys?

The following topics are discussed in this context:
- **Relationship between the adult and the attorney**
- **Involvement in the drafting of the *levenstestament***
- **Instructions, wishes and preferences of the adult**
- **The attorney's expectations**

Relationship between the adult and the attorney

Research questions: What is the relationship between the adult and the attorney? Why was this attorney chosen?
1. Can you tell me about your relationship to .... (name adult)?

2. Do you remember (approximately) when the *levenstestament* was made?

Involvement in the drafting of the levenstestament

Research question: Was the attorney involved in the drafting of the levenstestament? What did this involvement look like?

Follow-up question to the previous question
3. What can you tell me about how that went...?

4. What did you discuss with each other about the content of the *levenstestament*?

Instructions, wishes and preferences of the adult

Research questions:
- ***In what way is the attorney instructed regarding the adult's wishes and preferences***
- ***What powers are granted to the attorney?***
- ***Are supervisory and/or control measures included in the levenstestament?***

5. What have you discussed and agreed with each other regarding the role of attorney?
    - o What have you agreed with ... (name adult) about when you will act on his/her behalf?
    - o What will you arrange/take care of for ... (name adult) from then on if necessary?

The aim is to include in the conversation the topics on which provisions are included: financial matters, medical matters and/or personal matters, medical advance directives and, where possible, the way the attorney will take care of these matters.

Examples mentioned in the KNB checklist are:
- arranging tax matters
- personal care
- wishes in case the person goes to a care home or nursing home
- pets.

The second aim of this question is to explore the adult's instructions, preferences and wishes. Is there anything about this in the levenstestament? Or has the adult discussed this with the attorney?

The attorney's expectations

Research questions: What are the expectations and assumptions of the attorney regarding what is expected of him concerning the execution of the levenstestament?

6. How do you see your (future) role as an attorney?
   - o How do you envisage it if you will later act on behalf of ... (name adult)?

Representing someone can, of course, sometimes be difficult.

7. Can you tell me what you discussed/agreed on concerning this?
   - o What are you to do in situations where you would, for example, be in doubt about a decision?
   - o And in situations where you might have to make a difficult decision (referring to matters discussed previously, e.g. selling the family home)?

8. Has anyone else besides you been appointed as an attorney? If yes, can you tell me more about this?
   - o How will you jointly represent the interests of ... (name adult)?

Closing question

9. Is there anything else you would like to share that was not discussed during this interview?

Appendix 4: Interview schedule Attorney cohort 2 – interview study 'The levenstestament in practice'

Dutch interview schedule Attorney cohort 2
English translation interview schedule Attorney cohort 2

Interviewschema vertegenwoordiger – cohort 2

Aanwijzingen voor de interviewer

De interviewer neemt naar elk interview het volgende mee:

- Topiclijst interview
- Adres- en contactgegevens, respondentnummer (niet laten slingeren en los van elkaar bewaren)
- Een voice recorder, extra batterijen
- Extra kopie informatiefolder
- Informed consent formulier (4x)
- Notitieblok en pennen
- Twee enveloppen
- Bedankje

Instructie

De respondent heeft voorafgaand aan het interview een informatiefolder per post of e-mail ontvangen met als inhoud (samengevat):

- Doel van het onderzoek: studie naar de verwachtingen en ervaringen van gebruikers van het levenstestament en de verschillende partijen die bij de uitvoering van het levenstestament zijn betrokken
- Duur: 3 kwartier
- Toestemming respondent: het is aan de respondent om te beslissen over deelname, toestemming kan te allen tijde zonder opgaaf van redenen worden ingetrokken
- Opslag en bewaartermijn data: opslag op een beveiligde computer
- Gebruik geluidsopname
- Uitkomsten onderzoek: publicatie in open access tijdschriften

Bovengenoemde punten worden voorafgaand aan het interview kort doorgenomen met de respondent. Na beantwoording van eventuele vragen en bij akkoord vraag je de respondent om het informed consentformulier te ondertekenen. Een exemplaar gaat meteen in de envelop die je daarna direct dichtplakt. Het tweede exemplaar is voor de respondent.

N.B. In de praktijk wordt de persoon die als 'vertegenwoordiger' is aangewezen met verschillende termen aangeduid, zoals 'vertrouwenspersoon', 'gevolmachtigde', 'vertegenwoordiger'. Neem in het interview de term over die de respondent zelf gebruikt.

Na afloop checkt de interviewer het volgende:
- Is het respondentnummer ingesproken voorafgaand aan het interview?
- Informed consent ondertekend? (1 voor respondent, 1 mee terug)
- Bedankje overhandigd?
- Zijn de informed consent formulieren in een gesloten envelop gedaan?

Doel van dit interview is om een beeld te krijgen van de ervaringen van de gevolmachtigde met betrekking tot hetgeen er van hem verwacht wordt bij de uitvoering van het levenstestament. Heeft de gevolmachtigde een goed beeld van de wensen, voorkeuren en instructies van de volmachtgever? Is hij betrokken geweest bij de totstandkoming van het levenstestament? Weet hij/zij wat hem/haar te doen staat op het moment dat de uitvoering van het levenstestament in beeld komt? En hoe wordt hier vorm aan gegeven bij meerdere gevolmachtigden?

In dat kader wordt ingegaan op de volgende topics:
- **Relatie volmachtgever-gevolmachtigde**
- **Betrokkenheid bij de totstandkoming van het levenstestament**
- **Inwerkingtreding levenstestament**
- **Instructies, wensen en voorkeuren van de volmachtgever**
- **Ervaringen gevolmachtigde uitvoering levenstestament**

Relatie volmachtgever-gevolmachtigde

Onderzoeksvragen: Wat is de relatie tussen de volmachtgever en gevolmachtigde? Waarom is voor deze gevolmachtigde gekozen?

10. Kunt u mij vertellen wat uw relatie is tot ... (naam volmachtgever)?

11. Weet u nog (ongeveer) wanneer het levenstestament is opgesteld?

Betrokkenheid bij de totstandkoming van het levenstestament

Onderzoeksvraag: Is de gevolmachtigde betrokken geweest bij de totstandkoming van het levenstestament? Hoe zag deze betrokkenheid eruit?

Doorvragen op de vorige vraag:

12. Wat kunt u mij vertellen over hoe dat is gegaan....?

13. Wat hebben jullie over de inhoud van het levenstestament besproken met elkaar?

Inwerkingtreding levenstestament

14. Wanneer bent u (ongeveer) voor ... (naam volmachtgever) bent gaan handelen?
    - o Evt. doorvragen, hoe wist u dat het moment om te gaan handelen was aangebroken?
    - o Hoe was ... (naam volmachtgever) hier nog bij betrokken?
    - o Hoe heeft u de 'inwerkingtreding' van het levenstestament ervaren?

Instructies, wensen en voorkeuren volmachtgever

Onderzoeksvragen:

- ***Op welke wijze is instructie gegeven aan de gevolmachtigde omtrent de wensen en voorkeuren van de volmachtgever?***
- ***Welke bevoegdheden zijn aan de gevolmachtigde toegekend?***
- ***Zijn er in het levenstestament toezicht- en/of controlemaatregelen opgenomen?***
- ***Hoe houdt de gevolmachtigde rekening met de wil en voorkeuren van de volmachtgever?***

15. Hoe hebben jullie met elkaar afgesproken dat de rol van vertegenwoordiger zal zijn?
    - o Wat regelt u op dit moment voor ... (naam volmachtgever)?
    - o *Doorvragen op vraag 4*, u heeft net verteld dat... hoe houdt u hier bij de uitvoering van het levenstestament rekening mee?
    - o Hoe wordt .... (naam volmachtgever) hier nog bij betrokken?

Ervaringen gevolmachtigde uitvoering levenstestament

Onderzoeksvragen:

- ***Hoe gaat de gevolmachtigde om met de situatie waarin de wensen en voorkeuren van de volmachtgever afwijken van de wensen en voorkeuren die zijn neergelegd in het levenstestament?***
- ***Op welke wijze geeft de gevolmachtigde uitvoering aan de bevoegdheden die zijn neergelegd in het levenstestament?***
- ***Welke problemen worden door de gevolmachtigde ervaren m.b.t. acceptatie van het levenstestament door derden?***
- ***Tegen welke knelpunten lopen de gevolmachtigde, toezichthouders en derden aan?***
- ***Welke oplossingen/best practices zijn in de praktijk gevonden voor deze knelpunten?***

16. Wat zijn uw ervaringen met de uitvoering van het levenstestament?
    - o *Evt. doorvragen,* u vertelt net dat u ..... regelt of heeft geregeld voor ... (naam volmachtgever). Hoe kijkt u hier op terug? Waar bent u tegenaan gelopen? Evt. hoe heeft u dit opgelost?
    - o Hoe ziet u in de toekomst uw rol als vertegenwoordiger/gevolmachtigde voor u?

Iemand vertegenwoordigen kan natuurlijk soms best moeilijk zijn.

17. Kunt u me vertellen wat jullie hierover hebben afgesproken?
    - o Hoe hebben jullie het geregeld in situaties waarin u bijvoorbeeld twijfelt aan een beslissing?
    - o En in situaties waarin u misschien wel een moeilijke beslissing moet nemen (teruggrijpen op zaken die hierboven zijn genoemd, bijv. verkoop van het huis)?
    - o Wat zijn tot nu toe uw ervaringen met dit soort situaties? *Of* U vertelt net... hoe bent u hiermee omgegaan?

18. Is er naast u ook nog iemand anders als vertegenwoordiger aangewezen? Zo ja, kunt u mij hier iets meer over vertellen?
    - o Hoe behartigt u samen de belangen van ... (naam volmachtgever)?

Afsluiting/slotvraag

19. Is er nog iets dat niet in het interview aan de orde is gekomen, dat u nog graag aan mij/ons wilt vertellen?

Interview schedule list attorney – cohort 2[1]

Directions for the interviewer

The interviewer brings the following to each interview
- Interview topic list
- Address and contact details respondent, respondent number (keep this stored separately!)
- A voice recorder and extra batteries
- An extra copy of the respondent information leaflet
- Informed consent form (4x)
- Notepad and pens
- Two envelopes
- Chocolate bar for the respondent

Instruction interviewer

Before the interview, the respondent received an information leaflet by post or email with the following content (summarised):
- Purpose of the survey: this study explores the expectations and experiences of both adults and attorneys with the *levenstestament*
- Duration of the interview: approximately 45 minutes
- Informed consent: it is up to the respondent to decide whether to participate; consent can be withdrawn at any time without the respondent having to explain the reasons for withdrawal
- Storage and data retention period: storage on a secure computer
- Use of a recording device
- Research results: publication in open-access journals

The above points are briefly discussed with the respondent before the interview. Then, after answering questions and upon agreement, the interviewer asks the respondent to sign the informed consent form. One copy goes directly into the envelope, which the interviewer immediately seals. The second copy is for the respondent.

Note: In practice, the person designated as "attorney" is referred to by different terms, such as "trusted person", "attorney", or "representative". During the interview, please adopt the term used by the respondent.

1. This is an English translation of the original interview topic list, which was in Dutch. The free version of DeepL was used to translate this document.

After the interview, the interviewer checks the following:
- Was the respondent number recorded at the beginning of the interview?
- Was the Informed consent form signed? (1 for respondent, 1 for the research team)
- Thank you present handed over?
- Were the informed consent forms placed in a sealed envelope?

This interview explores the attorney's expectations of what is expected of him when executing the *levenstestament*.Does the attorney understand the adult's wishes, preferences and instructions well? Has he/she been involved in the drafting of the *levenstestament*? Does he/she know what to do when the execution of the *levenstestament* commences? And what are the arrangements in case there are multiple attorneys?

The following topics are discussed in this context:
- **Relationship between the adult and the attorney**
- **Involvement in the drafting of the *levenstestament***
- **Entry into force of the *levenstestament***
- **Instructions, wishes and preferences of the adult**
- **The attorney's experiences with the execution of the *levenstestament***

Relationship between the adult and the attorney

Research questions: What is the relationship between the adult and the attorney? Why was this attorney chosen?

1. Can you tell me about your relationship to .... (name adult)?

2. Do you remember (approximately) when the *levenstestament* was made?

Involvement in the drafting of the levenstestament

Research question: Was the attorney involved in the drafting of the levenstestament? What did this involvement look like?

Follow-up question to the previous question

3. What can you tell me about how that went...?

4. What did you discuss with each other about the content of the *levenstestament*?

Entry into force of the levenstestament

5. When (approximately) did you start acting for .... (name adult)?
   - o How did you know the time had come to start acting?
   - o How was ... (name adult) still involved in this?
   - o How did you experience the 'entry into force' of the *levenstestament*?

Instructions, wishes and preferences of the adult

Research questions:
- ***In what way is the attorney instructed regarding the adult's wishes and preferences?***
- ***What powers are granted to the attorney?***
- ***Are supervisory and/or control measures included in the levenstestament?***
- ***How does the attorney consider the adult's will and preferences?***

6. What have you discussed and agreed with each other regarding the role of attorney?
   - o What are you currently arranging for .... (name adult)?
   - o *Referring to answer question 4*: you just told me that .... How do you consider this when executing the *levenstestament*?
   - o How is .... (name adult) still involved in this?

The attorney's experiences with the execution of the levenstestament

Research questions:
- ***How does the attorney handle a situation where the adult's (current) wishes and preferences deviate from those recorded in the levenstestament?***
- ***How does the attorney execute the powers recorded in the levenstestament?***
- ***What problems do attorneys experience regarding the acceptance of the levenstestament by third parties?***
- ***What issues do attorneys encounter?***
- ***What solutions/best practices have been found for these problems?***

7. What are your experiences concerning the execution of the *levenstestament*?
   - o You just told me you arranged the following .... for (name adult). How do you reflect on this? What did you encounter? How did you solve this?
   - o How do you envisage your role as an attorney in the future?

Representing someone can, of course, sometimes be difficult.

8. Can you tell me what you discussed/agreed on concerning this?

- o What are you to do in situations where you would, for example, be in doubt about a decision?
- o And in situations where you might have to make a difficult decision (referring to matters discussed previously, e.g. selling the family home)?
- o What are your experiences thus far with these kinds of situations? *Or* You just told me that ... how have you dealt with this?

9. Has anyone else besides you been appointed as an attorney? If yes, can you tell me more about this?
   - o How do you jointly represent the interests of ... (name adult)?

Closing question

10. Is there anything else you would like to share that was not discussed during this interview?

Appendix 5: Country report Belgium

Comparative study on enduring documents

Country report Belgium

A. *General*

Brief general description of the legal system of Belgium

Belgium is a federal state composed of both communities and regions.[1] Although these communities and regions also have certain legislative and executive powers, the law concerning the protection of adults is a federal matter governed by the Belgian Civil Code.[2] Several languages are spoken in Belgium, including Dutch, French and German.

N.B. For this country report, I have studied literature available in Dutch.

1. **Give a brief account of the adult protection system in each country (e.g. state ordered protection measures, private remedies).**

With the Act of 17 March 2013, the Belgian legislator reformed the system of adult protection measures in Belgium. This reform aimed to ensure compliance with international human rights instruments, in particular the United Nations Convention on the Rights of Persons with Disabilities (UNCRPD), the Council of Europe Recommendation R(99)4 on Principles concerning the legal protection of incapable adults and the Council of Europe Recommendation CM/Rec(2009)11 on principles concerning continuing powers of attorney and advance directives for incapacity.[3] The new system of adult protection measures has been comprehensively organised in Book 1, Title IX of the Belgian Civil Code (BCC)

1. Van Overdijk & Pintens 2015, p. 442.
2. Van Overdijk & Pintens 2015, p. 442; Brouhns 2019.
3. Swennen 2014, pp. 4-5.

and, in terms of procedure, in the Belgian Judicial Code (BJC).[4] Chapter 2 of Title IX defines the phrase 'protected adults'. According to article 488/1 BCC, protection can be ordered for adults who, due to their state of health, are unable – wholly, partly or temporarily – to look after their financial or non-financial interests properly. Protection may only be ordered when this is required to protect the adult's interests. Swennen notes that article 488/1 BCC requires a link between the adult's state of health and his inability to care for his interests properly. In addition, protection must be necessary, which means that when the adult, for instance, is already receiving (informal) assistance, (further) protection could be unnecessary.[5] Article 488/2 BCC stipulates that protection of the adult's financial affairs is also possible in the case of prodigality.[6]

Title IX of Book 1 BCC distinguishes between two types of adult protection measures, namely, out-of-court or extrajudicial protection and court-ordered or judicial protection. As no. 2 discusses in more detail, the legal provisions on out-of-court protection included in Title IX BCC focus on one enduring document, namely the mandate agreement or *zorgvolmacht*. Out-of-court protection is to be considered the preferred alternative. The Belgian court or *vredegerecht* may only order judicial protection when the adult's interests cannot be sufficiently protected through out-of-court protection.[7] In Belgium, judicial protection consists of two components. The first component consists of a tailor-made assessment and determination by the court of the legal acts for which the adult is no longer legally capable of acting.[8] In line with the principle of proportionality, the court's assessment must be tailor-made, and protection must be as limited as possible.[9] To guide the court's assessment, article 492/1 BCC contains a list of legal acts concerning both financial acts (e.g. the acquisition of real estate) and personal acts (e.g. formal acknowledgement of a child). For each of these acts, the court must explicitly determine the adult's legal capacity to perform these acts.[10] The second component of court-ordered or judicial protection consists of the appointment of what is referred to as a *bewindvoerder* or administrator. Article 497 BCC makes clear that the role of the administrator is to look after the adult's interests. In this context, the administrator should promote the adult's autonomy as much as possible.[11] In line with this objective and the principles of proportionality and subsidiarity, the Belgian Civil Code distinguishes two forms of administration:

4. Swennen 2022, p. 1.
5. Swennen 2014b, pp. 13-17.
6. Swennen 2022, p. 1.
7. Article 492 BCC; Belgian House of Representatives, Parl. St. Kamer 2011-12, nr. 53-1009/10, p. 31; Swennen 2022, p. 2; Mosselmans & Van Thienen 2014, p. 92.
8. Article 492/1 BCC; Mosselmans & Van Thienen 2014, p. 104.
9. Swennen 2022, p. 2; Mosselmans & Van Thienen 2014, p. 104.
10. Swennen 2022, p. 2; Mosselmans & Van Thienen 2014, pp. 104-105; Swennen 2013a, p. 573.
11. Swennen 2003b, p. 609.

representation (*vertegenwoordiging*) and assistance (*bijstand*). Assistance is less intrusive than representation as it enables the adult to act with the agreement or consent of the administrator.[12] Article 492/2 BCC, therefore, stipulates that this form of administration is preferable to representation.[13] Another interesting feature of the Belgian system on adult protection is the appointment of a so-called 'trusted person' (*vertrouwenspersoon*). Article 501/1 BCC makes clear that the trusted person is appointed to support the adult, for example, by helping the adult to make his wishes and preferences known to the administrator.[14]

Infrastructure

In Belgium, the so-called *vredegerecht*, or justice of the peace, fulfils a key role. Article 1239 BJC makes clear that the *vredegerecht* is the competent court for all adult protection matters. Van Overdijk and Pintents note that this court may consider applications concerning the administration, conservation and disposal of the adult's property, the adult's health and medical care and the adult's personal welfare.[15] Section B of this country report discusses the court's authority in relation to the mandate agreement in more detail.

2. **Given the definitions of a 'continuing power of attorney' and an 'advance directive' in Council of Europe Recommendation 2009/11, describe the concept or concepts used in each country. What are the legal instruments?**

As discussed under No. 1, priority should be given to what is referred to as 'out-of-court protection'. In this regard, the provisions of article 489-490/2 BCC focus on one enduring document in particular, namely the mandate agreement or, more specifically, a mandate that has been granted by a legally capable adult with the specific aim to arrange the out-of-court protection of his financial and personal affairs.[16] This enduring document is, in practice, also known as a *zorgvolmacht*.[17] Article 14 of the Belgian Act on Patient's Rights clarifies that adults may also appoint an attorney for health and medical affairs. Wuyts notes that the appointment of such an attorney can be included in the *zorgvolmacht*. In this case, attention should, however, be paid to the requirements of the Act on Patient's

12. Article 491 under e and article 494 under e BCC; Mosselmans & Van Thienen 2014, pp. 126-127; Swennen 2013b, pp. 609-610.
13. The reader is for more information on the judicial protection measures referred to e.g. Bogaert, Rotthier, Van den Eenden & Wuyts 2020; Mosselmans & Van Thienen 2014; Swennen 2013a; Swennen 2013b.
14. Swennen 2022, p. 2; Swennen 2013b, p. 607.
15. Van Overdijk & Pintens 2015, p. 443.
16. Article 490 BCC.
17. Wuyts 2020, §70.

Rights, which – as a lex specialis – takes precedence over the generic provisions of article 489-490/2 BCC.[18]

In addition to the *zorgvolmacht*, there are other instruments the adult may use to make provisions for a future period of incapacity.[19] Wuyts refers to article 496 BCC, based on which legally capable adults can draw up an advance directive addressed to the court. Using such an advance directive, the adult may record his choice of representative in the event a judicial protection measure is deemed necessary. The adult can, in addition, include particular wishes, preferences and instructions in the advance directive, which are to be observed by the representative while executing his task.[20] Based on article 4 of the Belgian Law on Euthanasia, adults in Belgium also have the right to make a so-called advance directive for euthanasia.

N.B. Although, as the aforementioned makes clear, several enduring documents can be distinguished in Belgium, this country report focuses on the appointment of an attorney through the so-called 'zorgvolmacht'.

3. **What is the current source of law on enduring documents?**

Title IX of the Belgian Civil Code deals with the protection of adults. Articles 489-490/2 BCC of this title concern the provisions on the *zorgvolmacht*. Article 490/2 §1 BCC stipulates that unless otherwise specified by law, the *zorgvolmacht* is also subject to the provisions of articles 1984-2010 BCC concerning the (ordinary) mandate agreement.

4. **Give a brief history of the main developments of the law on enduring documents.**

With the Act of 17 March 2013, the Belgian legislator adopted a specific regulatory framework for what is generally known as the 'zorgvolmacht'.[21] Although before that time, it was already possible to make a *zorgvolmacht* – to which the provisions of article 1984-2010 BCC apply – the Belgian legislator considered it necessary to adopt a specific regulatory framework. With this legislative framework, the Belgian legislator sought to fulfil various objectives, namely: to create legal certainty; to prevent the misuse or abuse of the *zorgvolmacht* by the attorney as much as possible; to create awareness among adults and to motivate them to make

18. Wuyts 2020, §72.
19. Wuyts 2020, §71.
20. Wuyts 2020, §119.
21. In Dutch: Wet tot hervorming van de regelingen inzake onbekwaamheid en tot instelling van een nieuwe beschermingsstatus die strookt met de menselijke waardigheid.

a *zorgvolmacht*; to assign a more significant role to the social network of the adult; and, to reduce the workload of the courts.[22] The legislative framework on the *zorgvolmacht* was, on specific points, amended and supplemented with the Act of 21 December 2018, which entered into force on the 1st of March 2019. The Act of 21 December 2018 included an extension of the scope of affairs that can be included in the *zorgvolmacht*. Until 2019, the scope of the *zorgvolmacht* was restricted to the adult's financial affairs. As of 2019, it is also possible for adults to provide for their personal affairs through a *zorgvolmacht*.[23] The Act of 21 December 2018 also introduced the mandatory registration of the termination of the *zorgvolmacht* and an obligation for the attorney to inform the court of the termination of the *zorgvolmacht*.[24]

5. How does the specific legal regime concerning enduring documents relate to the (general) law on powers of attorney and other related legal figures?

Before the entry into force on the 1st of September of the 2013 Act introducing the *zorgvolmacht*, adults could make their own provisions for a future period of incapacity. This could be done using a mandate agreement (articles 1984-2010 BCC). As discussed under No. 3, with the 2013 Act, a specific regulatory framework was established for situations in which the mandate agreement would be used to provide for a future period of incapacity. The main difference between the ordinary mandate agreement regulated in articles 1984-2010 BCC and what is more generally known as the *zorgvolmacht* is that a valid *zorgvolmacht* needs to fulfil two requirements. Article 490 BCC stipulates that the *zorgvolmacht* must have the specific aim to provide for out-of-court protection and, in addition, must be registered.[25] To ensure that adults would not circumvent these and other requirements concerning the *zorgvolmacht*, the possibility of using the provisions of articles 1984-2010 to provide for a future period of incapacity was explicitly excluded by the Belgian legislator. The 2013 Act amended article 2003 BCC on the termination of mandate agreements. As of the 1st of September 2014, both ordinary mandate agreements and *zorgvolmachten* not meeting the requirements of article 490 BCC are terminated upon the adult's incapacity. Wylleman and Swennen note that this provision does not apply to mandate agreements made before the 1st of September 2014. These remain valid to date.[26]

6. Are there any recent proposals for reform in this area?

22. Belgian House of Representatives, Parl. St. Kamer 2011-12, nr. 53-1009/10, pp. 29-31; Wuyts 2020b, p. 235.
23. Belgian House of Representatives, Parl. St. Kamer 2018-19, nr. 54-3303/8, pp. 6-7.
24. Scheers & Scheers 2019, pp. 1522-1524.
25. Wylleman 2014, pp. 28-33.
26. Wylleman 2014, pp. 28-33; Swennen 2013, pp. 622-623.

No, an evaluation of the Act of 17 March 2013 – including the provisions on the *zorgvolmacht* – is scheduled to take place in 2023.[27]

7. **Are there statistics available on the number of (registered) enduring documents in each country? And if so, what are they?**

As No. 24 discusses in more detail, adults must register the *zorgvolmacht* in a register kept by the Royal Association of Belgian Notaries.[28] Based on information from this register, Wuyts provides an overview of the annual number of enduring documents registered from 2014 until the first quarter of 2020.[29]

Year	Number of zorgvolmachten registered
2014	1.522
2015	11.932
2016	19.038
2017	28.644
2018	37.312
2019	54.955
2020 (first quarter)	15.652

B. *Enduring documents and adult protection measures ordered by the court or an administrative authority*

8. **How do enduring documents relate to adult protection measures ordered by the court or an administrative authority? Is there a principle of subsidiarity in place?**

According to article 492 BCC, the court may only order an adult protection measure when and to the extent it determines that such a measure is necessary and the *zorgvolmacht* does not suffice. As the phrase 'to the extent' makes clear, the scope of the judicial protection measure should be as limited as possible. Article 492 BCC clarifies that the *zorgvolmacht* continues to apply insofar as it is compatible with the adult protection measure. The court must determine the conditions under which the *zorgvolmacht* may still be executed.[30]

27. Article 224 Act 17 March 2013.
28. Article 490(1) BCC.
29. Wuyts 2020b, pp. 224-265. In his report Wuyts provides information on the number of registered *zorgvolmachten,* the number of registered amendments of the *zorgvolmacht* and the number of registered terminations of the *zorgvolmacht*. These numbers have been taken together in the table presented in this country report. For an overview of the numbers on the different types of registrations see Wuyts 2020b, p. 245.
30. Wuyts 2020, §117.

9. **Is there an obligation for the court or the administrative authority to check whether an enduring document is in place?**

When the court is confronted with an application for an adult protection measure, the clerk's office must verify whether the adult has made a *zorgvolmacht*. This follows from article 1242 of the Belgian Judicial Code, stipulating that the clerk's office needs to verify whether a *zorgvolmacht*, a decision to terminate the *zorgvolmacht* or an advance directive containing the adult's instructions as to whom should be appointed as representative in the event a judicial protection measure is deemed necessary, has been registered in the register kept by the Royal Association of Belgian Notaries. If the clerk's office finds that a *zorgvolmacht* has been made, it subsequently asks the notary or the clerk's office of the court where the *zorgvolmacht* has been deposited to forward a certified copy of the document.[31]

10. **Can the measures ordered by the court or the administrative authority be combined with the enduring document?**

As discussed under no. 8, according to article 492 BCC, even in cases where the court finds that an adult protection measure is necessary, a *zorgvolmacht* continues to apply to the extent it can be considered compatible with the judicial protection measure. In this regard, the court determines the conditions under which the *zorgvolmacht* may still be executed. The aforementioned also follows from article 490/1 §2, according to which the court may order an adult protection measure in addition to the *zorgvolmacht*.

11. **Can the enduring document's content or the attorney's powers be changed or expanded by the court or any other institution? And if so, in what cases?**

According to article 490/2 §2 BCC, the court – in the context of a so-called 'alarm bell procedure' (discussed in more detail under no. 32) – may subject the execution of the *zorgvolmacht* by the attorney to the procedural requirements that apply in the event the court orders a judicial protection measure. According to Scheers, this could, for instance, include an obligation for the attorney to obtain the court's authorisation for specific actions or an obligation for the attorney to render account to the court.[32]

According to articles 490 and 490/2 §1 BCC, the attorney must follow the adult's wishes and preferences as recorded in the *zorgvolmacht*. However, Wuyts argues that the attorney can, when necessary, ask the court for permission to deviate

31. Wuyts 2020, §116.
32. Scheers 2014, pp. 214-216.

from these wishes and preferences if the adult – due to incapacity – can no longer indicate his current wishes and preferences.[33] Although no legal provision stipulates the aforementioned concerning the *zorgvolmacht*, Wuyts argues that the courts can apply article 499/1 §3 BCC by analogy. This legal provision concerns the wishes and preferences of the adult included in an advance directive addressed to the court and the court-appointed representative (discussed under no. 2). Article 499/1 §3 BCC makes clear that the courts may relieve the court-appointed representative of the obligation to observe the wishes and preferences recorded in the advance directive if circumstances have since then changed to such an extent that serious doubts arise as to the intention of the adult to have these wishes and preferences observed.

12. On which grounds are state-ordered measures applied, notwithstanding the presence of an enduring document?

Apart from article 492 BCC, stipulating that the court may only order an adult protection measure when and to the extent it finds that the *zorgvolmacht* does not suffice, the Belgian Civil Code does not contain any further specification concerning the grounds based on which the court may find that the *zorgvolmacht* does not suffice. This means that a wide margin of appreciation is granted to the courts when assessing whether the *zorgvolmacht* is sufficient. That being said, the court must substantiate a decision to order an adult protection measure notwithstanding the presence of a *zorgvolmacht*.[34] Although the Belgian Civil Code remains silent regarding the grounds on which the provisions of a *zorgvolmacht* can be considered insufficient, the Belgian government has provided some (broad) directions. In the context of the deliberations on the 2018 Act, the Belgian Minister of Justice noted that except in cases where objections arise regarding the attorney or situations where the execution of the *zorgvolmacht* is considered not in the interest of the adult, there are no reasons to disregard the *zorgvolmacht*.[35]

C. *Form and general content of the enduring document*

13. Are there any requirements as to the form of the enduring document?

As discussed under No. 5, according to article 490 BCC, a *zorgvolmacht* must have the specific aim to provide for out-of-court protection. In addition, the *zorgvolmacht* must be registered in a register kept by the Royal Association of Belgian Notaries. The law does not contain any further requirements regarding

33. Wuyts 2020c, pp. 126-127.
34. Wuyts 2020, §117. Wuyts refers in this regard to article 490/1 §2 BCC.
35. Wutys 2020, §117; Belgian House of Representatives, Parl. St. Kamer 2018-19, nr. 54-3303/8, pp. 26-27.

the form of the *zorgvolmacht*. However, De Feyter and De Nolf note that the registration requirement implies that the *zorgvolmacht* needs to be in writing.[36] In this regard, there are two options: the *zorgvolmacht* can be made in the form of a private document, or it can be made in the form of a notarial deed. The second form is needed if the adult wants to authorise the attorney for matters that, in principle, also require a notarial deed, for example, decisions concerning real estate, such as the sale of a house.[37]

14. **Is the enduring document unilateral or bilateral? Is a signature from the attorney a requirement?**

As noted under No. 2, the *zorgvolmacht* is a popular name for what is, in fact, a mandate agreement. This means that the *zorgvolmacht* is a bilateral document, which presupposes a mutual agreement between the adult and the attorney.[38] Although, according to article 1985 BCC, the attorney may also tacitly accept the *zorgvolmacht*, Verstraete notes that it is advisable that the attorney explicitly accepts the mandate agreement.[39] This is to avoid doubts about the formation of the *zorgvolmacht*. A signature is, in other words, advisable.

15. **Which matters (e.g. financial, health, welfare, personal) can be covered by the enduring document? Conversely, are there particular matters excluded?**

As noted under No. 4, with the Act of 21 December 2018, the legislator extended the scope of affairs that can be included in the *zorgvolmacht*. Since the 1st of March 2019, adults can include provisions concerning their property and financial affairs and their personal affairs in the *zorgvolmacht*.[40] Article 489 BCC also makes clear that the *zorgvolmacht* does not have to be restricted to acts of representation but may include provisions whereby the attorney is asked to manage the adult's affairs. The aforementioned means the adult can, for example, mandate the attorney to enter into agreements, such as an agreement to sell the house. He can also ask the adult to manage his bank account and pay the bills. The adult can also include in the *zorgvolmacht* a decision concerning his choice of a care home in case he can no longer stay home.[41]

Although the scope of affairs that can be included in the *zorgvolmacht* is considerably broad, there are two exceptions. First, with regard to certain matters,

36. De Feyter & De Nolf 2017, p. 6; see also Wuyts 2020, §84.
37. Wuyts 2020, §84; Van Moerkercke 2019, p. 16; De Feyter & De Nolf 2017, p. 6.
38. Verstraete 2019, pp. 168-172.
39. Verstraete 2019, pp. 168-172; see however differently Wuyts 2020, §85 who argues that the attorney must explicitly accept the *zorgvolmacht*.
40. Article 489 BCC.
41. Wuyts 2020, §72; Verstraete 2019, pp. 174-175.

the requirements of specific legislation have to be considered. Wuyts refers to the euthanasia act and the Belgian Act on Patient's Rights. These acts impose particular requirements – such as the requirement that an advance directive for euthanasia must be made in the presence of two adult witnesses – which, as *lex specialis*, take precedence over the regulation of the *zorgvolmacht*.[42] A second exception concerns certain acts considered 'highly personal acts', such as making a will or getting married. The adult cannot authorise the attorney to perform such acts on his behalf.[43]

16. What are the rules, regulations and practices concerning the entry into force of the enduring document?

It is for the adult to decide when the *zorgvolmacht* enters into force. Three options are in this regard distinguished:

1) immediately;
2) upon the incapacity of the adult; or,
3) a combination of the two options above.

Wuyts notes that when the adult decides on the second option, it is advisable that the *zorgvolmacht* clearly stipulates how the adult's incapacity is to be determined. It is, for instance, possible to require the written assessment of a doctor. Based on article 490/1 §2 BCC, the adult can also require the attorney to ask the court to determine the entry into force of the *zorgvolmacht*.[44] An example of the third option in which the *zorgvolmacht* enters into force both immediately and upon the incapacity of the adult is a situation in which the spouse who is appointed as an attorney may act immediately, and the children who are designated as substitute attorneys may act after a formal assessment in which the incapacity of the adult is established.[45]

17. Under which circumstances does the enduring document cease to have effect?

According to Wuyts and Verstraete, a distinction must be made between the termination of the *zorgvolmacht* and the termination of the out-of-court protection provided through the *zorgvolmacht*.[46] The termination of the *zorgvolmacht* in all cases results in the termination of the out-of-court protection.[47] However, this

42. Wuyts 2020, §73.
43. Wuyts 2020, §73 & §94; Verstraete 2019, pp. 174-175.
44. Belgian House of Representatives, Parl. St. Kamer 2018-19, nr. 54-3303/11, p. 6; Wuyts 2020, §82.
45. De Feyter & De Nolf 2017, p. 6.
46. Wuyts 2020, §111; Verstraete 2019, pp. 186-189.
47. Wuyts 2020, §111.

is not necessarily the case when it is the other way around, as explained in more detail below. Article 2003 BCC concerning the ordinary mandate agreement – which, according to article 490 §1 BCC, also applies to the *zorgvolmacht* – distinguishes four situations in which the mandate agreement ends.

1. *Revocation by the adult*

Article 2003 BCC stipulates that the mandate agreement, or the *zorgvolmacht*, ends when the adult revokes it. Article 490 BCC clarifies that only an adult with sufficient capacity can revoke the *zorgvolmacht*. In addition, adults for which an adult protection measure has been ordered – which can be combined with the *zorgvolmacht* – cannot revoke the *zorgvolmacht*.[48] As No. 26 discusses in more detail, the adult must register the termination of the *zorgvolmacht*. Article 490/2 §3 BCC clarifies that the out-of-court protection ends through this registration.

2. *Termination by the attorney*

According to article 2003 BCC, the attorney may end the mandate agreement. This does not necessarily have to result in the end of the out-of-court protection, as the adult may have appointed a substitute attorney who can take over the role of attorney. When this is not the case and the adult cannot make a new *zorgvolmacht*, the out-of-court protection ends as soon as the termination of the *zorgvolmacht* has been registered.[49]

3. *Death or bankruptcy of the adult or attorney*

The mandate agreement or *zorgvolmacht* ends upon the adult or attorney's death or bankruptcy.[50] Concerning the attorney, Verstraete mentions two additional circumstances under which a *zorgvolmacht* could end: when the attorney is subject to an adult protection measure or when the attorney falls under the scope of the restrictions included in article 490/1 BCC.[51] As No. 18 discusses in more detail, two restrictions are included in article 490/1 BCC concerning the choice of attorney. These restrictions that oppose the appointment of a person as an attorney also preclude the continuation of the appointment in the event the attorney has already started his task. Verstraete notes that this does not necessarily mean the end of the *zorgvolmacht* or the out-of-court protection when multiple attorneys have been appointed. However, it does mean the end of the *zorgvolmacht* in the event these attorneys are to act jointly.[52]

48. Verstraete 2019, pp. 186-189.
49. Article 490 §3 BCC; Wuyts 2020, §112.
50. Article 2003 BCC uses the Dutch phrase 'kennelijk onvermogen', which is hard to translate in English. Both Wuyts 2020, §112 and Verstraete 2019, p. 187 note that it includes bankruptcy and for convenience I have therefore used this term.
51. Verstraete 2019, pp. 186-189.
52. Ibid.

3. *Incapacity or prodigality of the adult or the attorney*
Article 2003 BCC clarifies that the *zorgvolmacht* does not end upon the adult's incapacity when the requirements of article 490 BCC (discussed under No. 13) have been met. The *zorgvolmacht* could end if the attorney comes into a situation as referred to in articles 488/1 BCC (incapacity) or 488/2 BCC (prodigality).[53] Once again, this does not necessarily have to end the out-of-court protection if the adult has appointed a substitute attorney.

In addition to these four situations, resulting in a termination of the *zorgvolmacht*, article 490/2 BCC distinguishes five situations in which the out-of-court protection ends. The out-of-court protection ends:

- when the requirements of article 488/1 BCC (incapacity) or 488/2 BCC (prodigality) are no longer met;
- when the termination of the *zorgvolmacht* by the attorney in accordance with article 490 BCC has been registered;
- when the revocation of the *zorgvolmacht* by the adult in accordance with article 490 BCC has been registered;
- when the adult or attorney has died or has been placed under an adult protection measure in accordance with article 492/1 BCC;
- through a decision of the court in accordance with article 490/2 §2 or article 490/1 §2.[54]

As indicated above, a termination of the out-of-court protection does not necessarily have to result in a termination of the *zorgvolmacht*. This is, for example, the case concerning the first bullet. Although the end of a temporary period of incapacity means that out-of-court protection is no longer necessary, it does not mean that the adult may no longer use the *zorgvolmacht* – which can also function as an ordinary mandate agreement – to ask the attorney to act on his behalf.[55]

D. The attorney

18. **Who can be appointed as an attorney? Are there restrictions concerning the choice of attorney (e.g. exclusion of certain people)?**

Regarding restrictions concerning the choice of attorney, article 490/1 § 1 BCC stipulates that the adult may not appoint a person subject to an adult protection measure or a person who, according to article 496/6 BCC, may not be appointed

53. Wuyts 2020, §114; Verstraete 2019, pp. 186-189.
54. See No. 10. In addition, to ordering an adult protection measure which is to complement the *zorgvolmacht*, the court may also order an adult protection which is to (completely) replace the *zorgvolmacht*.
55. Wuyts 2020, §115; Verstraete 2019, pp. 186-189.

as administrator.[56] Article 496/6 BCC includes a list of persons and legal entities who cannot act as administrators. For example, the management or staff members of the institution where the adult resides may not be appointed as administrators. In addition, persons who, based on article 32 of the Child Protection Law, have been deprived of parental authority cannot be active as administrators. Finally, article 496/6 BCC states that legal entities, in principle, cannot act as administrators unless it concerns a private foundation exclusively dedicated to ensuring the interests of the adult concerned.[57]

19. **Does the legal system allow for the appointment of more than one attorney? Can these attorneys act jointly, concurrently, separately or as substitutes?**

Both Wuyts and Wylleman note that the adult can appoint more than one attorney.[58] During the debate on the bill introducing the *zorgvolmacht*, it was noted in Parliament that the adult might appoint two or more attorneys to act jointly, concurrently or separately, or as substitutes.[59] Although Parliament, in the context of this debate, remained silent as to what these four different types might look like in practice, the four types are also distinguished in principle 4(2) of the Council of Europe Recommendation CM/Rec(2009)11 on Principles concerning continuing powers of attorney and advance directives for incapacity. In this regard, the explanatory memorandum attached to the Recommendation makes clear that an adult may require the attorneys to act and decide together (jointly); may appoint attorneys for different affairs, e.g. an attorney for financial matters and an attorney for health and medical matters (concurrently); may authorise attorneys to act and decide independently (separately); and, may appoint one or more substitute attorneys who are to replace the first-mentioned attorney in case this person is unable or unwilling to take up the task of attorney (substitutes).[60] It is also possible for the adult to combine one or more of the types mentioned above.[61] When more than one attorney is appointed, there is the risk that they may disagree on specific points, resulting in extreme cases in a conflict between the attorneys. The Belgian legislator has considered this through article 490/2 §1 BCC, stipulating that the court shall settle disputes between the attorneys based on what is deemed to be in the adult's interests. Before taking a decision, the court is obliged first to try and reconcile both parties.[62] Instead of leaving it to the court to

56. Wuyts 2020, §96; Wylleman 2014, pp. 34-37.
57. Verstraete 2019, p. 168-172; De Feyter & De Nolf 2017, p. 5.
58. Wuyts 2020, §96; Wylleman 2014, pp. 34-37.
59. Wuyts 2020, §96; Belgian House of Representatives, Parl. St. Kamer 2011-12, nr. 53-1009/10, p. 31.
60. Council of Europe, *Recommendation CM/Rec (2009)11 and explanatory memorandum*, Strasbourg: Council of Europe Publishing 2011, pp. 38-41.
61. Wuyts 2020, §97; Wylleman 2014, pp. 34-37.
62. Verstraete 2019, p. 189.

reconcile both parties, it is also possible for the adult to include in the *zorgvolmacht* a decision-making procedure for dealing with differences of opinion between the attorneys.[63]

20. **Is there a duty for the attorney to inform the court or any other administrative body if the appointment to act as an attorney is refused or discontinued?**

As discussed in more detail under No. 26, a decision to terminate the *zorgvolmacht* has to be registered in the register kept by the Royal Association of Belgian Notaries. Article 490 BCC clarifies that if the attorney wants to end his appointment resulting in the termination of the *zorgvolmacht*, it is his responsibility to inform the notary or the clerk's office where the *zorgvolmacht* has been registered of this decision. This obligation does not apply if the adult has appointed a substitute attorney who can take over the execution of the *zorgvolmacht*. The attorney must then inform his successor about the decision to discontinue his task.[64] Verstraete notes that the attorney has a duty of care to ensure that the substitute attorney can continue the execution of the *zorgvolmacht* without a hiatus.[65]

21. **Are there any rules or regulations regarding the attorney's role in line with, for example, article 12(4) UNCRPD and Principle 10 of the Council of Europe Recommendation 2009/11?**

As discussed under No. 1, the 2013 reform aimed to ensure compliance with international human rights instruments, including Council of Europe Recommendation CM/Rec(2009)11 on principles concerning continuing powers of attorney and advance directives for incapacity. This is particularly evident concerning Principle 10 of this recommendation, which appears to have been adopted by the Belgian legislator almost to the letter. According to article 490 BCC, the adult can include his wishes and preferences in the *zorgvolmacht*, and the attorney is, according to article 490/2 §1 BCC, obliged to observe these wishes and preferences as far as possible.[66] Article 490/2 §1 BCC makes clear that the attorney is, in addition, obliged to involve the adult as much as possible in the execution of the *zorgvolmacht*. The attorney must consult the adult – and, if applicable, a

63. Wuyts 2020, §98.
64. Belgian House of Representatives, Parl. St. Kamer 2018-19, nr. 54-3303/001, p. 22; Wuyts 2020, §112.
65. Verstraete 2019, p. 168.
66. Article 490 BCC uses the term 'principles', but discussion in Parliament has made clear that this term is to be understood as encompassing the adult's wishes and preferences concerning the execution of the *zorgvolmacht* (Belgian House of Representatives, Parl. St. Kamer 2011-12, nr. 53-1009/10, p. 39; see also Wuyts 2020, p. 124).

person appointed by the adult – at regular intervals and at least once a year.[67] According to article 490/2 §1 BCC, the attorney must keep his assets separated from the adult's assets. The bank accounts of the adult must be registered in the adult's name. Finally, according to article 1993 BCC, the attorney is obliged to render account.[68]

22. **Are there any limits as to the authorisations/responsibilities that can be given by the adult to the attorney (e.g. concerning personal decisions, such as making a will and deciding about donations)? Are there any rules concerning 'selbsteintritt'?**

As discussed under No. 15, there are certain 'highly personal acts' – such as making a will and getting married – for which the attorney cannot be authorised. However, the attorney can be authorised to donate on behalf of the adult. This requires an explicit power of attorney in which the adult must clearly stipulate the object, the beneficiary and the terms and conditions of the donation. According to Wylleman and Verstraete, this requirement should not be interpreted too rigidly; it suffices when the elements mentioned above are incorporated in such a way that they are determinable.[69] In this regard, Wylleman presents the example of a provision stipulating that all grandchildren are to receive an annual sum of €1000,- on New Year's Day.[70]

Although, in Belgium, an administrator is, in principle, not allowed to receive a donation from the adult concerned, this rule does not apply to attorneys. This means an attorney may receive a gift from the adult.[71] However, as no. 33 discusses in more detail, there are particular rules managing conflicts of interest, stipulating that the attorney may not act when there is a conflict of interest. A conflict of interest will generally be assumed when the attorney is the beneficiary of a donation. A so-called 'attorney ad hoc' may, in these instances, donate on behalf of the adult to the attorney.

23. **Does the legal system allow for the remuneration of the attorney?**

As discussed under No. 5, according to article 490/2 §1 BCC, the provisions of articles 1984 till 2010 BCC concerning the mandate agreement also apply to the *zorgvolmacht*. Article 1986 BCC makes clear that unless otherwise agreed by both the adult and the attorney, the attorney does not receive a salary. According to

67. Wuyts 2020, §98.
68. Wuyts 2020, § 102; Verstraete 2019, p. 169.
69. Verstraete 2019, p. 175; Wylleman 2014, p. 35.
70. Wylleman 2014, p. 35.
71. Wuyts 2020, §101; Verstraete 2019, pp. 170-172.

article 1999 BCC, the adult is, however, obliged to reimburse the costs the attorney encounters in the execution of his task. Wylleman notes that article 1999 BCC does not require the expenses to be 'necessary'. It is sufficient that they were useful.[72]

E. *Registration*

24. Are enduring documents registered? If yes, is registration voluntary or mandatory?

Article 490 BCC stipulates that the *zorgvolmacht* must be registered in the central register of the Royal Association of Belgian Notaries. Registration is, in other words, mandatory. A request to register the *zorgvolmacht* can be directed to the clerk's office of the court located at the place of residence or domicile of the adult. The adult can also ask the notary who has drafted the *zorgvolmacht* to register the *zorgvolmacht*. Both the clerk's office of the court and the notary are obliged to ensure that the *zorgvolmacht* is registered in the Central Register kept by the Royal Association of Belgian Notaries within 15 days.[73]

25. When does registration occur (e.g. registration directly after the enduring document has been made, registration upon entry into force, registration upon acceptance of the appointment by the attorney)?

The *zorgvolmacht* must be registered before the attorney starts or continues to act on behalf of the adult because the adult, due to incapacity, is no longer able to manage his own affairs (a *zorgvolmacht* may also enter into force immediately, in which case it functions as an ordinary mandate agreement until the moment of the adult's incapacity). In other words, although the adult is not obliged to register the *zorgvolmacht* directly after it has been made, he is strongly advised to do so.[74]

26. Are changes and terminations of enduring documents registered?

Article 490 BCC makes clear that a termination of the *zorgvolmacht* must also be registered. The obligation applies to both the adult upon revocation of the *zorgvolmacht* and to the attorney upon the termination of the *zorgvolmacht*. With the obligation to register the termination of the *zorgvolmacht*, the legislator wanted to enable the courts to check whether the *zorgvolmacht* presented by the attorney concerns a valid *zorgvolmacht*.[75] As discussed under No. 20, the attorney must

72. Wylleman 2014, pp. 34-37.
73. Wuyts 2020, §86; Verstraete 2019, pp. 182-183.
74. Wuys 2020, §85; Verstraete 2019, pp. 182-183.
75. Belgian House of Representative, Parl. St. Kamer 2018-19, nr. 54-3303/001, p. 22; Wuyts 2020, §112.

register the termination of the *zorgvolmacht* and inform the court when necessary, ensuring that the adult is not left without support and protection. According to article 490 BCC, the adult may also register changes concerning the *zorgvolmacht*. However, there does not seem to be an obligation to do so.

27. **Which parties can access the register? And to what extent do third parties have access (e.g. notification of the existence of an enduring document or access to the content of the enduring document)?**

Article 490 BCC stipulates that detailed regulation concerning the establishment, administration and consultation of the register will be provided for through a royal decree. This royal decree entered into force on the 1st of September 2014.[76] According to article 10 §2 of the decree, only notaries, the courts, the public prosecutor (in the course of his duties), the attorney and the adult may consult the information included in the register.[77] To do so, a request to consult the information must be submitted to the Royal Association of Belgian Notaries. Furthermore, article 8 of the decree clarifies that the register only contains information such as the adult's name, domicile, date and place of birth and information such as the name of the notary who has drawn up the deed or the court where the *zorgvolmacht* has been deposited. In other words, the register does not provide access to the content of the *zorgvolmacht*.

F. Capacity, supervision and control measures

28. **What is the legal consequence of the entry into force of the enduring document? Does the adult retain legal capacity?**

The adult retains legal capacity upon the entry into force of the *zorgvolmacht*.[78] However, according to Wuyts, adults can include a so-called 'restriction clause' in the *zorgvolmacht*. By doing so, the adult agrees he will no longer perform those legal acts for which he has authorised the attorney to act on his behalf.[79]

29. **Does the legal system provide protection against so-called 'ill-considered decisions' by the adult?**

76. In Dutch this decree is referred to as the: 'Koninklijk besluit houdende vaststelling van de regels inzake oprichting, beheer en raadpleging van het centraal register van lastgevingsovereenkomsten met het oog op het regelen van een buitengerechtelijke bescherming en van het centraal register van verklaringen betreffende de aanwijzing van een bewindvoerder of vertrouwenspersoon'.
77. Wuyts 2020, §86.
78. Wuyts 2020, §77.
79. Wuyts 2020, §95.

Since the adult remains legally capable of acting, the *zorgvolmacht* offers limited protection against so-called 'ill-considered decisions' taken by the adult. Both Wuyts and Verstraete, therefore, note that in situations where the adult is at risk of impoverishing himself or is the subject of abuse by third parties, a judicial protection measure seems more suited to protect the interests of the adult concerned.[80] In this regard, several experts interviewed in the context of this country report discussed the possibility of combining a *zorgvolmacht* with a judicial protection measure. As discussed under no. 1, the court can declare a person legally incapable of certain acts. The *zorgvolmacht* can then remain in force.

30. **How is the validity of the document ensured? Is the validity of the enduring document checked at the time the enduring document is made as to the capacity of the adult, freedom from undue influence, etc.?**

As discussed under No. 13, the *zorgvolmacht* can be made by the adult himself through a private document, or it can be made with the assistance of the notary in the form of a notarial deed. Verstraete rightly observes that a notarial *zorgvolmacht* offers more guarantees, as the notary can vouch for the correct date and signature on the *zorgvolmacht*. The notary is, in addition, obliged to verify whether the adult has the capacity to draw up the *zorgvolmacht*.[81] Doubts and disputes about the validity of the *zorgvolmacht* can be brought to the court's attention. Under article 490/1 §2 BCC, the court can ex officio or at the request of the adult, the attorney or any other interested party, take a decision on the entry into force or the execution of the *zorgvolmacht*.[82] In this regard, it is up to the person questioning the validity of the *zorgvolmacht* to prove that the conditions for a valid *zorgvolmacht* have not been met, for example, by providing the court with evidence that the adult lacked the capacity to make a *zorgvolmacht* at the time of signing.[83]

31. **What options are available to the adult concerning supervision and control of the execution of the enduring document?**

Adults may include provisions in their *zorgvolmacht* to ensure there is a form of supervision on the actions of the attorney in place. Wuyts provides several examples in this regard, such as:

- the appointment of multiple attorneys;
- the appointment of a supervisory attorney or 'trusted person', i.e. a person who supervises the actions of the attorney; is involved by the attorney in major decisions; assists the adult concerned in expressing his will and helps the adult

80. Wuyts 2020, §77; Verstraete 2019, pp. 166-167.
81. Verstraete 2019, p. 181.
82. Wuyts 2020, §106; Wylleman 2014, p. 38.
83. Wuyts 2020, §106.

to articulate how specific actions are experienced; and initiates the 'alarm bell procedure' upon signs that something is wrong;[84]
- an obligation for the attorney to consult the adult concerned and (other) family members regularly;
- an obligation for the attorney to inform and obtain the consent of, for example, the adult's children for actions such as the sale of the family home
- an obligation for the attorney to annually render account to, for example, the adult's children.[85]

32. **Is there any supervision of the attorney by the state (e.g. the court or another administrative body)? If so, are there any possibilities for these institutions to intervene in the execution of the enduring document (e.g. appointment of a third party to supervise the attorney)?**

As discussed under no. 30, the court can – under article 490/1 §2 BCC – ex officio or at the request of the adult, the attorney or any other interested party, take a decision on the entry into force or the execution of the *zorgvolmacht*.[86] In the context of this procedure, the court examines whether the conditions of article 488/1 or 488/2 BCC have been met, whether the *zorgvolmacht* is in accordance with the adult's interests and whether the attorney has accepted the authority conferred to him. If the court finds this is the case, the court orders the execution of the *zorgvolmacht* in accordance with article 490/2 BCC. If the court finds the abovementioned conditions have not been met, the court can order a judicial protection measure on top of the *zorgvolmacht* or entirely or partially replacing the *zorgvolmacht*.[87] The possibility for the court to intervene, ex officio, was added to article 490/1 §2 BCC through an amendment. This was done to ensure the prompt and efficient action of the court regarding out-of-court protection, providing the court with the tools to monitor and guide the attorney's actions where necessary.[88]

The Belgian legislator has also provided for a so-called 'alarm bell procedure', which can be used to bring (potential) situations of abuse or misuse of the *zorgvolmacht* to the court's attention.[89] Any interested party (family, neighbours, friends, etc.) can approach the court within the framework of the alarm bell procedure. According to Wuyts and Verstraete, professional actors such as bankers and notaries have a duty of care to inform the court when there are indications that the attorney is not acting in the interests of the adult concerned.[90] The court may –

84. See also Verstraete 2019, p. 173.
85. Wuyts 2020b, pp. 298-300 & pp. 311-312.
86. Wuyts 2020, §106; Wylleman 2014, p. 38.
87. Wuyts 2020, §106.
88. Wuyts 2020, §106; Belgian House of Representative, Parl. St. Kamer 2011-12, nr. 53-1009/7, pp. 1-2.
89. Wuyts 2020, §107; Verstraete 2019, p. 191.
90. Wuyts 2020, §107; Verstraete 2019, pp. 181-182.

when it finds the execution of the *zorgvolmacht* by the attorney is of such a nature that the adult's interests are adversely affected – partially or entirely terminate the *zorgvolmacht* and order a judicial protection measure instead. As discussed under no. 11, the court can also subject the execution of the *zorgvolmacht* to the procedural requirements that apply when a judicial protection measure is ordered. Examples are an obligation for the attorney to obtain the court's authorisation for particular actions (article 499/7 BCC) or an obligation to periodically render account to the court (499/14 BCC).[91]

33. Is regulation in place concerning (potential) conflicts of interest between the adult's and the attorney's interests?

Under a general principle of law, it is not possible in Belgium for the attorney to act as the counterparty of the adult concerned.[92] Article 490/2 §1 BCC makes this, concerning the *zorgvolmacht*, clear by stipulating that in the event there is a conflict of interest between the interests of the attorney and those of the adult concerned, the court shall appoint – ex officio, upon the request of the adult or any other interested party – a so-called 'attorney ad hoc'. The 'attorney ad hoc' temporarily acts in the place of the 'ordinary' attorney regarding those matters where a conflict of interests exists. The appointment of an attorney ad hoc can be left to the court's discretion. The adult can, however, also include the appointment of an attorney ad hoc in the *zorgvolmacht*.[93]

G. *Law in action*

34. What are considered the advantages and the disadvantages of enduring documents?

The majority of the experts interviewed in the context of this country report considered the main advantage of the *zorgvolmacht* to be that it enables adults to make their own provisions for a future period of incapacity, together with the family and without the interference of the state. This advantage is, indeed, also frequently mentioned in the literature. Van Moerkercke notes in this regard that it is for the adult to decide when the *zorgvolmacht* will enter into force. In addition, she notes that intervention by the court or any other administrative authority concerning the *zorgvolmacht* is not required in Belgium, meaning that everything can be discussed and decided within the family setting.[94] The main disadvantage of the *zorgvolmacht* is the risk of misuse or abuse of the *zorgvolmacht*. One of the

91. Wuyts 2020, §107; Scheers 2014, pp. 214-216.
92. This was confirmed in a case before the court in Antwerp (29-01-2019), see also Wuyts 2020, §98.
93. Wuyts 2020, §98.
94. Van Moerkercke 2019, p. 14.

experts noted that when the attorney lacks good intentions, this can stay under the radar for quite some time. Another concern is the risk of undue influence, where adults are unduly influenced by, for example, the prospective attorney to make a *zorgvolmacht*. This is, once again, a concern that is also frequently discussed in the literature. For instance, De Feyter and De Nolf outline the various risks, such as the risk that the attorney acts based on a *zorgvolmacht* which has not yet entered into force, has been revoked, or has not fulfilled the legal requirements as stipulated in article 490 BCC. In addition, they refer to situations where the attorney acts outside the remit of his powers and does not respect the wishes and preferences stipulated by the adult.[95] De Feyter and De Nolf note in this regard that if the *zorgvolmacht* fulfils the requirements of article 490 BCC, a third party, when acting in good faith, may assume that the attorney is acting on behalf of the adult.[96] Other disadvantages mentioned by the experts interviewed in the context of this country report include family disputes, situations in which the adult does not have any close relatives who can be appointed as an attorney, and cases in which an adult appoints an attorney who is not suited to the task.

Through an exploratory study – discussed in more detail under no. 35 – 27 professionals (lawyers, notaries, judges, etc.) were asked what the advantages and disadvantages of the *zorgvolmacht* are according to them. In this regard, the autonomy of the adult to choose his own attorney and to determine the scope of authority conferred to this attorney was considered an important advantage of the *zorgvolmacht*.[97] However, respondents of the exploratory study also mentioned several disadvantages and problems with the execution of the *zorgvolmacht*, such as a lack of specificity of the provisions included in the *zorgvolmacht*, resulting in some cases in a refusal of transactions by financial institutions; a lack of clarity concerning the entry into force of the *zorgvolmacht*; attorneys disregarding the provisions of the *zorgvolmacht* (such as a prohibition to donate on behalf of the adult); and more generally a lack of supervision and safeguards meaning the *zorgvolmacht*, according to some respondents, creates 'a false sense of security'.[98]

35. **How does the enduring document function/operate in practice? What works well and what does not? Are there or have there been any problems? How have these been dealt with? Is there any empirical research available on the questions mentioned above?**

Article 224 of the Act of 17 March 2013 stipulates that the application of this act must be evaluated in the ninth year following its entry into force. This evaluation

95. De Feyter & De Nolf 2017, p. 8.
96. De Feyter & De Nolf 2017, p. 8-9.
97. Wuyts 2020b, pp. 260-264.
98. Wuyts 2020b, pp. 260-264.

report must be sent to the Belgian Parliament in the tenth year following the entry into force. This means that the Act of 17 March 2013 is scheduled to be evaluated in 2023, and a report of this evaluation should be available in 2024.[99] In anticipation of this evaluation, an exploratory study – focusing particularly on the *zorgvolmacht* – was conducted by Wuyts in 2020.[100] This study explored whether the legislator's objectives regarding the zorgvolmacht had been achieved in practice.[101] In this regard, the study looked at the following themes:

1) the awareness of the possibility of making a *zorgvolmacht* among citizens and professionals;
2) the role of the social network;
3) the promotion of the adult's autonomy through the *zorgvolmacht*;
4) the primacy of the *zorgvolmacht* as a protection measure;
5) the enforceability of the *zorgvolmacht*;
6) the impact of time; and
7) the prevention of abuse.[102]

To explore these themes, an analysis of published case law and an analysis of the information registered in the central register kept by the Royal Association of Belgian Notaries were undertaken. In addition, interviews – 27 in total – were conducted with important stakeholders (lawyers, judges, notaries, financial institutions, and social services) in the Belgian district of Limburg.[103]

The study contains a thorough initial exploration of the regulatory framework on the *zorgvolmacht* and its application, based on which Wuyts presents a substantial number of recommendations. A comprehensive discussion of all these recommendations is beyond the scope of this country report. Therefore, I will confine myself here to highlight what I consider – within the scope of this country report – the most significant observations and recommendations. With regard to the first theme – the awareness of the possibility of making a *zorgvolmacht* – Wuyts' study shows that mere regulation of an enduring document does not automatically result in general awareness of the possibility of making an enduring document. Although in Belgium, the number of registered *zorgvolmachten* is still annually increasing, Wuyts argues that more can be done to make the general public aware of the possibility of making a *zorgvolmacht* and, more specifically, to provide both the public and professionals with correct information about the usefulness and consequences of making a *zorgvolmacht*.[104]

99. Wuyts 2020b, p. 237.
100. The results of this study were presented at a conference in December 2020 and in written form by means of the publication 'Zorgvolmachten: een zegen of een vloek?'.
101. See no. 4.
102. No. 36 discusses the observations and recommendations concerning the prevention of abuse.
103. Wuyts 2020b, pp. 240-244. These interviews were conducted by students at Hasselt University.
104. Wuyts 2020b, pp. 244-265 & pp. 316-318.

Concerning the second theme (the role of the social network), Wuyts notes that attorneys in Belgium often seem to belong to the social network of the adult concerned (e.g. the partner or the children). However, the appointment of an attorney belonging to the adult's family circle is not in all cases without problems. Wuyts highlights in this context the issue of family disputes, for example, in situations where the adult – to the dismay of the other children – singles out one of the children as an attorney. In some cases, this results in an application for a legal protection measure by family members who have not been appointed attorneys.[105] On the other hand, the appointment of all children can also lead to family disputes, for example, when the adult has authorised all his children to act separately, causing problems in situations where children act independently without consulting one another. Furthermore, *zorgvolmachten* in which the adult authorises all children to act jointly concerning all affairs – meaning the signature of all attorneys is required for all actions, even actions such as the payment of a bill – may result in practical problems with the implementation of the *zorgvolmacht*, for example when one of the children lives abroad.[106] This was, indeed, something also mentioned by one of the experts interviewed in the context of this country report. The proposed solution for the problems discussed above is to oblige the attorney to execute his charge clearly and transparently, for example, by avoiding cash payments that are considered less transparent.[107] To prevent further problems with the implementation of the *zorgvolmacht*, Wuyts also notes that it is important to ensure that attorneys are aware of their appointment and, in addition, that sufficient attention is paid to potential conflicts of interest.[108]

The third theme, addressed by Wuyts, concerns the promotion of the adult's autonomy. As discussed under no. 21, the Belgian legislator has tried through various provisions – such as the possibility for the adult to record his wishes and instructions addressed to the attorney and the obligation for the attorney to involve the adult in the execution of the *zorgvolmacht* – to promote the adult's autonomy. Wuyts concludes, however, that in practice, there is little attention to the execution of these provisions.[109] He notes, in this respect, that the belief in tailor-made protection and the workload this entails play an important role in the question of whether the autonomy of the adult, when it comes to the execution of the *zorgvolmacht*, is stimulated in practice.[110] Concerning the latter aspect (the workload), the task of providing adults with the assistance to formulate and include tailor-made wishes and instructions in the *zorgvolmacht*, in practice,

105. Wuyts 2020b, pp. 265-267 & pp. 318-319.
106. Ibid.
107. Ibid.
108. Ibid.
109. Wuyts 2020b, pp. 276-281 & pp. 319-320.
110. Wuyts 2020b, pp. 319-320.

appears to be a task too time-consuming for notaries. In another publication, Wuyts discusses several ideas to mitigate this problem. He mentions, for example, the possibility of encouraging adults to think about their wishes and instructions in advance – before the meeting with the notary – using a checklist or questionnaire containing examples of wishes and instructions that can be included in the *zorgvolmacht*.[111] As a next step, Wuyts also points out innovative developments such as 'legal tech' and 'legal design', which may allow clients to draft their own *zorgvolmacht* in advance. This *zorgvolmacht* can subsequently be sent to and discussed with the notary, enabling, according to Wuyts, a more targeted contribution by the notary to the process of making a *zorgvolmacht*.[112]

Regarding the fourth theme – the primacy of the *zorgvolmacht* as a protection measure – Wuyts notes that, in practice, the courts respect the primacy of the *zorgvolmacht*. In some cases, such as family disputes, the court imposes additional control measures, such as an obligation for the attorney to render account. The court may also mediate in a conflict or impose an evaluation period during which the court monitors the attorney's actions.[113] Even in situations where the *zorgvolmacht* does not provide for all necessary affairs, the courts respect the priority of the *zorgvolmacht*. An adult protection measure ordered by the courts is, in these instances, limited to matters that have not been included in the *zorgvolmacht*.[114] Concerning the fifth theme, Wuyts concludes that, in practice, there are few difficulties with the enforceability of the *zorgvolmacht*. However, a point of attention is, according to Wuyts, the privacy of the adult concerned. Financial institutions, for example, require a copy of the *zorgvolmacht* and proof of registration. However, these institutions do not have any interest in becoming acquainted with the adult's personal and medical preferences, which the adult may also have included in the *zorgvolmacht*. In this context, Wuyts proposes the introduction of so-called 'certificates', which only include the information relevant to the particular third party.[115] Another point of attention concerns the extent to which third parties, such as the family doctor or a nursing home, know the adult has made a *zorgvolmacht*. In this regard, Wuyts suggests that the adult – when making the *zorgvolmacht* – simultaneously determines who should be informed of the existence of the *zorgvolmacht*.[116]

With the sixth theme – the impact of time – Wuyts briefly touches upon one of the key issues of enduring documents. Over time, the adult's wishes and

111. Wuyts 2020c, pp. 96-97. Wuyts refers in this regard to the checklists and information materials which have been made publicly available in the Netherlands by the Dutch notariate.
112. Ibid.
113. Wuyts 2020b, pp. 281-291 & pp. 321-322.
114. Ibid.
115. Wuyts 2020b, pp. 291-294 & pp. 322-323; Wuyts 2020, pp. 281-291 & pp. 321-322.
116. Wuyts 2020b, pp. 291-294 & pp. 322-323.

preferences may change, and the question is whether adults are sufficiently aware of the impact time may have on their wishes and preferences. In this regard, Wuyts concludes that the number of amended *zorgvolmachten* is modest.[117] Furthermore, he concludes that adults do not always seem aware of the possibility of appointing another attorney or amending their *zorgvolmacht*. In some cases, adults are afraid to oppose the decisions or actions of their attorney, so they leave the *zorgvolmacht* intact.[118] Wuyts recommends, in this respect, that adults be informed about the impact of time and the possibilities to amend or terminate the *zorgvolmacht*. He furthermore advises that adults provide for so-called 'changed circumstances' through the *zorgvolmacht*.[119] For example, by including provisions in the *zorgvolmacht* stipulating in which circumstances the attorney may deviate from the adult's wishes and preferences. Another possibility, according to Wuyts, is to appoint one or more 'trusted persons' who can assess whether there are indeed changed circumstances and, in addition, what the impact of these changed circumstances is on the wishes and preferences of the adult.[120]

36. **Is there any information available on the number and type of cases where there has been (financial) abuse or misuse by the attorney?**

The study discussed under no. 35, provides insight into cases where there has been (financial) abuse or misuse by the attorney. Wuyts lists examples of abuse or misuse that have emerged in court cases and examples mentioned by respondents in the interviews. The examples mentioned by the respondents seem to boil down to the same thing, namely, a situation in which the attorney has used the adult's assets for purposes other than those intended.[121] This is discovered, for instance, when the bills of the care home are no longer paid by the attorney. Another example mentioned in the study concerned a situation in which a bank informed the court that an amount of €1000 was withdrawn by the adult daily, which was subsequently handed over to a person waiting outside.[122] Wuyts' study shows that objections to the person of the attorney may also arise on other grounds. He refers, in this regard, to a situation in which the attorney used the *zorgvolmacht* to protect his own interests against those of his brother and sister and a situation in which the attorney did not undertake any efforts to receive and become acquainted with the mail of the adult concerned and consequently did not pay the bills of the care home.[123] As the distinction between the terms 'abuse' and 'misuse' makes

117. Wuyts 2020b, pp. 294-297 & pp. 323-324.
118. Ibid.
119. Wuyts 2020b, pp. 323-324.
120. Wuyts 2020c, pp. 126-127.
121. Wuyts 2020b, pp. 302-305.
122. Ibid.
123. Wuyts 2020b, pp. 301-302, referring to a case before the court in Etterbeek (20-12-2018) and a case before the court in Gent (20-12-2019).

clear, situations in which the attorney acts contrary to the adult's interests are not in all cases intentional, as is also confirmed in Wuyts' study.[124] Wuyts notes that whether the attorney misuses the authority conferred to him can also be linked to discussions within the family about what constitutes 'good care' for the adult concerned.[125] In this regard, several respondents in the interviews emphasised communication, consultation and transparency as a means to avoid conflicts and problems with the execution of the *zorgvolmacht*.[126]

Although it falls beyond the scope of this question, it seems worthwhile to mention Wuyts' recommendations to prevent misuse or abuse as much as possible. According to Wuyts, more attention is needed for the 'alarm bell procedure'. Everyone should be informed about this procedure's existence through brochures, information campaigns and by including information in the *zorgvolmacht*.[127] He also recommends the adoption of an obligation for, e.g. banks to report suspicious transactions and adopting an obligation for the adult to include at least one control/supervisory mechanism in the *zorgvolmacht*. The attorney's responsibility to keep the adult's assets separate from his own assets should, according to Wuyts, be explicitly included in the *zorgvolmacht* to ensure the attorney is aware of this obligation.[128]

37. Are there any (mandatory) safeguards, and how have these been implemented in practice?

Two preventative, mandatory safeguards can, according to Wuyts, be distinguished.[129] First, there are certain restrictions concerning the choice of attorney. As discussed under no. 18, the adult may, for example, not appoint a person subject to an adult protection measure as an attorney. Second, as discussed under no. 25, the *zorgvolmacht* must be registered before the attorney may act on behalf of the adult. Changes and terminations of the zorgvolmacht must also be registered. In my opinion, a third preventative safeguard concerns the appointment of an 'attorney ad hoc', who is to act in the place of the ordinary attorney when there is a conflict of interests (see no. 33). As discussed in more detail under no. 32, a fourth safeguard includes the possibility of the court intervening, for instance, through the so-called 'alarm bell procedure'. The downside of this safeguard is, of course, that the misuse or abuse of

124. Wuyts 2020b, pp. 302-305.
125. Ibid.
126. Wuyts 2020b, pp. 312-315.
127. Wuyts 2020b, pp. 324-326.
128. Ibid.
129. Wuyts 2020, pp. 297-298.

the zorgvolmacht by the attorney may have already occurred and resulted in significant harm before action is taken by the court.[130]

Bibliography

J.P. Bogaert, K. Rotthier, E. van den Eenden & T. Wuyts, Handboek bescherming wilsonbekwamen. Zorgvolmacht en bewind na de wet van 21 december 2018, Mechelen: Wolters Kluwer 2020.

I. Brouhns, 'Legal systems in Belgium: overview', *Thomson Reuters Practical Law*, via: https://uk.practicallaw.thomsonreuters.com/w-019-2986?transitionType=Default&contextData=(sc.Default)&firstPage=true (last accessed: 01-04-2022)

L. De Feyter & E. De Nolf, 'Enkele praktische aandachtspunten bij de redactie van een zorgvolmacht, in het bijzonder in relatie met een Belgische bancaire instelling', *Vermogensplanning in de praktijk* 2017, no. 3, pp. 4-11.

A. van Moerkercke, 'De zorgvolmacht: hoe gedetailleerd moet dat zijn?', *Vermogensplanning in de praktijk* 2019, no. 3, pp. 14-19.

S. Mosselmans & A. van Thienen, 'Bescherming en bewind voor meerderjarigen in het licht van de wet van 17 maart 2013', *Tijdschrift voor Familierecht* 2014, no. 14, pp. 60-96.

C. van Overdijk & W. Pintens, 'Belgium', in: R. Frimston, A. Ruck Keene, C. van Overdijk & A. Ward, *The international protection of adults*, Oxford: Oxford University Press 2015, pp. 442-449.

D. Scheers & C. Scheers, 'Bescherming van meerderjarige onbekwamen: op maat van de praktijk', *Rechtskundig Weekblad* 2019, no. 39, pp. 1522-1532.

D. Scheers, 'Rechtsplegingen', in: P. Senaeve, F. Swennen & G. Verschelden (eds.), *Meerderjarige beschermde personen*, Brugge: Die Keure 2014, pp. 213-276.

F. Swennen, *FL-EUR Empowerment and Protection of Vulnerable Adults Quickscans – Belgium*, via https://www.fl-eur.eu/quick_scans/quick-scans (last accessed: 01-04-2022).

F. Swennen, 'Inleiding en historiek van de wet', in P. Senaeve, F. Swennen & G. Verschelden (eds.), *Meerderjarige beschermde personen*, Brugge: Die Keure 2014, pp. 3-7.

F. Swennen, 'Toepassingsgebied van de wet', in P. Senaeve, F. Swennen & G. Verschelden (eds.), *Meerderjarige beschermde personen*, Brugge: Die Keure 2014, pp. 11-21.

F. Swennen, 'De meerderjarige beschermde personen (Deel I), *Rechtskundig Weekblad* 2013, no. 15, pp. 563-576.

130. Ibid.

F. Swennen, 'De meerderjarige beschermde personen (Deel II), *Rechtskundig Weekblad* 2013, no. 15, pp. 602-623.

J. Verstraete, 'Krijtlijnen voor de zorgvolmacht', in: C. de Wulf, M. op de Beeck & J. Verstraete (eds.), Liber Amicorum Aloïs Van den Bossche, Brugge: die Keure 2019, pp. 163-193.

T. Wuyts, 'Zorgvolmachten: een zegen of een vloek?', in: W. Pintens & C. Declerck (eds.), *Patrimonium 2020*, Brugge: Die Keure 2020, pp. 235-323.

T. Wuyts, 'Een kritische doorlichting van (modellen inzake) zorgvolmachten', in: G. Verschelden (ed.), *Rechtskroniek van het Notariaat*, Herentals: Knops Publishing 2020, pp. 91-131.

T. Wuyts, 'Buitengerechtelijke bescherming', in: J.P. Bogaert, K. Rotthier, E. van den Eenden & T. Wuyts, Handboek bescherming wilsonbekwamen. Zorgvolmacht en bewind na de wet van 21 december 2018, Mechelen: Wolters Kluwer 2020.

A. Wylleman, 'Buitengerechtelijke bescherming', in: P. Senaeve, F. Swennen & G. Verschelden (eds.), *Meerderjarige beschermde personen*, Brugge: Die Keure 2014, pp. 23-48.

Parliamentary documents

- Belgian House of Representatives, Parl. St. Kamer 2011-12, nr. 53-1009/10.
- Belgian House of Representative, Parl. St. Kamer 2011-12, nr. 53-1009/7.
- Belgian House of Representatives, Parl. St. Kamer 2018-19, nr. 54-3303/001.
- Belgian House of Representatives, Parl. St. Kamer 2018-19, nr. 54-3303/8.
- Belgian House of Representatives, Parl. St. Kamer 2018-19, nr. 54-3303/11.

Experts interviewed

- Judge at the court in Kontich
- Judge at the court in Zandhoven
- Scholar and government official
- Lawyer
- Scholar and notary

Appendix 6: Country report England and Wales

Comparative study on enduring documents

Country Report England & Wales

A. General

Brief general description of the legal system of England & Wales

England and Wales are two of four countries (the others are Scotland and Northern Ireland) that comprise the United Kingdom. The United Kingdom has three separate legal systems. England and Wales follow the same legal system, English law.[1] English law has traditionally been characterised as a common law system rather than a civil law system. According to Van Overdijk, the essence of common law is 'that it is made by judges sitting in courts, applying legal precedent to the facts before them'. [2] Common law can, however, be changed and repealed by Parliament, and according to the doctrine of supremacy, legislation issued by Parliament takes precedence over the common law.[3] This has largely happened in relation to the adult protection system in England and Wales, as a comprehensive regulatory framework has been established through the Mental Capacity Act 2005.[4]

Abbreviations used:

–	MCA 2005	Mental Capacity Act 2005
–	LPA	Lasting power of attorney
–	EPA	Enduring power of attorney
–	OPG	Office of the Public Guardian

1. Van Overdijk 2015, p. 180.
2. Van Overdijk 2015, pp. 180-181.
3. Van Overdijk 2015, pp. 180-181; Rab 2021.
4. Van Overdijk 2015, pp. 183-184.

N.B. Where appropriate, this country report will refer to relevant legal provisions from the MCA 2005. This act uses the term 'donor' or 'P' to refer to the adult and 'donee' to refer to the attorney.

1. **Give a brief account of the adult protection system in each country (e.g. state ordered protection measures, private remedies).**

Measures and provisions

The Mental Capacity Act 2005 sets out for England and Wales how decisions should be made by and on behalf of adults when their capacity to make a specific decision is impaired.[5] The act is built upon five principles set out in section 1 of the MCA 2005, which according to Van Overdijk, emphasise the underlying objective of the act, which is the protection of adults who lack the ability to make specific decisions and to maximise the ability of adults who find themselves in such a situation, to participate in the decision-making process.[6] According to section 1 of the MCA 2005:

- A person must be assumed to have capacity unless it is established that he lacks capacity.
- A person is not to be treated as unable to make a decision unless all practicable steps to help him to do so have been taken without success.
- A person is not to be treated as unable to make a decision merely because he makes an unwise decision.
- An act done, or decision made, under this Act for or on behalf of a person who lacks capacity must be done, or made, in his best interests.
- Before the act is done, or the decision is made, regard must be had to whether the purpose for which it is needed can be as effectively achieved in a way that is less restrictive of the person's rights and freedom of action.

The starting point in England and Wales is the principle that a person must be assumed to have capacity unless it is proved otherwise.[7] An assessment of capacity should be decision-specific, and support should be provided to enable adults to make or contribute to making decisions about their lives.[8] Only when a person lacks capacity does the MCA 2005 allow a decision to be taken on that person's behalf. Important in this regard is the best interest principle of section 1(5) of the MCA 2005. Any act done or decision made on behalf of a person who lacks capacity must be in the best interests of the person concerned. In cases where the Court of Protection finds that an adult lacks the capacity to decide – and the adult has not made a lasting power of attorney or enduring power of attorney – the

5. Van Overdijk 2015, pp. 183-184.
6. Van Overdijk 2015, p. 192.
7. Terrell *et al.* 2018 p. 45.
8. Van Overdijk 2015, p. 192; see also Section 1 of the MCA 2005.

court can appoint a deputy to decide and act on behalf of the adult in relation to one or more particular matters (section 16(2) of the MCA 2005). The Court of Protection may also decide on behalf of the adult through a court order, which Ward defines as a 'single intervention designed to manage a specific event'.[9] An example is a court order for the sale of the family home or a court order admitting a person into long-term care.[10] Section 16(4) of the MCA 2005 makes clear that the best interests principle is – when it comes to the appointment of a deputy – also to be understood as a necessity requirement. The court is obliged to regard the principle that a court order is to be preferred to the appointment of a deputy and the principle that 'the powers conferred on a deputy should be as limited in scope and duration as is reasonably practicable in the circumstances'.[11]

Infrastructure

The infrastructure in England and Wales concerning the protection of adults falling within the scope of the MCA 2005 consists of:

A. The Court of Protection;
B. The Office of the Public Guardian.[12]

A. The Court of Protection

Section 45-56 of the MCA 2005 concern the legal provisions on the so-called Court of Protection. All areas of decision-making – financial and property decisions and decisions regarding personal welfare and healthcare – fall under the jurisdiction of this court.[13] The Court of Protection has several important functions, including making declarations on whether or not a person is capable of making a particular decision himself (section 15(1) of the MCA 2005).[14] Furthermore, sections 22 and 23 of the MCA 2005 stipulate the powers of the court in relation to lasting powers of attorney. Section B of this country report discusses these powers in more detail.

B. Office of the Public Guardian

Section 57-60 of the MCA 2005 deal with the so-called Public Guardian, an officer appointed by the Lord Chancellor. The Public Guardian has an office that works for him in carrying out the functions under the MCA 2005, making up the abbreviation of OPG (Office of the Public Guardian).[15] Section 58 of the MCA 2005 deals with the responsibilities of the Public Guardian. These are a mixture

9. Ward 2016, p. 167.
10. Lush & Bielanska 2019, p. 181; Ward 2016, p. 167.
11. Section 16(4) of the MCA 2005.
12. Lush 2019, p. 123.
13. Lush & Bielanska 2017, p. 180.
14. See for an exhaustive list of all main functions of the Court of Protection, Lush & Bielanska 2017, p. 181.
15. Stanyer 2017, p. 96.

of administrative, supervisory and investigatory responsibilities.[16] For example, concerning LPAs and EPAs, the Public Guardian is responsible for maintaining a register of LPAs and EPAs and investigating complaints about attorneys.

2. **Given the definitions of a 'continuing power of attorney' and an 'advance directive' in Council of Europe Recommendation 2009/11, describe the concept or concepts used in each country. What are the legal instruments?**

There are two types of power of attorney in England and Wales which are not revoked by the subsequent incapacity of the adult: the enduring power of attorney and the lasting power of attorney. Besides making a power of attorney, adults may draft a so-called 'advance decision to refuse medical treatment'.

Enduring power of attorney

With the Enduring Powers of Attorney Act 1985, it became possible to create an enduring power of attorney which remained in force after the adult had lost capacity.[17] Through an enduring power of attorney, adults could authorise one or more attorneys to take care of their property and financial affairs. Creating an enduring power of attorney for health and welfare affairs was impossible. The main difference between the enduring and lasting power of attorney, discussed below, is that enduring powers became effective as soon as they were granted unless the EPA specifically stated that the instrument would only take effect upon the mental incapacity of the adult.[18] The requirement to register the EPA arose upon the mental incapacity of the adult, and the EPA could function as an ordinary power of attorney in the meantime. Since 1 October 2007, it is no longer possible to create enduring powers of attorney. That said, enduring powers of attorney granted before 1 October 2007 remain valid. Provisions on the EPA have been included in Schedule 4 of the Mental Capacity Act 2005 to ensure a lawful operation of EPAs made before this date.[19]

Lasting power of attorney

According to section 9 of the Mental Capacity Act 2005, a lasting power of attorney is a power of attorney under which the adult confers on one or more attorneys the authority to make decisions about his property and financial affairs, his personal welfare or both. Like the enduring power of attorney, the lasting power of attorney is not revoked by the subsequent mental incapacity of the adult.

16. Stanyer 2017, p. 96.
17. Lush 2019, p. 134; Thurston 2015, pp. 2-3.
18. Thurston 2015, p. 4 & p. 33.
19. Ward 2016, p. 5.

Advance decisions to refuse medical treatment
Ward defines an advance decision to refuse medical treatment as 'a written or oral statement made by a person, aged 18 or over and with capacity to make it, to refuse consent to a medical treatment in anticipation of the event that he may, in future, lack capacity to make that refusal'.[20] The possibility of making such a document (often called a 'living will') already existed under common law and has been included in sections 24-26 of the MCA 2005. As the name makes clear, the provision relates only to the refusal of treatment.[21] However, this does not mean that it is not possible to record wishes and preferences concerning the treatment a person wishes to receive. Kitzinger and Kitzinger note that such an advance decision is also possible. However, such wishes and preferences are not legally binding.[22]

N.B. Although this country report addresses – under No. 4. – why the legislator deemed it necessary to replace the EPA with the LPA, the remainder focuses on the lasting power of attorney.

3. **What is the current source of law on enduring documents?**

The Mental Capacity Act 2005
Sections 9-14 of the MCA 2005 concern the lasting power of attorney. In addition to the MCA 2005, there are several so-called 'regulations', which for instance, include provisions on the prescribed form of the LPA (see no. 13). Examples are the Lasting Powers of Attorney, Enduring Powers of Attorney and Public Guardian Regulations 2007 and the Lasting Powers of Attorney, Enduring Powers of Attorney and Public Guardian Regulations 2015.

The Mental Capacity Act 2005 Code of Practice
Section 42 of the MCA 2005 stipulates that codes of practice must be issued to guide people with different duties and functions under the MCA 2005. The first Mental Capacity Act 2005 Code of Practice was issued on the 23rd of April 2007 and was supplemented by the Deprivation of Liberty Safeguards Code of Practice on the 3rd of November 2008.[23] The purpose of the MCA 2005 Code of Practice is to provide guidance and information on how the MCA 2005 works in practice. Section 42(4) of the MCA 2005 provides a list of people required 'to have regard' for the Code of Practice, including the 'donee of a lasting power of attorney'. The Code of Practice makes clear that the phrase 'to have regard to' is to be understood

20. Ward 2016, p. 386.
21. Ward 2016, p. 386; Brown *et al.* 2009, pp. 56-57. Both are referring to R (on the application of Burke) v. General Medial Council [2005] EWCA Civ 1003, § 55.
22. Kitzinger & Kitzinger 2016, pp. 4-5.
23. Lush & Bielanska 2017, pp. 376-377.

as: '[being] aware of the Code of Practice when acting or making decisions on behalf of someone who lacks capacity to make a decision for themselves, and they should be able to explain how they have had regard to the Code when acting or making decisions'.[24] Although the persons listed in section 42(4) of the MCA 2005 must have regard to the Code of Practice, the code does not impose a legal duty upon them to comply with it, and there are no specific penalties that can be imposed if they fail to have regard to it.[25] The Code of Practice should be viewed as providing guidance rather than instruction. That being said, if the relevant guidance in the Code of Practice has not been followed, the reasons for departing from it may need to be explained.[26] In this regard section 42(5) of the MCA 2005 stipulates:

> If it appears to a court or tribunal conducting any criminal or civil proceedings that—
> (a) a provision of a code, or
> (b) a failure to comply with a code,
> is relevant to a question arising in the proceedings, the provision or failure must be taken into account in deciding the question.

Common law and the Powers of Attorney Act 1971

Lush and Bielanska note that the LPA is subject to the common law of agency insofar as legislation, such as the MCA 2005, does not stipulate otherwise.[27] The LPA is, in addition, subject to section 1 (execution of powers of attorney), section 3 (proof of instruments creating powers of attorney) and section 5 (protection of donee and third persons where power of attorney is revoked) of the Powers of Attorney Act 1971.[28]

4. **Give a brief history of the main developments of the law on enduring documents.**

Through a power of attorney, a person can give another person the authority to act on his behalf and in his name. In England and Wales, the 'ordinary' power of attorney is automatically revoked when the adult loses capacity.[29] This means an ordinary power of attorney cannot be used to make provisions for future incapacity. Until 1986 the only option available for someone to be authorised to act on behalf of the adult was to submit an application to the Court of Protection to be appointed as what is nowadays referred to as a deputy.[30] Already in 1970,

24. The Mental Capacity Act 2005 Code of Practice, p. 2.
25. Lush & Bielanska 2017, p. 381.
26. The Mental Capacity Act 2005 Code of Practice, p. 1; Lush & Bielanska 2017, pp. 381-382.
27. Lush & Bielanska 2017, p. 3.
28. Ibid.
29. Lush & Bielanska 2017, p. 3 referring to Drew v. Nunn (1878) 4 QBD 661; Ward 2016, pp. 3-4.
30. Lush 2019, p. 133; Ward 2016, pp. 3-4.

the Law Commission of England and Wales noted that it would be desirable if there would be an instrument enabling the attorney to continue to handle the adult's affairs notwithstanding the latter's incapacity.[31] However, it was not until 1983 that the Law Society published the report *The Incapacitated Principal*, which proposed the introduction of the so-called 'enduring power of attorney'.[32] Through the Enduring Powers of Attorney Act 1985 – which entered into force on the 10th of March 1986 – this instrument was introduced in England and Wales, enabling adults to make provisions for their financial and property affairs.[33] The Enduring Powers of Attorney Act 1985 was repealed and replaced by the Mental Capacity Act 2005, which introduced the lasting power of attorney. Ward notes that a number of problems with the EPA were reasons to design the LPA. These included problems with the registration of EPAs and the widespread assumption that some attorneys abused the authority granted to them through the EPA. With the introduction of the LPA, it became possible for adults to make provisions for their welfare and health affairs in addition to their financial and property matters.[34]

5. **How does the specific legal regime concerning enduring documents relate to the (general) law on powers of attorney and other related legal figures?**

As noted under no. 4, under common law, an ordinary power of attorney is automatically revoked upon the mental incapacity of the donor. This principle follows from the notion that 'an act done by a person's agent [attorney] is to be treated as one done by the person himself, so that an agent [attorney] does not have authority to do what his principal cannot himself do'.[35] In other words, adults in England and Wales can only use an LPA to make provisions for future incapacity.

6. **Are there any recent proposals for reform in this area?**

Lush and Bielanska note that there is increasing attention to digitalisation. They refer in this respect to the development of a digital tool by the OPG which can be used to make an LPA online.[36] This development is not welcomed by everyone. Indeed, Lush and Bielanska note that 'there is concern amongst the legal profession and some judges with the ease at which an LPA can be created'.[37] One of the experts interviewed in the context of this country report noted that it is essential

31. Ward 2016, p. 4.
32. Law Commission 1983.
33. Ward 2016, p. 5.
34. Ward 2016, pp. 9-10; See for a more detailed discussion of the reasons to introduce the LPA Lush & Bielanska 2017, pp. 10-15.
35. Law Commission 1983, p. 7.
36. https://www.lastingpowerofattorney.service.gov.uk/home (last accessed: 01-04-2022).
37. Lush & Bielanska 2017, p. 23.

to design a process allowing people time to reflect on the decisions that must be made. A recent public consultation on the modernisation of LPAs shows that the OPG is continuing its efforts in search of what they call a 'safer, simpler and fit for the future' lasting power of attorney.[38]

7. **Are there statistics available on the number of (registered) enduring documents in each country? And if so, what are they?**

Referring to the statistics published in the OPG's Annual Reports, Lush and Bielanska provide an overview of the annual number of LPAs registered from 2009 to 2016.[39] Supplemented by the figures from the Annual Reports of 2017 and 2018, the figures for the period 2009-2018 are as follows[40]:

Accounting year 1 April – 31 March	Number of LPA's registered	Number of EPA's registered
2009-2010	98.400	17.600
2010-2011	162.000	18.200
2011-2012	183.000	16.000
2012-2013	229.000	17.000
2013-2014	295.000	16.000
2014-2015	395.000	15.000
2015-2016	533.000	13.792
2016-2017	635.540	12.778
2017-2018	759.976	11.019
2018-2019	739.650	9.432

38. OPG, *We want to hear from you on modernising LPAs*, 16-09-2021, via: https://publicguardian.blog.gov.uk/2021/09/16/we-want-to-hear-from-you-on-modernising-lpas/ (last accessed: 31-03-2022); OPG, *Modernising lasting powers of attorney consultation – what happens next?*, 09-12-2021, via: https://publicguardian.blog.gov.uk/2021/12/09/modernising-lasting-powers-of-attorney-consultation-what-happens-next/ (last accessed: 31-03-2022).
39. Lush & Bielanska 2017, p. 25.
40. Office of the Public Guardian, *Annual Report and Accounts 2017-2018*, p. 6, via: https://www.gov.uk/government/publications/office-of-the-public-guardian-annual-report-and-accounts-2017-to-2018 (last accessed: 22-07-2019); Office of the Public Guardian, *Annual Report and Accounts 2018-2019*, via: https://www.gov.uk/government/publications/office-of-the-public-guardian-annual-report-and-accounts-2018-to-2019 (last accessed: 22-07-2019). The Annual Report of 2018-2019 only contains the combined number of registered LPA's and EPA's, the OPG has kindly provided me with the number of registered LPA's and EPA's.

B. Enduring documents and protection measures ordered by the court or an administrative authority

8. How do enduring documents relate to adult protection measures ordered by the court or an administrative authority? Is there a principle of subsidiarity in place?

A principle of subsidiarity can be inferred from section 16 of the MCA 2005 in conjunction with section 1 of the MCA 2005. Section 16 of the MCA 2005 concerns the court's powers to make decisions and appoint so-called deputies, i.e. a person appointed by the court to take care of the adult's personal welfare and/or property and affairs. Section 16(2) of the MCA 2005 stipulates that the court may appoint a deputy 'to make decisions on P's behalf in relation to the matter or matters'. When doing so, the court must adhere to the provisions of the MCA 2005 and, in particular, sections 1 and 4 of this act, encompassing the principles that apply for the purpose of the act (section 1) and the concept of best interests (section 4). Section 1(6) of the MCA 2005 states:

> Before the act is done, or the decision is made, regard must be had to whether the purpose for which it is needed can be as effectively achieved in a way that is less restrictive of the person's rights and freedom of action.

9. Is there an obligation for the court or the administrative authority to check whether an enduring document is in place?

Although such an obligation is nowhere stipulated as such, the court is – as discussed under no. 8 – obliged to ensure that the interests of the adult are protected in a way that restricts the rights and freedom of action of the adult concerned as little as possible (section 1(6) of the MCA 2005).

10. Can the measures ordered by the court or the administrative authority be combined with the enduring document?

According to Ward, there may be circumstances where both an attorney and a deputy act for the same person.[41] Ward refers in this regard to the case of Public Guardian v. Marvin.[42] In this case, the Public Guardian made an application to revoke two LPAs, i.e. an LPA for property and financial affairs and an LPA for health and welfare. As a result, the LPA for property and financial matters was revoked, and the former attorney was appointed as deputy to act jointly with a

41. Ward 2016, p. 419.
42. Public Guardian v. Marvin [2014] EWCOP 47.

professional deputy.[43] However, revocation of the health and welfare LPA was not deemed necessary, thus creating a situation where both an attorney and a (professional) deputy acted for the same person.

11. Can the enduring document's content or the attorney's powers be changed or expanded by the court or any other institution? And if so, in what cases?

According to section 23(1) of the MCA 2005, the Court of Protection 'may determine any question as to the meaning or effect of a lasting power of attorney or an instrument purporting to create one'.[44] Linked to this Schedule 1, section 11 of the MCA provides that:

> (2) Sub-paragraph (3) applies if it appears to the Public Guardian that the instrument contains a provision which—
> (a) would be ineffective as part of a lasting power of attorney, or
> (b) would prevent the instrument from operating as a valid lasting power of attorney.
> (3) The Public Guardian—
> (a) must apply to the court for it to determine the matter under section 23(1), and
> (b) pending the determination by the court, must not register the instrument.
> (4) Sub-paragraph (5) applies if the court determines under section 23(1) (whether or not on an application by the Public Guardian) that the instrument contains a provision which—
> (a) would be ineffective as part of a lasting power of attorney, or
> (b) would prevent the instrument from operating as a valid lasting power of attorney.
> (5) The court must—
> (a) notify the Public Guardian that it has severed the provision, or
> (b) direct him not to register the instrument.
> (6) Where the court notifies the Public Guardian that it has severed a provision, he must register the instrument with a note to that effect attached to it.

As this provision makes clear, the court may sever ineffective or illegal provisions from the LPA. The court can do so before registration of the LPA, but also when the OPG has already registered an LPA.[45] Referring to various court cases, Lush and Bielanska provide several examples of provisions the court has severed. For instance, in the case of Re Norris, the court severed a provision whereby the adult tried to authorise the attorney to handle the financial affairs of the adult's daughter since an LPA cannot be used to authorise the attorney to manage the affairs of

43. In this regard the exceptional nature of the case was emphasized and it was noted that this decision should not be regarded as 'setting a precedent for other cases in which the court finds having to revoke the appointment of an attorney under an LPA'.
44. Lush & Bielanska 2017, p. 190.
45. Lush & Bielanska 2017, pp. 190-191; Schedule 1, section 19 of the MCA 2005.

another person. Another example concerns the case of Re Hart, in which the court severed a provision whereby the adult had tried to add something to the EPA of his wife.[46]

The Court of Protection also has several powers in relation to the operation of the LPA, but only in the event, the adult lacks the capacity to decide and act himself. In this regard, sections 23(2), (3) and (4) of the MCA 2005 stipulate:

> (2) The court may—
> (a) give directions with respect to decisions—
> (i) which the donee of a lasting power of attorney has authority to make, and
> (ii) which P lacks capacity to make;
> (b) give any consent or authorisation to act which the donee would have to obtain from P if P had capacity to give it.
> (3) The court may, if P lacks capacity to do so—
> (a) give directions to the donee with respect to the rendering by him of reports or accounts and the production of records kept by him for that purpose;
> (b) require the donee to supply information or produce documents or things in his possession as donee;
> (c) give directions with respect to the remuneration or expenses of the donee;
> (d) relieve the donee wholly or partly from any liability which he has or may have incurred on account of a breach of his duties as donee.
> (4) The court may authorise the making of gifts which are not within section 12(2) (permitted gifts)

12. On which grounds are state-ordered measures applied, notwithstanding the presence of an enduring document?

Section 22(4) and (5) of the MCA 2005 stipulate that:

> (4) The court may—
> (a) direct that an instrument purporting to create the lasting power of attorney is not to be registered, or
> (b) if P lacks capacity to do so, revoke the instrument or the lasting power of attorney.
> (5) If there is more than one donee, the court may under subsection (4)(b) revoke the instrument or the lasting power of attorney so far as it relates to any of them.

Section 22(3) of the MCA 2005 makes clear that the court may revoke the LPA or direct that the LPA is not to be registered in the event:

46. See Lush & Bielanska 2017, pp. 823-837 for these and other examples.

- Subsection (4) applies if the court is satisfied—
  - (a) that fraud or undue pressure was used to induce P—
    - (i) to execute an instrument for the purpose of creating a lasting power of attorney, or
    - (ii) to create a lasting power of attorney, or
  - (b) that the donee (or, if more than one, any of them) of a lasting power of attorney—
    - (i) has behaved, or is behaving, in a way that contravenes his authority or is not in P's best interests, or
    - (ii) proposes to behave in a way that would contravene his authority or would not be in P's best interests.

Referring to several court cases, Lush and Bielanska list the following examples of situations in which the court removed the attorney and cancelled the LPA:

- a situation in which the attorney exceeded the authority to make gifts (see no. 22), did not pay the bills and kept the adult short of money;
- a situation in which the attorney severely restricted the contact between the adult and other family members;
- a situation in which the attorney was not giving effect to the adult's current wishes and preferences;
- a situation in which the attorney had failed to keep account and had used the adult's funds to benefit himself;
- a situation in which there was a conflict between the attorneys, impeding the adult's best interests.[47]

C. *Form and general content of the enduring document*

13. **Are there any requirements as to the form of the enduring document?**

Section 9(3) of the MCA 2005 stipulates the following:

> An instrument which—
> (a) purports to create a lasting power of attorney, but
> (b) does not comply with this section, section 10 or Schedule 1, confers no authority.

Schedule 1, section 1 of the MCA 2005 stipulates that a prescribed form must be used to create a lasting power of attorney. These prescribed forms have been set out in the LPA, EPA & PG Regs 2007 and subsequent changes have been made in

47. Lush and Bielanska 2017, pp. 254-255 referring to JL (Revocation of Lasting Power of Attorney [2014] EWCOP 36; Public Guardian v. AW and DH [2014] EWCOP 28; SAD and ACD v. SED, District Judge Glenworth, case no. 12791319; Public Guardian v. DA, YS and ES [2015] EWCOP 41; Public Guardian v. PM and SH [2016] EWCOP 25; See also Stanyer 2017, p. 107 where are other examples are provided.

the LPA, EPA & PG Regs 2009 and the LPA, EPA & PG Regs 2015.[48] Two different forms can be distinguished. With the LP1H form, an LPA for health and care affairs can be made, and with the LP1F form, an LPA for financial matters can be made.[49] Both forms can be accessed and downloaded from the Office of the Public Guardian website.[50]

The 2015 forms consist of the following 15 sections:

- Sections 1-7 can be considered the core of the form containing the personal details of both the adult and the attorney(s), as well as the decisions of the adult as to how attorneys are to act (jointly and/or severally, see no. 19), when attorneys can make decisions (immediately after registration or upon the incapacity of the adult), which people are to be notified upon registration (see no. 16) and finally the preferences and instructions according to which the attorney(s) should act;
- section 8 contains certain prescribed information which has to be read by both the adult, the attorney(s) and the certificate provider (see no. 30);
- section 9 contains the signature of the donor;
- section 10 contains the signature of the certificate provider (see no. 30);
- section 11 contains the signature of the attorney(s);
- sections 12-15 concern the application to register the LPA.[51]

Notwithstanding the requirement that the LPA must be made in a prescribed form, schedule 1, section 3 of the MCA 2005 stipulates that:

> 1) If an instrument differs in an immaterial respect in form or mode of expression from the prescribed form, it is to be treated by the Public Guardian as sufficient in point of form and expression.
> 2) The court may declare that an instrument which is not in the prescribed form is to be treated as if it were, if it is satisfied that the persons executing the instrument intended it to create a lasting power of attorney.[52]

14. Is the enduring document a unilateral or bilateral document? Is a signature from the attorney a requirement?

Section 8 of the LP1F and LP1H form states the following: 'In sections 9-11, you [referring to the adult], the certificate provider (see no. 30), all your attorneys

48. Terrell *et al.* 2018, p. 429; Lush & Bielanska 2017, pp. 105-107.
49. Ward 2016, p. 212.
50. https://www.gov.uk/government/publications/make-a-lasting-power-of-attorney (last accessed: 01-04-2022).
51. Terrell *et al.* 2018, p. 430.
52. See also Lush & Bielanska 2017, pp. 188-190; Stanyer 2017, pp. 160-161.

and your replacement attorneys must sign this lasting power of attorney to form a legal agreement between you (a deed)'. A signature from the attorney is, in other words, required. The attorney has to complete section 11 of the forms in the presence of a witness (LPA, EPA & PG Regs 2007, reg 9(6)).[53] With his signature, the attorney confirms that he has read the prescribed information in section 8 of the LPA form.[54]

15. **Which matters (e.g. financial, health, welfare, personal) can be covered by the enduring document? Conversely, are there particular matters excluded?**

As to the scope of the lasting power of attorney, section 9(1) of the MCA 2005 states:

> A lasting power of attorney is a power of attorney under which the donor ("P") confers on the donee
> (or donees) authority to make decisions about all or any of the following—
> (a) P's personal welfare or specified matters concerning P's personal welfare, and
> (b) P's property and affairs or specified matters concerning P's property and affairs,
>
> and which includes authority to make such decisions in circumstances where P no longer has capacity.

The expression 'personal welfare' in section 9(1)(a) has not been defined in the MCA 2005. However, examples of decisions in this regard have been given in section 7.21 of the MCA 2005 Code of Practice. These include decisions about where the adult should live and with whom, decisions about the adult's day-to-day care, and decisions about the adult's personal correspondence and papers.[55] With regard to decisions on life-sustaining treatment, the adult needs to expressly state in the LPA that he wants the attorney to have this authority.[56] In relation to 'property and affairs' (section 9(1)(b)), section 64(1) of the MCA 2005 defines the word 'property' as 'anything in action and any interest in real or personal property'.[57] Examples of decisions relating to property and affairs can be found in section 7.36 of the MCA 2005 Code of Practice. These include buying or selling a property, paying private medical care, residential care or nursing home fees, and paying the adult's mortgage, rent and household expenses. The adult can, of course, place restrictions on both the personal welfare and the property and financial decisions the attorney will be able to make.

53. Lush & Bielanska 2017, p. 121.
54. Lush & Bielanska 2017, p. 120.
55. Lush & Bielanska 2017, p. 222.
56. Section 11(8) MCA 2005.
57. Lush & Bielanska 2017, p. 221.

There are so-called 'excluded decisions' where the attorney cannot make a decision on behalf of the donor. Excluded decisions that have been mentioned explicitly in the MCA 2005 include the following:

- Decisions relating to family relationships, such as consenting to marriage or a civil partnership (section 27(1) MCA 2005);
- Decisions relating to the treatment of the adult's mental disorder in cases where the adult has been detained under the Mental Health Act 1983 for treatment (section 28(1) MCA 2005);
- Decisions relating to voting at an election for any public office (section 29(1) MCA 2005).[58]

In addition, the attorney cannot make decisions which are required by statute to be made by the adult personally, such as making a will or the right to conduct litigation. Nor decisions excluded by the common law of agency, which according to Lush and Bielanska, include decisions where a statute requires the evidence of the adult's signature or where the adult's competency to act arises by virtue of his holding an office.[59]

16. What are the rules, regulations and practices concerning the entry into force of the enduring document?

As discussed in more detail under no. 25, the LPA must be registered by the adult or the attorney(s) before it may be used. The adult may name up to five persons to be notified when an application to register the LPA is made. These named persons can object to the registration and, consequently, the entry into force of the LPA. Objections can only be based on one of the grounds specified on Form LP3 of the Office of the Public Guardian.[60] In this regard, a distinction is made between so-called factual objections, such as the death of the adult or the attorney, and prescribed objections, such as an allegation that the LPA has not been validly made because the adult at the time lacked the capacity to make an LPA or was unduly influenced to do so.[61] The named person must object within three weeks of receiving word that an application for registration has been made.[62] In the context of the law in action component of this comparative study, an employee of the OPG was asked if the possibility to name a person is regularly used in practice. According to internal research conducted in 2017, 83% of the adults in the sample

58. Lush & Bielanska 2017, pp. 223-224.
59. Lush & Bielanska 2017, pp. 224-225.
60. https://www.gov.uk/government/publications/make-a-lasting-power-of-attorney (last accessed 01-04-2022).
61. Ward 2016, pp. 13-14.
62. Lush & Bielanska 2017, p. 61.

did not choose to name any persons, 13% of the adults named one person and 4% of the adults named two persons.

17. Under which circumstances does the enduring document ceases to have effect?

Lush and Bielanska distinguish five situations in which an LPA – subject to the provisions relating to joint and several appointments and replacement attorneys – ends.

1. *Revocation by the adult*

According to section 13(2) of the MCA 2005, the adult may revoke the LPA at any time when he has the capacity to do so. The adult can do so:

- Explicitly, through a deed of revocation; or
- Implicitly, through conduct inconsistent with the continuation of the LPA (such as making a new LPA).[63]

The adult is advised to choose the first option (a deed of revocation) to ensure the LPA is revoked.

2. *Disclaimer by the attorney*

According to section 13(6) of the MCA 2005, the attorney may disclaim his appointment as an attorney, in which case he resigns or renounces his appointment.[64] Regulation 20(1) of the LPA, EPA & PG Regs 2007 stipulates that a prescribed form has to be used to disclaim the appointment.[65] According to regulation 20(2) of the LPA, EPA & PG Regs 2007, the attorney must send the completed form to the adult and a copy to the Public Guardian and any other attorney who, for the time being, is appointed under the LPA. The phrase 'for the time being' indicates that the attorney is not obliged to inform a replacement attorney, even though the disclaimer might trigger the replacement attorney's authority to act.[66] Sections 13(5)(b) and 13(7) of the MCA 2005 make clear that the disclaimer by the attorney will revoke the LPA unless the attorney is replaced under the terms of the LPA (a replacement attorney) or in case the attorney is one of two or more persons who have been appointed to act jointly and severally in respect of any matter, and after the disclaimer, there is at least one remaining attorney.

63. Lush & Bielanska 2017, p. 246-247; Ward 2016, pp. 376-377.
64. Lush & Bielanska 2017, p. 248.
65. Lush & Bielanska 2017, p. 248; LPA 005 form titled 'Disclaimer by a proposed or acting attorney under a Lasting Power of Attorney'.
66. Lush & Bielanska 2017, p. 249; Ward 2016, pp. 378-379.

3. Revocation by operation of law
Section 13 of the MCA lists several events which lead to a revocation of the LPA. These are:
- The adult's bankruptcy (section 13(3) of the MCA 2005), which will revoke the LPA in so far as it relates to the property and financial affairs of the adult;
- The attorney's bankruptcy (section 13(5) and (6)(b) of the MCA 2005), which will revoke the LPA in so far as it relates to the property and financial affairs of the adult, unless the exceptions of section 13(7) of the MCA 2005, discussed above, apply;
- The winding-up or dissolution of a trust corporation (section 13(5) and (6)(b) of the MCA 2005) in cases where the attorney is a trust corporation unless the exceptions of section 13(7) of the MCA 2005 apply;
- The adult's death (Regulation 22 of the LPA, EPA & PG Regs 2007);
- The attorney's death (section 13(5) and (6)(b) of the MCA 2005), unless the exceptions of section 13(7) of the MCA 2005 apply;
- The attorney's incapacity (section 13(5) and (6)(c), unless the exceptions of section 13(7) of the MCA 2005 apply.

4. Revocation by the Court of Protection
Under section 22(4) of the MCA 2005, the Court of Protection may order that an LPA not be registered or, if the adult lacks the capacity to do so, revoke the LPA. Section 22(3) of the MCA 2005 lists the events in which the Court of Protection may do so. This is the case when fraud or undue pressure was used to induce the adult and/or when the attorney has behaved, is behaving or intends to behave in a way that is contrary to his authority or is not in the best interests of the adult.

5. Dissolution or annulment of a marriage or civil partnership
Sections 13(6)(c) and 13(11) provide that a dissolution or annulment of a marriage or civil partnership between the adult and the attorney will terminate the appointment of the attorney unless the LPA has stipulated otherwise.[67]

In addition to these five situations in which an LPA ceases to have effect, Thurston distinguishes a sixth situation. Section 9(4) of the MCA and the prescribed form permit the conferral of a general or limited authority. In the exceptional case that the LPA only confers authority for one transaction, the authority conferred by the LPA will terminate when the transaction has been completed.[68]

67. Lush & Bielanska 2017, pp. 252-253; Ward 2016, p. 381.
68. Thurston 2015, pp. 312-313.

D. *The attorney*

18. **Who can be appointed as an attorney? Are there restrictions concerning the choice of attorney (e.g. exclusion of certain people)?**

Sections 10(1) and (2) of the Mental Capacity Act 2005 state:

> (2) A donee of a lasting power of attorney must be—
> (a) an individual who has reached 18, or
> (b) if the power relates only to P's property and affairs, either such an individual or a trust corporation.
>
> (3) An individual who is bankrupt or is a person in relation to whom a debt relief order is made may not be appointed as donee of a lasting power of attorney in relation to P's property and affairs.

This means that persons under 18 cannot be appointed as an attorney. Lush and Bielanska note that the position concerning enduring powers of attorney differed slightly. In theory, it was possible to appoint a minor as an attorney, who subsequently had to wait until he was of age before he could execute the instrument. This is not the case with the lasting power of attorney, where the appointment of a minor is prohibited.[69] According to section 10(1)(b) MCA 2005, a trust corporation can be appointed as attorney of an LPA for property and financial affairs but not as attorney of an LPA for personal welfare. The Mental Capacity Act refers with regard to the meaning of 'trust corporation' to section 68(1) of the Trustee Act 1925:

> '"Trust corporation" means the Public Trustee or a corporation either appointed by the court in any particular case to be a trustee or entitled by rules made under subsection (3) of section four of the Public Trustee Act, 1906, to act as custodian trustee.'[70]

Section 10(2) of the MCA 2005 stipulates that an individual who is bankrupt or subject to a debt relief order may not be appointed as attorney of an LPA for property and financial affairs. However, according to Lush and Bielanska, this does not disqualify someone who has been bankrupt in the past.[71] The MCA 2005 also does not allow the appointment of an office-holder as an attorney. The individual's name must be given if a professional is appointed attorney. A job title or the name of a firm is insufficient.[72]

69. Lush & Bielanska 2017, p. 45.
70. Section 68(1) Trustee Act 1925; see for more information Lush & Bielanska 2017, pp. 45-48.
71. Lush & Bielanska 2017, p. 48.
72. Lush & Bielanska 2017, pp. 48-49.

The MCA 2005 does not contain other restrictions. However, the MCA Code of Practice states in section 7.10 that:

> 'A paid care worker (such as a care home manager) should not agree to act as an attorney, apart from in unusual circumstances (for example, if they are the only close relative of the donor).'

19. **Does the legal system allow for the appointment of more than one attorney? Can these attorneys act jointly, concurrently, separately or as substitutes?**

Section 10(3) of the MCA 2005 clarifies that more than one attorney may be appointed. According to section 10(4), attorneys may be appointed to act:

(a) jointly,
(b) jointly and severally, or
(c) jointly in respect of some matters and jointly and severally in respect of others.

When attorneys are to act 'jointly', all must agree to decisions made and acts performed on behalf of the adult. Ward notes that such an arrangement enables one attorney to oversee the other attorney's actions, thus providing a safeguard against abuse.[73] However, disadvantages should also be considered, such as when attorneys cannot work together or when an attorney is unavailable to sign an important document due to illness or holiday, causing a delay. Another disadvantage is that when attorneys have been appointed to act jointly, a failure concerning one of them to comply with the requirements of sections 10(1) and 10(2) of the MCA 2005 prevents the LPA from being created. The same goes for situations where the joint appointment is terminated for one of the reasons listed in section 13(6) MCA 2005 unless the adult has chosen a replacement attorney.[74] This is not the case in situations where the attorneys are to act jointly and severally or where in other words, decisions can be taken together or independently by the attorneys. The last option, appointing attorneys to act jointly regarding some matters and jointly and severally regarding others, requires the adult to stipulate in the LPA which decisions must be made in a certain way. The adult might, for example, specify that decisions such as the buying or selling of a house or a decision concerning life-sustaining treatment need to be made jointly, whereas other decisions can be made severally.[75] Ward notes that many problems have arisen concerning this third option, in some cases leading to a severance of restrictions by the Court of Protection as these were considered ineffective and

73. Ward 2016, p. 188.
74. Ward 2016, p. 188 & 190; Lush & Bielanska 2017, pp. 52-54.
75. Ward 2016, p. 189.

unworkable.[76] In cases where the adult has not specified whether the attorneys are to act 'jointly' or 'jointly and severally', it is assumed the adult intended the attorney to act jointly.[77] Lush and Bielanska indicate, however, that this provision may have become less relevant in practice as the prescribed form asks the adult to indicate (by way of ticking a box) how he wishes the attorney to act.[78]

20. **Is there a duty for the attorney to inform the court or any other administrative authority if the appointment to act as an attorney is refused or discontinued?**

Section 7.58 of the MCA 2005 Code of Practice clarifies that the attorney, in addition to his statutory duties under the MCA 2005, is subject to specific duties under the law of agency. One of these duties includes the attorney's duty 'not to give up the role without telling the adult and the court'.[79] Section 7.50 of the MCA 2005 Code of Practice states that an attorney 'can withdraw from the appointment if they ever become unable or unwilling to act'. If the LPA has been registered, the attorney must follow the correct procedures for withdrawing. Section 7.66 of the MCA 2006 Code of Practice clarifies that both the adult and the Office of the Public Guardian must be notified. The OPG has provided a form on their website titled 'Disclaimer by a proposed or acting attorney under a lasting power of attorney', which can be used in this regard.[80]

21. **Are there any rules or regulations regarding the attorney's role in line with, for example, article 12(4) UNCRPD and Principle 10 of the Council of Europe Recommendation 2009/11?**

Section 9(4) of the MCA 2005 stipulates that:

> The authority conferred by a lasting power of attorney is subject to—
> - the provisions of this Act and, in particular, sections 1 (the principles) and 4 (best interests), and
> - any conditions or restrictions specified in the instrument.

As section 9(4) under a of the MCA 2005 makes clear, the attorney is obliged to act in accordance with the provisions of the MCA 2005, in particular section 1 listing the principles of the act (see no. 1) and section 4 on best interests. Section 1(3)

76. Ward 2016, p. 189. See for a list of examples of court decisions in this regard Lush & Bielanska 2017, pp. 859-862.
77. Section 10(5) MCA 2005.
78. Lush & Bielanska 2017, p. 51.
79. Section 7.58 MCA Code of Practice; Ward 2016, p. 192.
80. https://www.gov.uk/government/publications/disclaim-a-lasting-power-of-attorney (last accessed: 01-04-2022).

of the MCA 2005 stipulates that 'a person is not to be treated as unable to make a decision unless all practical steps to help him do so have been taken without success'. The attorney is, in other words, obliged to assist the adult in making his own decisions.[81] Chapter 3 of the MCA 2005 Code of Practice provides information on the steps the attorney can take in this respect. Lush and Bielanska note that the attorney should, for instance, consider whether the adult has received the relevant information to make a decision, whether the information has been presented in such a way as to make it easier for the adult to understand it and whether the aspects of time and place have considered in enabling the adult to make a decision.[82] If the adult lacks the capacity to decide himself, the attorney may decide on behalf of the adult.[83] Section 1(5) of the MCA 2005 clarifies that the attorney, in this event, must act in the best interests of the adult concerned. Section 4 of the MCA 2005 outlines how the attorney is to determine the adult's best interests:

> (1) In determining for the purposes of this Act what is in a person's best interests, the person making the determination must not make it merely on the basis of—
> (a) the person's age or appearance, or
> (b) a condition of his, or an aspect of his behaviour, which might lead others to make unjustified assumptions about what might be in his best interests.
> (2) The person making the determination must consider all the relevant circumstances and, in particular, take the following steps.
> (3) He must consider—
> (a) whether it is likely that the person will at some time have capacity in relation to the matter in question, and
> (b) if it appears likely that he will, when that is likely to be.
> (4) He must, so far as reasonably practicable, permit and encourage the person to participate, or to improve his ability to participate, as fully as possible in any act done for him and any decision affecting him.
> (5) Where the determination relates to life-sustaining treatment he must not, in considering whether the treatment is in the best interests of the person concerned, be motivated by a desire to bring about his death.
> (6) He must consider, so far as is reasonably ascertainable—
> (a) the person's past and present wishes and feelings (and, in particular, any relevant written statement made by him when he had capacity),
> (b) the beliefs and values that would be likely to influence his decision if he had capacity, and
> (c) the other factors that he would be likely to consider if he were able to do so.
> (7) He must take into account, if it is practicable and appropriate to consult them, the views of—

81. Lush & Bielanska 2017, pp. 236-237.
82. Lush & Bielanska 2017, p. 237; see also the MCA 2005 Code of Practice, chapter 3.
83. Ibid.

(a) anyone named by the person as someone to be consulted on the matter in question or on matters of that kind,
(b) anyone engaged in caring for the person or interested in his welfare,
(c) any donee of a lasting power of attorney granted by the person, and
(d) any deputy appointed for the person by the court, as to what would be in the person's best interests and, in particular, as to the matters mentioned in subsection (6).

Further guidance on determining what is in the adult's best interests is provided in chapter 5 of the MCA 2005 Code of Practice. Article 4(9) of the MCA 2005 clarifies that there is sufficient compliance with section 4 if the attorney reasonably believes that he decides and/or acts in the bests interests of the adult concerned.[84] In addition to adhering to the provisions of the MCA 2005, the attorney is, according to Section 9(4) under b of the MCA 2005, obliged to act in accordance with the adult's preferences and instructions as recorded in the LPA.[85] Article 42(4) of the MCA 2005 makes clear that the attorney is obliged to have regard for the provisions included in the MCA 2005 Code of Practice.[86] In section 7.58 of this Code of Practice, an overview is presented of the duties the attorney has under the law of agency:

> An attorney appointed under an LPA is acting as the chosen agent of the donor and therefore, under the law of agency, the attorney has certain duties towards the donor. An attorney takes on a role which carries a great deal of power, which they must use carefully and responsibly. They have a duty to:
> - apply certain standards of care and skill (duty of care) when making decisions
> - carry out the donor's instructions
> - not take advantage of their position and not benefit themselves, but benefit the donor (fiduciary duty)
> - not delegate decisions, unless authorised to do so
> - act in good faith
> - respect confidentiality
> - comply with the directions of the Court of Protection
> - not give up the role without telling the donor and the court.
>
> In relation to property and affairs LPAs, they have a duty to:
> - keep accounts
> - keep the donor's money and property separate from their own.[87]

84. Lush & Bielanska 2017, p. 239.
85. Lush & Bielanska 2017, p. 233.
86. Lush & Bielanska 2017, p. 241.
87. See for a discussion of these duties in more detail section 7.59-7.68 of the MCA 2005 Code of Practice and Thurston 2005, chapter 9.

Section 8 of the LPA form reminds the attorney of his legal rights and responsibilities.[88]

22. **Are there any limits as to the authorisations/responsibilities that can be given by the adult to the attorney (e.g. with regard to personal decisions, such as making a will and deciding about donations)? Are there any rules concerning 'selbsteintritt'?**

In addition to decisions that the attorney cannot make on behalf of the adult – the so-called 'excluded decisions' mentioned in no. 15 – some decisions come with certain restrictions. There are four important restrictions concerning the personal welfare LPA. First of all, under a personal welfare LPA, an attorney can only make decisions concerning the adult's welfare if the adult lacks the capacity to make these decisions himself.[89] This is in contrast to an LPA for financial decisions, where the adult may stipulate that the attorney may act as soon as the LPA has been registered.[90] Second, the attorney is subject to the provisions of sections 24, 25 and 26 of the MCA 2005 concerning advance decisions to refuse treatment. An important restriction following from these provisions is that the attorney cannot consent to treatment if the adult has made an advance decision refusing that treatment. However, section 25(2)(b) MCA 2005 clarifies that if an LPA gives the attorney the power to give or refuse consent for specific treatment and this LPA is of a later date than the advance decision, the advance decision is not considered valid. In that case, the restriction does not apply as it is assumed the adult has changed his mind.[91] A third restriction concerns decisions about life-sustaining treatment, defined in section 4(10) of the MCA 2005, as 'treatment which in the view of a person providing health care for the person concerned is necessary to sustain life'. According to section 11(8), the attorney can only consent to or refuse life-sustaining treatment when the adult has expressly stated in the LPA that he wants the attorney to have this authority.[92] A fourth restriction concerns the use of restraint, which is only allowed in limited circumstances and where the conditions of section 11 of the MCA 2005 have been fulfilled.

Concerning property and financial affairs, there is an important restriction regarding gifts. Gifts are allowed to the extent permitted by section 12(2) of the MCA 2005:

> The donee may make gifts:

88. Stanyer 2017, pp. 157-158.
89. Section 11(7)(a) MCA 2005.
90. Stanyer 2017, pp. 154-155.
91. Lush & Bielanska 2017, p. 227.
92. Lush & Bielanska 2017, p. 227.

> (a) on customary occasions to persons (including himself) who are related to or connected with the donor, or
>
> (b) to any charity to whom the donor made or might have been expected to make gifts,
>
> if the value of each such gift is not unreasonable having regard to all the circumstances and, in particular, the size of the donor's estate.

Section 12(3) of the MCA 2005 makes clear that the phrase 'customary occasions' is to be understood as occasions such as anniversaries of birth, marriage or the formation of a civil partnership or 'any other occasion on which presents are customarily given within families or among friends or associates'.[93] Considering all circumstances and the size of the adult's estate, the value of gifts must be reasonable. This means that a gift of £100,- to a grandson on his birthday may be perfectly reasonable when the adult's assets are £100.000 or more. However, it will not be considered reasonable when the adult does not have much.[94]

The adult may restrict the attorney's authority to make gifts but cannot authorise the attorney to go beyond the limits of section 12 of the MCA 2005.[95] There are several cases in which the Court of Protection has severed provisions circumventing section 12 of the MCA 2005.[96] The attorney may make gifts to himself, but only, as section 12(2) of the MCA 2005 stipulates, on customary occasions, such as the attorney's birthday.[97] If the attorney wishes to make a gift that does not fall within the scope of section 12(2) MCA 2005, an application can be made to the Court of Protection. The court may, according to section 23(4) MCA 2005, 'authorise the making of gifts which are not within section 12(2) (permitted gifts)'.

23. Does the legal system allow for the remuneration of the attorney?

According to Ward, the presumption concerning professional attorneys is that they charge or are being remunerated for their services by the adult. Such a presumption does not exist concerning lay attorneys. Without a suitable clause, they can only claim expenses.[98] According to section 7.59 of the MCA Code of Practice, attorneys may have a different duty of care depending on whether the attorney is paid for his services or is a member of a profession:

---

93. Section 12(3) MCA 2005.
94. Thurston 2015, p. 232.
95. Thurston 2015, p. 232; Stanyer 2017, p. 157.
96. See e.g. Re Wheatley (an order of the Senior Judge made on 31 January 2011); Re Careford (an order of the Senior Judge made on 16 February 2011); Re Burdock (an order of the Senior Judge made on 2 July 2012). See Lush & Bielanska 2017, appendix H13, p. 839-844 for other examples.
97. Thurston 2015, p. 232.
98. Ward 2016, pp. 182-183.

- 'Attorneys who are not being paid must apply the same care, skill and diligence they would use to make decisions about their own life. An attorney who claims to have particular skills or qualifications must show greater skill in those particular areas than someone who does not make such claims.
- If attorneys are being paid for their services, they should demonstrate a higher degree of care and skill.
- Attorneys who undertake their duties in the course of their professional work (such as solicitors or corporate trustees) must display professional competence and follow their profession's rules and standards.'

E. *Registration*

24. Are enduring documents registered? If yes, is registration voluntary or mandatory?

A lasting power of attorney may only be used once registered with the Office of the Public Guardian, and registration can therefore be considered mandatory in England and Wales.[99] That being said, the LPA is not required to be registered immediately. It can also be registered at a later date. Once registered, the attorney can use an LPA for financial affairs as an ordinary power of attorney unless the LPA has been restricted to when the adult has lost capacity.[100]

25. When does registration occur (e.g. registration directly after the enduring document has been made, registration upon entry into force, registration upon acceptance of the appointment by the attorney)?

Registration can take place immediately after the execution of the LPA but also at a later date. However, the LPA may not be used until registered with the Office of the Public Guardian.[101] Both the adult and the attorney(s) may submit an application to register the LPA. In cases where two or more attorneys have been appointed to act jointly, the application has to be made by all the attorneys.[102] The adult can name up to five persons to be notified of an application to register the LPA.[103] These 'named persons' must be informed by the applicant, i.e. either the adult or the attorney(s). The Office of the Public Guardian will ensure notification has occurred upon receiving the registration request and will notify both the adult and the attorney of the receipt of an application to register the LPA.[104] Both the

99. Section 9(2)(b) MCA 2005; Lush & Bielanska 2017, pp. 162-163; Ward 2016, p. 232.
100. Ward 2016, p. 221 & 233.
101. Ward 2016, p. 232; Lush & Bielanska 2017, p. 125.
102. Lush & Bielanska 2017, p. 126.
103. Lush & Bielanska 2017, p. 61.
104. Lush & Bielanska 2017, pp. 127-128, see also pp. 132-133.

adult, the attorney and the named persons can object to the registration of the LPA. The attorney(s) and the named person(s) are required to do so in a period of three weeks upon receiving word from either the Office of the Public Guardian (attorney) or the applicant (named person) that an application for registration has been made.[105]

26. Are changes and revocations of enduring documents registered?

Both changes or alterations and revocations of the LPA are registered. Lush and Bielanska list several circumstances in which the OPG is obliged to cancel the registration of the LPA. An example is the revocation of the LPA by the granter (regulation 21 of the Lasting Powers of Attorney, Enduring Powers of Attorney and Public Guardian Regulations 2007). In addition, there are also several instances in which the Court of Protection may direct the OPG to cancel the registration, for example, when it determines that the requirements for creating the LPA have not been met or when it determines that the LPA has been revoked or has otherwise come to an end.[106]

MCA 2005 Schedule 1, part 4 (sections 21-25) deals with so-called alterations of LPAs. The OPG must enter these alterations as soon as possible in the register and attach a note to the LPA to that effect. The alterations mentioned in MCA 2005, Schedule 1 are: the partial revocation or suspension of an LPA as a result of bankruptcy (section 21); termination of appointment of the attorney which does not revoke the LPA (section 22); replacement of the attorney (section 23) and the severance of ineffective provisions in the LPA (section 24).

27. Which parties can access the register? And to what extent do third parties have access (e.g. notification of the existence of an enduring document or access to the content of the enduring document)?

An application to search the register can be made using form OPG100.[107] Two different types of searches can be distinguished: a so-called 'first tier' and 'second tier' search.[108] Information received after a first-tier search includes: the name of any attorney(s), whether the LPA or EPA refers to 'property and affairs' or 'personal welfare', the date the LPA or EPA has been made and if applicable, the date the LPA or EPA was revoked. Enquiries made with the OPG – as part of the law in action component of the comparative study – revealed that anyone could

105. Lush & Bielanska 2017, p. 61.
106. Lush & Bielanska 2017, pp. 171-172.
107. https://www.gov.uk/government/publications/search-public-guardian-registers (last accessed 01-04-2022).
108. Stanyer 2017, p. 99.

make a request as long as the person in question can provide the adult's name, date of birth and address. Requests are, in practice, submitted by various people and entities, such as local authorities, solicitors, the NHS, banks, the police, and care home organisations. On average, the OPG receives around 8.000 requests to search the LPA/EPA and deputy register monthly.[109] Stanyer notes that although the Data Protection Act usually applies to information held by the OPG, it does not apply to the information you can access in a first-tier register search.[110] This is different concerning the so-called second-tier search. This type of search will reveal additional information relating to the adult. The OPG considers each application before deciding whether the additional information will be released.[111] Stanyer notes that the information provided by the OPG, in the context of a second-tier search, varies according to the individual circumstances of the case.[112]

F. *Capacity, supervision and control measures*

28. **What is the legal consequence of the entry into force of the enduring document? Does the adult retain legal capacity?**

The adult retains legal capacity upon the entry into force of the LPA. This follows from section 1 of the MCA 2005. Section 1 sets out the principles that underly the purpose of the Act:

- A person must be assumed to have capacity unless it is established that he lacks capacity.
- A person is not to be treated as unable to make a decision unless all practicable steps to help him to do so have been taken without success.
- A person is not to be treated as unable to make a decision merely because he makes an unwise decision.
- An act done, or decision made, under this Act for or on behalf of a person who lacks capacity must be done, or made, in his best interests.
- Before the act is done, or the decision is made, regard must be had to whether the purpose for which it is needed can be as effectively achieved in a way that is less restrictive of the person's rights and freedom of action.[113]

As the first bullet stipulates, a person must be assumed to have capacity unless it is shown that he has not. Section 2 of the MCA 2005 clarifies that capacity is decision- and time-specific.[114] This means that although a person may, at a

109. This information was obtained in 2019.
110. Stanyer 2017, p. 100.
111. Stanyer 2017, p. 100.
112. Stanyer 2017, p. 100.
113. Section 1 of the MCA 2005.
114. Ward 2016, p. 38.

particular moment, lack capacity concerning, for example, a significant financial decision, he may be perfectly able to decide on another matter. The second bullet clarifies that before a person is treated as unable to make a decision, all practicable steps to help him make this decision must have been taken in vain. Chapter 3 of the MCA 2005 Code of Practice provides guidance on the steps to help a person make a decision. About timing the Code of Practice notes, for example:

> Try to choose the time of day when the person is most alert – some people are better in the mornings, others are more lively in the afternoon or early evening. It may be necessary to try several times before a decision can be made.

As indicated under no. 21, section 9(4) of the MCA 2005 stipulates that the attorney is required to act according to these principles. This implies that unless the LPA (for property and financial affairs) directs him otherwise, he is not to decide if the adult has the capacity to make a decision himself.[115]

29. Does the legal system provide protection against so-called 'ill-considered decisions' by the adult?

The third bullet of the list of principles of section 1 of the MCA 2005, included under no. 28, stipulates that a person is not to be treated as unable to make a decision merely because he makes what is in the MCA 2005, referred to as an 'unwise decision'. Section 2.10 of the MCA 2005 Code of Practices notes in this regard:

> 'Everybody has their own values, beliefs, preferences and attitudes. A person should not be assumed to lack the capacity to make a decision just because other people think their decision is unwise. This applies even if family members, friends or healthcare or social care staff are unhappy with a decision.'

However, section 2.11 of the MCA 2005 Code of Practice also states that where a person 'repeatedly makes unwise decisions that put them at significant risk of harm or exploitation or makes a particular unwise decision that is obviously irrational or out of character', there might be a need for further investigation. In doing so, the person's past decisions and choices should be considered. Lush and Bielanska refer in this regard to the case of Re S; D v R and S [2012] COPLR Con Vol 1112, at § 43:

115. See no. 24, once registered the attorney may use the LPA for financial affairs straightaway as an ordinary power of attorney, unless the LPA has been restricted to when the adult has lost capacity.

'The significance of section 1(4) must not, however be exaggerated. The fact that a decision is unwise or foolish may not, without more, be treated as conclusive, but it remains in my judgment, a relevant consideration for the court to take into account in considering whether the criteria of inability to make a decision for oneself in section 3(1) are satisfied. **This will particularly be the case where there is a marked contrast between the unwise nature of the impugned decision and the person's former attitude to the conduct of affairs when his capacity was not in question** [emphasis added].'[116]

30. How is the validity of the document ensured? Is the validity of the enduring document checked at the time the enduring document is made as to the capacity of the adult, freedom from undue influence, etc.?

An adult must have the capacity to make an LPA.[117] A so-called 'certificate provider must confirm this'. Section 10 of the LPA form requires this certificate provider to confirm that at the time of signing:

- 'the donor understood the purpose of this LPA and the scope of the authority conferred under it
- no fraud or undue pressure is being used to induce the donor to create this LPA
- there is nothing else which would prevent this LPA from being created by the completion of this instrument.'[118]

Regulation 8 of LPA, EPA & PG Regs 2007 clarifies whom the adult can choose as the certificate provider. In this context, two categories are distinguished: the adult may choose a person who has known him personally for at least two years to act as a certificate provider, or the adult may ask a professional, such as a health care professional, a barrister or lawyer, or a social worker to act as certificate provider.[119] Regulation 8(3) of LPA, EPA & PG Regs 2007 also includes a list of persons who may not act as certificate providers. The list comprises the adult's family members, the designated attorney(s), the attorney's family members and the director and staff of the care home where the adult resides.[120]

31. What options are available to the adult concerning supervision and control of the execution of the enduring document?

116. As cited by Lush & Bielanska 2017, p. 40.
117. Ward 2016, p. 11.
118. https://www.gov.uk/government/publications/make-a-lasting-power-of-attorney (last accessed: 01-04-2022); See also Schedule 1, section 2(1) under e of the MCA 2005; Lush & Bielanska 2017, pp. 90-91 & 116-118; Ward 2016, pp. 11-12.
119. See for a list of examples Regulation 8(2) of the LPA, EPA & PG Regs 2007 and Lush & Bielanska 2017, pp. 93-97.
120. Lush & Bielanska 2017, pp. 97-98.

Adults can include a form of supervision on the attorney's actions in the LPA. The adult can, first of all, appoint more than one attorney to act on his behalf.[121] Secondly, the attorney can include preferences and instructions addressed to the attorney in the LPA (section 7 of the LPA forms).[122] The distinction between 'preferences' and 'instructions' is as follows. Preferences are not legally binding but should be considered by the attorney. Instructions are legally binding on the attorney and must be followed to the letter.[123] The adult cannot require the attorney to obtain the consent of a third person – a person not appointed as an attorney – for specific actions. The court has previously severed such instructions (see no. 11).[124] Referring to the MCA Code of Practice, Thurston notes that the adult could also appoint a person to audit the accounts of the adult periodically.[125] In this regard, section 7.39 of the MCA Code of Practice notes that:

> 'Donors may like to appoint someone (perhaps a family member or a professional) to go through their accounts with the attorney from time to time. This might help to reassure donors that somebody will check their financial affairs when they lack capacity to do so. It may also be helpful for attorneys to arrange a regular check that everything is being done properly. The donor should ensure that the person is willing to carry out this role and is prepared to ask for the accounts if the attorney does not provide them. They should include this arrangement in the signed LPA document. The LPA should also say whether the person can charge a fee for this service.'

32. **Is there any supervision of the attorney by the state (e.g. the court or another administrative body)? If so, are there any possibilities for these institutions to intervene in the execution of the enduring document (e.g. appointment of a third party to supervise the attorney)?**

Safeguarding concerns can be raised with the Office of the Public Guardian. According to Section 58 of the MCA 2005, the Office of the Public Guardian is responsible for dealing with 'representations (including complaints) about the way in which a donee [attorney] of a lasting power of attorney or a deputy appointed by the court is exercising his powers'. Section 14.14 of the MCA Code of Practice notes in this regard:

121. Ward 2016, p. 187.
122. Stanyer 2017, pp. 156-157.
123. Ibid; see also the LPA forms – https://www.gov.uk/government/publications/make-a-lasting-power-of-attorney (last accessed: 01-04-2022);
124. Lush & Bielanska 2017, p. 235; Ward 2016, p. 189; See also Re Reading (Lush & Bielanska 2017, pp. 834-835). The adult can, however, stipulate that in the event there in the event there is a disagreement between the attorney for property and financial affairs and the attorney for health and welfare affairs, the decision of the latter prevails (Re Scott).
125. Thurston 2015, p. 277.

> 'The Public Guardian will not usually get involved once somebody has registered an LPA – unless someone is worried about how an attorney is carrying out their duties. If concerns are raised about an attorney, the OPG works closely with organisations such as local authorities and NHS Trusts to carry out investigations.'

Regulations 44 and 46 of The Lasting Power of Attorney, Enduring Powers of Attorney and Public Guardian Regulations 2007 provide the Office of the Public Guardian with the authority to investigate the attorney's actions.[126] Based on regulation 44, the OPG can direct a so-called Court of Protection Visitor to visit the attorney and report to the OPG.[127] According to regulation 46, the OPG may require the attorney to provide information or produce specified documents when it appears to the OPG that the attorney has behaved or may be behaving in a way that contravenes his authority or is not in the best interests of the adult.[128] If the OPG finds grounds for concern, the OPG may apply to the Court of Protection and request the revocation of the LPA and the appointment of a deputy instead of the attorney (see no. 12).[129]

33. Is regulation in place concerning (potential) conflicts of interest between the adult's and the attorney's interests?

According to section 7.58 of the MCA 2005 Code of Practice (see no. 21), the attorney has the fiduciary duty not to take advantage of his position and not to benefit himself, but benefit the adult. Furthermore, section 7.60 of the MCA 2005 Code of Practice stipulates:

> A fiduciary duty means attorneys must not take advantage of their position. Nor should they put themselves in a position where their personal interests conflict with their duties. They also must not allow any other influences to affect the way in which they act as an attorney. Decisions should always benefit the donor, and not the attorney. Attorneys must not profit or get any personal benefit from their position, apart from receiving gifts where the Act allows it, whether or not it is at the donor's expense.

Notwithstanding the aforementioned, Thurston notes that the attorney can obtain the court's consent for acts that benefit himself or someone other than the adult.[130] Thurston refers to section 23(2) of the MCA 2005, which stipulates that the court

126. Stanyer 2017, p. 227.
127. Lush & Bielanska 2017, pp. 174-175.
128. Stanyer 2017, p. 227.
129. Stanyer 2017, p. 106.
130. Thurston 2015 pp. 281-282.

may 'give any consent or authorisation to act which the donee [attorney] would have to obtain from P if P had capacity to give it'.[131]

G. *Law in action*

34. **What are considered the advantages and the disadvantages of enduring documents?**

Lush and Bielanska note the following advantages of the LPA:
- LPAs are relatively cheap, and through a simple procedure, the adult can prepare in advance for the possibility of mental incapacity at some time in the future.
- LPAs respect the adult's authority by allowing him to choose the person(s) who is/are to manage his affairs in the future.
- LPAs provide the opportunity for a smooth and seamless transition in managing the adult's affairs. Lush and Bielanska point out that it is often difficult to determine precisely the point at which the adult lacks capacity. LPAs allow the attorney to step in gradually.
- Lush and Bielanska note that LPAs legitimise community practice. They argue that before it was possible to make an enduring power of attorney, it was common practice for attorneys to continue using an ordinary power of attorney even though, technically, it had been revoked by the adult's incapacity.
- LPAs avoid the stigma of a formal assessment of capacity and the bureaucracy, delay and expense of court proceedings.[132]

The most striking advantage mentioned by Lush and Bielanska is that LPAs give greater freedom of action to the attorney. In this regard, they note:

> 'The argument that EPA's and LPA's provide greater autonomy to the donor has generally been overstated. The person who really does benefit from enhanced autonomy is the attorney, because of the absence of the constraints that would be imposed upon him if he were a court-appointed deputy.'[133]

Ward notes the following disadvantages or risks associated with the making of an LPA:
- The attorney misuses the LPA or does not have the necessary skills to act as an attorney;
- The LPA may further aggravate family conflicts;

131. Ibid.
132. Lush & Bielanska 2017, p. 4.
133. Lush & Bielanska 2017, p. 4.

- Problems when dealing with banks in case the adult and attorney have concurrent authority to make decisions concerning financial and property affairs;
- Privacy concerns as once the LPA has been registered, anyone can make a so-called 'first tier search' (see no. 27);
- The occurrence of a significant change in the circumstances of the adult after the LPA has been registered and the adult neglects to make a new LPA;[134]

35. **How does the enduring document function/operate in practice? What works well and what does not? Are there or have there been any problems? How have these been dealt with? Is there any empirical research available on the questions mentioned above?**

Several (research) studies have been conducted in England and Wales, looking at various aspects of how the LPA operates in practice. These studies seldom provide quantitative information but are often qualitative or provide anecdotal information.

Research on the 'customer base' of the LPA and the process of execution

In 2014 a quantitative and qualitative study looking into the potential customer base of the lasting power of attorney was conducted by Beckett *et al.* at the behest of the Office of the Public Guardian. Beckett *et al.* found a lack of awareness of the LPA among potential customers; 45% of the respondents in the quantitative survey had never heard of the LPA or knew nothing about it.[135] Moreover, upon being informed of the possibility of making an LPA, only 34% of the respondents were interested in making an LPA at some stage.[136] Beckett et al. distinguished several reasons for adults not to make an LPA, including so-called 'attitudinal and emotional barriers', such as the adult's belief that they would not lose capacity, and so-called 'relevance barriers', such as the belief that their relatives would be able to manage without an LPA.[137] Other barriers included 'practical barriers', such as the adult not having someone they could nominate to act as an attorney; 'information barriers' reflecting a lack of awareness of the LPA; and 'process barriers', such as the costs of registering an LPA.[138]

A small-scale study looking at the experiences with LPAs for financial affairs

In 2018, a local (West of Berkshire) small-scale qualitative study looking into the experiences of people with dementia and their partners and carers in obtaining

134. Ward 2016, pp. 165-166.
135. Beckett *et al.* 2014, p. 5.
136. Ibid.
137. Beckett *et al.* 2014, pp. 6-7.
138. Ibid.

and administrating an LPA for financial and property affairs was conducted by the Research Institute for Consumer Affairs (RICA). The research study consisted of two group discussions: one group consisting of people with dementia (3 participants) and one group consisting of carers or partners of people with dementia (3 participants). Using a semi-structured framework, the researchers explored the participants' knowledge and experience of the LPA. The same questions were used for both group discussions to examine the issues from two perspectives.[139] The researcher found difficulties in administering LPAs in some instances, as not all businesses (such as banks, utilities and agencies) have staff at points of contact who are fully aware of LPAs and their administration.[140] The participants in the second group discussion, carers or partners of people with dementia, indicated that they experienced a burden of responsibility associated with the LPA. It was noted that having two or more attorneys could alleviate some of this burden, but participants also indicated that taking up the responsibility of being an attorney is not suited to everyone.[141] Although the participants of group discussion 1 indicated that they experienced a sense of relief once the LPA was in place, all participants also indicated that the time after diagnoses can be difficult as both the person with dementia and carers and relatives are coming to terms with the diagnosis.[142] Researchers suggested that further research should look into the experiences and motivations of people who are newly diagnosed with dementia and do not have an LPA in place.[143]

Post-legislative scrutiny of the MCA 2005

In 2013, the House of Lords established a committee to conduct a so-called post-legislative scrutiny of the Mental Capacity Act 2005 and to examine whether the act was working as Parliament intended.[144] In a report presented in March 2014, the Committee presented its findings and recommendations based on 15 public evidence hearings and 216 written submissions from both organisations and individuals with experience with the MCA 2005.[145] Concerning LPAs, the Committee expressed concern that LPAs are not recognised or understood in practice in all cases.[146] In this context, problems with banks' acceptance of the LPA were mentioned, but also a lack of knowledge and awareness of LPAs in the medical and care sector. In addition, several experts expressed concern about attorneys' lack of awareness and knowledge of their rights and duties.[147] Based

139. Rica 2018, p. 7-8.
140. Rica 2018, p. 3, 13 & 17.
141. Rica 2018, p. 3, 11 & 18.
142. Rica 2018, p. 3, 17 & 18.
143. Rica 2018, p. 19.
144. House of Lords, Select Committee on the Mental Capacity Act 2005, 2014, p. 22.
145. Ibid.
146. House of Lords, Select Committee on the Mental Capacity Act 2005 2014, p. 72.
147. House of Lords, Select Committee on the Mental Capacity Act 2005 2014, p. 73.

on the above, the committee made the following recommendations, which also provide a clear reflection and summary of the problems identified in the report:

'191. As with other aspects of the Mental Capacity Act, low levels of awareness have affected implementation of the provisions relating to Lasting Powers of Attorney. Awareness needs to be raised among the general public of the benefits of Lasting Powers of Attorney in order to encourage greater take-up, especially for Health and Welfare matters. We support the initiatives of the Public Guardian to improve take-up by simplifying the forms and reducing the cost of registration, as well as identifying other barriers to take-up.

192. We recommend that the Government, working with the independent oversight body recommended in chapter 4, and the Office of the Public Guardian:

- address the poor levels of understanding of LPAs among professional groups, especially in the health and social care sector, paying specific attention to the status of Lasting Powers of Attorney in decision-making;
- consider how best to ensure that information concerning registered Lasting Powers of Attorney can be shared between public bodies, and where appropriate with private sector bodies such as banks and utilities;
- issue guidance to local authorities that their new responsibilities for provision of information in relation to care contained in the Care Bill should include information on Lasting Powers of Attorney;
- consider how attorneys and deputies faced with non-compliance by public bodies or private companies can be supported in the absence of specific sanctions;
- review the apparent anomalies in the current arrangements with regard to successive replacement attorneys, and the status in England of Scottish Powers of Attorney.'[148]

Research on financial abuse of people lacking mental capacity

Insight into how the LPA functions or operates in practice may be found by studying the cases that the Court of Protection hears. This has been done by Daley *et al.* in a study focusing on the financial abuse of people lacking mental capacity.[149] The insights provided by this study concerning financial abuse will be discussed under no. 36. The study, however, also provided insights into other problems with the LPA in practice, predominantly the role of family conflicts. In their study, Daley et al. looked at 34 court cases heard in the Court of Protection between 1 January and 9 November 2015. In 23 of these cases, they found clear indications of family disputes, such as disputes about who should act as an attorney or disputes about how the attorney had handled the affairs of the adult.[150] Daley *et al.* note, in this regard, that the role of attorney can have a negative side-effect,

148. House of Lords, Select Committee on the Mental Capacity Act 2005 2014, pp. 74-75; see also Lush & Bielanska 2017, pp. 21-22.
149. Daley *et al.* 2017.
150. Daley *et al.* 2017, p. 82.

namely that it further exacerbates a bad relationship or that it creates suspicions or conflicts where none existed in the past:

> 'Having to take responsibility for the property and financial affairs of a relative, often a parent, seems sometimes to have one or other of two negative impacts – that it poisons pre-existing relationships further, or that it precipitates bad feeling where none existed in the past.'[151]

In addition to family disputes, Daley et al. found that attorneys are insufficiently aware of their rights and duties in some cases. In this regard, they note:

> 'Individuals do not always remember the information that has been provided to them, but there seems to be too little information provided to them about their role as attorneys when LPAs are first registered. Better information – including warnings about the implications of failing to exercise their duties properly – might head off difficulties that crop up when LPAs are put into effect.'[152]

36. Is there any information available on the number and type of cases where there has been (financial) misuse or abuse by the attorney?

In a study conducted by Daley *et al.* looking at the financial abuse of people lacking mental capacity, Daley et al. distinguish two sources of information which provide insight into the nature and extent of financial abuse in the context of an LPA.[153] The first source concerns reports of complaints or allegations of abuse against attorneys, registered with the Office of the Public Guardian. The second source concerns cases heard by the Court of Protection on breaches of duties by the attorney, cases where an application for the revocation of the LPA has been made and cases where an LPA has been contested.[154] Daley et al. note that data from these sources cannot provide a total picture of all possible and actual misuse and abuse by attorneys, as not all situations will come to the attention of the OPG or the Court of Protection.[155] However, although the data from these sources do not provide information on the number of cases, it does provide information on the nature and type of cases where there has been financial misuse or abuse by the attorney.

Concerning the first category, as discussed under no. 32, a concern about an attorney or deputy can be reported to the Office of the Public Guardian. Information is available on the number of safeguarding referrals the Office of the

151. Daley *et al.* 2017, p. 85.
152. Daley *et al.* 2017, p. 97.
153. Daley *et al.* 2017, p. 26.
154. Ibid.
155. Daley *et al.* 2017, p. 31.

Public Guardian receives. In 2017-2018 the Office of the Public Guardian received 5245 safeguarding referrals, of which 1886 were accepted for investigation by the investigation unit of the OPG. In addition, 3156 referrals were signposted to other agencies, such as the police and public authorities.[156] Safeguarding referrals come from several sources, such as relatives, local authorities, care homes and financial institutions.[157] In its 2017-2018 annual report, the OPG released the following numbers showing the referrals made by different sources[158]:

Referral source	Referrals made	Accepted for investigation
Relative	2122	593
Local authority	1221	595
Attorney/deputy	324	116
Solicitor/other professional	268	84
OPG	168	112
Bank	152	113
Client/donor	117	27
Third-party	146	55
Whistleblower	80	21
Police	85	32
Other sources	359	138

The 2015/2016 annual report provides typical examples of cases the OPG looked at in that year, including undervalued house sales, the client's home being sold to the attorney, creating fraudulent LPA's and large financial sums transferred from the client's bank account to another bank account.[159] As part of this comparative study, a staff member of the OPG was asked whether, four years later (a list with questions was sent in 2019), these cases were still considered typical examples of cases investigated by the OPG. Such was the case. Additional examples included inappropriate gifting of the adult's money by the attorney, improper loans, a refusal to engage with medical professionals and the adult lacking the capacity to have made the LPA.

Concerning the second category, as discussed under no. 12, the Court of Protection may revoke an LPA or direct that it is not to be registered when fraud or undue

156. OPG 2017-2018, p. 16.
157. Office of the Public Guardian, *Annual Report and Accounts 2015-2016*, p. 15, via: https://www.gov.uk/government/publications/office-of-the-public-guardian-annual-report-and-accounts-2015-to-2016 (last accessed: 01-04-2022).
158. OPG 2017-2018, p. 16.
159. Office of the Public Guardian, *Annual Report and Accounts 2015-2016*, p. 15, via: https://www.gov.uk/government/publications/office-of-the-public-guardian-annual-report-and-accounts-2015-to-2016 (last accessed: 01-04-2022).

pressure has been used to induce the adult to make an LPA or when the attorney has behaved, is behaving or is proposing to behave in a way that contravenes his authority or is not in the adult's best interests (section 22 of the MCA 2005). Examples of situations where the court found this was the case have already been mentioned under no. 12. In their study, Daley et al. looked at 34 cases heard in the Court of Protection between 1 January and 9 November 2015, intending to study the characteristics of financial abuse by attorneys and deputies.[160] In 18 of these 34 cases, the court was confronted with a situation in which the attorney allegedly had breached his authority or had failed to act in the bests interests of the adult concerned.[161] Based on these cases, Daley et al. provide a list of common examples which either raise suspicions or indicate misbehaviour by the attorney or the deputy:

- 'failure to provide accounts to the Court or OPG;
- arrears in the payment of care home fees;
- failure to provide the donor, resident in a care home, with a weekly personal allowance;
- no separation of the attorney and donor's funds (co-mingling);
- spending on purchase of or repairs to property not the donor's;
- holding donor's money in an account in own name;
- gifting to self and own family above permissible levels;
- unjustified and false claims as to why the donor's money had been spent;
- chaotic incompetence in managing the property and financial affairs of the person lacking capacity.'[162]

Daley et al. further note that misuse of the adult's assets not in all cases resulted from what is referred to as 'a fraudulent impulse'. In some cases, it seemed grounded in 'naïve incompetence, bitter intra-family disputes or the pressure of personal problems'.[163]

37. Are there any (mandatory) safeguards, and how have these been implemented in practice?

Lush describes the following characteristics of the LPA, of which the majority also seem to act as some form of safeguard:

1) A prescribed form;
2) 5 people to be notified if desired;
3) Certificate of capacity;

---

160. Daley *et al.* 2017, p. 70. Important to note here, is that the 32 of these cases had been dealt with by the same judge (Daley *et al.* 2017, p. 73).
161. Daley et al. 2017, p. 72.
162. List cited from Daley *et al.* 2017, p. 73.
163. Daley et al. 2017, p. 73. See also pp. 79-80.

4) Registration LPA by OPG;
5) Objections to registration;
6) Limited authority to make gifts;
7) Ongoing role COP;
8) Revocation by the donor.[164]

Ad 1 and 2) As discussed under no. 13, the LPA must be made in a prescribed form. There are two forms, one for financial affairs and the other for health and care decisions. Both forms include a section (section 8) with certain prescribed information, which the adult, the attorney(s) and the certificate provider must read to ensure that the adult is aware of the effects of making an LPA and that the attorney is aware of his rights and responsibilities.[165] The adult may include in his LPA the names of up to five people to be notified if an application to register an LPA is submitted to the OPG (see no. 16 and no. 25).[166]

Ad 3) As discussed in more detail under no. 30, the valid execution of an LPA requires the involvement of a certificate provider. The certificate provider discusses the LPA with the adult, makes sure the adult understands what he is about to do and makes sure there is no undue influence concerning the signing of the LPA.[167]

Ad 4 and 5) As discussed under no. 24, an LPA may only be used once the OPG has registered it. Registration can have a deterrent effect on people with bad intentions, as was also noted by the Law Commission in its report on Mental Capacity:

> 'A process of registration involving a public body will undoubtedly discourage some people who might abuse powers which remain in the private domain and will provide a point of reference for those who have queries or concerns about the status of a particular document.'[168]

Linked to this, Lush and Bielanska list several circumstances in which the OPG must refrain from registering the LPA. This is the case when:
- the LPA is not in the prescribed form and/or has not been correctly executed;
- the LPA which has been sent to the OPG for registration is not the original instrument nor a certified copy of it;
- the court of protection has already appointed a deputy for the adult;
- an attorney or named person has objected to the registration of the LPA;

164. Lush 2019, p. 139-140.
165. Lush 2019, p. 134 & 139.
166. Lush 2019, p. 139.
167. Stanyer 2017, p. 158.
168. Lush & Bielanska 2017, p. 162 citing Law Commission 1995, § 7.30.

– the adult has objected to the registration of the LPA.[169]

As discussed under no. 16 and no. 25, the adult, the attorney and the so-called named persons can object to the registration of the LPA. Lush notes that with the possibility of raising concerns with the OPG regarding how the attorney is exercising his powers – which is open to everyone – (see no. 32), the objection process seems to be largely superseded.[170]

Ad 6) As discussed under no. 22, there are important restrictions regarding gifts the attorney may perform on behalf of the adult.

Ad 7 and 8) Lush notes that although there is no direct supervision by the Court of Protection, the court still has a 'corrective function'.[171] The court of protection can, for instance, revoke the LPA when fraud or undue pressure has been used to induce the adult to make an LPA (see no. 17). When the adult still has the capacity to do so, the adult himself can also – at any time – revoke the LPA.

38. **Is there anything else of interest not included in the answers above?**

– As discussed under no. 13, In England and Wales, there are two prescribed forms to make an LPA: a form for the instrument intended to create a property and financial affairs LPA and a form for the instrument designed to create a health and welfare LPA. In the consultation paper 'Lasting Powers of Attorney – forms and guidance', the Department for Constitutional Affairs gave the following reasons for prescribing two forms rather than one or three forms:

> We consider a single form would be too cumbersome in practice and confusing for those simply wishing to make an LPA in relation to one area or the other. A single form for both types of LPA could be misleading as an LPA for property and affairs can be used when the donor has capacity and when the donor lacks capacity, whereas an LPA for personal welfare can only be used when the donor lacks capacity.
>
> We considered creating a third form for use when someone wishes to appoint the same person as an LPA with powers in respect of their personal welfare and property and affairs. However we do not think that this is desirable. For example, a donor may want to include particular instructions about his or her healthcare on their personal welfare LPA but they would not wish

169. Lush & Bielanska 2017, p. 170-171.
170. Lush 2019, p. 140.
171. Lush 2019, p. 136.

> this information to be seen by financial institutions who are following the property and affairs LPA.[172]

In the Netherlands, property and financial affairs and health and welfare affairs are frequently included in the same document if the adult wants to make a 'levenstestament' for both matters. Unfortunately, this means that information on the health and welfare wishes of the adult is currently also visible for financial institutions such as banks, which often require the attorney to submit the whole document. This is not desirable as the information on health and welfare affairs does not concern financial institutions. Therefore, it seems a best practice to separate both elements.

- Family conflicts (see no. 34) and disputes between attorneys may hinder the execution of the LPA by the attorney. Mediation is in the MCA 2005 Code of Practice presented as a means that might effectively resolve conflicts.[173] The OPG has twice conducted a pilot study to examine whether mediation can be of added value in resolving issues with court-appointed deputies and attorneys. In the 2019/2020 annual report, the OPG concluded the following:

> 'From the end of 2018 throughout 2019, we carried out a pilot of using mediation in investigations in certain circumstances, in cases where the parties agreed to this. The pilot and evaluation is now complete. We will not be pursing the pilot further at this time as the findings demonstrated limited success in preventing cases going to Court.'[174]

Bibliography

A. Beckett, K. Leary, L. Cumming & G. Davies, *The Future of Lasting Power of Attorney. A research report for the Office of the Public Guardian*, Ipsos MORI 2014.

A. Brown, P. Barber & D. Martin, *The Mental Capacity Act 2005. A guide for practice,* Exeter: Learning Matters Ltd 2009.

G. Dalley, M. Gilhooly, K. Gilhooly, P. Harries & M. Levi, *Financial Abuse of People Lacking Mental Capacity. A Report to the Dawes Trust,* Brunel University London 2017.

J. Kitzinger & C. Kitzinger, *Increasing understanding and uptake of Advance Decisions in Wales,* A report for the Public Policy Institute for Wales, 2016.

172. Lush & Bielanska 2017, pp. 107-108 citing 'Department for Constitutional Affairs, Lasting powers of Attorney – forms and guidance (CP 01/06)', 20 January 2006.
173. Ward 2016, p. 189; Code of Practice MCA 2005 Code of Practice.
174. Office of the Public Guardian, *Annual Report and Accounts 2019-2020,* p. 21, via: https://www.gov.uk/government/publications/office-of-the-public-guardian-annual-report-and-accounts-2019-to-2020 (last accessed: 01-04-2022).

The Law Commission, *The Incapacitated Principal*, London 1983, accessible via: https://www.lawcom.gov.uk/project/the-incapacitated-principal/ (last accessed: 01-04-2022).

D. Lush, 'Adult Guardianship and Powers of Attorney in England and Wales', in: L. Ho & R. Lee, *Special Needs Financial Planning. A Comparative Perspective*, Cambridge University Press 2019, pp. 117-148.

D. Lush & C. Bielanska, *Cretney & Lush on Lasting and Enduring Powers of Attorney*, London: LexisNexis 2017.

OPG, *We want to hear from you on modernising LPAs*, 16-09-2021, via: https://publicguardian.blog.gov.uk/2021/09/16/we-want-to-hear-from-you-on-modernising-lpas/ (last accessed: 01-04-2022).

OPG, *Modernising lasting powers of attorney consultation – what happens next?*, 09-12-2021, via: https://publicguardian.blog.gov.uk/2021/12/09/modernising-lasting-powers-of-attorney-consultation-what-happens-next/ (last accessed: 01-04-2022).

Office of the Public Guardian, *Annual Report and Accounts 2019-2020*, p. 21, via: https://www.gov.uk/government/publications/office-of-the-public-guardian-annual-report-and-accounts-2019-to-2020 (last accessed: 01-04-2022).

Office of the Public Guardian, *Annual Report and Accounts 2018-2019*, via: https://www.gov.uk/government/publications/office-of-the-public-guardian-annual-report-and-accounts-2018-to-2019 (last accessed: 01-04-2022).

Office of the Public Guardian, *Annual Report and Accounts 2017-2018*, p. 6, via: https://www.gov.uk/government/publications/office-of-the-public-guardian-annual-report-and-accounts-2017-to-2018 (last accessed: 01-04-2022).

Office of the Public Guardian, *Annual Report and Accounts 2015-2016*, p. 15, via: https://www.gov.uk/government/publications/office-of-the-public-guardian-annual-report-and-accounts-2015-to-2016 (last accessed: 01-04-2022).

C. van Overdijk, 'England and Wales', in: R. Frimston, A. Ruck Keene, C. van Overdijk & A. Ward, *The international protection of adults*, Oxford: Oxford University Press 2015, pp. 179-216.

S. Rab, 'Legal systems in the UK (England and Wales: overview)', *Thomson Reuters Practical Law*, via: https://uk.practicallaw.thomsonreuters.com/5-636-2498?transitionType=Default&contextData=(sc.Default) (last accessed: 01-04-2022)

Rica, *Financial lasting power of attorney – experiences from people with dementia and their partners*, 2018, published on: www.rica.org.uk.

A. Stanyer, *Financial abuse of older clients: law, practice and prevention*, London: Bloomsbury 2017.

M. Terrell, C. Bielanska, J. Holmes & R. Frimston, *A Practitioner's Guide to the Court of Protection*, London: Bloomsbury 2018.

J. Thurston, *A Practitioner's Guide to Powers of Attorney*, London: Bloomsbury 2015.

C. Ward, *Lasting Powers of Attorney. A Practical Guide*, London: The Law Society 2016.

Legislation, parliamentary documents and jurisprudence

- Mental Capacity Act
- LPA, EPA & PG Regs 2007
- LPA, EPA & PG Regs 2009
- LPA, EPA & PG Regs 2015
- The Mental Capacity Act 2005 Code of Practice, accessible via https://www.gov.uk/government/publications/mental-capacity-act-code-of-practice (last accessed 01-04-2022).
- House of Lords Select Committee on the Mental Capacity Act 2005, *Mental Capacity Act 2005: post-legislative scrutiny*, 2014.
- R (on the application of Burke) v. General Medial Council [2005] EWCA Civ 1003.
- Drew v. Nunn (1878) 4 QBD 661.
- Public Guardian v. Marvin [2014] EWCOP 47.
- JL (Revocation of Lasting Power of Attorney [2014] EWCOP 36.
- Public Guardian v. AW and DH [2014] EWCOP 28.
- SAD and ACD v. SED, District Judge Glenworth, case no. 12791319.
- Public Guardian v. DA, YS and ES [2015] EWCOP 41.
- Public Guardian v. PM and SH [2016] EWCOP 25.
- Re Wheatley (an order of the Senior Judge made on 31 January 2011).
- Re Careford (an order of the Senior Judge made on 16 February 2011).
- Re Burdock (an order of the Senior Judge made on 2 July 2012).

Experts interviewed

- Solicitor
- Barrister & researcher
- Solicitor & researcher

N.B. An Office of the Public Guardian employee was kind enough to answer a set of questions in writing.

Appendix 7: Country report Germany

Comparative study on enduring documentsCountry report Germany

A. *General*

Brief general description of the legal system of Germany

Germany is a federal republic consisting of 16 states (Länder), approximately 400 districts (Landkreise or Stadtkreise) and municipalities (Städte and Gemeinden). According to article 30 of the German Constitution (Grundgesetz), both legislation and administration is a matter for the Länder, except when it is otherwise provided for or permitted in the German Constitution.[1] The law concerning the protection of adults is a federal matter governed by the German Civil Code.[2]

1. **Give a brief account of the adult protection system in each country (e.g. court-ordered protection measures, private remedies).**

Measures and provisions

In 1990, Germany undertook a fundamental reform of its adult protection system. With the *Betreuungsgesetz* – which entered into force on 1. January 1992 – major changes were incorporated into the German Civil Code, resulting in the abolition of judicial incapacitation (*Entmündigung*) and the guardianship institutions of tutorship (*Vormundschaft*) and curatorship (*Gebrechlichkeitspflegschaft*).[3] Instead, a new two-tier system was introduced, with enduring documents (tier one) on the one hand and the statutory system of *Betreuung* or custodianship (tier two) on the other.[4] As no. 2 discusses in more detail, three enduring documents can be distinguished in Germany: the *Vorsorgevollmacht*, the *Patientenverfügung*, and the *Betreuungsverfügung*. The regulatory framework for these instruments (tier one) is discussed in more detail in the remainder of this country report. The regulatory

1. Lipp & Ward 2015, p. 375.
2. Lipp & Ward 2015, p. 377.
3. Brosey 2020, pp. 199-200; Dethloff 2021, p. 1; Lipp & Ward 2015, p. 376.
4. Brosey 2020, p. 199; Lipp 2016-1, p. 1.

framework concerning tier two – the *Betreuung* – can be found in the Book 4 of the German Civil Code (GCC) on Family Law (§1896 onwards) and, as far as procedure is concerned, in the Family Procedure Act (*Gesetz über das Verfahren in Familiensachen und in den Angelegenheiten der freiwilligen Gerichtsbarkeit*).[5] According to §1896 GCC, the custodianship court or *Betreuungsgericht* can appoint a custodian or *Betreuer* 'if a person of full age, by reason of a mental illness or a physical, mental or psychological handicap, cannot as a whole or in part take care of their affairs'.[6] The *Betreuungsgericht* can do so at the request of the adult concerned or ex officio.

The system, introduced with the *Betreuungsgesetz,* is based on the principles of autonomy and necessity.[7] According to the necessity principle, the court may only appoint a *Betreuer* if necessary. As no. 8 discusses in more detail, according to §1896(2) GCC, a *Betreuung* is unnecessary if the adult's affairs are already looked after by an attorney authorised through a *Vorsorgevollmacht*.[8] Moreover, a *Betreuung* must be person-centred and tailored to the adult's need for support, protection and representation.[9] In the old system, according to Lipp, guardianship and legal incapacity were inseparable and like two sides of the same coin.[10] However, this changed with the *Betreuungsgesetz*. The court's decision to appoint a *Betreuer* no longer affects the adult's legal capacity. In this regard, Brosey notes that 'legal capacity is generally a question of a concrete situation and of the adult's current capability in this situation and not of a status as a result of a court decision'.[11] Protection is provided in principle through the general rules of private law (§104 and §105 GCC).[12] §104(2) GCC stipulates that 'a person is incapable of contracting if the person is in a state of pathological mental disturbance, which prevents the free exercise of will, unless the state by its nature is a temporary one'.[13] That being so, according to §1903 GCC, the court may impose a so-called reservation of consent (*Einwilligungsvorbehalt*). This reservation of consent limits the adult's legal capacity to the extent that the adult needs the custodian's consent to engage in financial transactions.[14] The court may only impose such a reservation of consent when 'this is necessary to prevent a substantial danger for the person

5. Dethloff 2021, p. 1.
6. Translation via: https://www.gesetze-im-internet.de/englisch_bgb/englisch_bgb.html#p0027.
7. Brosey 2020, pp. 200-201.
8. Dethloff 2021, pp. 1-2.
9. Brosey 2020, p. 203; Lipp & Ward 2015, p. 377.
10. Lipp 2016-1, p. 3.
11. Brosey 2020, p. 201.
12. Dethloff 2021, p. 2.
13. Translation via: http://www.gesetze-im-internet.de/englisch_bnoto/englisch_bnoto.html#p0518 (last accessed 01-05-2022).
14. Lipp 2016-1, pp. 3-4.

under custodianship or their assets'.[15] A *Betreuung* does not necessarily equate to representation but can be an element of *Betreuung*. According to Brosey, the term *Betreuung* could be translated as legal caretaking or legal caring.[16] The above-mentioned principle of necessity applies not only to the appointment of the custodian but also to the actions of this custodian, who should only act when necessary.[17] The custodian must support the adult in making his own decisions and respect the adult's rights, will and preferences. Representation, which involves making decisions on behalf of the adult, is only possible as a last resort.[18]

Although the *Betreuungsgesetz* of 1992 already led to significant changes in the German system promoting the right to autonomy of adults, the ratification of the United Nations Convention on the Rights of Persons with Disabilities (UNCRPD) inspired a further reform process. In 2015, the German Ministry of Justice and Consumer Protection commissioned a research project, which resulted in the report 'Qualität in der rechtlichen Betreuung'.[19] According to Brosey, the research project examined the implementation of the *Betreuungsgesetz* in practice. It also explored what the guiding principles for quality should be and, linked to that, whether there are structural deficits and, if so, what the underlying causes for these deficits are.[20] The study found, among other things, that while both professional and non-professional court-appointed custodians are aware of the importance of the adult's right to autonomy and self-determination, in practice, it is not easy to actually support adults in exercising these rights.[21] Brosey indicates that for professional custodians, this may have to do with the hours available to support the adult.[22] Concerning non-professional custodians, Brosey notes that insufficient use is made of the information, advice and support provided by so-called *Betreuungsvereine* (see below for more information).[23] These observations are only a tiny part of what constitutes a substantive report. Based on the findings of this report, the Ministry of Justice and Consumer Protection began the reform process 'Selbstbestimmung und Qualität im Betreuungsrecht' in 2018.[24] This reform process resulted in a new law coming into force on 1. January 2023. The new law further strengthens the adult's right to autonomy and introduces the

15. §1903 GCC. Translation via: http://www.gesetze-im-internet.de/englisch_bnoto/englisch_bnoto.html#p0518 (last accessed 01-05-2022).
16. Brosey 2020, p. 200.
17. Brosey 2020, p. 203.
18. Brosey 2020, pp. 205-206.
19. Bundesministerium der Justiz und für Verbraucherschutz 2018.
20. Brosey 2020, p. 200 & p. 207.
21. Brosey 2020, p. 211.
22. Brosey 2020, p. 211; See also Bundesministerium der Justiz und für Verbraucherschutz 2018, p. 599, which, in addition, notes that concepts and methods to support the adult are lacking.
23. Brosey 2020, p. 211; See also Bundesministerium der Justiz und für Verbraucherschutz 2018, p. 598.
24. Brosey 2020, p. 211.

possibility for spouses to represent each other ex-lege in medical matters (§1358 GCC-new).[25] However, as no. 6 discusses in more detail, the new law does not lead to significant changes in the regulation of the *Vorsorgevollmacht*.

Infrastructure

A key role is fulfilled in Germany by the so-called *Betreuungsgericht* or court. Section B of this country report discusses the court's authority in relation to the *Vorsorgevollmacht* in more detail. In addition, Germany has so-called *Betreuungsbehörde*, authorities responsible at the local level for specific matters concerning adult protection. For example, concerning the *Vorsorgevollmacht*, the *Betreuungsbehörde* play a role in verifying the adult's signature through a so-called *Beglaubigung* (see no. 13). Finally, so-called *Betreuungsvereine* (custodianship organisations) play a role in the recruitment, support and training of voluntary custodians.

2. **Given the definitions of a 'continuing power of attorney' and an 'advance directive' in Council of Europe Recommendation 2009/11, describe the concept or concepts used in each country. What are the legal instruments?**

In Germany, three enduring documents can be distinguished: the *Vorsorgevollmacht*, the *Patientenverfügung* and the *Betreuungsverfügung*. As no. 4 discusses in more detail, the possibility of making a *Vorsorgevollmacht* has been made available within the framework of the existing law. In other words, the term *Vorsorgevollmacht* is a word used in practice to refer to a situation in which the adult uses a *Vollmacht* or ordinary power of attorney to authorise one or more attorneys to act on his behalf in the event of his incapacity.[26] In addition to the *Vorsorgevollmacht*, adults can make a *Betreuungsverfügung* and a *Patientenverfügung*. With a *Betreuungsverfügung*, the adult can record his wishes regarding the choice of a custodian in case the court deems a custodianship necessary. The adult can also record his wishes on how the custodianship should be carried out in the *Betreuungsverfügung*.[27] Through a Patientenverfügung, the adult can specify which medical treatment he consents to or refuses in case of incapacity.[28]

With the following table (translated by RSR), Zimmerman has provided a clear overview of the aforementioned private law instruments and their relationship to the public law instrument of the *Betreuung*.[29]

25. For a more extensive discussion of futher changes, see Brosey 2022.
26. Zimmerman 2017, p. 38; Lipp 2009, p. 56.
27. Zimmerman 2017, p. 213; see also §1901c GCC from which a definition of the *Betreuungsverfügung* can be derived.
28. Zimmerman 2017, pp. 224-225; see also §1901a GCC from which a definition of the *Patientenverfügung* can be derived.
29. Zimmerman 2017, p. 40; Spalckhaver 2009, p. 96-97.

Vorsorgevollmacht	Betreuungsverfügung	Patientenverfügung
A *Vollmacht* granted by the adult to make provisions for a future period of incapacity.	An advance directive in which the adult expresses who should be appointed in the event the court deems *Betreuung* necessary and, in addition, expresses how the *Betreuung* is to be carried out.	An advance directive concerning future medical treatment when the patient is no longer capable of expressing or giving consent to treatment.
The *Vorsorgevollmacht* often, but not always, makes a *Betreuung* unnecessary.	The *Betreuungsverfügung* does not make a *Betreuung* unnecessary but presupposes it.	The *Patientenverfügung* does not make a *Betreuung* unnecessary but does not necessarily require a *Betreuung* either.

N.B. Although several enduring documents can be distinguished in Germany, this country report focuses on the appointment of an attorney through the so-called Vorsorgevollmacht.

3. What is the current source of law on enduring documents?

As discussed under no. 2, the term *Vorsorgevollmacht* is a term that has emerged in practice to refer to a situation in which the adult uses an ordinary power of attorney or *Vollmacht* to make provisions for a future period of incapacity. However, Lipp notes that the term *Vorsorgevollmacht* is not entirely accurate as it only draws attention to the *Vollmacht*, i.e. the conferral of authority to an attorney to act on behalf of the adult. Although the *Vollmacht* is an essential component of the *Vorsorgevollmacht*, according to Lipp and Spalckhaver, it is the so-called *Vorsorgeverhältnis* or *Grundverhältnis* – a basic agreement between the adult and the attorney stipulating how the *Vollmacht* should be used – that forms the basis of the *Vorsorgevollmacht* as an instrument intended to provide for a future period of incapacity.[30] Lipp notes that the *Grundverhältnis* will, in most cases, be based on the legal construct of the non-remunerated *Auftrag* (mandate) or the remunerated *Geschäftsbesorgungsvertrag* (agency agreement).[31] The aforementioned means that the *Vorsorgevollmacht* is subject to the provisions on the ordinary power of attorney (§164-§181 GCC). In addition, depending on the *Grundverhältnis*, the provisions on the *Auftrag* (§662-§674 GCC) or the *Geschäftsbesorgungsvertrag* (§675-675b GCC) can apply. Finally, Section 3, title 2 of the German Civil Code, containing provisions on custodianship or *Rechtliche Betreuung*, includes several provisions which bear direct relevance to the *Vorsorgevollmacht*, such as §1896 II GCC, from which a principle of subsidiarity (see no. 8) can be inferred.

30. Lipp 2009, p. 56; Spalckhaver 2009, pp. 96-97.
31. Lipp 2009, p. 56; see also Zimmerman 2017, pp. 108-109. This country report uses the English translations of the terms *Auftrag* and *Geschäftsbesorgungsvertrag* provided by Lipp (2015).

4. **Give a brief history of the main developments of the law on enduring documents.**

As noted under no. 2 and no. 3, the *Vorsorgevollmacht* has been developed within the framework of the existing law on ordinary powers of attorney (*Vollmacht*) and agency agreements (e.g. *Auftrag*). Lipp notes that, as such, the *Vorsorgevollmacht* has been acknowledged since the introduction of the German Civil Code in 1900.[32] In other words, in theory, adults in Germany already, for over 120 years, have the possibility to provide for a future period of incapacity through a *Vorsorgevollmacht*. Yet it was not until 1990 that the German legislator, with the *Betreuungsgesetz*, stipulated that priority should be given to provisions – such as the *Vorsorgevollmacht* – organised by adults themselves.[33] With the *Betreuungsgesetz*, the German legislator also provided a form of supervision in the form of the so-called *Überwachungsbetreuung* (see no. 32).[34] The law of 1990 has been amended and complemented four times (1999, 2005, 2009 and 2013). Significant changes and additions concerning the *Vorsorgevollmacht* were the adoption of §1904 and §1906 GCC in 1999. Although, in practice, the *Vorsorgevollmacht* was regularly used to make provisions for financial and property matters, it was less clear whether the *Vorsorgevollmacht* could also be used to make provisions for personal and medical matters. With §1904 and §1906 GCC, the German legislator confirmed this is the case if the adult has expressly stipulated this in the *Vorsorgevollmacht*.[35] In 2005, the German legislator extended the authority of the *Betreuungsbehörden* and *Betreuungsvereine* (see no. 1) to advise and support the attorney in the execution of his task.[36] *Betreuungsbehörden* were also given the authority to authenticate *Vorsorgevollmachten* (see no. 13).[37] Parallel with the changes and adjustments in 2005, a legal framework was created in 2004 for a central register in which both notarial and private *Vorsorgevollmachten* can be registered.[38]

5. **How does the specific legal regime concerning enduring documents relate to the (general) law on powers of attorney and other related legal figures?**

As discussed under no. 2 and no. 3, the *Vorsorgevollmacht* has been developed within the framework of the existing law on the *Vollmacht* and other legal constructs – such as the *Auftrag* or the *Geschäftsbesorgungsvertrag* – which can form the basis of the *Vorsorgeverhältnis* or *Grundverhältnis*, i.e. the underlying relationship between the adult and the attorney.

32. Lipp 2016-2, p. 2; Lipp & Ward 2015, p. 379.
33. §1896 GCC.
34. Lipp 2009, pp. 2-3.
35. Deinert 2017, p. 59.
36. Müller & Renner 2018, p. 6.
37. Müller & Renner 2018, p. 7.
38. Müller & Renner 2018, p. 8.

6. Are there any recent proposals for reform in this area?

As discussed under no. 1, a major reform process of the *Betreuungsgesetz* has taken place and a new law is scheduled to enter into force on 1 January 2023. Part of the reform process was an interdisciplinary discussion process consisting of four specialised working groups. Although the *Vorsorgevollmacht* was not a central theme of the reform process, the third working group discussed some selected issues, including the risk of abuse of the *Vorsorgevollmacht* and problems with the effectiveness and acceptance of the *Vorsorgevollmacht* in practice. The working group concluded that the *Vorsorgevollmacht* should remain a low-threshold, private, autonomous instrument and that legal restrictions on the right of self-determination should only be adopted to the extent necessary to avert danger to the adult concerned.[39] Therefore, at most, selective legislation was considered necessary. Although the working group deemed it important to improve the quality of the advice and guidance provided to adults and attorneys – particularly concerning the risk of abuse – legislative action was not considered the appropriate means to achieve this.[40] The German legislator adopted this advice, and consequently, the new law does not change much in the current regulation of the *Vorsorgevollmacht*.[41] A new §1820 GCC brings together various provisions concerning the *Vorsorgevollmacht*, such as the conditions for the appointment of a supervisory attorney (see no. 32) and the revocation of the *Vorsorgevollmacht*. Where relevant, this country report addresses the changes that will occur with the entry into force of the new law.

7. Are there statistics available on the number of (registered) enduring documents in each country? And if so, what are they?

As no. 24 discusses in more detail, Vorsorgevollmachten can be registered in the so-called *Zentrale Vorsorgeregister*. This register is kept by the *Bundesnotarkammer*, the Federal Chamber of Notaries in Germany).[42] Based on the information presented in the annual reports of the *Zentrale Vorsorgeregister*, the following

39. Bundesministerium der Justiz und für Verbraucherschutz, *Der interdisziplinäre Diskussionsprozess des Bundesministeriums der Justiz und für Verbraucherschutz „Selbsbestimmung und Qualität im Betreuungsrecht" – Erste Ergebnisse*, 12 August 2019, via https://www.bmj.de/SharedDocs/Downloads/DE/Themen/VorsorgeUndPatientenrechte/20190812_Diskussionsprouess_Betreuungsrecht_erste-Ergebniss.pdf?__blob=publicationFile&v=1 (last accessed: 01-05-2022);
40. Ibid.
41. Deutscher Bundestag, *Entwurf eines Gesetzes zur Reform des Vormundschafts- und Betreuungsrechts*, 19/24445, 18.11.2020, pp. 150 & 244-247, via https://www.bmj.de/SharedDocs/Gesetzgebungsverfahren/DE/Reform_Betreuungsrecht_Vormundschaft.html (last accessed: 01-05-2022).
42. §78a of the Federal Code for Notaries.

overview concerning the annual number of registered enduring documents can be given.[43] In 2020, almost 5 million enduring documents were registered.[44]

Year	Number of registered Vorsorgeverfügungen*
2005	125.885
2006	147.931
2007	170.362
2008	181.233
2009	187.462
2010	218.832
2011	290.789
2012	335.746
2013	421.962
2014	370.375
2015	382.292
2016	383.891
2017	390.207
2018	382.029
2019	393.092
2020	390.437

* As discussed under no. 2, three different enduring documents can in Germany be distinguished (the Vorsorgevollmacht, the Patientenverfügung and the Betreuungsverfügung). The annual number of registered documents presented in the table above includes the annual number of registered Vorsorgevollmachten; the annual number of registered Vorsorgevollmachten combined with a Patientenverfügung, a Betreuungsverfügung or both; and the annual number of registered Betreuungsverfügungen. It is not possible to register an 'isolated' Patientenverfügung in the Zentrale Vorsorgeregister. The number of 'isolated' Betreuungsverfügungen is relatively small (in 2020: 0,6% of all registered documents; in 2019: 0,4% of all registered documents).

B. Enduring documents and adult protection measures ordered by the court or an administrative authority

8. How do enduring documents relate to adult protection measures ordered by the court or an administrative authority? Is there a principle of subsidiarity in place?

43. Bundesnotarkammer Zentrales Vorsorgeregister, Jahresbericht 2020, 2019, 2018, 2017, 2016, 2015, 2014, 2013, 2012, 2011, 2010, 2009, 2008, 2007, 2006, 2005, via https://www.vorsorgeregister.de/footer/jahresbericht-und-statistik (last accessed: 08-04-2022).
44. Bundesnotarkammer Zentrales Vorsorgeregister, Jahresbericht 2020, via https://www.vorsorgeregister.de/footer/jahresbericht-und-statistik (last accessed: 08-04-2022).

A principle of subsidiarity can be inferred from §1896(2) of the German Civil Code, which states:

> 'A custodian may be appointed only for groups of tasks in which the custodianship is necessary. The custodianship is not necessary to the extent that the affairs of a person of full age may be taken care of by an authorised person who is not one of the persons set out in section 1897 (3), or by other assistants for whom no legal representative is appointed, just as well as by a custodian.'[45]

What is referred to as a custodianship (*Betreuung*) is deemed unnecessary when the affairs can be handled by the attorney 'just as well' or even better than by the custodian.[46] According to Lipp and Zimmerman, §1896(2) GCC not only has the aim to ensure that the adult's right to autonomy and self-determination are as much as possible respected but also has the aim to relieve the burden placed on the courts and the public purse by avoiding (unnecessary) custodianships.[47]

9. **Is there an obligation for the court or the administrative authority to check whether an enduring document is in place?**

Such an obligation follows from §1896(2) of the German Civil Code mentioned under no. 8. Based on §6 of the Regulation on the Central Register of Lasting Powers of Attorney (*Verordnung über das Zentrale Vorsorgeregister*), courts can obtain information from the *Zentrale Vorsorgeregister* through an automated search procedure. In 2020, the courts in 205.049 cases requested information from the central register.[48] In addition to the obligation to check whether a *Vorsorgevollmacht* is in place, courts, according to §278 II (2) of the Family Procedure Act (Gesetz über das Verfahren in Familiensachen und in den Angelegenheiten der freiwilligen Gerichtsbarkeit – FamFG), also have an obligation to make adults aware of the possibility to make a *Vorsorgevollmacht*:

> 'The court shall instruct the person concerned on the possible course of the proceedings. In suitable cases it shall inform the person concerned of the possibility of a lasting power of attorney, its substance, and the possibility of his registration with the Central Register of Lasting Powers of Attorney (zentrales Vorsorgeregister) pursuant to section 78a (2) of the Federal Regulation on Notaries (Bundesnotarordnung). The court shall discuss with the person

45. Translation via: https://www.gesetze-im-internet.de/englisch_bgb/englisch_bgb.html#p0027.
46. Zimmerman 2017, p. 39.
47. Zimmerman 2017, p. 39; Lipp 2009, p. 28.
48. Bundesnotarkammer Zentrales Vorsorgeregister, Jahresbericht 2020, via https://www.vorsorge register.de/footer/jahresbericht-und-statistik (last accessed: 08-04-2022).

> concerned the scope of duties and the question of which person or agency should be considered as custodian.'[49]

The court is only obliged to inform adults within the context of a pending curatorship procedure. Zimmerman notes in this respect that in these circumstances, it will often no longer be possible for the adult to make a *Vorsorgevollmacht* since the adult will generally already be experiencing a decline in decision-making capabilities.[50]

10. Can the measures ordered by the court or the administrative authority be combined with the enduring document?

Kurze notes that a co-existence of a *Vorsorgevollmacht* and a *Betreuung* for the same matters is not possible. However, a combination is possible if the *Betreuung* concerns matters which cannot be included in the *Vorsorgevollmacht* (e.g. representation in an application procedure for the adoption of a person of full age – §1768(2) GCC) or matters which the adult has not included in the *Vorsorgevollmacht* and for which the court deems support for the adult necessary.[51]

11. Can the enduring document's content or the attorney's powers be changed or expanded by the court or any other institution? And if so, in what cases?

Two situations have been identified in the literature that affect the attorney's power to act on behalf of the adult. First, as no. 32 discusses in more detail, the court can appoint a so-called *Kontrollbetreuer* or supervisory custodian to supervise the attorney's actions and enforce the adult's rights under the basic agreement. Second, as no. 21 discusses in more detail, the attorney must follow the adult's instructions included in the basic agreement of the *Vorsorgevollmacht* (§665 GGC). Nedden-Boeger notes, however, that the attorney – when he wants to deviate from the instructions of the adult and can no longer ask the adult for his permission to do so – can request the court to appoint a custodian or *Betreuer* whose specific purpose is to determine whether a deviation from the adult's instructions should be allowed.[52]

12. On which grounds are state-ordered measures applied, notwithstanding the presence of an enduring document?

49. Translation via: http://www.gesetze-im-internet.de/englisch_famfg/englisch_famfg.html#p1411.
50. Zimmerman 2017, p. 40.
51. Kurze 2018, pp. 49-59 & pp. 295-296.
52. Nedden-Boeger 2019, p. 89.

Zimmerman lists the following situations where the court can order a custodianship despite the *Vorsorgevollmacht*:

1) The court is not aware of the *Vorsorgevollmacht*. Although the court must check the register (see no. 9), registration is not mandatory in Germany (see no. 24), meaning there can be situations in which the court is unaware of the adult's *Vorsorgevollmacht*.
2) The *Vollmacht* was not made to provide for a future period of incapacity, making it an ordinary *Vollmacht* and not a *Vorsorgevollmacht*.
3) The *Vorsorgevollmacht* is invalid, for example, because the adult at the time lacked the capacity to make the *Vorsorgevollmacht*.
4) Due to doubts about the validity of the *Vorsorgevollmacht,* there are problems with the acceptance of the *Vorsorgevollmacht* by third parties.
5) The *Vorsorgevollmacht* does not cover all matters the court deems support necessary, making a (partial) custodianship necessary.
6) The requirements concerning the form have not been met. For example, specific affairs require a so-called *Beglaubigung* (see no. 13).
7) The attorney does not act or is unsuited to the task.
8) There are concerns about abuse.
9) It concerns a matter for which representation through a *Vorsorgevollmacht* is not possible (see no. 10 and 15).
10) The nominated attorney may not act as such (see no. 18).[53]

C. *Form and general content of the enduring document*

13. Are there any requirements as to the form of the enduring document?

Concerning the *Vollmacht*, §167 GCC stipulates:

> a. Authority is conferred by declaration to the person to be granted authority, or to the third party in relation to whom the authority is to have effect.
> b. The declaration is not required to be in the form laid down for the legal transaction to which the authority relates.

As §167(2) GCC makes clear, there are, in principle, no formal requirements regarding the form of the *Vollmacht*. This means that the authority to act on behalf of the adult can, in theory, be granted orally. However, Zimmerman notes that, in practice, such a *Vorsorgevollmacht* will not be accepted by third parties because the authority conferred to the attorney is not verifiable.[54] In other words, a *Vorsorgevollmacht* in written form is advisable. The written form is, in

53. Zimmerman 2017, pp. 191-198.
54. Zimmerman 2017, p. 50-51. See also Kurze 2018, p. 91 & pp. 96-97.

particular cases, also required, for instance, when the adult wishes to authorise the attorney to consent to an examination of the adult's state of health or medical treatment of the adult.[55] In some cases, in addition to the written form, a so-called *Beglaubigung* of the *Vorsorgevollmacht* is required, for example, when the adult through the *Vorsorgevollmacht* wants to enable entries in the land register (*Grundbuch*).[56] Through a *Beglaubigung*, a notary or a *Betreuungsbehörde* verifies the identity of the adult and confirms that the signature on the *Vorsorgevollmacht* is that of the adult concerned.[57] A *Beglaubigung* must be distinguished from a *Beurkundung*. With the latter, a notary not only verifies the identity of the adult but also examines the will of the adult concerned and makes sure the adult is aware of the consequences of the *Vorsorgevollmacht*. The notary also assumes responsibility for an unambiguous and effective formulation of the *Vorsorgevollmacht*.[58] Kurze points out that a *Beurkundung* will rarely be a formal requirement for a *Vorsorgevollmacht*.[59] Therefore, he notes that it depends on the case's circumstances whether an adult should opt for a *Beglaubigung* or a *Beurkundung* of the *Vorsorgevollmacht*. The advantage of a *Beurkundung* of the *Vorsorgevollmacht* is that duplicates of the *Vorsorgevollmacht* can be issued at a later date, which may be useful since third parties, in some cases, require the official document before accepting the authority conferred to the attorney.[60]

14. Is the enduring document unilateral or bilateral? Is a signature from the attorney a requirement?

As discussed under no. 3, the *Vorsorgevollmacht* includes both a conferral of authority to an attorney to act on behalf of the adult (*Vollmacht*) and a so-called *Vorsorgeverhältnis* or basic agreement between the adult and the attorney stipulating how the *Vollmacht* should be used.[61] According to Lipp, the basic agreement will, in most cases, be based on the legal construct of the *Auftrag* (mandate) or the *Geschäftsbesorgungsvertrag* (agency agreement). These are bilateral agreements.[62] However, Kurze notes that such an agreement does not have to be in writing – which, according to him, is rarely the case – but can also be concluded by oral declaration or implied action.[63] As the aforementioned makes

55. §1904(5) GCC and §126 GCC, see also §1906 SCC; Kurze 2018, pp. 96-97; Zimmerman 2017, pp. 51-52.
56. Zimmerman 2017 pp. 51-52.
57. Kurze 2018, pp. 92-93.
58. Zimmerman 2017, pp. 52-53.
59. A conferral of authority to conclude credit agreements on behalf of the adult (*Verbraucherkreditverträgen*), which requires a *Beurkundung*. However, Kurze notes that such an authority will rarely be included in the *Vorsorgevollmacht*.
60. Kurze 2018, pp. 96-97.
61. Lipp 2009, p. 56; Spalckhaver 2009, pp. 96-97.
62. Kurze 2018, p. 118.
63. Kurze 2018, pp. 195-196.

clear, the attorney's signature is not required. The *Vollmacht* is a unilateral act and also does not require the attorney's signature.[64]

15. **Which matters (e.g. financial, health, welfare, personal) can be covered by the enduring document? Conversely, are there particular matters excluded?**

Both financial, personal and medical affairs can be included in the *Vorsorgevollmacht*. Although until 1999, it was unclear whether the adult could authorise the attorney to act on his behalf in medical matters, the German legislator has confirmed with §1904(5) GCC that the adult has this possibility.[65] As noted under no. 13, the *Vorsorgevollmacht* must have the written form when it includes medical matters. §1904(5) GCC further stipulates that if the adult wishes to authorise the attorney to decide on his behalf on an examination of the adult's state of health, medical treatment or an operation, the adult must expressly include these matters in the *Vorsorgevollmacht*.[66] The attorney requires the court's approval when a (medical) decision may lead to the adult's death or long-term severe injury to the adult's health.[67] This approval is not required if the attorney and the physician agree on the course of action to take.[68] According to §1906(5) GCC, the adult may also authorise the attorney to decide that the adult should be placed in a custodial facility. The same formal requirements mentioned above – *Vorsorgevollmacht* must be in writing and clearly stipulate the attorney's authority – apply. In addition, the attorney cannot exercise this authority at his discretion. Only when one of the grounds of §1906(1) GCC has been met – e.g. when there is a risk, due to the adult's mental state, that the adult will take his own life or cause significant damage to his own health – can the adult be placed in a custodial facility. In addition, the attorney requires the approval of the court to make this decision.[69] The adult cannot authorise the attorney to perform other highly personal acts, such as making a will or getting married, on his behalf.[70]

16. **What are the rules, regulations and practices concerning the entry into force of the enduring document?**

It is up to the adult when the *Vorsorgevollmacht* enters into force. Lipp notes that no mandatory registration or approval by a public authority is required for the *Vorsorgevollmacht* to become operational.[71] Instead, the adult can decide that the

64. Kurze 2018, p. 86; Zimmerman 2017, pp. 54-55.
65. Zimmerman 2017, p. 66; Lipp 2009, p. 57.
66. Zimmerman 2017, pp. 66-67.
67. §1904(1) and (2) GCC.
68. Zimmerman 2017, p. 69; §1904(4) GCC.
69. §1906(2) GCC; Zimmerman 2017, p. 73.
70. Zimmerman 2017, p. 75.
71. Lipp 2016-2, p. 9.

Vorsorgevollmacht enters into force immediately or at a specified time in the future (e.g., the adult's incapacity). Adults who choose the second option are advised to include a provision in the basic agreement stipulating when the attorney can use the authority conferred to him. Although, in theory, adults also have the option of granting a conditional power of attorney (*Vollmacht*), whereby the attorney is given the power to act on behalf of the adult at a specific time in the future, in practice, this is not advisable. Both Zimmerman and Müller and Renner note that a conditional power of attorney in practice leads to problems with the acceptance of the *Vorsorgevollmacht* by third parties – such as banks and the German land registry office – who require proof that the conditions for the entry into force of the *Vollmacht* have been met.[72] By including a clause on the entry into force of the *Vorsorgevollmacht* in the basic agreement between the adult and the attorney, problems with the acceptance of the *Vorsorgevollmacht* can be avoided.[73]

17. Under which circumstances does the enduring document cease to have effect?

The following situations can be distinguished in which the *Vorsorgevollmacht* ceases to have effect:

1. *Revocation of the Vorsorgevollmacht by the adult*

The adult can revoke the *Vorsorgevollmacht* at any time if he still has the capacity to do so.[74] Whether the adult has capacity is determined according to the general rules of private law (§104 and §105 GCC). According to §168 GCC, the revocation of the *Vorsorgevollmacht* is subject to the same conditions as the granting of the *Vorsorgevollmacht* (see no. 13). This means that the adult can revoke the *Vorsorgevollmacht* orally. However, Zimmerman notes that the written form is advisable for evidentiary purposes.[75] The revocation should be addressed to the attorney. If this is not possible (e.g. because the adult is unaware of the attorney's whereabouts), the adult can apply to the local district court (*Amtsgericht*) to have the *Vorsorgevollmacht* declared invalid (§176 GCC).[76]

2. *Revocation of the Vorsorgevollmacht by the court or the court-appointed custodian*

According to §1908i(1) GCC in conjunction with §1846 GCC, the court may take the measures necessary in the interests of the adult concerned, including the revocation of the *Vorsorgevollmacht*. However, the court can only do so in

72. Müller & Renner 2018, pp. 94-97 & pp. 100-101; Zimmerman 2017, pp. 56-57.
73. Müller & Renner 2018, pp. 100-101.
74. Zimmerman 2017, pp. 144-145.
75. Zimmerman 2017, p. 148.
76. Zimmerman 2017, p. 148 & p. 157.

'urgent cases' if a *Betreuer* has not yet been appointed and the revocation of the *Vorsorgevollmacht* cannot be delayed.[77] The *Vorsorgevollmacht* can also be revoked by a court-appointed custodian (*Betreuer*) or a court-appointed supervisory custodian, a so-called *Kontrollbetreuer* (see no. 32). However, the court must expressly state that the court-appointed (supervisory) custodian is authorised to do so; such authority cannot be implied.[78] Furthermore, the court may only grant the court-appointed (supervisory) custodian the power to revoke the *Vorsorgevollmacht* if there are severe and well-founded concerns that the attorney could endanger the welfare of the adult concerned and other measures do not appear suitable to avert this danger.[79] In this regard, the appointment of a supervisory custodian to monitor the actions of the attorney is preferable, if possible.[80]

3. *Death of the adult or the attorney*

§673 GCC on the mandate (*Auftrag*) and §675 GCC on the agency agreement (*Geschäftsbesorgungsvertrag*) stipulate that in case of doubt, the mandate or agency agreement ends with the death of the attorney. In other words, the basic agreement underlying the *Vorsorgevollmacht* ends. According to §168 GCC, this means that the *Vorsorgevollmacht* also ends.[81] The *Vorsorgevollmacht* does not necessarily have to end with the death of the adult. The adult can stipulate that the *Vorsorgevollmacht* will remain in force even after his death.[82]

4. *Insolvency of the adult or the attorney*

Pursuant to §117 of the Insolvency Act (*Insolvenzordnung*), a *Vorsorgevollmacht* concerning the adult's financial assets, expires upon the commencement of insolvency proceedings. As the preceding makes clear, this concerns only the assets of the insolvent estate. This means that the *Vorsorgevollmacht* can remain in force for matters not pertaining to the adult's financial estate, such as personal and medical matters.[83] Insolvency of the attorney does not automatically lead to the termination of the *Vorsorgevollmacht*. However, according to Zimmerman, the attorney's insolvency justifies the termination of the basic agreement. According to §168 GCC, this results in the termination of the *Vorsorgevollmacht*.[84]

77. Zimmerman 2017, p. 155.
78. Zimmerman 2017, pp. 150-152 referring to BGH NJW 2015, 3657 and BGH NJW 2015, 3557.
79. Zimmerman 2017, p. 152 referring to BGH NJW 2015, 3572.
80. Ibid.
81. Zimmerman 2017, pp. 159-160.
82. See for more information Zimmerman 2017, pp. 161-167; Müller & Renner 2018, pp. 247-249.
83. Zimmerman 2017, p. 160.
84. Ibid. N.B. when no substitute attorney has been appointed by the adult.

D. *The attorney*

18. Who can be appointed as an attorney? Are there restrictions concerning the choice of attorney (e.g. exclusion of certain people)?

As discussed in more detail under no. 8, according to §1896(2) GCC, *Betreuung* is not necessary if the adult's affairs can be handled by the attorney as well or even better than by the *Betreuer*. However, as §1896(2) GCC also makes clear, this principle of subsidiarity does not apply when the adult has appointed as an attorney a person falling under the scope of §1897(3) GCC. According to §1897(3) GCC:

> 'A person who is in a situation of dependence or in another close connection to an institution, a home or another establishment to which the person of full age has been committed or in which he lives may not be appointed custodian.'[85]

According to Zimmerman, the purpose of this provision is to avoid conflicts of interest between the interests of the institution and those of the adult.[86] Therefore, persons under the scope of §1897(3) GCC cannot be appointed as *Betreuer*. As §1896(2) GCC makes clear, the German legislator also intended to discourage the appointment of such persons as an attorney. However, Müller and Renner argue that the appointment of such a person does not make the *Vorsorgevollmacht* invalid.[87] In this respect, they note that a statutory prohibition should have been formulated more clearly. In addition, they argue that such a prohibition – and thus the invalidity of the *Vorsorgevollmacht* – would lead to legal uncertainty, as third parties would not be able to ascertain if an attorney falls within the scope of §1897(3) GCC and, in other words, whether they are dealing with an invalid *Vorsorgevollmacht*. Finally, they indicate that §1896(2) GCC should not prevent the appointment of an attorney with whom there was already a relationship of trust before the adult's admission to the institution.[88] On this latter point, the German legislator seems to agree with Müller and Renner. In the reform law that will enter into force on the 1. January 2023 (see no. 6), a new §1816(6) GCC makes clear that the above prohibition does not apply if there is no concrete risk of a conflict of interests in the case concerned.[89] With §1816(6) GCC-new, the German legislator has also widened the range of persons considered unsuitable to act as a *Betreuer* or an attorney because of potential conflicts of interest. §1816(6) GCC new

85. Translation via: https://www.gesetze-im-internet.de/englisch_bgb/englisch_bgb.html#p0027 (last accessed: 01-05-2022).
86. Zimmerman 2017, p. 92.
87. Müller & Renner 2018, pp. 88-89.
88. Ibid.
89. https://www.bmj.de/SharedDocs/Gesetzgebungsverfahren/DE/Reform_Betreuungsrecht_Vormundschaft.html (last accessed 01-05-2022).

stipulates that 'a person who is in a relationship of dependency or in another close relationship with an institution or service provider involved in the care of the adult cannot be appointed as *Betreuer*'.[90] This includes, for example, persons employed by organisations providing outpatient care.[91]

In addition to the restriction (or discouragement) referred to above, there is a restriction concerning the appointment of so-called professional attorneys. According to both Lipp and Kurze, the management of the adult's financial, medical and personal affairs includes legal services.[92] Under the German Legal Services Act (*Rechtsdienstleistungsgesetz*), legal services outside 'family, neighbourly or similarly close personal relationships' (§6) can only be provided by an authorised person, which in the context of the *Vorsorgevollmacht* means that only solicitors (*Rechtsanwälte*) can be appointed as attorney.[93]

19. **Does the legal system allow for the appointment of more than one attorney? Can these attorneys act jointly, concurrently, separately or as substitutes?**

The adult may appoint more than one person to act as attorney and direct these attorneys to act jointly, concurrently, separately or as substitutes. Concerning the latter, however, it is important to note that although possible in theory, not all of these options seem feasible in practice. Müller, Renner, and Zimmerman note that practical difficulties can arise when attorneys must act jointly, meaning all decisions must be made together. Zimmerman notes, for example, that the attorney's task may become cumbersome, as every bank transfer requires two or more signatures, even for a small amount. Problems can also arise in the event of a conflict between the attorneys, which means that the attorneys can block each other's actions.[94] Therefore, the German notariate recommends that adults grant an unlimited power of attorney to each attorney and include restrictions – for instance, that specific important, clearly defined decisions must be taken together – in the basic agreement between the adult and the attorney.[95] Problems can also arise when the appointment of a substitute attorney is included in the external power of attorney (*Vollmacht*). In this respect, Müller, Renner, and Zimmerman

90. Bundesgesetzblatt 2021, Part 1, Nr. 21 (12-05-2021), p. 893, viahttps://www.bmj.de/SharedDocs/Gesetzgebungsverfahren/DE/Reform_Betreuungsrecht_Vormundschaft.html (last accessed: 01-05-2022) (translation by RSR).
91. Deutscher Bundestag, *Entwurf eines Gesetzes zur Reform des Vormundschafts- und Betreuungsrechts*, 19/24445, 18.11.2020, p. 244, via https://www.bmj.de/SharedDocs/Gesetzgebungsverfahren/DE/Reform_Betreuungsrecht_Vormundschaft.html (last accessed: 01-05-2022).
92. Kurze 2018, pp. 239-241; Lipp 2016-2, p. 4.
93. Ibid. See however also Müller & Renner 2018, pp. 91-93 who provide a more nuanced view.
94. Zimmerman 2017, pp. 87-88.
95. Müller & Renner 2018, p. 227; Zimmerman 2017, pp. 87-88.

note that it is not easy to clearly define the conditions under which the substitute attorney may act.[96] Subsequently, it may be difficult for the substitute attorney to demonstrate that he now has the authority to act on behalf of the adult, which may cause problems with the acceptance of the *Vorsorgevollmacht* by third parties, such as banks. Therefore, once again, the notariate recommends granting an unlimited power of attorney to each attorney and including restrictions – in this context, a hierarchy as to who should act when – in the basic agreement between adult and attorney.

20. Is there a duty for the attorney to inform the court or any other administrative body if the appointment to act as an attorney is refused or discontinued?

There is no obligation as such to inform the court. However, if the attorney wishes to terminate the basic agreement underlying the *Vorsorgevollmacht*, the declaration of intent to terminate the basic agreement cannot be directed to the adult if the adult lacks capacity.[97] In this event, the attorney must request the court to appoint a *Betreuer*, after which the attorney can address the termination of the *Vorsorgevollmacht* to this *Betreuer*.[98]

21. Are there any rules or regulations regarding the attorney's role in line with, for example, article 12(4) UNCRPD and Principle 10 of the Council of Europe Recommendation 2009/11?

Lipp, Spalckhaver, Müller and Renner note that the adult may include provisions in the basic agreement between the adult and the attorney, regulating the rights and duties of the attorney.[99] In addition, the general provisions on the *Auftrag* (mandate) apply. According to Lipp, the duties and obligations of the attorney are modelled upon the duties and obligations of the court-appointed *Betreuer*. He seems to derive this from §1896(2) GCC (discussed under no. 8), according to which the appointment of a *Betreuer* is unnecessary when an attorney can take the place of the *Betreuer*.[100] Consequently, according to Lipp, the attorney's task is 'to assist and represent the grantor [adult] on the one hand, and to protect him from inflicting harm onto himself or his property on the other'.[101] The adult can make this general duty more concrete by including specific provisions in the basic agreement. The adult can, for example, stipulate that the attorney is obliged

96. Müller & Renner 2018, p. 226-227; Zimmerman 2017, pp. 83-84.
97. §131 GCC.
98. Kurze 2018, pp. 231-232; Zimmerman 2017, p. 111.
99. Müller & Renner 2018, pp. 215-219; Lipp 2016-2, p. 7; See for an extensive overview of the provisions that can be included in the basic agreement, Spalckhaver 2009, pp. 267-313.
100. Lipp 2016-2, pp. 7-8.
101. Ibid.

to consult the adult or a supervisory attorney (see no. 31) before taking certain important decisions, such as a decision on the sale of the house.[102] In addition, the adult can include wishes and instructions in the *Vorsorgevollmacht*. The attorney is obliged to follow the adult's instructions. This follows from §665 GCC, according to which the attorney may only deviate from the adult's instructions if he may assume that the adult 'would approve of such deviation if he were aware of the factual situation'.[103] Kurze notes that the aforementioned does not mean the attorney must follow the adult's instructions blindly. According to Kurze, the attorney must weigh the instruction's purpose and the adult's interests.[104] In this regard, Lipp refers to situations in which an instruction might prove harmful to the adult.[105] The adult can also include specific supervisory or control provisions in the basic agreement (see also no. 31). An example is the obligation for the attorney to render account. In this regard, §666 GCC does provide the statutory starting point. According to this section, the attorney is – upon request – obliged to keep the adult informed about the management of his affairs. In addition, the attorney is obliged to render account. However, through the basic agreement, the adult and the attorney may derogate from this statutory provision and organise the duties included in §666 GCC differently or waive these altogether.[106]

22. **Are there any limits as to the authorisations/responsibilities that can be given by the adult to the attorney (e.g. concerning personal decisions, such as making a will and deciding about donations)? Are there any rules concerning 'selbsteintritt'?**

As discussed under no. 15, the adult cannot authorise the attorney to perform certain highly personal acts, such as making a will or entering into a marriage or divorce.[107] However, the attorney can be authorised to make gifts on behalf of the adult.[108] A power of attorney (*Vollmacht*), in principle, includes the power to donate on behalf of the adult unless the adult expressly excludes this. As no. 33 discusses in more detail, the attorney may donate to himself when the restriction of §181 GCC is removed.[109] The fact that the attorney has the power to donate and, in other words, *can* donate does not automatically mean that the attorney *may* donate. Müller and Renner note in this regard:

102. Müller & Renner 2018, p. 216; Spalckhaver 2009, pp. 275-276.
103. §665 GCC, translation via: https://www.gesetze-im-internet.de/englisch_bgb/englisch_bgb.html#p0027 (last accessed: 01-05-2022).
104. Kurze 2018, p. 211).
105. Lipp 2016-2, p. 8.
106. Spalckhaver 2009, pp. 287-290.
107. Müller & Renner 2018, p. 127 & pp. 143-144; Zimmerman 2017, p. 75.
108. Kurze 2018, p. 65; Müller & Renner 2018, pp. 125-126.
109. Zimmerman 2017, p. 77.

> 'Of course, there is a difference between being able to give and being allowed to give. This must be assessed on a case-by-case basis, whereby the attorney may by no means do everything that he or she can legally do. The donee also bears the burden of proof that the gift was given to him and that he may keep it.'[110]

Müller and Renner advise clients to include arrangements in the *Vorsorgevollmacht* about the extent to which the attorney may donate.[111] Opinions differ in the literature as to whether it is wise to allow the attorney to donate on behalf of the adult. Zimmerman argues that given the risk of abuse, it would be wise to exclude the possibility of donating in *Vollmacht*.[112] However, Kurze notes that this could lead to problems with banks' acceptance of the Vorsorgevollmacht, which could refuse to execute a transfer because they cannot check whether it is a donation. According to Kurze, banks cannot be burdened with an obligation to review every transaction, meaning the *Vollmacht* becomes partially unusable if gifts are excluded.[113] Kurze notes that restrictions – such as an exclusion of specific donations or a regulation where gifts need to be authorised by a second attorney – are best included in the basic agreement between the adult and the attorney.[114]

23. Does the legal system allow for the remuneration of the attorney?

As discussed under no. 3, the *Grundverhältnis* or basic agreement of the *Vorsorgevollmacht* is, in most cases, based on the legal construct of the non-remunerated *Auftrag* (mandate) or the remunerated *Geschäftsbesorgungsvertrag* (agency agreement).[115] The adult can use the agency agreement to include provisions on the attorney's remuneration in the *Vorsorgevollmacht*. Both Zimmerman, Müller, and Renner note that the adult would do well to determine the amount of the attorney's remuneration clearly.[116] In this regard, Zimmerman gives several directions on how this can be determined, for example, by aligning the remuneration with the compensation received by a custodian.[117] Regardless of the type of basic agreement (mandate or agency agreement), §670 GCC clarifies that the adult must reimburse the attorney's expenses, such as travel and telephone costs.[118]

110. Müller & Renner 2018, p. 126 (translation by RSR).
111. Ibid.
112. Zimmerman 2017, p. 77.
113. Kurze 2018, p. 65.
114. Ibid.
115. Lipp 2009, p. 56.
116. Müller & Renner 2018, p. 218; Zimmerman 2017, p. 119.
117. Zimmerman 2017, pp. 119-123.
118. Zimmerman 2017, p. 113.

E. *Registration*

24. **Are enduring documents registered? If yes, is registration voluntary or mandatory?**

Registration is voluntary in Germany, an adult may register his *Vorsorgevollmacht* in the so-called *Zentrale Vorsorgeregister*, but there is no obligation to do so. The *Zentrale Vorsorgeregister* is kept by the *Bundesnotarkammer* (the Federal Chamber of Notaries in Germany).[119] Registration can be completed online via the website vorsorgeregister.de or by downloading and completing the appropriate forms and sending these by post. Both a notarised *Vorsorgevollmacht* and a privately drafted *Vorsorgevollmacht* can be registered.[120] However, the adult has to register the Vorsorgevollmacht; his attorney cannot do so. Alternatively, the adult may ask a professional such as a notary or a lawyer, to register the *Vorsorgevollmacht* on his behalf.[121] In 2020, 82,4% of the registered *Vorsorgevollmachten* were registered by notaries, 5,6% by lawyers and 8,6% by adults themselves.[122]

25. **When does registration occur (e.g. registration directly after the enduring document has been made, registration upon entry into force, registration upon acceptance of the appointment by the attorney)?**

As registration is voluntary, it is up to the adult to decide when to register the *Vorsorgevollmacht*. Zimmerman notes that the value of the *Vorsorgevollmacht* increases when it can be located quickly when needed.[123] In other words, the adult is advised to register the *Vorsorgevollmacht* directly after it has been made.

26. **Are changes and terminations of enduring documents registered?**

According to §5 of the *Verordnung über das Zentrale Vorsorgeregister* (VRegV), changes, revocations and terminations of the *Vorsorgevollmacht* can be registered. Again, however, there is no obligation to do so.[124]

27. **Which parties can access the register? And to what extent do third parties have access (e.g. notification of the existence of an enduring document or access to the content of the enduring document)?**

119. §78a of the Federal Code for Notaries.
120. Müller & Renner 2018, p. 270; Zimmerman 2017, p. 141.
121. Kurze 2018, p. 481.
122. Bundesnotarkammer Zentrales Vorsorgeregister, Jahresbericht 2020, via https://www.vorsorge register.de/footer/jahresbericht-und-statistik (last accessed: 08-04-2022).
123. Zimmerman 2017, p. 140.
124. Zimmerman 2017, p. 143.

In Germany, only the courts – specifically the *Betreuungsgerichte* and the *Beschwerdegerichte* (the court of second instance) – can request information from the register.[125] The register does not provide access to the content of the *Vorsorgevollmacht*. Under §78a (2) of the Federal Code for Notaries, only specific details are registered:

> Details concerning the following may be included in the Central Register of Lasting Powers of Attorney:
> 1. the donor,
> 2. the attorneys,
> 3. the power of attorney and its content,
> 4. suggestions regarding the choice of carer,
> 5. wishes regarding the provision of care and
> 6. the proposer.[126]

This is specified further in the *Verordnung über das Zentrale Vorsorgeregister* (VRegV). This regulation makes clear that concerning the adult (donor), data such as the adult's surname, date of birth and place of birth can be registered. Information on the content of the *Vorsorgevollmacht* can consist of general information on whether the *Vorsorgevollmacht* relates to financial matters, health and personal matters or both.[127] As indicated, the register does not provide access to the content of the *Vorsorgevollmacht*. The adult can keep the *Vorsorgevollmacht* himself or ask a relative or professional, such as a lawyer or notary, to keep the document for him. According to §1901c GCC, the person keeping the *Vorsorgevollmacht* is obliged to notify the court of the *Vorsorgevollmacht* as soon as he learns that proceedings for the appointment of a *Betreuer* have been initiated. The court can subsequently require a copy to be submitted.

F. Capacity, supervision and control measures

28. What is the legal consequence of the entry into force of the enduring document? Does the adult retain legal capacity?

The adult retains legal capacity upon the entry into force of the *Vorsorgevollmacht*. This means that the adult can continue to act simultaneously with the attorney. According to Zimmerman, in some cases, this can significantly disrupt the attorney's work.[128] The German legislator has considered the above in the context

125. Zimmerman 2017, p. 143.
126. Translation via: http://www.gesetze-im-internet.de/englisch_bnoto/englisch_bnoto.html#p0518 (last accessed 09-11-2020). The phrase 'carer' is used here to refer to a so-called 'Betreuer'
127. §1 VRegV.
128. Zimmerman 2017, p. 109.

of the *Betreuung*. Under §1903 GCC, the court can – insofar as necessary to avert a substantial danger to the adult or the adult's assets – order a so-called *Einwilligungsvorbehalt*, which means that the adult needs the consent of the *Betreuer* for actions that fall under the responsibility of the *Betreuer*. However, such an *Einwilligungsvorbehalt* is not possible in the context of the *Vorsorgevollmacht*. Kurze considers this an omission and argues that an *Einwilligungsvorbehalt* should also be made available concerning the *Vorsorgevollmacht*.[129]

29. **Does the legal system provide protection against so-called 'ill-considered decisions' by the adult?**

See the answer to no. 28. Protection is provided through the general rules of private law. As discussed under no. 1, §104(2) GCC stipulates that 'a person is incapable of contracting if the person is in a state of pathological mental disturbance, which prevents the free exercise of will, unless the state by its nature is a temporary one'.[130] §105 GCC clarifies that a contract concluded under these circumstances is void.

30. **How is the validity of the document ensured? Is the validity of the enduring document checked at the time the enduring document is made as to the capacity of the adult, freedom from undue influence, etc.?**

As discussed under no. 13, there are few formal requirements concerning the form of the *Vorsorgevollmacht*. Only in some instances – for example, when the adult wants to enable entries in the land register – is a so-called *Beglaubigung* by a notary or *Betreuungsbehörde* required. This means that adults do not have to use the services of a professional, such as a notary, to make a *Vorsorgevollmacht*, but can also make a *Vorsorgevollmacht* in the form of a private document. The German government has made available a form that adults can use.[131] As the preceding makes clear, there are few safeguards ensuring the validity of the *Vorsorgevollmacht*. Concerns about the validity of the *Vorsorgevollmacht* can be brought to the court's attention. Nedden-Boeger notes that the court must then confirm whether the signature on the *Vorsorgevollmacht* is that of the adult.[132] However, for doubts as to whether the adult had the capacity to make the *Vorsorgevollmacht*, the following applies. It is for the person questioning the adult's

129. Kurze 2018, p. 296.
130. Translation via: http://www.gesetze-im-internet.de/englisch_bnoto/englisch_bnoto.html#p0518 (last accessed 01-05-2022).
131. https://www.bmj.de/SharedDocs/Downloads/DE/Service/Formulare/Vorsorgevollmacht.html?nn=6425014&cms_dlConfirm=true (last accessed: 01-05-2022).
132. Nedden-Boeger 2019, p. 87.

capacity to prove that the adult lacked the capacity to make the *Vorsorgevollmacht* at the time of signing.

31. **What options are available to the adult concerning supervision and control of the execution of the enduring document?**

Adults can include a form of supervision in the *Vorsorgevollmacht*. Zimmerman mentions, for instance, the possibility of appointing several attorneys to act jointly in important matters such as decisions regarding real estate. Adults can also include an obligation in their *Vorsorgevollmacht*, requiring the attorney to obtain the consent of others who have not been appointed as an attorney – for example, the attorney's siblings – for important decisions, such as the sale of the house.[133] According to Müller, Renner, and Schwab, adults can appoint a so-called *Überwachungsbevollmächtigter* or supervisory attorney to supervise the attorney's actions.[134] However, Müller, Renner, and Schwab also note that such supervisory mechanisms in practice do not seem very popular as they signal an inherent contradiction between trust and supervision. It is psychologically difficult for a person to give someone their trust while at the same time taking certain precautions that signal that the attorney does not have the adult's complete confidence after all.[135]

32. **Is there any supervision of the attorney by the state (e.g. the court or another administrative body)? If so, are there any possibilities for these institutions to intervene in the execution of the enduring document (e.g. appointment of a third party to supervise the attorney)?**

Under §1896(3) GCC, the court can appoint a so-called *Kontrollbetreuer* or supervisory custodian. A *Kontrollbetreuer* is tasked with supervising the attorney and enforcing the adult's rights under the basic agreement vis-à-vis the attorney.[136] As with all appointments of a *Betreuer*, the appointment of a *Kontrollbetreuer* must be necessary. This necessity is assessed on a case-by-case basis.[137] The current provision – §1896(3) GCC – of the German Civil Code only focuses on the task of the *Kontrollbetreuer* and remains silent as to when the court may appoint a *Kontrollbetreuer*. This will change when the new reform law enters into force on 1. January 2023 (see no. 6). A new §1820 of the German Civil Code will stipulate that the court may deem the appointment of a *Kontrollbetreuer* necessary when 1) the adult, due to illness or disability, is no longer able to exercise his or

133. Zimmerman 2017, pp. 170-172.
134. Müller & Renner 2018, p. 228; Schwab 2009, pp. 117-118.
135. Ibid.
136. Zimmerman 2017, pp. 173-174; Lipp 2016-2, p. 9.
137. Lipp 2016-2, p. 9.

her rights towards the attorney, and 2) there are concrete indications that the attorney is not managing the affairs of the adult in accordance with what has been agreed or in accordance with the declared or presumed will of the adult.[138] §1820 GCC-new will establish what already applies based on the case law of the *Bundesgerichthof* (the Federal Court of Justice in Germany).[139] Referring to case law, both Müller and Renner and Zimmerman note that the court may only appoint a *Kontrollbetreuer* when 1) there is a valid – i.e. the adult had capacity at the time the *Vorsorgevollmacht* was made – and not revoked *Vorsorgevollmacht*, 2) the adult no longer has the capacity to supervise the actions of the attorney himself, 3) there is a concrete need to monitor the actions of the attorney, 4) a *Kontrollbetreuung* is a sufficient and suitable intervention to ensure the necessary supervision.[140] Müller, Renner, and Zimmerman note that an indication of a concrete need for supervision of the attorney's actions is a situation in which the adult, who can no longer revoke the *Vorsorgevollmacht*, attempts to revoke the *Vorsorgevollmacht* and thus expresses his lack of trust in the attorney.[141]

33. Is regulation in place concerning (potential) conflicts of interest between the adult's and the attorney's interests?

According to §181 GCC:

> 'An agent may not, unless otherwise permitted, enter into a legal transaction in the name of the principal with himself in his own name or as an agent of a third party, unless the legal transaction consists solely in the performance of an obligation.'[142]

The preceding means that the legal starting point is that the attorney cannot act as a counterparty to the adult in question. Kurze notes that this statutory prohibition is intended to prevent a conflict of interest.[143] However, as §181 GCC itself makes clear, there are two situations in which self-contracting is nevertheless permitted. Firstly, legal transactions which 'consist solely in the performance of an obligation' are allowed. Zimmerman refers in this context to a situation in which the adult has taken out a loan from the attorney. The attorney may then repay this loan to

138. Bundesgesetzblatt 2021, Part 1, Nr. 21 (12-05-2021), p. 894, viahttps://www.bmj.de/SharedDocs/Gesetzgebungsverfahren/DE/Reform_Betreuungsrecht_Vormundschaft.html (last accessed: 01-05-2022) (translation by RSR).
139. Deutscher Bundestag, *Entwurf eines Gesetzes zur Reform des Vormundschafts- und Betreuungsrechts*, 19/24445, 18.11.2020, p. 246, via https://www.bmj.de/SharedDocs/Gesetzgebungsverfahren/DE/Reform_Betreuungsrecht_Vormundschaft.html (last accessed: 01-05-2022).
140. Müller & Renner 2018, p. 229-232; Zimmerman 2017, pp. 174-175.
141. Ibid.
142. Translation via: http://www.gesetze-im-internet.de/englisch_bnoto/englisch_bnoto.html#p0518 (last accessed 01-05-2022).
143. Kurze 2018, p. 130.

himself from the adult's assets.[144] Payment of expenses – e.g. travel costs – are another example.[145] The adult can also exempt the attorney from the prohibition to enter into an agreement with himself. The adult's permission does not require a specific form; it can be given expressly or implicitly. However, it is up to the person who claims that the adult has permitted him to self-contract, to prove this is the case.[146]

G. *Law in action*

34. What are considered the advantages and the disadvantages of enduring documents?

Zimmerman notes the following advantages of the *Vorsorgevollmacht*:

- There is almost no state interference in the adult's private life. However, according to Zimmerman, this is only partly an advantage, namely concerning medical and personal matters. In Germany, family members cannot represent each other without a legal basis, such as a *Vorsorgevollmacht* or a *Betreuung*.[147] In this respect, Zimmerman notes that it can be humiliating for the spouse of the adult concerned if he or she cannot make a decision for the other spouse.[148] According to Zimmerman, the advantage of state interference is that it can prevent the abuse of the *Vorsorgevollmacht*, which is particularly relevant in financial matters.[149]
- The adult is free to determine the scope of the matters included in the *Vorsorgevollmacht* and free to choose his attorney.
- With a *Vorsorgevollmacht*, time-consuming and expensive court proceedings can be avoided.
- Contrary to the *Betreuung*, the *Vorsorgevollmacht* can also function before the adult's incapacity and after his death (*Vorsorgevollmacht über den Tod hinaus*).[150]

Zimmerman notes the following disadvantages of the *Vorsorgevollmacht*:

- There is no adequate judicial supervision of the attorney. Zimmerman notes that the attorney can sell the adult's family home and take out loans without the court's supervision, making abuse situations difficult to avoid.
- There are inadequate safeguards to confirm that the adult had capacity when drafting the *Vorsorgevollmacht*.

---

144. Zimmerman 2017, p. 80.
145. Kurze 2018, p. 131; Zimmerman 2017, p. 80.
146. Kurze 2018, p. 132.
147. Zimmerman 2017, p. 37. N.B. This will change with the entry into force of the new law on 1. January 2023 (see no. 1).
148. Zimmerman 2017, p. 42.
149. Ibid.
150. Zimmerman 2017, pp. 42-43.

- There is insufficient protection against 'ill-considered decisions'; a so-called *Einwilligungsvorbehalt* or reservation of consent (see no. 1 and 28) is not possible.
- There is uncertainty as to whether the attorney will become and remain active.
- In situations of divorce or conflicts, adults frequently forget to revoke the *Vorsorgevollmacht*, resulting in cases where an 'unwanted person' is authorised to act on behalf of the adult.[151]

35. **How does the enduring document function/operate in practice? What works well and what does not? Are there or have there been any problems? How have these been dealt with? Is there any empirical research available on the questions mentioned above?**

Little empirical information is available on how the *Vorsorgevollmacht* functions in practice. Annually, the *Bundesnotarkammer* publishes a report with information on the number of registered *Vorsorgevollmachten* (see no. 7), the content of the *Vorsorgevollmacht* (e.g. whether it also includes a *Betreuungsverfügung* or a *Patientenverfügung*), who has registered the *Vorsorgevollmacht* (notaries, lawyers or private persons) and information on the number of cases in which the court has submitted a request for information.[152] The 2020 annual report shows that in the majority of cases (82,4%), a request to register the *Vorsorgevollmacht* is submitted by a notary. In 86,3% of all cases, a *Vorsorgevollmacht* also included a *Betreuungsverfügung* and in 74,7% of all cases, also a *Patientenverfügung*. In 2020, the courts in 205.409 cases requested information from the register, and in 9,6% of all cases, such a request for information was successful.[153] Apart from the annual reports, the most recent empirical study seems to be an evaluation study of the second amendment act (see no. 4) carried out by Köller and Engels in 2009. This study aimed to explore whether the aims of the amendment act – which included strengthening the *Vorsorgevollmacht* to avoid the need for a *Betreuung* – had been achieved in practice.[154] In the context of the *Vorsorgevollmacht*, Köller and Engels looked at information provided by the *Bundesnotarkammer*.[155] These findings are not discussed here, as more recent information is – as discussed above – available. In addition, Köller and Engels looked at information provided by the courts. In this regard, Köller and Engels looked at the number of cases in which a *Betreuung* was not necessary because the adult had made a *Vorsorgevollmacht*. This was the

151. Zimmerman 2017, pp. 43-45.
152. Bundesnotarkammer Zentrales Vorsorgeregister, Jahresbericht 2020, 2019, 2018, 2017, 2016, 2015, 2014, 2013, 2012, 2011, 2010, 2009, 2008, 2007, 2006, 2005, via https://www.vorsorgeregister.de/footer/jahresbericht-und-statistik (last accessed: 08-04-2022).
153. Bundesnotarkammer Zentrales Vorsorgeregister, Jahresbericht 2020, via https://www.vorsorgeregister.de/footer/jahresbericht-und-statistik (last accessed: 08-04-2022).
154. Köller & Engels 2009, pp. 42-43.
155. Köller & Engels 2009, pp. 213-216.

case in 8310 cases in 2006 compared to 5634 cases in 2004 (an increase of 47%). Köller and Engels also looked at the number of cases in which the attorney had asked for the court's approval under §1904(5) GCC or §1906(5) GCC. In 2006, the court's approval was requested in 5310 cases compared to 3610 cases in 2006 (an increase of 47%).[156] Köller and Engels also tried to get an impression of active *Vorsorgevollmachten*. Based on a survey study of elderly homes and care homes, Köller and Engels looked at the number of adults living in a home represented by an attorney. In 2008, this was the case for a third of the adults living in a care home for older people.[157] Of these adults, 67% were represented by one or more of the adult's children, 13% by other relatives, 10% by the partner, 6% by a non-relative and 4% by a brother or sister of the adult.[158]

The information discussed above is outdated and says little about the current state of affairs since, for example, the number of active *Vorsorgevollmachten* and linked to this, the number of cases in which a *Betreuung* is unnecessary, may have increased significantly. This may be different for the information provided in the study regarding the grounds for the appointment of a *Betreuer*, even though the adult has made a *Vorsorgevollmacht*. As part of their study, Köller and Engels interviewed experts – including judges – on the disadvantages of *Vorsorgevollmachten*. In this context, the risk of abuse by the attorney and problems with the acceptance of the *Vorsorgevollmacht* due to, for example, the multitude of forms were considered disadvantages.[159] In addition, Köller and Engels asked the courts – through a survey – to provide information about the grounds to order a *Kontrollbetreuung*, an ordinary *Betreuung* or the replacement of an attorney. When asked how often problems with asset management or problems within the family are the reason to appoint a *Kontrollbetreuer*, 56% of the courts (N=170) indicated that problems with asset management are often a reason to order a *Kontrollbetreuung* and 32% of the courts indicated that problems within the family are often a reason to order a *Kontrollbetreuung*.[160] The courts were also asked about the reasons for ordering a *Betreuung* despite the adult having a *Vorsorgevollmacht*. Reasons mentioned in this regard included: the *Vorsorgevollmacht* not covering all affairs for which assistance was considered necessary, problems with the acceptance of the *Vorsorgevollmacht*, the factual or legal inability of the attorney to act on behalf of the adult or the court not being aware of the *Vorsorgevollmacht* in the context of the proceedings.[161] Finally, Köller and Engels also inquired about the reasons for replacing an attorney with a *Betreuer*. In this respect, the courts indicated that problems with the asset

156. Köller & Engels 2009, pp. 216-218.
157. Köller & Engels 2009, pp. 221-224 & 227-228.
158. Köller & Engels 2009, pp. 229-230.
159. Köller & Engels 2009, p. 232.
160. Köller & Engels 2009, p. 233-235.
161. Köller & Engels 2009, p. 235-236.

management of the adult, the attorney being overburdened, the factual or legal inability of the attorney to act for the adult and problems within the family were reasons to replace an attorney.[162]

The findings of the study by Köller and Engels are supplemented in this country report by the comments of practitioners, both in the literature on the *Vorsorgevollmacht* and in the interviews conducted as part of the law in action component of the comparative study. An analysis of problems and potential solutions from a solicitor's perspective is presented by Kurze. Although Kurze acknowledges that his observations are not based on empirical data and are therefore subjective, he also indicates that his observations are not only based on his own experiences but also on a study of relevant court cases and literature and information provided by solicitors, notaries, employees of *Betreuungsbehörden* and judges.[163] Kurze addresses in his contribution the risk of misuse and abuse of *Vorsorgevollmachten*, whereby he notes that although reliable empirical data are missing, there are sufficient indications for the existence of this problem. He refers in this regard to the – in his opinion – increasing number of court cases dealing with, for instance, *Kontrollbetreuungen* and the revocation of donations.[164] This is also the impression of the experts interviewed in the context of this comparative study. Such misuse or abuse, according to Kurze, frequently occurs within a setting of familial conflicts. It is not easy for the adult, a new representative – such as a *Betreuer* or new attorney – or the adult's heirs to ensure that justice is done when such misuse or abuse occurs. To date, there is still discussion about the legal nature of the *Vorsorgeverhältnis*, the basic agreement between the adult and the attorney. Although there seems to be general agreement that the basic agreement concerns a mandate agreement (*Auftrag*), Kurze notes that the applicability of the provisions on the *Auftrag* frequently needs to be demonstrated before the court, especially before the courts in the first instance.[165] In addition, it is difficult for the adult or his heirs to obtain the necessary information (e.g. bank statements) to build a case against the (former) attorney.[166] The aforementioned makes cases before the court difficult and complex. Kurze discusses potential factors that can cause familial conflicts and the misuse or abuse of *Vorsorgevollmachten*. In this regard, he notes that attorneys often underestimate their task and that current actions and instruments – such as the court's intervention – seem insufficient and inadequate to resolve conflicts.[167] According to Kurze, a third factor concerns the frequently poorly drafted *Vorsorgevollmachten*, where the basic agreement between

162. Köller & Engels 2009, p. 236-237.
163. Kurze 2018, p. 48.
164. Ibid.
165. Kurze 2018, pp. 49-50.
166. Kurze 2018, p. 49.
167. Kurze 2018, p. 50.

the adult and the attorney is rarely regulated.[168] On the one hand, this means, for example, that the (extensive) statutory provisions on rendering account apply, while, on the other hand, the attorney is unaware of the obligation to do so. Kurze notes that the lack of explicit provisions on donations and reimbursement for the attorney in a basic agreement also leads to conflicts and advances the intentional or unintentional abuse of the *Vorsorgevollmacht*.[169] The avoidance of (extensive) basic agreements was also confirmed by the experts interviewed in the context of this comparative study, whereby not all experts agreed about the necessity to do so.

Kurze suggests several directions as possible solutions to the problems mentioned above. First, he notes that professionals should advise attorneys to act openly. This can be done, for example, by allowing others (e.g. siblings) who have not been appointed attorneys to view the online banking environment to check the attorney's transactions. Such social control can prevent distrust.[170] Second, Kurze notes that attention should also be paid to a better design of *Vorsorgevollmachten*.[171] This can be done by involving a legal professional, who ensures that the *Vorsorgevollmacht* is tailored to the specific situation of the adult and includes details on the rights and obligations of the attorney. In addition, clear instructions concerning the appointment of multiple attorneys should be included in the *Vorsorgevollmacht*. Kurze also highlights the importance of notaries keeping an eye on the adult's capacity to make a *Vorsorgevollmacht*, particularly in situations in which there is a risk the adult might be unduly influenced (e.g. when the attorney approaches the notary with a request to make a *Vorsorgevollmacht*).[172] Third, Kurze notes that mediation – so-called *Vorsorgemediation* – might be a possible way forward to solve conflicts.[173]

36. Is there any information available on the number and type of cases where there has been (financial) abuse and/or misuse by the attorney?

Apart from the reasons mentioned under no. 35 to order a *Kontrolbetreuung* or a *Betreuung*, I have not been able to find empirical information on the number and type of cases in which there has been (financial) abuse or misuse of the *Vorsorgevollmacht* by the attorney. Indeed in their opinion on the bill of the new *Betreuungsgesetz*, which will enter into force on 1 January 2023, the organisation VorsorgeAnwalt noted that the government's strong focus on the *Betreuung* had led to a neglect of the problems with the *Vorsorgevollmacht*. The organisation

168. Ibid.
169. Ibid.
170. Kurze 2018, p. 51.
171. Kurze 2018, p. 52.
172. Kurze 2018, p. 52.
173. Ibid.

VorsorgeAnwalt, therefore, recommended that the government further address the problems with the *Vorsorgevollmacht*, among other things, by stimulating research into the abuse and misuse of the *Vorsorgevollmacht*.[174]

37. Are there any (mandatory) safeguards, and how have these been implemented in practice?

There are two preventative safeguards. First, as discussed under no. 15, the attorney requires the court's authorisation for certain important healthcare decisions if there is a dispute between the attorney and the physician about the adult's wishes. Moreover, the court's authorisation is under §1906 GCC required when the attorney wants to place the adult in a closed ward or deprive him of his liberty.[175] A second preventative safeguard can be found in §1896(2) GCC in conjunction with §1897(3) of the German Civil Code. As discussed under no. 18, the German legislator has sought to discourage the appointment of persons working in an institution where the adult has been placed. This is to prevent situations in which the interests of the adult and the institution for which the attorney works become conflated. A third retrospective safeguard concerns the court's appointment of the supervisory *Betreuer* (see no. 32). However, the effectiveness of this safeguard is debated. Schwab notes in this respect that the measure is based on the assumption that cases that require supervision will come to the court's attention, whereas it is doubtful this will be the case in all instances.[176]

The draft law on the new *Betreuungsgesetz*, which enters into force on 1 January 2023, shows that the German legislator made a conscious decision to refrain from adopting further safeguards, such as requirements regarding the form of the *Vorsorgevollmacht*, mandatory registration or requirements regarding proof of capacity when granting the *Vorsorgevollmacht*. Based on the advice obtained as part of the discussion process mentioned under no. 6, the German legislator concluded that it would not create further barriers for both the adult and the attorney concerning the granting and implementation of the *Vorsorgevollmacht*.[177]

174. VorsorgeAnwalt e.V., *Stellungnahme des VorsorgeAnwalt e.V. zum Entwurf eines Gesetzes zur Reform des Vormundschafts- und Betreuungsrechts*, 10-08-2020, via https://www.bmj.de/SharedDocs/Gesetzgebungsverfahren/DE/Reform_Betreuungsrecht_Vormundschaft.html (last accessed: 01-05-2022).
175. Lipp 2016-2, p. 10.
176. Schwab 2009, pp. 115-117.
177. Deutscher Bundestag, *Entwurf eines Gesetzes zur Reform des Vormundschafts- und Betreuungsrechts*, 19/24445, 18.11.2020, pp. 244-245, via https://www.bmj.de/SharedDocs/Gesetzgebungsverfahren/DE/Reform_Betreuungsrecht_Vormundschaft.html (last accessed: 01-05-2022).

38. Is there anything else of interest not included in the answers above?

According to §1908f GCC, one of the tasks of a *Betreuungsverein* is to provide advice and support to the attorney.[178]

Bibliography

D. Brosey, 'Aspects of the discussion regarding the reform of the German legislation of Betreuung in light of the UN-CRPD', *Julgar* 2020, vol. 41, pp. 199-212.

D. Brosey, 'Mehr Selbstbestimmung für Menschen mit rechtlicher Betreuung. Ein Überblick zur Refrom des Betreuungsrechts', *TUP – Theorie und Praxis der Sozialen Arbeit* 2022, no. 3, pp. 221-229.

Bundesministerium der Justiz und für Verbraucherschutz, *Qualität in der rechtlichen Betreuung*, Köln: Bundesanzeiger Verlag 2018.

H. Deinert, 'Sachgerechte Stärkung der Vorsorgevollmacht – Aber wie?', *BtPrax* 2017-2, pp. 59-65.

N. Dethloff, *FL-EUR Empowerment and Protection of Vulnerable Adults Quickscans – Germany*, via https://www.fl-eur.eu/quick_scans/quick-scans (last accessed: 01-04-2022).

R. Köller & D. Engels, *Rechtlichen Betreuung in Deutschland. Evaluation des Zweiten Betreuungsrechtsänderungsgesetzes*, Köln: Bundesanzeiger Verlag 2009.

D. Kurze, *Vorsorgerecht. Vollmacht, Patientenverfügung, lebzeitige Verfügungen*, München: C.H. Beck 2017.

D. Kurze, 'Tätigkeit des Vorsorgebevollmächtigten aus anwaltlicher Sicht', *BtPrax* 2018-2, pp. 47-53.

V. Lipp, 'Vorbemerkungen', in: V. Lipp, *Handbuch der Vorsorgeverfügungen*, München: Verlag Franz Vahlen 2009, pp. 1-5.

V. Lipp, 'Staatlicher Erwachsenenschutz und private Vorsorge ', in: V. Lipp, *Handbuch der Vorsorgeverfügungen*, München: Verlag Franz Vahlen 2009, pp. 7-29.

V. Lipp, 'Instrumente privater Vorsorge', in: V. Lipp, *Handbuch der Vorsorgeverfügungen*, München: Verlag Franz Vahlen 2009, pp. 51-60.

V. Lipp & A.D. Ward, 'Germany', in: R. Frimston, A. Ruck Keene, C. van Overdijk & A. Ward, *The international protection of adults*, Oxford: Oxford University Press 2015, pp. 375-385.

178. Zimmerman 2017, p. 41.

V. Lipp (1), *Legal Protection of Adults in Germany – An overview*, revised version (11 January 2016) of a lecture held at the University of Leuven on 10. February 2015, via: https://www.bgt-ev.de/fileadmin/Mediendatenbank/Themen/Einzelbeitraege/Lipp/Lipp_Legal_Protection_Adults.pdf (last accessed: 01-05-2022).

V. Lipp (2), *Going Private: "Vorsorgevollmacht" as an Alternative to Legal Guardianship for Adults*, revised version (11 January 2016) of a lecture held at the Tokyo Bar Association on 22. February 2014, via: https://www.bgt-ev.de/fileadmin/Mediendatenbank/Themen/Einzelbeitraege/Lipp/Lipp_Vorsolgevollmacht_as_an_Alternative.pdf (last accessed: 01-05-2022).

G. Müller & T. Renner, *Betreuungsrecht und Vorsorgeverfügungen in der Praxis*, München: Carl Heymanns Verlag 2018.

C. Nedden-Boeger, 'Die Vorsorgevollmacht in der betreuungsgerichtlichen Praxis', *BtPrax* 2019-3, pp. 87-91.

J. Spalckhaver, 'Die Vorsorgevollmacht und das ihr zugrunde liegende Rechtsverhältnis als umfassende Vorsorgeregelung', in: V. Lipp, *Handbuch der Vorsorgeverfügungen*, München: Verlag Franz Vahlen 2009, pp. 95-105.

J. Spalckhaver, 'Inhaltliche Gestaltung des Vorsorgeverhältnisses', in: V. Lipp, *Handbuch der Vorsorgeverfügungen*, München: Verlag Franz Vahlen 2009, pp. 260-313.

D. Schwab, 'Vorsorgevollmacht, die ideale Lösung?', in: W. Bayer & E. Koch (eds.), *Aktuelle Fragen des Familienrechts*, Baden-Baden: Nomos 2009, pp. 111-125.

W. Zimmerman, *Vorsorgevollmacht, Betreuungsverfügung, Patientenverfügung für die Beratungspraxis*, Berlin: Erich Schmidt Verlag 2017.

Experts interviewed
- Lawyer
- Notary

Appendix 8: Country report Switzerland

Comparative study on enduring documents

Country Report Switzerland

A. General

Brief general description of the legal system of Switzerland

Switzerland is a federal state with three political levels: the federal government, the cantons and the communes. The cantons have a strong autonomous standing, as article 3 of the Constitution, in conjunction with article 43a of the Constitution, makes clear. Article 3 reads: 'The Cantons are sovereign except to the extent that their sovereignty is limited by the Federal Constitution. They exercise all rights that are not vested in the Confederation'.[1] According to article 43a of the Constitution, the federal government is only to undertake 'tasks that the Cantons are unable to perform or which require uniform regulation by the Confederation'.[2] Over time, the federal government has assumed more and more tasks that were previously the cantons' responsibility. Civil law, criminal law, criminal procedure and, more recently, civil procedure have been codified. However, the legislative power regarding public and administrative law has remained with the cantons.[3] As a result, in some cases, federal and cantonal competencies may overlap. This is the case concerning the system of adult protection measures in Switzerland. The measures have been laid down in the Swiss Civil Code and thus codified at the federal level. However, these measures are ordered by governmental authorities, and the procedure in this regard is considered public law and therefore falls within the competence of the cantons.[4] Several languages are spoken in Switzerland,

1. English translation of the Federal Constitution of the Swiss Confederation, via: https://www.fedlex.admin.ch/eli/cc/1999/404/en (last accessed: 23-03-2022).
2. Ibid.
3. Aebi-Müller & Magliana 2015, p. 387; Thommen 2018, p. 19.
4. Aebi-Müller & Magliana 2015, p. 387.

including German, French and Italian. For most Swiss inhabitants, German is the primary language.

N.B. For this country report, I have studied literature available in the German language.

1. **Give a brief account of the adult protection system in each country (e.g. state ordered protection measures, private remedies).**

Measures and provisions

The general norms on legal capacity are outlined in Articles 11-19 of the Swiss Civil Code (SCC). A closer reading of these provisions makes clear that when it concerns the Swiss concept of capacity, a distinction has to be made between what has been defined by the Committee on the Rights of Persons with Disabilities as 'legal standing' and 'legal agency'.[5] According to article 11 SCC, every person has legal capacity in the sense of legal standing (*Rechtsfähigkeit*) or the 'ability to hold rights and duties'. Articles 12 and 13 SCC make clear that legal capacity in the sense of legal agency (*Handlungsfähigkeit*) or the ability to exercise rights and duties is reserved for those who have attained the age of majority (18) and are capable of judgement (*Urteilsfähigkeit*). A person is considered capable of judgement (*Urteilsfähig*) if he or she 'does not lack the capacity to act rationally by virtue of being under age or because of a mental disability, mental disorder, intoxication or similar circumstances'.[6] According to case law, *Urteilsfähigkeit* or discernment comprises both the ability to make an independent decision and to understand the meaning and consequences of this decision and the ability to act in accordance with this decision, including the ability to withstand undue influence.[7] Discernment is case-specific; an assessment of a person's capacity to act should be carried out in relation to the decision or act at hand.[8]

Representation is needed if a person lacks the capacity to act concerning a specific decision.[9] A new law on the protection and representation of adults was enacted in Switzerland in 2013, replacing the previous system of *Vormundschaft* that had been in place since 1912. As is shown schematically below, this new law (articles 360-456 SCC) differentiates between what is referred to as '*behördliche Massnahmen* and *nichtbehördliche Massnahmen*.[10] *Behördliche Massnahmen* are authoritative measures ordered by the Swiss adult protection authorities

5. United Nations Committee on the Rights of Persons with Disabilities, *General Comment No. 1. Article 12: Equal Recognition before the law*, 2014, p. 3.
6. Article 16 SCC – English translation of the Swiss Civil Code, via: https://www.fedlex.admin.ch/eli/cc/24/233_245_233/en (last accessed: 23-03-2022).
7. Fankhauser 2018, p. 190; Aebi-Müller & Magliana 2015, p. 389; BGE 124 III 5 no. 1a.
8. Fankhauser 2018, p. 199, Aebi-Müller & Magliana 2015, p. 389.
9. Aebi-Müller & Magliana 2015, p. 389.
10. This table is based on the table as presented by Hausheer, Geiser & Aebi-Müller 2018, p. 463.

(*Kinder- und Erwachsenenschutzbehörde*). These will not be discussed in detail in this country report.[11] The latter concern the provisions on enduring documents (Vorsorgeauftrag and Patientenverfügung), which the adult himself can make, and the default – ex-lege – provisions for statutory representation by relatives.[12]

			Article(s) in the Swiss Civil Code
Behördliche Massnahmen	State-ordered adult protection measures	Begleitbeistandschaft	393
		Vertretungsbeistandschaft	394
		Vermögensverwaltungsbeistandschaft	395
		Mitwirkungsbeistandschaft	396
		Kombinierte Beistandschaft	397
		Umfassende Beistandschaft	398
		The Adult Protection Agency has the authority to undertake specific actions to avoid a 'Beistandschaft' (Erforderliche Vorkehren der Erwachsenschutzbehörde)	392
		Hospitalisation for treatment or care (Fürsorgerische Unterbringung)	426-439
Nichtbehördliche Massnahmen	Statutory (ex-lege) measures	Representation by the spouse or registered partner	374-376
	Provisions that the adult himself can make	*Vorsorgeauftrag*	360-369
		Patientenverfügung	370-373

The right to autonomy and self-determination has, according to Aebi-Müller and Bienz, been placed at the core of the new protection system. Key in this regard is the principle of proportionality; measures may not interfere more or less in the life of the adult concerned than is needed to achieve the pursued objective, which is to provide sufficient protection to ensure that the personal and/or property rights of the person are protected.[13] From this principle of proportionality, a so-called *Stufenfolge* or sequence of steps follows. This sequence of steps starts at the bottom with the *nichtbehördlichen Massnahmen*, where there is no or limited state involvement as the adult or his relatives ensure adequate protection is in

11. The reader is for more information referred to for example H. Hausheer, T. Geiser & R.E. Aebi-Müller, *Das Familienrecht des Schweizerischen Zivilgesetzbuches*, Bern: Stämpfli Verlag 2018, pp. 521-526.
12. Aebi-Müller & Magliana 2015, p. 391.
13. Aebi-Müller & Bienz 2011, pp. 58-59; see also: Hausheer, Geiser & Aebi-Müller 2018, pp. 464-465.

place. The sequence of steps continues with the *Begleitbeistandschaft*, the least intrusive state-ordered adult protection measure which does not result in a loss or limitation of legal capacity. It ends at the top with the *Umfassende Beistandschaft*, the most intrusive state-ordered adult protection measure resulting in a full deprivation of legal capacity (*Handlungsfähigkeit*).[14] In addition to the principle of proportionality and the sequence of steps, the principle of subsidiarity is a third important foundation principle of the new adult protection system. According to this principle, measures may only be ordered when the negative consequences of the inability of the adult to act and decide cannot be managed any other way. Aebi-Müller and Bienz note that this principle explicitly underlines the significance of the *nichtbehördliche Massnahmen*, such as the representation by a family member and the provisions that can be taken by the adult himself (*Vorsorgeauftrag* and *Patientenverfügung*).[15] However, Biderbost stresses that the principle is not limited to the enduring documents in the Swiss Civil Code. He argues that measures should also be avoided when sufficient protection is ensured by an ordinary power of attorney (*Vollmacht*) or agency contract (*Auftrag*) (which does not end upon the adult's incapacity) or through a so-called joint bank account.[16] Hausheer *et al.* note that sufficient protection may also be ensured through support and assistance offered by relatives of the person concerned, support by non-governmental, non-profit organisations such as churches or support from state social welfare institutions.[17]

Infrastructure

The Kindes- und Erwachsenenschutzbehörde (KESB), or the adult protection authority, fulfils a key role in Switzerland. According to article 440 SCC, every canton must appoint at least one adult protection authority (APA).[18] The adult protection authorities are, in principle, responsible for all tasks concerning the protection of adults, apart from any exceptions stipulated by law. Concerning enduring documents, the adult protection authority is, for instance, responsible for the entry into force of the *Vorsorgeauftrag* (article 363 SCC – discussed in more detail under no. 16) and the clarification of the *Vorsorgeauftrag* on minor points (article 363 SCC – discussed in more detail under no. 11). The adult protection authorities are, in addition, obliged to intervene when the interests of the

14. Hausheer, Geiser & Aebi-Müller 2018, pp. 465-466. The 'Fürsorgerischen Unterbringung' is not included in the 'Stuffenfolge' as this is a different type of measure compared to the other measures.
15. Aebi-Müller & Bienz 2011, p. 59;
16. Biderbost 2019, pp. 104-105.
17. Hausheer, Geiser & Aebi-Müller 2018, pp. 466-467.
18. Aebi-Müller & Magliana 2015, p. 390.

adult concerned are no longer sufficiently protected through the *Vorsorgeauftrag* (article 368 SCC – discussed in more detail under no. 32).[19]

2. **Given the definitions of a 'continuing power of attorney' and an 'advance directive' in Council of Europe Recommendation 2009/11, describe the concept or concepts used in each country. What are the legal instruments?**

With the entry into force of the new law on adult protection in 2013, the Swiss legislator introduced two enduring documents in Switzerland, namely the *Vorsorgeauftrag* and the *Patientenverfügung*.

Article 360(1) SCC defines the *Vorsorgeauftrag* as follows:

> 'A person with capacity to act may instruct a natural person or legal entity to take responsibility for his or her personal care or the management of his or her assets or to act as his or her legal agent in the event that he or she is no longer capable of judgement.'[20]

Article 370(1) and (2) SCC define the *Patientenverfügung* as follows:

> 1) 'A person who is capable of judgement may specify in a patient decree which medical procedures he or she agrees or does not agree to in the event that he or she is no longer capable of judgement.
> 2) He or she may also designate a natural person who in the event that he or she is no longer capable of judgement should discuss the medical procedures with the attending doctor and decide on his or her behalf. He or she may issue instructions to this person.'[21]

As article 370 SCC clarifies, two different forms of the *Patientenverfügung* can be distinguished. The first type concerns a *Patientenverfügung* in which the adult records which medical treatment is under certain conditions desired or refused. The second type involves a *Patientenverfügung* in which the adult designates an attorney or 'trusted person' to make decisions regarding medical treatment on the adult's behalf.[22] The adult may combine both forms of the *Patientenverfügung* and can, in both cases, also include specific wishes or

19. See Hausheer, Geiser & Aebi-Müller 2018, pp. 471-472 for an extensive list of the tasks of the adult protection authorities.
20. Article 360(1) SCC – English translation of the Swiss Civil Code, via: https://www.fedlex.admin.ch/eli/cc/24/233_245_233/en (last accessed: 23-03-2022); See also: Botschaft zur Änderung des Schweizerischen Zivilgesetzbuches (Erwachsenenschutz, Personenrecht und Kindesrecht) 2006, p. 7012.
21. Article 370(1) and (2) SCC – English translation of the Swiss Civil Code, via: https://www.fedlex.admin.ch/eli/cc/24/233_245_233/en (last accessed: 23-03-2022); See also: Botschaft zur Änderung des Schweizerischen Zivilgesetzbuches (Erwachsenenschutz, Personenrecht und Kindesrecht) 2006, p. 7012.
22. Hausheer, Geiser & Aebi-Müller 2018, pp. 503-504.

instructions in the Patientenverfügung that the doctors and/or the attorney must consider.[23] Although the adult may appoint a legal person when it concerns a *Vorsorgeauftrag*, only a 'natural person' can be designated as an attorney when it involves a *Patientenverfügung*.[24] Langenegger and Jungo note that the adult can combine the *Vorsorgeauftrag* and the *Patientenverfügung* in the same document when it concerns the appointment of a 'natural person'.[25]

Although this is not included as an 'official instrument' in the Swiss Civil Code, Fassbind notes that the adult may also draw up an advance directive addressed to the adult protection authority, in which the adult records his wishes regarding his choice of a representative if a 'Beistandschaft' is deemed necessary. The adult protection authority is, according to article 401(1) SCC obliged to follow the adult's wishes when the proposed person is suitable and prepared to accept the appointment.[26]

N.B. Although, as the aforementioned makes clear, several enduring documents can be distinguished in Switzerland, this country report focuses on the appointment of an attorney through the so-called 'Vorsorgeauftrag'.

3. What is the current source of law on enduring documents?

Articles 360-369 of the Swiss Civil Code concern the provisions on the *Vorsorgeauftrag*. Article 365 SCC makes clear that unless otherwise stipulated by law, the *Vorsorgeauftrag* is also subject to the provisions on the agency contract (*Auftrag*) in the Code of Obligations:

> 'The appointee shall represent the client in accordance with the advance care directive and fulfil his or her duties with due care in accordance with the provisions of the Code of Obligations on agency contracts.'[27]

4. Give a brief history of the main developments of the law on enduring documents.

---

23. Ibid.
24. Article 370(2) SCC; Hausheer, Geiser & Aebi-Müller 2018, p. 504.
25. Jungo 2018, pp. 2127-2128; Langenegger 2015, p. 57; see also: Botschaft zur Änderung des Schweizerischen Zivilgesetzbuches (Erwachsenenschutz, Personenrecht und Kindesrecht) 2006, pp. 7025-7026.
26. Fassbind 2017, p. 233; Article 401(1) SCC – English translation of the Swiss Civil Code, via: https://www.fedlex.admin.ch/eli/cc/24/233_245_233/en (last accessed: 23-03-2022).
27. Article 365(1) SCC – English translation of the Swiss Civil Code, via: https://www.fedlex.admin.ch/eli/cc/24/233_245_233/en (last accessed: 23-03-2022); see also: Jungo 2018, p. 2117; Hrubesch-Millauer & Jaussi 2013, p. 33; Aebi-Müller & Bienz 2011, p. 75.

Before the enactment of the new adult protection law in 2013, there was already a demand for instruments enabling adults to make their own provisions for future incapacity. *Patientenverfügungen* already played a role in medical practice and were subject to cantonal health legislation. The scope of this instrument was, however, assessed differently throughout Switzerland.[28] In addition to the use of *Patientenverfügungen*, a practice arose in which the Swiss instruments of the *Vollmacht* (power of attorney) and the *Auftrag* (agency contract) were used as instruments of anticipatory decision-making. However, the answer to the question of whether these instruments could be used in the event of the adult's incapacity was controversial. The Swiss Federal Court, in part, removed this legal uncertainty by ruling that a person could grant a power of attorney which would remain in force upon the adult's incapacity.[29] The Swiss federal government subsequently rephrased articles 35 (*Vollmacht*) and 405 (*Auftrag*) of the Code of Obligations to incorporate the court's ruling.[30] Notwithstanding the judgment of the Federal Court and the subsequent rephrasing of articles 35 and 405 of the Code of Obligations, legal uncertainty remained. Jungo notes that some scholars still rejected the notion that powers of attorney could remain in force upon the adult's incapacity.[31] The legal uncertainty concerning the use of the *Vollmacht* and the *Auftrag* as anticipatory decision-making instruments led in 2006 to the proposal of two new enduring documents: the *Vorsorgeauftrag* and the *Patientenverfügung*. According to the Swiss government, adopting these instruments would remedy the unsatisfactory legal situation (*Vollmacht* and *Auftrag*) and create uniformity throughout Switzerland (*Patientenverfügung*).[32] From the parliamentary papers, it becomes clear that the Swiss federal government also considered the use of the *Vollmacht* and the *Auftrag* as enduring documents undesirable as these instruments provide the attorney with the opportunity to act on behalf of the adult before the incapacity to act occurs.[33]

5. **How does the specific legal regime concerning enduring documents relate to the (general) law on powers of attorney and other related legal figures?**

As discussed under no. 4, already before 2013, there was a demand for enduring documents and the instruments of the *Vollmacht* (article 32 and further of the Code of Obligations) and the *Auftrag* (article 394 and further of the Code of Obligations)

28. Botschaft zur Änderung des Schweizerischen Zivilgesetzbuches (Erwachsenenschutz, Personenrecht und Kindesrecht) 2006, p. 7012.
29. BGE 132 III 222.
30. Hausheer, Geiser & Aebi-Müller 2018, pp. 491-492.
31. Jungo 2018, p. 2111.
32. Botschaft zur Änderung des Schweizerischen Zivilgesetzbuches (Erwachsenenschutz, Personenrecht und Kindesrecht) 2006, p. 7012.
33. Botschaft zur Änderung des Schweizerischen Zivilgesetzbuches (Erwachsenenschutz, Personenrecht und Kindesrecht) 2006, p. 7012.

were used to make provisions for a future period of incapacity. With the entry into force of the new adult protection law and the introduction of the *Vorsorgeauftrag*, two questions concerning the instrument of the *Vollmacht* and the *Auftrag* arose. The first question concerns the validity of *Vollmachten* and *Aufträge* drafted before the enactment of the new law in 2013. Hrubesch-Millauer and Jaussi, Langenegger and Schmid argue that these *Vollmacht*en and *Aufträge* can remain in force. In this context, it is irrelevant whether the *Vollmacht* takes effect upon the incapacity of the adult or remains in force upon the incapacity of the adult. Nor does it matter whether incapacity occurs before or after 1 January 2013.[34] The second question concerns the validity of *Vollmachten* and *Aufträge* – with the objective to provide for a future period of incapacity – drafted after the entry into force of the new law in 2013. In this respect, a distinction must be made between *Vollmachten* and *Aufträge*, which enter into force upon the incapacity of the adult and *Vollmacht*en and *Aufträge*, which remain in force upon the incapacity of the adult. It is undisputed that the first alternative is no longer possible as the *Vorsorgeauftrag* applies as a lex specialis.[35] However, the second alternative – *Vollmachten* and *Aufträge*, which remain in force upon the adult's incapacity – is also possible under the new adult protection law.[36] According to article 397a of the Code of Obligations, the attorney must notify the adult protection authority of the adult's incapacity when such a notification seems appropriate to safeguard the adult's interests.

6. Are there any recent proposals for reform in this area?

No

7. Are there statistics available on the number of (registered) enduring documents in each country? And if so, what are they?

Statistics on the number of adult protection measures are published annually by the 'Konferenz für Kindes- und Erwachsenenschutz' (KOKES). These statistics show that in 2018, the number of people with a protection measure amounted to 94.359.[37] These protection measures concerned the various *behördliche Massnahmen* discussed above. As no. 16 and 24 discuss in more detail, *Vorsorgeaufträge* can be registered and must be validated before they come into effect. Unfortunately, I

34. Langenegger 2015, p. 48; Hrubesch-Millauer 2014, pp. 1290-1291; Schmid 2014, p. 295; See however differently Jungo (2018, p. 2115) who argues that in the event a *Vollmacht* – made before 1 January 2013 – is intended to take effect upon the incapacity of the adult and such incapacity occurs after 1 January 2013, the *Vollmacht* must comply with the requirements of article 363 SCC.
35. Biderbost 2019, p. 108; Jungo 2018, p. 2116; Langenegger 2015, pp. 49-50; Hrubesch-Millauer & Jaussi 2014, p. 1291.
36. Biderbost 2018, pp. 106-107; Jungo 2018, pp. 2115-2116; Langenegger 2015, p. 49.
37. https://www.kokes.ch/de/dokumentation/statistik/aktuellste-zahlen/medienkonferenz-050920 19 (last accessed: 23-03-2022).

have not been able to find official statistics on the total number of *Vorsorgeaufträge* that have been drawn up, registered or validated in Switzerland. However, both the adult protection authority in Basel-Stadt and Zürich have been kind enough to provide me with the number of Vorsorgeaufträge registered and validated at their office. These statistics give an impression of the number of registered and validated *Vorsorgeaufträge* on a local level.

Number of validated Vorsorgeaufträge KESB Basel-Stadt

Year	2013	2014	2015	2016	2017	2018
Number of registered *Vorsorgeaufträge*	157	209	315	616	695	794
Number of validated *Vorsorgeaufträge*	1	2	5	10	26	29

Number of validated Vorsorgeaufträge KESB Zürich

Year	2013	2014	2015	2016	2017
Number of registered *Vorsorgeaufträge*	40	43	105	163	182
Number of validated *Vorsorgeaufträge*	20	6	10	14	30

At the behest of the Swiss organisation Pro Senectute, a survey study was conducted in 2017 by the GFS-Zürich research institute.[38] The survey focused on the awareness of the *Vorsorgeauftrag* and the *Patientenverfügung* among the Swiss population and the number of people who had made a *Vorsorgeauftrag* or *Patientenverfügung*. One thousand two hundred people completed the survey through computer-assisted telephone interviewing (CATI), and the study was considered representative of the Swiss population. Only half (48%) of the respondents were familiar with the possibility of making a Vorsorgeauftrag; 65% were aware of the possibility of making a *Patientenverfügung*. Furthermore, 12% of the respondents indicated they had made a *Vorsorgeauftrag*, compared to 22% who had made a *Patientenverfügung*.[39] The study was repeated in 2021 and again conducted by the GFS-Zürich research institute at the behest of Pro Senectute. The study found a significant increase in the awareness of enduring documents; 65% of the respondents were familiar with the possibility of making a *Vorsorgeauftrag*, compared to 82% who were aware of the option to create a *Patientenverfügung*.[40]

38. Pro Senectute, *Selbstbestimmen bei Urteilsunfähigkeit – Zahlen und Fakten*, 2017; Pro Senectute, *Medienmitteilung 'Nur jede zehnte Person in der Schweiz hat bei Urteilsunfähigkeit vorgesorgt'*, 2017; A. Umbricht (GFS-Zürich, Markt- & Sozialforschung, *Telefonische Omnibus-Befragung zur persönliche Vorsorge*, 2017, accessible via: https://gfs-zh.ch/nur-jede-zehnte-person-in-der-schweiz-hat-bei-urteilsunfaehigkeit-vorgesorgt/ (last accessed: 23-03-2022).
39. Ibid.
40. Pro Senectute, *Medienmitteilung 'Wunsch nach Selbstbestimmung ist stärker als Druck durch Corona'*, 2021; A. Umbricht & J. Yin (GFS-Zürich, Markt- & Sozialforschung, *Telefonische Omnibus-*

B. *Enduring documents and adult protection measures ordered by the court or an administrative authority*

8. **How do enduring documents relate to adult protection measures ordered by the court or an administrative authority? Is there a principle of subsidiarity in place?**

The adult protection authority is obliged to respect the arrangements (*Vorsorgeauftrag* and/or *Patientenverfügung*) made by the adult insofar as these are sufficient to protect the adult's interests.[41] This follows from article 389 SCC, titled 'subsidiarity and proportionality':

> 1. The adult protection authority shall order a measure if:
>   a. support for the person in need offered by his or her family, other closely related persons or private or public services is or proves to be insufficient;
>   b. where the person in need is no longer capable of judgement, he or she has failed to make any or sufficient arrangements for his or her own care and the statutory measures are insufficient.
> 2. Any official measure must be necessary and suitable.[42]

9. **Is there an obligation for the court or the administrative authority to check whether an enduring document is in place?**

In principle, it is the adult's responsibility to ensure that authorities and organisations, such as the adult protection authority or the bank, are aware of the existence of the *Vorsorgeauftrag*.[43] However, when making a *Vorsorgeauftrag*, one can opt to have it registered with the Civil Register Office. If a person chooses to do so, both the fact that a *Vorsorgeauftrag* has been made and where it is kept are registered.[44] Upon receiving notification that a person is no longer capable of judgement (*Urteilsfähig*), the adult protection authority has to initiate proceedings to examine the necessity of an adult protection measure. In this regard, the adult protection agency has to check, under article 363(1) SCC, with the Civil Register Office whether or not the adult has made a *Vorsorgeauftrag*:

Befragung zur persönliche Vorsorge, 2021, accessible via: https://gfs-zh.ch/bekanntheitszunahme-bei-vorsorgedokumenten/ (last accessed: 23-03-2022).

41. Biderbost 2019, pp. 103-104; Hausheer, Geiser & Aebi-Müller 2018, p. 491.
42. Article 389 SCC – English translation of the Swiss Civil Code, via: https://www.fedlex.admin.ch/eli/cc/24/233_245_233/en (last accessed: 23-03-2022); see also: Hausheer, Geiser & Aebi-Müller 2018, p. 491.
43. Hausheer, Geiser & Aebi-Müller 2018, p. 495.
44. Article 361(3) SCC.

> 'Where the adult protection authority learns that a person is no longer capable of judgement, but it is unaware if there is an advance care directive, it shall enquire at the Civil Register Office.'[45]

Büttner and Fountoulakis note that although the person concerned may also choose other means to inform the adult protection authority of the existence of the *Vorsorgeauftrag* (for example, by asking the attending physician or relatives to inform the adult protection authority), the duty of the adult protection authority to check whether a *Vorsorgeauftrag* is in place, is limited to obtaining the corresponding information from the Civil Register Office and if no entry is reported, to asking people closely related to the adult, such as family members, if a *Vorsorgeauftrag* is in place.[46]

10. **Can the measures ordered by the court or the administrative authority be combined with the enduring document?**

As discussed in more detail under no. 16, the adult protection authority is, according to article 363(2) SCC, obliged to verify – upon the entry into force of the *Vorsorgeauftrag* – if further adult protection measures are required. For instance, the adult protection authority can deem an additional adult protection measure necessary when the *Vorsorgeauftrag* only partially covers the affairs for which an adult protection measure is considered necessary.[47]

11. **Can the enduring document's content or the attorney's powers be changed or expanded by the court or any other institution? And if so, in what cases?**

The adult protection authority may interpret the provisions of the *Vorsorgeauftrag* and add clarifications or adjustments on minor points. According to Jungo, there are two stages in which the adult protection authority can exercise this authority. First, as will be discussed in more detail under no. 16, before the entry into force of the *Vorsorgeauftrag*, the adult protection authority has to establish whether the attorney accepts the *Vorsorgeauftrag*. If this is the case, a certificate is subsequently issued detailing the scope of the attorney's mandate. Jungo argues that already in this phase, the provisions of the *Vorsorgeauftrag* must be interpreted, and clarifications and adjustments made to determine the scope of the attorney's mandate.[48] Second, in some cases, a further explanation or clarification of the *Vorsorgeauftrag* is required after the entry into force. In these cases, article 364

45. Article 363(1) SCC – English translation of the Swiss Civil Code, via: https://www.fedlex.admin.ch/eli/cc/24/233_245_233/en (last accessed: 23-03-2022).
46. Büttner & Fountoulakis 2015, pp. 511-512.
47. Hausheer, Geiser & Aebi-Müller 2018, p. 493; Jungo 2018, p. 2146.
48. Jungo 2018, p. 2151-2156.

SCC provides a remedy. The attorney may turn to the adult protection authority and request a (further) interpretation or clarification of the provisions of the *Vorsorgeauftrag*. However, the adult protection authority may, in this second phase, also act ex officio or at the request of persons closely related to the adult if this is considered necessary to protect the adult's interests (article 364 in conjunction with article 368(1) SCC).[49]

From the parliamentary memorandum on the amendment of the Swiss Civil Code regarding the protection of adults, it follows that the objective of article 364 SCC has been to avoid an (additional) state-ordered adult protection measure in cases where the *Vorsorgeauftrag* is unclear on minor points. The memorandum refers to situations where circumstances may have changed unexpectedly since the entry into force of the *Vorsorgeauftrag*, leaving the attorney uncertain about how to act and jeopardising the continuance of care.[50] The adult protection authority should, as much as possible, act in accordance with the (actual) will of the adult when interpreting and clarifying the provisions of the *Vorsorgeauftrag*.[51] Clarifications or adjustments are only possible on minor points and may not result in creating new tasks for the attorney. If the adult has been intentionally silent on a particular subject, adjustments concerning this subject are not possible.[52] As an example of a situation in which a clarification or adjustment is possible, Jungo refers to a situation in which the adult provides the attorney with a general mandate to organise his or her financial assets. The adult subsequently includes a list of most financial assets, except one or two, such as a bank account. Nothing further is said about this bank account, for example, the appointment of another attorney to take care of this bank account. Suppose this at a later stage causes problems concerning the bank's acceptance of the *Vorsorgeauftrag*. In that case, the adult protection authority may decide to add the bank account to the list of financial assets if it was clearly the adult's intention that the attorney would take care of all financial assets.[53]

12. On which grounds are state-ordered measures applied, notwithstanding the presence of an enduring document?

As discussed under no. 1, the principle of subsidiarity plays a significant role in the Swiss legal system on adult protection. Article 389(1) SCC makes clear that preference should be given to provisions taken by the adult himself, such

49. Hausheer, Geiser & Aebi-Müller 2018, p. 501.
50. Botschaft zur Änderung des Schweizerischen Zivilgesetzbuches (Erwachsenenschutz, Personenrecht und Kindesrecht) 2006, p. 7028.
51. Jungo 2018, pp. 2152-2154.
52. Jungo 2018, p. 2155.
53. Jungo 2018, p. 2155. This example also came up in the conversations with experts from two adult protection authorities.

as the *Vorsorgeauftrag* and the *Patientenverfügung* (see also no. 8). The adult protection authority should, in addition, refrain from ordering an adult protection measure, when adequate support and assistance are provided by relatives, other persons close to the adult and public services, such as churches and social welfare institutions.[54] In this regard, the Swiss legislator has noted that adult protection measures are only to be ordered when the care of the adult cannot be adequately ensured by any other means.[55] An example of a situation in which an adult protection measure, notwithstanding the presence of a *Vorsorgeauftrag*, can be necessary has already been discussed under no. 10, namely a situation in which the *Vorsorgeauftrag* only partially covers the affairs of the adult for which protection is deemed necessary. If, in that case, there is also no or insufficient support provided by one of the actors mentioned above, the adult protection authority may order an adult protection measure.[56] As discussed under no. 1, when ordering an adult protection measure, the adult protection authority has to consider the principle of proportionality. This also becomes apparent from article 389(2), stipulating that any measure must be necessary and suitable.[57]

C. *Form and general content of the enduring document*

13. **Are there any requirements as to the form of the enduring document?**

As to the form of the *Vorsorgeauftrag*, article 361 SCC states the following:

> 1) The advance care directive must be executed in holographic form or publicly authenticated.
> 2) A holograph advance care directive must be handwritten, dated and signed by the client from beginning to end.[58]

This means the adult has two options regarding the form of the *Vorsorgeauftrag*. The *Vorsorgeauftrag* must either be 1) publicly authenticated or 2) handwritten from beginning to end, dated and signed by the adult. These requirements aim to prevent the adult from acting unwisely and precipitately.[59] A publicly authenticated *Vorsorgeauftrag* is drafted by what is in German referred to as an *Urkundsperson*. Who may act as *Urkundsperson* is determined by cantonal law.[60]

---

54. Biderbost 2019, pp. 103-104.
55. Botschaft zur Änderung des Schweizerischen Zivilgesetzbuches (Erwachsenenschutz, Personenrecht und Kindesrecht) 2006, pp. 7042-7043.
56. Schmid 2014, p. 276.
57. BGE 140 III 49.
58. Article 361 SCC – English translation of the Swiss Civil Code, via: https://www.fedlex.admin.ch/eli/cc/24/233_245_233/en (last accessed: 23-03-2022).
59. Jungo 2018, p. 2129-2130.
60. Hausheer, Geiser & Aebi-Müller 2018, pp. 494-495.

In most cases, this person will be a notary.[61] The *Urkundsperson* has to advise the adult, establish the identity of the adult and assess whether the content of the *Vorsorgeauftrag* truly reflects the adult's wishes.[62] The adult may also choose to draft the *Vorsorgeauftrag* himself. In this case, it has to be handwritten from beginning to end. A *Vorsorgeauftrag*, prepared on a computer or dictated by someone else, is invalid. With this requirement, the Swiss federal government hoped to avoid situations where the adult would simply sign a document drafted by a third person without being aware of the content.[63]

Without these formal requirements, a *Vorsorgeauftrag* cannot be validly executed. However, according to Hausheer *et al.*, this does not prevent the adult protection authority from taking the content of the non-validly executed *Vorsorgeauftrag* into account as information regarding the adult's wishes.[64]

14. Is the enduring document unilateral or bilateral? Is a signature from the attorney a requirement?

The *Vorsorgeauftrag* can be characterised as both a unilateral and a bilateral document, depending on its phase. Jungo notes that in the first instance – until the attorney accepts his appointment – the *Vorsorgeauftrag* is a unilateral declaration of intent (*Willenserklärung*) in which the adult stipulates who is to take care of his affairs in the event of his future incapacity.[65] As no. 17 discusses in more detail, the adult can – when he is still capable of judgement or *Urteilsfähig* – at any time withdraw this *Willenserklärung*. This changes as soon as the adult becomes incapable of judgement or *Urteilsunfähig*.[66] When this occurs, the adult protection authority is, according to article 363 SCC, obliged to verify whether the *Vorsorgeauftrag* can enter into force (see no. 16). If the conditions for the entry into force of the *Vorsorgeauftrag* are fulfilled, the adult protection authority enquires whether the attorney is prepared to take on the task of attorney. For the *Vorsorgeauftrag* to become binding on the attorney, a declaration of acceptance by the attorney is required. This declaration of acceptance creates a legal relationship comparable to a contract, in other words, a bilateral agreement.[67] Schmid argues that the *Vorsorgeauftrag* concerns a special type of agreement or in German 'einer

61. Botschaft zur Änderung des Schweizerischen Zivilgesetzbuches (Erwachsenenschutz, Personenrecht und Kindesrecht) 2006, p. 7026.
62. Hausheer, Geiser & Aebi-Müller 2018, pp. 494-495; Schmid 2014, pp. 285-287.
63. Botschaft zur Änderung des Schweizerischen Zivilgesetzbuches (Erwachsenenschutz, Personenrecht und Kindesrecht) 2006, p. 7026.
64. Hausheer, Geiser & Aebi-Müller 2018, pp. 494-495.
65. Jungo 2018, pp. 2117-2118; See also Schmid 2014, pp. 277-279.
66. Jungo 2018, pp. 2118-2119.
67. Ibid.

erwachsenenschutzrechtlichen Rechtsfigur eigener Art'.[68] He notes that the general rules of contract law, in various ways, have been modified by the adult protection law. There is, for instance, no reciprocity in the declarations of intent. The adult does not necessarily have to address his declaration of intent (*Willenserklärung*) to the prospective attorney. The attorney does not have to declare acceptance to the adult but to the adult protection authority.[69]

15. Which matters (e.g. financial, health, welfare, personal) can be covered by the enduring document? Conversely, are there particular matters excluded?

Article 360(1) and (2) SCC stipulate the following concerning the affairs that can be included in the *Vorsorgeauftrag*:

> 1) A person with capacity to act may instruct a natural person or legal entity to take responsibility for his or her personal care or the management of his or her assets or to act as his or her legal agent in the event that he or she is no longer capable of judgement.
> 2) He or she must define the tasks that are to be assigned and may issue instructions on how these tasks are to be fulfilled.[70]

Three elements are included in article 360(1) SCC, namely the financial affairs of the adult, the personal affairs of the adult and the authority to represent the adult. As discussed under no. 2, the adult may include a *Patientenverfügung* in the *Vorsorgeauftrag*, which means that the adult can also make provisions for health and medical affairs. However, the adult can only appoint a natural person as an attorney for health and medical matters.[71] The adult can assign the abovementioned tasks cumulatively or alternatively and limit the *Vorsorgeauftrag* to specific affairs or legal transactions.[72] As no. 22 discusses in more detail, the adult cannot authorise the attorney to perform certain highly personal acts – such as making a will or filing for a divorce – on his behalf. Although article 360(1) SCC distinguishes the authority to represent the adult (*Rechtsvertretung*) as a separate element, Jungo notes that in most cases, the power to represent the adult is a necessary condition for the proper execution of the *Vorsorgeauftrag*. Jungo, therefore, argues that if the adult does not include such an authority

---

68. Schmid 2014, pp. 278-279.
69. Ibid.
70. Article 360(1) and (2) SCC – English translation of the Swiss Civil Code, via: https://www.fedlex.admin.ch/eli/cc/24/233_245_233/en (last accessed: 23-03-2022).
71. Jungo 2018, pp. 2127-2128; Langenegger 2015, p. 57; see also: Botschaft zur Änderung des Schweizerischen Zivilgesetzbuches (Erwachsenenschutz, Personenrecht und Kindesrecht) 2006, pp. 7025-7026.
72. Botschaft zur Änderung des Schweizerischen Zivilgesetzbuches (Erwachsenenschutz, Personenrecht und Kindesrecht) 2006, p. 7025; Hausheer, Geiser & Aebi-Müller 2018, pp. 492-493; Jungo 2018, pp. 2128-2129.

(*Vertretungsbefügnis*) in the *Vorsorgeauftrag*, this authority is granted by operation of law based on article 365(1) SCC.[73] Langenegger notes that although a detailed description is recommended, the adult should describe, at least in general terms, the duties assigned to the attorney.[74] As discussed under no. 11, the adult protection authority may add clarifications or make adjustments on minor points when there are uncertainties regarding the scope of the authority conferred to the attorney.

16. What are the rules, regulations and practices concerning the entry into force of the enduring document?

Article 363 SCC sets out the conditions for the entry into force of the *Vorsorgeauftrag*:

1) Where the adult protection authority learns that a person is no longer capable of judgement, but it is unaware if there is an advance care directive, it shall enquire at the Civil Register Office.
2) If there is an advance care directive, the adult protection authority shall verify if:
   1. the directive has been validly executed;
   2. the requirements for its effectiveness are met;
   3. the appointee is fit for his or her duties; and
   4. if further adult protection measures are required.
3) If the appointee accepts the advance care directive, the authority shall advise him or her of his or her obligations under the provisions of the Code of Obligations on agency contracts and issue him or her with a formal document stating his or her powers.[75]

As article 363(2) SCC clarifies, the adult protection authority decides whether the *Vorsorgeauftrag* can enter into force. There are four elements the adult protection authority must verify in what is referred to as a process of validation (*Validierung*). The adult protection authority must, first of all, examine whether the *Vorsorgeauftrag* has been validly made. This means that 1) the requirements of article 361 SCC concerning the form of the *Vorsorgeauftrag* must have been met, 2) that the adult had legal capacity (*Handlungsfähigkeit*) to draw up the *Vorsorgeauftrag* – meaning the adult was both of age and capable of judgement (*Urteilsfähig*) – and 3) that the content of the *Vorsorgeauftrag* is not contrary to the

73. Jungo 2018, p. 2128; see also Hrubesch-Millauer & Jaussi 2014, p. 1284.
74. Langenegger 2015, p. 55; Botschaft zur Änderung des Schweizerischen Zivilgesetzbuches (Erwachsenenschutz, Personenrecht und Kindesrecht) 2006, p. 7025.
75. Article 363 SCC – English translation of the Swiss Civil Code, via: https://www.fedlex.admin.ch/eli/cc/24/233_245_233/en (last accessed: 23-03-2022).

law.[76] Jungo notes that with respect to the assessment of the adult's capacity at the time of drafting, the adult protection authority may assume that the adult had the capacity to draft the *Vorsorgeauftrag* (*Urteilsfähigkeit*) unless there is evidence indicating otherwise.[77]

In the second place, the adult protection authority must assess whether the requirements for the entry into force of the *Vorsorgeauftrag* are met. The *Vorsorgeauftrag* can only enter into force when the adult concerned is no longer capable of judgement (*Urteilsunfähig*) regarding the affairs included in the *Vorsorgeauftrag*.[78] There is no prescribed course of action for the adult protection authorities to assess the adult's capacity. Büttner and Fountoulakis note that a physician's assessment is often requested in practice.[79] Jungo notes that – besides the requirement that the adult must be *Urteilsfähig* – there must also be a so-called *Sorgebedürftigkeit* or a need for care. In this respect, a *Vorsorgeauftrag* is only effective when the attorney has a task to perform. If there is no need – or no longer any need – for support or representation concerning the matters included in the *Vorsorgeauftrag* – e.g. the *Vorsorgeauftrag* contains the order to sell the family home, but the family home has already been sold – the *Vorsorgeauftrag* is ineffective because it is without purpose.[80]

Suppose the Vorsorgeauftrag has been validly executed, and the requirements for its effectiveness have been met. In that case, the adult protection authority must – in third place – examine whether the attorney is suited to the task at hand. This assessment should be based on objective criteria as much as possible.[81] The attorney must have the capacity (*Handlungsfähigkeit*) to act on behalf of the adult.[82] In addition, the (professional) competencies of the attorney must be sufficient for the task at hand. In this regard, the difficulty and scope of the assignment affect the suitability of the person nominated as an attorney. Büttner and Fountoulakis note, for instance, that the management of complex financial investments requires different knowledge and skills than the management of an ordinary pension.[83] The attorney must be willing to take on the role of attorney and must be able to do so in terms of time and location.[84] The attorney must also be a reliable and honest person. To assess this, in practice, the adult protection authority checks whether

76. Jungo 2018, pp. 2141-2142.
77. Jungo 2018, p. 2142.
78. Hausheer, Geiser & Aebi-Müller 2018, p. 497; Jungo 2018, p. 2143.
79. Büttner & Fountoulakis 2015, pp. 517; see also Jungo 2018. p. 2144.
80. Jungo 2018, p. 2144.
81. Jungo 2018, p. 2145; Büttner & Fountoulakis 2015, p. 515.
82. Büttner & Fountoulakis 2015, p. 515.
83. Büttner & Fountoulakis 2015, pp. 514-515.
84. Jungo 2018, p. 2145.

the attorney has any criminal records and whether the attorney appears in the bankruptcy and insolvency register.[85]

Article 363(3) stipulates that if the attorney accepts the appointment, the adult protection authority must inform the attorney about his rights and duties and issue a formal document confirming the appointment of the attorney, a so-called *Legitimationsurkunde*.[86] The attorney can use this document to identify himself to third parties as the person responsible for the adult's affairs. Furthermore, according to article 363(2) under 4 SCC, the adult protection authority must consider whether an additional adult protection measure is necessary. This may be the case if the adult protection authority finds that the *Vorsorgeauftrag* has not been validly executed, if the *Vorsorgeauftrag* only partly covers the affairs for which an adult protection measure is considered necessary, or if the attorney only accepts part of the authority conferred to him.[87]

17. Under which circumstances does the enduring document cease to have effect?

Hausheer *et al.* distinguish three situations in which the *Vorsorgeauftrag* ceases to have effect.

1. *Revocation by the adult or the adult protection authority*

According to article 362 SCC, the adult may at any time – when he has the capacity (*Urteilsfähigkeit*) to do so – revoke the *Vorsorgeauftrag*. The adult can revoke the *Vorsorgeauftrag* through one of the ways prescribed for drafting the *Vorsorgeauftrag* (see no. 13) or by physically destroying the document.[88] Article 362(2) SCC clarifies that if the adult makes a new *Vorsorgeauftrag* without explicitly revoking the previous *Vorsorgeauftrag*, the new *Vorsorgeauftrag* replaces the previous one unless the adult intended the new *Vorsorgeauftrag* to be an addition to the old *Vorsorgeauftrag*.[89] Hausheer *et al.* note that the adult may include in the *Vorsorgeauftrag* a so-called *Befristung* or time limitation. In this context, the adult may, for instance, stipulate that the *Vorsorgeauftrag* will only enter into force if incapacity arises within a certain period of time, or the adult may specify that the *Vorsorgeauftrag* will only remain in force for a certain period after the onset of incapacity.[90] If the adult is *Urteilsunfähig* or no longer capable of judgement, revocation of the *Vorsorgeauftrag* by the adult is no longer possible. However, the

85. Büttner & Fountoulakis 2015, p. 515.
86. Jungo 2018, p. 2148.
87. Jungo 2018, p. 2416.
88. Article 362(2) and (3) SCC; Hausheer, Geiser & Aebi-Müller 2018, pp. 495-496.
89. Article 362(2) SCC – English translation of the Swiss Civil Code, via: https://www.fedlex.admin.ch/eli/cc/24/233_245_233/en (last accessed: 23-03-2022).
90. Hausheer, Geiser & Aebi-Müller 2018, pp. 496-497.

adult protection authority can, in the framework of, for example, article 368 SCC (see no. 32), revoke the *Vorsorgeauftrag*.[91]

2. *The Vorsorgeauftrag ceases to apply by operation of law*

Article 369(1) SCC stipulates that if the adult concerned regains capacity or becomes *Urteilsfähig* again, the *Vorsorgeauftrag* ceases to apply. Hausheer *et al.* note that if the adult concerned, at a later stage, again becomes incapable of judgement or *Urteilsunfähig*, without having revoked the *Vorsorgeauftrag*, it enters into force again.[92] The *Vorsorgeauftrag* also ceases to apply upon the death of the adult unless the adult has stipulated otherwise.[93]

3. *Disclaimer by the attorney*

Based on article 363(2) SCC, the adult protection authority must enquire whether the attorney accepts the appointment. The attorney may, of course, refuse the appointment.[94] As no. 20 discusses in more detail, a notice period of two months applies when the attorney terminates an ongoing appointment. Only in certain circumstances may the attorney terminate his appointment immediately. In either case, the attorney must notify the adult protection authority of the termination. If there is no replacement or substitute attorney, the *Vorsorgeauftrag* ceases to apply.

D. *The attorney*

18. **Who can be appointed as an attorney? Are there restrictions concerning the choice of attorney (e.g. exclusion of certain people)?**

Article 360(1) SCC stipulates that:

> 'A person with capacity to act may instruct a natural person or legal entity to take responsibility for his or her personal care or the management of his or her assets or to act as his or her legal agent in the event that he or she is no longer capable of judgement.'[95]

The adult may appoint a natural person or a legal entity to act as an attorney. Concerning the latter, the adult may, for example, appoint as his attorney a bank, a trust company or a stakeholder organisation (in Switzerland, e.g. Pro Senectute). According to Jungo, the adult cannot appoint a legal entity when the attorney's

91. Hausheer, Geiser & Aebi-Müller 2018, pp. 495-496.
92. Hausheer, Geiser & Aebi-Müller 2018, p. 496.
93. Ibid.
94. Hausheer, Geiser & Aebi-Müller 2018, p. 497.
95. Article 360(1) SCC – English translation of the Swiss Civil Code, via: https://www.fedlex.admin.ch/eli/cc/24/233_245_233/en (last accessed: 23-03-2022).

responsibilities extend to decision-making regarding medical matters. In this case, only a natural person can be appointed since more personal management of affairs is considered important when it concerns medical decision-making.[96] The attorney must have the capacity to act (*Handlungsfähigkeit*), which means he must have attained the age of majority and be capable of judgement (*Urteilsfähig*).[97] The adult does not have to mention the attorney by name. It must, however, be clear whom the adult wants to appoint as his attorney. Jungo gives the following example: the adult may indicate that he wants to appoint 'his eldest son' or 'the director of the elderly care home X' as an attorney. However, using the general phrase 'an employee of bank X' is insufficient.[98] As discussed in more detail under no. 16, the adult protection authority is, according to article 363 SCC, obliged to assess the suitability of the nominated attorney upon the entry into force of the *Vorsorgeauftrag*. Langenegger notes in this respect that the adult would be well advised also to consider the future suitability of the person appointed as attorney.[99]

19. Does the legal system allow for the appointment of more than one attorney? Can these attorneys act jointly, concurrently, separately or as substitutes?

The adult may appoint more than one person to act as his attorney. The adult may direct the attorneys to act jointly or concurrently.[100] If the adult directs the attorneys to act concurrently, he must regulate the position of each attorney by clearly assigning each attorney individual tasks and competencies.[101] The attorneys are to act jointly if the adult does not specify any distribution of tasks and competencies. Of course, this will not always be convenient in practice, for example, when one of the attorneys spends time abroad. According to Langenegger, article 402 of the Code of Obligations allows the adult to determine that the attorneys may authorise each other to act separately.[102] Article 360(3) SCC makes clear that the adult may also appoint a substitute attorney:

> 'He or she may provide for a replacement for the event that the appointee is not suitable for the tasks, does not accept the mandate or terminates the mandate.'[103]

---

96. Jungo 2018, p. 2123; Botschaft zur Änderung des Schweizerischen Zivilgesetzbuches (Erwachsenenschutz, Personenrecht und Kindesrecht) 2006, pp. 7025-7026.
97. Jungo 2018, p. 2123.
98. Hausheer, Geiser & Aebi-Müller 2018, p. 493; Jungo 2018, p. 2124.
99. Langenegger 2015, p. 53.
100. Jungo 2018, p. 2127; Botschaft zur Änderung des Schweizerischen Zivilgesetzbuches (Erwachsenenschutz, Personenrecht und Kindesrecht) 2006, p. 7025.
101. Langenegger 2015, p. 53; See also article 360(2) SCC.
102. Langenegger 2015, p. 53; Jungo 2018, p. 2127.
103. Article 360(3) SCC – English translation of the Swiss Civil Code, via: https://www.fedlex.admin.ch/eli/cc/24/233_245_233/en (last accessed: 23-03-2022).

20. **Is there a duty for the attorney to inform the court or any other administrative authority if the appointment to act as an attorney is refused or discontinued?**

As discussed under No. 16, the adult protection authority must, under art. 363 SCC, validate the *Vorsorgeauftrag*. Part of the validation process is an assessment of the suitability of the attorney. In this regard, the adult protection authority has to ascertain whether the intended attorney is prepared to act as an attorney. Concerning the termination of an ongoing appointment by the attorney, article 367 SCC stipulates:

1) 'The appointee may terminate the advance care directive at any time subject to giving two months' written notice to the adult protection authority.
2) For good cause, the appointee may terminate the directive without notice.'[104]

In other words, the attorney must notify the adult protection authority when the appointment is discontinued. There is a notice period of two months, which means that if the attorney wants to terminate his appointment by the first of November, he has to make sure the adult protection authority receives his notice on the first of September. The notice period of two months has been included to give the adult protection period sufficient time to assess the necessity of an adult protection measure. Art. 367 SCC stipulates that in certain circumstances, the attorney may terminate his appointment with immediate effect. Jungo provides the following examples of such circumstances: a not foreseeable conflict of interest; due to the poor health of the attorney; and improper behaviour by the adult or his relatives.[105]

21. **Are there any rules or regulations regarding the attorney's role in line with, for example, article 12(4) UNCRPD and Principle 10 of the Council of Europe Recommendation 2009/11?**

According to article 365(1) SCC, the attorney must represent the adult according to the adult's wishes, preferences and instructions, recorded in the *Vorsorgeauftrag*.[106] The attorney may not act beyond the scope of the authority conferred to him and must inform the adult protection authority in the event transactions have to be carried out which are not covered by the *Vorsorgeauftrag*.[107] According to Hrubesch-Millauer and Jaussi, the attorney must also contact the adult protection authority if there are ambiguities or uncertainties concerning the content of the

104. Article 367 SCC – English translation of the Swiss Civil Code, via: https://www.fedlex.admin.ch/eli/cc/24/233_245_233/en (last accessed: 23-03-2022).
105. Jungo 2018, pp. 2168-2169.
106. Hausheer, Geiser & Aebi-Müller 2018, pp. 498-450.
107. Article 365(2) SCC; Hrubesch-Millauer & Jaussi 2013, p. 34.

Vorsorgeauftrag.[108] As discussed under no. 11, the adult protection agency can, in these instances, interpret the *Vorsorgeauftrag* and add clarifications on minor points.

Article 365 SCC makes clear that, in addition to the legal provisions on the *Vorsorgeauftrag*, the attorney is also obliged to act in accordance with the provisions of the Code of Obligations on agency contracts (*Auftrag*). Again, article 397 of the Code of Obligations confirms that the attorney must act following the adult's instructions.[109] The attorney, in addition, has a duty of care and is obliged to put the interests of the adult first and to refrain from doing anything that could harm the adult.[110] As no. 33 discusses in more detail, the attorney's authority is restricted when there is a conflict of interest unless the adult has explicitly authorised the attorney to perform the transaction concerned.[111] When determining the duty of care, professional attorneys such as notaries and lawyers are, according to Hrubesch-Millauer and Jaussi, subject to higher standards.[112] According to article 398(3) of the Code of Obligations, the attorney is, in principle, obliged to act himself. Finally, according to article 400 of the Code of Obligations, the attorney also must render account to the adult or – when the adult is no longer able to supervise the actions of the attorney – to the adult protection authority in the context of article 368(2) SCC (see no. 32).[113]

22. **Are there any limits as to the authorisations/responsibilities that can be given by the adult to the attorney (e.g. concerning personal decisions, such as making a will and deciding about donations)? Are there any rules concerning 'selbsteintritt'?**

According to both Langenegger and Jungo, attorneys are, by law, obliged to disregard the adult's wishes, preferences and instructions when these are contrary to the law. This includes situations in which the adult's wishes and instructions provide for representation in highly personal matters, such as making a will or filing for a divorce. [114] In other words, the adult cannot authorise the attorney to perform such highly personal acts on his behalf. However, opinions differ in the literature concerning whether and how the attorney can be authorised to donate on behalf of the adult. This debate centres around whether article 396(3) of the Code of Obligations

108. Hrubesch-Millauer & Jaussi 2013, p. 34.
109. Hrubesch-Millauer & Jaussi 2013, p. 35.
110. Article 398(1) and (2) of the Code of Obligations – English translation of the Swiss Code of Obligations via: https://www.fedlex.admin.ch/eli/cc/27/317_321_377/en (last accessed: 23-03-2022); Hausheer, Geiser & Aebi-Müller 2018, p. 499; Hrubesch-Millauer & Jaussi 2013, p. 35.
111. Hrubesch-Millauer & Jaussi 2013, p. 35.
112. Ibid.
113. Hrubesch-Millauer & Jaussi 2013, p. 36.
114. Jungo 2018, p. 2128; Langenegger 2015, p. 59.

also mutatis mutandis – based on article 365 SCC (see no. 21) – applies to the *Vorsorgeauftrag*.

Article 396(3) of the Code of Obligations stipulates that:

> 'The agent [attorney – RS] requires special authority to agree a settlement, accept an arbitration award, contract bill liabilities, alienate or encumber land or make gifts.'[115]

Based on article 365 SCC in conjunction with article 396(3) of the Code of Obligations, Hopf argues that the adult must explicitly authorise the attorney to perform the acts mentioned in article 396(3) of the Code of Obligations.[116] Hopf goes on to argue that to authorise the attorney to donate on his behalf, the adult must clearly specify the amount and the beneficiary of the donation.[117] Jungo disagrees with the aforementioned and argues that – contrary to the ordinary *Auftrag* – the *Vorsorgeauftrag*, in principle, includes an authorisation to perform the acts mentioned in article 396(3) of the Code of Obligations.[118] This follows, according to Jungo, from article 396(2) of the Code of Obligations which, mutatis mutandis, stipulates that the *Vorsorgeauftrag* includes the authority to carry out such transactions as are required for the execution of the *Vorsorgeauftrag*.[119] Hrubesch-Millauer and Jaussi consider the discussion mentioned above irrelevant since, according to article 240(2) of the Code of Obligations, 'the assets of a person who lacks the capacity to act may be used only to make customary occasional gifts'.[120]

23. Does the legal system allow for the remuneration of the attorney?

The adult may include instructions concerning the attorney's remuneration in the *Vorsorgeauftrag*. When the *Vorsorgeauftrag* is silent as to the subject of remuneration, the adult protection authority may, according to article 366 SCC, in cases where this seems justified given the duties of the attorney or in cases where the attorney is usually remunerated for his services, decide on the appropriate remuneration that is to be provided to the attorney.

115. Article 396(3) of the Code of Obligations – English translation of the Swiss Code of Obligations via: https://www.fedlex.admin.ch/eli/cc/27/317_321_377/en (last accessed: 23-03-2022).
116. Hopf 2013, p. 146.
117. Ibid.
118. Jungo 2018, pp. 2158-2159.
119. Article 396(2) Swiss Code of Obligations (English translation of the Swiss Code of Obligations, via https://www.fedlex.admin.ch/eli/cc/27/317_321_377/en, last accessed 23-03-2022).
120. Hrubesch-Millauer & Jaussi 2013, p. 35.

E. Registration

24. Are enduring documents registered? If yes, is registration voluntary or mandatory?

As noted under No. 9, the adult can register the *Vorsorgeauftrag* with the Civil Register Office. Registration is voluntary. Following article 361(3) SCC, only the fact that a *Vorsorgeauftrag* has been made and the place where it is kept can be registered:

> 'On request, the Civil Register Office shall record in the central database the fact that a person has executed an advance directive and the place where it is kept. The Federal Council shall issue the required provisions, in particular on the access to the data.'[121]

In other words, the content of the *Vorsorgeauftrag* is not recorded in the register. The Civil Register Office keeps a register for *Vorsorgeaufträge* within the framework of an existing system (Infostar).[122] Several adult protection authorities also allow the adult to deposit a copy of the *Vorsorgeauftrag* at their office.[123]

25. When does registration occur (e.g. registration directly after the enduring document has been made, registration upon entry into force, registration upon acceptance of the appointment by the attorney)?

Registration occurs at the adult's request after the *Vorsorgeauftrag* has been made. Since, as discussed in more detail under no. 16, validation of the *Vorsorgeauftrag* by the adult protection authority is required before the entry into force of the *Vorsorgeauftrag*, one could argue that at this point there is, once again, some form of registration.

26. Are changes and revocations of enduring documents registered?

According to article 23a of the Civil Status Decree (*Zivilstandsverordnung*), changes and revocations of the *Vorsorgeauftrag* can also be registered.

27. Which parties can access the register? And to what extent do third parties have access (e.g. notification of the existence of an enduring document or access to the content of the enduring document)?

121. Article 361(3) SCC – English translation of the Swiss Civil Code, via: https://www.fedlex.admin.ch/eli/cc/24/233_245_233/en (last accessed: 23-03-2022).
122. Jungo 2018, p. 2132.
123. Langenegger 2015, p. 59.

The adult protection authority has access to the information registered in the Infostar system of the Civil Register Office. As discussed under no. 9, only the fact that a *Vorsorgeauftrag* has been made, as well as the place where it is kept, are registered.[124]

F. *Capacity, supervision and control measures*

28. What is the legal consequence of the entry into force of the enduring document? Does the adult retain legal capacity?

As discussed in more detail under no. 1, articles 12 and 13 SCC make clear that legal capacity (*Handlungsfähigkeit*), in principle, is reserved for those who have attained the age of majority and are capable of judgement (*Urteilsfähig*). As discussed under no. 16, the *Vorsorgeauftrag* can only enter into force when the adult concerned is no longer capable of judgement (*Urteilsfähig*) concerning the affairs included in the *Vorsorgeauftrag*.[125] Considering articles 12 and 13 SCC, this could mean that the adult for these affairs is also no longer *Handlungsfähig*—however, Hausheer *et al.* and Frankhauser note that *Urteilsfähigkeit* is a 'relative' concept. Therefore, an assessment of the adult's capacity should be conducted in relation to the decision or act at hand.[126] Consequently, it seems opportune to not automatically assume *Handlungsunfähigkeit* – and *Urteilsunfähigkeit* – when the *Vorsorgeauftrag* enters into force. Even more so since – as no. 35 discusses in more detail – in practice, a pragmatic approach is adopted regarding the requirement that the adult must be *Urteilsunfähig* before the *Vorsorgeauftrag* enters into force.[127]

That being said, certain consequences result from the entry into force of the *Vorsorgeauftrag*. The adult is – when no longer capable of judgement (*Urteilsunfähig*) – no longer able to revoke the *Vorsorgeauftrag* (see no. 17). In addition, the adult protection authority is, according to article 449c SCC, obliged to inform the civil register office when a *Vorsorgeauftrag* becomes effective for a person 'permanently lacking capacity of judgement'.[128] The parliamentary explanation on this article clarifies that this is because, according to Article 2 of the Federal Act on Political Rights, the adult is considered ineligible to vote.[129]

124. Hausheer, Geiser & Aebi-Müller 2018, p. 495; Jungo 2018, p. 2132.
125. Hausheer, Geiser & Aebi-Müller 2018, p. 497; Jungo 2018, p. 2143.
126. Frankhauser 2018, p. 199; Hausheer, Geiser & Aebi-Müller 2018, p. 497.
127. See also Langenegger (2015, p. 56) who notes that even if the adult makes a comprehensive *Vorsorgeauftrag* – covering all affairs – the adult remains *Handlungsfähig* when the adult is still capable of judgement (*Urteilsfähig*).
128. Article 449c SCC – English translation of the Swiss Civil Code, via: https://www.fedlex.admin.ch/eli/cc/24/233_245_233/en (last accessed: 23-03-2022).
129. Botschaft zur Änderung des Schweizerischen Zivilgesetzbuches (Erwachsenenschutz, Personenrecht und Kindesrecht) 2006, p. 7082.

29. Does the legal system provide protection against so-called 'ill-considered decisions' by the adult?

According to Swiss case law, capacity or *Urteilsunfähigkeit* cannot be inferred merely from an unwise act or decision.[130] In this context, Frankhauser notes that a legal act that is in itself unwise does not indicate that a person is incapable of judgement (*Urteilsunfähig*), just as, conversely, a legal act that seems reasonable and sensible is not a sign that a person is capable of judgement (*Urteilsfähig*).[131] However, Frankhauser goes on to note that an unwise decision can be an indication of *Urteilsunfähigkeit* when the underlying motivation for the act or decision in question is incomprehensible from all points of view.[132]

30. How is the validity of the document ensured? Is the validity of the enduring document checked at the time the enduring document is made as to the capacity of the adult, freedom from undue influence, etc.?

As discussed under no. 13, two options exist to make a *Vorsorgeauftrag*. The *Vorsorgeauftrag* can either be publicly authenticated or handwritten from beginning to end. As discussed above, public authentication of the *Vorsorgeauftrag* is performed by a so-called *Urkundsperson*, in most cases, a notary. This *Urkundsperson* must establish the adult's identity and assess the adult's capacity to make a *Vorsorgeauftrag*.[133] The *Urkundsperson* is, in addition, obliged to determine whether the content of the *Vorsorgeauftrag* truly reflects the wishes and preferences of the adult.[134] Less protection – concerning the validity of the *Vorsorgeauftrag* – seems to be offered with the second option, a handwritten *Vorsorgeauftrag*. As discussed under no. 13, by asking the adult to write the document from beginning to end by hand, the Swiss federal government hoped to avoid situations where the adult would sign a document drafted by another person without being aware of the content.[135]

31. What options are available to the adult concerning supervision and control of the execution of the enduring document?

Adults may include a form of supervision on the attorney's actions in their *Vorsorgeauftrag*. Schmid and Langenegger point out that the adult can, for instance, appoint a so-called supervisory attorney, i.e. a person the adult appoints to

130. See e.g. BGE 55 II 157;
131. Frankhauser 2018, p. 200.
132. Ibid; see also BGE 124 III 5, S17.
133. Hausheer, Geiser & Aebi-Müller 2018, pp. 494-495; Schmid 2014, pp. 285-286.
134. Ibid.
135. Botschaft zur Änderung des Schweizerischen Zivilgesetzbuches (Erwachsenenschutz, Personenrecht und Kindesrecht) 2006, p. 7026.

supervise the attorney's actions.[136] The adult can also oblige the attorney to submit periodical reports to an auditor (in German: *Revisionsstelle*), who is to inform the adult protection authority in case of misuse or abuse of the *Vorsorgeauftrag* by the attorney.[137] This second form of supervision was frequently mentioned by the experts interviewed in the context of this country report. According to Schmid, a so-called *Urkundsperson* (see no. 30) must inform the adult about the possibility of including the provisions mentioned above in the *Vorsorgeauftrag*.[138]

32. **Is there any supervision of the attorney by the state (e.g. the court or another administrative body)? If so, are there any possibilities for these institutions to intervene in the execution of the enduring document (e.g. appointment of a third party to supervise the attorney)?**

The adult protection authority must intervene when the adult's interests are endangered or no longer protected.[139] This follows from article 368 SCC, which stipulates that:

> 1) 'If the interests of the client are endangered or no longer protected, the adult protection authority may take the required measures ex officio or at the request of a closely associated person.
> 2) It may in particular issue the appointee [attorney – RS] with instructions, order the appointee to file an inventory, regular accounts and reports or revoke all or some of his or her powers.'[140]

The adult's interests are considered endangered when the attorney misuses or abuses the authority conferred to him, but also when the adult's interests are no longer adequately safeguarded because the attorney remains passive, acts negligently or inattentively.[141] The adult protection authority has several options when it finds the conditions of article 368(1) SCC have been met. Jungo notes that the adult protection authority must consider the principles of subsidiarity and necessity when deciding which course of action to take. Measures must be necessary and proportionate. In this regard, Jungo distinguishes between 1) measures within the framework of the existing *Vorsorgeauftrag*, 2) measures in addition to the *Vorsorgeauftrag* and 3) measures revoking the *Vorsorgeauftrag*.[142] Based on article 368(2) SCC, the adult protection authority can oblige the attorney

136. Langenegger 2015, p. 54; Schmid 2014, p. 285; See also Hrubesch-Millauer & Jaussi 2013, p. 37.
137. Langenegger 2015, p. 54.
138. Schmid 2014, p. 285.
139. Jungo 2018, p. 2170; Hrubesch-Millauer & Jaussi 2013, p. 36.
140. Article 368 SCC – English translation of the Swiss Civil Code, via: https://www.fedlex.admin.ch/eli/cc/24/233_245_233/en (last accessed: 23-03-2022).
141. Jungo 2018, pp. 2170-2171; Hotz 2011, p. 112.
142. Jungo 2018, pp. 2171-2172.

to submit an inventory and periodic (financial) reports. The adult protection authority can also issue particular instructions concerning the execution of the *Vorsorgeauftrag*. Jungo argues that the adult protection authority may withdraw or restrict the adult's instructions – as recorded in the *Vorsorgeauftrag* – when this is considered in the adult's interests. This is, however, only permissible when the meaning and 'spirit' of the *Vorsorgeauftrag* remain preserved.[143] Jungo provides the following example of such a situation:

> 'If, for instance, the adult has instructed the attorney (for financial reasons) not to involve an advisor for the management of the adult's assets, but the management of the adult's assets has become considerably complicated because the adult has inherited several majority shareholdings in companies, the adult protection authority may instruct the attorney to engage an advisor for the management of these majority shareholdings if this is in the adult's interests and is considered consistent with the adult's will had the adult known about the subsequent inheritance.'[144]

In the event the interests of the adult are no longer (sufficiently) protected through the *Vorsorgeauftrag*, the adult protection authority may order an additional measure such as a 'Fürsorgerische Unterbringung' or a 'Beistandschaft' (see no. 1).[145] Finally, the adult protection authority can also – wholly or partly – revoke the powers of the attorney and/or – fully or partially – terminate the *Vorsorgeauftrag*.[146] Although not included in article 368(2) SCC, both Hausheer *et al.* and Jungo note that the adult protection authority may also oblige the attorney to request the authorisation of the adult protection authority for specific actions.[147]

33. Is regulation in place concerning (potential) conflicts of interest between the adult's and the attorney's interests?

Article 365(2) and (3) stipulate:

2) Where transactions must be carried out that are not covered by the advance care directive, or if the appointee has an interest in a matter that conflicts with that of the client, the appointee shall notify the adult protection authority immediately.
3) In the event of a conflict of interest, the powers of the appointee cease to apply by law.[148]

143. Ibid.
144. Jungo 2018, pp. 2171-2172.
145. Hausheer, Geiser & Aebi-Müller 2018, p. 502; Jungo 2018, p. 2172.
146. Jungo 2018, pp. 2172-2173; Hrubesch-Millauer & Jaussi 2013, p. 36.
147. Hausheer, Geiser & Aebi-Müller 2018, p. 502 referring to article 416 SCC; Jungo 2018, p. 2173.
148. Article 365(2) and (3) SCC – English translation of the Swiss Civil Code, via: https://www.fedlex.admin.ch/eli/cc/24/233_245_233/en (last accessed: 23-03-2022).

In other words, the attorney may not act if there is a conflict of interest and must notify the adult protection authority if this is the case. The adult protection authority can subsequently order a *Beistandschaft* for the affair.[149] Both Jungo and Schmid note that the aforementioned only applies if the adult has not consciously accepted the conflict of interest in question.[150] In this regard, Schmid argues that if the adult has acknowledged and accepted the conflict of interest through the *Vorsorgeauftrag*, then the attorney may still act and does not have to report to the adult protection authority unless the adult protection authority has ordered otherwise in the context of, for instance, article 368 SCC (see no. 32).[151]

G. *Law in action*

34. What are considered the advantages and the disadvantages of enduring documents?

Jungo summarises the advantages of the *Vorsorgeauftrag* as follows: the adult can exercise his right to autonomy and self-determination in three respects. Firstly, the adult can determine who acts on his behalf. Secondly, the adult can determine which matters the attorney will manage on his behalf, and thirdly, the adult can establish guidelines according to which the attorney must decide and act.[152] Fassbind argues that, in particular, adults with substantial financial assets and complex financial portfolios benefit from making a *Vorsorgeauftrag*.[153] He notes in this regard that with a *Beistandschaft*, the consent of the adult protection authority is required for certain acts the state-appointed representative wants to perform on behalf of the adult, such as – for an ordinary person – unconventional investments. Obtaining this consent can take a while because the adult protection authority, not in all cases, will have the knowledge and experience to deal with complex financial requests and might even have to involve an external specialist to assess a request. In addition, a decision by the adult protection authority might not produce the desired and necessary outcome for the strategy that the adult would have wanted the attorney to pursue.[154] Using a *Vorsorgeauftrag*, the adult can ensure that his assets are managed according to his wishes and preferences.

The risk of misuse or abuse is considered a significant disadvantage of the *Vorsorgeauftrag*. Fassbind notes in this regard that the *Vorsorgeauftrag* can serve as a means to cause considerable financial damage to the adult with impaired capacity.

149. Hausheer, Geiser & Aebi-Müller 2018, p. 498; Botschaft zur Änderung des Schweizerischen Zivilgesetzbuches (Erwachsenenschutz, Personenrecht und Kindesrecht) 2006, p. 7028.
150. Jungo 2018, p. 2162; Schmid 2014, pp. 290-292.
151. Schmid 2014, p. 291.
152. Jungo 2018, p. 2114.
153. Fassbind 2017, pp. 220-222 & pp. 229-233.
154. Ibid.

In this regard, there is a risk that assets are disposed of in an uncontrolled manner or that exorbitant compensation is charged for the fulfilment of tasks that do not require specialist knowledge.[155] Another disadvantage is that the *Vorsorgeauftrag* is, in some cases, propagated in connection with what is referred to as 'KESB-basing', i.e. the appeal to avoid state interference – interference by the adult protection authorities (KESB) – by making a *Vorsorgeauftrag*.[156] This is seen as a disadvantage because, in such cases, a *Vorsorgeauftrag* is made for the wrong reasons. Firstly, as discussed under no. 16, the involvement of the adult protection authorities cannot be avoided.[157] Secondly, the decision to make a *Vorsorgeauftrag* should depend on individual factors, such as the availability of a suitable attorney. This can sometimes rule out the *Vorsorgeauftrag* as the best alternative. Langenegger, therefore, argues that the undifferentiated propagation of the *Vorsorgeauftrag* as an 'always better because self-determined solution' is misplaced.[158]

35. **How does the enduring document function/operate in practice? What works well and what does not? Are there or have there been any problems? How have these been dealt with? Is there any empirical research available on the questions mentioned above?**

Few empirical studies have addressed how the *Vorsorgeauftrag* functions in practice. The studies that have been conducted are exploratory. In addition to the studies mentioned under no. 7, Büttner and Fountoulakis conducted a quantitative analysis of the *Vorsorgeaufträge* validated by the adult protection authorities in the canton of Bern.[159] Their study also looked at the experiences of the adult protection authority Bern Mittelland Süd. Based on these experiences, Büttner and Fountoulakis present examples of cases which the adult protection authority Bern Mittelland Süd has encountered. Several of these examples are discussed below, supplemented with the experiences of the experts interviewed as part of the law-in-action component of this comparative study and the observations presented by scholars and practitioners in the literature on the *Vorsorgeauftrag*.

A first problem concerns *Vorsorgeaufträge* that have been made by adults, who at the time lacked the capacity – *Urteilsfähigkeit* – to do so. Fassbind notes that

155. Fassbind 2017, p. 219.
156. See e.g. D. Gerny, 'Angst vor der Kesb lässt die Zahl von Vorsorgeaufträgen in die Höhe schiessen', *Neue Zürcher Zeitung* 01-03-2019, via: https://www.nzz.ch/schweiz/kesb-angst-loest-run-auf-vorsorgeauftraege-aus-ld.1463125?reduced=true; M. Genova, 'Angst vor Fremdbestimmung: in der Ostschweiz wächst die Zahl der Vorsorgeaufträge', *Tagblatt* 05-05-2019, via: https://www.tagblatt.ch/ostschweiz/angst-vor-fremdbestimmung-in-der-ostschweiz-waechst-die-zahl-der-vorsorgeauftraege-ld.1116127 (last accessed: 23-03-2022).
157. Fassbind 2017, pp. 238-239.
158. Langenegger 2015, p. 45.
159. Büttner & Fountoulakis 2015.

it is not uncommon for adult protection authorities to be confronted with a validation request quite soon after the adult has made the *Vorsorgeauftrag*.[160] Rather than abuse, a lack of information lies, according to Fassbind, at the root of this problem. He refers, in this regard, to situations in which relatives of the adult are concerned that without a *Vorsorgeauftrag*, they will not be able to continue their care of the adult and subsequently urge the adult to make a *Vorsorgeauftrag* although the adult lacks the capacity to do so. These situations can be avoided by ensuring that both adults and relatives are informed in good time about how and when the *Vorsorgeauftrag* can be used to make provisions for the future.[161] Büttner and Fountoulakis also address this problem but zoom in on the question of whether there is merit in the argument that a person, on the one hand, no longer has the capacity to carry out specific affairs but, on the other hand, does have the capacity to entrust the handling of these affairs to another person through a *Vorsorgeauftrag*.[162] Büttner and Fountoulakis argue that the aforementioned argument cannot be sustained. They note that the requirement that the adult must have the capacity to make a *Vorsorgeauftrag* presupposes the ability to assess the importance of entrusting the prospective attorney with the affairs included in the *Vorsorgeauftrag*. In this regard, the adult must be able to understand the complexity and the scope of the matters included in the *Vorsorgeauftrag*.[163] The adult protection authority Bern Mittelland Süd, faced with such a case, thus ruled that it could not validate the *Vorsorgeauftrag*. However, to respect the adult's autonomy as much as possible, it subsequently examined whether the prospective attorney could act as a representative in the context of a *Beistandschaft*.

A second problem concerns the adult's capacity – *Urteilsfähigkeit* – when the *Vorsorgeauftrag* enters into force. Several interviewed experts noted that the requirement that the adult must be *Urteilsunfähig* – or no longer capable of judgement – before the *Vorsorgeauftrag* can enter into force (see no. 16) is not always practicable. In this respect, it is pointed out that *Urteilsunfähigkeit* is often preceded by *Hilfsbedürftigkeit*, a phase whereby the adult can still act and decide but requires the assistance of others to do so.[164] In practice, the adult protection authorities adopt a pragmatic approach concerning the requirement that the adult must be *Urteilsunfähig* before the *Vorsorgeauftrag* may enter into force. Fassbind notes that the adult protection authority might, for instance, decide to validate the *Vorsorgeauftrag* somewhat prematurely in a situation in which the adult – although still being *Urteilsfähig* to a certain extent – is no longer in a state of health that enables him to cope with day-to-day administrative

160. Fassbind 2017, p. 224.
161. Fassbind 2017, pp. 224-225.
162. Büttner & Fountoulakis 2015, pp. 525-527.
163. Ibid, see also Jungo 2018, p. 2122; Langenegger 2015, p. 51.
164. Biderbost 2019, pp. 101-102.

and legal matters.[165] The alternative would be a partial entry into force of the *Vorsorgeauftrag*. Within the framework of this country report, three experts from different adult protection authorities have been interviewed. All three experts indicated that in their experience, the *Vorsorgeauftrag* never partially enters into force. In some instances, adults are advised to use an ordinary power of attorney (*Vollmacht*) or agency contract (*Auftrag*) to make provisions for the phase preceding *Urteilsunfähigkeit*. Fassbind notes, however, that a *Vollmacht*/ *Vorsorgeauftrag*-construction is not without problems because such constructions sometimes cause confusion in practice and meet resistance from, for example, banks.[166] To avoid the issues above, the Swiss legislator could change the law to allow – similar to the *Beistandschaft* – the entry into force of the *Vorsorgeauftrag* when the adult protection authority establishes that the adult is *Hilfsbedürftig*.[167]

A third area of interest linked to which several problems can be identified concerns the role and position of the attorney. A first problem, in this regard, involves the absence of a suitable person to be appointed as an attorney, which could prevent the adult from making a *Vorsorgeauftrag*.[168] A second problem concerns situations where the adult's choice of attorney or attorneys proves problematic. This can, for instance, occur when the adult appoints an older person as an attorney – such as a brother or sister – who, when the *Vorsorgeauftrag* enters into force, is physically unable to take care of the adult's affairs.[169] The execution of the *Vorsorgeauftrag* can also become problematic when the adult appoints more than one attorney but fails to clearly delineate the tasks of these attorneys resulting, for instance, in conflicts between the attorneys.[170] Fear of disputes can also result in the attorney taking on only part of the authority conferred through the *Vorsorgeauftrag*. Büttner and Fountoulakis refer in this regard to a case at the adult protection authority Bern Mittelland Süd, where the attorney only wanted to accept part of the authority conferred through the *Vorsorgeauftrag*.[171] The attorney – the daughter of the adult concerned – did not want to take on the responsibility for certain legal transactions for fear of (later) conflicts with her siblings. In this case, a solution was found using article 392(2) SCC, whereby the adult protection authority can entrust a third party – in this case, the attorney – with a specific task. This reduced the risk of conflict as the adult protection authority had examined and approved the legal transactions in question.[172]

165. Fassbind 2017, p. 223.
166. Fassbind 2017, pp. 223-224; see also Biderbost 2019, p. 97 & pp. 108-109.
167. Fassbind 2017, pp. 223-224.
168. Walser Kessel 2015, p. 357; see also Büttner & Fountoulakis 2015, p. 521.
169. Büttner & Fountoulakis 2015, pp. 527-529; Walser Kessel 2015, p. 357.
170. Fassbind 2017, p. 229.
171. Büttner & Fountoulakis 2015, pp. 529-530.
172. Ibid.

A fourth point of interest concerns the involvement of the adult protection authority through, among other, the validation process. There are both advantages and disadvantages linked to this involvement. An advantage is that the adult protection authority – as discussed under no. 11 – has the authority to interpret the provisions of the *Vorsorgeauftrag* and add clarification or adjustments on minor points. Both Büttner and Fountoulakis and Fassbind provide examples of situations in which such an interpretation or clarification is necessary. Büttner and Fountoulakis discuss a case at the adult protection authority Bern Mittelland Süd in which the adult protection authority had to interpret a handwritten *Vorsorgeauftrag* that was very difficult to read.[173] Fassbind gives an example of a *Vorsorgeauftrag* in which the instruction addressed to the attorney on how to handle the adult's financial affairs was formulated in too general a manner which led to problems with the acceptance of the *Vorsorgeauftrag* in practice.[174] Linked to this, one of the interviewed experts, working at an adult protection authority, noted that interpretation and clarification of the *Vorsorgeauftrag* often occur with the acceptance of the *Vorsorgeauftrag* by third parties in mind. The adult protection authority can, in other words, promote the acceptance of the *Vorsorgeauftrag* in practice. At the same time, the adult protection authority seems to have made itself indispensable in ensuring the acceptance of the *Vorsorgeauftrag* in practice. Fassbind notes in this regard:

> 'Enduring documents are not accepted, nor are representatives, without the state's approval in the form of an official stamp on a piece of paper – purely because of the existing liability risks. Not only the liability risks of the banks but also the tendency of the courts to interpret the banks' duty of care broadly (in dubio pro small savers) contributes to the necessary involvement of the state. Experience has shown that nothing works in practice without official documents. Banks cover their risks, no matter what the law says.'[175]

Fassbind goes on to note that a tendency to pass risks – in particular liability risks – to the state has emerged, which, in his opinion, cannot be considered the objective of an instrument intended to promote self-determination.[176] Another disadvantage of the involvement of the adult protection authority is that the validation process takes time.[177] Jungo notes that this may result in a 'competency gap' between the onset of incapacity (*Urteilsunfähigkeit*) and the entry into force of the *Vorsorgeauftrag*.[178] The adult can prevent such a 'competency gap' through

173. Büttner & Fountoulakis 2015, pp. 530-531.
174. Fassbind 2017, p. 227.
175. Fassbind 2017, p. 234 (translation by RS); see also Biderbost 2019, p. 97 & pp. 108-109.
176. Fassbind 2017, p. 235-236.
177. Büttner & Fountoulakis 2015, pp. 513.
178. Jungo 2018, p. 2144.

an ordinary *Vollmacht* or *Auftrag*. However, as discussed above, the acceptance of these instruments can, in practice, prove problematic.

36. **Is there any information available on the number and type of cases where there has been (financial) abuse or misuse by the attorney?**

I have not been able to find (empirical) studies on the number and type of cases where there has been (financial) abuse or misuse of the *Vorsorgeauftrag* by the attorney. However, the experts interviewed in this comparative study's law-in-action component have been asked about their experiences with misuse and abuse. The experts noted that, so far (the interviews were conducted in 2019), they have seen few situations of misuse or abuse of the *Vorsorgeauftrag*. Examples of cases where the adult protection authority was extra alert include a situation where the invoices from the care home had not been paid and a situation in which the adult protection authority was confronted with a validation request quite soon after the adult had made the *Vorsorgeauftrag*.

37. **Are there any (mandatory) safeguards, and how have these been implemented in practice?**

Several preventive safeguards can be distinguished. First, to ensure that it is the adult who has made the *Vorsorgeauftrag*, article 361(1) and (2) SCC (discussed under no. 13) stipulate that the *Vorsorgeauftrag* must either be publicly authenticated or handwritten from beginning to end. Second, as discussed under no. 16, the *Vorsorgeauftrag* must be validated by the adult protection authority. With this validation process, the adult protection authority checks the validity of the *Vorsorgeauftrag*, as well as whether the conditions for the entry into force of the *Vorsorgeauftrag* have been met, whether the attorney is up to the task at hand and whether additional adult protection measures are necessary. A third preventive safeguard concerns article 365(2) and (3) SCC (see no. 33), which stipulate that the attorney may not act when there is a conflict of interest and must notify the adult protection authority. A fourth safeguard is provided by article 368 SCC, according to which the adult protection authority may intervene when the interests of the adult concerned are endangered or no longer protected (see no. 32).

38. **Is there anything else of interest not included in the answers above?**

In Switzerland, representatives appointed through a *Beistandschaft* can receive support from the adult protection authorities. An interesting development is that several adult protection authorities have also made this support available for attorneys appointed by a Vorsorgeauftrag.[179]

Bibliography

R.E. Aebi-Müller & S. Bienz, 'Vorsorgeauftrag und Patientenverfügung in der Schweiz', in: M. Löhnig, D. Schwab, D. Henrich, P. Gottwald, I. Kroppenberg, *Vorsorgevollmacht und Erwachsenenschutz in Europa*, Bielefeld: Verlag Ernst und Wrener Gieseking 2011, pp. 57-86.

R.E. Aebi-Müller & M. Magliana, 'Switzerland', in: R. Frimston, A. Ruck Keene, C. van Overdijk & A. Ward, *The international protection of adults*, Oxford: Oxford University Press 2015, pp. 386-394.

Y. Biderbost, 'Erwachsenenschutz: Subsidiarität über alles?!', in: R. Arnet, P. Eitel, A. Jungo & H.R. Künzle (eds.), *Der Mensch als Mass. Festschrift für Peter Breitschmid*, Zürich: Schulthess Juristische Medien 2019, pp. 91-111.

P. Breitschmid & I. Matt, 'Im Vorfeld des *Vorsorgeauftrags*: Wirrungen um die (altrechtliche) Vorsorgevollmacht (BGE 134 III 385 ff.), *Pflegerecht-Pflegewissenschaft*, 2012-4, pp. 223-234.

J. Büttner & C. Fountoulakis, 'Der *Vorsorgeauftrag*: erste Erfahrungen aus der Praxis – Zahlen und Fallbeispiele von den Berner Erwachsenenschutzbehörden', *FamPra* 2015-2, pp. 507-535.

R. Fankhauser, 'Art. 12', in: T. Geiser & C. Fountoulakis (eds.), *Basler Kommentar. Zivilgesetzbuch I*, Basel: Helbing Lichtenhahn Verlag 2018, pp. 168-180.

R. Fankhauser, 'Art. 13', in: T. Geiser & C. Fountoulakis (eds.), *Basler Kommentar. Zivilgesetzbuch I*, Basel: Helbing Lichtenhahn Verlag 2018, pp. 180-183.

R. Fankhauser, 'Art. 16', in: T. Geiser & C. Fountoulakis (eds.), *Basler Kommentar. Zivilgesetzbuch I*, Basel: Helbing Lichtenhahn Verlag 2018, pp. 189-206.

P. Fassbind, '*Vorsorgeauftrag* in der Praxis. Risiken und Nebenwirkungen', in: R. Fankhauser, R.E. Reusser & I. Schwander (eds.), *Brennpunkt Familienrecht, Festschrift für Thomas Geiser zum 65. Geburtstag*, Zürich/St. Gallen: Dike Verlag 2017, pp. 217-241.

H. Hausheer, T. Geiser & R.E. Aebi-Müller, *Das Familienrecht des Schweizerischen Zivilgesetzbuches*, Bern: Stämpfli Verlag 2018.

M. Hopf, 'Neues Erwachsenenschutzrecht und *Vorsorgeauftrag*. Regelungsmöglichkeiten und Wirkungen für die Vorsorgebeauftragten', *Der Schweizer Treuhänder* 2013-3, pp. 145-150.

S. Hotz, 'Zum Selbstbestimmungsrecht des Vorsorgenden de lege lata und de lege ferenda – Die Vorsorgevollmacht de lege ferenda', *Zeitschrift für Kindes- und Erwachsenenschutz* 2011, pp. 102-115.

179. See e.g. PriMA BS – Die neue Beratungsstelle für private Beistandspersonen und für Vorsorgebeauftragte, accessible via: https://www.bs.ch/nm/2019-prima-bs--die-neue-beratungsstelle-fuer-private-beistandspersonen-und-fuer-vorsorgebeauftragte-wsu.html (last accessed: 23-03-2022).

S. Hrubesch-Millauer & M. Jaussi, 'Vorsorgeauftrag – Pflichten und Haftung des Beauftragten', *Plädoyer* 2013-1, pp. 33-39.

S. Hrubesch-Millauer & M. Jaussi, 'Instrumente der Vermögenssorge – das Verhältnis des Vorsorgeauftrags zum einfachen Auftrag und zur Vollmacht', *AJP/PJA* 2014-10, pp. 1281-1296.

A. Jungo, 'Art. 360', in: in: T. Geiser & C. Fountoulakis (eds.), *Basler Kommentar. Zivilgesetzbuch I*, Basel: Helbing Lichtenhahn Verlag 2018, pp. 2109-2129.

A. Jungo, 'Art. 361', in: in: T. Geiser & C. Fountoulakis (eds.), *Basler Kommentar. Zivilgesetzbuch I*, Basel: Helbing Lichtenhahn Verlag 2018, pp. 2129-2132.

A. Jungo, 'Art. 362', in: in: T. Geiser & C. Fountoulakis (eds.), *Basler Kommentar. Zivilgesetzbuch I*, Basel: Helbing Lichtenhahn Verlag 2018, pp. 2133-2137.

A. Jungo, 'Art. 363', in: in: T. Geiser & C. Fountoulakis (eds.), *Basler Kommentar. Zivilgesetzbuch I*, Basel: Helbing Lichtenhahn Verlag 2018, pp. 2137-2150.

A. Jungo, 'Art. 364', in: in: T. Geiser & C. Fountoulakis (eds.), *Basler Kommentar. Zivilgesetzbuch I*, Basel: Helbing Lichtenhahn Verlag 2018, pp. 2150-2156.

A. Jungo, 'Art. 365', in: in: T. Geiser & C. Fountoulakis (eds.), *Basler Kommentar. Zivilgesetzbuch I*, Basel: Helbing Lichtenhahn Verlag 2018, pp. 2156-2163.

A. Jungo, 'Art. 366', in: in: T. Geiser & C. Fountoulakis (eds.), *Basler Kommentar. Zivilgesetzbuch I*, Basel: Helbing Lichtenhahn Verlag 2018, pp. 2163-2167.

A. Jungo, 'Art. 367', in: in: T. Geiser & C. Fountoulakis (eds.), *Basler Kommentar. Zivilgesetzbuch I*, Basel: Helbing Lichtenhahn Verlag 2018, pp. 2167-2169.

A. Jungo, 'Art. 368', in: in: T. Geiser & C. Fountoulakis (eds.), *Basler Kommentar. Zivilgesetzbuch I*, Basel: Helbing Lichtenhahn Verlag 2018, pp. 2170-2173.

A. Jungo, 'Art. 369', in: in: T. Geiser & C. Fountoulakis (eds.), *Basler Kommentar. Zivilgesetzbuch I*, Basel: Helbing Lichtenhahn Verlag 2018, pp. 2174-2176.

KOKES, *KOKES-Statistik 2018 / Bestand Erwachsene*, 2019, accessible via: https://www.kokes.ch/de/dokumentation/statistik/aktuellste-zahlen/medienkonferenz-05092019

E. Langenegger, 'Art. 360', in: D. Rosch, A. Büchler & D. Jakob (eds.), *Erwachsenenschutzrecht. Einführung und Kommentar zu Art. 360ff. ZGB und VBVV*, Basel: Helbing Lichtenhahn Verlag 2015, pp. 43-58.

Pro Senectute, *Medienmitteilung 'Wunsch nach Selbstbestimmung ist stärker als Druck durch Corona'*, 2021.

Pro Senectute, *Selbstbestimmen bei Urteilsunfähigkeit – Zahlen und Fakten*, 2017.

Pro Senectute, *Medienmitteilung 'Nur jede zehnte Person in der Schweiz hat bei Urteilsunfähigkeit vorgesorgt'*, 2017.

J. Schmid, '*Vollmachten* und *Vorsorgeauftrag*', in: *Stiftung Schweizerisches Notariat, Nachlassplanung und Nachlassteilung*, Zürich: Schultess Juristische Medien 2014, pp. 259-300.

M. Thommen, *Introduction to Swiss Law*, Berlin-Bern: Carl Grossmann Publishers 2018.

A. Umbricht & J. Yin (GFS-Zürich, Markt- & Sozialforschung, *Telefonische Omnibus-Befragung zur persönliche Vorsorge*, 2021, accessible via: https://gfs-zh.ch/bekanntheitszunahme-bei-vorsorgedokumenten/

A. Umbricht (GFS-Zürich, Markt- & Sozialforschung, *Telefonische Omnibus-Befragung zur persönliche Vorsorge*, 2017, accessible via: https://gfs-zh.ch/nur-jede-zehnte-person-in-der-schweiz-hat-bei-urteilsunfaehigkeit-vorgesorgt/

United Nations Committee on the Rights of Persons with Disabilities, *General Comment No. 1. Article 12: Equal Recognition before the law*, 2014.

C. Walser Kessel, 'Der Vorsorgeauftrag. Einige praktische Überlegungen', *Der Schweizer Treuhänder* 2015-5, pp. 355-358.

Parliamentary documents and jurisprudence
- Botschaft zur Änderung des Schweizerischen Zivilgesetzbuches (Erwachsenenschutz, Personenrecht und Kindesrecht) 2006
- BGE 124 III 5
- BGE 132 III 222
- BGE 140 III 49
- BGE 55 II 157
- BGE 55 II 157

Newspaper articles
- D. Gerny, 'Angst vor der Kesb lässt die Zahl von Vorsorgeaufträgen in die Höhe schiessen', *Neue Zürcher Zeitung* 01-03-2019, via: https://www.nzz.ch/schweiz/kesb-angst-loest-run-auf-vorsorgeauftraege-aus-ld.1463125?reduced=true;
- M. Genova, 'Angst vor Fremdbestimmung: in der Ostschweiz wächst die Zahl der Vorsorgeaufträge', *Tagblatt* 05-05-2019, via: https://www.tagblatt.ch/ostschweiz/angst-vor-fremdbestimmung-in-der-ostschweiz-waechst-die-zahl-der-vorsorgeauftraege-ld.1116127

Experts interviewed
- Employee of the adult protection authority Basel-Stadt
- Employee of the adult protection authority Luzern
- Employee of the adult protection authority Zürich
- Employee of Alzheimer Schweiz
- Physician
- Nurse practitioner